More Advance Praise for *The Strategist*:

"Bartholomew Sparrow has written a superb biography of Brent Scowcroft, a smart, honorable, and highly capable man who was the national security advisor for both Presidents Ford and Bush 41. As this book makes clear, it's a great misfortune that Bush 43 did not employ Scowcroft in that same role, as he saw from the start that invading Iraq would turn the Middle East into a cauldron and seriously damage America's standing around the world."

—JOHN J. MEARSHEIMER, R. WENDELL HARRISON DISTINGUISHED
SERVICE PROFESSOR OF POLITICAL SCIENCE, UNIVERSITY OF CHICAGO

"Although overshadowed by the more flamboyant figures of Henry Kissinger and Zbigniew Brzezinski, Brent Scowcroft is considered by many foreign policy professionals as the ideal national security advisor—self-effacing, an honest broker, and highly competent. And now he has a biography that does him justice and brings together his personal life, his multiple roles in the government, and the history he helped to make. Sparrow's fascinating account sheds a great deal of light on the man and his tumultuous times."

—ROBERT JERVIS, ADLAI E. STEVENSON PROFESSOR OF INTERNATIONAL
POLITICS, COLUMBIA UNIVERSITY

"Every American knows the name and the career of past presidents. Little attention is given to individuals who should have been president—for either party. Brent Scowcroft's contributions—as national security advisor to two presidents, as a military leader, and a public official—are unmatched. Sparrow's book documents over half a century of contributions as a public intellectual with a style that encourages trust and respectful dialogue among concerned citizens. This man is the model of a great American."

—JOHN DEUTCH, INSTITUTE PROFESSOR, MIT, FORMER DIRECTOR
OF CENTRAL INTELLIGENCE, DEPUTY SECRETARY OF DEFENSE, AND
UNDERSECRETARY OF ENERGY

"From Kennedy to Obama, Brent Scowcroft was probably the most respected, admired, and successful national security advisor. In this comprehensive, judicious, and thoughtful biography, Bartholomew Sparrow beautifully illuminates the qualities of mind and character that contributed to Scowcroft's unique stature."

—Melvyn P. Leffler, Edward Stettinius Professor of American History, University of Virginia

THE STRATEGIST

BRENT SCOWCROFT

and THE CALL
of NATIONAL SECURITY

— *the* —

STRATEGIST

BARTHOLOMEW SPARROW

PublicAffairs
New York

Published in the United States by PublicAffairs™, a Member of the Perseus Books Group
All rights reserved.
Printed in the United States of America.

Book Design by Trish Wilkinson
Set in 11 point Adobe Garamond Pro

Library of Congress Cataloging-in-Publication Data
Sparrow, Bartholomew H., 1959–
The strategist : Brent Scowcroft and the call of national security / Bartholomew Sparrow.—First edition.
        pages cm.
Includes bibliographical references and index.
    ISBN 978-1-58648-963-2 (hardcover)—ISBN 978-1-58648-964-9 (electronic)
1. Scowcroft, Brent. 2. National Security Council (U.S.)—Officials and employees—Biography. 3. National security—United States—History—20th century. 4. National security—United States—History—21st century. 5. United States—Military policy—History—20th century. 6. United States—Military policy—History—21st century. 7. Generals—United States—Biography. 8. United States. Air Force—Officers—Biography. 9. United States—Foreign relations. 10. Strategy—United States. I. Title. II. Title: Brent Scowcroft and the call of national security.
E840.8.S38S63 2015
353.1'224092—dc23
[B]

                                                              2014028318

First Edition

10 9 8 7 6 5 4 3 2 1

To Christopher Grant Sparrow

Contents

Photo insert between pages 262–263

Preface

"**DON'T ATTACK SADDAM,**" read the headline of a *Wall Street Journal* op-ed on Thursday, August 15, 2002. The twelve-hundred-word opinion piece argued that the invasion and occupation of Iraq would be "very expensive" and have "very serious" and "bloody" consequences. It cautioned that a campaign against Iraq would divert the United States from the real war against terrorism for an "indefinite period" and that such a war, if conducted without full international support, would strain relations between the United States and other countries. And without "enthusiastic international cooperation," especially on intelligence, it was by no means clear the United States could win the global war against terrorism.[1]

The op-ed argued that Saddam Hussein was first and foremost a "power-hungry survivor" who had little cause to join with Al Qaeda and that he could be deterred just like other aggressors. It warned, too, that should the United States attack Iraq, the ensuing war could "swell the ranks of terrorists," sidetrack US foreign policy from grappling with the more important Israeli-Palestinian conflict, and possibly "destabilize Arab regimes in the region" (the irony being that "one of Saddam's strategic objectives" was precisely such destabilization).

The argument—which proved to be sadly prescient—echoed those made by other opponents of the war, chiefly on the political left. Which is what made the identity of its author so startling. The op-ed had been written by a retired US Air Force lieutenant general, a former military assistant under President Richard Nixon, and the US national security advisor under presidents Gerald Ford and George H. W. Bush—the seventy-seven-year-old Brent Scowcroft.* He was a long-standing, loyal Republican, a highly

---

* Brent Scowcroft's name has no middle initial, and the first syllable of his surname rhymes with "snow."

regarded Washington insider, and a man widely admired for his judiciousness and discretion.

By most measures, Scowcroft's op-ed seemed grossly out of character. It rejected the war plans being formulated by President George W. Bush, who was the son of Scowcroft's close friend and former boss and who had himself appointed Scowcroft as the chairman of the President's Foreign Intelligence Advisory Board (PFIAB, pronounced *piffy-ab*). It directly criticized Scowcroft's protégée, national security advisor Condoleezza Rice, who'd worked under Scowcroft from 1989 to 1991. And it sharply challenged the views of other friends and former associates of Scowcroft, including Vice President Dick Cheney (secretary of defense under George H. W. Bush) and deputy national security advisor Stephen Hadley (Scowcroft's colleague in the Ford and Bush administrations and a former principal of the Scowcroft Group, Scowcroft's consulting firm). For a man known for his quiet diplomacy—the consummate Washington insider—this act of public disagreement was a shocking gesture. No wonder Leslie Gelb, president of the Council on Foreign Relations and a former editor of the *New York Times* editorial page, called the op-ed "very brave."[2]

Scowcroft immediately became the most serious critic of the Bush administration's plans to overthrow Saddam Hussein. The editorial opened the door for other foreign policy experts, including former secretary of state Lawrence Eagleburger, former national security advisor Samuel "Sandy" Berger, Senator Richard Lugar, and Marine Corps Gen. Anthony Zinni, to come out publicly against the administration. Other military leaders spoke out in Army and Navy professional journals, and former secretary of state Henry Kissinger and former national security advisor Zbigniew Brzezinski each offered muted criticisms of the "how" of the administration's plans, though not of the "why." Ten days later, former secretary of state James Baker wrote an op-ed cautioning against any rash action directed at Iraq and urging that the United States "do it in the right way."[3]

A front-page article in the *New York Times* the day after Scowcroft's op-ed called it evidence of a deep split within the Republican Party, and a lead story in *Time* magazine questioned whether the GOP was at war with itself.[4]

The White House fought back. The Bush team's philosophy on dissent was a simple one: "Either you're for us or you're against us." Scowcroft had crossed the line. Vice President Cheney gave two prominent and strongly worded speeches articulating the administration's position, and Bush's other senior advisers, White House supporters, and surrogates published their own op-eds, appeared on television and radio, held press conferences, gave interviews, and made public appearances in which they emphatically reasserted the need to remove Saddam from power, all implicitly rebutting Scowcroft's arguments.

Most media coverage and most of the American public soon rallied behind the president, and on March 20, 2003, the United States went to war with Iraq.

If any man ever had the right to proclaim "I told you so," Brent Scowcroft, in the disastrous aftermath of the invasion, would have had that right. But he never said it—not even after the weapons of mass destruction claimed as justification for the attack proved illusory, not even after the Bush administration grossly mismanaged the invasion and the occupation, and not even after the US presence grew increasingly unpopular at home and around the world, with casualties climbing and the cost in dollars skyrocketing. Nor did Scowcroft distance himself from the Bush administration—even after Bush declined to renew Scowcroft's term as chair of the PFIAB in 2004. Instead, he slowly reestablished his ties with the administration, and in February 2007 he testified before the US Senate to defend the administration's proposed troop surge in Iraq.[5]

Rather than denouncing the war and rejecting the administration that had attacked him for daring to dissent, Scowcroft quietly assisted the Bush White House during its second term in office. President Bush revamped his foreign policy team and attempted to restart the Middle East peace process. He and secretary of state Condoleezza Rice began to work more closely with other countries on issues of mutual concern. And after the 2006 midterm election, Bush appointed Scowcroft's former deputy national security advisor and good friend Robert Gates as secretary of defense.

With the election of Democrat Barack Obama in 2008, Scowcroft continued to offer the White House advice. Secretary of state nominee Hillary Clinton, prospective UN ambassador Susan Rice, and president-elect Obama all consulted with Scowcroft during the presidential transition period and early in the presidency—Scowcroft's impeccable Republican credentials and deep ties to the Bush family notwithstanding. President Obama appointed US Army Gen. James Jones, a friend of Scowcroft's (and someone Obama didn't know well), as his national security advisor.[6]

These twists and turns, which might seem strange in the career of a more conventional player of the Washington power game, reflect the unique role that Brent Scowcroft has occupied as arguably the United States' leading foreign policy strategist of the last forty years. Over the period encompassing the last fifteen years of the Cold War, the years up to September 11, 2011, and the post-9/11 period through the final withdrawal of US forces from Iraq and Afghanistan, no other official or analyst has consistently had such a profound impact on the national security policy of the United States. For many in Washington, Brent Scowcroft is a pillar of the foreign policy community and a global strategist par excellence.

But he is a strategist with a small *s*. Scowcroft views the international scene the way a great chess player views the board: he has a clear objective, has analyzed the evidence available, and has charted a prudent course in pursuit of his goals while recognizing both the uncertainty of others' responses and the often incalculable consequences that any action he might take could have. As one former colleague and friend put it, "one of his great skills . . . is [as] as strategic thinker. What I mean by that is . . . he instinctively does not look at any issue in a vacuum, as self-contained; every issue has tentacles. And he's very good at (a) remembering that there are tentacles, (b) discerning them, and (c) tracing out their connections to other issues."[7]

The strategist may not alter the nature of the game by formulating sweeping new theories of political change or grand summaries of the course of history—but he plays the game set before him, using the pieces available, with insight, skill, and occasionally brilliance. He recognizes the moving parts in a complex situation, sees how the pieces fit together, and devises the most appropriate response, considering not just the military element but also the economic and political aspects of a problem. "He'd see the necessary integration of the tools of American power, not just military power," Lee Hamilton says. "And he had a keen sense of the limitations of military power."[8]

Knowledge of other countries, of other political leaders, and of what has gone before is critical to understanding the properties and trajectories of those moving parts and how they mesh with the tools of American power. "This is where I believe in the importance of history," Scowcroft says. The study of history has taught him about "how countries behave" and has helped him to remain objective about people, events, institutions, and forces—their origins, their likely interactions, and the possible future results.[9]

Of course, being a strategist in the realm of international policy ultimately involves more than just thinking strategically. A would-be strategist without access to the levers of power and the ability to wield them skillfully is merely an armchair theorist, like a military analyst who never leads a battalion or a campaign consultant who simply kibitzes from the sidelines.

We think of George Kennan as a great international strategist because of his 1946 "Long Telegram," written while he was chargé d'affaires at the US embassy in Moscow, and his 1947 *Foreign Affairs* article, "The Sources of Soviet Conduct," published while he was director of policy planning under secretary of state George C. Marshall. These two writings provided the conceptual underpinnings that largely guided United States policy toward the Soviet Union for the four decades of the Cold War. By contrast, the decades Kennan spent writing at the Center for Advanced Study at Princeton and in retirement, when US policy makers all but ignored his analyses and prescriptions, may be significant and interesting to intellectual historians, but they add little to his résumé as a strategist.[10]

Similarly, Henry Kissinger is famous (if controversial) for his strategic vision—formulated in partnership with President Richard Nixon—in regard to détente and SALT, the opening of China, and the United States' disengagement from Vietnam, as well as for the private advice he has given George H. W. Bush,* George W. Bush, and other US presidents. It is the moments when Kissinger helped shape the course of world history that elevate him to the status of strategist, however, and not the quality and volume of the analyses of US foreign policy that he has published in his many books and other writings.

Strategy, then, inevitably has an operational component. For this reason, Scowcroft has observed that national security strategies will either "succeed or fail depending on whether they are implemented effectively. Too often a brilliant strategy can flounder for lack of resources or agencies' commitment to implementing the president's decisions."[11] Because of his skill at getting his strategies implemented, Scowcroft has helped to shape the national security policies of six US presidents—those of Gerald Ford and George H. W. Bush most directly, but also those of Nixon, Reagan, George W. Bush, and Obama. That long-standing influence reflects the confidence officials throughout the government have in him and his credibility with other participants in the world of global policy.

Three qualities in particular have enabled Scowcroft to earn this credibility. One is his integrity in the cause of public service. He has been able to remain his own person even as he has been selfless in the service of the US

---

*George H. W. Bush, the nation's forty-first president, was known as "George Bush" during his own political career, up to the mid-1990s. The text adopts the current usage.

Army, the Air Force, a series of US presidents, and the broader interests of the United States itself. He is careful in his use and analysis of information, thoughtful in his judgments of others, objective in his evaluation of evidence, and confident in his conclusions. He has an internal gyroscope with respect to his judgments regarding national security, as one colleague noted, one not readily influenced by factors external to the events and individuals at hand. He speaks truth to power, a longtime friend, Gen. Amos "Joe" Jordan, says—a quality, Jordan points out, that doesn't always make him very popular. Scowcroft says what's on his mind, Leslie Gelb observes, and he'll speak up if he disagrees.[12]

A second crucial element in Scowcroft's makeup is his ability to reach out to multiple audiences and diverse constituencies at the same time. This capacity to bridge professions, connect specializations, and link policy subsystems—to communicate with different "knowledge communities," to phrase it another way—is what anthropologists sometimes call "multivocality."[13]

Scowcroft has shown himself to be fluent in at least four foreign policy "languages." As a retired Air Force general and an expert on weapons systems, strategic forces, and military organization, Scowcroft is heeded by military and Defense Department personnel, defense policy experts, members of Congress specializing in national security affairs, and Pentagon reporters. As a student of the history and theory of international relations, Kissinger's deputy, national security advisor to two presidents and the author of articles, reports, newspaper op-eds, and books on multiple aspects of US national security, Scowcroft's advice is followed by foreign policy experts, diplomats, journalists, and academics writing on the presidency, national security, and international relations. As a probing consumer of intelligence, a former intelligence officer, and former chairman of PFIAB, he is respected and trusted by officials in the intelligence community. And as the head of a successful international business consulting firm and a leader of prestigious boards that connect business and policy communities (such as the Atlantic Council and the Aspen Strategy Group), Scowcroft is heeded by policy makers and business leaders in the United States and overseas. The ability to understand and connect these varied disciplines is part of what makes Scowcroft unique.

The third quality that accounts for Scowcroft's effectiveness is his quiet personality. Unlike many ambitious policy experts, military officers, and Washington politicians, he prefers to act without fanfare, often letting others receive the acclaim for initiatives he helped devise. He is also extremely discreet, always ready to listen but slow to talk, a quality that leads some to call him "secretive," others very "compartmentalized" or "taciturn." As one former colleague remarks, Scowcroft has "survived in Washington by forgetting an awful lot, or appearing to." Such self-control is highly valued in the nation's capital, and uncommon.[14]

These personal traits, together with the quality of his mind and his unusual work ethic, have enabled Scowcroft to be extraordinarily effective as a policy expert. There are "lots of very, very smart people" in the nation's capital, another former associate observes, but "rarest of all in Washington is judgment"—especially "great judgment" like that consistently exhibited by Scowcroft.[15]

Despite his contributions as a strategist, Scowcroft's low profile has been a hallmark of his life.[16] Most journalists, historians, and analysts of late twentieth-century and early twenty-first-century US foreign policy have paid Scowcroft little direct attention, while writing at length about more outspoken public officials such as Dick Cheney, Henry Kissinger, Colin Powell, Condoleezza Rice, and Donald Rumsfeld. Even the biographies of Richard Nixon, Gerald Ford, and George Bush do not devote much attention to Scowcroft's contributions. And the same can be said of the many memoirs written by former presidents, members of Congress, cabinet officials, and other high-ranking office holders.

This is what Scowcroft has wanted. He has deliberately avoided the attention of the mass media, and his rare forays into public view—whether through interviews, newspaper articles, books, or speeches—have always been designed with specific purposes or specialized audiences in mind. Only occasionally does he appear on national television, and rarely does he attempt to persuade the broader American public of his views. Neither does he trumpet his own accomplishments. Not until 2013, at the age of eighty-eight, did Scowcroft start work on his memoirs, and they remain unfinished as of this writing.[17] As Condoleezza Rice observes, while her mentor and former boss is "one of the most important people in the second half of the twentieth century in terms of foreign policy . . . you would not pick him out of a lineup, right?"[18]

However, because of Scowcroft's prominent role in US foreign policy, a study of his life offers an insider's perspective on many of the critical developments of the last four decades. Many of the events in which Scowcroft participated helped to define the evolution of the United States' international role: the opening of diplomatic relations with China, the US withdrawal from South Vietnam, the handling of the nuclear arms race, the

Iran-contra scandal, the Tiananmen Square massacre and the emergence of China as an economic and political superpower, the reunification of Germany and the end of the Cold War, the 1991 Persian Gulf War, the collapse of the Soviet Union, the establishment of the North American Free Trade Association (NAFTA), and the United States' invasion of Iraq and the start of the war on terror after the attacks of September 11, 2001.

A study of Scowcroft's life also touches on other significant though less heralded events in US and world history: the reform of military education at West Point in the late 1940s, the British financial crisis in the fall of 1976, President Bush's near-disastrous trip to China in February 1989, the failed coup against Panama's Manuel Noriega in October 1989, the reforms of the intelligence community in the mid-1970s, and the growing role of former high-level US officials as international business consultants over the past few decades. By necessity, then, any book-length account of the life and career of Brent Scowcroft must include a history of US national security policy in the post–World War II era.

The Scowcroft story further provides a valuable perspective on the all-important matter of *how* American foreign policy is decided and carried out. We may speak of this as the NSC process, since it centers on the national security advisor and the staff of the National Security Council. It involves the recruitment and placement of personnel; the management of interagency relations; the determination of which governmental agencies or units and which officials are to decide, coordinate, and implement policy; and the handling of public relations between the presidency, Congress, and the media with respect to national security policy. This book accordingly reviews Scowcroft's relationships with his bosses, associates, and subordinates who worked with him as part of the NSC process in shaping US national security over the past fifty years—and, in the process, sheds light on the influence of personal factors on the course of history. It gives particular attention to two former national security advisors, both friends of his. One is his immediate predecessor in office, Henry Kissinger; the other is his former protégée, Condoleezza Rice. How each performed as national security advisor and interpreted the NSC process illuminates the different roles that national security advisors may play across presidential administrations and brings Scowcroft's own choices and actions into fuller relief.

Brent Scowcroft generally exercised his power in subtle, nonobvious ways, quietly influencing policy through the force of his insights and his talent for persuasion. Scowcroft's strategic vision can nonetheless be discerned from his statements, his writings, and his actions both in and out of office.

First and foremost, he is deeply concerned with protecting and advancing American interests. He is what international relations theorists would call a realist. At the same time, he is an internationalist because he sees the United States and most of the rest of the world as having congruent and ultimately reconcilable interests and values.[19] Yet Scowcroft also believes that the achievement of multilateral cooperation depends on strong US leadership in NATO, the United Nations, and other institutions. Finally, we can see Scowcroft as an optimist, because he believes that his voice matters and that reason can prevail in international relations. In this book, I try to show how these core values—realism, internationalism, nationalism, and a fundamental optimism—have informed what Scowcroft has done in his various roles, inside and outside government.

In late 2006, when I first approached General Scowcroft about writing his biography, he expressed some doubt. After a ninety-minute conversation at his Washington office—a meeting that was as much his interview of me as my interview of him—he said he would cooperate. He allowed me access to his academic records and his Air Force personnel files, and he helped me contact many of the people I wanted to interview, encouraging them to share with me what they knew. Most important, Scowcroft himself agreed to talk with me on a regular basis. Our on-the-record interviews—most by telephone, some in person—averaged between thirty and forty-five minutes, with a few running over an hour. They continued through early May 2014. I am deeply grateful to General Scowcroft for his assistance, as well as to the many others who gave generously of their time (see the acknowledgments).

Although *The Strategist* is an authorized biography, it is an independent work of scholarship and analysis (and in no sense a preview of Scowcroft's own memoirs). General Scowcroft did not try to impose his own views on what I would write or otherwise dictate the content of the book. The interpretations, judgments, and conclusions are therefore my responsibility, as are any errors and omissions contained herein.

Bartholomew Sparrow
August 2014

— PART I —

Air Force Officer

════

We must not forget the self-confidence that is instilled by the military training and career: those who are successful in military careers very often gain thereby a confidence that they readily carry over into economic and political realms. . . . Whatever the case may be with individuals, as a coherent group of men the military is probably the most competent group now concerned with national policy; no other group has the training in co-ordinated economic, political, and military affairs; no other group has the continuous experience in the making of decisions; no other group so readily "internalizes" the skills of other groups nor so readily engages their skills on its behalf; no other group has such ready access to world-wide information.

—C. WRIGHT MILLS, *THE POWER ELITE*[1]

1

JUNCTION CITY

SHORTLY AFTER BREAKFAST one morning, Mark Twain's westbound stage-coach overtook a Mormon emigrant train just past Independence Rock in southeastern Wyoming. "Dozens of coarse-clad and sad-looking men, women and children" trudged along, Twain wrote in *Roughing It*, "dusty and uncombed, hatless, bonnetless, and ragged." Traveling the eight hundred miles from Florence, Nebraska Territory—now "Historic Florence" in Omaha, Nebraska—to Independence Rock had taken Twain's stagecoach eight days and three hours. It had taken the Mormon wagon train eight long, exhausting weeks to cover the same distance.[2]

However bedraggled and trail-worn the Mormon men, women, and children may have appeared to Twain as he looked out from his stagecoach, their trek to Salt Lake City would be a success. All 150 people survived, and all thirty-three wagons arrived intact on September 2, 1861, eighty-seven days after leaving Omaha on June 7.[3] Leading the Pingree Company was twenty-four-year-old Job Pingree, a tall, dark-haired, dark-eyed man originally from Worcestershire, England. Pingree was "captain," as the leaders of the Mormon wagon trains were called, and he was returning to Utah after spending a year and a half back in his native country.

Pingree's was one of several overland wagon trains making the trek that summer. Between 1847 and 1868, almost 50,000 Mormons arrived in Salt Lake City in a total of 7,453 wagon trains, according to the records kept by the Latter-day Saints. About 90,000 Mormons in all emigrated to the United States between 1840 and 1890, almost all of them going to or ending up in Utah, with the overwhelming majority of them coming from Europe. By 1890, the territory's population had surpassed 210,000, nearly all of them Mormon. As the historian of religion John G. Turner observes, Brigham Young, the leader of the Church of Latter-day Saints, was responsible for "the organization and settlement of more people than anyone else in American history."[4]

Less than a month after leading his company to Salt Lake City, Pingree married one of the Saints—that is, a member of the Church of Jesus Christ of Latter-day Saints—traveling under his charge: Esther Hooper, a twenty-two-year-old woman also from Worcestershire. Job and Esther settled in Ogden, a town nestled at the base of the Wasatch Mountains, forty miles north of Salt Lake City and ten miles east of the Great Salt Lake.

The area around Ogden, like much of Utah, is open, majestic country. But also like much of Utah, it is unforgiving, arid land. Yet through years of effort Mormon settlers managed to clear the land, divert and channel water for irrigation, and plow the hard, dry soil. Gradually they turned the harsh terrain into productive farmland.

Like other Mormon towns in what are now the states of Nevada, Wyoming, Idaho, and Utah, Ogden benefited from its location along the routes being traversed by tens of thousands of forty-niners heading west (and fewer returning east). An extensive trade developed between the Mormon farmers and entrepreneurs and the often-desperate gold seekers.[5]

Pingree was one of Ogden's first residents, and he became a successful merchant, a prosperous banker—he cofounded the Pingree National Bank—and a large landowner. He opened the Ogden Co-operative Store in the summer of 1866, the first cooperative in Utah and a predecessor of Zion's Co-operative Mercantile Institution, which was established in 1868 by Brigham Young in Salt Lake City (ZCMIs were later opened throughout the Utah Territory).[6] Job and Esther had fourteen children and two infants who were stillborn.

But Pingree already had a wife, a woman by the name of Mary Morgan Pingree, with whom he had had seven children. In fact, Pingree would marry three more times before he died in 1928 (although only his first two wives bore him children).

For Joseph Smith, the founder of the Church of Jesus Christ of Latter-day Saints, for Brigham Young, and for other Mormon leaders, the possession of multiple wives was a manifestation of belief and constituted a reward to the faithful. As a practical matter, though, polygamy was also a measure of worldly success, since caring for more than one spouse, having many children, and keeping more than one household demanded more resources—sometimes a great deal more. And Pingree, who had twice led wagon trains through the Great Plains and over the Rockies into the Salt Lake Valley and who had become one of Ogden's early leaders, had revealed himself to be a dedicated Saint.

For his dedication, US federal agents arrested Pingree along with other leading Ogden citizens in 1885, following the passage of the Edmunds

Anti-Polygamy Act of 1882. On one of their "polyg hunts," US deputy marshals seized Pingree while he having dinner with his second wife, Esther, and their children, fined him, and imprisoned him briefly for being a "cohab."[7]

Job Pingree was Brent Scowcroft's great-grandfather, and Esther Hooper Pingree, Pingree's second wife, was his great-grandmother; Job and Esther's eldest child, Ellen Pingree, was his father's mother.[8]

Making the overland trek to the Salt Lake Valley thirteen years before Pingree was another of Scowcroft's great-grandfathers, Richard Ballantyne. Born in Whitridgebog, Roxburgshire (now part of the Scottish Borders council area), Ballantyne grew up working on his parents' farm, began working as a baker, and then owned and operated a bakery. He became an elder in the Presbyterian Church before converting to Mormonism at the age of twenty-five. In 1843, he and his siblings left Scotland for the United States and, after stops in Liverpool, New Orleans, and St. Louis, met up with their fellow Mormons in Nauvoo, Illinois, shortly before they would all be driven away by mobs and Joseph Smith would be assassinated. Ballantyne himself was kidnapped for a short period in the summer of 1846 and held hostage before LDS leaders negotiated his release. Ballantyne was subsequently ordained a Seventy—a member of the inner council that Brigham Young established to serve as the equivalent to the Twelve Apostles—and made a high priest of the Church.

After a short, harsh migration in 1846 from Nauvoo, across Iowa Territory, and to the east bank of the Missouri, Brigham Young and the Mormon faithful spent almost two years in the grim Winter Quarters, where an estimated 550 Mormons died.[9] Then in late May 1848, Ballantyne, his mother, his sister (a second sister had married one of the Mormon leaders), and his new twenty-year-old wife, Huldah Maria Clark (known as Maria), joined the 1,220-person Brigham Young Company for the trek across the high plains and over the Rockies to the Intermountain West. Only a few days after leaving Council Bluffs, Maria gave birth to a son, and Richard and Maria completed the journey with the nursing infant.

Ballantyne lived a remarkable life as a devout Mormon and an early Ogden settler. In 1849, just one year after arriving in Salt Lake City, he established the first Mormon Sunday school. He then went on a difficult three-year mission to India, leaving his young wife and family behind. Upon his return to the United States in 1855 he led his own 402-person company, the Ballantyne Company, in forty-five wagons from Mormon Grove in Kansas Territory—a settlement that no longer exists but was originally four miles west of Atchison, Kansas—to Salt Lake City, where, to great fanfare, they were greeted by Erastus Snow and Heber Kimball, both Apostles of the Mormon Church, and Brigham Young.[10]

Young rewarded Ballantyne by enjoining him to take a second wife. Ballantyne chose Mary Pearce, a twenty-seven-year-old woman from his company. Ballantyne's biographer writes that he was uncomfortable taking a second wife but believed he should do what Young and other Church leaders asked of him.[11] Maria believed it was her duty as a Saint to accommodate Richard. Less than two years later, Ballantyne married again. His third wife was Caroline Sanderson (also spelled "Sandersen"), a Norwegian woman who had come to Utah in 1855. Mary, in turn, accepted the new spouse.

Throughout his life Ballantyne dutifully agreed to do whatever Brigham Young and the Church asked of him. So when Young asked Ballantyne in 1860 to relocate to Ogden and open a general merchandise store, Ballantyne willingly moved up to Ogden, accompanied by his three wives and their children.[12] Just one year later Young requested that Ballantyne sell his store—already very successful—and take his wives and all his children to Eden Township, east of Ogden, to start a farm. So he did.

The pattern would be repeated. Over the next two decades Ballantyne helped build a toll road and a railway through Weber and Echo Canyons; he assisted subcontractors on other railroads; he built canals; he served as a Weber County commissioner for fourteen years; he sat on the Ogden city council; he became the editor and publisher of a local newspaper, the *Ogden Junction*; and he bought a lumber company and then a brickyard. He then lost his businesses and two homes because of the depression of 1893.[13]

Ballantyne's foremost legacy was the Mormon Sunday school system. He founded the first Sunday school in Weber County, was the first to introduce music to Sunday schools, made Sunday school available to the deaf and blind, and began a system for qualifying Sunday school teachers, among other efforts on behalf of religious instruction for Mormon children. Ballantyne died in 1898, highly respected and deeply revered by the residents of Ogden and among Mormons more generally. His wives Maria, Mary, and Caroline, twenty-two children, and more than one hundred grandchildren survived him.[14]

Richard and Caroline Ballantyne were the parents of Thomas Henry Ballantyne, Scowcroft's grandfather, and the grandparents of Lucile Ballantyne Scowcroft, Brent's mother.

The most famous of Scowcroft's great-grandfathers was John Scowcroft. Scowcroft grew up in Lancashire, England, and in 1861, at the age of seventeen, converted to Mormonism. When he was thirty-six, he, his wife,

Mary Fletcher Scowcroft, and their five surviving children left for America and Utah.

Having learned the confectionary business in Lancashire, Scowcroft set up his own bakery and candy store in 1881, within a year of arriving in Ogden. Three years after that, he turned his business into a retail grocery and dry goods store, and three years later he added shoes, hardware, and household goods to his product list. By 1893, the now-incorporated Scowcroft & Sons—John gradually brought his sons Joseph, Willard, Heber, and Albert into the business—was doing half a million dollars in annual sales, an immense volume at the time. The company moved to a large five-story building in downtown Ogden and expanded further by adding men's clothing to its offerings. It also began to engage exclusively in the wholesale business.

The growth of Scowcroft & Sons dovetailed with Ogden's rise as "Junction City." Ogden was the site where the two rival transcontinental railroads met, the Union Pacific coming from the east and the Central Pacific from the west. Ogden, then, was where all railroad passengers had to disembark to change trains when traveling across the country. Freight trains kept their own railcars and only had to switch locomotives and crews; Ogden had a series of railroad turntables built to accommodate ever bigger and more powerful locomotives.

Passengers and freight soon began arriving in Ogden from directions other than east or west. Trains began running on the Utah Central line on January 10, 1870, thereby connecting Ogden with Salt Lake City. (Utah Central was to be the only American railroad line built by a religious organization.[15]) A year later, construction started on the narrow-gauge Utah Northern, which reached north to Logan, Utah, in 1874 and Silver Bow, Montana, in 1880. The narrow-gauge Denver and Rio Grande Western railroad, heading northeast from Ogden, was completed in 1883.

By the 1920s a total of seven separate railroads (four steam and three electric) joined in Ogden, with five of them constituting "the largest systems [in the] region." Hence Ogden's other nickname, "Crossroads of the West," and the boast of the town's leaders: "You can't go anywhere without coming to Ogden."[16]

Southern Pacific's one thousand employees constituted the largest workforce of any railroad company in the country and the biggest share of Ogden's four thousand railroad employees. With dozens of freight trains coming through every day—an average of 70 in the early 1910s, and up to 140 a day, including as many as 62 passenger trains in the 1940s—the Ogden depot and surrounding rail yards grew to encompass hundreds of acres. The rail yard area became filled with warehouses, livestock pens, grain silos, and icing equipment for refrigerated cars (for the shipment of fruits and vegetables and the products of meatpacking companies such as Swift and Armour). A whole section of Ogden's Union Station was set aside for handling the mail, the most profitable part of the railroad business.[17]

With dozens of passenger trains arriving every day, a thriving and gritty downtown sprang up around the railroad station, complete with hotels, restaurants, bars, and brothels, all teeming with clients. Below street level, the city had a hidden world consisting of underground tunnels and inter-connecting basements that were used for gambling, smoking opium, and, during Prohibition, smuggling liquor. Ogden had sixty-five different gambling establishments in the years between 1940 and 1944, for instance, and more than its share of saloonkeepers and prostitutes. Al Capone is re-ported to have declared that Ogden—referred to as "Little Chicago" during Prohibition—was too wild a town for him.[18]

The result was that Ogden's civic culture clashed with that of the rest of Utah. In 1889, Ogden became the first town in Utah Territory to have its mayor's office captured by the Liberal Party, which ran on the separation of church and state. The new city administration proceeded to rename the city streets, replacing the names honoring Mormon leaders such as Brigham Young, Joseph Smith, and Franklin D. Richards with the names of US presidents. "Ogden Americanized," proclaimed one newspaper.[19]

The population of Ogden grew steadily, increasing from fifteen thousand residents in 1890 to twenty-six thousand in 1910, thirty-three thousand in 1920, and forty thousand by 1940.[20] Many famous Americans would call Ogden their hometown, among them Bernard DeVoto, the famous writer and historian; Marriner Eccles, the Utah banker and budget director under President Franklin D. Roosevelt (although Eccles was born in Logan, Utah); and the Browning family of gunsmiths.

Ogden proved to be an optimal site for Scowcroft & Sons and its line of wholesale grocery and dry goods products, which it sold under the Blue Pine Foods label. Weber County had the agricultural resources—the water supply, wheat, sugar beets, dairy, poultry, livestock, tomatoes, peas, lima beans, carrots, peaches, cherries, and other fruits and vegetables, plus the nearby salt—and the manufacturing, canning, bottling, meatpacking, mill-ing, iron foundries, and other facilities to support the firm's booming busi-ness. Other needed materials or ingredients could be brought in by train.[21]

The company became one of the city's best-known businesses, and John Scowcroft became very wealthy. He organized the local chamber of com-merce, known as the "Weber Club," and served as its first president. He was a director of the Ogden Sugar Company, which he founded with a former mayor, David Eccles (Marriner Eccles's father and Ogden's first million-aire), as well as of the Utah State Bank. And he built a grand home that he named Lancaster; it was designed by the same architect who designed Ogden City Hall, the Utah Loan and Trust Building, and the remodeled Broom Hotel, which was Ogden's finest hotel at the time.

When John Scowcroft died in 1902, his sons took over the business. They oversaw the completion of a huge warehouse in downtown Ogden— itself containing eleven separate warehouses within its walls—and the company became one of the largest wholesalers in the vast area stretching between Omaha and San Francisco. Scowcroft & Sons offered teas, spices, extracts, coffee, and other grocery and household items under its Blue Pine and Kitchen King labels. Its best-known product was Never Rip Overalls, which in 1909 the company produced at the rate of two thousand pairs per day. By 1914, Scowcroft & Sons had 250 employees making just overalls, work pants, and work shirts.[22]

John Scowcroft's eldest son, Heber, married Ellen Pingree on January 10, 1890, and the young couple's son, James, was born in 1892. Ellen died eight years later. James Scowcroft, who went by Jim, served for four years as a Mormon missionary in Japan before returning to Ogden in 1915 to help run the family business. He eventually succeeded his father as the manager of Scowcroft & Sons, and the business thrived in the 1910s and 1920s. Seeking to adjust to the depressed market conditions of the 1930s, Scow-croft & Sons would get out of manufacturing and move into the retail gro-cery business, opening large grocery stores—what Scowcroft described as the "forerunner of supermarkets"—under the name American Food Stores in Utah, Wyoming, and Idaho. In 1958 Scowcroft & Sons would be sold to the Mayfair Corporation.[23]

Back in 1915, though, the first thing Jim Scowcroft did upon returning from Japan was to marry his high-school sweetheart, Lucile Ballantyne, on Wednesday, August 18. Her father, Thomas Ballantyne, was a "big, tough man," in Brent Scowcroft's description, who served as a police officer, as an Ogden City marshal, and then as a deputy sheriff. Lucile herself, though, was a warm, personable, and very pretty young woman: trim, petite, and brown-eyed, with dark curly hair. Jim, for his part, was of medium height (five feet eight inches tall) and a similarly compact build. The couple was "popular in Ogden society," the Ogden *Standard Journal* reported, with "a host of warm friends," and the fact that Jim and Lucile were married in the Mormon Temple in Salt Lake City was indicative of their good standing among the Saints. Both were twenty-three years old.[24]

Immediately after the wedding and their honeymoon in California, Jim and Lucile moved to Idaho Falls. They lived there for several years, where he represented Scowcroft & Sons, before they returned to Ogden, where Jim became manager of Blue Pine Foods.[25] Brent was born ten years after their wedding, on March 19, 1925, the youngest of three children and the couple's only son.

Brent was small for his age, shy, and extremely bright. Cheerful and engaging, he easily made friends among the kids in his neighborhood and the children at school. He attended the local schools: Polk Elementary, Mount Ogden Middle School, and the brand-new Ogden Central High School (built in 1938). Brent's homeroom teachers took an interest in him, and he recalled that he liked his teachers.

Brent loved sports and roamed outdoors with his friends, especially around the foothills of the Wasatch Mountains, which began only five blocks east of where his father had built their home, at 2735 Taylor Avenue on a large corner lot in the eastern part of town. He also played baseball, joined the Boy Scouts, played a little golf, and practiced the piano for eight years (hating "every minute of it," including the recitals).

A precocious child, Scowcroft loved to read. One of his older sisters called him "a speed reader before we knew what speed reading was." Among the books he read as a young teenager were Plutarch's *Lives* and Edward Gibbon's *The Decline and Fall of the Roman Empire*. Because of Brent's reading ability and obvious intelligence, his elementary school principal wanted him to skip some grades, but his father rejected the idea. Jim Scowcroft worried that Brent, who was already short and slight for his age, would not be able to participate in organized sports if he had to compete against older and much bigger boys.[26] But Brent ran track in high school—the 100-yard dash, 4-by-100-yard relay, 220-yard dash, and 4-by-220-yard relay—and placed well in many of his meets. When he was a junior in high school, his 4-by-220 relay team won the state championship.[27]

Jim Scowcroft and Brent had a close, easy relationship. He was an attentive and loving father, and his son reciprocated. When Jim was on a business trip to Chicago, for instance, his ten-year-old son wrote:

Dear Daddy,
If you happen to pass where you got my Draw-Mor set please get me
some paper. I took Mother to Will Rogers today.
    Your Pal
    Guess Who?

P.S. Don't forget to get some candy for Mother and hurry home. A happy birthday, too. I'll kiss Mother for you. We will come down to the train to meet you Saturday morning. Don't try to fool us by coming home on the taxi like you did last spring.

His list of particulars on "How I would like to work," which he wrote down when he was eleven, speaks to his character:
Summer

1. making fires
2. cuting [*sic*] the lawn
3. Watering the grass

Fall

1. raking leaves
2. put them around the flowers

Winter

1. cleaning the terrase [*sic*]
2. cleaning the walk
3. clearing the drive
4. clearing the front and back stairs[28]

Scowcroft was liked and respected by his school classmates. "Brent Scowcroft's good humor and cheerful grin have made him well known to all of the students," two girl reporters wrote for the Ogden high school newspaper. He became the president of the small Ogden High School Ski Club; he was tapped to join an exclusive high school society, the Stagg Club; he was secretary of the Golf Club; he attended dances and other social events; and he excelled in the high school ROTC program. His summer job during his high school years was loading boxes at the Blue Pine Foods warehouse.[29]

During the summers, when not working, Brent played outdoors, swam, and went vacation for two weeks each year with his family, usually driving out to La Jolla, California, their favorite destination, where he would sometimes golf. Other years, he and his parents and sisters would go to different national parks or, as they did once, drive across the country to see Niagara Falls, visit New York City, and also look at colleges.[30] Since he made almost all A's in high school—nothing lower than a B—and graduated in the top 10 percent of his 650-student senior class, he could go to almost any college he wished.

Reflecting back on his upbringing, Scowcroft wryly observed that his idyllic childhood gave him a highly distorted view of his fellow humans: not once did he remember hearing his parents fight. On the contrary, he recalled that his mother and father loved each other deeply, and he never remembered feeling any tension at home. Raised in a setting that gave him a sense of utter security, Brent was a well-behaved child, never getting into trouble either at home or at school.

Scowcroft's personal background exemplified a comment attributed to George Will: that Mormonism is the "most American" of religions, since Mormons have been highly successful at both establishing a strong community of believers and achieving material success.[31] Jim Scowcroft thought his son might grow up to be a college professor and study international relations; Brent himself thought he would become a chemist.[32]

He found another calling instead.

2

SURVIVING HELL ON THE HUDSON

AT THE AGE of twelve, Brent Scowcroft read the book *West Point Today.* Its detailed, flattering, and amusing account of the culture and challenges of cadet life seized Scowcroft's imagination. He dreamed of attending the US Military Academy with its tight discipline, its singular community, and "the air in general."[33]

The following summer, Brent's parents took their thirteen-year-old son east to visit West Point, where their older daughter Janice's fiancé also happened to be a cadet. Brent once more fell in love, this time viscerally, with the imposing campus, the fortress-like granite buildings overlooking the Hudson, and the mess-hall lunch, courtesy of a tour offered by his future brother-in-law. In his book *Absolutely American,* David Lipsky captures the timeless image that has captivated generations of cadets:

> You enter the Academy through a Military Police checkpoint and pass rows
> of stately granite buildings until you're on a green hill above the river. On
> a clear spring day you can look across to the rolling treetops of the Hudson
> Valley . . . and feel that God himself has issued you a uniform and notebook
> and sent you to one of the most crisply beautiful places on earth to study
> the practice of war.[34]

Young Brent caught the bug. Even though his parents also took him to see Princeton, Swarthmore, and Harvard on their trip, he remained intent on going to West Point, becoming an Army officer, fighting for his country, and "being a part of something bigger than you are."[35]

It would be hard to overstate how much the Second World War influenced Brent. He was in the ninth grade when the war began in Europe, and he remembered sitting by the radio with his mother and father two years later when they heard the news about Pearl Harbor. The fighting continued throughout his high school years, pervading virtually every aspect of

American society, and affected Ogden especially because of the large number of troop trains passing through and the huge increase in rail freight.
For a boy of Brent's interests and ideals, the war and its corollary, military
life, became an overwhelming reality. He joined the Ogden High School
Reserve Officer Training Corps and dedicated himself to drilling exercises
and classes in military science and tactics. He was a captain of the Ogden
High School ROTC his junior year, and as a senior he was picked to be
"cadet colonel"—the ROTC regimental commander in charge of inspect-
ing and reviewing the five-hundred-student regiment (which included students from other high schools). World War II "very much changed my
perspective," Scowcroft allowed, and it probably "enhanced the appeal of
West Point."[36]

An essay Brent wrote in the fall of 1939, following his trip east with his
parents, signaled the intensity of the young teenager's focus on military affairs and suggested his patriotic sentiments:

> I think every American citizen should be thinking how thankful they ought
> to be. We life in a land where we are not afraid that our neighbor will shoot
> us in the back. We are about three thousand miles from the nearest hostile
> nation in any country.
>
> We have very peaceful neighbors. Take the boundaryline between the
> United States and Canada. The only way anyone can tell he has crossed the
> boundary is a stone monument by the roadside. Now go over into Europe.
> Take the boundary between France and Germany. There are thousands of
> soldiers there. Hundreds of outposts, forts, and underground strongholds.
>
> Also the United States is free from fear of any other nation pouncing
> upon it without a minute's notice. We are not living in fear of any enemy
> bombers coming over here and bombing our strongholds and flying over
> the cities dropping their messages of death upon the citizens.
>
> I think that especially now in this great European crisis every American
> should be very happy and thankful that they live in America.[37]

The essay's comparison of North America with Europe and its assessment
of the threat of foreign attack point to Scowcroft's analytical abilities, even as
a ninth grader. Its references to "boundaryline," "strongholds," and "enemy
bombers . . . dropping their messages of death" indicate his deep interest in
strategic issues. And the title, "Our America," signals his strong identity with
the United States. The essay underscores, too, just how utterly shocking the
Japanese attack on Pearl Harbor would be for him two years later.

Although Jim Scowcroft didn't want his son to join the military—certainly not with World War II raging—he never let Brent know of his reservations or tried to dissuade him.[38] In early 1943 Brent applied to the US Military Academy with a letter of endorsement from Utah senator Elbert Thomas, and was accepted. However, the appointment arrived just two days before the USMA admissions office was supposed to receive Scowcroft's grades and application materials. Not having his grades in hand, the Army required that Brent take the full written exam, which had an English section, a mathematics section, and a new West Point Aptitude Test. Scowcroft was still taking his high school solid geometry course when he sat for the test, however, and so he failed the solid geometry and algebra portion of the admissions exam. Written petitions by Senator Thomas and his father failed to get the Army to budge.[39]

But when Brent turned eighteen in March 1943—four months after Congress lowered the draft age to eighteen—Uncle Sam came calling. Scowcroft was drafted and given five months to report. On August 5, 1943, he enlisted as a reservist, and on August 20 he began US Army basic training at Fort Douglas, on the eastern edge of Salt Lake City, next to the University of Utah campus. Less than two weeks later, he learned that he'd been admitted to West Point through its college preparatory program.[40] He accepted, turning down offers from the University of Utah, the University of Colorado, and Stanford.

The Army assigned Scowcroft to the United States Military Academy preparatory school at Lafayette College, a private four-year liberal arts and engineering school in Easton, Pennsylvania. The purpose of the one-year USMA preparatory program is to train promising high school graduates—all have to be enlisted personnel who, for one reason or another, did not qualify for direct admission into West Point—in the necessary physical, academic, and military skills to qualify for subsequent admission to the USMA.[41]

Before leaving Utah, Scowcroft was made a Mormon elder. The status of "elder," the higher-order Melchizedek priesthood, is conferred on young men leaving for missionary work or military service. All young Mormon men are eligible to hold the priesthood in their church, and about 80–90 percent of observant Mormon youth and 40–50 percent of all Mormons go on missions. (Scowcroft admitted that the idea of a mission didn't appeal to him then, and that had he stayed in Utah or had he attended a regular four-year college, he wouldn't have gone on one.[42])

In late August, Scowcroft took a troop train east, accompanying soldiers from the 10th Mountain Division, and on September 1, 1943, he started classes at the USMA preparatory program at Lafayette College. He and the other students lived in crowded converted fraternity houses, since the war had depleted Lafayette of most of its male students. (Most of the young women enrolled at Lafayette College stayed on during the war, as they did in other coed colleges and universities across the country.) Reveille for the USMA prep students was at 6:00 A.M., followed by a completely prescribed curriculum of coursework, extensive military training exercises (including marching drills in the snow), and demanding physical and athletic activities. Only about a third of the 250 candidates finished the program.[43]

Despite the busy routine, the high female-to-male ratio at Lafayette helped keep the USMA prep students' morale high. On weekends, prep students in good standing were given Saturday afternoons and Sundays off, and Scowcroft would hitchhike a ride to New York City, "prowl around" with his friends, and often attend plays and musicals (including *Othello* and *Oklahoma!*). And he went out with Vickie, an attractive brunette. In the description of Edwin Robertson II, one of Brent Scowcroft's classmates and friends who was also in the USMA class of 1947 (and was later promoted to major general), it was "a pretty relaxed year."[44]

Scowcroft's time at Lafayette coincided with that of two other young men who would later play important roles in his life. One was Frank Church, the future Democratic senator from Idaho and chairman of the Senate Select Committee to Study Governmental Operations with Respect to Intelligence Activities, better known as the Church Committee. The other was Henry Kissinger, who was studying basic engineering. (He "ate books," his roommate recalled, mumbling criticism—"rumbling" criticism might be more apt, given Kissinger's *basso profondo*—as he read. He would then explode with an outraged, German-accented "BULL-SHIT" and tear the author's reasoning apart.)[45]

Both men were in the Army Specialized Training Program (ASTP), as the US Army had contracted with Lafayette, along with thirty-five other US colleges and universities, to train tens of thousands of enlisted men in engineering, medicine, foreign languages, dentistry, veterinary science, and other specialties that the Army and the Army Air Corps desperately needed. Overseeing the 140,000 men in the three-dozen ASTP programs around the country was Colonel Herman Beukema, the head of the Department of Economics, Government, and History at West Point. Beukema, too, would later play a significant role in Scowcroft's life.[46]

In March 1944, Scowcroft retook the US Military Academy's entrance exam, and this time passed the math and English portions and did well on the new West Point Aptitude Test. He completed his prep program at Lafayette College on June 19, 1944.

On July 1, after a two-week leave, he began life at the US Military Academy, where "every new arrival, without distinction, is dumped unceremoniously into the hopper of the West Point machine that four years later grinds him out as the finished product," Kendall Banning writes in *West Point Today.* "Those four years are, without much doubt, the toughest four years to be found in any educational institution in the world. Tough not only in the academic requirements but more particularly in the uncompromising and unceasing discipline. . . . The toughest period of all covers the first two months."[47] Scowcroft's time there was no exception.

THE WAR RAGING in western and eastern Europe, in North Africa and the Middle East, and in the Far East and southwest Pacific transformed the United States of Scowcroft's childhood. The astounding mobilization of resources and personnel, the great internal migration within the forty-eight states, the tremendous advances in science, industry, and technology, and the many new public policies instituted by Congress and the Roosevelt administration profoundly changed the national economy, the federal government, and American political culture.[48]

By contrast, the serene and postcard-perfect West Point campus appeared fixed in time. The imposing stone and red-brick buildings, the monuments and memorials, the impeccable grounds sloping down to the broad Plain (the parade grounds at the center of the USMA campus), and the time-honored customs and rituals of West Point all continued seemingly undisturbed. The cadets still ran across campus between classes. They still turned out en masse, impeccably dressed and arrayed in rows and lines, to march in the scheduled parades. They were still almost all Caucasian and almost all from the middle or upper middle class. West Point carried on its love affair with Army football, rendezvousing each Saturday in the fall. And the campus still had horses and stables in a world where armor reigned supreme. As one common saying had it—only partially in jest—West Point represented two hundred years of tradition unimpeded by progress.[49]

But appearances may deceive. West Point's venerable traditions obscured the drastic changes being forced upon it by the Second World War. In mid-1942 Congress legislated an increase in the size of the student body to almost 2,500 cadets—a 37 percent increase—and Congress further stipulated that all cadets were to graduate in three years' time, effective beginning in the fall of 1942.[50]

With thousands of cadets already enrolled at West Point, Army officials had to find ways to collapse the four-year curriculum into three years. They decided that the original class of 1943 would graduate a semester early, that the original class of 1944 would take abbreviated versions of Second Class (junior) and First Class (senior) courses, and graduate a year early, and that the remaining underclassmen and subsequent classes of cadets would simply graduate in just three years (since Army officials also determined that cadets now needed fewer course credits with which to graduate). The Second Class (or junior year) was effectively eliminated. The Army cut back, too, on classes in English, social science, and military history—although it did offer more classes in Russian and Portuguese, since the Soviet Union and Brazil were now US allies. And the cadets had to be in class more days each year, with fewer days allotted for their winter and summer furloughs.[51]

Before World War II, West Point didn't separate its training of cadets for the Army proper from those going into the Army Air Corps (with the Army Air Forces officially replacing the Army Air Corps in 1941, although the Air Force personnel continued to be referred to as the Army Air Corps). Beginning in 1942, however, the Army made Third Class cadets (sophomores) choose between being "Air Cadets" or "Ground Cadets"—up until then, all cadets were educated as Ground Cadets, without being labeled as such—thus splitting each class in half after the Fourth Class (the plebe or freshman year). Both the Air Cadets and the Ground Cadets would finish in three years, but the former would be able to graduate as accredited pilots, which involved many extra hours of special courses, flying lessons, and summer training.[52]

Making this new and intensive Air Cadet program possible was the construction of Stewart Field, which was dedicated on August 25, 1942. Stewart Field was a former dairy farm located eleven miles northwest of West Point and outside of the town of Newburgh, and it served as a second West Point campus for all intents and purposes, complete with barracks for the Air Cadets and the Women Air Cadets, officers' quarters, classrooms, a library, a hospital, aircraft hangars, radio facilities, a motor repair shop, roads, walkways, and dozens of other buildings.

The war also caused West Point to expand its training facilities for the Ground Cadets. Congress authorized money for the Army to buy 10,300 acres around Popolopen Lake, immediately west of and adjacent to the West Point campus, and the new land provided extensive areas for artillery training and for rifle, pistol, and machine gun ranges. The Popolopen Lake tract further ensured an adequate water supply for West Point, supplementing Lusk Reservoir. In fact, in 1945 and 1946 part of the new Popolopen Lake tract housed a German POW camp.[53]

Once the war began to wind down, the Army began to reverse West Point's wartime changes. In the summer of 1944, the USMA stopped dividing the corps into Air and Ground Cadets, discontinued its program allowing cadets to graduate as certified pilots, and returned to its usual four-year curriculum. But with the war still going in mid-1944, the Army kept its accelerated, three-year curriculum for one-half of the new class arriving in July 1944. Half were to graduate in June 1947, and the other half in June 1948. Brent Scowcroft and his most famous classmate, Alexander Meigs Haig, were both in the three-year cohort.[54]

The nineteen-year-old Brent Scowcroft arrived at West Point on July 1, 1944. His open face had a ruddy complexion, a domed forehead, well-spaced and deep-set brown eyes, wide cheeks, a narrow nose that widened to the nostrils, a flat mouth with thin lips, and a square jaw. The Army's medical records listed him as standing 5'7¾" in his socks and weighing 140 pounds.[55] And because cadets were sorted into their companies by height (a practice since discontinued), Scowcroft was assigned to Company B, Regiment 2 (B2), which had cadets between 5'8" and 5'9" tall.

Company B was notoriously tough on plebes, with one of the worst reputations for hazing. After "Beast Barracks"—the grueling, spirit-breaking six weeks of basic training, an almost nonstop regimen of calisthenics, rifle instruction, lessons on the honor system, athletics, and other required introductory exercises—regular classes began. The challenges Scowcroft now faced were ones he was less prepared for, more psychological than physical or academic. "It was, well, a bit like I imagined hell was," Scowcroft told an Army interviewer in 2012. "It was a really transforming experience. I had never gone through anything like this before, and I hardly knew what was happening."

One of Company B's favorite kinds of hazing was "clothing formation" (which was also practiced by other companies). Plebes, who lived on the fourth floor, had to assemble on the first floor. They were then sent back upstairs to change into new uniforms and come down for inspection. They were then ordered back upstairs to change their uniforms once again and immediately reassemble on the ground floor, and so on, for a total of five or six changes of uniform. For forty-five to sixty minutes, depending on how fast the plebes were and how merciless the upperclassmen felt, Scowcroft and his fellow B2 plebes had to race up and down the stairs at breakneck speed and repeatedly change into and out of their various uniforms—full dress, regular dress, athletic dress, evening dress (complete with white collar and cuffs), and others—in no particular order. These and other humiliations were standard fare for "Hell on the Hudson," or what West Point cadets in later years crudely described as "a $50,000 education, shoved up the ass a nickel at a time."[56]

Scowcroft found this and the other forms of hazing "extremely uncomfortable" and "humiliating" (although none involved physical contact). The upperclassmen, he said, "made life miserable." But at the time, he mainly thought about how he could survive, get along, and do well. Decades later, Scowcroft was philosophic about the "traumatic" West Point introduction. It was, "in retrospect, a useful experience because it pulled me out of a privileged environment in which I had been raised with loving parents and threw me into an environment where I was overstressed constantly and just struggling to keep my head above water." It taught Scowcroft how not to lose control and be self-disciplined. "It was a tremendous lesson," he said, "one of the most valuable," and it marked his "transition to a very different kind of life."[57]

As a Fourth Class and then Third Class cadet, Scowcroft was under constant scrutiny from the First Class cadets. Upperclassmen could enter cadets' always-unlocked rooms for inspection at any time, without knocking, and they monitored underclassmen in the halls, during meals, in chapel, and at other times. If the inspections turned up anything irregular, then the cadet received demerits. Scowcroft received demerits for a number of infractions, among them ones for not properly shining his shoes to a glistening sheen (four times), leaving lights burning unnecessarily (three times), not caring properly for the butt, bore, and operating rod of his rifle (once each, respectively), leaving the top of his locker dusty (twice), talking before "Take Seats" at dinner (twice), wearing his trousers too long (twice), sleeping without pajamas (twice), and having his collar unattached at breakfast (once).[58] However, because Scowcroft received relatively few demerits, he never had to march in the courtyard or face more extreme punitive measures.

The single exception came in Scowcroft's senior year at West Point, when he was confined to the campus from noon on May 15, 1947, until 9:00 P.M. on May 27. The charge was hazing: that on the evening of December 20, 1946, he didn't sufficiently supervise the plebes under his charge. The fact was that Scowcroft was giving a party for the First Class cadets in the company, and to introduce the party he made it appear as though the plebes were in a hazing formation. This was what he was penalized for. But rules were rules, and the tactical officer overseeing the company was charged with enforcing them. Fortunately, the punishment was meted out informally: Scowcroft was never brought before a disciplinary board, never charged with any infractions, and received no demerits for the incident.[59]

Helping Scowcroft overcome his loneliness and survive the upperclassmen's cruelties were his weekly letters home to his parents (which all cadets were expected to do and which, Scowcroft added, was "a lot for me") and his attendance with a handful of other cadets at the Sunday afternoon Latter-day Saints church services held in the basement of the Protestant chapel at West Point. The LDS chapel group formed what was in effect a small support group, allowing him to meet six to eight other cadets of a similar religious background, "let his hair down," and escape from the harassments of plebe life. For example, Scowcroft got to know fellow Mormon Amos "Joe" Jordan, who was a year ahead of him and ended up following a career path somewhat parallel to his own—named a Rhodes Scholar, receiving a PhD from Columbia University, teaching for twenty years at West Point, and serving under defense secretaries James Schlesinger and Donald Rumsfeld in the mid-1970s.[60]

Also helping to alleviate Scowcroft's feelings of isolation and easing his adjustment to cadet life was his affiliation with Army football. Immediately after arriving at West Point Scowcroft decided to try out for intercollegiate track and ice hockey, but he wasn't good enough to make either freshman team. So he decided to manage the football C (plebe) squad.[61] Although he loved football, he couldn't play at the intercollegiate level because of his small size. Being the football team manager was the next best thing, and it gave Scowcroft another group of cadets to be around. Given the additional time and travel commitments that went with the position, being the football team manager spared him some of the routine and unpleasant jobs plebes normally do, such as guard duty at the barracks, the mess hall, academic buildings, and the camps they visited.[62]

In the summer after his plebe year, the summer of 1945, the war in Europe was over, but Scowcroft and his classmates were still fully expecting to be called into active service, since it wasn't clear how much longer the war in the Pacific would last—and because war had been their reality since 1939. So it came as a shock when, in mid-August 1945, while Scowcroft was training with 18 mm mortars at Pine Camp in upstate New

York (renamed Fort Drum in 1951) and about to enter the Third Class, he learned the war was over. He wondered if he'd made a stupid career choice: what was the point of being an Army officer and fighting for his country if there was no war?[63]

But Scowcroft had adjusted successfully to life at West Point. He'd become very good at learning how to divide his time among different activities and doing each of them extremely well. (In fact, it was in the ten-minute break between classes—assuming that the classes weren't in buildings across campus—that he learned to take catnaps on the fly.[64]) He continued to apply himself to his coursework as a sophomore and then as a senior, and to manage the Army football teams. He also continued to play tennis, volleyball, soccer (center halfback), and water polo ("water soccer" at West Point, where he was goalie). And as a senior, or First Classman, he worked as a ski instructor on the new ski slope German POWs had built while they were incarcerated in the Popolopen Lake area in 1945 and 1946. Although he and his classmates knew the German POWs were being held nearby, neither Scowcroft nor his friends had any direct interaction with them.[65]

As a sophomore, Scowcroft managed the B squad football team, and as a senior—there was no junior year in the three-year curriculum—he managed the powerhouse A squad that went undefeated in the 1946 season, as it had in 1944 and 1945. This was the Army football team of "Mr. Inside," Doc Blanchard, winner of the Heisman Trophy in 1945, and "Mr. Outside," Glenn Davis, winner of the Heisman Trophy in 1946, the Associated Press's 1946 Male Athlete of the Year, the Walter Camp Award, and the Maxwell Award. The 1946 Army–Notre Dame football game in New York—a 0–0 tie played in Yankee Stadium and a classic in the history of college football—was the only game Army didn't win outright in its three-year run as an undefeated team.

Scowcroft admitted he did not work as hard as he could have. He fell in love with the game of bridge and spent most of his evenings as a First Classman playing cards with fellow students. He wasn't used to intensive studying and didn't feel compelled to do so at West Point. High grades had always come easy for him, and Company B "sort of looked down on high achievers."[66] Although he didn't graduate in the top 10 percent of his class, he did well, earning his highest marks in social science (economics, international relations) and English (writing, public speaking, and research), and his lowest grades, Cs, in math and physics. Scowcroft's single highest grade came in his physical education class during his last year, helped by the fact that he worked out in the gym each day after classes. He ended up graduating a respectable 87th out of a class of 310. Alexander Haig ended up 214th—and was the first in the class to make general. Their class of 1947 was the last class required to take equestrian training; after they graduated, West Point's hundreds of horses were auctioned off, and the stables were cleared out except for a handful of mascot mules.

Scowcroft's relatively high academic rank meant that he could join almost any branch of the Army he wanted. Engineering had the highest prestige, but it held little appeal for him. Although he considered artillery and infantry, he and several close friends—along with a third of their classmates—decided to join the Army Air Corps. He'd go to flight school and become a fighter pilot.[67]

On the morning of June 3, 1947, Scowcroft was commissioned a second lieutenant in the US Army. A few hours later, he received his United States Military Academy diploma from Gen. Dwight D. Eisenhower, one of his heroes; this would remain one of the proudest moments of his life.[68]

Scowcroft assumed he would put in his four years in the Army Air Corps—the five-year obligation for service academy graduates didn't go into effect until 1964, with the class of 1968—and then go back to civilian life, to Ogden, and to Scowcroft & Sons.[69]

That was not how things worked out.

3

CRASH LANDING

SHORTLY BEFORE 1:30 P.M. on Thursday, January 6, 1949, on a cold, sunny winter's day, 2nd Lt. Brent Scowcroft almost died. Shortly after he'd taken off from Grenier Field to rendezvous with other pilots for a dogfight training exercise in the skies over central New Hampshire, another pilot jumped Scowcroft's F-51H Mustang, quickly bearing down on him from behind. Scowcroft throttled up his aircraft, only to watch the propeller speed run past the red line. Although he didn't know it at the time, the engine governor had given out, causing the propeller to rotate too fast and breaking a connecting rod. Coolant was leaking from his dead engine and he was rapidly losing airspeed.[70]

He turned his F-51 back toward the base and desperately tried to nurse the engine to life, but to no avail. And without power, the F-51 glided "like a rock."[71] Scowcroft had to make a snap decision: he could either bail out or attempt to make an emergency landing. Only two thousand feet off the ground, he immediately realized he didn't have enough altitude or time to use his parachute, and so he began to look for a suitable clearing in which to crash-land the aircraft. Spotting an open area, he used the little speed he had left to make it over a stand of trees. He retracted the landing gear, tightened his safety belt, and started to bring the plane down. The last thing he remembered was a feeling of relief that'd he made it to the clearing.

Scowcroft regained consciousness later that day in a hospital bed. He'd hit the ground at 100 mph after first skimming the trees and then hitting some telephone cables—tearing a few loose in the process—before passing under some streetlight wires. Once the aircraft hit the ground, it bounced into a small stone bridge, with the collision knocking the engine off the fuselage. The F-51 came to rest in a shallow frozen marsh near Route 28, just north of the town of Londonderry, about five miles southeast of downtown Manchester.

Scowcroft was lucky to survive. His plane could have easily caught fire or exploded upon crashing, and he missed by barely a hundred yards colliding with a Boston & Maine passenger bus with twenty-one people on board. Because he'd been in constant radio contact with the Grenier control tower, emergency crews arrived at the crash site within minutes. They rushed him to the base hospital, where doctors found a broken vertebra in Scowcroft's middle back and a chipped vertebra in his lower back. The crash also left Brent with a three-and-a-half-inch gash in his scalp and cuts and bruises on his face, arms, and chest. Lt. Scowcroft "miraculously escaped death," the Manchester *Union Leader* reported the next day.[72]

Scowcroft had been assigned to the 97th Fighter Squadron of the 82nd Fighter Group and was training as a "fire wing," tasked to protect a Strategic Air Command bomber. Scowcroft's billet at Grenier Air Force Base followed nine months of basic flight training (October 1947 through June 1948) at Randolph Field in San Antonio and three months at Williams Field in Chandler, Arizona (July 1 through October 8, 1948), where he earned his pilot's rating (and remembered getting up at 4 A.M. to fly liquid-cooled engines because it was "hot as hell"). Because he graduated into the Army Air Forces several months before the next pilot training course started at Randolph, he spent the months from July to October at Lackland Air Force Base outside San Antonio, helping teach Air Force basic training to new recruits.[73]

Scowcroft had loved flying. Even the training exercises were fun and exhilarating, especially by comparison with the drudgery of West Point. Now the crash and the ensuing twenty-five months would reshape Scowcroft's life.

Within twenty-four hours, Air Force authorities transferred Scowcroft to Murphy Army Hospital in Waltham, Massachusetts, and put him in a plaster jacket that required that he be manually turned over every six hours. Doctors told him he'd never be able to fly again, and the Air Force suspended Scowcroft's pilot's wings indefinitely—standard practice following a crash, though it angered Scowcroft.[74]

Scowcroft's career as a pilot had come to an abrupt end. He wouldn't be able to fly in Korea or later in the Cold War. Worse still, the crash threw his military career and his own life plans into a spin. Scowcroft hadn't previously given his career much thought. He enjoyed the discipline and camaraderie of military life, and loved to fly. But he figured he'd sooner or later return to the family business, since he knew he'd be warmly welcomed back at Scowcroft & Sons (although he and his father had never directly broached the subject).[75] Now, however, Scowcroft realized he wasn't all that excited about investing his energy in and devoting his life to the wholesale food business. He wasn't sure what he would do. Too quickly, everything had become very serious.

While Scowcroft was recuperating at Murphy Army Hospital and still thinking about his military career and life goals, he received some good news. On February 8, he discovered he was to be promoted to first lieutenant. Four days later, that bit of welcome information lost all significance: on February 12—barely a month after the crash—Scowcroft learned his father had died of a heart attack.

Jim Scowcroft had suffered from chronically high blood pressure and had had other health problems as well, including a case of dysentery contracted decades earlier during his Mormon mission in Japan. And the year before, he'd had a small stroke. Even so, Scowcroft, his mother, two sisters, and extended family were hardly ready for James Scowcroft to pass away at the age of fifty-seven.

And Brent, encased in a plaster cast that covered his whole upper body, was hardly ready to travel to Ogden. The Air Force flew him out nonetheless, so he could attend his father's funeral—an extremely cold and uncomfortable trip in a military transport plane. Scowcroft remained in Ogden for a month, grieving with his mother, sisters, and other relatives and settling family affairs. The plaster cast allowed him to walk around, but since it was winter, he mostly stayed indoors. He and his mother, sisters, and other members of the extended family tried to comfort each other as best they could as the days passed and the pain slowly subsided.[76]

Brent's mother was "unbelievably devastated" by her husband's death, her son said. Lucile Scowcroft never recovered from the loss, remaining depressed for the rest of her life. She kept the family home after her husband's death and lived there until 1968, when at the age of seventy-six she moved into a nearby condominium.[77] Brent stayed in close touch with her over the years and called, wrote, or visited whenever his intense schedule permitted.

Neither Lucile nor her children inherited much. Jim had borrowed money in the 1940s to buy out the shares of Scowcroft & Sons held by other members of the Scowcroft family, and when he died he still owed money to other family members—debts that his estate then had to settle. Jim's older cousin Fletcher Scowcroft took over the management of Scowcroft & Sons until the business was sold, nine years later.[78]

In March 1949, after a month in Ogden, Scowcroft headed back to Murphy Army Hospital. On his way back east, flying via New York, he

suddenly experienced nausea and intense abdominal pain. The Army immediately moved him to Fort Jay Army Hospital on Governors Island, where
he was diagnosed with appendicitis and operated on. A week later, while
recovering from the appendectomy, Scowcroft once again felt severe nausea
and began to take on a jaundiced appearance. This time Army doctors diagnosed him with hepatitis, apparently contracted from a blood transfusion
given immediately after the crash. The appendicitis, it so happened, was an
early indication of hepatitis B.[79]

Scowcroft stayed at Fort Jay Army Hospital until April, when Army
doctors removed his body cast and put him in a back brace. They then
transferred him to the Hepatitis Center at Valley Forge Army Hospital—
the largest Army hospital in the United States at the time—in Phoenixville,
Pennsylvania, five miles west of Valley Forge National Historic Park.[80]

While at Valley Forge and while still in his back brace, Scowcroft received
more news—this time good news. He received a letter from Col. Herman
Beukema, the head of the Department of Social Sciences at the US Military
Academy, inviting him to return to West Point to teach economics.[81]

Colonel Beukema, who was a tall man with a long, lean face, prominent
cheekbones, and light-colored eyes, had spent thirteen years as a field artillery officer when the Army asked him to teach at the US Military Academy.
He was an extremely committed teacher whom the Army promoted to full
professor after only two years of teaching; he had a first-class intellect, and
he was a superb administrator. Thanks to his extraordinary ability, he'd
been chosen to run the Army Specialized Training Program (1942–1944),
which educated 140,000 men at thirty-six US colleges and universities in
engineering, medicine, foreign languages, dentistry, veterinary science, and
other specialties desperately needed by the Army and Army Air Corps.

Indicative of Beukema's standing in the Army was his handling of
Maj. Gen. Maxwell D. Taylor. Taylor, who was USMA superintendent
from 1945 to 1949, turned out not to be a good fit with the West Point
faculty and staff, and soon wore out his welcome. So Beukema told Eisenhower, Beukema's former classmate and Army chief of staff at the time,
"You tame him or we will." Taylor was transferred.[82]

At West Point, Beukema began an extensive effort to reform the education of US Army officers. He wanted faculty members in the Department
of Social Sciences who would broaden the cadets' horizons and prepare
them to be effective leaders under the new conditions of the postwar world.
So he needed more than academic achievers on his faculty; he sought men
of character (they were all men at the time, of course), leaders who could

serve as role models for the cadets and inspire them. Despite Scowcroft's undistinguished grades, he had impressed Beukema and Colonel George "Abe" Lincoln, the deputy department head.

Part of what Beukema did as department head was to keep tabs on those cadets who met his criteria for serving as potential teachers of economics, political science, history, or geography. He then had First Classmen fill out a form asking if they'd like to come back as instructors. After the cadets graduated, Beukema and his successors as department head would gauge officers' level of interest, their individual strengths, and the department's needs, and might then invite a selected few back to teach.

Scowcroft had expressed interest in coming back to teach on the department's questionnaire. Beukema, in turn, had been impressed by Scowcroft, and he and Col. Lincoln wanted the young officer to return.[83]

Scowcroft would also be admitted to graduate school under an informal arrangement the Army had established with a handful of elite universities. The promising officers selected for this program were admitted without having to apply formally, and the Army paid for their education. The officers would then return to West Point for three-year teaching rotations before heading back into the Army—or, in Scowcroft's case, back to the Army Air Corps.[84]

If teaching economics didn't much interest Scowcroft, going back to West Point to teach did—whatever the subject. While he was lying in the Murphy, Fort Jay, and Valley Forge hospitals for hours, days, and weeks on end, Scowcroft had come to realize that he wanted to learn about military strategy, planning for war, intelligence, and other dimensions of US national security.[85] Going to graduate school and teaching at West Point would help him achieve these goals, which were also consistent with his father's wish that he be an intellectual.

Scowcroft's transfer to Valley Forge Army Hospital in March 1949 had another life-changing consequence. Among those caring for him was 1st Lt. Marian Horner, a pretty, petite, outgoing, dark-haired, and dark-eyed Air Force nurse who was known as "Jackie" to her friends (who couldn't resist the wordplay evoking the nursery rhyme). Jackie was two years older than Brent, a Roman Catholic from Syracuse, New York, and a graduate of the St. Francis Hospital School of Nursing in Pittsburgh. She had joined the Army Nurse Corps in 1945, was transferred to the Army Air Forces shortly thereafter, and then began working at Valley Forge. The Army Air Forces had named her "Outstanding Nurse" at Valley Forge Army Hospital, an honor indicative of her great competence, positive attitude, and strong work ethic.[86]

Brent found Jackie immensely attractive, and she began to visit Brent whenever she could. Her vivacity complemented and leavened his reserve; he respected her abilities—he assumed she'd eventually become a medical doctor—and admired her character. Although Scowcroft recognized he "was more hard-driving" and "much more of an outdoors person than she was," he found her to be a "really good" person, and they fell in love.[87]

In July 1949 Army doctors judged Scowcroft's prognosis to be "excellent" and predicted he would be out of the hospital in three months' time. But Scowcroft's back failed to heal, so in January 1950 Army surgeons fused together three of his lower vertebrae as a substitute for the single crushed vertebra. Five months later, in May 1950, he still hadn't recovered from the surgery and continued to have a stiff back, making it difficult for him to bend forward and even more difficult—and painful—to bend backward.[88] And because the Army was scheduled to close its Valley Forge hospital in 1950 (it actually stayed open because of the Korean War and would remain in service until 1975), Scowcroft was transferred to St. Albans Naval Hospital on Long Island, about two miles north of what is now John F. Kennedy International Airport.

At St. Albans, Scowcroft slowly recovered, although he was temporarily set back in August 1950 with a kidney stone. He must have been feeling a little better, though, because in December 1950 he proposed to Jackie—who accepted.

———

BEUKEMA AND THE Air Force arranged for Scowcroft's admission to graduate school at Columbia University for the study of economics, set to begin in January 1952. But because Scowcroft was released from St. Albans in March 1951, the Army assigned him to Mather Air Force Base, a bombardier training facility just east of Sacramento, for the ten-month interim. The plan was for Scowcroft to train student navigators and student bombardiers, which would also allow him to accumulate the necessary flying hours to requalify him for his pilot's rating.[89]

Once Scowcroft was at Mather, however, the Air Force delayed his reappointment to flying duty until that November—a "dithering" and "wasting-away of time," in his description—notwithstanding the fact that in May 1951 the medical examining board had cleared him to fly. So instead of flying, which he'd very much looked forward to doing, Scowcroft was assigned to assist the supervision of the bachelor officers' and visiting officers' quarters. Scowcroft was miserable. Worse, he and Jackie, who had been transferred to Walter Reed Army Hospital, were a continent apart, and their frequent telephone conversations offered little solace.[90]

When the Air Force finally allowed Scowcroft to again take up the controls, only a few months remained before he was to begin graduate school. He nonetheless relished being back in the cockpit. He flew whenever he could during his last few weeks at Mather, both single-engine planes and twin-engine propeller aircraft. But as much as Scowcroft loved flying, no longer did he view it as his career; it was now an enjoyable pastime, an avocation rather than his vocation. Neither did Jackie think Brent should make flying the center of his Air Force career.[91]

For all of Scowcroft's frustrations while being stationed at Mather, his Officer Effectiveness Reports (the periodic evaluations that superior officers filled out to rate their subordinates; later called Officer Efficiency Reports) started to reflect the exceptional qualities Beukema and other West Point faculty had seen in him, and they suggested the new seriousness with which he pursued his career. Scowcroft's supervisors gave him the highest ratings possible in several categories, among them "setting a good example," "getting cooperation," "giving instruction," "taking responsibility," "solving problems," demonstrating "good judgment," complying with orders, showing loyalty, and being "fair and scrupulous." They judged him "open-minded and cooperative" and someone who clearly earned the "esteem and respect of his associates."[92]

At the end of the year, Scowcroft would leave California for Columbia University and New York. But first, he and Jackie got married. With their tight schedules (and with Jackie's parents both deceased), they didn't consider a wedding in Pennsylvania or Utah. In September, he flew down to Sumter, South Carolina, where Jackie was stationed. The two were wedded on Monday, September 17, 1951, in a small Catholic ceremony. Scowcroft's mother and two West Point classmates stationed at nearby Shaw Air Force Base attended the wedding. So did one of Jackie's close friends, a nursing colleague, who served as her maid of honor. No notice of the mixed-faith wedding appeared in the Ogden *Standard-Examiner*—a reflection of how life's pressures can disrupt the traditions of even a close-knit Mormon family such as the Scowcrofts.

In December, Brent and Jackie moved to New York, where they leased a small apartment in suburban Bronxville. Although Jackie resigned her Air Force nurse's commission upon marriage—she'd earlier been promoted to captain and outranked her fiancé—she remained committed to nursing and began to take classes at Columbia University's Teachers College toward a bachelor's degree in nursing education. Every morning Jackie and Brent would take the train down into the city.[93]

The twenty-six-year-old first lieutenant registered for graduate classes in Columbia's Department of Public Law and Government (as the Department of Political Science was then called) and dutifully enrolled in economics classes. But he also took courses in history, geography, and other disciplines over his eighteen months in residence. Making a particular impression was an international relations class, one in which guest lecturers would come up from Washington, DC each week.[94]

Scowcroft joined a close-knit group that included half a dozen other Army officers in his public law and government classes, but he didn't spend much time with the other graduate students. He recognized that the Army graduate students were "sort of a different species." "We knew where we were going," he said, both "more focused" and "probably a little older." And he generally preferred to study at home. As a serious student and newlywed, he had little cause to join his classmates in the coffeehouses or taverns in Morningside Heights or elsewhere in the city.[95]

Scowcroft loved graduate school. For the first time, he found learning enjoyable, even fascinating. Whereas West Point had been mostly rote learning, his graduate classes challenged him to think in much broader terms and engage on a more abstract level. Scowcroft was now more mature, more motivated, more receptive to new ideas, and better able to appreciate the broader relevance of his studies.[96]

Graduate school exposed Scowcroft to a sophisticated realm of ideas and a larger intellectual universe; it challenged him. What's more, his classes and teachers provided him with the tools to think about the development of the remarkable events that the nation had just lived through: the origins and outcomes of the Second World War, the new international order arising from Bretton Woods, the establishment of the United Nations, the Korean War, and the emergence of the Cold War. Especially compelling for Scowcroft was thinking about the potential for and dangers of nuclear weapons and figuring out the logic of their use. While he had always kept up with current events and closely followed the news, now he was learning the history and theory to make sense of it all.[97]

Professor William T. R. Fox, a prominent member of the Public Law and Government Department, took Scowcroft under his wing. Fox, a reserved but friendly man, had studied under Hans Morgenthau, one of the founders of the new academic discipline of international relations at the University of Chicago. Fox had edited *World Politics* for several years, helped establish the Yale Institute of International Studies (whose faculty included such notable scholars as Nicholas Spykman, Arnold Wolfers, and Ted Dunn), and had coined the term *superpower*.[98]

Fox was a prominent member of the realist school of foreign policy, a philosophy with which Scowcroft would later be associated. Realism, according to E. H. Carr and Hans Morgenthau, its two founders, is about the survival of states in a fundamentally anarchic world—one in which no overarching authority exists to enforce international agreements. Realism focuses on how states gain power, acquire wealth, and otherwise improve their position in a world of ambitious rival states, each of which must forge its own path in order to survive and further its interests. Scowcroft's years in graduate school gave him his first extended exposure to this important school of thought, which would help shape his approach to foreign policy challenges for decades to come.

Scowcroft also took classes with Professor Frank Tannenbaum, a renowned scholar of Latin American history and labor movements and a student of liberalism. He would invite Scowcroft and six or seven of his other students to his home, where they would talk over drinks. Whereas Fox was a realist, Tannenbaum focused on "the threads of human history," the importance of emotion, and the fact that people did not simply pursue their narrowest interests. He exposed the young graduate student to a more humanistic world.[99]

Although he described himself as "80 percent realist," Scowcroft didn't necessarily identify himself as a realist as such.[100] He never believed that realism wholly captured the history of American foreign policy or the motivations for US foreign policy decisions, nor did he think the prescriptions derived from realism were always the ones to follow.

Providing another perspective was Leland Goodrich, who taught international law. Goodrich wrote on the United Nations Charter, UN policies, and the UN's global role. Like Tannenbaum, Goodrich was something of an idealist and provided Scowcroft with a "fundamentally different outlook" on international relations—one that stayed with him, alongside Morgenthau's and Fox's realism and Tannenbaum's humanitarianism.[101]

But it was Professor Fox who supervised Scowcroft's MA thesis, "The Struggle for Trieste," which he described as "workmanlike" and "well written." Fox observed perceptively that the thesis's relative analytical weakness (as compared with its strength on the descriptive side) was the product of Scowcroft's regimented undergraduate training at the USMA and not an indicator of Brent's ability or promise. On the contrary, Fox regarded him as a serious student capable of further graduate study should he so choose.[102]

Scowcroft received his master's degree in June 1953, and in July he returned to his alma mater, first as an instructor in the Department of Social Sciences (1953–1954) and then an assistant professor (1954–1957).

Scowcroft's new path in life, shaped by the near-fatal crash he'd survived, now seemed clear. Instead of being in the cockpit, he'd be in the classroom.

4

SOLDIER–SCHOLAR

WHEN HE RETURNED to West Point in July 1953, Captain Scowcroft was pleasantly surprised to find he didn't have to teach economics. Thanks to another teacher's departure, he'd be teaching Russian history instead, one of the few electives the cadets could take and one of the subjects Scowcroft had studied at Columbia.

Scowcroft threw himself into his role as a member of the social sciences faculty with intelligence, dedication, and good humor. He was passionate about Russian history and cared for the cadets in his twelve-to-twenty-person sections. He used a combination of lecture and the Socratic question-and-answer method in his classes, methods that were similar to those he'd experienced as a cadet. He also participated in a new experimental language program for learning how to speak Russian, and voluntarily wrote a report that analyzed how the Russian history course could be further improved.

He taught two other electives, Modern European History and America and Contemporary Foreign Governments, in subsequent semesters. His supervising officer commented that Scowcroft was "a most skillful instructor" who obtained "a willing and enthusiastic response from the cadets he teaches." And a colleague noted that he was known to be "exceptionally hard working, bright," and a "great teacher."[103]

Scowcroft contributed outside the classroom in other ways. In March 1954 he took the Cadet Debating Team to Brooklyn College, and he joined a national group of academics to judge debates at the National Invitational Debate Tournament in April 1954.[104] He spent the summer of 1954 reviewing and selecting book chapters and journal articles for inclusion in *Readings in the History of Russia*, a reader for the sixty students in the advanced Russian history classes. Then, in his second year at West Point, he worked as assistant officer in charge of the Rhodes Scholar committee, encouraging interested cadets to apply, helping them though the application process, and conducting numerous personal interviews. Three cadets were selected as Rhodes Scholars in 1954–1955, the most ever selected from West Point in a single year and a high number for any college or university.

Scowcroft also served as a roundtable chairman for West Point's annual Student Conference on United States Affairs (SCUSA) in his second, third, and fourth years at the USMA. SCUSA, which began at West Point in 1949, was a "very big deal," a three-day conference that drew hundreds of students from colleges and universities around the United States to discuss contemporary issues and attend panels led by dozens of leading civilian and military experts. SCUSA was where Scowcroft first met the slightly younger Harvard PhD Zbigniew Brzezinski.[105]

Scowcroft's investment in the Russian language program, his work with Rhodes Scholar candidates, and his help with SCUSA reflected his keen sense of duty as well as his ability to work efficiently with minimal supervision.

Brent and Jackie lived in the so-called Gray Ghost faculty housing at West Point—recently constructed two-and three-bedroom duplex wood-frame townhomes. Jackie, a devout Catholic, ran a Catholic Sunday school program together with Ruth Gorman, the wife of Brent's officemate Paul Gorman. "Very capable, outgoing, and pleasant," Jackie was "a pillar of the Catholic parish," Paul Gorman said. Joe Jordan's wife, Polly, was also "fast friends" with Jackie, and Joe described her as "very warm, outgoing," someone who "never shirked at pitching in with help." (Scowcroft credited Joe for taking "my eastern wife under his wing and [telling] her about being a western wife.") Not only did Jackie help other Catholic wives, but she assisted Mormon spouses with their religious services as well. She also continued to practice her nursing, often making trips down to New York City to work as a visiting nurse. Fridays were movie nights for Jackie and Brent.[106]

Scowcroft shared an office with three other young instructors on the second floor of the West Academic Building, overlooking the Plain. He was popular with his fellow faculty members, personable, and respected. When he had something to say, his colleagues paid attention—no doubt because of what one of his contemporaries described as the "uncommon ease, fluency, and confidence" with which he spoke, in combination with his seriousness. "His speeches always got a great deal of attention," Gorman said.[107] Indicatively, he was chosen to be West Point's representative at the annual meeting in New York City of the Academy of Political Science in the fall of 1953 and at a conference on academic freedom in the USSR in the spring of 1954, also in New York City.[108]

Yet Scowcroft didn't fully participate in the office jokes and banter. Despite his friendly and collegial personality, he wasn't one of the boys. He was slightly older than his colleagues and also outranked them, since he'd been promoted to captain in April 1953; his officemates were all lieutenants. He'd also been accepted into the PhD program at Columbia University, so in the 1954, 1955, and 1956 winter semesters, he drove down once a week to Columbia, a ninety-mile round trip, for his course work; none of his officemates were then in graduate school. Scowcroft was Air Force, too, whereas almost all of his department colleagues were Army. And the flying imposed extra demands on his time, since he had to drive up to Stewart Field to fly the trainers and log the hours needed for him to maintain his pilot's rating.[109]

Scowcroft's most distinguishing quality was his reserve. More inclined to listen than to speak, he kept his own counsel—a quality reinforced by his crash, the two years he had spent in military hospitals, and his father's death, sobering events that imparted a gravitas uncommon among young men. So if he was in some ways younger than his twenty-eight years, in other ways he was older. To some, he came across as aloof.[110]

Scowcroft's superior officers, Lt. Col. Charles Cannon and Colonel Beukema, remarked on Scowcroft's unusual qualities, particularly his exceptional sense of duty and moral integrity.[111] "Captain Scowcroft is a quiet, serious-minded, and ambitious young officer," Colonel Cannon wrote after Scowcroft's first two semesters teaching at West Point. "Habitually neat, orderly, and courteous, he maintains a dignified and superior military bearing." He showed "a maturity of thought and grasp of academic problems uncommon in officers of his grade and service."[112] Cannon and Beukema both remarked on Scowcroft's ability to work confidently, highly efficiently, and enthusiastically. With the exception of ambition, though, these aren't qualities typical of men still in their twenties.

Scowcroft's Officer Effectiveness Reports soon became "firewalled," or close to it, meaning that all of the marks on his reports were lined up on the far right side of the form. This superior performance put Scowcroft in a special group sometimes referred to as the "5 percenters"—officers in the top 5 percent of their cohort, selected for their potential as Army and Air Force officers. As one Army officer said a bit blasphemously, these "water walkers" were men who "could breeze right by Jesus Christ like he was in a rowboat and they had hydroplanes for shoes."[113]

The fact that the young social sciences faculty was full of 5 percenters was the result of design. Both Beukema, who was department head until

1954, and Col. George "Abe" Lincoln, Beukema's immediate successor, were strongly committed to reforming how Army officers were being trained. They wanted to make the social sciences curriculum more rigorous, more personalized, and better suited to motivating officers to think for themselves.[114]

By cultivating the brightest faculty possible at West Point and undertaking additional reforms, Beukema and Lincoln sought to inculcate what David Cloud and Greg Jaffe in their book *The Fourth Star* refer to as a wellspring of unconventional thinking and a culture of unabashed elitism.[115] And once a member of the elite social sciences faculty corps, an officer always remained a member.[116] Army generals Wesley Clark, Barry McCaffrey, and Daniel Christman, among others, had studied under Lincoln and then gone back to teach. Army generals John Abizaid, George Casey, Peter Chiarelli, and David Petraeus—the subjects of Cloud and Jaffe's *The Fourth Star*—had also returned to the Department of Social Sciences to teach. To this day, the department continues to try to "identify future Scowcrofts," in the words of department head Col. Michael Meese.[117]

Colonel Lincoln, like Beukema, exemplified the soldier-scholar. An owlish-looking man with a long, rectangular face, a large nose, fleshy jowls, and horn-rimmed glasses, he had been a Rhodes Scholar, had served as one of General Marshall's star aides, had been an adviser and confidant to General Eisenhower, and had been promoted to a general officer at the young age of thirty-eight. Lincoln had also been the Army's representative on the State-War-Navy Coordinating Committee—the predecessor of the National Security Council—and participated in the decision to use the atomic bomb against Japan.[118]

Yet soon after helping to decide the fate of Germany and Japan, establish NATO, and create the Department of Defense, he made an "extraordinary" decision, as Gen. Andrew Goodpaster described it: Lincoln calculated "he could contribute more to the national security of the United States not by progressing to the rank of four star general, but instead by abandoning his first star and returning to West Point to teach as a colonel." Lincoln's scholarly stature within the community of foreign-policy experts was such that he corresponded with and commented on papers by Paul Nitze, Henry Kissinger, Frank Barnett, and other prominent academics and public intellectuals. It was when Kissinger came down from Harvard to lecture at West Point that he and Scowcroft first met, in fact.[119]

Lincoln followed Beukema in wanting to make the Department of Social Sciences the "institutional engine" of the reform of Army education.[120] He realized that future Army leaders needed to understand the full scope of the challenges that the United States would face when mobilizing for total war. He saw that US Army officers would have to be capable of working in alliances with foreign military and civilian leaders, and that they had to be able to appreciate the difficulties accompanying the occupation of foreign countries and the challenges of dealing with peoples who espoused contrasting ideologies and differing faiths. In other words, the cadets needed to learn a lot more than physics, applied math, and engineering if they were going to be prepared for the world that awaited them; they needed to learn comparative politics, international relations, economics, and foreign languages.[121]

Lincoln and Beukema sought to encourage their students to study a few selected subjects and specific regions of the world. The Department of Social Sciences accordingly began to offer more electives and to require each cadet to write a short thesis. When Scowcroft returned to the USMA in the fall of 1953, he observed there was "not nearly so much rote memory" required as when he had been in a cadet.[122]

Scowcroft's very presence at West Point testified to Beukema's and Lincoln's efforts to foster a broad-minded and cerebral environment, since one of their initiatives for reducing the intellectual gap between West Point and the best civilian colleges and universities was to appoint more faculty who were either working on their doctorate or already had their PhD in hand.[123] They wanted their top students to have theoretical knowledge so that they wouldn't be treated as second-class citizens or "knuckle-draggers" at academic conferences. Interestingly, of those whom Beukema and Lincoln invited back, "relatively few . . . came from the top of the class." Rather, they were "very much picked for personality"—for their ability to serve as officer role models.[124]

As a result of these reforms, numerous officers recruited by Beukema and Lincoln began to flow through the academic pipeline, studying politics, economics, geography, or international relations. In 1956, for instance, a total of eighteen Army officers were enrolled in graduate programs at Columbia, Harvard, Princeton, and Yale.[125] Beukema and Lincoln supervised their handpicked officer corps by keeping in touch with their academic colleagues at the institutions training their officers. They corresponded with several of Scowcroft's Columbia professors, including Fox, Tannenbaum, and John Wuorinen in the Department of History. They were likewise acquainted with many of the faculty at Harvard, Princeton, and Yale.[126]

Beukema and Lincoln's reforms had their disadvantages. Because of the high proportion of young instructors and assistant professors rotating through the Department of Social Sciences, the few permanent members of the department's faculty had to become, in effect, full-time administrators. They had to evaluate cadets whom the department might want to bring back to teach and correspond with graduate school administrators to ensure that their selected officers would be admitted and then make satisfactory progress. The department head and his deputy also had to coordinate the curriculum with the constantly rotating officer faculty as well as supervise their junior colleagues, and then see to their officers' placement in the Army (and in the Air Force until 1959, when the Air Force Academy was completed). The administrative load was a heavy one.

Lincoln served as a role model, a mentor, and almost a father figure for Scowcroft, encouraging him and advising him on curricular matters and other issues. Scowcroft was "a particularly brilliant and dedicated officer," Lincoln wrote in his Officer Efficiency Report, "a stabilizing and leadership influence in an officer group, poised, cheerful, considerate, and farsighted." And when Lincoln asked Scowcroft during his third year if he'd stay a fourth—a request to which Scowcroft replied he wasn't sure, because he feared that another year at West Point would hurt his career—Lincoln assured him he'd take care of things. Scowcroft stayed on.[127]

Scowcroft credited Lincoln with furthering his intellectual and professional development and inspiring by example. In Scowcroft's eyes, Lincoln behaved the way someone who held an important administrative position should behave: he was thoroughly competent, he was curious and broadminded, and he was in control of his ego.[128] (Lincoln was also the mentor for another of Scowcroft's heroes, Andrew Goodpaster.[129]) Later, when Lincoln was head of President Nixon's Office of Emergency Preparedness (the predecessor to the Federal Emergency Management Agency, FEMA) and Scowcroft was deputy national security advisor, they talked to each other regularly.[130]

For Scowcroft's next assignment, the Army personnel office offered him a Japan-based billet as a pilot for troop transport aircraft, part of the Military Air Transport Service (now the Air Mobility Command). Flying Army personnel around the world held little appeal for Scowcroft, though, so he asked the personnel office for a position that would match his interests in strategic issues and Russian history and use his Russian-language skills. His dream job was a position at the US embassy in Moscow. The Army couldn't find an opening for him in the Soviet Union, but it was able to offer him a position as assistant air attaché to the US embassy in Belgrade— the senior US Air Force officer in Yugoslavia. The job involved collecting air intelligence of strategic or tactical value, advising the US ambassador on aviation issues, and representing and establishing goodwill for the US Air Force in Yugoslavia.[131]

To prepare for the job, the Army assigned Scowcroft to the USAF Special Activities Squadron at Fort Myer in Arlington, Virginia. So in August 1957 Brent and Jackie moved to a small rented apartment in Washington, DC, where he began taking classes at the Strategic Intelligence School, studying the fundamentals of strategic intelligence, the work of an attaché, security defense, photography, and intelligence collection.

Scowcroft also studied Serbo-Croatian at Georgetown University's School of Languages and Linguistics, with Jackie joining him in order to be prepared for living in Belgrade. In September 1958, she gave birth to their daughter, Karen.[132]

In the spring of 1959, the Air Force sent Scowcroft on temporary assignments at the Air Command and Staff College at Maxwell Air Force Base and the Aeronautical Chart and Information Center in St. Louis, Missouri, for further intelligence training.[133] In April 1959, Scowcroft was promoted to major, and in late May, Brent, Jackie, and their eight-month-old daughter left for Yugoslavia.[134]

Scowcroft looked forward to the assignment. Trieste, Italy, the subject of Scowcroft's master's thesis, lay just across Yugoslavia's northwestern border, on the Adriatic. Yugoslavia itself represented an experiment in communism. Under the rule of Marshal Josip Broz Tito, Yugoslavia was turning toward a workers' management model of industry and away from Soviet-style communism. Tito, because of his break with Stalin and the Soviet bloc in 1948, was a heretic in the international communist community. He was thereby the beneficiary of US foreign aid, including military assistance in the form of air and ground equipment and agricultural aid that allowed Yugoslavia to become more self-sufficient in wheat and corn.[135] Scowcroft had reason to think that the experience of living and working in Yugoslavia would be able to provide him with unusual insights into both Yugoslavia and communism, given that the Belgrade-Moscow relationship dominated Yugoslavia's foreign policy.[136]

As an "intelligence staff officer"—the Army's official title for the assistant air attaché position—Scowcroft was responsible for organizing confidential missions for gathering, evaluating, and reporting air intelligence on Yugoslavia and, when possible, Eastern bloc countries. Scowcroft adapted quickly, worked hard, and learned a lot. He dedicated himself to mastering Serbo-Croatian, using the language whenever possible and taking personal language lessons on the side. Although beset with provocations and "myriads of minor problems," Scowcroft was still able to develop new intelligence sources and to obtain important intelligence that other attachés had not previously recognized. His supervising officer noted that Scowcroft was "cool and observant," showed "great perception of the intelligence collection targets," and displayed "ingenuity, skill and tenacity in devising methods of collecting intelligence under the most adverse situations." Scowcroft performed his duties with "outstanding understanding, intelligence, skill, and judgment," and he had an "iron will."[137]

Scowcroft had other responsibilities. He had to maintain an inventory of all top-secret documents at the US embassy and ensure they were all properly logged, inventoried, handled, and, if necessary, destroyed. As the Air Force's representative, he was also in charge of the embassy's supply account. So he had to supervise a small Yugoslavian staff and fly to Wiesbaden, Germany, at least once a month to refresh the embassy's supplies. Scowcroft excelled in this capacity as well—the first time in his life he'd held a significant supervisory or administrative position—transforming a poorly organized office into a well-functioning and efficient one by the force of his example. Scowcroft's superiors in the embassy and Air Force noticed, and they respected and trusted the young assistant air attaché. By the end of Scowcroft's two-year tour, the visiting inspector had only words of praise for how well the supply account was being managed.[138]

A smaller part of his job—apart from his attendance at diplomatic functions—was flying the US ambassador and other VIPs around Yugoslavia. (In fact, while in Yugoslavia, Scowcroft made it a point to fly at every opportunity, whether to take US State Department or military officials around the country or to train on his own to keep up his pilot's rating and make up for his lost time in the air because of the crash.) In this way Scowcroft became acquainted with George Kennan, who served as US ambassador to Yugoslavia from 1961 to 1963. Decades later, when Scowcroft was Bush's national security advisor and the Cold War was winding down, Scowcroft invited Kennan down to the White House on several occasions to discuss US-Soviet relations and possible changes in the United States' strategic mission.[139]

In his memoirs, Kennan describes the Belgrade embassy staff in some detail—although the passage probably says as much about Kennan's passion for writing, his delight in description, and his willingness to paint in bold strokes as about the embassy staff:

> These were men of a different generation than my own. They had come up in a different sort of bureaucratic environment; less human, less personal,

vaster, more inscrutable, less reassuring. Some of them tended initially, to be wary, correct, faithfully pedantic, but withdrawn and in a sense masked. The studied absence of color, in personality and colored thought, had become a protective camouflage. But of course they were real people underneath, and in most instances very valuable and intelligent ones, in some instance highly competent and even talented. . . . They viewed me, I suspect, with a certain amused astonishment, enjoyed the rhetorical melodrama of my numerous telegraphic conflicts with the Department of State, were intrigued by the unorthodox reactions to the work they performed and the experiences they reported to me, and were aware—as I like to think—of the genuine respect and affection in which I came to hold them. For me, in any case, the Belgrade experience would have been worth it for the association with them alone.[140]

Much of this description could apply to Scowcroft. But rather than viewing Kennan with "a certain amused astonishment," he considered him "a breath of fresh air," Scowcroft later said. Kennan was an ambassador who brought intellectual interest to what could have been a dull, hardship assignment in a then-impoverished country.[141]

While at the embassy, Scowcroft also began research for his doctoral dissertation.[142] US-Yugoslavian relations were then entering a difficult phase. Tito hosted the Belgrade Conference of nonaligned nations while Scowcroft was in Yugoslavia—a bold maneuver that induced Soviet leader Nikita Khrushchev to reach out to Tito and invite him to Moscow. The result was a rapprochement between the Soviet Union and Yugoslavia.[143] But the US government declared a "Captive Nations Week" in the same period—and the list of nations included Yugoslavia. The declaration thus implied that the United States was committed to overthrowing Tito's regime, and a year later Congress stopped all aid to Yugoslavia and withdrew its most-favored-nation trade status.

Amid these changes in US-Yugoslavian relations and the increasingly ideological American domestic politics, Scowcroft asked William Fox how he could best profit from his time in Belgrade. Fox suggested that he research the influence of ideology on US foreign policy as a potential dissertation topic and use Yugoslavia as his case study.[144]

Scowcroft and other embassy employees had only limited exposure to current information, however, since they were living in a controlled environment: the only radio broadcasts they received were from Voice of America, they were without television, and the Pentagon and State Department cables mostly handled intelligence and top-secret traffic specific to Yugoslavia and the Balkans.[145]

Scowcroft found living in Yugoslavia highly instructive, as he had hoped. Most significant was that it altered his view of communism, giving him a fresh appreciation for the fact that Russia lacked natural boundaries that might protect it from invasion. Since Russia had long been vulnerable to invasion, he didn't find it at all surprising that Russian leaders sometimes tried to improve their security by extending their borders and by acquiring more territory within which they could maneuver.

He thus concluded that Soviet ideology—Marxism-Leninism, Stalinism, or other variants of communism—was essentially the servant of nationalism and Russia's own geopolitical insecurity. Scowcroft didn't deny that the Soviets were intent on military expansion and that it was fully consistent with communist ideology, but in his assessment the expansion was mostly being done in the cause of protecting the Russian heartland. He didn't think the Soviet Union was intent on world domination or that there was anything inherent "in the Slavic soul," as he put it, that necessitated the Soviet Union's geographical expansion.[146]

Although Scowcroft does not comment on how his study of Russian history and Soviet Communism accorded with McCarthyism and the Red Scare of the early- and mid-1950s, it would seem that the relatively junior and insulated positions he held during those years sheltered him from American national politics and the political climate of the period.

As much as Scowcroft liked his Yugoslavia assignment, Jackie "hated" it. Although Jackie had learned enough Serbo-Croatian to get around, she was more of a homebody than was her husband. She also had a baby girl to take care of and was living far away from her family and friends. Making things worse, the Yugoslavian secret police would harass the Scowcrofts' servants, making them report on everyone who visited the major each week. (Scowcroft, for his part, assumed as a matter of course that his phone was tapped and that the house was bugged.)[147]

The Scowcrofts returned to Washington in late August 1961. The Army assigned Brent to the Armed Forces Staff College in Norfolk—now the Joint Forces Staff College and part of the National Defense University—where he was to attend an intensive twenty-two-week program on joint and combined operations. Classes covered such subjects as the interrelationship of the military branches, the principles of joint command, the strategic, tactical, and logistical dimensions of joint command, and the organization and planning required for combined operations.[148]

Scowcroft excelled. He impressed the faculty as broadly intellectual, highly analytical, and very capable, and he appeared to enjoy mixing with students from the other services. He didn't find the Joint and Combined Operations program particularly challenging, though, probably because of his previous graduate studies, teaching experience, and work in Yugoslavia.[149]

An unfortunate side effect of having to attend classes full-time was that Scowcroft was unable to fly enough hours—a minimum of eight hours a month and one hundred hours a year—to keep his pilot's rating. So despite the fact he was judged to be "a cool and skillful" and "extremely competent pilot" whose "interest and active participation in flying [were] exemplary," he had to turn in his pilot's wings on January 1, 1962—along with a wristwatch, two flying jackets, coveralls, two helmets, and other issued equipment. Despite his initial choice as a West Point graduate, his training with the Army Air Corps, his demonstrated love of flying, and his evident skill, he never made senior pilot or, therefore, command pilot.[150]

In late 1961 the Army asked Scowcroft to fill in for Brig. Gen. Wesley Posvar, the head of the Department of Political Science in the new Air Force Academy in Colorado Springs, who would be on leave studying for his doctorate at Harvard. Scowcroft would be an associate professor from January 1962 through June 1962, serve as the deputy department head for the 1962–1963 academic year, and the acting department head in 1963–1964.[151]

Scowcroft welcomed the assignment, and following a two-week course on counterinsurgency at the State Department Foreign Service Institute, he and his family moved out to Colorado in January 1962. At the Air Force Academy he was chairman of First Class instruction, oversaw the two capstone classes on international relations and on defense policy, edited a new edition of the Air Force's *Readings in Defense Policy,* and was responsible for interviewing, evaluating, and selecting new instructors, advising the officer-instructors on their graduate education, and planning the curriculum. Scowcroft quickly gained the respect of the twelve instructors who were teaching the First Class courses.

On May 21, 1962, at the end of Scowcroft's first semester at the Air Force Academy, Professor Fox accepted his revised dissertation proposal (he'd submitted a draft of his dissertation proposal earlier that spring). Scowcroft spent the summer of 1962 at Columbia University working on his doctoral dissertation. He then returned to the Air Force Academy to serve as deputy department head.

His promotion brought additional responsibilities. Besides continuing as the chairman of First Class instruction for the nearly six hundred cadets who were taking courses in international relations and defense policy and the dozen instructors teaching the courses, he helped formulate department policy. He supervised course directors and instructors. He represented the department at faculty meetings, where he could act with the authority of the department head if he had to. He also helped the department head, Col. William McDonald, supervise and guide the Third Class political science classes and plan the Cadet Assembly (attended that year by secretary of state Dean Rusk).

In the summer of 1963, Scowcroft returned to Washington, DC, to do more work on the dissertation. He, Jackie, and their daughter lived in a small apartment in the Meridian Park neighborhood, and during the week Scowcroft would hole up in the Library of Congress, researching and writing. He continued working on the dissertation once he got back to Colorado Springs, finding time at night or on weekends. "Agony" was Scowcroft's description of the writing process.[152] Later that fall, he submitted a final draft to his committee for their approval.

Upon his return to Colorado Springs, Scowcroft was promoted to professor and began his role as the acting head of the Department of Political Science. Whereas he had previously taught three courses each semester, he now taught only one. He impressed the dean of the faculty, Brig. Gen. Robert F. McDermott, as a highly "dedicated, sincere, loyal, and hard working" officer who was always concerned about the mission above his own welfare.[153]

Scowcroft had also been able to boost morale among the political science faculty "higher than it had ever been," McDermott pointed out.[154] This was no small feat, since the new Air Force Academy still had its rough edges and was still developing its guiding principles. In recognition of his "outstanding leadership, knowledge, and initiative" on behalf of the Political Science Department and the Air Force Academy, Scowcroft was awarded an Air Force Commendation Medal.[155]

=====

ALTHOUGH SCOWCROFT LIKED being a professor and enjoyed academic life, he was "too restless" to stay long at the US Air Force Academy or at any other teaching job. He worried he'd stagnate; he'd seen some of his professors at Columbia, "eminent names in their field"—not Fox or Tannenbaum, he volunteered—come into the classroom, deliver the same lecture they had given for the past ten or fifteen years or so, take questions, and then leave. He feared a merely routine job. He wanted assignments that demanded a wide range of skills, involved a variety of activities, and exposed him to new and important challenges. Above all, he wanted to be closer to the formation of US national security policy.[156] So even as Scowcroft thrived in Colorado Springs, he wasn't eager to stay on.[157]

Scowcroft was promoted to lieutenant colonel in July 1964. That same summer, the Air Force assigned him to a high-level staff position at Air Force headquarters in the Pentagon, just as his superior officers had recommended. Scowcroft, Jackie, and their daughter moved back to Washington. Jackie took moving households in stride—as her niece later observed, she could "put up with anything" for the sake of her family—and wherever she went, she took with her the ability to cook "the best beef stroganoff in the world."[158]

Scowcroft's presence in the Pentagon was unusual. His stellar military record was unaccompanied by any line assignments. He hadn't flown in a fighter squadron during the Korea War or led any fighter or bomber wings in Vietnam, Thailand, or elsewhere in Southeast Asia. Neither had he led any Air Force squadrons in Great Britain, Germany, or other countries with US air bases. Nor had he commanded Air Force training facilities, flight operations, or missile installations. (By way of comparison, Edwin Robertson, Scowcroft's classmate at West Point and in flight school in Texas and Arizona, fought in South Korea, served as vice commander of a tactical fighter wing in Vietnam, commanded a tactical fighter wing in Germany, was vice commander of the Sixteenth Air Force in Spain, and commanded the Chanute Technical Training Center in Illinois.[159]) Scowcroft's only command assignment had been as an administrator—as the deputy head and then acting head of the Air Force Academy's Political Science Department.

Scowcroft appreciated the fact that his commanding officers were willing to treat him differently. The Air Force "always made exceptions for me," he recognized. It "always supported me" and "was very tolerant of a maverick."[160] It didn't hurt that he had what in Air Force slang was called a "40 lb. cranium."

Scowcroft was in this sense following in the steps of one of his heroes, Gen. Andrew Goodpaster, who had been one of Eisenhower's most trusted foreign policy advisers and later served under Presidents Kennedy, Johnson, and Nixon. Goodpaster was also a West Point graduate who earned a PhD in international relations and was an extremely capable and highly effective officer.[161]

Over the next six years, however, Scowcroft's life as a soldier-scholar would end. He was about to become a "blue suiter"—one of the many senior Air Force officers at the Pentagon distinguished by their blue Air Force uniforms.[162] He would have to dedicate his considerable talents to the bureaucratic needs of the Air Force, Office of the Joint Chiefs of Staff, and Office of the Secretary of Defense—the next stage in an education that would ultimately lead him to the very top of the national security apparatus.

5

BLUE SUITER

THE PERSON WHO had the greatest influence on Scowcroft's development as a strategist wasn't George Lincoln, Herman Beukema, or any of his other West Point or Air Force Academy teachers. Neither was he William Fox, Frank Tannenbaum, or any of Scowcroft's other Columbia professors. Nor was he any of the leaders Scowcroft would work with during his later career, such as Andrew Goodpaster, Henry Kissinger, or Richard Nixon. Rather, he was an extremely smart, very energetic, and highly respected Air Force major general by the name of Richard A. Yudkin.[163]

General Yudkin, six years older than Scowcroft, was a graduate of the Army Command and General Staff College at Fort Leavenworth—whose alumni include Dwight Eisenhower, Andrew Goodpaster, Omar Bradley, and Douglas MacArthur—and the Air Command and Staff College at Maxwell Air Force Base in Alabama. In author Fred Kaplan's description, he was "rotund, Jewish, bookish, a bachelor with no hobbies or interests outside the Air Force." (He was also "semi-bald," Scowcroft added.) What made Yudkin's stellar Air Force career that much more exceptional was the fact that he was nonrated: he'd never qualified as a pilot, but had risen through the ranks by virtue of the quality of his mind. By the mid- to late 1960s, Yudkin had become the "intellectual master" of a new generation of Air Force staff officers who studied nuclear warfare.[164]

Together with the Air Force chief of staff, Gen. Thomas D. White, Yudkin established the single integrated operations plan (SIOPS) for US strategic forces, replacing the old plan that had simply aggregated the plans of the various service branches, leading to redundancy and illogic. Yudkin had also worked closely with the RAND Corporation, where he'd supervised James Schlesinger. When Scowcroft began working for him, Yudkin had just returned from serving in NATO and was deputy director of advanced planning at Air Force headquarters.[165]

In mid-1964 Scowcroft relocated to Washington following his two and a half years at the Air Force Academy. He bought a modest two-story brick house in Bethesda, Maryland, just north of the District, and Jackie began working part-time as a nurse. Their daughter attended the local Bethesda elementary school.[166]

The Air Force assigned Scowcroft to the Directorate of Doctrine, Concepts, and Objectives, where he filled two separate positions—first with the Policy Planning Studies Program (1964–1965), then with Long Range Planning (1965–1966). In both jobs, Scowcroft worked on sensitive projects involving the Air Force's future force structure. One of his assignments, for instance, was to determine the optimal balance in the United States' nuclear arsenal between the number and type of Strategic Air Command bombers and the number and configuration of intercontinental ballistic missiles (ICBMs).

In order to develop and design concepts that could be applied to future aerospace operations, Scowcroft had to elicit, coordinate, and evaluate proposals from Air Force staff agencies as well as from the industrial, scientific, and academic communities, including the RAND Corporation. This meant that he had to help Yudkin and others in the Air Force assess how the Air Force's contributions to national security meshed with other governmental, cultural, and societal factors. Scowcroft then had to integrate these analyses into the Air Force's and the Joint Chiefs of Staff's long-range plans, draft comprehensive reports on these assessments, and brief senior officers.[167]

Scowcroft applied his usual intelligence and initiative to his responsibilities. He coordinated with the policy expert, academic, and industrial communities. He negotiated with representatives from the State and Defense Departments. He expanded the Air Force's contacts with the research and academic communities through written correspondence and by attending conferences. And he prepared and staffed out—that is, assigned groups of officers to execute—proposals that recommended how to improve the joint functions of the Air Force's plans for future operations.[168]

He learned quickly, and the longer he worked with Doctrine, Concepts, and Objectives, the more responsibilities he took on. Among his accomplishments was the preparation of Part II of *USAF Planning Concepts,* which provided long-range direction and guidance, projecting as many as fifteen years ahead. He was the project manager for three policy planning studies done by academic scholars under contract with the Air Force, which, according to his superior officer, constituted "important reference documents for strategy and policy formation in both [the] Department of Defense and . . . the State Department." He was also "assigned the task of developing a rationale and methodology to improve the capability of the Air Staff to deal with issues of critical importance to the Air Force."[169]

Scowcroft's success as a staff officer grew in part from his ability to balance the qualities of independence, initiative, and self-confidence with those of loyalty and discipline. In pursuit of his objectives and those of his superior officers, he could be creative, resourceful, and even entrepreneurial in his dealings with the military bureaucracy. At the same time, he was a team player. With his cheerful and straightforward demeanor, his quiet leadership, and the force of his own example, he was able to disarm or deflect almost all potential personal clashes or bureaucratic conflicts. He was also completely loyal to the Air Force. So when his superior officers decided on a course of action, Scowcroft could be counted on to carry it out.

Navigating the contrary currents in the Pentagon during the 1960s wasn't easy. Many in the military strongly disliked secretary of defense Robert McNamara and those who surrounded him, and the feeling was mutual. Scowcroft's West Point classmate Gen. Robertson described the period as "extremely disagreeable," "an era of total arrogance . . . by young, bright, or maybe even brilliant, members of the McNamara staff."[170] Fortunately, Scowcroft didn't join the Pentagon until after the Kennedy administration (although McNamara himself stayed on through February 1968).

The overall atmosphere in Washington was toxic. "I didn't like the way we, within the military, treated our own people," Robertson remarks. "I certainly didn't like the way I was treated by the civilians on the Secretary of Defense staff." Furthermore, it was a "difficult period in the Washington area anyway because of the beginnings of the anti-war movement" and because life "was becoming more and more difficult" for military personnel living in the area.[171] Worse, as H. R. McMaster and Thomas E. Ricks point out, the top brass were themselves compromised, with Gen. Maxwell Taylor, Gen. William Westmoreland, Gen. Earle Wheeler, and others willing to go along with what Kennedy and Johnson and their advisers wanted. Even two of Scowcroft's own mentors, Col. George Lincoln and Gen. Goodpaster, had their analyses pushed aside by their fellow military officers. Scowcroft, though, said that these issues did not affect him much and that he did not experience them personally.[172]

Scowcroft dealt with these conflicts by compartmentalizing. Once his superiors at Air Force Headquarters, the Office of the Secretary of Defense, or the Joint Chiefs of Staff received his reports, his job was done. Scowcroft then accepted the decisions that were subsequently made, irrespective of his former positions.[173] He did not complain, question, or challenge the decisions made or attempt to maneuver around them. Nor did he passively resist his superiors' decisions by delaying implementing them or ignoring them—tactics officials often use to avoid taking actions that run contrary to their own preferences.

This ability to divorce his own ego from his professional performance distinguished Scowcroft from most other blue suiters and policy experts. It was a quality that caused Scowcroft's colleagues to see him as both the quintessential team player and an independent-minded officer of impeccable integrity. People trusted him. They recognized he was acting on behalf of the Air Force, the Department of Defense, the Joint Chiefs, or the president of the United States, whichever the case might be, and not trying to enhance his own reputation or feather his own nest. He succeeded at appealing to his colleagues' better angels.

In all these ways, Scowcroft could be considered the ideal "staff man," as described by NSC staff member Jeanne W. Davis in her paper "The Role of the Coordinative Staff Officer":

> The coordinative staff man must accept the fact that his responsibility greatly exceeds his authority; indeed, the staff officer has no authority in his own right, but only that which he acquires as an extension of the official personality of the executive he serves. A good staff man can usually work with this shadow authority, rarely if ever finding it necessary to invoke the authority of his principal. Indeed, a demand by a staff officer for exercise of authority by his executive to force compliance with his wishes is a confession of weakness and ineptitude. Given this fact, the wise staff officer comports himself in his dealing with others in the manner best designed to persuade them to do his will. The staff man cannot afford the luxury of temperament. It can never be said of a staff man that "he's a so-and-so but he gets results." In staff work, a "so-and-so" does not get results.[174]

In recognition of Scowcroft's "singularly distinctive accomplishments" in the period from September 1964 to July 1967, the Air Force in December 1971 would award him the Legion of Merit. "Lt. Col. Brent Scowcroft," the citation read, "distinguished himself by exceptionally meritorious conduct in the performance of outstanding service to the United States." His "exemplary ability, diligence, and devotion to duty . . . were instrumental factors in the resolution of many complex problems of major importance to the Air Force." Earlier that year, in March, he received the Joint Chiefs of Staff Identification Badge, an award given for his "important and loyal service in a position of responsibility in support of the Joint Chiefs of Staff."[175]

If Scowcroft got results, it also meant that he heeded the authority of his ultimate superiors, persons such as Air Force General Curtis LeMay, who was appointed Air Force vice chief of staff in 1957 and chief of staff in 1961, and other Air Force leaders. Scowcroft did not regard questioning the Air Force leadership, whether that of LeMay; Gen. Thomas S. Power, the commander-in-chief of the Strategic Air Command from 1957–1964; or of other military and civilian leaders, as consistent with his role as a military officer. Nor was it part of his personality.

Scowcroft admitted he found neither staff position very stimulating. Notwithstanding his noteworthy achievements, Scowcroft thought that neither job really seemed to affect US national security policy at the end of the day—and both involved extensive paperwork and speechwriting. The best thing about being at Air Force headquarters, Scowcroft said, was being able to work closely with Richard Yudkin.[176]

Yudkin was a genuine mentor to Scowcroft, someone who taught him how to be an effective staff officer and policy adviser and who cared about his professional development and future career.[177] Yudkin had exacting standards. He was extremely hardworking. And he expected those associated with him to abide by those same standards. He set an example of how to manage national security issues and to administer personnel.[178]

Scowcroft learned how the Defense Department and the military establishment operated, thanks to Yudkin's stature in the Air Force and to his many contacts throughout the Air Force, industry, and the research community. He began to see how it was possible to get things done in the vast, intricate, and politically fraught bureaucratic environment of defense policy. Perhaps even more important, Yudkin was farsighted and got Scowcroft to think rigorously about the relationship between the Air Force's strategic bombing and its tactical missions. He "gave me a feel for the whole of the NATO mission, the whole issue of alliances, and raised my sights in a very interesting way," Scowcroft said. For example, he caused Scowcroft to rethink what the Italian military theorist Giulio Douhet had said about what kind of bombing was appropriate. (Douhet believed that command of the air meant victory because of the offensive potential of air power, its use in total war against an opponent, and its damaging effects on enemy morale—to the detriment of air defense and the use of air power for tactical support for ground or sea operations.)[179]

Scowcroft's relationship with Yudkin was similar to his later relationship with Henry Kissinger. Yudkin and Kissinger were both highly accomplished, extremely demanding, and had great affection for Scowcroft. However, Yudkin was the more patient of the two, the more generous with his time, the more hands-on as a teacher, and he served as Scowcroft's mentor for a longer period. He was "more influential than Kissinger," Scowcroft said. "He actually told me how to get things done, how to think." What's more, he brought Scowcroft to the attention of Air Force leaders, thereby helping to prepare the way for his subsequent promotion to colonel and, eventually, general officer.[180]

After Scowcroft had submitted his dissertation, he learned that his advisory committee wanted him to cut its length in half.[181] The news did not wholly surprise him, as he had deliberately erred on the side of writing too inclusively, knowing that he normally wrote too sparely for most readers' tastes. But this meant that it had to be rewritten, in effect. Somehow, using odd hours and weekends, he managed to find the time to do it, submitting a final draft in the fall of 1966.[182]

"Congress and Foreign Policy: An Examination of Congressional Attitudes Toward the Foreign Aid Programs to Spain and Yugoslavia" compared congressional policy toward Spain and Yugoslavia during the Cold War. The dissertation started from the premise that the United States *had* to cooperate with Yugoslavia and Spain out of strategic necessity, even though both countries had governments antithetical to American democratic values: Spain had a fascist government under the dictatorship of Generalissimo Francisco Franco, and Yugoslavia had a Marxist government under Marshal Tito. Yet Spain was vital to European and Western security and had three major US Air Force bases, just as Yugoslavia formed a bulwark against Soviet domination in Eastern Europe and the Balkans.[183]

Since Spain and Yugoslavia had undemocratic governments with contrasting ideologies, Scowcroft sought to determine how Congress's foreign aid to the two differed. After analyzing years of roll call votes and congressional testimony, he discovered that Congress voted on a more ideological basis with respect to socialist Yugoslavia than it did with Falangist Spain. Congress protected aid to Spain under Franco and defended its aid program against what some members of Congress perceived as the hostility of the executive branch, whereas it cut funding and restricted foreign aid to Yugoslavia. He found, too, that congressional conservatives were more influential in setting US foreign policy than liberals (and this was before "liberal" and "conservative" in American politics became almost synonymous with "Democratic" and "Republican"). Religious and southern conservatives in Congress were especially influential, particularly when foreign aid issues became tinged with emotional and ideological overtones. Congress was more conservative on US foreign aid decisions than was the executive branch, he also discovered—even during Republican presidencies. Nor were members of Congress likely to be persuaded by White House arguments based on pragmatic considerations or on the United States' national interests.[184]

Scowcroft defended the dissertation in April 1967, and he received his PhD in political science from Columbia University on June 6, 1967, at the age of forty-two.[185]

For the 1967–1968 academic year, Yudkin and other Air Force leaders recommended that Scowcroft attend the National War College. Classes there would prepare him for a joint staff appointment by increasing his knowledge of the many components of the national security establishment and rounding out his education. He would then be ready to be promoted to general officer.[186]

Attending the National War College held little appeal for Scowcroft. He felt he had already spent too much time in classrooms, not to mention the added research and writing he'd done for his PhD in international relations. So he turned down Yudkin's offer the first time, but accepted it the second time around. He ended up being glad he went, as he found the whole experience "extremely broadening."[187]

The National War College, located at Fort Lesley J. McNair in southeast Washington, DC, represents the pinnacle of postgraduate training for US military officers. Each year, the NWC selects outstanding military officers from the four services along with highly rated officials from the Department of State, the CIA, the Treasury Department, the Department of Commerce, and other federal agencies. It then trains them to plan national security policy and formulate grand strategy. The 140 military officers and federal officials chosen for the intense ten-month program are typically the most senior officials attending any of the military's postgraduate programs.[188] Army Gen. Wesley Clark, Adm. Elmo Zumwalt, Army Gen. Colin Powell, USMC Gen. Anthony Zinni, Air Force Gen. Norton A. Schwartz (President Obama's first Air Force chief of staff), and USMC Gen. James L. Jones (Obama's first national security advisor) were all graduates of the National War College, as was Scowcroft's one-time officemate Paul Gorman.

The premise of the NWC's forty-three-week curriculum is that the students are members of the National Security Council staff who have been directed to come up with policies that meet the United States' strategic requirements. The program therefore teaches students the comprehensive skills needed for planning national policy, securing the resources for implementing strategy, and exercising the joint and combined high-level policy, staff, and command functions. The students learn about the complex scientific, political, psychological, and social factors that influence US national security and the United States' capacity to wage warfare successfully. By attending with others from throughout the government, students are supposed to become familiar with the roles, functions, and missions of the other military services and other government departments and agencies. The expectation is that the seminar discussions will cause students to say, "Well, I never thought of looking at it that way."[189]

Scowcroft's classes were arranged in a sequence of blocks, with each class lasting from seven days to six weeks. The introduction to the ten-month course of study was a four-week "statement of the problem"; the second part, which lasted twenty-four weeks, featured separate classes on "the facts bearing on the problem"; and the final thirteen weeks incorporated a three-week overseas field trip.[190]

Scowcroft's courses included US Military Capability and Strategy, the International Environment and US Interests in the World Today, National Security Policymaking, and Problems of Subversive Insurgency, as well as courses on "free Europe," the Western Hemisphere, the Communist states, and other regions of the world. The classes included lectures, discussions, group projects, field trips, and guest lectures by prominent academics, high-ranking military officers, well-known journalists, and leaders from the business world, the intelligence community, and the defense industry.

Scowcroft's capstone field trip was a journey with a small group of classmates from March 20 to April 8, 1968, to the Middle East, including Israel, Turkey, Lebanon, and Iran, with additional stops in Pakistan, India, and Spain. (Other groups took trips to Africa, the Far East, or Europe.) Scowcroft found his first trip to the Middle East "fascinating" and "extremely enlightening." Not only did he get a sense of the culture, climate, and life in an area of the world new to him, but he met with top policy makers and military leaders from various countries—including an hour-and-a-half visit with the shah of Iran.[191]

If Scowcroft didn't find the readings and class discussions particularly challenging or innovative—not surprising, perhaps, considering his extensive academic experience—the "most important thing" that the National War College provided him, he said, was that he "got to know the people from the other services" and "understand other perspectives."[192] The experience enabled him to build relationships with others across the government—in the Navy, Marine Corps, Coast Guard, State Department, and CIA, as well as in the two branches he was already familiar with, the Army and the Air Force. Later, when Scowcroft was working in the White House and needed to speak with someone in a particular department or agency, he often used contacts he had made at the NWC.[193]

Scowcroft's required research paper, titled "Deterrence and Strategic Superiority," described and illustrated the problems with measuring and operationalizing the concept of strategic superiority. Because of the varying definitions of the term, Scowcroft warned, policy makers who used the phrase uncritically risked dangerously oversimplifying complex problems. Scowcroft later published the paper in the foreign policy journal *Orbis*.[194]

Being at the National War College further allowed Scowcroft to become acquainted with General Goodpaster, who was commandant in the 1967–1968 academic year (Yudkin, who was friends with Goodpaster, introduced the two of them). Scowcroft admired Goodpaster's careful and thoughtful approach to problems. He appreciated his patient and respectful handling of people. And he liked Goodpaster's quiet and unobtrusive style: reserved, highly disciplined, deliberate in speech, unflappable, and self-confident. Scowcroft saw that Goodpaster didn't put himself before others and wasn't manipulative. Goodpaster let the ideas speak for themselves, rather than advocating them dogmatically; he was "gentle and intellectual," in Scowcroft's description, "not forceful and not bragging." He felt that they both "thought very much alike."[195] Scowcroft and Goodpaster later worked together on the Atlantic Council in the late 1970s and the 1980s, and they remained in touch when Scowcroft was national security advisor under President George H. W. Bush.[196]

But they had their differences. Goodpaster would become a member of the Committee on the Present Danger—something Scowcroft later said he didn't know about Goodpaster—and close to Edward Teller, Albert Wohlstetter, James Schlesinger, Caspar Weinberger, and other hardcore anti-Soviet hawks, many of them associated with 1980s neoconservatism. Goodpaster would also be an early supporter of the Strategic Defense Initiative ("Star Wars"), whereas Scowcroft, as we shall see, remained a skeptic.

———

SCOWCROFT RETURNED TO the Pentagon, where he held three offices in quick succession: country director for Ecuador, Peru, Bolivia, and Paraguay in the Western Hemisphere Region in the Office of the Assistant Secretary of Defense on International Security Affairs (1968–1969); deputy assistant for National Security Council matters in the Directorate of Plans (1969–1970); and special assistant to Air Force Gen. John W. Vogt in the Office of the Joint Chiefs of Staff (1970–1971).

In the first job, Colonel Scowcroft—he was promoted on July 1, 1968—helped design and execute US military policy regarding Ecuador, Peru, Bolivia, and Paraguay (as well as for Latin America more generally). The position incorporated many separate responsibilities, just as he preferred. As the liaison to the air forces of these four friendly Latin American countries, all of which used US-made equipment, Scowcroft implemented military arms sales and monitored their execution, helped plan joint exercises, and coordinated policy and practices with the personnel of their respective air forces (many of whom were US-trained). Not that the late 1960s was an easy period for US relations with most Latin American countries.

The job also required Scowcroft to help formulate diplomatic and military strategy on sensitive and complex matters involving the United States' security interests in the four countries and the region. He had to recommend Defense Department positions on proposals originating from the State Department. Scowcroft was further responsible for managing important special projects involving US policies in Latin America, drafting studies for the National Security Council (the most significant a study of overall US policy toward Latin America), and consulting daily with his counterparts in other US agencies and the military attachés of Latin American governments.[197]

As deputy to the special assistant for Vietnamization from 1969 to 1970 in the Directorate of Plans, Scowcroft's next job was to oversee the US Air Force's component of the Vietnamization program. The purpose of Vietnamization was to transfer the burden of the war to the South Vietnamese through the withdrawal of US forces, replacement of American personnel by South Vietnamese personnel, and transfer of US equipment to the South Vietnamese armed forces—the Vietnamese army (ARVN), air force (VNAF), navy (VNN), and marines (VNMC). Although the Vietnamization policy had originated under defense secretary Robert McNamara and President Johnson in 1967, Nixon made it the United States' top priority in 1969 and the centerpiece of his plan for "peace with honor." Vietnamization stood as the chief manifestation of Nixon's (and Kissinger's) strategy of the United States working more through allied governments in lieu of acting directly on its own so as to reduce the costs of US foreign engagement.[198]

Air Force leaders handpicked Scowcroft for the job of integrating and uniting all of the Vietnamization efforts for the secretary of the Air Force and the Air Force chief of staff. The fact that he had little guidance about how to proceed and little direct supervision gave him further opportunity to use his initiative. Scowcroft could define the scope of operations, decide how different functions would be divided, and determine who would play what roles in the transfer of US Air Force matériel and military operations to the VNAF. He then supervised the handover of US Army aviation units—helicopters, equipment, and maintenance operations—to newly activated VNAF helicopter squadrons. He oversaw the transfer of C-123 cargo planes to the VNAF (USAF instructors, meanwhile, trained Vietnamese pilots to fly the C-123s as well as C-5s). He started the relinquishing of air base commands to VNAF officers and directed the redeployment of US Air Force and Army aviation personnel.

He also represented the Air Force in all Joint Chiefs decisions regarding Vietnamization. Some of these decisions involved psychological warfare. In order to boost South Vietnamese morale, for instance, the Air Force and other services established Operation Limelight, which the US Air Force history office described as "a public affairs program designed to lift the VNAF's *esprit de corps* of the troops and give more recognition to their performance and progress."[199]

Particularly impressive about Scowcroft's performance was his ability to assemble almost overnight a staff consisting of personnel from different Air Force agencies and forge them into an effective and responsive organization. He organized a series of comprehensive briefings for the relevant units within the Air Force and for other agencies in order to coordinate the extensive transfers. And because of his ability to collaborate effectively with others, his efforts were quickly recognized and readily accepted throughout the Pentagon.[200]

By objective indicators, the Air Force's Vietnamization program was highly successful—especially in consideration of the fact that Nixon's decision to speed up the training and equipping of the South Vietnamese military imposed significant additional demands on the Air Force and Joint Chiefs of Staff. The VNAF expanded from 19,000 people in late 1968 to 45,000 in early 1970 and 64,000 by 1973. The recruiting and training of VNAF pilots and specialists grew in parallel, and US Air Force mobile training teams helped to upgrade Vietnamese maintenance and logistics facilities.[201] As a result, the VNAF participated in a much larger share of all air operations in South Vietnam during 1969, according to a history produced by the Joint Chiefs of Staff, with total VNAF sorties rising from 54,900 in the first quarter of 1969 to 73,700 in the last quarter. And by 1970, the US command in South Vietnam rated the VNAF combat performance on a par with that of American units.[202]

As a practical reality, however, in terms of South Vietnam actually becoming militarily self-reliant, Vietnamization was a failure. It would not have been necessary—or even possible—without the previous "Americanization" of the war in the late 1950s and early 1960s because of the vulnerabilities of the government of South Vietnam under Ngo Dinh Diem. Yet Americanization had the perverse effect of depriving the Vietnamese armed forces of the experience and responsibility they needed to successfully defend South Vietnam and wage war against the North Vietnamese.[203]

So when Vietnamization began in 1967, it was a cynical exercise almost certainly doomed to failure, since the South Vietnamese air force, like other components of the South Vietnamese military, was neither sufficiently trained nor sufficiently motivated to succeed in taking over from the US armed forces. However great the quality and quantity of US matériel, the VNAF, like the South Vietnamese army, navy, and marine corps, suffered from a number of serious problems. Among them were problems of morale (low pay and desertions), a deficiency in leadership (the low quality and shortage of leaders), poor training (the lack of standardization, the low quality of instructors, and weak logistical support), and inadequate maintenance (the shortage of sufficiently experienced personnel, since military equipment cannot function without regular high-quality maintenance).[204]

Without much experience, with little professionalism, and with corruption rampant among the Vietnamese military and the civilian government, the South Vietnamese armed forces were ill positioned to benefit from Vietnamization. Nixon, Kissinger, and their top military and civilian advisers knew these facts full well, and few US officials actually believed the South Vietnamese would be able to hold their own against the North. However, they hoped at least to buy some time to separate a peace agreement from the eventual withdrawal of all US support of South Vietnam. To prop up the regime long enough to establish this "decent interval," the administration was expanding US military activities in Cambodia and, on occasion, massively bombing North Vietnam even as it transferred equipment and withdrew US forces.[205] Thus, the "decent interval" later established through the 1973 Hanoi peace agreement pointed to the discrepancy between American rhetoric and the uncomfortable facts on the ground.

Vietnamization was but a fig leaf for defeat, the historian Robert Dallek writes. Scowcroft conceded that he "thought it was an uphill battle all along" and that "the overall outcome was against it succeeding" (although he added that the overall strategy was not of his own doing).[206] As one Pentagon official put it, "Vietnamization was like getting nine women pregnant in order to have a baby in one month."[207]

Scowcroft may have had his own ideas about how the war should be run, but as an Air Force colonel and staff officer, he knew his views did not matter. Years later, though, Scowcroft expressed his doubts about the US government's policies. While he believed in the basic merits of the war and the containment doctrine that was the war's underlying rationale, he also believed that a whole generation of US political and military leaders had behaved irresponsibly. They had never thoroughly, methodically, and dispassionately deliberated over exactly what the United States hoped to accomplish in Vietnam, he said, and never determined precisely what steps the United States should take to achieve its goals.[208]

At the time, though, Scowcroft enjoyed the challenges posed by Vietnamization, especially compared to the drudgery of the paperwork and speechwriting required in his previous Pentagon assignments. "In a way I enjoyed Vietnamization. I had to deal with the real world and real problems," he noted. He was a professional military officer with a job to do, and by all accounts he did it superbly. "There was not a single incident of failure in a serious of high priority tight suspense actions," Scowcroft's supervising officer reported. His personnel ratings were consistently "absolutely superior" and his growth potential was considered "unlimited."[209]

In his next assignment, Scowcroft worked as the special assistant to the Air Force vice chief of staff, Lt. Gen. John Vogt. In this role, Scowcroft set up and managed the agenda for the meetings of the Joint Chiefs of Staff, attended the meetings, sitting in the back of the room, and afterward tasked the Joint Chiefs' decisions to the relevant offices and organizations within the Pentagon. He also ensured that the Joint Chiefs' practices and programs were militarily sound as well as consistent with their stated objectives and the United States' larger interests. One of his other responsibilities was to brief the deputies in charge of operations and the Air Force chief of staff before they went into their meetings. Another was to process "a whole bunch of study requirements for issues around the world" for the Nixon administration. As a result, he was constantly engaged in monitoring, evaluating, and executing the Joint Chiefs' policies. He judged his position to be the single most important job in the Office of the Joint Chiefs of Staff.[210]

In acknowledgment of Colonel Scowcroft's "singularly distinctive accomplishments" between March 1970 and December 1971, he received the Air Force's Distinguished Service Medal. The award cited Scowcroft's "penetrating analyses and consistently sound judgment and advice on matters developed for consideration of the Joint Chiefs of Staff dealing with the most significant aspects of our military posture and national strategic policy."[211]

Scowcroft nonetheless found the tasks involved in his three previous positions overly bureaucratic and uninspiring—not unlike his previous assignments under General Yudkin. It wasn't as if he felt his work for the Air Force, Department of Defense, and Joint Chiefs of Staff was unimportant or that he wasn't proud of his efforts and accomplishments. It was just that none of the jobs involved major issues or ideological disputes. He viewed his staff duties as being essentially managerial positions in which he had to administer ongoing operations and handle existing problems. In this sense he was a blue suiter par excellence: doing the staff work necessary to keep the Air Force, Defense Department, and Joint Chiefs of Staff functioning well.[212] However, it was not much fun.

Despite his lack of enthusiasm for high-level staff work, Scowcroft's supervising officers—now all generals, of course—commented consistently on his inquisitive intelligence, his manifest brilliance, and his uncommon ability to grow in stature as his responsibilities increased. They likewise appreciated Scowcroft's cordiality and ability to get along with others. General Vogt, in particular, was impressed, reporting that Scowcroft assisted him "in an absolutely outstanding manner" and describing him as extremely dedicated, completely loyal, and very hardworking.[213] More impressive still, none of Scowcroft's supervising officers, among the most senior officers in the Air Force, was able to determine a ceiling on his capacity for additional responsibilities. They unanimously recommended his promotion to brigadier general.

Scowcroft was himself confident he would receive his first star, since his two predecessors in the Office of the Joint Chiefs had also become general officers. And while he didn't know what his next assignment would be, he assumed he'd be assigned another important Pentagon position.[214] But Vogt had other plans for his forty-six-year-old assistant. He wanted him to replace Maj. Gen. James "Don" Hughes as military assistant to President Nixon.[215]

Although Scowcroft was surprised at Vogt's offer, it came at an opportune moment. For some time he'd been thinking about retiring from the Air Force. Not only did he not care for the staff work, but it was while he was a lieutenant colonel—from 1964 to 1968—that for the first time in his career he had not been promoted at the earliest opportunity, and he began to wonder if he'd ever make general. Certainly the odds were against him: out of a hundred newly commissioned second lieutenants, a third make colonel, and only two make brigadier general. As of June 1967, Scowcroft had put in his twenty years, qualifying for retirement. He figured it might be time to go into business and to start making some money.[216]

As the White House military assistant, however, Scowcroft realized he would face very different challenges and have very different responsibilities. So he agreed to the offer, and on November 17, 1971, the White House announced that Col. Brent Scowcroft would be the new military assistant to the president. Remarkably, Scowcroft would never again work for the Air Force, the Joint Chiefs of Staff, or the Department of Defense.[217]

Unfortunately, Brent's mother was unable to witness her son's transfer to the White House or, in just three months' time, his promotion to brigadier general. On September 3, 1970, Lucile Scowcroft died from breast cancer at the age of seventy-nine. She'd had breast cancer in the mid-1960s and had had a mastectomy; the cancer went into remission for a time, only to recur.[218]

Vogt's selection of Scowcroft as the White House military assistant and Kissinger's later choice of Scowcroft as his deputy were not accidents. General Hughes had recommended that Scowcroft replace him as military assistant, since it was known that Lt. Gen. Alexander Haig, Kissinger's deputy national security advisor, wanted to return to the Army.[219] Hughes further calculated that Scowcroft, once he was in position as Nixon's military assistant, had the intelligence, academic training, administrative savvy, and personality to attract Kissinger's attention.[220] Both Hughes and Vogt wanted an Air Force officer to serve as Kissinger's right-hand man, since the deputy national security advisor was the first to brief the president each morning and was in constant contact with the commander in chief. He would be well placed to learn of developments vital to Air Force interests, such as diplomatic breakthroughs or early drafts of the federal budget.[221] If Scowcroft became Kissinger's new deputy, Hughes and Vogt figured they would be kept apprised of Kissinger's plans. Like the other Air Force and other military leaders, they both feared and distrusted Kissinger because of his unpredictable foreign policy and his apparent influence over the president. They, along with other Air Force leaders, especially disliked having the national security advisor tell them how many and what kind of missiles or bombers they could have.[222]

Hughes's and Vogt's scheming was not unusual within the Nixon administration. Haig had been providing top Army generals and defense secretary Melvin Laird with information on Kissinger's activities and plans. Navy officers serving on the NSC staff had been found eavesdropping on Kissinger's conversations and then passing along information to the chief of Navy operations, Adm. Elmo Zumwalt. And in December 1971, just before Scowcroft started his new job, the news broke that Navy Yeoman Charles Radford, who was on the NSC staff, had been spying for Adm. Thomas Moorer, the chairman of the Joint Chiefs of Staff. For months, Radford had been taking thousands of secret papers from Kissinger's burn bag, papers Kissinger had not shared with the military, and delivering them to Admiral Moorer. (Nixon, upon finding out, decided not to take any formal action or punitive measures, because, as Scowcroft explains, the Defense Department wasn't leaking information.)[223]

Air Force leaders wanted their own man as Kissinger's deputy. They didn't want another Army officer, much less—God forbid!—a Navy man. And Hughes and Vogt calculated that the best way to get their man selected as deputy national security advisor was to station him inside the White House as military assistant to the president. Nixon, meanwhile, had heard of Scowcroft's superlative performance at Air Force headquarters and the Office of the Joint Chiefs, and was happy to accept Vogt's and Hughes's recommendation.[224]

Colonel Scowcroft was to be the Air Force's White House spy. At least, that was the plan.

— PART II —

The Nixon and Ford Administrations, 1972–1977

⎯⎯⎯⎯

All morning they made their way southeastwards down the strait between Canada and the United States, taking continuous bearings through the periscope, keeping a running plot at the chart table and changing course many times. They saw little change on shore, except in one place on Vancouver Island near Jordan River where a huge area on the southern slopes of Mount Valentine seemed to have been burned and blasted. . . . [I]n it no vegetation seemed to grow although the surface of the ground seemed undisturbed. . . .

Soon after midday they were off Port Townsend and turning southwards into Puget Sound. They went on . . . and in the early afternoon they came to the mainland at the little town of Edmonds, fifteen miles north of the centre of Seattle. They were well past the mine defenses by that time. From the sea the place seemed quite un-damaged, but the radiation level was still high.

—NEVIL SHUTE, *ON THE BEACH*

6

MILITARY ASSISTANT
TO THE PRESIDENT

SECRET SERVICE AGENTS surrounded the dingy twenty-year-old light blue Mercedes sedan with a cracked and curled leather dashboard they found parked on West Executive Avenue the morning of December 15, 1971. No one knew whose car had been left on the White House grounds, and it was about to be towed—until White House officials discovered it belonged to Col. Brent Scowcroft, who had parked it there that morning after driving in for his first day of work as President Nixon's new military assistant.[1]

The pale, short, and slightly built man didn't impress his new colleagues. He claimed to be an Air Force colonel, but he was wearing a nondescript civilian suit. His open and friendly face, receding hairline, and cordial demeanor gave his new colleagues further reason to think he would be a pushover. And they laughed when he naively asked for a White House organizational chart so as to make sense of his new responsibilities. Those with government experience know that formal titles reveal little about anyone's actual role, since the exact responsibilities and actual importance of any assistant or deputy are notoriously particularistic and protean. But for Scowcroft, who was used to the military's rigid hierarchies and organizations, the presidential system came as "an enormous change, an enormous shock."[2]

Other White House officials were underwhelmed upon meeting Nixon's new military assistant. When Lawrence Eagleburger, then a member of Kissinger's NSC staff, first met the soft-spoken and pleasant-mannered Scowcroft, he considered him a Caspar Milquetoast. Frank Carlucci, then with the Office of Management and Budget, later recalled having seen no signs of Scowcroft's "brainpower and strategic sense." And Nixon aide Col. Jack Brennan thought that the new military assistant seemed like a "small, meek-looking guy." He "fools you a little bit initially," as Representative Lee Hamilton later noted. "He doesn't try to impress you."[3]

Scowcroft's new teammates soon realized that he was no pushover. And he quickly earned the respect and affection of US Marine Corps Sgt. Warren "Bill" Gulley and the other staff members who worked in the White House Military Office in the East Wing, right next to the First Lady's suite.[4] Scowcroft had "no ideology [and] no ego," Gulley said, calling him "a fish I hadn't worked for before" and the "closest thing to a patriot" he'd ever encountered.[5]

Scowcroft's new colleagues appreciated the fact that their boss wasn't impressed by his White House position, awed by prestigious titles, or intimidated by officials with higher rank. Nor did he flatter or curry favor with those who had more seniority—a refreshing contrast to most other ambitious aides. He seemed to respect people no matter their position or fame. Most important, Scowcroft was utterly committed to fulfilling his duties as well as he could and to serving the president of the United States. In this role, he was much more of a bureaucrat or even a "fixer"—someone who could be counted on to handle touchy or tricky problems with skill and discretion—than a policy maker.

The new military assistant continued to drive his old Mercedes to the White House for another several days, refusing the offer of a car and driver. But Scowcroft eventually accepted the fact that he needed the secure communications accompanying the car and driver, since one of his roles was as an emergency action officer in the Office of Emergency Management (forerunner of the Federal Emergency Management Agency), and he had to be available at any time.

President Lyndon B. Johnson had created the position of military assistant. Previously, four military aides, one from each service branch, had jointly managed the Defense Department's White House assets. It was LBJ's idea to elevate one aide above the others and put him in charge. As the highest-ranking military officer on the White House staff, the military assistant would be responsible for all of the Defense Department's personnel and equipment dedicated to the service of the president and his family, advisers, other White House staff, and guests.

These assets included the Presidential Airlift Group, operated by the Air Force, which consists of the various aircraft used by the president, the vice president, cabinet secretaries, other officials, family members, and guests. They included the White House's fleet of thirteen or so helicopters (Marine Helicopter Squadron One) operated by the Marine Corps. They included the motor pool of cars and limousines, operated by the Army, as well as the White House Communications Agency, which sets up and secures the president's communications in the White House and while traveling, operated by the Army Signal Corps. And they included the presidential yacht *Sequoia* and other boats used by the White House, Camp David, the White House mess and dining facilities, the White House social aides, and the White House doctors and medical staff (the White House Medical Group) as well as Bethesda Naval Hospital, all of which are operated by the Navy. And they included the Special Programs Office, in charge of the emergency bomb shelters. In short, the military assistant managed many of the programs, processes, and staff that kept the American presidency in operation.

Despite the fact that the White House Military Office, with about two thousand employees, constitutes by far the largest group of staff in the White House, it remains almost entirely out of view to visitors, the public, and even White House officials and staff, since the officers and enlisted men and women working for the president are spread across different offices, do not wear their military uniforms, and serve a wide variety of functions.[6] What is more, the sizable budget of the Military Office is buried within the Pentagon budget and divided among separate accounts spread across the four military services. Hiding these dollar figures from public view dissuades politicians and reporters from grandstanding in front of their colleagues and television by announcing "the president and his staff spend $500,000 a year on telephone calls," for instance, or declaring "presidential air travel cost $6,000,000 to U.S. taxpayers in the first half of the year alone."[7]

The size of the budget dedicated to the US president and his entourage was another LBJ legacy. Lyndon Johnson and then Richard Nixon were the first presidents to insist upon the luxurious accommodations that later presidents, their families, their advisers, and their guests have come to take for granted—and that the American public, the press corps, and other politicians now expect of the office.

Johnson and Nixon also used US government assets for their private residences. President Johnson used funds from the White House Military Office to finance work at his ranch in Johnson City, Texas, fifty miles west of Austin. He had US government property and gifts shipped down to Texas, installed an airplane runway, converted a hangar into a movie theater, and had other improvements done. LBJ also used US government airplanes to take four secret trips down to a 110,000-acre ranch in Chihuahua that he leased from former Mexican president Miguel Alemán—in the process violating US and Mexican customs regulations, FAA regulations, and rules on presidential travel outside the United States, among other restrictions.[8]

When Nixon assumed office, he had work done on his Key Biscayne compound to suit it for presidential use and fixed up his San Clemente house. He had Camp David transformed into a luxurious retreat and elegantly redecorated the White House. Twice he rebuilt the interior of Air Force One. (H. R. "Bob" Haldeman, Nixon's chief of staff, had done the original redesign, but because there was no way to go from one end of the plane to the other without walking through the First Lady's cabin, the president insisted on a second redesign.) Both Johnson and Nixon made use of extra funds tucked away in Pentagon budgets as well as a secret fund—since discontinued—for exceptional projects.[9]

The journalists and political scientists who wrote in the mid-1970s about the "imperial presidency" were referring to the executive's increase of power relative to the other branches of government, but they could have just as easily been commenting on the luxury now associated with the White House and other presidential facilities. The presidential scholar Richard E. Neustadt made precisely this point in his classic study *Presidential Power*, when he wrote of the "extraordinary self-indulgence" of presidents Johnson and Nixon.[10]

It was Scowcroft's job as military assistant to run this small empire. Therefore, much of his attention was taken up by efforts to ensure that President Nixon's accommodations were up to snuff. And Nixon's chief of staff, Bob Haldeman, was his boss, with oversight of all the improvements and other projects. Scowcroft had to spend much of his time appeasing Haldeman, a demanding, hard-nosed man who, when he saw the slightest thing that needed attention—whether in the White House, aboard Air Force One, at Camp David, or elsewhere—was quick to telephone Scowcroft or dash off a memorandum. Not only did the chief of staff micromanage, he complained constantly and bullied; Scowcroft was by no means the only victim of his bullying.

Scowcroft saw to it that his boss's requests, however trivial, were quickly carried out. At Nixon's Key Biscayne compound (the "Florida White House"), for instance, Haldeman had Scowcroft do an assortment of jobs—fixing loose boards along the edge of the helicopter pad, getting dead car batteries replaced, installing a pair of outdoor stereo speakers at one of the villas, and checking to see that that same villa was equipped with an AM/FM radio. He ensured there was TV reception aboard Air Force One and that movie cassettes could be viewed in flight. He supervised the delivery of a new Boeing 707 as a backup Air Force One, and ordered a fleet of new presidential helicopters. He planned routes for the *Sequoia* to take on the Washington waterways for when the president was entertaining—including one-way trips with helicopter-ride returns—and supervised the remodeling of Camp David. Scowcroft also had to decide who would receive dining privileges at the well-subsidized White House Mess (a much sought-after status symbol), set the food prices, and scheduled the seatings for meals.[11]

Scowcroft handled the arrangements for state events as well. He had to oversee the logistics of President Harry Truman's funeral in Independence, Missouri, on December 28, 1972, as well as the details of President Nixon's motorcade for his second inauguration on January 20, 1973. And when Leonid Brezhnev gave the president of the United States a new Volga 70 hydrofoil—which Scowcroft had ridden during the June 1972 US-Soviet summit in Moscow—the military assistant saw to its docking in Baltimore harbor and its eventual destination.[12]

Despite the mundane nature of many of these tasks and despite Haldeman's frequent complaints and harsh memoranda, Scowcroft invariably remained poised, cordial, and professional. He accepted responsibility for any problems that arose and didn't let Haldeman, whom he described as a "very, very difficult" person, get to him. Because of his perseverance, professionalism, and ability not to personalize matters, he was able to say in good faith that he "got along all right" with Haldeman.[13]

Other aspects of Scowcroft's job as military assistant took him in wholly different directions. Scowcroft's most impressive performance may have been in an uncomfortable, poignant role: his responsibility for corresponding and meeting with the parents, families, and loved ones of US servicemen in Vietnam who had been taken as prisoners of war (POWs) or who were missing in action (MIAs). Although this part of his job didn't take up a great deal of his time, "it was very stressful," he said, and "very complicated."[14]

When family members of POWs and MIAs wrote to President Nixon, Kissinger, or other administration officials about their sons (there were no women in combat at the time), Scowcroft's assignment was to draft letters in response, often in Nixon's or Kissinger's name. In some cases, the families would request a visit with the president, and Scowcroft would see to the arrangements so that groups of POW or MIA families (the Forgotten Americans Committee of Kansas, Inc., for example) could meet with Nixon. He also corresponded with families and Defense Department officials about getting POWs home.

Making Scowcroft's job particularly difficult was the fact that family members of POWs and MIAs were, as a rule, demanding and insistent. They strongly—and justifiably—believed the US government owed them a great debt for what Scowcroft later described as "the most agonizing and anguishing experience for many of these persons."[15] Many of the POWs fortunate enough to be released from prison in North Vietnam suffered from serious and long-lasting injuries that were both physical and psychological. And almost no MIAs were ever found.

Dealing with the families of the POWs and MIAs forced Scowcroft to draw upon personal reserves of compassion and to consider the many dimensions of patriotism. Scowcroft had to be diplomatic, tactful, and politically savvy. No one wanted the loss of his or her loved one to be in vain, yet different survivors took different lessons from their losses. Some became more supportive of the United States and the Vietnam War, while a number came to consider the war a terrible, tragic mistake; still others had different reactions.[16] The POW-MIA problem "was a very sensitive issue and much more sensitive at the time than people [today] realize," Scowcroft said, a matter that at once reflected and distilled the public's attitudes on the Vietnam War. It was "a big political issue," he emphasized, "not just an emotional one."[17]

Scowcroft fulfilled these delicate responsibilities with thoroughness, patience, and kindness. He gave the POW-MIA families more time and attention than he had to, and more than his predecessors had given.[18] Gen. Don Hughes had taken a tough approach to the POW and MIA survivors so as to shelter President Nixon; so had Marvin Watson, LBJ's military assistant. Scowcroft, in contrast, made himself accessible to the families of the POWs and MIAs and was gentle with, sympathetic to, and considerate of the survivors. He wrote detailed and personalized letters in reply to those who wrote to the White House.

It was while working on the POW issue that Scowcroft met Ross Perot, the colorful, opinionated business leader who would mount eccentric third-party presidential candidacies in 1992 and 1996. The two of them "became fairly good friends," Scowcroft later recalled. Perot "was very helpful [with the POW issue], but only to a point. He wanted to be more helpful and play a bigger role, and the White House didn't want him to."[19]

Scowcroft was also able to get Nixon himself involved.[20] Sergeant Gulley recollected one incident that showed Scowcroft's willingness to go the extra mile. In 1972—Gulley didn't remember exactly when—a Florida man wrote in to request that his father be buried in Arlington National Cemetery (the kind of random letter that Gulley and others in the White House Military Office termed "moon mail"). This man's father had been a Good Humor man during the Second World War, bicycling around the docks with a small refrigerator and distributing ice cream free to the sailors.

Since burial in Arlington was restricted to those who had served in the military, Gulley responded to the man by writing that his father didn't qualify for burial at Arlington. The two went back and forth, until the man, fed up, wrote Gulley saying that he was flying up to Washington National Airport with his father's body. He threatened to throw the body over the fence, "embarrass the hell out of everyone," and have Gulley fired. Gulley thought the man was bluffing, so he ignored him; he heard nothing more, and thought that was end of it.

A few years later, with President Ford in office, the man again wrote Gulley. In the letter, he revealed that General Scowcroft had met him at National Airport, given him a letter personally signed by President Nixon— not by robo-pen—and invited the man's father to be buried at Baltimore National Cemetery, another veterans cemetery. But the man was writing Gulley because he still wanted his father to be buried in Arlington. When Gulley asked Scowcroft about the man's story, Scowcroft said, "Yeah," and volunteered nothing more. Gulley knew of no other officer or White House official who would have gone to such trouble.[21]

Another incident, recounted by journalist Neil Sheehan in his book *A Bright Shining Lie*, reveals Scowcroft's combination of toughness and poise. Col. John Paul Vann's middle son, Jesse, wanted to protest the war by giving one-half of his torn draft card to President Nixon at a White House ceremony following his father's state funeral at Arlington. He planned to put the other half of the card on his father's coffin. Of course, mutilating a draft card was a federal crime. Vann's eldest son, John Allen, told Scowcroft what Jesse intended to do, and said that their family didn't know how to stop him. So at the ceremony, Scowcroft sought Jesse out. He was easy to spot: the young man, who had shoulder-length blond hair, was wearing purple slacks and two-tone golf shoes. Scowcroft drew Jesse aside and calmly told him, "Whatever you think about the war and whatever you want to do about it, this ceremony is to honor your father. There is no way you can do this and not ruin the ceremony. Unless you promise us you won't give your draft card to the president, we'll have to cancel the ceremony."

Scowcroft's calm demeanor impressed Jesse, and he realized he'd be acting selfishly if he proceeded as he planned. "Okay, okay," he promised. But Scowcroft kept his eye on Jesse throughout the ceremony.[22]

Years later, when he was working as deputy national security advisor, Scowcroft was still in touch with a few of the POW and MIA wives.[23]

Because of these dealings with POW-MIA families, Scowcroft got to know Nixon in a private, nonpolitical setting. He came to appreciate an unexpected side of the man—the reflective, sensitive, and compassionate Dr. Jekyll who coexisted with the devious, embittered, and vindictive Mr. Hyde described by former aides and political writers and revealed on the White House tapes.

George H. W. Bush captured Nixon's divided personality in a letter to his sons in the summer of 1974, three weeks before the president's resignation. "He is enormously complicated. He is capable of great kindness . . . [and] he holds people off some," Bush observed. "But I've been around him enough to see some humor and to feel some kindness." On the other hand, Bush added, "he has enormous hang-ups. He is unable to get close to people. It almost like he's afraid to be reamed in some way—people who respect him and want to be friends get only so close—and then it is clear— no more!"[24]

Scowcroft got to know all these sides of Nixon. He also discovered that Nixon was a very shy man. After the president made difficult decisions, for instance, he "would go hole up in Camp David and wouldn't talk to anybody." And he anguished over his actions. "Was it the right decision? Would it work?"[25]

Nixon's Mr. Hyde was very real, and the president's personality clearly had serious and damaging consequences for his administration. But Scowcroft recognized that Nixon was also a tortured soul and that in most situations he was profoundly insecure. He saw that the president would often lapse into tough-guy, "macho" talk among his inner circle of aides and that he easily became paranoid. Nixon was ill at ease with himself and, with rare exception, everyone else. He "never let his hair down altogether," Scowcroft recalled. Nixon made it hard for people to love him, and because of that, Nixon also made it difficult for members of Congress, reporters, and the American public to rally to him.[26]

Scowcroft appreciated Nixon's kindness and humanity during their visits together with the families of the POWs and MIAs and when listening to his conversations with the survivors. He became fond of Nixon and got to see something of and to appreciate his better, less-seen side. (Before Scowcroft had met Nixon, he "was not a particular fan of his." He was unsympathetic to how Nixon had made his political career and to "the whole notion of the internal communist menace.") Furthermore, Scowcroft could almost always tell when Nixon was being serious and when he was only posturing. Yet the president almost always had a double agenda, Scowcroft observed— and when Nixon was dealing with him directly, he conceded, he couldn't always discern the other agenda. Scowcroft could "never be quite sure about Nixon."[27]

Nixon, in turn, became acquainted with his military assistant and grew to have confidence in him as an intellectual, a person of discipline, and a thoughtful man of substance. And he came to trust Scowcroft in a way he trusted few others.

Scowcroft was also responsible for the White House advance team—the crews who preceded presidential trips and coordinated presidential visits with the local officials where the visit would take place. This was a particularly important responsibility on sensitive trips abroad, such as those to Beijing, Warsaw, and Moscow.

The most important part of presidential travel was the president's physical security. The Secret Service had to coordinate with the local police or security forces and work out the security details for his public appearances, for any travel within that city or country, and for his housing. The same applied to medical care: Scowcroft had to line up a local staff of available physicians and other emergency personnel, as well as find and approve of nearby hospitals.

The advance team was also responsible for presidential communications. The White House military office therefore had to arrange for a wiring crew and electricians—who sometimes had to secure a power source—so that the president could have a secure telephone system available wherever he was, whether immediately upon landing in a foreign city or in the president's and senior staff's hotel suites or guesthouses. For example, during President Carter's August 1978 raft trip with family members down the Salmon River in Idaho, the communications personnel had to set up secure telephone stations on a series of mountaintops running parallel to the Carters' route down the river. (Not that everything always went smoothly. During the administration of George H. W. Bush, for instance, Scowcroft was on a secure telephone line with defense secretary Dick Cheney when a strange voice suddenly came on the line. Inexplicably, it was the hotel operator.)[28]

Another part of the advance team had responsibility for the president's limousine and for any other cars needed for ground transportation. If the president was going to a large city and didn't want to shut down the city with a motorcade, the military office would transport three helicopters by Air Force cargo so that the president and his entourage could fly from the airport directly to their ultimate destination. To make things easier for regular travelers, as well as safer for himself, the president didn't always fly to the most obvious airports. In Los Angeles, for instance, he might use the Long Beach Airport or the Burbank-Glendale-Pasadena Airport (now the Bob Hope Airport), rather than Los Angeles International Airport.[29]

One of Scowcroft's first trips as head of the advance team was with President Nixon on his famous visit to Beijing in February 1972. He had to oversee the president's daily schedule, review all of the arrangements, and plan for any contingencies. He had to check the schedule and itinerary for First Lady Pat Nixon and the other women accompanying the president in the event that Nixon and his advisers were occupied and the women needed to make separate plans. Scowcroft also had to make the final decision if an issue couldn't be worked out between the Secret Service and the local security forces or between the respective countries' medical personnel. Because of his role, Colonel Scowcroft was the highest-ranking US military officer to visit the People's Republic of China (PRC) since 1949.[30]

At the time of Nixon's visit, China—then almost universally known as Communist China or "Red China"—was still isolated internationally and recovering from the horrific Cultural Revolution. It was impoverished, bleak, barely industrialized, and extremely fearful of the Soviet Union. This was the context for Nixon's path-breaking visit, which heralded the beginning of the warming of US-China relations. (National security advisor Henry Kissinger had already visited China secretly in July, October, and December 1971 to set up Nixon's historic journey.)[31]

As a result of Nixon's visit, the United States and China established understandings that would set the course of US-China relations for the next forty years. According to what would become known as the 1972 Shanghai Communiqué, the United States was to neutralize Soviet threats against China, keep China current on developments regarding the Strategic Arms Limitation Treaty (SALT) and other significant negotiations and agreements with the USSR, offer China the same trade status as the Soviet Union, agree not to discuss US-China relations with the USSR, and agree not to pressure China to join the Geneva Disarmament Conference. President Nixon also agreed to withdraw two-thirds of US forces from Taiwan after the conclusion of the Vietnam War and not to support Taiwanese independence. The United States further promised to dissuade Japan from intervening in Taiwan and Korea and from expanding its military. And the United States and China both renounced the use of force against the other as well as against other states, and both agreed that neither country would try to dominate Asia.[32]

This was tremendous progress, given that the United States and the PRC had not previously had any diplomatic relations. Nixon's visit sparked an increase in trade between the two states and, in particular, in the sale of US arms and technology to China, including M48 tanks and C-54 transport aircraft.[33] The Shanghai Communiqué marked a significant change in the strategic terrain of the all-consuming Cold War. And while Scowcroft was responsible only for the president's safety and for the logistics of the visit, it marked the beginning of a special relationship between Scowcroft and China that would span the rest of his career.

Less than two months later, Scowcroft headed a small advance team to prepare for a ten-day visit by President Nixon and his twenty-five-person delegation to Moscow for a summit with Soviet leader Leonid Brezhnev. The Soviet Union was an ally of North Vietnam at the time, and by engaging with the Soviet leadership Nixon wanted to gain some leverage in US negotiations with the North Vietnamese—despite the fact that the summit came at a bad time, right after the Nixon administration had renewed its bombing of North Vietnam and had mined Haiphong harbor. The visit marked the first time a US president had traveled to the Soviet Union since Franklin D. Roosevelt visited Yalta in the Crimea in February 1945.

By most counts, the summit was a success. It resulted in several political, economic, and cultural agreements between the United States and the Soviet Union. Most important, Nixon and Kissinger's diplomacy paved the way for the separate, difficult negotiations that resulted in the first Strategic Arms Limitation Treaty. SALT put ceilings on the numbers of different types of nuclear weapons allowed and, as a result, slowed the escalating Cold War arms race.

Thus, the Moscow summit marked the beginning of détente—a thaw in the Cold War mean to promote a spirit of mutual coexistence, reverse the demonization of the Soviet Union, and establish a way to manage an extremely dangerous relationship. But since détente first and foremost revolved around arms control, one effect of détente was to make weapons systems sought-after chips in US-Soviet negotiations. "We have to have these [weapons] systems if we're to be able to bargain away the Soviet systems," Scowcroft said in reference to arms control negotiations.[34] The implication was that the United States needed to keep developing new weapons so it could accumulate additional bargaining chips for use in negotiations.

Despite détente and the opening of China, the administration made little progress on the dominant foreign policy issue of the era, the war in Vietnam. And coinciding with Nixon's foreign policy breakthroughs were the rumblings from Watergate. Nixon and his advisers had already begun to cover up the break-ins at the Democratic National Committee headquarters in the Watergate apartment complex.[35] Watergate and the Vietnam War would haunt and ultimately wreck the Nixon presidency. Scowcroft witnessed these developments as well.

Scowcroft enjoyed being military assistant. He liked the variety of tasks and challenges involved, he appreciated learning firsthand how the White House and the federal government functioned, and he enjoyed the opportunity to solve practical problems, especially with the resources of the

US military and the General Services Administration at his disposal. And by all accounts he was extraordinarily conscientious, highly efficient, and immensely capable in this role. For example, Henry Kissinger—generally stingy with praise—thanked Scowcroft in writing for his "superb support" during his "trip to Moscow, Munich, London and Paris" and commented that "every aspect of the myriad of complicated logistical and communications arrangements was flawlessly handled by your people."[36]

In acknowledgment of Scowcroft's "singularly distinctive accomplishments" and his "exceptionally meritorious service in a duty of great responsibility," President Nixon, the secretary of the Air Force, and the Air Force chief of staff awarded Scowcroft the Distinguished Service Medal. Scowcroft was cited for his "rare degree of tact and diplomatic skill in dealing with officials of the highest levels of the United States government, political personages, industrial figures, and foreign dignitaries . . . In addition, the manner in which he initiated and carried out the many sensitive and confidential duties related to the Office of the Presidency reflected a high order of judgment, discretion, and personal integrity."[37] And it was during his tenure as military assistant that Scowcroft received his first star as a brigadier general, on March 1, 1972.

He served as military assistant for barely twelve months. In October 1972, Kissinger asked Scowcroft to be his new deputy national security advisor; Alexander Haig, who currently held that position, had his sights on becoming the Army vice chief of staff. In January 1973, Scowcroft started working in the West Wing, in a small office right next to Kissinger's corner office. (Scowcroft retained the title of military assistant until August 1973, when Brig. Gen. Richard L. Lawson took over; in the months when Scowcroft nominally held both jobs, Sergeant Gulley effectively acted as Nixon's military assistant.)

Vogt and Hughes had figured right: Scowcroft's skill, intelligence, and tact had attracted Kissinger's notice. With his appointment as the deputy national security advisor, Scowcroft's dream of being able to help shape national policy was one big step closer to being realized.

7

KISSINGER'S DEPUTY

AT LEAST THREE members of Henry A. Kissinger's National Security Council staff thought they should be selected as the next deputy national security advisor. The Pentagon gave Kissinger its own list of candidates to choose from, and General Haig wanted an Army officer to replace him. But Kissinger wanted someone else—someone who wasn't already on his NSC staff and who wasn't already a part of the high-level Pentagon bureaucratic game. He wanted someone he could rely upon, someone who would be loyal and who had integrity.[38]

While he was traveling to Vietnam, France, the Middle East, and other overseas destinations, Kissinger realized Haig wasn't always being straight with him. Rather than neutrally conveying information between Kissinger and the president, Haig was ingratiating himself with Nixon and influencing the message. "Things happened," Scowcroft recalled, "that shouldn't have been happening."[39]

Alexander Haig had many outstanding qualities. He had performed heroically as a soldier in Vietnam. He had superb staff skills, and for five years he had served as the supreme Allied commander in Europe. Kissinger found him extremely valuable during Nixon's first term in office, since he "disciplined" the national security advisor's own "anarchic tendencies." Haig was able to establish "coherence and procedure" among the NSC staff, Kissinger writes in his memoirs, and he essentially viewed Haig as a "partner." Haig was, moreover, "strong in crisis," "decisive in judgment, skillful in bureaucratic infighting, [and] indefatigable in his labors." And he put in longer hours than anyone else in the White House, arriving at seven in the morning and remaining until midnight, usually seven days a week, year after year.[40]

Yet Haig also had a "sixth sense for bureaucratic gamesmanship," one White House official commented, which led him to "indicate to the powers that be that he is their man." But at the center of that power structure is the president of the United States, not the national security advisor. And

Nixon found Haig a valuable ally in his complicated and often competitive relationship with Kissinger. Nixon regarded Haig as being "steady, intelligent, and tough," and ensured his promotion to two-star, three-star, and finally four-star general "with unmatched rapidity." He then "used Haig to pick up the pieces after Kissinger's fiascoes, as in Haig's two visits to [South Vietnamese president] Nguyen Van Thieu to hammer Saigon into acquiescence to the Paris peace agreements," the military and foreign policy historian John Prados reports. Haig was able to achieve a comfortable working relationship with Nixon, whereas there was "more daylight on substance and more personal tension" in Nixon's relationship with Kissinger.[41]

So Kissinger had ended up feeling distrustful of the smart and hardworking but politically slippery Haig. Meantime, he'd gotten to know Brent Scowcroft while on presidential flights together, including several clandestine missions, such as the April 1972 trip to Moscow and the secret visits to Paris to meet with North Vietnamese negotiator Le Duc Tho. "I would provide the airplane and make sure it was taken care of in Paris," Scowcroft said, "and that's how [Kissinger] really got to know who I was."[42] Kissinger found Scowcroft to have a solid grasp of strategic doctrine, discovered he could talk knowledgably about European and Russian history, and appreciated his understanding of the US government and the federal bureaucracy. Kissinger saw that Scowcroft was at once very well informed, extremely smart, immensely competent, and wholly trustworthy—precisely the sort of person he wanted to have as his new deputy. Kissinger said he wanted someone "intellectually who was my equivalent and comparable," and in Scowcroft he found precisely that.[43]

Nixon's military assistant had a further quality that impressed Kissinger: his courage. The national security advisor witnessed Scowcroft's willingness to stand up to Bob Haldeman, the "fearsome, domineering chief of staff" (Kissinger's words), when he'd enough of Haldeman's bullying. One day in early 1972 aboard Air Force One—the date and even the cause of the incident are unclear—Scowcroft took exception to Haldeman's unreasonable point of view on an issue, and the two went at it. Strong words flew, and soon the two men were face-to-face, inches apart. Neither budged for what seemed hours—although probably only a minute or two elapsed—until Haldeman backed away from the considerably shorter and more slightly built Scowcroft. It took courage, Kissinger said, because "the military representative at the White House is a replaceable post." "That's the man I want," Kissinger decided.[44]

In mid-October, Kissinger spoke to President Nixon and Haldeman about appointing Scowcroft as his new deputy. Nixon was happy to let

Kissinger make his own choice, and Haldeman, to his credit, said it "would be a superb idea."[45]

Yet when Kissinger asked Scowcroft if he would like to be his deputy, he was taken aback by Scowcroft's response. The military assistant told Kissinger—already an international celebrity—that he'd "think about it," since he already had a good job and since he knew the national security advisor wasn't an easy person to work for.[46]

In the end, of course, Scowcroft accepted Kissinger's invitation. But his nonchalant reaction to the offer—one that most ambitious people in Washington would have seized immediately—foreshadowed the unique quality of their relationship.[47]

General Hughes and General Vogt had gauged correctly that Kissinger would pick Scowcroft as his new deputy—but they'd also misjudged their man: Scowcroft wasn't going to be their spy. Once Scowcroft began working for the White House, his allegiance shifted to his civilian bosses.[48] And playing the role of informer didn't suit Scowcroft's loyal and straightforward personality. Indicatively, when Haldeman hinted to Scowcroft that he should provide President Nixon with information about Kissinger on the sly—as Haig had done—Scowcroft brushed him off.[49]

=====

SCOWCROFT WAS RIGHT in thinking that Kissinger would not be easy to work for. In fact, before Scowcroft began working as deputy national security advisor, Nixon saw to it that Haig fully informed "him on the Kissinger problem," Haldeman later reported. Yet by virtue of his tact, his professionalism, and his ability not to take things personally, Scowcroft succeeded remarkably well in a job that required him to loyally serve two powerful, strong-willed principals—Kissinger and President Nixon—while remaining his own man.[50]

Kissinger and Scowcroft ended up operating in tandem for four years: the years of Nixon's truncated second term in office and the shortened Ford administration. Kissinger served as national security advisor from January 1969 to November 1975 and as secretary of state from April 1973 to January 1977. He held both offices from April 1973 to November 1975, and for about 90 percent of that time, Scowcroft was de facto national security advisor and managed the NSC staff.[51]

As a rule, Kissinger was "very abrasive to his subordinates," recalled Admiral Moorer, and he would "frequently belittle them or demean them in public." As one anonymous source told Marvin Kalb and Bernard Kalb (two of Nixon's biographers), it was "a case of control or castrate" with Kissinger. Jack Brennan, who was Nixon's military aide in the White House and then his chief of staff in San Clemente, remarked that when one of Kissinger's assistants had a nervous breakdown from "working so hard, . . . Kissinger boasted about it." And Lawrence Eagleburger called him "a miserable son of a bitch," because when Kissinger first became national security advisor "he was so lacking in confidence" that he was "very, very tough" on his staff." He demanded that his staff "get there at 6:30 and leave at 11:00, 11:30, and be there Saturday and Sunday." But the longer Kissinger was in office and the more confident he became, Eagleburger observed, the more his "miserable" qualities were mitigated by his virtues.[52]

Yet Kissinger had great respect for Scowcroft. Not only did his deputy obviously possess considerable expertise and ability, but he couldn't be intimidated. Although Kissinger sometimes verbally abused and terrified his subordinates—NSC staff members Eagleburger, Haig, and Helmut Sonnenfeldt were all favorite targets—he didn't yell at Scowcroft. One day he tried. Kissinger lost his temper—Scowcroft couldn't remember exactly why—and began screaming at his secretary, who broke down in tears. He then turned to Scowcroft and began yelling at him, standing right up against him, chest to chest. But Scowcroft just stood there, silent, until the slightly taller and heavier Kissinger suddenly stopped in midsentence and said, "Scowcroft, one day I'll find a way to get to you." He never did.[53]

Nor did he really want to. Kissinger never berated, belittled, or badmouthed Scowcroft, unlike how he treated others—presidents Nixon and Ford included. In return, Scowcroft almost never deviated from his courteous, poised, and good-natured self.[54] He had the good sense to wait out his boss's flashes of anger, which blew over quickly, without engaging him. He had the knack, too, of knowing when and how to offer suggestions or ask questions and when to be silent. And when Kissinger solicited his advice, Scowcroft listened carefully and replied thoughtfully. He "was particularly good at pointing out weaknesses in [the] conventional wisdom."[55]

Considerate of Kissinger's pride and sensitive to his vulnerabilities, Scowcroft avoided openly questioning his judgment or challenging him in meetings or in front of the president. Instead, he waited until they were alone together or among a few trusted colleagues to question assumptions, make objections, and offer suggestions.

One tactic Scowcroft used was to ask Kissinger whether he wanted a briefing paper. If he said yes, Scowcroft would compose a short memo that considered the issue from another angle or looked at a perspective previously overlooked—often nudging Kissinger in the direction he wanted. "Most of the time Brent got his way," Eagleburger said, although "not always." Given that "being Kissinger's deputy was not an easy task," this was no small achievement, Eagleburger noted, adding, "Many times, he and I would connive to change Henry's mind."[56] In fact, Scowcroft was better at handling Kissinger intellectually and temperamentally than anyone else in the government.

Not only did Scowcroft have the motivation, stamina, and discipline to put in grueling hours, but he had an immense amount of what we would now identify as "emotional intelligence." As a result, Scowcroft became Kissinger's "other self," the author John Hersey observed. Kissinger may have had "intellectual disdain" for nearly everyone around him, Lt. Col. Robert "Bud" McFarlane remarked—including most members of Congress, many reporters and political writers, and the two presidents under whom he served—but he held Scowcroft in high regard.[57] Florence Gantt, who was Kissinger's and Scowcroft's personal assistant at the NSC, said she got the feeling that Kissinger never learned to respect others, but that he "had a lot of respect" for the deputy national security advisor. Winston Lord, another NSC aide and later US ambassador to China, also spoke of the "enormous respect" Kissinger had for Scowcroft.[58]

Moreover, Kissinger said that when the two of them were working on national security issues together, he couldn't remember which contributions were his and which were Scowcroft's (except for when Kissinger was traveling, as during the Middle East shuttle diplomacy of 1973 and 1974).[59] It is possible Kissinger was being overgenerous, of course, since Eagleburger, Sonnenfeldt, NSC staff member Peter Rodman, and others all made valuable contributions to Kissinger's decision making; nonetheless, the remark suggests how close the two of them were and how well each complemented the other.[60]

The two men were quite different, to be sure. Whereas Kissinger was excitable, impatient, impetuous, self-centered, and occasionally malicious, Scowcroft was calm, patient, cautious, modest, and typically caring. Kissinger was perpetually concerned with intrigue, which was second nature to him, and strongly focused on obtaining his objectives, even when that meant using people. "During the worst days of Watergate," McFarlane reported, "I knew that [Kissinger] was capable of undermining Al Haig in a conversation with Nixon one moment, and then hanging up and calling Haig to disparage Nixon in turn. He would make commitments to senators or congressmen, then call the President to rip apart the position to which he had just committed."[61] That the ends justified the means went without saying.

Kissinger's self-consciousness and insecurity made him highly sensitive to how others in the White House corridors and in the press perceived him. He had a famously thin skin and spent considerable time and energy talking to and meeting with journalists to counteract any unfavorable reports or perceived slights. "He was a junkie for public praise," one of his biographers writes, "and almost maniacal about guarding his reputation." McFarlane, too, noted that "not only was Kissinger demanding and dogmatic," he was "distrustful, hypocritical, routinely dishonest and abusive to his friends. He [was] an extremely vain man, apparently without solid spiritual anchors, who was as absorbed with how he would be perceived by future generations as he was with his genuine commitment to sound policy." He "went at his job with a Spenglerian view of humankind," McFarlane said, as if "his role was to exploit the vulnerabilities of others as each situation demanded, by fair means or foul, to accomplish what he thought was right."[62]

Although this might seem harsh, the transcripts of Kissinger's telephone calls confirm McFarlane's judgment about Kissinger's egotism and mercurial nature. The phone calls offer dozens of examples of his shrewd, charming, purposeful, and disingenuous conversations with colleagues, members of Congress, and numerous reporters, a handful of columnists and editors, and a few publishers. Kissinger, Nixon speechwriter William Safire observed acidly, had an extraordinary "ability to project childlike anguish at the reaction of others to action he had recommended with cold precision."[63]

Scowcroft was by no means ignorant of Kissinger's personality and treatment of others, but he also recognized his brilliance, incisive mind, strategic sense, charisma, and rare talent. Kissinger was two years older, had been a Harvard professor with a brilliant academic record, was the author of a bestselling 1957 book on nuclear warfare (*Nuclear Weapons and Foreign Policy*), and thought in broad, conceptual terms. Scowcroft appreciated the fact that Kissinger never looked at problems or solutions in isolation, but rather in conjunction with other factors. He admired Kissinger's "unbelievable capability" at bringing the different threads of problems and solutions together and then calculating one, two, and three years ahead.[64]

Scowcroft had his own well-developed sense of military strategy and world history. He was also brilliant at questioning and evaluating the merits of new ideas and policy options as well as a superb bureaucratic operator who knew how to put concepts into practice. But unlike Kissinger, Scowcroft said, he was better at reacting to and evaluating ideas than he was at dreaming them up; that was why he liked to hire people smarter than himself. "I don't have a quick, innovative mind," he claimed. "I don't auto-matically think of good new ideas. What I do better is pick out good ideas from bad ideas."[65]

Besides learning strategy from Kissinger, Scowcroft learned how to handle reporters. A master at dealing with the press, Kissinger frequently spoke by phone or over meals with leading reporters, columnists, editors, and publishers, including Stewart Alsop, Jack Anderson, Ben Bradlee, Wil-liam F. Buckley, Rowland Evans, Max Frankel, Bernard Gwertzman, Rich-ard Hottelet, Marvin Kalb, Ted Koppel, Joseph Kraft, Don Oberdorfer, Dan Rather, James Reston, William Safire, Frank Stanton, C. L. Sulzberger, and Sander Vanocur. For Bob Schieffer, Kissinger was a "gargantuan per-sonality" who was "funny" and "could play the press . . . like a violin." It was "just remarkable," to Schieffer, "how good he was at it. And he never stopped. He never stopped. And, I mean, there was no detail too small."[66] Suggestive of Kissinger's stature, both Hugh Sidey of *Time* magazine and Katharine Graham, the publisher of the *Washington Post*, sometimes de-ferred to Kissinger, with Sidey at one point clearing a story with him and with Graham on another occasion telling him, "I was so scared . . . I'll come running over on my knees."[67]

Since Scowcroft had little experience with journalists, Kissinger initially had him brief just one person, the columnist Joseph Alsop. He later added Meg Greenfield, a *Newsweek* columnist and editorial page editor for the *Washington Post*, and then others to the list of those he wanted his deputy to brief. Eventually Scowcroft came to have weekly meetings with a half dozen or so Washington writers, either on background or off the record, in which he'd explain what the president had decided or was thinking of doing. He became more familiar with the press and came to appreciate how important press relations were. But he never became as deeply connected with the media as Kissinger was. Telephone records show that about half of Kissinger's calls were to journalists, a percentage that increased after the 1972 elections, when the Watergate investigations heated up.

To describe Kissinger solely in terms of his self-absorption and instru-mental use of others does injustice to his complexity. Kissinger scheduled frequent meetings with his staff—especially after first taking office—listened attentively, and frequently consulted with his subordinates, which is why he sought to hire the best talent possible.[68] And while he expected and demanded that those on his staff work long hours and perform to the highest standards, he worked extremely hard himself. Underappreciated, too, was Kissinger's intellectual honesty with respect to other people's ideas and options, as Walter Isaacson, one of his biographers, observes. Far from wanting to have yes-men around him, Kissinger enjoyed intellectual debate and tolerated, even sought, criticism and disagreement, so long as those who disagreed with him argued with subtlety and rigor.[69]

Witty, brilliant, and charming—especially in pursuit of the approval or agreement of others—Kissinger could be seductive. But because he had the capacity to appear as a different person to different audiences and could say different things to those different audiences, he acquired a reputation for duplicity and untruthfulness.[70] He could be charismatic as well as cruel, inspiring as well as insulting, bold as well as petty, and creative as well as prejudiced. He could be funny, endearing, self-deprecating, and playful, just as he could be rude, abrupt, self-aggrandizing, and intolerant. And when circumstances seemed to be deteriorating, he had a "well-timed sense of humor that he [used] to break the 'tension spell' and then in the next few moments to get the best out of people, their best thinking."[71] If others often found Kissinger extremely difficult to take, he made things happen. People wanted to be around him; he was exciting. For all of Kissinger's ambition, ego, arrogance, and guile, Scowcroft's NSC colleagues and presidents Nixon and Ford appreciated Kissinger's ability to conceive of grand designs, his diplomatic imagination, and his lofty aspirations to worthy goals, such as ending the US-Soviet arms race.[72] Those who couldn't stomach him or his policies, such as NSC staff members Anthony Lake, Roger Morris, and Morton Halperin, simply quit.[73]

Notwithstanding Kissinger's complex and sometimes difficult personality, Scowcroft very much admired him.[74] Further cementing their relationship was their convergence on foreign policy positions. In terms of international relations theory, both were realists—if Kissinger more than Scowcroft—as were Nixon and others on the NSC staff, such as Eagleburger, Sonnenfeldt, and Rodman. Specifically, Kissinger and Scowcroft believed that the United States, as the hegemon (that is, the dominant global actor), had to balance its rivals and suppress threats to the world order, whether through its own actions or through joint actions with its allies. Both agreed, too, that the United States had the burden of leading the free world against the Soviet Union or any coalition of communist or communist-allied states that might contest US global interests.

Scowcroft and Kissinger further recognized the limits of diplomacy and were skeptical of what United States could expect from other governments. They took the world as it was, with its violence, political repression, cruelty, ethnic and racial prejudices, and dysfunctional governments. They were thus wary of the capacity of ideals, shared norms, or international institutions to serve as guidelines for international relations or to constrain the behavior of other states. The practical implication of realism was that the US government had to have the means to either act on its own or ensure that its alliances with other states could safeguard its national security. In a world of many shades of gray, replete with deep ambiguities, difficult compromises, unhappy trade-offs, and half-truths, the United States needed to be able to engage in careful, discreet, and judicious foreign policy making, while being willing to take initiative on its own when necessary. Accordingly, Scowcroft and Kissinger both strongly believed in the prerogatives and privileges of the executive branch, which could afford the United States the leeway it needed to make and enact foreign policy in its best interests.

In this world of complexity and ambiguity, the United States needed a national security policy that was pragmatic, nuanced, and discreet. It couldn't afford a policy based on absolute standards of human rights, on moral ideals, or on crystal-clear transparency, like the ideals expressed by President Woodrow Wilson in his speeches. As for the idea that Americans knew the one path to righteousness and therefore could impose their norms and principles on other states, realists believed this to be shortsighted and even arrogant. Thus, the vigorous pursuit of universal values such as human rights or democratic government risked being unpractical and backfiring on the United States.

This sort of realpolitik tended to be out of step with American values, however. Americans pride themselves on their commitment to democracy and freedom, and most have little patience for the finer points of strategy and geopolitics.[75] Yet these finer points were exactly what Kissinger and Scowcroft offered an American public looking for accessible truths and moral reassurance.

Most students of the Nixon and Ford presidencies underestimate Scowcroft's importance. With the exceptions of Bob Woodward and Carl Bernstein, Walter Isaacson, and John F. Osborne, most of those who have written about the period focus exclusively on Kissinger. If they mention Scowcroft, they variously describe him as a "pliable technician," "Kissinger's loyal deputy," "Kissinger's protégé," or his "errand boy." Robert T. Hartmann, President Ford's chief political adviser and former congressional chief of staff, calls Scowcroft a "typical staff" type, and author Neil Sheehan refers to him as a "career staff officer." The most critical label him a "Kissinger clone." Kissinger himself did not do very much to correct the misperception; Scowcroft plays only a minor role in his multivolume memoirs.[76]

These descriptions are correct in one sense: Scowcroft *was* Kissinger's "loyal deputy" and "protégé" when he first began working as deputy national security advisor. Scowcroft conceded as much. He said he was unprepared for his new responsibilities upon taking office, since he hadn't previously served on the NSC staff or held a policy-making position. So for the nine months up to September 1973, when Kissinger became secretary of state, Scowcroft *was* essentially a staff officer, deferential to and solicitous of his boss (although the records of their telephone conversations suggest their relationship was more consistently even-handed than the edited transcripts of their in-person conversations would seem to indicate).

Scowcroft would duck out of meetings in the Oval Office to fetch maps. He would write up Kissinger's notes and forward them to the president. He would draft memos, make calls, or do research on Kissinger's behalf. Sometimes these duties weren't very pleasant. After Ford took office, for instance, Scowcroft had to tell his mentor and hero, General Andrew Goodpaster, that he was being relieved of his position as supreme Allied commander in Europe (SACEUR) to make way for Al Haig. Once Ford made the decision, he asked Kissinger to inform Goodpaster. "Kissinger in turn looked squarely at Scowcroft, who then picked up the telephone and called his good friend," the military historian Robert S. Jordan reports. Goodpaster "was not at all pleased with the news."[77]

Upon first becoming deputy national security advisor, Scowcroft wasn't involved in setting national security policy. He'd been trained to serve his superiors and to assist them in achieving their goals, not to concern himself with the whats and whys. But to describe Scowcroft as Kissinger's loyal aide *is* misleading for the reason that their relationship evolved over the course of Nixon's shortened second term and the two and a half years of the Ford presidency. Kissinger himself considered Scowcroft far more than his staff officer. "I didn't need a staff officer," said Kissinger. Rather, national security policy "was an amalgam," he said, and "when we were together I did not do anything without consulting him, without bringing him into the discussion."[78]

Scowcroft's responsibilities gradually expanded beyond military and strategic affairs to encompass diplomacy, economics, intelligence, and other matters, and once Kissinger was appointed secretary of state in September 1973, Scowcroft became the one briefing the president, seeing him often several times a day for up to thirty minutes each time, and managing the NSC staff during an extremely difficult period in US foreign relations.[79]

A brief exchange between Scowcroft and Kissinger in early 1974 suggests the shifting terms of their relationship. When Kissinger found out that Scowcroft was invited to a black-tie dinner with the ambassadors from the Organization of American States, he remarked, "Oh, are you invited to that? That's a little more above your level." Scowcroft merely replied, "I understand that."[80] The conversation hints at Kissinger's insecurity, his jealousy of Scowcroft's privileges, and his concern over appearance. But it also suggests his deputy's calm, modesty, and self-possession. Scowcroft didn't apologize, explain himself, or crack a joke at Kissinger's expense. He simply admitted Kissinger's point and phrased his reply so as to defuse any status anxiety his boss may have had.

Scowcroft understood the need to reassure and soothe Kissinger. He would affirm him by saying after something Kissinger decided, "That's terrific, just terrific." Or, when Kissinger said of an action, "We cannot do this now," he affirmed his judgment by responding, "Oh no. That would be the worst possible thing to do."[81] When Kissinger, in reference to his characterization of a particular policy, for instance, asked, "Brent, have I exaggerated?" Scowcroft said, "You have bent over backward."[82] Neither did Scowcroft contradict or try to tone down Kissinger's more caustic remarks, whether directed at CIA director William Colby, German chancellor Helmut Schmidt, defense secretary James R. Schlesinger, or others.[83] Instead, he usually commiserated, remained silent, or moved on to another subject.

The two never quite became peers during the Nixon and Ford years; Scowcroft said he always regarded Kissinger as his boss. But the longer Scowcroft worked in the West Wing, the more responsibilities he took on, the more independent he became, and the more confident he felt in his own judgment. In early 1975, for instance, Scowcroft recommended that Ford veto the 1975 foreign aid bill on the grounds that almost $500 million in the bill was to go to Israel, with none for any Arab states—despite the fact that Israel had reneged on a promise to return to Egypt two oil fields and two strategic passes it held in the Sinai. Ford vetoed the bill without telling his secretary of state, shocking Kissinger, who had wanted the bill passed. (When Senator Hubert Humphrey asked the president why he had vetoed the bill, Ford said, "Hubert, you don't seem to understand; I am the President." US diplomat Robert Oakley reports that Kissinger, who was also in the room, "turned purple.") Over the following days, Scowcroft worked closely with Representative Otto Passman to revise the bill—again without direct input from Kissinger.[84]

But differences between the two men were few. Kissinger trusted Scowcroft, something that didn't come easily to him. When Kissinger married Nancy Maginnes on Saturday, March 30, 1974, he asked Scowcroft to be his best man.

Scowcroft's subsequent promotion to national security advisor on November 2, 1975, marked another shift in the terms of their relationship. In this stage, which lasted until January 20, 1977, the end of the Ford presidency, Scowcroft became Kissinger's near equal. Part of the reason was that Kissinger's star had started to descend. SALT II and détente had become increasingly controversial among Republicans and across the country as the Republican Party swung to the right and as Ford's own advisers—Donald Rumsfeld, Robert Hartmann, and others—tried to distance the president from Kissinger and the disgraced Nixon White House. But it was also because of Scowcroft's emergence in his own right as an adviser to the president and a policy maker.

The claim that Scowcroft was merely Kissinger's loyal deputy thus has to be understood in context of their evolving relationship. Scowcroft may have been "very quiet" and almost invisible to those outside the government, as the *New York Times* initially described him, but he could also be "very forceful," as the *Times* also pointed out. And by no means was he bland, unemotional, retiring, or unwilling to contradict the boss, contrary to the image of a typical staff officer.[85] In short, the description of Scowcroft as Kissinger's "loyal aide" doesn't capture Scowcroft's true role. There were good reasons why Kissinger described their relationship as a "full partnership."[86] In their book *The Final Days*, Woodward and Bernstein rightly observe that Scowcroft had perhaps as much influence on US foreign policy at this time as any White House official or cabinet member apart from Kissinger and the president.[87]

————

IN THE YEARS following World War II, as the Cold War grew in scale and complexity, the position of national security advisor rose in prominence. US presidents needed more and more help formulating, enacting, and implementing national security policy. And they needed help managing the ever-larger cast of people, agencies, and departments involved with foreign policy, military planning, international economic policy, and grand strategy.

The accretion of power in the president's assistant for national security affairs and the NSC staff was an uneven process. The text of the 1947 National Security Act, best known for establishing the Central Intelligence Agency, for creating the Air Force as a separate military service, and for unifying the services under a single secretary of defense, makes no mention of a "national security advisor." However, it did establish the National Security Council, which Navy Secretary James Forrestal (later the first secretary of defense) perceptively considered the most important feature of the proposed legislation.[88]

Yet the National Security Act only mentioned a civilian executive secretary to be appointed by the president, and the position of "assistant to the president for national security affairs"—the official title of the present-day national security advisor—was reserved for the chairman of the Committee on Foreign Intelligence (one of the several committees to be established within the NSC).[89] For the first NSC executive secretary, President Truman appointed Rear Adm. William "Sid" Souers, an intelligence expert and the former head of the Central Intelligence Group (the successor to the wartime Office of Strategic Services and the immediate precursor of the CIA). Souers mainly assisted Truman on intelligence issues, however, and played only a limited role in the administration. He saw himself as an "anonymous servant" whose role was to help the president in any way possible, which mostly meant fostering interagency cooperation on policy planning, rather than participating in policy decisions.

For advice and options on foreign policy, military affairs, and grand strategy, Truman chiefly relied on his two secretaries of state, Dean Acheson and George C. Marshall. However, Truman did use the NSC as an "intimate forum" during times of crisis, and began to convene regular meetings to "develop, discuss, and coordinate" policy relating to the Korean War.[90]

President Eisenhower, who had extensive experience with a military staff system, established an "elaborate interagency structure" for handling foreign policy decision making, with General Andrew Goodpaster as the executive secretary responsible for coordinating policy among the secretary of state, secretary of defense, director of central intelligence, and others. Goodpaster, who had Eisenhower's complete trust, took it on himself to gather and vet different policy options for the president. Once Eisenhower decided upon a policy, Goodpaster was the one who ensured the policy got implemented. By presenting policy options with equal advocacy and without imparting his own preferences, Goodpaster set the model of the "honest broker" in foreign policy management.

It was Robert Cutler, in 1953, who became the first official to be given the title of assistant to the president for national security affairs. Cutler served in that role for two years, and then returned in 1957 for another two-and-a-half-year stint in the post. Yet Eisenhower, like Truman, chiefly relied on his secretary of state, John Foster Dulles, for advice on diplomacy, military policy, and other matters of US national security.

President John F. Kennedy ultimately gave the national security advisor position its current recognizable form as the president's chief administrator with respect to national security and his confidential adviser.[91] Kennedy appointed McGeorge Bundy as his assistant for national security affairs, and Bundy, together with his small staff, oversaw the administration's organization and handling of information and decisions on national security. An extremely able man, Bundy was impartial when presenting different recommendations and analyses to the president, just as Goodpaster had been with Eisenhower. Also like Goodpaster, Bundy organized and coordinated national security affairs and ensured that JFK's decisions were carried out. At the same time, Bundy was closer to the president than Souers or Cutler had been.

Kennedy relied on defense secretary Robert McNamara for advice more than he did on his capable but passive secretary of state, Dean Rusk. But he relied on Bundy even more. It was Bundy who had the president's ear, who was the closest intellectually and by disposition, and who—in another NSC innovation—began setting Kennedy's "action agenda" of current foreign policy issues. Bundy foreshadowed the role played by such national security advisors as Kissinger, Zbigniew Brzezinski, Scowcroft, and others, who have been both coordinators or guarantors of the president's policies being carried out and their counselors and personal agents.[92] Bundy was also the first presidential assistant for national security affairs to have a West Wing office.

Advances in technology under JFK further enhanced the national security advisor's growing role. After the Bay of Pigs fiasco, the White House installed real-time communications in the new Situation Room, providing twenty-four-hour command and control capabilities for all US military posts, American embassies, and US departments and agencies. The national security advisor position thus took its present-day shape. Perhaps indicative of the effectiveness of the NSC process under Kennedy and Bundy was the fact that the thirty-three-member Executive Committee convened during the Cuban missile crisis produced no leaks.[93]

Lyndon B. Johnson's use of the national security advisor marked a step backward to some degree. Although President Johnson initially retained Bundy upon taking office, LBJ didn't mesh well with his Harvard-affiliated national security advisor, and in early 1966 he replaced Bundy with Walt W. Rostow. Although LBJ deliberately avoided bestowing the title of national security advisor on Rostow, Rostow had Bundy's job, in essence. He attended White House meetings on national security, made decisions about how to handle the information flow, and presented LBJ with policy options.

In contrast to Bundy, however, who saw it as his duty to ask questions and maintain intellectual skepticism, Rostow unequivocally supported the president on Vietnam. A brilliant economic historian and policy analyst, Rostow was supremely confident of his own judgment and impervious to criticism. He did not function as an honest broker; his strong views biased the information as well as the range and quality of policy options presented to LBJ. As a result, Rostow's influence on LBJ didn't translate to a commensurate influence on national security policy across the federal government.[94]

Rostow's proximity to the president and influence on national security decision making nonetheless set an example followed by his successor, Henry A. Kissinger. Kissinger stands as the single most influential and most celebrated national security advisor in US history and in many ways defined the position. He "broke the mold," as Kissinger's personal assistant later put it.[95]

Kissinger became national security advisor in January 1969, when Nixon first took office—noteworthy in itself, since Kissinger had been closely associated with New York governor and rival Republican presidential candidate Nelson Rockefeller—and he had Nixon's full support in centralizing information and decision making within the national security advisor's office and the NSC. He proceeded to establish the Washington Special Actions Group (WSAG) in May 1969, the Verification Panel (for arms negotiations) in July 1969, and the Vietnam Special Studies Group in September 1969. He chaired all three groups. By creating these groups, Kissinger in some ways returned to the administrative formality of the Eisenhower administration; in other ways, he also retained Bundy and Rostow's roles as presidential advisers who exceeded the influence of official cabinet members. Kissinger oversaw an expanded NSC staff that included about eighty professionals and staff as well as dozens more—off the NSC budget—detailed to his staff.[96] Like Bundy, he was very close to the president and became his chief adviser with respect to US foreign policy and military affairs.

Further helping Kissinger concentrate decision-making power in his hands was his skill at bureaucratic maneuvering and his penchant for secrecy. He was notorious for not sharing information with the secretary of state, defense secretary, and others in the government—including his own aides—with the result that other government actors, especially in the military, sought to develop their own White House sources (hence the spying). Nixon gave Kissinger wide discretion and let him control policy making at the expense of secretary of state William Rogers and defense secretaries Melvin Laird and then James R. Schlesinger. If Kissinger didn't create the secrecy of the Nixon White House, he "certainly manipulated and profited" from it, one of his biographers, Jussi Hanhimäki, observes.[97]

But by collapsing the national security advisor and secretary of state into one position, Nixon—and later Ford—defeated the purpose of the national security advisor role. By overshadowing the Department of State and constantly battling with the Department of Defense, Kissinger undermined the idea of the national security advisor as an honest broker of competing interests and ideas. The role of the national security advisor and the NSC during those years "was probably not as useful or valuable as later," Scowcroft observed—though, as deputy national security advisor under Nixon and Ford, he played a more important role than he probably would have otherwise because of the very changes Kissinger put in place.[98]

In the role of deputy national security advisor, Scowcroft's assiduous work habits became even more pronounced. Informed that Kissinger needed no more than five hours of sleep a night, Scowcroft began to sleep even less—though he had to nap more, curling up on his small office couch, to survive his own seven-day workweeks of ninety to a hundred hours. Scowcroft was at the White House almost every day of the year in the mid-1970s, except when traveling with the president. During crises, he'd stay up until two or two-thirty in the morning or simply remain at the White House around the clock, except for brief trips home to visit Jackie.[99]

Scowcroft's desk at the White House was stacked high with papers—nine separate stacks, each between ten and thirty-six inches high, which rendered him almost invisible when he sat behind the desk. However, the most important papers stayed on the coffee table, and Scowcroft worked on these while seated in his armchair, where he could be seen. All of the papers would be put away in the evening, with secretaries collecting and locking them up in five drawer safes and then putting them out again the next morning, all in exactly the same order.[100]

Scowcroft recognized he was "routinely slow" at moving paper. He wanted to read documents carefully, study them thoroughly, and mark them up. If a report or memo was urgent, he'd have the author put a little red circle on it; some memos would have three or four red circles on them. But Scowcroft said he never remembered any president ever complaining about his deliberate pace.[101]

He worked out of a small office in the West Wing, next door to Kissinger's corner office, up until November 1973, two months after Kissinger was appointed secretary of state. Scowcroft then moved into the national security advisor's larger office.[102] To make the most of his time, he almost always took lunch in his office, brought up from the White House Mess (his favorite meal was Thursday's Mexican lunch). And he always had a cup of black coffee on hand, even in late afternoon or early evening.[103]

This is Woodward and Bernstein's description of Scowcroft in their book *The Final Days:*

The small man with thinning hair and a scholarly, meek look sat behind the cluttered desk in the West Wing of the White House. His slightly rumpled suit, inexpensive white Dacron shirt, and drooping black socks seemed out of place in the exquisitely furnished office. Around him were the historic keepsakes of five years of whirlwind diplomacy. Contemporary art hung on the walls, and marvelous Oriental rugs lay on dark-blue wall-to-wall carpeting. Foot-high stacks of papers bulged from folders marked "Top Secret." They were piled all across the desk.

It was the office of Henry A. Kissinger, Secretary of State of the United States and national-security adviser to the President. The gentleman sitting at Kissinger's desk was Air Force [General] Brent Scowcroft, one of the Nixon Administration's most powerful men.[104]

Others noticed Scowcroft's clothes. Kissinger's (and later Scowcroft's) personal assistant, Florence Gantt, laughed about how Scowcroft dressed upon arriving at the White House. "We had a joke about Air Force One, he wore high water jeans," his personal assistant recalled. "So for Christmas, we got him a track suit for Air Force One. Neat, very neat. For golfing attire we teased him about his plaid pants." But as Scowcroft spent more time in the White House, "his wardrobe got better," Gantt observed.[105]

Scowcroft and his staff knew they were putting in longer hours than anyone else in the White House because early in the morning and late at night they wouldn't see any other lights on in the West Wing or the Old Executive Office Building. Weekends were particularly productive for Scowcroft and the NSC staff, since he could catch up on the memoranda that had arrived during the week and compose his own messages. So the stacks on Scowcroft's desk would shrink to a more manageable size over the weekend, only to slowly and ineluctably grow again after Monday morning rolled around.

Scowcroft expected his staff to perform. He wanted polished and complete memoranda, "perfect in form and substance," Bud McFarlane, Scowcroft's NSC assistant, said. And he assumed the staff would put in long hours, show total dedication, and exert their utmost efforts on behalf of the president and the United States. But whereas Kissinger demanded perfection and became outraged when he found mistakes, Scowcroft was patient and almost always maintained his cordial demeanor. And rather than having his staff members rewrite memoranda that required it, he'd often simply have his secretarial staff help rewrite them or rewrite them himself. Some thought him "patient to a fault."[106]

While he rarely got mad, he did get upset if someone leaked information or acted without clearing it with him. When one of his secretaries took it upon herself to organize his piles of office papers by subject, he threatened to fire her. (He relented, but refused to speak to the offending secretary for weeks.) This was a rare outburst, however. Gantt could easily tell when he was angry. He'd stay quiet and merely glare at the culprit. Scowcroft simply "didn't get flustered," Gantt said; it was "just incredible"—especially in contrast to Kissinger, who was "was a terror in the office."[107]

Scowcroft's NSC staff appreciated his simple decency in how he treated people and experienced firsthand his puckish and self-effacing sense of humor. When Gantt presented him with notes that required an action on his part, she generally gave him options labeled A, B, and C, occasionally including "Other" as a fourth choice. One time, when asked about scheduling a meeting, he wrote in his own additional option, "When pigs fly," and checked that. Bill Gulley, Scowcroft's aide and good friend, noted that many of those on the NSC staff and many of the "efficient and good-looking secretaries" in the office adored him.[108] Rose Mary Woods (known simply as Rose to Scowcroft and others in the White House), who was particular about her likes and dislikes, loved Scowcroft—and disliked Kissinger. For Maria Downs, the White House social secretary, Scowcroft was a "jewel," her "Little General." The White House secretaries called him "Babycakes."[109]

Bud McFarlane described him as "concerned as a boss and generous." He told of one occasion when Scowcroft, concerned that McFarlane wasn't getting enough time away from the office, conspired with McFarlane's wife to get airline tickets to Nantucket and arrange for a friend to drive them to the airport. When McFarlane protested, his wife called Scowcroft, who then ordered his aide not to come back to work.[110]

Scowcroft was the most popular and most beloved senior official in the Ford administration, with the exception of deputy chief of staff and then chief of staff Dick Cheney—who, Gulley said, was equally well liked. ("The Cheney I knew always had a lopsided smile on his face," press secretary Ron Nessen writes. "He was relaxed around reporters, trading jokes and gossip with them," and "close friends" with many of them.) For Bob Schieffer, Cheney was "the single best staff person I ever worked with." He was "straightforward. He was open. He didn't tell us any dirty laundry, but he was very accessible." Gulley, who'd served in five presidencies, described Cheney and Scowcroft as being as close as any two senior presidential advisers he had ever seen.

Scowcroft's demanding work schedule eased up a little when he traveled with the president. He might then be able to take in a ballgame, go skiing (as with President Ford at Vail), play golf, or enjoy some other kind of break. However, when he was paired with Jack Nicklaus in a celebrity golf tournament, his performance made Gulley, then serving as Ford's military assistant, the "most embarrassed [he'd] been in his life"; Scowcroft was nothing but a "whacker," Gulley said.[111]

Notwithstanding his promotions to major general on October 1, 1973, and then lieutenant general on August 16, 1974, Scowcroft continued to live in the house in Bethesda with Jackie and their daughter, Karen, who was now a teenager. Karen would remain an only child, though Scowcroft says that he and Jackie would have liked to have another.[112]

While he was at the Pentagon, Scowcroft had made time to play squash and practice pistol shooting (and won a prize for his shooting). But he now had no spare time for exercise. So he began to run around his Bethesda neighborhood at night, usually after the late evening news and sometimes as late as midnight. Scowcroft was no jogger, however; he ran seven-minute miles—like "a gazelle," Gantt said when she saw him once—as though he were still running high school track. The late-night runs gave Scowcroft a chance to clear his mind, he said; he was able sort things out, plan speeches, and give the ideas swimming around his head a chance to incubate.[113] And then he'd get up at 4:45 A.M. so that he could be in the office by six.

Brent Scowcroft would get little rest in the mid-1970s, as the nation careened through the Watergate scandal, Nixon's resignation, the end of the Vietnam War, and a seemingly endless parade of other problems and crises.

8

WHITE HOUSE UNDER SIEGE

BRENT SCOWCROFT BEGAN working as deputy national security advisor at the start of Richard Nixon's second term in office—which also marked the beginning of the end of the Nixon presidency. The process was a long and painful one. Although the Watergate burglars were caught breaking into the Democratic Party offices in the Watergate apartment complex on June 17, 1972, the story was slow to develop, with only the *Washington Post* and then the *New York Times* investigating. The scandal broke open in March 1973 when James A. McCord, one of the four men arrested in the Watergate break-in, wrote to Judge John Sirica claiming that the now-indicted burglars had lied at the behest of John Dean, counsel to the president, and John Mitchell, the attorney general. On April 20, 1973, Nixon fired Dean, and aides John Ehrlichman and H. R. Haldeman resigned. On May 22, 1974, Scowcroft learned that Nixon had lied about the cover-up in his statement eleven months previously, on June 23, 1973. On July 31, 1974, Scowcroft found out from chief of staff Alexander Haig that there was a problem with the White House tapes.[114] And on August 9, 1974, Nixon resigned from office.

Watergate damaged the US government's foreign policy, hampered its ability to act in Vietnam, eroded the momentum for SALT II, and disrupted the prospects for a stable US-Soviet relationship.[115] Besides hurting Nixon's effectiveness internationally, it weakened his political power domestically vis-à-vis Congress, the press, and the public. It also depressed the president psychologically, sapping his energy and diverting his attention from governing.

Solitary by nature, Nixon became even more reclusive and withdrawn as the scandal worsened and spread—so much so that over the "last sixteen months" of the Nixon presidency, William L. Stearman of the NSC staff recalled, "Al Haig was the President of the United States." Because Nixon "was so totally wrapped up in Watergate . . . he was a part-time president at best." Haig was running "the day-to-day operations," Stearman observed, and making most of the decisions. And everyone in the White House "more or less assumed this was the case," he added. Special prosecutor Leon Jaworski called Haig the nation's "thirty-seventh-and-a-half president" in light of his role in the period before Nixon's resignation.[116]

Haig himself remembered the White House officials being "stressed to the limit" during the last weeks and months of the Nixon presidency, with most of them simply "seeing [their] way through . . . holding things together" as best as they could.[117]

In consequence, as the Watergate scandal grew increasingly serious and as Haig played an ever larger role running the government, Scowcroft began working more and more closely with Nixon's chief of staff.

The two had an unusual relationship. They were former classmates and fellow junior faculty members at West Point; Haig had been brought back as a tactical officer, responsible for the day-to-day command and discipline of the corps of cadets. Scowcroft said that he and Haig were "very close" when they first overlapped in the White House. Haig helped keep Scowcroft informed, since Kissinger often kept important information from his deputy (and everyone else, for that matter). And when the relationship between Kissinger and Haig soured, Scowcroft and Haig still "had a relationship there that worked very well," one that allowed for a "gradual evolution" of Scowcroft's responsibilities as deputy national security advisor, Scowcroft noted. He conceded he was able to interact with Haig "in a more benign and more nuanced way" than could Kissinger.

Yet Scowcroft and Haig were also wary of each other, as Walter Isaacson reports in his biography of Kissinger. Haig was suspicious of his classmate and protective of his position, and Scowcroft didn't fully trust or feel comfortable with Haig.[118] Scowcroft admits they had a complicated relationship; he and Haig were each a little uncertain and somewhat distrustful of the other. Scowcroft describes Haig and him as getting along "okay"—not a great endorsement.[119]

Besides elevating Haig to de facto president, Watergate exacerbated Nixon and Kissinger's tense, difficult, and in many ways perverse relationship.[120] Each man was insecure, socially awkward, and, from his own perspective, an outsider (although the longer Kissinger held office the more he shed his social awkwardness and outsider status). Nixon resented Kissinger's celebrity and his tendency to take credit for the administration's achievements; Nixon didn't allow Kissinger to give his first televised press conference until mid-1972 or make his first on-the-record speech until April

1973, lest he be outshined. Conversely, Kissinger thought Nixon took undue credit for what Kissinger himself had accomplished.

Scowcroft was caught in the middle. "Richard Nixon is perhaps the most complicated personality that I have ever encountered," he commented, "a mixture of compulsions, fears, and so on." Neither was "Henry Kissinger . . . a simple personality," he added. "And the interaction of the two was quite a burden for me, who frequently found myself in between them. The two of them admired each other, but each was jealous of the other. Watching them operate was awesome. Dealing between the two of them, as I had to do, was a very complicated human process."[121]

Scowcroft thought that both men were brilliant—imaginative, unpredictable, and ambitious to reshape the course of American history. He regarded Nixon as the better global strategist, someone who was "a deep thinker" as well as "quite wise."[122] Nixon was the first US president to use diplomacy to take advantage of the split between the Soviet Union and China; later he fully approved of Scowcroft and Bush's response to the Tiananmen Square massacre, and he quickly reached out to Russia after the collapse of the Soviet Union to help steer it toward a path of integration within the larger international community.

Yet to speak of a Nixon-Kissinger rift, as some did, was too strong a claim, in Scowcroft's view. Each man needed the other for his continued political success, at least until Nixon's final days in office. Moreover, they were intellectually compatible, they implicitly trusted each other's judgment, and they usually found ways to accommodate each other.[123]

One such accommodation was deciding what position Scowcroft would have in the administration. In May 1973, after Haldeman's forced resignation as chief of staff, Nixon wanted to appoint Scowcroft to that role, but according to Rose Mary Woods, Kissinger wouldn't agree to release him. It wasn't Nixon's style to force the issue, so Haig got the job instead.[124]

Watergate propelled Scowcroft into serving as a go-between for Nixon and Kissinger and collaborating more with Haig. The scandal affected him in other ways, too. Well before Nixon resigned, Scowcroft and Lawrence Eagleburger developed a fourteen-step plan for a potential presidential transition, Woodward and Bernstein reported in *The Final Days*. Separately, Kissinger telephoned fourteen key foreign ambassadors and initiated presidential messages to the leaders of thirty-seven foreign countries to ensure the continuity of US foreign policy. Fearful of what a desperate Nixon might do, Kissinger and Haig also arranged for the US military to clear any presidential commands with them before carrying them out.[125]

As the president became more removed from governing, Scowcroft, who was one of the few people Nixon trusted, sometimes received odd late-night demands from him. After a martini or two, Nixon "would order all sorts of unusual things to be done—which I didn't do—and the next morning he'd've forgotten all about it." While the president didn't drink much, Scowcroft said, "alcohol affected him strongly." So he knew to essentially ignore Nixon "when he got in that kind of a mood." And the next day, the president almost always "never mentioned the evening before."[126]

Another weird—and famous—nighttime incident involved Kissinger, who told Scowcroft and Eagleburger that late one evening Nixon had asked him to kneel down with him and pray, which they did. Kissinger said the president was slurring his words and that Nixon asked him not to tell let anyone know "I was not strong."[127]

The day before he resigned, Nixon called Scowcroft and two or three others—Scowcroft didn't identify them—to plan "some mundane thing that he wanted done. . . . It was a real human tragedy," in his description. Nixon "was trying to maintain the spirit of normalcy" when his world was crashing down around him. Scowcroft learned the next day, on August 6, that the president didn't have the votes in the Senate to defeat the resolution for impeachment.[128] That spelled the end of his administration.

On September 8, a month after the resignation, President Ford pardoned Nixon for any crimes he might have committed in connection with the Watergate scandal. The controversial decision put an end to Ford's honeymoon with Congress, the press, and the American public. It's possible that some sort of a deal between Ford and Nixon had been brokered through Haig or arranged by Ford's legal aide, Philip Buchen. The vice president and Haig discussed the president's power to pardon in a meeting on August 1, 1974, when Ford found out that Nixon planned to resign, but there is no hard evidence of any sort of deal. To Ford, Scowcroft, and other White House officials, the pardon made sense and was the right thing to do given the circumstances.[129]

Despite Scowcroft's position as an insider within the Nixon White House and his close relationship with the president, he escaped being tarnished by the Watergate scandal. Not so Henry Kissinger.[130] Because of the wiretaps he'd put on the telephones of his NSC aides (such as Morton Halperin) and staff members in the office of the secretary of defense, Kissinger came under attack for having his own secret taping system. (Scowcroft said he knew about the "dead key" that allowed secretaries and others—such as him—to listen in on Kissinger's phone conversations. The secretaries would

then type transcriptions of these "telcons," which Kissinger sometimes edited.)[131] There was speculation, too, that the secretary of state had known of
the break-ins (including an earlier one on May 28, 1972) and the cover-up
much earlier than he admitted, through David Young, one of his former
aides who co-managed the political intelligence unit known as the "White
House Plumbers."

But despite the increased criticism being directed at Kissinger and the
White House, Nixon's resignation initially gave Kissinger even more power.
Whereas Nixon usually had the upper hand when dealing with Kissinger,
Ford, with his limited foreign policy experience, usually deferred to his
secretary of state. And given his role as de facto national security advisor
and his close relationships with both Kissinger and Ford, Scowcroft also
acquired more influence on US foreign policy.

President Ford had gotten to know Scowcroft through a series of weekly
one-on-one briefings, up to two hours in length, given by the deputy national security advisor to Ford when he was vice president. These afternoon
tutorials had begun in October 1973 at President Nixon's request, following Vice President Spiro Agnew's resignation, and covered a range of complex topics in international politics and US national security. Their purpose
was to educate Ford, since the new vice president had mostly focused on
budgetary and domestic issues when he was a member of Congress. Although Kissinger had started off doing the briefings, Scowcroft soon took
over and handled virtually all of them from November 1973 through early
August 1974.[132]

Scowcroft conducted the tutorials "with phenomenal intensity," according to White House witnesses. But rather than merely lecture Ford, he had
the NSC staff draft short papers, no more than twelve pages in length, on
major issues such as arms control, US-Japan policy, human rights, and specific European allies. Each week, he assigned a paper for Ford to read and
digest in advance of their meeting. Scowcroft would brief Ford on what
had happened around the world that week that affected the United States,
then lead a discussion about the issue covered by that week's paper. In this
way the vice president grew familiar with the context and development of
national security policy, came to learn some of the ins and outs of current
events, and acquired a working knowledge of the "personalities and idio-
syncrasies of the principal actors in foreign affairs."[133]

The informal tutoring forged a close bond between the two, one that
strengthened further once Ford became president, since Scowcroft now
went in to see him three or four times a day for up to a half hour at a time,

gave him daily memos on pressing issues, and, when solicited, offered him advice. In a difficult time, the national security expert John Prados writes, Scowcroft was "a rock of stability."[134]

Scowcroft recognized that his relationship with Ford was much closer than the one he had had with Nixon. It was hard for anyone to get close to Richard Nixon, even his wife, Pat. Ford was much less complicated than his predecessor. He'd never sought the White House; in fact, he probably would have been content to stay on as House minority leader and perhaps become Speaker of the House before retiring from Congress and perhaps taking up another occupation.[135] After being thrust into the presidency, Ford initially planned not to run for election in his own right, changing his mind only to avoid being a lame-duck president for a full two and a half years.[136]

Rather than an "imperial president," Ford was personally modest, down-to-earth, and plainspoken. He was also convivial, relaxed, comfortable with himself, and, like Scowcroft, secure enough not to let Kissinger's "huge personality" bother him. Both he and Scowcroft had grown up in middle America, were moderate to conservative Republicans, and were deeply patriotic. As they got to know each other, Ford came to greatly respect Scowcroft's first-rate intellect, independent thinking, and utter reliability.[137] Scowcroft, in turn, became very fond of Gerald Ford. And after the Ford presidency, the two stayed close. Ford was "a very warm, good-hearted human being," Scowcroft said, and "a very dear friend."[138] Their personal bond helped them forge an effective policy partnership.

———

EVEN APART FROM Watergate, the mid-1970s were a period of enormous conflict and crisis in American society and in US foreign policy. The issues were many: the continuing war in Vietnam; strained US-Soviet relations and the deterioration of détente; a crisis in the intelligence community; turmoil in Europe over economics, party politics, and terrorist organizations such as the Irish Republican Army and the Baader-Meinhof Gang; and the Yom Kippur War, the OPEC embargo, and the first oil crisis of 1973, followed by a period of high inflation, large commodity price increases, and, briefly, wage and price controls.

These crises were played out against a domestic backdrop of political polarization. Americans' trust in the federal government plummeted. Whereas 76 percent of the public had trusted the government "almost always" or "most of the time" in 1964, according to public opinion surveys conducted by the National Election Study, by 1974 only 36 percent of Americans trusted their "government in Washington to do what is right." Once Americans lost that trust, they never regained it.[139]

Democrats in Congress acted boldly against Nixon and then Ford. Congress passed the War Powers Resolution in 1973, designed to prevent future presidents from waging undeclared wars like that in Vietnam. They passed revisions to the Freedom of Information Act to force improved access to executive branch materials. They enacted the Privacy Act in 1974, allowing Americans to inquire what information federal agencies had on them in their files. They passed the Hughes-Ryan Amendment, also in 1974, which required the president to inform Congress of all covert operations. And they passed the Congressional Budget and Impoundment Control Act over Nixon's veto, thereby giving rise to the budget reconciliation procedure (what is now just termed "reconciliation," since it has been applied to non-budget-related legislation as well), which gave Congress enhanced control over federal spending.

In 1974, the so-called Watergate babies—the seventy-five Democrats and thirteen Republicans elected as new members of the Ninety-Fourth Congress—gave the Democrats majorities in both houses of Congress. Washington Senator Henry "Scoop" Jackson and other hawkish Democrats were joined in their opposition to the Ford administration by Albert Wohlstetter, Paul Nitze, and other prominent foreign policy experts, military strategists, and staunch anticommunists. Many later became members of the Committee on the Present Danger (CPD) and eventually "neoconservatives" (the term was coined in 1973 but wasn't in widespread use until the 1980s). Helping the CPD and their allies were key members of the press, particularly syndicated columnist Robert Novak and *New York Times* columnist and former Nixon speechwriter William Safire.

The Ford White House had to swim against these fierce political currents. Scowcroft recalled that he and his colleagues had a "very defensive attitude" and that they took on a "bunker mentality." Events, he said, were "weighing us down." The Ford administration's difficulties were exacerbated by its own internal divisions. Holdovers from the Nixon administration, including Kissinger and Scowcroft, favored détente, US-Soviet arms control agreements, closer US-China ties, and US internationalism. Other officials who had been with Ford when he was vice president and a congressman, including Robert Hartmann, Ford's chief speechwriter, were more skeptical of the Soviet Union, more protective of Nationalist China, and less internationalist. Meanwhile, those surrounding Donald Rumsfeld (who served as Ford's White House chief of staff and then as his secretary of defense)—a group that included press secretary Ron Nessen and deputy chief of staff Dick Cheney—were more pragmatic than the Hartmann group and less ideological.[140]

Scowcroft kept away from controversy and out of public view, devoting his efforts to US-Soviet relations, Vietnam, problems in the Middle East, Angola and other countries in southern Africa, intelligence, and relations with US allies with respect to SALT, NATO, and conventional arms control. Kissinger still dominated the conceptualization and formulation of US foreign policy and grand strategy. But Scowcroft was someone who could efficiently handle difficult national security issues because of his adeptness as a bureaucratic operator, a quality that had first become evident during his years as an up-and-coming Air Force officer collecting aeronautical intelligence in Yugoslavia and ensuring the success of the US Air Force's component of Vietnamization.

Scowcroft's capacity as a strategist—that is, a strategic thinker with the power to directly influence US foreign policy and national security by having his hands on the levers of government—would emerge for the first time in the mid-1970s. It would become increasingly evident the longer he worked on national security policy at the highest levels. But Scowcroft was a policy implementer and bureaucratic operator—a "fixer"—before he became a strategist.

Even in the Yom Kippur War that began on October 6, 1973, Scowcroft's chief role was logistical. When the war started, Kissinger was in New York and Scowcroft was in Washington, where he served as an important back channel to Israeli Ambassador Simcha Dinitz and Soviet Ambassador Anatoly Dobrynin. With Israel fighting on two fronts—against Egypt across the Suez and through the Sinai, and against the Syrians in the Golan Heights—the Israelis immediately petitioned the United States for resupply of armaments. Kissinger and Nixon agreed to a limited resupply, and the Israelis sent over an unmarked El Al 747 to pick up Sidewinder air-to-air missiles, bomb racks, and ammunition.

But Kenneth Rush in the State Department, William Clements in the Defense Department, and Nixon himself resisted any extensive resupply. The president wanted to be tough; he was confident that the Israelis would win ("Thank God," he said), and he bemoaned the fact that now they would "be even more impossible to deal with than before."

By the fourth day of fighting, however, it was clear that Israel was in serious trouble. The Israeli forces had suffered extraordinary losses, on the order of forty-nine airplanes (including fourteen Phantom F-4s) and five hundred tanks, and they were running out of equipment and ammunition. Israeli leaders weren't even sure they could hold on.

In a White House meeting early on October 9, the gruff and defiant Ambassador Dinitz insisted on an extensive resupply and hinted at an Israeli nuclear response against Egyptian and Syrian targets. Kissinger and Nixon changed their minds, promising that the United States not only would begin a modest resupply but also would eventually replace all lost Israeli matériel—so long as both parties agreed to keep it quiet.[141] At about the same time, and making the administration's decision much easier, the Soviets had started a massive airlift to Syria using some twenty Soviet transport aircraft.[142]

Yet Kissinger insisted on using chartered planes rather than Air Force cargo planes, against the wishes of the Defense Department, because he didn't want the United States associated with an Israeli humiliation of Arab states. However, the fleet of civilian aircraft that Scowcroft coordinated with Israel ultimately wouldn't undertake the mission because of the perceived danger. Neither did the Pentagon insist that they do so.

When the news reached the White House of the delay in resupplying Israel, they switched to USAF planes. But even then there were more delays. Scowcroft described Schlesinger as being unhelpful (calling the defense secretary "my chief foot-dragger") in finding USAF cargo planes to lend to the effort.[143] Nonetheless, under Operation Nickel Grass, the US government transported a total of over 22,000 tons of supplies, including almost 9,000 tons before the end of the war, in 567 missions; El Al planes flew another 5,500 tons with 170 flights. The first planes arrived on October 13, to the great relief of the Israelis, delivering more in one day than the Soviet aircraft had brought to Syria in the previous four days combined. By the end of the war, Israel received dozens of aircraft of different sorts, 200 tanks, 250 armored personnel vehicles, massive quantities of 105 mm, 155 mm, and 175 mm ammunition, and new tube-launched, optically tracked, wire-guided (TOW) missiles from the airlifts as well as sealifts that continued after the cease-fire on October 25, 1973.

When Israeli forces surrounded the Egyptian Third Army in the Sinai on October 19, the Soviets sent Kissinger a message saying they wanted to negotiate a cease-fire. So he flew to Moscow—on the same evening as the Watergate crisis that came to be called the "Saturday Night Massacre," with the firing of White House special prosecutor Archibald Cox and the resignations of attorney general Elliott Richardson and deputy attorney general William Ruckelshaus. Kissinger didn't want the plenary negotiating authority Nixon had given him, for he "didn't want to be in the firing line as making the agreement by himself," the deputy national security advisor noted. Kissinger's reasoning was that he wanted to have more time—the delay of going back and forth to the president—so the Israelis could improve their position. When Kissinger and the Soviets quickly negotiated a cease-fire, the Israelis weren't happy, since they had not been able to destroy the Third Army, but for Kissinger, "turning an Arab setback into a debacle" didn't represent a "vital interest" for the United States.[144]

When the Soviets wanted to send in their troops after the cease-fire and there was evidence of a Soviet airlift fleet, Kissinger decided to raise the military alert level from DEFCON 2 to DEFCON 3—not to prepare for war, but to send a clear signal that the Soviets couldn't mistake. The last thing the United States wanted, Scowcroft noted, was Soviet troops in the Middle East. After checking that the cable traffic raising the military alert level had been seen, Kissinger called Dobrynin and gave him the message. Dobrynin said that the airlift planes had never contained troops, and that it was "all a big mistake." Perhaps, but the Soviets had known of the Egyptian attack in advance, according to Robert Gates (a CIA analyst at the time), and even though this era was the high-water mark of détente, they hadn't seen fit to warn the United States.[145]

It was over the course of the subsequent negotiations that Scowcroft got to know and respect Egyptian leader Anwar El Sadat. (At one point, Nixon gave Sadat a ride in the helicopter he and Scowcroft were using, Marine Corps One.) Egypt ended up throwing out the Soviets, perhaps because, in Scowcroft's words, Sadat "was tired of the highhandedness of the Russians."[146]

In the mid-1970s, Kissinger, Nixon, and Ford repeatedly depended on Scowcroft to quietly resolve difficult issues or sensitive problems in US national security policy. Prominent among such delicate issues were foreign military sales.

"I wanted you to meet General Scowcroft," Kissinger told Saudi Arabia's foreign minister in June 1974 at the Royal Guest Palace in Saudi Arabia. "He handles all the sensitive business in the White House for the President and me." In this instance, "the sensitive business" was the sale of TOW antitank missiles to Saudi Arabia and Kuwait.[147] A year earlier, when Kissinger and Schlesinger discussed getting military equipment to Egypt in April 1973, Kissinger had told the secretary of defense to "let [Gen. John A.] Wickham and Scowcroft work out a $180 million package."[148] In August of the same year, when the Defense Department had questions about the sale of British-made Rolls-Royce engines, Kissinger told Schlesinger, "Brent will work it out with you . . . [and] one of the guys at ISA" (the Department of Defense's Office of International Security Affairs, which handled the US military's cooperation with and sales to foreign governments).[149] And when the CIA found out in early 1974 that Soviet advisers had been seen around Damascus, Syria, in increased numbers and that Syria was transferring large amounts of supplies to front-line units, Kissinger checked with Scowcroft to see if the Pentagon had shipped the agreed-upon matériel to the Israelis. Scowcroft assured him that it had.[150]

Arms sales such as these represented an important part of US foreign policy, since selling weapons to other countries empowered those countries and enabled them to serve as the United States' surrogates. They could thereby provide the White House with significantly cheaper and more convenient military and strategic options than would be available were the United States to act on its own. For example, US arms sales to Taiwan might raise the cost to China of intervening militarily, for instance, just as the sale of US military technology to China could improve its position vis-à-vis the Soviet Union (depending on the type, quality, and sophistication of the weapons). In the same way, weapons sales to Israel and its Arab neighbors had to be approved with an eye toward their impact on regional politics and the United States' larger strategic interests.

Foreign military sales also allowed US manufacturers to reduce their per-unit costs, provided them with more revenues and profits, and enabled US defense contractors to grow. This in turn facilitated investment in the R&D necessary for the next generation of weapons. And with the defense industry being big business, employing tens of thousands of workers and having a strong lobbying arm, members of Congress consider weapon sales important politically.

Furthermore, US presidents and their top advisers often agree to sell arms to countries to curry favor with their heads of state, even if those countries might not seem to need the weaponry.[151] As a result, high-level diplomacy between top US and foreign officials, personal chemistry, and simple persuasion also play a role in determining US foreign weapons sales.

With all these factors in play, arms sales quickly get very complicated—hence Scowcroft's close involvement. In working to facilitate the deals, he had to take into account diplomatic relations, international economics, intelligence, and crisis management issues involving several different departments and agencies within the US government, all within the broader context of Cold War politics and the global and regional balance of power.

For example, the United States had a "close defense relationship" with Iran in the mid-1970s. As a result, Scowcroft had to work closely with Carlyle E. Maw, under secretary for international security assistance in the Department of Defense, to sort out the issues involved in "trying to coordinate our arms sales with our foreign policy," as Kissinger explained to President Ford and the secretary of defense.[152]

One of these issues was that the United States was helping Iran develop a nuclear power program that would provide the United States with $6.4 billion in sales of reactor components, fuel supplies, and services. But the United States had the right to determine how any plutonium was to be produced and how it was to be reprocessed, fabricated, or stored, and it reached an agreement with Iran on civilian uses of nuclear power.[153] The US government also allowed Pratt & Whitney of United Technologies to coproduce aircraft engines with Iran, permitted the sale to Iran of 222 Harpoon antiship missiles, approved of the construction of two liquefied natural gas facilities in Iran that would export gas to the United States (though they were never built), and agreed to the sale to Iran of Bell helicopters, F-14s, F-16s, and Spruance-class naval destroyers. These military sales to Iran not only benefited US defense contractors but also gave the Ford administration some additional influence with respect to OPEC's oil pricing and other issues in the Middle East—at least until the shah was toppled from power.

What held with Iran was more broadly true with respect to the Persian Gulf as a whole, where the United States was concerned about the stability of the Gulf states and the outside influence exerted by European states, the Soviet Union, and Japan. Issues of arms supply and training, military bases and their installation, technology transfer, and co-production of equipment all factored in, along with economic policies and regional relationships.[154] Equally complex arrays of concerns were involved in such disparate issues as military deals with Japan in the wake of the Lockheed bribery scandal, the provision of nuclear fuel to India for its Tarapur power plant, and payment to the Philippine government for the use of military bases in that country.[155]

Scowcroft thus had to balance the attractiveness of weapons sales with other considerations. His principal concern was "losing technology to the wrong hands, whether Soviet or non-original recipients," according to Bud McFarlane, his former NSC military aide. So when defense secretary Dick Cheney told McFarlane that forward-looking infrared radiometer (FLIR) or thermal imaging capacity was to be included on airplanes that the United States was selling to Israel, "Brent lost it." Even though "it was a done deal," according to Cheney, and even though the Israeli ambassador insisted the

United States "had to do this," Scowcroft refused. The technology had high strategic value, he pointed out, and "even some units of the USAF" weren't equipped with FLIR.[156]

With Israel, as with other countries, Scowcroft had to weigh the United States' overall interests against the internal politics of the purchasing country when negotiating and approving arms sales. Scowcroft and the Ford administration consequently restricted the sale of some weapons to the Israelis because they could be regionally destabilizing (such as Pershing missiles), technologically compromising (such as FLIR-equipped aircraft), or still in R&D (such the CBU-84, an air-delivered land mine).[157]

Arms sales could also be politically controversial when US military equipment sold overseas was used for the suppression of domestic populations, deployed aggressively against third parties not considered adversaries of the United States, or employed against the United States itself. Indicatively, when Kissinger, Scowcroft, and President Ford were preparing for the first presidential debate between Ford and Democratic candidate Jimmy Carter, Kissinger asked what Schlesinger—who'd joined the Carter side—could bring up against Ford, and Scowcroft answered, "Arms sales."[158]

In managing these and other delicate matters, Scowcroft was exceptionally effective. One reason was the fact that his "agenda was the president's agenda," as a widely experienced NSC staff member put it. While it might seem that this should be taken for granted, in reality presidential assistants and other staff sometimes give pride of place to their own favored policies or personal political prospects, not those of the president.[159] After he resigned, Nixon confided to Bill Gulley that he couldn't remember being as comfortable around any other military general as he was with Scowcroft. Nixon never doubted that Scowcroft's loyalty lay with him.[160]

Nixon and Ford therefore occasionally used Scowcroft for diplomatic purposes, despite the fact that this was usually the State Department's domain. For example, when President Ford and Kissinger were discussing what to do about the situation with Turkey and Cyprus in early July 1975, Ford noted that Representative John Brademas, a Democrat from Indiana, and former national security advisor Walt Rostow wanted to get involved. Kissinger immediately responded, "I think it is better if Brent handles this, so we won't have too many different cooks in the broth."[161] Another time, after he became national security advisor, Scowcroft had to coordinate contingency plans with respect to Cuba and the presence of Soviet pilots.[162]

So Scowcroft's unique combination of intelligence, knowledge, tact, self-confidence, and loyalty made him especially valuable and effective as a fixer for the Nixon and Ford administrations. But Scowcroft also had larger concerns to worry about, including the SALT nuclear weapons treaty and other aspects of US-Soviet relations, attacks from the right on the two administrations' foreign policy, and threats from Congress against the intelligence community. In the years of the Ford administration, these problems would test Scowcroft's talents to the fullest.

9

SALT, DÉTENTE, AND THE
INTELLIGENCE WARS OF THE SEVENTIES

THE BIGGEST CHALLENGE the new Ford administration faced in foreign policy was to negotiate the second round of the Strategic Arms Limitations Treaty (SALT II) to control the costs and dangers of the spiraling nuclear arms race. Scowcroft's primary role was to see to it that the president's policy was coordinated and carried out. But he also served as Ford's and Kissinger's adviser on strategic issues and military affairs, and the longer he worked in the White House, the more he served as an equal partner in guiding US national security policy.

With SALT set to expire in October 1977, President Nixon had arranged to meet with Soviet general secretary Leonid Brezhnev at Vladivostok on November 23 and 24, 1974, following stops in Japan and South Korea. SALT II was more complex than SALT because the United States and Soviet Union had asymmetrical forces built under different concepts—differences that had become increasingly pronounced under SALT. The Soviets now led in the number of launchers and mega-tonnage, whereas the United States had more warheads, since it had many more missiles with multiple warheads (MIRVs). The Soviets were proceeding rapidly on four new types of ICBMs, and the United States was developing the B-1 bomber, the Trident nuclear submarine, and an anti-ballistic-missile system (ABM).[163]

That same asymmetry of US-Soviet nuclear forces made the administration a ready target for criticism from hard-line anti-Soviets and political conservatives. Sen. Henry Jackson pointed out that SALT put no limits on the numbers of heavy bombers or MIRVed missiles, since it simply froze the total number of sea- and land-based ICBMs at 2,360 for the Soviet Union and 1,710 for the United States. Scoop Jackson, Paul Nitze, political scientist and commentator Jeane Kirkpatrick, and other politicians, newspaper pundits, and military experts feared that Soviet Union could overtake the United States if it had more missiles with multiple warheads and built more long-range bombers.

Given these criticisms and the upcoming 1976 presidential elections, Ford kept to Nixon's plan to meet at Vladivostok (actually at a secluded spa just outside the port city on the Sea of Japan). He wanted to use the summit to secure agreements on the number of nuclear delivery vehicles (missiles, bombers, and submarines) and the number of missiles with multiple warheads, which could serve as the foundation for SALT II.

The meeting largely succeeded. After hours of negotiations, Ford and Brezhnev agreed to establish a ceiling of 2,400 nuclear delivery vehicles each and to limit the number of missiles with multiple warheads to 1,320 each. They further agreed not to build more nuclear missile silos or to enlarge their existing missile silos by more than 15 percent, and they agreed to ban testing and deployment of sea- and ground-launched cruise missiles with ranges greater than six hundred kilometers. Air-launched cruise missiles with a range greater than six hundred kilometers would be included under the ceiling on nuclear delivery vehicles. Brezhnev also agreed to drop the demand that European and Communist Chinese nuclear weapons and US bombers based in Europe also be factored in. Neither did the United States have to stop production of the Trident submarine or cancel plans for the B-1. The agreement, if approved, was to last until 1985.

The president was delighted with the Vladivostok summit, since the long hours of difficult negotiations had led him to believe that the Soviets would never agree to numerical equality in ballistic missiles. The summit exceeded his expectations, he writes in his memoirs.[164]

But the Vladivostok agreement had to be approved by the Senate if there was to be a SALT II—and, as a practical matter, the Pentagon also had to sign off. On both points the administration met with failure.

Scowcroft, who'd advised Ford and Kissinger during the summit, observed that the US Joint Chiefs were "tending toward signing the Vladivostok position and exempting cruise missiles and Backfire." Keeping the cruise missiles off the table helped the United States, while excluding the Backfire, a Soviet medium-range bomber, presumably helped the USSR. (The Soviets denied it was a long-range bomber; US experts said it had such capability with in-flight refueling.) Kissinger, for his part, dreaded taking the agreement to the Senate. "I am not anxious for an agreement," he said, "because it just gets me into a brutal fight with [Senator] Jackson." Scowcroft agreed, saying, "Jackson will attack it no matter what."[165]

Scoop Jackson, chairman of the Senate Armed Services Committee Sub-committee on Arms Control, would twice seek the Democratic presidential nomination, and in 1968 he had declined Nixon's offer to become secretary of defense (the job went to Melvin Laird). Jackson now joined with other Democratic hawks and Republican conservatives, as well many in the Pentagon, in attacking the Vladivostok agreement. He contended the deal would allow the Soviet Union to produce an intercontinental delivery vehicle, the Backfire, while the United States had to give up the Tomahawk cruise missile. The agreement, he contended, eliminated any incentive for the United States to improve its weapon systems, while the Soviet Union would gain parity and the potential to achieve superiority over the United States. Meanwhile, critics on the left pointed out how high the new weapons ceilings were and that they represented little constraint on the arms race. Lacking the support he needed, Ford backed away from the Vladivostok agreements and SALT II. The Backfire and cruise missile issues never got resolved, and SALT II would die under the Carter administration.[166]

Meanwhile, the Ford administration was suffering other blows. Less than two months after the Vladivostok meetings, on January 3, 1975, the Jackson-Vanik Amendment became law. Members of Congress had been outraged to learn that shortly after 1972 summit, the Soviet Union had imposed an exit tax on Soviet emigration. Although the tax was relatively insignificant, given the other practices of the Soviet police state, it induced Jackson and Representative Charles Vanik to attach an amendment to a trade bill that would deny most-favored-nation trade status, credits, and other economic benefits to any "non-market economy" that inhibited the right to emigrate. Kissinger and Scowcroft believed that the Jackson-Vanik Amendment interfered with US-Soviet relations and tied their hands in dealing with the Soviets. They further contended that it jeopardized détente by using crude legislative clout where quiet diplomacy would be more effective.[167]

In fact, emigration from the Soviet Union had increased in recent years, but after the passage of the Jackson-Vanik Amendment, it began to fall. Not until December 2012 was Jackson-Vanik repealed.[168]

In mid-1975, the administration came under more fire from anti-Soviet conservatives when the Soviet dissident novelist and Gulag survivor Aleksandr Solzhenitsyn came to visit the United States. AFL-CIO president George Meany invited Ford to a June 30 banquet in honor of Solzhenitsyn. A week later, Sen. Jesse Helms and Sen. Strom Thurmond also separately invited President Ford to meet with Solzhenitsyn.

John "Jack" Marsh, Ford's congressional liaison, Rumsfeld, and Cheney all advised the president to accept the invitation and attend the dinner. But

Kissinger and Scowcroft "strongly argued against it," fearing that if Ford met with Solzhenitsyn—a private citizen whom European leaders had refused to agree to meet—it would sabotage the upcoming negotiations with the Soviets at the Helsinki conference, only a few weeks away. Ford accepted his advisers' suggestion and declined to see Solzhenitsyn. Notwithstanding the dissident's great personal courage and devout Christianity, the president considered Solzhenitsyn—who opposed détente and East-West coexistence and disdained American popular culture and Western consumerism—arrogant and "a goddamned horse's ass." But when the news leaked that the president wouldn't be meeting with Solzhenitsyn, the resulting uproar caused Ford to reverse his decision and invite Solzhenitsyn to the White House after the Helsinki conference. Solzhenitsyn said he was too busy.[169]

Ford paid a heavy political price. "That refusal to see the most powerful witness against Soviet tyranny," Cheney later remarked, "became a centerpiece of the conservative foreign policy against Ford."[170]

Conservatives and human rights advocates likewise vigorously criticized Ford, Kissinger, and the administration for the president's participation in the Conference on Security and Cooperation in Europe (CSCE). Since the 1950s, Soviet leaders had wanted their European and US counterparts to recognize the boundaries established after the Second World War. US presidents had seen no advantage in doing so until the early 1970s under Nixon, when the Soviets made concessions with respect to the status of West Berlin, agreed to meet with US and European officials in Vienna on mutual and balanced force reduction (MBFR), and embarked on détente.[171]

So in 1973 President Nixon had begun to make plans for a CSCE conference to be held in Helsinki in two years' time. Thirty-five countries were to be represented, as well as the Vatican, which would make the Helsinki meeting the largest gathering of European states since the 1815 Congress of Vienna. Kissinger approved of the conference, insofar as the United States needed to support its European and NATO allies and demonstrate the administration's commitment to staying engaged in international affairs. Although the CSCE results (which were essentially all negotiated in advance of the meeting—hence its title, the Helsinki Final Act) recognized the post–World War II boundaries, they were "not wholly what the Soviets wanted," as Kissinger noted. They did nothing to undermine NATO and were largely permeated with the philosophical assumptions shared by "the West's open societies."[172]

The CIA's analysis stated, "In summary, the agreements that will be signed in Helsinki touch on virtually all areas of critical interest to Europe. But they will not have a decisive impact on European events, and the future course of detent in Europe will be much more affected by West European and US cooperation," by "the possible emergence of new leadership in Moscow," and by the "growth of East-West economic interdependence," among other factors.[173]

The Helsinki Final Act itself, to which all of the attendees agreed, laid out a set of recommendations in four categories, or "baskets": (1) the observation of boundaries and respect for human rights, (2) improved cooperation on economic issues, (3) support for human rights, media information, and free movement of people and ideas, and (4) instruments for monitoring compliance and scheduling future conferences. If the Soviets benefited more from the first two baskets, the West had more to gain from the third and fourth, which had the potential to undermine the legitimacy of the Soviet police state and ultimately endanger the Soviet Union.[174]

In the end, Kissinger was ambivalent about the Helsinki Final Act, and by the time of the meeting he was at pains to distance himself from the accords. He feared the Soviets were using the CSCE in an attempt to weaken the European commitment to NATO. He also thought the accords were a "bunch of crappy ideas," especially the third basket on human rights. "A lot of conservatives are screaming that the Security Conference is sanctifying the Soviet presence in Europe," he told the writer William F. Buckley. "The Conference wasn't our idea. It isn't something I'm proud of. Our instructions to our men was to stay ½ step behind the Europeans. . . . The territorial integrity issue is something they have gone over for years. It isn't in our interests," he added, "to build up something that isn't that important."[175]

The CIA, too, was ambivalent, concerned that the Soviets were trying to use the Helsinki accords to split the United States from its European allies. According to Ford's briefing book for the conference, prepared by the NSC staff, Soviet officials perceived the CSCE as means by which "the Soviet Union hope first to freeze the political map of Europe and thereby extend its political influence westward."[176]

By contrast, Scowcroft was firmly committed to the Helsinki conference. Not only did he appreciate that the United States' European allies very much wanted the CSCE conference, but he thought it could help unite the West, ease East-West tensions, and provide extra impetus to the ongoing SALT negotiations. Furthermore, the Helsinki meeting could show that the administration cared about human rights, contrary to the accusations of both the right and the left.[177] Scowcroft realized that the agreement didn't change political and strategic realities in Europe, but he saw it as constituting a promising step. This wasn't so much an ideological issue for Scowcroft, since he viewed Soviet motives from a perspective of their own national security, but a matter of practical diplomacy: the Helsinki accords would strengthen US relations with Europe and improve the United States' and the West's positions vis-à-vis the Soviet Union and Eastern Bloc at minimal cost.

With this larger, longer-term picture in mind, Scowcroft ended up at the last minute drafting a speech for the president to deliver at Andrews Air Force Base just before his departure for Bonn, Warsaw, and then Helsinki. A speech had already been drafted by Hartmann and Ford's speechwriting staff, though because the speechwriters hadn't consulted with the NSC (ostensibly because Kissinger had never informed the White House how the United States and the Ford administration stood to gain from the Helsinki conference), the speech had negative, hostile overtones.

When Scowcroft saw it, he realized that he had to write a completely separate speech if the president was going to salvage the CSCE conference for the purposes of the United States' international diplomacy. It spoke of President Ford's "mission of peace and progress," of the hopes of the people of Eastern Europe that depended upon "increased cooperation and stability between the East [and] the West," and of the United States' support "for the aspirations for freedom and national independence of peoples everywhere." The Helsinki accords, Scowcroft wrote, constituted a "forward step for freedom."[178] Ford chose to deliver Scowcroft's speech.

In the conference's closing ceremony, Ford reemphasized the same ideas. "These principles are not clichés or empty phrases," he stated. "We take this work and these words very seriously. We will spare no effort to ease tensions and to solve problems between [the United States and the Soviet Union]," he said, "but it is important that [Secretary Brezhnev] realize the deep devotion of the American people and their government to human rights and fundamental freedoms and thus to the pledges that this conference has made regarding the freer movement of people, ideas, and information."[179]

For Scowcroft, the "great achievement" of the Helsinki accords "was that it started the process that undermined Moscow's ability to dominate its neighbors." With the Helsinki Final Act, party secretary Leonid Brezhnev committed the Soviet Union to an international agreement that recognized that "the participating states will respect each other's sovereign equality and individuality . . . including in particular the right of every state to juridical equality, to territorial integrity, and to freedom and political independence." As Ford points out in *A Time to Heal*, the Soviet leader was effectively renouncing the Brezhnev Doctrine, which claimed the right of the Soviet Union to intervene militarily so as to protect existing communist governments, as with its intervention in Czechoslovakia in 1968.[180] What's more, the United States and the other member states agreed to West Germany's proposal that it be allowed to peacefully change its borders as long as both East Germany and West Germany were in agreement.

The US delegation in Helsinki, unfortunately, made no further progress toward resolving the sticky issues in the SALT negotiations—specifically, the status of the Soviet Backfire bomber and the US cruise missiles. But the Helsinki Final Act put into play the very forces that would eventually end the Cold War.[181] In just fifteen years' time, Germany would be reunified, Poland and other Eastern bloc states would be independent, the Baltic nations would be free, and the Soviet Union would be on its way to oblivion. Even in the short run, the CSCE agreements seemed to have an effect: in the months following Helsinki, Soviet authorities began to allow ethnic Germans to leave Poland as well as the Soviet Union for West Germany. The Soviets began to provide advance notice to European countries of Warsaw Pact military exercises and to invite the attendance of European observers to those exercises. And they began to allow more Soviet Jews to emigrate.

Nonetheless, those on the right in both American political parties likened the CSCE to Yalta. They didn't care for it beforehand, and they didn't approve of it afterward. "Don't go," editorialized the *Wall Street Journal*. Governor Ronald Reagan declared that "all Americans should be against it," and others—even including some White House aides—joined in openly condemning the Helsinki Final Act.

After the conference, Congress established the Commission on Security and Cooperation in Europe, consisting of twelve members of Congress and three executive officials charged with monitoring compliance with the Helsinki Final Act. Congress would at once impel the administration to move aggressively on human rights and keep tabs on the Soviet Union's progress with respect to human rights.[182]

Besides displeasing hard-line members of Congress, conservative Republicans, and Washington pundits, the summit angered ethnic groups representing various Eastern European countries. Prior to the CSCE meeting, they threatened to vote against Ford in 1976 should he go to Helsinki, and they were hostile now that he had signed the Helsinki Final Act—this despite the crowds in Poland, Yugoslavia, and Romania who enthusiastically cheered President Ford during his East European tour. Ford's approval ratings fell after the CSCE conference.

Unhappiness over Helsinki, SALT, détente, and the fall of Vietnam fed a wider perception of US weakness. "The United States now faces its first defeat in 200 years of independent history" stated the London-based *Financial Times*. One German writer wondered about the United States' commitment to freedom: "The Americans did nothing to interfere with the erection of the Berlin Wall" fifteen years after the post–World War II division of Germany. "Now, 30 years later, I am convinced they would not go to war if the Soviets decided to straighten out what they would doubtlessly call a 'cold war abnormality' and made an overnight grab for West Berlin."[183] And James Schlesinger—after he was dismissed from his position as secretary of defense—wrote of other nations' perceptions of America's waning strength, not only among European countries but also China and in Latin America.[184]

This rightward shift and the mobilization of Democrats, Republicans, and much of the Beltway community against Nixon's foreign policy was the product of design. In two famous articles published in 1974, Albert Wohlstetter argued that the United States was declining vis-à-vis the Soviet Union, and the Defense Department assisted the spread of such perceptions by leaking relevant materials to Senator Jackson and a cross section of columnists of various political persuasions, including Rowland Evans and Robert Novak, Jack Anderson and Les Whitten, Joseph Kraft, James Kilpatrick, Tom Wicker, Anthony Lewis, and William Safire.

Some began to organize around their belief that the United States was falling behind. In July 1974—perhaps earlier—Paul Nitze, Eugene Rostow, Admiral Elmo Zumwalt, and a handful of others began to get together to map out a strategy for shifting US foreign policy. Two years later, Rostow gathered like-minded people at the Metropolitan Club in New York City to set up the National Emergency Committee on Foreign and Defense Policy. Rostow, Nitze, Richard Pipes, Jeane Kirkpatrick, journalist Midge Decter, and Richard Perle, then an aide to Senator Jackson, planned on raising funds from the "Scaifes and the Richardson Foundation," to use the media, to publish articles in specialized journals, and to enlist prominent policy makers, experts, scientists, and academics to warn of the grave threats facing the United States as a result of recent US presidents' attempts to negotiate with and appease the Soviet Union.[185]

Less than two months later, on May 11, 1976, Rostow and Nitze formalized what they had started by forming the bipartisan Committee on the Present Danger. Other members of the committee included Gen. Andrew Goodpaster and Scowcroft's former superior officer Gen. John Vogt. Much later Scowcroft said he hadn't realized either man was a member.[186]

To some degree, Scowcroft shared in this rightward shift. By the time he wrote about the US-Soviet relationship in the late 1970s, following the Ford presidency, he had come to realize that the Soviets regarded détente as a tactic, not an end in itself, and that they played strategic hardball. He recognized that Nixon and Kissinger had oversold the benefits of SALT and détente, even if both were still worth pursuing. And though Scowcroft was by no means a member of the Committee on the Present Danger, he was as dedicated to containing the Soviet Union as anyone else. However, Scowcroft's opposition was based on the threat posed by Soviet military capabilities, views shaped by his study of Russian history and his observations from being in Yugoslavia rather than his ideological differences. He also firmly believed that US presidents had to have the wherewithal to maneuver politically, acquire information, conduct espionage, and embark on covert operations without being under the prying eyes of Congress and the press.

Meanwhile, the administration faced as least as strong a threat from the Democrat-controlled Congress and the political left. This threat to the presidency became perhaps most apparent at the end of 1974 and over the next fourteen months, with revelations about systematic abuses by the CIA.

FLYING OUT TO Vail on December 22 for the 1974 Christmas holidays, President Ford read a *New York Times* front-page article by Seymour Hersh about how the CIA had engaged in massive domestic spying in the 1950s and 1960s. Ford contacted the director of central intelligence (DCI), William Colby, who partly confirmed the story but also said it overstated the CIA's culpability (the same thing Colby had told Hersh). It was then that Colby told the president of the "skeletons" or "family jewels"—an extensive set of top-secret documents on improper behavior by the CIA that had been compiled by agency officials at the request of DCI James R. Schlesinger (on Nixon's directive) in early 1973.[187]

Among the family jewels were records concerning the CIA's wiretapping of more than 9,900 American citizens, keeping files on a hundred thousand Americans, opening Americans' first-class mail, infiltrating domestic antiwar and black activist groups, and conducting psychological experiments on civilians—all legally prohibited. Among the CIA's other improper surveillance activities were illegal breaking and entering at of the premises of two former CIA employees, the placement of wiretaps on two newspaper columnists, and the physical surveillance of three former CIA employees and five reporters (Jack Anderson and two of Anderson's staff members as well as Brit Hume and a *Washington Post* reporter). The CIA had also recruited paid informants among Washington-area dissident groups, opened the mail of those corresponding between the United States and "certain communist countries" (namely, the Soviet Union and the People's Republic of China), and recruited people to infiltrate US dissident groups for the purpose of collecting foreign intelligence.[188]

Not only did these revelations cast doubt on the capabilities and competence of the CIA and intelligence community, but they further damaged the administration, shifting the balance of power away from the executive branch and toward the legislative. For many in the press and among the public, it appeared the whole national security apparatus had gone awry and that US presidents and their advisers weren't minding the shop—and hadn't been doing so for decades.

Although the CIA had been created by Congress via the National Security Act of 1947, the intelligence community hadn't been subject to close scrutiny up to this point. Now that was about to change. Congress could assert its ultimate control and subject the agency to its investigations. The CIA had violated the trust of Congress and the American public; its "secrecy," John Ranelagh writes in *The Agency*, "was the mask for disgrace." Nixon had been right not to trust the CIA—except that Nixon himself had relied on the organization to infiltrate the antiwar movement, to help him in Watergate, and to act against President Salvador Allende in Chile. By so doing, Nixon himself further damaged the reputation of the agency.[189]

Ford and his advisers had several immediate objectives. They wanted to escape any taint of a cover-up. They wanted to ensure that the CIA's misdeeds weren't repeated. They wanted to limit the damage to the CIA. And they hoped, by moving quickly, to avoid any intrusive congressional investigations.

The day after the story broke, Kissinger advised Rumsfeld that the White House needed to act fast "to head off, if possible, a full-blown congressional investigation outside of the normal legislative channels." President Ford agreed. As a member of the intelligence subcommittee of the House Appropriations Committee, Ford had been among the few members of Congress privy to CIA secrets. He'd also served on the Warren Commission, which investigated the assassination of President Kennedy, and in the aftermath of the Bay of Pigs disaster, he'd come out in defense of DCI Allen Dulles and the CIA.[190]

Eight days later, with Executive Order 11828 of January 4, 1975, President Ford established an eight-member independent commission, chaired by Vice President Rockefeller, to investigate the CIA's domestic operations and make recommendations as to how the agency should be administered. It had three months to produce its report—a short period designed to preempt the findings of any congressional investigations. But its chief objective, Rumsfeld noted, was to be "a damage-limiting operation for the President."[191]

Meanwhile, CBS News's Daniel Schorr reported that the CIA had been involved with at least three assassination attempts, targeting Fidel Castro of

Cuba, Rafael Trujillo of the Dominican Republic, and Patrice Lumumba of the Congo. Ford himself generated the story—perhaps intentionally, perhaps not—by telling reporters about the CIA's dark secrets at an off-the-record White House luncheon. Additional stories then broke on the CIA's complicity in coups in Guatemala, Iran, the Congo, Brazil, and Indonesia. With the assassinations of John F. Kennedy, Martin Luther King Jr., Robert F. Kennedy, and Malcolm X still fresh in American memory, the revelation of foreign assassinations at the behest of US government officials resonated uncomfortably.[192]

Reporters and their editors and producers figured they had another Watergate on their hands. And when the Rockefeller Commission finished its work in the summer of 1975, after being granted a two-month extension, the press believed there'd been yet another cover-up, since the commission's report drew no conclusions about CIA assassination attempts, merely referring to allegations of such attempts.[193]

On January 27, 1975, the Senate voted 82–4 to create the Select Committee to Study Governmental Operations with Respect to Intelligence Activities, also known as the Church Committee after its chairman, Idaho senator Frank Church. Just a few weeks later, the House of Representatives created a similar committee under the leadership of New York congressman Otis Pike.

Scowcroft had no alternative to being involved in the investigations, especially since the national security advisor had formal oversight of intelligence and covert actions. But to handle Congress's growing demands for classified documents, chief of staff Don Rumsfeld created the Intelligence Coordinating Group, with Michael Raoul-Duval, a White House lawyer, as its executive director. Members of Congress and their staffers also worked through White House counsel Philip Buchen. Scowcroft was therefore spared the day-to-day challenge of responding to Congress's demands for documents. The congressional investigations nonetheless took up some 25–30 percent of his time on top of his already huge workload.[194]

Scowcroft became caught up in three aspects of the intelligence mess in particular. One involved deciding how to respond to congressional requests—whether to release classified information, to redact classified documents before handing them over, or to provide paraphrased versions of those same documents. He wanted to manage the release of information that could hurt the CIA, degrade the effectiveness of the intelligence community, and handicap national security policy—and possibly that of succeeding presidents. And to Scowcroft's dismay, the information was being leaked. He didn't blame the reporters or editors who printed the leaks.

"The real problem is the people who are leaking the material to the press," he told President Ford. "They are the ones we have to go after."[195]

Chief among the newspapers' sources was DCI William Colby—making Colby the second part of the CIA scandal Scowcroft had to handle.

Colby had had an outstanding record in World War II, in postwar Italy, and then in Vietnam with the controversial Phoenix program (which arrested, interrogated, tortured, and eventually killed thousands of suspected Viet Cong). Scowcroft, who worked closely on intelligence issues as deputy national security advisor, said he had gotten to know Colby "quite well." But after the disclosure of the "family jewels" and with the investigations by the Church and Pike Committees, Colby decided to come clean. He made thirty-two trips to Capitol Hill to testify over a twelve-month period, revealing many of the CIA's activities (although he did withhold information on the CIA's human sources and its proprietary technology). Colby also said he intended to hand CIA documents over to Senator Church—even though Ford, Kissinger, Scowcroft, the president's general council, and others in the administration hadn't yet agreed whether they should submit the documents.[196]

Scowcroft did not understand how Colby could side with Congress rather than the executive branch. "Bill really became a tortured soul in this period. He saw his life and his life's work crumbling," Scowcroft told Colby's son, Carl Colby. "I often wondered if Bill was not expiating his sins, starting with the Phoenix program and whatever had gone wrong in it that he felt responsible for." Scowcroft said he thought Colby was "always deeply disturbed by the Phoenix program" and that the "Phoenix program wrenched him fundamentally." He also mentioned "the tragedy of [Colby's] daughter," who died as a young adult from a combination of epilepsy and anorexia nervosa. "Maybe, like Job, he had to atone," Scowcroft continued. "I would never say he fell apart. But it was a very traumatic period and I think he could be excused for feeling overwhelmed at times."[197] He thought that Colby was behaving "very, very differently" from the person he had earlier known. Colby, he concluded, was a "troubled man."[198]

Kissinger had a stronger reaction. Upon learning that Colby intended to give files to members of Congress, including ones the Church Committee hadn't even asked for, Kissinger was enraged. "Goddamn Colby," he exclaimed. "They charge him with shoplifting; he confesses to murder." To Colby himself, Kissinger joked, "Bill, you know what you do when you go up to the Hill? You go to confession."[199]

What Scowcroft and Kissinger regarded as betrayal, however, others saw differently. The *Washington Post*'s Walter Pincus saw Colby as being committed to uphold the oath he had taken to protect the Constitution. Rumsfeld thought Colby felt caught between the legislative and executive branches. And Bob Woodward figured that Colby believed that the administration he served and the laws he followed had both lost their moral authority.[200] As one CIA official later put it, "The tragedy was that he believed."[201]

For his part, Colby regarded Scowcroft as being fiercely loyal "to the Presidential command structure."[202] And he was right. Scowcroft's concern with Colby derived from his larger concern with protecting executive privilege. Both the Church and Pike Committees "were undermining the executive branch," Scowcroft said, and "were doing so in an unthoughtful way." The congressional investigations amounted to a "witch hunt" and were "extremely stressful," he said, given "everything else that was going on." So whereas "Colby wanted to have open files," Scowcroft wanted "to protect records" and didn't allow Colby to take all that he wanted—although he "allowed him to look at particular ones." Together with chief of staff Dick Cheney, Scowcroft considered Congress to be "taking advantage of the weak executive."[203]

Scowcroft, like Kissinger, was also very much opposed to Colby's actions and White House leaks:

> Kissinger: On this intelligence business, I want you to know I think I cannot tolerate junior people testifying on policy issues. Nor am I willing to follow Colby's precedent of letting them paw through cables. Then there is this NSA [National Security Agency] stuff coming out.
> President: Can't we prosecute?
> Scowcroft: Yes. I am suggesting we look into that. There is a more damaging article by Tad Szulc in *Penthouse.*
> Kissinger: It is disastrous. We have no secrets left.[204]

(The Szulc article accused the Federal Republic of Germany, with US involvement, of conducting secret NATO-sponsored intermediate-range nuclear missile and cruise missile tests in Zaire, the former Belgian Congo.)

As a realist and as a military man who believed in centralized control, Scowcroft felt it was essential to defend the US intelligence community against its critics on Capitol Hill and in the press. For Scowcroft, Colby's faith in the wisdom of Americans' representations in Congress was foolhardy, a recipe for degrading the influence of the executive branch and for weakening the ability of the United States to act overseas. Scowcroft believed that the president had preeminent authority over US foreign policy and national security and that allowing interference from Congress was unwise, especially at this crucial moment in the life-and-death struggle between the West and the East. Such interference would slow down decision making, produce leaks, and gum up the works. If the Church Committee decided to "publish a report at all," in Scowcroft's view, it would be "irresponsible."[205]

Not everyone in the Ford administration agreed with Scowcroft and Kissinger. Robert Hartmann, Jack Marsh, Philip Buchen, and others thought that stonewalling Congress would be counterproductive, and they argued for more cooperation.[206] They often had the president on their side. And if Scowcroft got to "spend five minutes with the president," Bud Mc-Farlane observed, Marsh and Hartmann would then spend "thirty minutes with the President." Scowcroft thus learned to pick his fights, realizing that the president wasn't as adamant as he was about protecting executive privilege, with McFarlane once remarking that "Brent didn't back me up" with respect to records McFarlane had stored in the White House basement and which Marsh wanted to turn over to over to Congress. But Ford had limited political capital, and Scowcroft was most likely aware of how far he could—and should—push the president.[207]

Toward the end of Colby's tenure as DCI and following his repeated trips to the Hill, members of Congress—perhaps in response to a ground-swell of reaction among many Americans and more cautionary coverage in the press—began to pull back. The CIA may have made errors, but almost everyone agreed it didn't warrant being dismantled. By the time the Church Committee released its two-foot-thick report in May 1976, the rush to condemn the CIA had somewhat abated. For one thing, it had become obvious that the CIA's misdeeds had a bipartisan pedigree. Colby and the Church Committee both discovered that both John and Robert Kennedy were implicated in the CIA's illegalities, as were LBJ and other Democrats. These revelations greatly diminished the value of the scandal as a weapon of partisanship. Then the assassination of the CIA station chief in Greece in December 1975, followed by Ford's statement about it in his 1976 State of the Union address, fueled a backlash against the attacks on the CIA.

Perhaps reflecting this altered climate, the Church Committee ended up taking moderate positions in its report and succeeded in keeping the report secret. (By contrast, the Pike Report was leaked to the press, with major portions published in the *Village Voice*.) Contrary to Church's declaration in the Senate that the CIA was a "rogue elephant"—a statement many saw as grandstanding spurred by Church's own presidential ambitions—his committee made no such claim in its report. The Church Committee found serious errors, abuses, and oversights, but nothing of a gross or systematic nature. Rather, everything the CIA had done had been in accordance with explicit or implicit instructions from the White House.[208]

The intelligence scandal prompted Scowcroft to figure out how the White House could reform the intelligence system to improve its functioning. This was the third part of his involvement with the crisis in the intelligence community. When the Rockefeller Commission finished its report, Scowcroft ordered a comprehensive study of the organization and management of the entire intelligence community to be led by Donald Ogilvie, the associate director of the Office of Management and Budget. The report was to follow up on the findings of the Rockefeller Commission, include a report on foreign policy and intelligence compiled by Under Secretary of State Robert Murphy, and follow up on the "decision book" that Michael Raoul-Duval had spent six months producing for Dick Cheney, which sorted out the functions of the intelligence agencies. Scowcroft's hope was to get the administration out ahead of the issue before either of the congressional reports forced its hand.

Scowcroft then met with the president and his top advisers on January 6 and February 16, 1976, where Ford agreed with Scowcroft, Bush, Buchen, Marsh, and attorney general Edward H. Levi to define the intelligence agencies in terms of their public charters and to vest control in the DCI. (By contrast, Rumsfeld, deputy secretary of defense Robert Ellsworth, and chairman of the Joint Chiefs of Staff Gen. George S. Brown wanted to leave line authority to other agencies.)[209]

In a two-hour meeting on January 10, 1976, with the president and his chief foreign policy advisers (including Colby, who stayed on as DCI for another few months), Scowcroft addressed a number of key issues. He discussed the sharing of information between the foreign intelligence community and the FBI, whether the president should have an independent intelligence adviser, and how covert action proposals should be handled. He also made recommendations as to how the leadership of the intelligence community should be improved, how intelligence should be consolidated, and how analysis and production of intelligence should be realigned. He also discussed whether covert action should be separated from the CIA, and he speculated about the major reorganization options for the community.[210]

Five weeks later, on February 18, in an effort to get ahead of the issue and spare the intelligence community further damage, the president released the administration's plans to "strengthen our foreign intelligence capability" to "gather and evaluate foreign intelligence and conduct necessary covert action." In a special message to Congress of February 18, Ford announced that in order to conduct intelligence activities "in a Constitutional and lawful manner, never aimed at our own citizens," and to establish an effective process to prevent abuses, he was issuing an omnibus executive order (EO 11905) based on twenty of the thirty recommendations in the Rockefeller Commission report and on Duval's "decision book." In order to get other reforms passed, the president asked members of Congress to draft legislation that would protect individuals, concentrate supervision of intelligence in Congress, and discourage leaks on foreign intelligence.[211]

The establishment of the new ground rules for intelligence essentially retained oversight in the National Security Council, following the original 1947 National Security Act. Now, however, the president's assistant for national security affairs—the national security advisor—would be in control. Intelligence planning was to originate with the NSC, which was to conduct semiannual policy reviews of foreign intelligence activities and to manage and control the foreign intelligence community through the Committee on Foreign Intelligence, which was to consist of the DCI, the deputy secretary of defense for intelligence, and the deputy assistant to the president for national security affairs.

Covert actions were to be reviewed and recommended by a new Operations Advisory Group, consisting of the national security advisor (chair), the secretary of state, the secretary of defense, the DCI, and the chairman of the Joint Chiefs, with the attorney general and the head of the Office of Management and Budget as observers. General oversight of the CIA was to be conducted by the Intelligence Oversight Board (IOB), a three-person subgroup of the President's Foreign Intelligence Advisory Board (PFIAB), which would receive and consider reports on a quarterly basis, review the practices and procedures of the intelligence community, and make periodic reports. EO 11905 specified the distinct responsibilities of the Central Intelligence Agency, Federal Bureau of Investigation, National Security Agency, and Defense Intelligence Agency, among other agencies, and prohibited or severely restricted the collection of information on US citizens, opening mail, infiltrating domestic groups, and physical or electronic surveillance of US citizens, among other activities. It also put explicit restrictions on surveillance both personal and electronic, experimentation, and assassinations.[212]

Ford wanted to clean house, but he refused "to be a party to the dismantling of the CIA and other intelligence agencies." Critics in fact claimed that the new organizational structure served to heighten presidential involvement in agency activities and reinforced the barriers between the executive and legislative branches.[213] According to *Newsweek* magazine, the biggest winner was George H. W. Bush, the newly appointed DCI, since the director of central intelligence now oversaw the intelligence budgets (together with the assistant secretary of defense and the deputy national security advisor). And Scowcroft, as national security advisor, now chaired the Operations Advisory Group (which was essentially a reconstituted version of the 40 Committee, which oversaw US covert activities during the Nixon and Ford administrations). Meanwhile, to the satisfaction of Scowcroft, Cheney, Rumsfeld, Bush, and other national security hawks, Ford sent Congress a bill that imposed criminal and civil penalties on government employees who disclosed information involving "intelligence sources and methods."[214]

Despite this effort to respond to and defuse the CIA scandal, the Ford administration couldn't escape further controversy on intelligence. The infamous Team B exercise was the brainchild of critics on the political right who were unhappy with the CIA's National Intelligence Estimates. At the suggestion of physicist John Foster, Adm. George Anderson, the PFIAB chairman, requested that an outside group of experts be convened to evaluate the CIA's National Intelligence Estimates. Specifically, there were to be three separate external review panels on air defense, missile accuracy, and strategic objectives. Then-DCI Colby rejected Anderson's proposal, although he tried to appease the critics by ordering an analysis of the agency's track record on air defense, missile accuracy, and strategic objectives. However, since the analysis was conducted by active and recently retired CIA personnel, it didn't mollify the critics.[215]

In late 1976, DCI Bush agreed to Anderson's request. And while personnel within CIA were split on the advisability of the exercise, Scowcroft and Kissinger signed off on the competitive analysis. Kissinger, for one, thought that an external review might do some good and offer the CIA some alternatives. Scowcroft, by then national security advisor, told interviewers in 1999 for his oral history at the University of Virginia's Miller Center that he enthusiastically supported the Team B exercise. Speaking more recently, he said he hadn't think it could hurt to try the exercise, and his deputy, William Hyland, had agreed. He may also have been willing to go along with Bush in the hope of allaying further criticism of the CIA.[216]

The Team B analysis of the Soviet threat was charged with duplicating the CIA's in-house National Intelligence Estimate while making different initial assumptions about Soviet decision makers. The experiment was to disclose to what degree the two estimates differed based on their distinct premises. The staff of the IOB recommended the members of Team B.

To serve as chairman of Team B, Bush selected Richard Pipes after others declined. Pipes was a Russian specialist at Harvard, a staunch conservative, and a Polish émigré. Pipes and the IOB together chose the other members of Team B, and they selected older, experienced individuals, including academics, scientists, and former military officers and government officials.[217]

Team B came to grim conclusions about the military dangers posed by the Soviet Union, conventional and nuclear alike, and soundly trounced the much younger, less experienced officials the CIA selected to explain and defend its own analysis. The competitive process seemed to vindicate the critics of the CIA's intelligence estimates: that the threat from the Soviet Union was much worse than the agency had led the White House and Congress to believe.

Unfortunately, the effect of the leak of the Team B report was to further polarize the country. Some observers believed that the Ford administration had been dissembling—that the president was deliberately obscuring the risks of détente and the extent of Soviet gains thanks to the SALT I agreement. Others considered the Team B enterprise the fruit of a right-wing effort to undermine international diplomacy and perpetuate the Cold War. Interestingly, when the Team B exercise became controversial, both Ford and Kissinger complained about how Team B had been set up.[218]

Scowcroft said his only objection to the Team B exercise was that someone leaked its findings to the press, since Team B's report was intended for the White House's internal use only. Although he also noted that Team B was "somewhat excessive" and depicted the Soviets as monsters, he largely agreed with the harsh report. Speaking after the much later collapse of the Soviet Union, he acknowledged that the Soviets remained a military threat until the very end. They were "deploying system after system at what would for us be enormous cost, and at a rate we couldn't begin to match—partly because of our politics. . . . Were [these systems] as good as ours? No, but they were okay," he said. "We tended to solve our problems of physics with exquisitely designed systems, thus very temperamental systems. The Soviets didn't take that approach . . . so they overwhelmed physics with brute force. That's why their weapons were bigger. They didn't depend on this exquisite timing of the primer and so on." At sea, however, "they never did match us, but . . . in ICBMs they were good."[219]

As the intelligence controversies vividly illustrate, by the mid-1970s America was becoming more and more ideologically divided. On one hand, the failure in Vietnam, the revelations about the CIA, the stench of Watergate, and the controversy over the Nixon pardon bolstered the Democratic Party and the political left, leading to the election of Jimmy Carter as president and strengthening Democratic control of Congress. On the other hand, the defeat in Vietnam, the rise of the Soviet Union as a military adversary, and the perceived failure of the Nixon-Kissinger foreign policy gave rise to a resurgent conservative movement on the right. These conflicting currents meant that Scowcroft and the Ford administration had to work within an extremely challenging political climate.

Intelligence remained an abiding interest for Scowcroft, and two years after leaving office he expressed some of his ideas on intelligence in an article published in 1979 in the *Naval War College Review*:

> Intelligence is one of our vital tools in preserving our security. And our security is a prerequisite for the advancement of the ideals for which we stand. . . . Our opponents will not hesitate to employ any means to advance their cause. Intelligence is by its nature an unpleasant amoral business and there have perhaps been times when our practitioners may have been inclined to play the game for its own sake. On balance, however, when one considers the requirements for secrecy, compartmentation, the numbers of people involved, and the need for flexible operating rules, the amazing thing to me is not that there were mistakes, but that so very little [over] so long a period did go wrong. In any event, it is vital that a few aberrations not blind us to the absolute requirements for a strong aggressive intelligence organization if we are to survive. In my opinion we have hurt ourselves badly, both substantively and procedurally. Just imagine the effort the Soviets would have been willing to expend to acquire the evidence of our intelligence operations that was spread across the front pages of our newspapers during the recent investigations. If we cripple our ability to compete in this vital, but arcane field we hurt only ourselves, and of course delight our opponents.[220]

Scowcroft would himself later serve as the chairman of PFIAB and would once again be in a position to reform the intelligence community. The next time, however, the central problem wouldn't be errors of commission, as when the CIA engaged in illegal domestic spying and planned foreign assassinations, but errors of omission—its failure to adapt organizationally after the end of the Cold War and its inability to foresee and prevent the terrorist attacks of September 11.

10

MANAGING FAILURE
The Last Days of Vietnam

ON APRIL 23, 1975, before a youthful crowd of forty-five hundred at Tulane University, President Gerald R. Ford announced that the Vietnam War was over. "Today," the president proclaimed, "America can regain the sense of pride that existed before Vietnam, but it cannot be achieved by refighting a war that is finished as far as America is concerned." The crowd erupted in "a jubilant roar" and "nearly raised the roof with whoops and hollers," the *New Republic*'s White House correspondent wrote.[221] In less than a week, thousands of Americans and tens of thousands of Vietnamese would be evacuated from Saigon as the North Vietnamese Army closed in on the capital city.

Had Ford consulted Brent Scowcroft about the speech, his de facto national security advisor probably would have urged him to take a less negative, less defensive tone about the war. Later Scowcroft said that the president had strayed "off the reservation," led on by his political advisers and by his chief speechwriter, Robert Hartmann, in particular. The president was sincere in his desire to get the United States out of Vietnam and to be done with the war. But over the next few weeks, Ford joined Scowcroft and Kissinger in blaming Congress for America's failure in Vietnam, arguing it had sold out a faithful ally by cutting off the funds for South Vietnam.[222] The president might have wanted to avoid refighting the war, but a prolonged national debate about assigning responsibility for America's worst military defeat and determining the lessons to be drawn from it was inevitable—and arguably necessary. The defeat scarred Scowcroft and his colleagues throughout the military and the government as well as millions of ordinary Americans. Following Watergate, it was "another traumatic experience."[223]

In the meantime, however, there were urgent practical problems to be dealt with in connection with America's departure from Vietnam, and these challenges fell into Scowcroft's lap. He was a jack-of-all-trades during the final weeks of the United States' presence in Vietnam, juggling multiple responsibilities and handling competing demands from different departments and agencies across the government. If he "wasn't the manager," he said, he certainly had a finger "on the pulse of what everyone else was doing." He was the "emergency guy," the person who exerted ultimate oversight and determined, "Well, we need to do this," or "Well, we need to get another helicopter to go in." His job was to ensure that the United States' actions meshed as well as they could, so as to meet the president's goals. He was at the center of operations during this last phase of the war, and his actions were integral to the ultimate outcome.[224]

On the face of it, this was not so different from what Scowcroft had done as a Pentagon staff officer or as the White House military assistant: managing complex operations. What did make it different, though, was the scale. Scowcroft now had to stay on top of the whole national security system, not just the Air Force or the presidency. And again he excelled. Two close observers of the Ford White House wrote that it was because of Scowcroft's impressive performance during the evacuation of Saigon that the president later chose him to succeed Henry Kissinger as national security advisor.[225]

For most Americans, the end of America's war in Vietnam is symbolized by the iconic photograph of a Huey helicopter being loaded with passengers on top of a Saigon building—not the US embassy roof, contrary to common belief, but an apartment building used to house Americans (the journalist Tim Weiner identifies it as a CIA safe house).[226] But if that photograph suggests the desperation of those final helicopter evacuations, it gives little hint of their mammoth scale. One hundred and thirty thousand Vietnamese left South Vietnam that April, ten times the number that the State Department had planned for. In the final phase alone, in just over fourteen hours' time, Marine helicopters lifted out almost 8,000 US military personnel, South Vietnamese, and their dependents—about 5,600 from Tan Son Nhut airport, another 2,206 from the roof and courtyard of the US embassy in Saigon, and dozens more from other locations.[227]

This is all the more impressive since the Ford administration had failed to appreciate the seriousness of the situation in Vietnam until mid-March; up until then, its attention had been overwhelmingly focused on Israel, Egypt, and the broader Middle East.[228] But by March 17, the latest North Vietnamese military offensive had put the communists in a "very strong" military position, in the words of Wolfgang Lehmann, the deputy US ambassador in Saigon. The communists took Ban Me Thuot, a strategically significant town in the central highlands, captured the ancient imperial city of Hue, took the coastal city of Da Nang, and then began to advance on Saigon. Nonetheless, as late as March 28, CIA director William Colby predicted that the South Vietnamese would be able to control the Saigon area until 1976, and even North Vietnam's own political and military leaders didn't expect to complete their conquest of South Vietnam until the next year.[229]

Yet soon US officials could not avoid the grim reality facing them: the unexpectedly rapid advance of the North Vietnamese army, coupled with the sudden collapse of the ARVN. The Washington Special Actions Group, consisting of the second-rank officials from each of the national security agencies, such as State, Defense, Joint Chiefs of Staff, and the CIA, met on April 2 and decided to immediately begin the evacuation of South Vietnam. Chartered World Airways flights, Air Force C-130s and C-141s, and Air America started flying Americans and South Vietnamese out of Saigon's Tan Son Nhut airport on a steady basis, with the USAF planes taking off at a rate of three per hour. In the eight days before the airport became inoperable (April 21–28), the Air Force alone lifted out more than forty thousand Americans and Vietnamese.[230]

Helping to make the extraordinary evacuation possible was the fact that North Vietnam eased up on its attack on Saigon. On April 19, Kissinger, via Soviet ambassador Anatoly Dobrynin, asked Brezhnev for his help in obtaining a two-week halt of hostilities in the cause of "finally ending the Vietnam tragedy." Hanoi responded to the Soviet request on April 24, essentially agreeing to a cease-fire for the final week of the evacuation. North Vietnamese leaders hoped the United States would help fund the postwar reconstruction and redevelopment of Vietnam, providing assistance of about $1 billion a year over five years, as Kissinger had offered to North Vietnamese premier Pham Van Dong in February 1973 following the Paris accords. Now, however, the White House was no mood to seriously consider providing aid to Hanoi (and denied having made any such offer, with Scowcroft himself at first refusing to provide a copy of Kissinger's letter to Dong).

Nonetheless, the North Vietnamese followed through on the cease-fire promise. As one North Vietnamese major general explained, "We didn't want to do anything that would involve Americans in the fight. Therefore, we did not touch the Americans or shoot at them at all. We just wanted the Americans to leave the country as soon as possible." The Soviet ambassador sent Scowcroft a message saying that "the leadership of Vietnam favors the establishment of good relations with the United States," and— on Moscow's recommendation—a separate statement that there was "no animosity toward the United States in Vietnam and they seek the same from the American side."[231]

So the evacuation of Saigon proceeded. Like the Vietnam War itself, it was both a demonstration of extraordinary courage and resolve and an ignominious failure. Thousands of Americans and many South Vietnamese acted heroically and selflessly during those final weeks of near chaos, among them State Department, Defense Department, and intelligence officials, Marine Corps soldiers and officers, Marine helicopter pilots and crews, Air America pilots and crews, and many South Vietnamese civilians and military personnel. The United States thereby avoided what could have been a horrible disaster. As the NSC official Richard Smyser noted, "I can at least say that we did do the decent thing to get the people help."[232]

At the same time, the evacuation of Saigon was a disaster in some fundamental respects. As Smyser also pointed out: "It was obvious that we couldn't help them all." Hundreds of thousands of Vietnamese who wanted to leave could not. These were the people who didn't make it on board USAF transport aircraft or the CIA's Air America flights, who couldn't reach the helicopters, who were unable to make it onto the US embassy grounds, or who could not escape by boat. Many simply did not have the political clout, military standing, personal ties, cash and other valuable possessions, good looks—many dancers and bar girls were among those taken out—or other assets that allowed them to get out.[233]

Timing was one reason for this failure. The Ford administration and the US ambassador to South Vietnam, Graham Martin, delayed the evacuation in an attempt to keep the South Vietnamese government intact as long as possible. Ambassador Martin, CIA station chief Tom Polgar, and Secretary Kissinger hoped to be able to negotiate a settlement with North Vietnam in order to buy more time, even if only to explore the possibility of forming a neutral coalition government.[234] Yet by delaying the evacuation until the North Vietnamese army was nearing Saigon, the Ford administration ended up leaving hundreds of thousands, if not millions, of Vietnamese behind.[235] In the end, Ford, Kissinger, and Scowcroft muddled through, grappling with a situation that was beyond their capacity to manage.

The sheer numbers were daunting. As of mid-April, about 4,000 Americans remained in Saigon, according to the US embassy and NSC's calculations, and they figured there were another 90,000 relatives of US citizens who likely wanted to leave. There were also 17,000 local employees of the US government and their 120,000 relatives, whom Ambassador Martin had promised he'd evacuate. On April 7 Martin wrote Scowcroft that the

United States owed protection to about 175,000 people, among them "local national employees, in-laws of US citizens, Vietnamese employees of American concerns, including the communications media, American foundations, and volunteer agencies, religious leaders, and Western educated professionals" in the employment of the Thieu government. A week later, Kissinger, too, spoke of an "irreducible list" of 174,000 people.[236] The government of South Vietnam had about 600,000 employees of its own, too, together with their dependents—and all of them would be vulnerable to reprisals after the fall of Saigon.

A total of 2 to 3 million people thus had a legitimate claim for being evacuated or a good reason to fear for their safety should they stay in South Vietnam.[237] But hundreds of thousands of Vietnamese were unable to get out and faced reprisals at the hands of the invading communist forces.[238] Making matters worse, the North Vietnamese knew all about these people because, in their haste to flee, South Vietnamese officials hadn't destroyed their files at the Joint General Staff and National Police headquarters, which named those who'd collaborated with the US military or with the CIA. (These were duplicates of the CIA's own files that US embassy officials incinerated.)[239]

In any event, the fear of reprisals against the South Vietnamese resisters proved to be well founded. After the North Vietnamese army gained control of Saigon on April 30, the communists moved hundreds of thousands of South Vietnamese to "reeducation" facilities—in effect, grim concentration camps. While most were held for less than a year, about two hundred thousand people were detained for years under conditions of extreme hardship. Although the historical record is murky, the combined numbers of those who were executed and those who disappeared—about sixty-five thousand people—seems to match the estimated number of high-risk South Vietnamese the United States was unable to take out. Some high-ranking military officers and government officials did not wait to be captured and took their own lives.[240]

It could have been much worse. Contrary to what many US officials had predicted, there was no bloodbath or systematic slaughter in Vietnam, as there had been in Cambodia under Pol Pot and the Khmer Rouge, in China under Mao during the Cultural Revolution, or in the Soviet Union under Stalin. Still, the evacuation marked an inglorious end for the United States, and Scowcroft characterized the fall of Saigon as "a tragedy."[241]

How did it come to this?

═══

THE NIXON ADMINISTRATION had opened US diplomatic relations with the People's Republic of China in 1972 partly in the hope that the new ties with China would provide leverage on North Vietnam and Cambodia with respect to the war, then at its height. But China wasn't much help to the United States with either country, and by late 1974 the situation in Vietnam was worse than it had been after January 27, 1973, the date when the Paris peace agreement between Kissinger and Le Duc Tho was finalized. The main reason was that the North Vietnamese themselves, under the leadership of General Secretary Le Duan, refused to deviate from their goal to unify Vietnam. If the Soviets and the Chinese were to retain their influence among Third World nations and uphold their revolutionary credentials, they had little choice but to support North Vietnam's ambitions.

North Vietnamese leaders were emboldened, too, by the fact that by October 1974, they had "concluded that South Vietnam could no longer count on American support and that the potential for a renewed U.S. intervention was extremely remote."[242] So they decided to embark on a two-year military offensive, the General Offensive, General Uprising campaign, to conquer South Vietnam and reunite Vietnam—with their only opposition being South Vietnam. In the wake of the Paris accords and then Watergate, South Vietnam was essentially on its own (except for the resupply of US equipment and some assistance from the US embassy and the Defense Attaché Office). The ARVN thus had to radically adjust the way it fought, since its soldiers had been trained with and were accustomed to using almost unlimited supplies. By April 1975, South Vietnamese soldiers would reportedly go into battle with one or two grenades rather than a half dozen, and artillery batteries were only allowed to fire one round before getting permission to fire additional rounds—even as the South Vietnamese forces usually had more supplies than they could use and left huge amounts of equipment behind when they retreated.[243]

Brent Scowcroft was hardly responsible for the United States' Vietnam strategy or for the fact that by early 1975 the very existence of South Vietnam was in doubt. He had not started working as Kissinger's deputy until the Paris peace talks with Hanoi were almost completed, and he had not been a party to Nixon's decisions to "Vietnamize" the war, to invade Cambodia, and to bomb Hanoi and Haiphong in 1972 (Operation Linebacker II). Upon taking office, Scowcroft said he had little confidence in South Vietnam and "no faith in the North."[244]

But Scowcroft wasn't simply a silent partner. The more he, Kissinger, and Nixon worked together, especially after Kissinger became secretary of state, the more Scowcroft participated in decision making. Scowcroft and Kissinger "had worked together a long time and their thoughts were similar," Robert Hartmann observed. The deputy national security advisor substituted for Kissinger at meetings when he was out of town, served as a go-between with the president when the president was on the road, drafted memos and press releases on his behalf, and kept his boss informed. "Scowcroft was aware of what he didn't have to show Kissinger," Hartmann noted, "and what he had [to] show Kissinger."[245]

But assessing Scowcroft's role in Vietnam policy is difficult because of his style as an administrator and presidential adviser. Not only did he prefer to do things quietly, but he liked to discuss issues and make decisions in person rather than in writing.[246] For a trusted aide like Scowcroft, communicating orally was faster and more efficient than writing, and every bit as effective. It was also safer. Memoranda can be leaked. They can die on someone's desk, get killed through editing or redrafting, or be undermined or counteracted by other memoranda. But the scant written record means that Scowcroft's historical role and political influence are scarcely visible in the archival record—or in journalists' and historians' accounts.[247]

What the Vietnam records do show, however, is Scowcroft's clear position within the White House's inner circle. Even as military assistant, he knew about Operation Menu—the secret bombing of Cambodia in 1969–1970, together with the falsification of reports at President Nixon's orders (the White House even deliberately misled the Air Force chief of staff).[248] And as Kissinger's deputy, Scowcroft facilitated policy making in several ways. He relayed messages from President Thieu and Le Duc Tho to Kissinger, and vice versa. He and his staff tracked violations by the North Vietnamese and South Vietnamese governments of the January 27, 1973, Vietnam peace agreement. He provided Kissinger with a list of US military options against Laos and North Vietnam in April 1973, following up on those presented by Adm. Thomas Moorer.[249] And he had his own back-channel correspondence with Ambassador Martin (back-channel because the communications went directly to and from the NSC rather than through the State Department).

Scowcroft also contributed with his tactical and operational knowledge. In 1972, for instance, he advised it would be better to bomb Laos sooner rather than later. In late 1973, he informed Kissinger that the Douglas A-1s could lay mines, but that the LTV A-7 Corsairs could not, since they had trouble flying at night.[250] He informed Kissinger and his State Department aides that South Vietnam lacked the ability to mine North Vietnamese harbors, and in early 1975 he recommended moving B-52s to Guam so that they could be available to bomb the advancing North Vietnamese army if need be.[251] And he advised the head of the Office of Management and Budget to take into account a number of factors with respect to foreign assistance to Vietnam and Cambodia in 1975, including food aid; a "10% increase in ammunition for the dry season"; the replacement of "very critical equipment lost in combat, to include artillery pieces, M113 armored personnel carriers"; landing craft and patrol boats "for the Mekong supply route"; and helicopter gunships.[252]

Scowcroft occasionally took jabs at other US officials, particularly at the defense secretary. When discussing the Cambodia bombing, he pointed out that Schlesinger sought a lower sortie rate for air strikes against Cambodia because he was "worried about his press position" and "credibility." Scowcroft thought that this explained why Schlesinger shied away from taking strong positions on Vietnam and Indochina notwithstanding his hard-line positions on the Soviet Union and continuing SALT negotiations.[253]

As much as Scowcroft was in Nixon's inner loop of advisers, his one-on-one conversations with Nixon on Vietnam were not so much dialogues as they were occasions for Scowcroft to serve as the president's sounding board or as a source of reassurance. Nixon was very proud of his own judgment on foreign policy and not inclined to let others influence his thinking (much less to reveal that others had influenced his thinking). The tenor of the conversations seems to suggest that Nixon was never quite sincere when asking Scowcroft for advice and that his and Scowcroft's conversations involved little genuine back-and-forth.[254]

But Scowcroft essentially agreed with Nixon as well as with Kissinger. Like them, he believed that the United States had to be strong in the face of the threats posed by the Soviet Union, Red China, and international communism. He believed in the fundamental importance of preserving "an American image of reliability," and he subscribed to the domino theory. It was in the United States' "cardinal" interest "*not* to be a Paper Tiger," as McGeorge Bundy had put it in 1965; the United States could not afford to "have it thought that when we commit ourselves we really mean no high risks." Like Bundy, as well as LBJ, Nixon, Kissinger, and other Cold War hawks, Scowcroft believed that "the way to peace" lay "over the hard road of determination," whether the enemy was the Axis Powers of World War II or the Soviet Union, "It has been so since 1940 for us all."[255] "Fundamentally, I do believe in power," Scowcroft said, "and the exercise of power."[256]

Like Nixon and Kissinger, Scowcroft saw the fate of Vietnam as intimately connected with the full range of Cold War conflicts, symbolic and real.[257] Credibility was (almost) everything for Kissinger and Scowcroft. Thus, in a March 24 meeting on congressional funding for South Vietnam and Cambodia, when Kissinger and his aides discussed the symbolic reasons for maintaining US support for Cambodia, Kissinger speculated that the "contempt" the Chinese had for the United States "must be total at this point"—that is, with the unimpeded advance of the North Vietnamese on Saigon.[258]

Scowcroft also shared with Nixon and Kissinger a deep resentment of Congress's interference in US foreign policy. Scowcroft and Kissinger particularly condemned Congress for its refusal in late 1974 and 1975 to consider how its reductions in funding South Vietnam would undermine the Saigon government, affect the capacity of the American presidency, and ramify internationally. In several meetings with Ford and Kissinger, Scowcroft spoke of Congress's intransigent and destructive behavior.

Although Congress had appropriated $700 million for Vietnam in fiscal year 1975—July 1974 through June 1975—that amount represented only one-half of the previous year's $1.4 billion budget. So in January 1975, President Ford requested $522 million in supplemental funds to assist South Vietnam; the sum was later reduced to $300 million. For Scowcroft, the smaller, reduced amount was a "reasonable approach which will meet minimal requirements" that "should be submitted . . . probably at the same time as the request for Cambodia."[259] Yet not only did the House Democratic Caucus refuse on March 12, 1975, to commit any more money, but Congress's foreign aid bill of March 25 contained $2.7 billion *less* than the White House had requested. And the new legislation didn't provide any funds for either Vietnam or Cambodia.[260]

Also on March 12, Ban Me Thuot fell to the communists. President Nguyen Van Thieu then surprised his Army generals—and also the NVA—by ordering them to fall back. Although the retreat was to have consolidated the South Vietnamese army around more defendable positions, the ARVN generals were unprepared for the order to withdraw their forces, and soldiers and civilians alike, faced with the advancing communist forces, fled.[261] The North Vietnamese quickly proceeded to seize Hue on March 26, and on March 30 they captured Da Nang, fifty miles to the southeast.

Learning of the imminent arrival of the North Vietnamese, ARVN officers and soldiers, public officials, policemen, and civilians panicked. Some military officers used their own helicopters to rescue their families and flee south. Others used their guns to force their way on board the ships evacuating people from Da Nang. "There have been terrible mob scenes," Colby reported, "both at the airport where [civilians] stormed loading aircraft and at the port where they jammed ships." Other soldiers and officers left the field en masse to find their families rather than leave them behind in the provinces. But only fifty thousand of the more than two million who'd crowded into Da Nang were able to leave by sea.[262]

The others escaped by land. But with the few roads leading south becoming packed with hundreds of thousands of refugees and retreating army troops, all of these people became easy targets. The communists succeeded in killing tens of thousands of them. The ARVN ended up abandoning about $5 billion worth of US aircraft, tanks, ammunition, and other matériel on the front lines, on the roadsides, and in weapons depots in Da Nang, Cam Ranh Bay, and elsewhere (all told, the United States sent $28.5 billion in military and economic aid to the South Vietnam regime between 1953 and 1975).[263] "Law and order [had] broken down completely," William Colby reported. The situation was "almost impossible."[264]

With the North Vietnamese forces advancing much faster than either Hanoi or Saigon had expected, the situation in South Vietnam became acute. One hundred and twenty-five Vietnamese Air Force planes were able to flee to U-Tapao and other bases in Thailand—many of the aircraft filled with refugees—and much of the Vietnamese navy was also able to escape, eventually making it to Subic Bay in the Philippines. But ARVN personnel, officials of the Thieu government, and others who had worked for the US and South Vietnam governments were trapped. "It was frantic, a mess," Scowcroft told *Newsweek*.[265]

In this the context, Thieu wrote an "eyes only" letter on March 25 to President Ford. It read, in part:

> As I am writing to you, the military situation in South Vietnam is very grave and is growing worse by the hour.
>
> The serious disequilibrium in the balance of forces in favor of the North Vietnamese as well as their strategic advantages, accumulated over the past two years, have led to the present critical situation. . . . Saigon itself is threatened.
>
> It has become evident that it would be extremely difficult for us to contain the advance of the communist forces and to hold the line in order to push back the invaders.

Thieu blamed the United States for the retreat. Ford had quietly promised South Vietnam adequate support immediately after he took office, but with Congress tying his hands, the president couldn't deliver on his promise. Nor was Ford above deceiving Thieu about how much the administration could help, telling him in late 1974 that "American policy remains unchanged" and promising to "make every effort to provide you with the assistance you need." Yet after the Nixon pardon and the passage of the Jackson-Vanik Amendment, Ford and others in his administration recognized that Congress would not be cooperating with the administration on US aid to Vietnam—a realization confirmed in a meeting of the Senate Foreign Relations Committee with Ford, Kissinger, Scowcroft, and other presidential advisers on January 8, 1975.[266]

Scowcroft agreed with the South Vietnamese president. He thought Congress's refusal to provide funds had caused the morale of the South Vietnamese army to plummet. It wasn't so much that the Vietnamese armed forces no longer had the manpower and equipment—although the paucity of supplies was a problem, as we have seen. It was more a matter of "spirit and commitment," in Scowcroft's assessment. In his view, the psychological effects of Congress's refusal reverberated among the South Vietnamese and "perpetrated the collapse" that ultimately led to the disintegration of the ARVN's command and control.[267]

Scowcroft believed that had a significantly larger budget been approved, "quite possibly" something could have been worked out. He thought there was "a decent chance to make it work after the Paris Accords"—at least up until Congress cut back its funding.[268] Although Scowcroft had no specific scenario in mind, it's certainly *conceivable* that the Vietnam War could have ended differently. For Scowcroft, "there was always a big question in my mind, could we have made it work; did the Congress pull the plug?" "So who knows?" he wondered. "History doesn't reveal its alternatives."[269]

When the Senate Foreign Relations Committee decided on April 18 to recommend just $200 million for the evacuation of Saigon and humanitarian relief, Scowcroft couldn't contain his bitterness. "It is lovely," he sarcastically said to Kissinger. "They are proposing $200 million for humanitarian assistance." "It is unbelievable," Scowcroft added. "It sums up the worst of what went on in the meeting" between the president's advisers and members of the Senate Foreign Relations Committee. "Well, Indochina is gone," Kissinger responded, "but we'll make [Congress] pay for it. In my whole testimony today, I said 25 times that it was Congress' fault."[270]

Later that year, Kissinger observed, "We are living in a nihilistic nightmare. It proves that Vietnam is not an aberration but our normal attitude." He had Congress's failure to support South Vietnam in mind.[271] Both

Kissinger and Scowcroft spoke of Congress's rejection of additional funding for South Vietnam as the immediate cause of defeat, and looked no further than that—not at the military, not at the State Department, not at White House advisers (Kissinger himself most prominently), and not at American presidents.[272]

Yet with the decent interval that Kissinger and Nixon had created with the Paris Accords and the formal withdrawal of US forces, the United States had essentially committed to leaving Vietnam—something Scowcroft was well aware of. Neither Kissinger, nor President Nixon, nor Al Haig, nor Admiral Zumwalt believed the peace would last, in fact, notwithstanding the fact that Kissinger and Nixon triumphantly presented the Paris Accords to the American public.[273]

Survivors from both the North Vietnamese and South Vietnamese armies have attested to the fact many ARVN units fought vigorously to defend what remained of South Vietnam against the advancing communist divisions, despite their logistical handicaps and waning morale, especially around Xuan Loc. However, that same commitment wasn't apparent among South Vietnamese government officials or its civilians. "No spirit of support or sacrifice has been summoned," wrote one reporter. "No crowds of Saigonese collected blood or money or food for the soldiers, or helped care for the sick and wounded in the hospitals, or offered their services for the refugees," observed another. "No swarms of volunteers appeared at recruiting stations. No civilians built barricades or filled sandbags or dug antitank ditches. Nor were they asked to." Ultimately, "the Saigon regime could find no reserve of will largely because it had no relation to its own people," the reporter, Arnold Isaacs, found. "Its leaders could conceive [of] useless appeals to the United States for the return of B-52s, but not to their countrymen for a common effort at survival."[274]

The United States did provide some measure of assistance to the South Vietnamese military in these last weeks. The defense attaché's office loaded a propane-fueled CBU-55 bomb—the deadliest non-nuclear bomb in the US arsenal—on a South Vietnamese airplane, which then dropped the CBU-55 over North Vietnamese divisional army headquarters just outside the town of Xuan Loc. The massive fireball killed hundreds of North Vietnamese almost instantaneously, either through suffocation—because of the propane suddenly consuming all the oxygen in the air—or through incineration. It was the only time the United States deployed the CBU-55 in Vietnam. Both Radio Hanoi and China protested vehemently, accusing the United States of a military atrocity. The United States also supplied dozens of deadly fifteen-thousand-pound "daisy cutter" bombs to the South Vietnamese air force, which dropped them around Xuan Loc.[275]

The president, his aides, and US military leaders knew the bombing was only a stopgap measure. "Vietnam [was] falling to pieces," in the words of David Hume Kennerly, Ford's prize-winning photographer. Kennerly agreed with the State Department's William Hyland that Vietnam was a lost cause. "I don't care what the generals tell you," Kennerly told the president after visiting Vietnam with Army chief of staff Frederick C. Weyand in April, "they're bullshitting if they say that Vietnam has got more than three or four weeks left."[276]

The growing issue confronting Ford, Kissinger, Scowcroft, Schlesinger, Ambassador Martin, and Joint Chiefs chairman General George S. Brown (who succeeded Admiral Moorer in July 1974) now became how to evacuate Saigon. In early April the planning began in earnest. "Timing is of utmost importance," the State Department reported to Scowcroft, adding that "for maximum success the implementation must begin promptly after intelligence sources have indicated Saigon is doomed—and before it is too late to be effective." Since the evacuation would most likely leave South Vietnam without any effective political and military governing authority, the White House wanted to start the evacuation only when absolutely necessary. Yet the more it delayed, the less the chance that all US officials, American citizens, and high-risk Vietnamese needing to leave Saigon would be able to get out safely. Fundamentally related to the matter of timing was, therefore, the matter of "sufficient speed," since the logistics of the evacuation depended on which assets—ships, helicopters, cargo planes, commercial aircraft—were available, in what numbers, and when.[277]

The timing and speed of the operation depended, in turn, on more basic questions. Who was to be evacuated? How many were to be taken out? And what was their order of priority? It was assumed that virtually all US citizens would leave (some missionaries, humanitarian volunteers, and contractors excepted), but it wasn't obvious to US officials which and how many South Vietnamese were to be evacuated. Defense secretary Schlesinger and some members of Congress wanted to evacuate few, if any, South Vietnamese. In many of his decisions on the evacuation, the president was given the option to leave all South Vietnamese (or those South Vietnamese remaining, as the case may be) behind to face the North Vietnamese.

Ford, Scowcroft, and Martin—who were joined by Kissinger, if to a lesser degree—chose another path. They agreed to take out as many high-risk Vietnamese as possible, a number that "could be anywhere from 10,000 to 75,000 people," Dean Brown remarked. (Ford appointed Brown, a former ambassador to Jordan and Cyprus, to manage the humanitarian portion of Operation Frequent Wind, the final stage of the evacuation).[278] Yet it still was not clear what proportion of those in the high-risk category would be evacuated, since the assumption was that not everyone who qualified as high-risk could be taken out.

Another factor Ford's advisers had to consider was how the US government was going to protect those being evacuated, as well as the flight crews and the soldiers helping get people out, since Congress had prohibited US forces in Vietnam from engaging in further conflict. Would extra forces need to be brought in? How was the US military to respond when attacked by hostile fire? And would some in the South Vietnamese military who opposed the Americans' departure resist and obstruct the evacuation?

In addition, Ford's top military and civilian advisers had to decide on a policy for those rescued at sea, since many South Vietnamese were fleeing by boat. What resources should the United States spend on rescuing the boat people, especially if most were not in the high-risk category? How was the administration going to handle the thousands of refugees? Where were these people to be housed, fed, processed, and eventually located?

Scowcroft and his NSC staff, Bud McFarlane in particular, were responsible for overseeing and coordinating almost all phases of the evacuation. They monitored how many Americans and Vietnamese US forces took out each day, using figures from the Saigon embassy and Department of Defense, so as to calculate how many people remained to be evacuated. They coordinated actions with the State Department and the Pacific Command. Mostly, they simply tried to impose a modicum of order on what Scowcroft called a "confusing, crazy" mess.[279]

Notwithstanding Scowcroft's hope that the United States would be able to continue to support the Thieu government, he recognized by late March that there was very little the Ford administration could do.[280] Under the circumstances, Scowcroft advocated evacuating "as many as possible," believing the United States had a "moral obligation" to those who worked for the US government and to US contractors. He also believed that Washington's management of the evacuation would affect the United States' international reputation: "Other nations will see in our handling of this issue how the U.S. deals with the people of a country which has long been involved with us."[281]

The administration feared that the Americans still in Saigon would effectively become hostages. DCI Colby and embassy officials warned that some South Vietnamese held the position that the "evacuation of Americans should not be permitted unless guarantees for their own safety [were] made." Americans might be subject to "reprisals" if the United States attempted to evacuate US citizens "without taking along friendly South Vietnamese." The South Vietnamese might even "fire on anyone trying to leave."[282]

Based on some combination of these different factors, Ford decided to evacuate as many as possible, including the South Vietnamese dependents of American personnel, the high-risk Vietnamese along with their families and other dependents, and others who had assisted or collaborated with the United States.[283]

Scowcroft gave Ford immense credit for this decision, especially since members of the Senate Foreign Relations Committee had unanimously recommended that the last US forces be withdrawn "as fast as possible." Ford had "nothing to gain" politically by refusing to abandon the Vietnamese, Scowcroft pointed out, while he had "everything to lose" had the evacuation led to US casualties or a subsequent military engagement with the North Vietnamese. It was, he later wrote, "perhaps Ford's finest hour. It was a tough, lonely decision made with great courage."[284]

With the North Vietnamese about to overrun Saigon, Kissinger and Scowcroft depended on Ambassador Martin's presence on the ground and relied on his judgment of the situation. Martin was among the last to accept the reality that the battle to save South Vietnam was lost. As late as April 25, well after the White House, Department of Defense, and intelligence officials realized how hopeless the situation was, Martin cabled Kissinger and Scowcroft that "the will to fight was still there," that Hanoi could "no longer mass superior force," and that the Republic of Vietnam's air force, which was equipped with Northrop F-5s and other US aircraft, would, "for the first time, be able to meet the enemy in equal force." Scowcroft thought Martin had broken down and gone "off the deep end."[285] Perhaps the fact that Martin's own adopted son had been killed while serving as a Marine in Vietnam colored the ambassador's analysis, intensifying his unwillingness to admit that the war was lost.

Scowcroft nonetheless found Martin "extreme[ly] useful" and "a stabilizing factor" in the midst of "a very hectic period," offering a consistent message: "Don't get out. Hang in there." Scowcroft thought that Martin gave the administration perspective and recognized that he "helped me a lot in trying to figure out how slow we could go, how fast we had to go because Schlesinger at that time was pushing to get his troops out."[286] Even when he and Kissinger had serious disagreements with Martin, the urgency of the situation and the politics of the moment made it impossible to fire the ambassador.

So, paradoxically, Kissinger and Scowcroft allowed Martin considerable discretion, despite the fact that they considered his analysis of the situation in Vietnam fundamentally inaccurate—and even sometimes referred to him as "the madman."[287] On April 19, Scowcroft cabled Martin, advising him to use his "own judgment" in moving out "Vietnamese in the high-risk category." He assured the ambassador that neither he nor Kissinger was going to "second guess" him; Martin himself had to be "the judge on when and how fast to move such high-risk elements as CIA assets and so forth." Scowcroft ended the message by writing, "Thank God you are out there."[288]

Martin nevertheless attempted to stall the evacuation as long as he could and tried to delay the closing of the defense attaché's office, the withdrawal of US military forces, and the shutting down of the South Vietnamese government. When push came to shove, he and CIA Station Chief Polgar were even willing to sacrifice President Thieu for the sake of making any kind of deal that could allow the South Vietnamese government and Martin's "little empire"—as Scowcroft called it—to survive.[289]

On April 21, after Martin told Thieu it was time to leave, the South Vietnamese president resigned and was flown to Taipei, where his brother was ambassador (Thieu's wife had already left for Taiwan). On April 28, after a weeklong interregnum during which the vice president was in charge, Duong Van Minh (known as "Big Minh") became president of South Vietnam. The next morning, the situation deteriorated further. The South Vietnamese army began to disband and the North Vietnamese shelled Tan Son Nhut airport—the center of the US military presence in South Vietnam—littering the runway with the debris of destroyed aircraft and wrecked trucks.

When Schlesinger heard the news that the airport was inoperable, he called Scowcroft, yelling at him, "For Christ's sake, let's go to the helos." Ford checked with Kissinger and agreed: "We have no choice but to send in the helicopters, get our Americans out, and try to save as many friends as we can," Ford told Scowcroft. So Scowcroft ordered Martin and the Seventh Fleet to begin Option IV—Operation Frequent Wind (before April 15 known as Operation Talon Vise). Thirty minutes later, Armed Forces Radio in Saigon played "White Christmas," signaling that the final evacuation was under way. Some South Vietnamese had their own name for the operation: "The Running."[290]

Over the final two days of April, seventy-one helicopters made 689 sorties staffed by 865 Marines.[291] As long as Americans remained at the embassy, Martin knew, the helicopters would keep flying. So he used the flights to evacuate dependents and other at-risk Vietnamese, even as hundreds of Americans at the embassy remained to be evacuated. To Kissinger, Scowcroft, and the Joint Chiefs, Martin's insistence on evacuating Vietnamese against explicit orders to the contrary was insubordinate. "Graham gave me an initial headcount of several hundred that included both Americans and Vietnamese," McFarlane reports in his memoirs, "and we started the [last set] of sorties." Once the helicopters lifted off, however, "Graham reported back" and gave McFarlane "a number that was more than we had started with." Since McFarlane "knew what [Graham] was doing," and since he agreed with "his desire to evacuate as many Vietnamese as possible," he didn't pass anything along. After a while, "Henry caught on," and he became very upset when his military assistant admitted that Martin "was padding things a bit and bringing out more Vietnamese."[292]

The usually calm Scowcroft snapped. "UNDERSTAND THERE ARE STILL ABOUT 400 AMERICANS IN EMBASSY COMPOUND," he cabled Martin. "YOU SHOULD ENSURE THAT ALL, REPEAT ALL, AMERICANS ARE EVACUATED IN THIS OPERATION ASAP."

Furious, the ambassador gave as good as he got:

Perhaps you can tell me how to make some of these Americans abandon their half-Vietnamese children, or how the president would look if he ordered this. . . .

Am well aware of the danger here tomorrow and I want to get out tonight. But I damn well need at least 30 CH-53s [Sikorsky Sea Stallion helicopters] or the equivalent to do that. Do you think you can get president to order CINCPAC [Office of the US Commander in Chief Pacific] to finish job quickly? I repeat, I need 30 ch-53s and I need them now.[293]

Less than two hours later Martin sent another "flash" (high-priority) message to Scowcroft: "Since my last message nineteen, repeat 19, CH-46s [Boeing Sea Knight tandem-rotor helicopters] have come and gone. They carry about two-fifths of CH-53 capacity. I needed thirty CH-53 sorties capacity. I still do. Can't you get someone to tell us what is going on?[294]

As the waves of helicopters scurried back and forth between the US embassy and the US fleet, Martin kept boarding Vietnamese, even though embassy staff, US Marines, and others waited at the mission. "Brent Scowcroft had promised me fifty more of those big helicopters," Martin recalled. "We had taken the Vietnamese and the Koreans to whom we had made a promise, we carefully counted them and brought them across the wall into the inner compound. We had no intention of bringing the people we had left in the outer compound. We were going to bring these other people out—some of them were cabinet ministers and so on."[295]

Many wouldn't get out. The word in the White House and in the Pentagon was that Martin was "always going to have 2,000 more." "No matter how many helicopters left, the estimate of the number of evacuees remaining never changed," one helicopter squadron commander said. "It was like trying to empty a 'bottomless pit.'" Military leaders already held Martin responsible for delaying the evacuation, and they now (rightly) suspected that he was deliberately withholding Americans so he could evacuate more Vietnamese.[296]

For his part, Martin blamed Scowcroft for not ordering enough helicopter sorties so he could evacuate all of the Vietnamese still at the embassy. "Actually we very carefully calculated the whole bloody business, taking ninety at a time, and with what Scowcroft had promised me—well, God knows if you can't count on the President's national security advisor, who the hell do you count on?"

But the decision wasn't Martin's to make. The White House and Joint Chiefs had decided that time was up. Recounted Martin, "Suddenly we got this message that everything was off. 'The next helicopter is coming; please come out.'" After receiving the news, he cabled Scowcroft, "Plan to close mission Saigon approximately 0430. . . . Due to necessity to destroy [communications] gear, this is the last Saigon message to SecState."[297]

At 4:42 A.M. on April 30, the ambassador, pale, suffering from insomnia, unsteady on his feet, and still recovering from a recent medical operation, was helicoptered from the embassy. Additional helicopters rescued the remaining few Americans. The final CH-46 and its escort of Cobra gunships landed just before 8:00 A.M.—in full daylight—to pick up the last eleven Marines. As the last Marines quickly climbed the stairs up to the embassy roof, desperate South Vietnamese raced up behind them. And as the Marines hastily boarded the one waiting helicopter, the first Vietnamese to reach the roof made a dive for the helicopter as it began to lift off.[298]

About four hundred Vietnamese who were crowded in the embassy courtyard and whom Martin or other US officials had promised to evacuate were stranded. For the US officials and Marines taking the last few helicopters, the scene was excruciating: although orders were orders, many of them had worked for years with the South Vietnamese, and they felt responsible for abandoning them.[299]

At about noon on April 30, the lead tank from the 324th Division of the North Vietnamese army crashed through the gates to the presidential palace in Saigon. Big Minh was placed under arrest, and the US embassy was ransacked not long afterward. All of Vietnam was in communist hands.[300]

Soon after Martin landed on the USS *Blue Ridge*, Kissinger cabled him his appreciation: "I am sure you know how deeply I feel about your performance under the most trying circumstances. My heartfelt thanks." In the same telegram, Scowcroft wrote, "Graham, you were superb."[301]

THE EVACUATION CRISIS was the most severe leadership test Brent Scowcroft had faced in his career. Throughout, he was constantly in touch with Kissinger and frequently with the president. He spoke often with Schlesinger and others in the Department of Defense as well as with Ambassador Martin, Wolfgang Lehmann, Tom Polgar, and President Thieu, whether by telephone or cable. He also worked closely with Adm. Noel Gayler, commander in chief of the Pacific Command.[302] And he was "able to knock heads together at CINCPAC and with the fleet commanders when critical bottlenecks showed up," John Prados reported, not losing sight of what the US hoped to achieve.[303]

Scowcroft ran the situation room "for a long, exhausting day of one emergency after another." And with the twelve-hour time difference between Washington and Vietnam, he was often up most of the night and sometimes all night during those final days. To others in the White House, he appeared "frail and exhausted."[304] In contrast to Kissinger, who "grew increasingly irate and short-tempered" as the evacuation drew to a climax, Scowcroft kept his poise. Hartmann, who disliked the holdovers from the Nixon White House, especially Kissinger, appreciated Scowcroft's "tireless and unflappable" personality. It was similar to that of President Ford himself, who "always tended to calm" during crises.[305]

Still, Scowcroft found the end of the Vietnam War greatly disturbing. Having dealt with hundreds of families of POWs and MIAs in his role as military assistant and having himself been confined to military hospitals for two years, he couldn't view the episode and the suffering it involved from twenty thousand feet, as Kissinger did.

The end of the Vietnam War was in many ways a microcosm of the multifaceted history of the failed US involvement in Indochina. "It was," admitted Scowcroft, "a miracle we got out."[306] What Scowcroft does not say is that the North Vietnamese themselves very much wanted the United States and its South Vietnamese collaborators out; that's why they were willing to agree to a de facto week-long ceasefire. What he also leaves unmentioned are the significant mistakes and great costs that accompanied the evacuation.

The evacuation of Saigon highlighted the interservice rivalries that had hobbled the US military throughout the war. Bureaucratic battles interfered with the planning, orchestration, and conduct of the operations, and departments and agencies worked at cross-purposes with the "lines of responsibility . . . unclear," Arnold Isaacs reported in his book *Without Honor*. "Everybody thought everybody else was in charge until somebody wanted to do something" one military official stated, "and then somebody would disapprove it." Right until the end, the war featured "mutual incomprehension and mistrust among the various U.S. agencies." Worse, Ford and his top advisers were "disastrously slow to set any clear direction."[307]

William Clements, deputy secretary of defense from 1973 to 1977, described the evacuation as "a damn poor performance by everybody concerned," with the worst problem being the "absolutely miserable" communications. The Joint Chiefs performed terribly, Clements said, notwithstanding the weeks of planning they'd done. And nonmilitary agencies performed just as poorly: on Guam, for instance, only ninety Immigration and Naturalization Service officials were sent to process the twenty thousand Vietnamese who'd arrived on the island since early April, causing a backlog of thousands of refugees.[308]

Some of the responsibility falls on Ambassador Martin. Martin conceded his responsibility for how the evacuation developed because of his ceaseless attempts to try to find a way for the government of South Vietnam to survive. But Kissinger and Scowcroft also bore some responsibility. Not only did they stand by Martin until the very end, however upset they may have been with him at times, but they also placed top priority on delaying the fall of South Vietnam as long as they could, in the cause of upholding the credibility of the United States.

Of the three, Scowcroft was the most practical-minded, the least emotional, and the most accepting of the fall of South Vietnam. In his view, having lost the war, the United States simply had to manage the withdrawal as best as it could.[309] For Kissinger, the loss of South Vietnam hit deeper. It called into question his years of diplomatic maneuvering and policy making, and it focused new scrutiny on his autocratic style, "his penchant for the virtuoso performance," and his "addiction to secrecy," in the description of CIA officer Frank Snepp.[310] Kissinger's management style especially alienated Schlesinger and the Defense Department, Colby and the CIA, and important members of Congress on whom the Nixon and Ford administrations ultimately depended. The fact that the secretary of state told other White House officials he wanted to "avoid running all around town and giving the impression that there will be a total bug-out" suggested his frustration at how the war ended.[311]

The Vietnam War also revealed long-standing divisions within the White House itself. Kissinger, Scowcroft, Martin, and other anticommunist hawks refused to concede South Vietnam till the bitter end, while James Schlesinger, Ron Nessen, and Robert Hartmann all recommended that the United States cut its losses in Vietnam. Eventually, Ford came to agree with Schlesinger and his political advisers, which led to his Tulane speech declaring the end of the war.

But even with that speech, the internal squabbling did not end. When a reporter asked the president after the speech if Kissinger had approved of his address, Ford exclaimed, "No!" Quickly, Hartmann interrupted: "Mr. President, we did circulate this speech as we always do . . . and I believe that General Scowcroft signed off on it." Hartmann was covering for his boss, since Scowcroft had never seen the speech. But Scowcroft and Kissinger had been partly misled by the fact that Ford gave another speech in New Orleans that same day, at the Navy League. When Kissinger had asked Scowcroft to check with Ford's assistants about the speech, Ford's staff reassured him there would be nothing in it that would "surprise or disturb Kissinger," John F. Osborne reported in his book *White House Watch: The Ford Years*.[312]

The next morning Kissinger went to Oval Office "in a fine temper," demanding an explanation. So Ford summoned Hartmann and asked him why Kissinger didn't know about the speech. Hartmann describes the scene in his memoirs:

> "Well, we circulated it to General Scowcroft, [Hartmann replied] and we didn't know for sure whether he'd seen it or not, but his initials are just as good as anybody's in this room." And the President knew and I knew that this line [about the ending of American involvement in the Vietnam War] wasn't in there at the time. But Kissinger didn't know that. . . . And then Henry ranted and raved and said, "This has got to stop. I can't hold my head up in front of all these ambassadors with a major statement like this and I don't know about it. I've just lost face." So when he got through, the President looked over at me and said, "Well I think it's a misfortunate

misunderstanding; the system slipped up somehow. Just be sure, Bob, that this never happens again."

Hartmann made sure he "looked properly cowed and repentant" and said, "Yes sir." The meeting adjourned.[313]

Hartmann knew he could blame Scowcroft and get away with it, since neither the president nor Kissinger would question Scowcroft's judgment. In any case, Kissinger was being disingenuous: in speeches on April 5 and April 23, he had essentially said the same thing: "The Vietnam debate has run its course. The time has come for restraint and compassion."[314] (Interestingly, Gerald Ford doesn't write about the Tulane speech in his memoir, *A Time to Heal*.)

Beyond the divisions within the White House and the military lay deeper splits in the political system. From Kennedy through Nixon, presidents suspected that America's Vietnam policy could not work in the long run. But each administration chose to put off the reckoning by simply perpetuating the US presence in Vietnam; no president wanted to be the one who "lost Vietnam."[315] While congressional majorities agreed to what the president and Pentagon asked, as the United States poured more and more personnel, matériel, and money into South Vietnam, Congress became increasingly isolated from the policy-making process. Members of Congress were not informed of or included in the Paris peace talks, for example, and the 1973 peace agreement was never approved by Congress.[316]

The Watergate scandal certainly played a role in the conclusion of the Vietnam debacle. According to NSC staff member William L. Stearman, had Nixon not been preoccupied with Watergate, "he would have resumed bombing" after the North Vietnamese began violating the Paris accords. Lawrence Eagleburger similarly observed, "Had it not been for Watergate, the administration could have carried on a substantially more effective response to the North Vietnamese violations of the agreement." Eagleburger went so far as to say that it was entirely likely that the North Vietnamese, because they "read us very well," would not have undertaken "the final invasion of South Vietnam, I think with the proper analysis that we would not react, had it not been for Watergate." Scowcroft's analysis aligns with Stearman's: he had no doubt that "had it not been" for "the growing constraints of Watergate and what it was beginning to mean," Nixon would have restarted a bombing campaign when the North Vietnamese began to use the Ho Chi Minh Trail to resupply the insurgence in the South in March, 1973. In fact, this is precisely what Nixon, Kissinger—and possibly also Scowcroft—planned for that March and April. But "Watergate sapped any resolve that Nixon may have had to bomb again," Larry Berman concludes.[317]

But by 1975, after years of being lied to and misled, after Watergate, and after all those thousands of deaths and all those billions of dollars, a majority in Congress now joined the public and the press in doubting the wisdom of the Vietnam War.[318] American presidents had cried "wolf" too many times. Congress would not go along anymore—making the fall of Vietnam only a matter of time.

If Congress had gone along and provided more funding, it might have delayed the fall of the South Vietnam regime, but by late 1974, the fate of South Vietnam was almost inevitable. It is virtually impossible to come up with a plausible alternative history to the end of the South Vietnamese regime—and an end that would more likely come sooner than later. But the secretary of state, national security advisor, and president were all too happy to blame Congress as the proximate cause of the Vietnam defeat. To the extent to which Scowcroft still blames Congress, moreover, he would seem to be ignoring the reasons behind Nixon's and Kissinger's "decent interval" and to be taking congressional behavior out of its larger context: the evolution of American public opinion and the shift in presidential-congressional relations in the late 1960s and early 1970s.

═══

LESS THAN TWO weeks after the evacuation, in response to a request from President Ford, Kissinger drafted a memo outlining the lessons he took from the Vietnam War.

One lesson was that "American political groups will not long remain comfortable in positions that go against their traditional attitudes." In particular, Kissinger claimed that liberal Democrats were incapable of supporting for any significant length of time "a war against a revolutionary movement." So the "liberal Democrats" were able to accept Vietnam under Kennedy, but "withdrew from it under President Johnson" and subsequent Republican administrations.

Kissinger also pointed out the need for accurate reporting in the press and by US officials. He noted the "absolute importance of focusing our own remarks and the public debate on the essentials" (that is, on what we now call "controlling the narrative"). He emphasized how much "consistency" mattered, since members of Congress and members of the public applied different standards at the beginning of the war in comparison to toward the end.

He observed, too, that the US military was not suited for a war that was at once "a revolutionary war fought at knifepoint during the night within villages" and a conventional "main force war."

In the end, however, Kissinger contended that the United States could be proud of its accomplishments in Southeast Asia. The United States had saved Indonesia from going communist, he argued. "We paid a high price but we gained ten years of time," he wrote, "and we changed what then appeared to be an overwhelming momentum."[319]

Around the same time, Scowcroft received a memo from the State Department, "Lessons from Viet-Nam"—one that he himself may have commissioned—that reached opposite conclusions. Rather than treating consistency as being of essential importance, the United States needed to "avoid confusing constancy with inertia." In 1954 and up to the early 1960s the United States faced a monolithic communist bloc, the report observed, and the "activist, outward-looking" climate of the time held that "American resources and American expertise could solve any problem anywhere." But by the late 1960s, the Vietnam War had come to be perceived as "unjust and unwinnable" by the American public, a situation in which US foreign policy "outstripped the national consensus." The US government would have been better off seeking a political settlement in 1968 rather than waiting until 1972. As the conditions of the war and as the political climate changed, so, too, should have American policies.

Rather than blaming liberal Democrats or other domestic groups, the State Department's memorandum observed that successive presidential administrations had made the mistakes of employing short-term rationales, excluding Congress from planning, and failing to explain how the United States' vital national interests were at stake. Furthermore, the United States had failed to adequately assess its allies' tenacity and sense of purpose, since "in the final analysis" South Vietnam was "unable to mobilize effectively the support of its people in the face of an implacable, disciplined enemy." Instead, the United States had "consistently underestimated the tenacity and sense of purpose of Hanoi" and overestimated its ability to break the communists' will—determination that Kissinger acknowledged by saying that the North Vietnamese were "the toughest in the world to deal with."[320]

The report concluded by remarking—once more, contrary to Kissinger— that the United States had "been badly burned in Viet-nam." The war was not an episode of which the United States should be proud.[321]

It might be pointless to "refight" the Vietnam war. But the dueling memos made it clear that the lessons of Vietnam were radically different depending on the perspective of the person drawing those lessons. The division is probably just as stark today, with some continuing to believe that Congress caused the United States to lose Vietnam, others arguing that Watergate played a critical role in weakening Nixon's political capital, and others asserting that by the early 1970s the war was unwinnable.

What was certain, however, was that the fall of Vietnam represented a psychic wound to America's self-image. But within a few weeks, the Ford administration would get an unexpected chance at payback—an opportunity to restore the United States' reputation and to demonstrate that America remained committed to international leadership. The president and his advisers would make the most of the opportunity.

11

WE MEAN BUSINESS

ON MONDAY, MAY 12, 1975, at 5:12 A.M., fewer than two weeks after the American evacuation from Vietnam, officers in the White House Situation Room learned that the US merchant ship *Mayaguez* had been boarded and seized by armed Khmer Rouge forces in international waters off Cambodia. Lt. Gen. Brent Scowcroft received the call at home at 5:17 A.M., just as he was getting ready to leave for work. Because the military officers and State Department officials staffing the White House situation room had few details, Scowcroft chose not to telephone either President Ford or Secretary Kissinger. Scowcroft found out more at his 7:00 A.M. intelligence briefing, and at 7:40 A.M., during the regular morning intelligence briefing, he told the president what he knew.[322]

Khmer Rouge forces in five US-made Swift Boats, teenagers mostly, had fired upon and captured the *Mayaguez* and its crew of forty Americans just after three o'clock in the afternoon (2:00 A.M. Washington time). A ten-thousand-ton, five-hundred-foot-long, thirty-one-year-old ship owned by Sea-Land Services, Inc., the *Mayaguez* was making its way from Hong Kong to the Thai port of Sattahip when it was stopped and boarded by the communists near a small island about sixty miles from the Cambodian mainland.

The *Mayaguez* had been reconfigured to handle shipping containers after three previous lives (and three previous names) as a cargo ship. It was the first-ever American container ship—that is, the first US-flagged merchant vessel dedicated to transporting individual, prefilled container boxes capable of being stacked, inventoried, and loaded onto trucks and trains.[323] One Cambodian said that when they seized the vessel with its 274 containers, they thought they might find evidence the ship was on a spying mission or carried weapons and munitions.

The Khmer Rouge had taken over Cambodia from the Lon Nol government barely four weeks earlier, on April 17. The Khmer Rouge quickly began to hunt down and execute members of the former regime as well as to assert its claims over territorial waters, especially over the waters around islands also claimed by Vietnam, where Shell and Mobil had discovered rich oil deposits.[324] These claims had led to incidents involving Cambodian forces and boats belonging to Thailand, South Korea, South Vietnam, and Panama.[325] Now an American ship had been seized. The *Mayaguez* had been in what the United States deemed international waters within eight miles of Poulo Wai, one of the islands also claimed by Vietnam, when it was boarded and captured. The Khmer Rouge kept the *Mayaguez* at Poulo Wai for only a few hours before moving it to a spot off Koh Tang (Tang Island), a three-mile-long, narrow island lying thirty miles southeast of the port of Kompong Som (Sihanoukville) on the Cambodian coast.

Coming so soon after the demoralizing fall of South Vietnam and loss of Cambodia, the seizure of the *Mayaguez* posed a serious international relations challenge to the president and his advisers. How the United States responded would send an all-important signal to America's adversaries and the rest of the world. As Ford later recalled, editors of major newspapers worldwide were starting to question the United States' resolve to support its allies and its commitment to defend their mutual interests in the aftermath of its "humiliating" retreat from South Vietnam and Cambodia.[326] Kissinger was adamant: the administration could not let the incident go unpunished without seeming to concede that United States was in decline. The president agreed.

During the four NSC meetings convened over the four days and three nights of the crisis, the president, Kissinger, James Schlesinger, Nelson Rockefeller, chief of staff Donald Rumsfeld, Brent Scowcroft, and others repeatedly emphasized the importance of international perceptions.[327] As Kissinger put it at the Tuesday night NSC meeting, "We should do something that will impress the Koreans and Chinese."[328] Scowcroft defined the challenge in even broader terms, making clear that the global reputation of the Ford presidency and the United States was front and center. "Our objectives," Scowcroft said, "must be the recovery of the crew and ship in such a fashion as to make clear that the United States will not tolerate violence to its interests and remains able to act decisively as a free world leader."[329]

A second, more immediate challenge was to save the ship's crew. With the Khmer Rouge condemning the "bourgeois" business and professional classes, beginning to purge members of the former Lon Nol government, and starting to impose its brutal vision of a communist utopia, Ford and his advisers imagined the worst. No one, Scowcroft in particular, wanted a repeat of the

1968 incident in which North Korean forces had captured the USS *Pueblo*, a US intelligence-gathering ship, and held the crew captive for nearly a year before their release. (Afterward, the North Korean government proclaimed "another great victory of the Korean people who have crushed the myth of the mightiness of the United States imperialism to smithereens.")[330]

The president and his advisers dreaded the possibility that the *Mayaguez* crew might become political hostages. If the crew were removed to the mainland, the State Department's Lawrence Eagleburger wrote, "their recovery would have been virtually impossible—unless the Cambodians decided to release them—after who knows how many months and how much agony and humiliation."[331] This concern appears to have been first and foremost in the mind of President Ford, himself a former Navy officer.

A third challenge presented by the capture of the *Mayaguez* was one of presidential leadership. In office only nine months, Ford faced a skeptical, Democratic-controlled Congress and a critical American public, only 39 percent of whom approved of Ford's performance in office. The *Mayaguez* crisis would be the "first real test" of his leadership, Robert Hartmann told him: "What you decide is not as important as what the public perceives."[332]

Complicating matters was the fact that any military action taken by the US government would trigger for the first time the 1973 War Powers Act, with its requirements that Congress be notified of any military action before it was undertaken and as it proceeded. Furthermore, the 1970 Cooper-Church Amendment barred the US government from further air operations in Cambodian airspace—in any airspace outside Vietnam, in fact—without congressional approval.[333] Ford didn't want to compromise his executive authority by acknowledging the constitutionality of the War Powers Act, but at the same time he didn't want to provoke a constitutional controversy by ignoring or directly challenging Congress. So he wanted to concede as little as possible, declaring at one NSC meeting that he'd decide how the United States responded "irrespective of Congress."[334]

As the crisis unfolded, Brent Scowcroft was at the nexus where US foreign policy, intelligence, military operations, international diplomacy, and domestic politics came together. He ensured that all intelligence sources were brought to bear on the situation, placing an orbiting satellite in the right spot, monitoring radio transmissions in the Khmer dialect, and checking that regular aircraft reconnaissance was up and running.[335] He served as the link between Ford and the rest of the government, communicating orders from the commander in chief to the military and relaying information from the military to the White House. He reminded those attending the

NSC meetings of important relevant facts, kept the discussions focused on the decisions needing to be made, and translated the discussion and Ford's statements into specific actions.

In the first NSC meeting on the *Mayaguez*, Vice President Rockefeller set the tone by strongly advocating a "show of force." For the outspoken Rockefeller, it was obvious what the United States had to do: the seizure demanded a "violent response. The world should know that we will act and that we will act quickly. . . . If they get any hostages, this can go on forever."[336]

Schlesinger agreed. The United States should "attack and sink the Cambodian Navy . . . after we have our ship and our people out, in order to maximize the punishment." Kissinger, too, welcomed "the opportunity to prove that others will be worse off if they tackle us, and not that they can return to the status quo." It was "not just enough to get the ship's release," Kissinger said; the United States "should seize the island, seize the ship, and hit the mainland. I am not thinking of Cambodia, but of Korea and of the Soviet Union and of others. It will not help you with the Congress if they get the wrong impression of the way we will act under such circumstances."[337]

The administration's subsequent military plan was dedicated to communicating the message that the United States was not to be trifled with. The plan was a hybrid of the options presented to the president by General David C. Jones, the acting chairman of the Joint Chiefs (the regular chairman, Gen. George S. Brown, was in Europe on business). It had three parts: a ground assault on Koh Tang, an air attack on the Cambodian mainland, and the physical recapture of the *Mayaguez*.

If concern about international perceptions dominated Ford's decision making, then the safety of the *Mayaguez* crew logically came second. For this reason, Ford approved the military plan despite the great risk it entailed. From late Monday, May 12, through late Wednesday, May 14—that is, for almost the entire duration of the crisis—the White House and Pentagon were never actually certain where the *Mayaguez* crew was. But time was of the essence. The White House wanted to act quickly to lessen the chance that the crew would be taken hostage and that more Cambodian forces would be mobilized. The tight scheduling put Ford, Kissinger, Rockefeller, Rumsfeld, and Scowcroft at odds with Schlesinger and General Jones, who wanted to move more deliberately.

Thanks in part to the fast timetable, the ground assault was a near disaster. It was premised on an erroneous CIA report that the crew of the *Mayaguez* had been taken ashore on Koh Tang—even though DCI Colby and others had evidence that some or all of the ship's crew had been moved to

Kompong Som. "I don't think the Americans are [on Koh Tang]," deputy secretary of defense William Clements said in Wednesday's NSC meeting. "They could be," Kissinger replied. "The problem is that we do not know that they are not there." But he conceded the White House didn't have good intelligence "about the crew's whereabouts and movement," and then added, "Taking the island if they are not there is easier to explain than failing to take it if they are."[338] Thus, despite the fact that neither the Pentagon nor the CIA could confirm that the *Mayaguez* crew was on Koh Tang, Ford decided to go ahead and "seize the island."

Unfortunately, no one knew how many Khmer Rouge soldiers were on Koh Tang or what arms they had. The generally accepted intelligence estimate used by Ford was one hundred troops, but Schlesinger gave an estimate of sixty at an NSC meeting, while other intelligence reports put the number at no more than twenty.[339] Yet there was no attempt to reconcile or test the assumptions behind the inconsistent intelligence estimates.[340] Worse, the Defense Intelligence Agency's larger estimate of 150 to 200 troops—which turned out to be the most accurate—was never communicated to Air Force Lt. Gen. John Burns, who was the local commander of the operation, or to any of the US Marine Corps officers involved with the situation.[341]

The rule of thumb in the Marines is to go in with at least a three-to-one ratio of attackers to defenders, but the first wave of Marines, 150 troops, was only 50 percent larger than the estimated enemy force of 100. And the actual number able to land and engage the Cambodians was only 110 Marines—essentially a one-to-one ratio.[342] Worse, it turned out that the Cambodians were armed with mortars, small arms, and light and heavy machine guns.

The ground assault was further handicapped by the fact there were only sixteen helicopters available (eight CH-53s and eight HH-53s) to transport the Marines from the U-Tapao military base in Thailand, 190 nautical miles (200 statute miles) away—and to get to U-Tapao, the helicopters had to be relocated from the Seventh Air Force Headquarters at Nakhon Phanom, in northeastern Thailand on the Laos border. Unfortunately, during the relocation of the helicopters from Nakhon Phanom to U-Tapao late Tuesday night (local time), one of the CH-53s crashed, killing nineteen air force security policemen and all four crew members.[343]

Complicating matters was the fact that half of the helicopters being deployed for the ground assault were unsuited to the mission. The Air Force versions of the CH-53 were designed for passenger and cargo transport, and were less heavily armored and not as well equipped for battle as the US Marines' HH-53, the Jolly Green Giant.[344]

When the first wave of Marines went in at sunrise on Thursday morning, May 15, three helicopters immediately drew heavy fire and went down. Not until six hours later did the second wave of Marines land on the beaches. Because a total of eight helicopters had been downed or incapacitated, further waves of Marines were canceled.

The Marines nonetheless managed to secure part of the island, but faced with a well-armed enemy, they chose not to try to capture the island. American military leaders then decided to evacuate, but this was a problem: there were "insufficient helicopter assets available to lift all personnel prior to darkness," the Department of Defense summarized.[345] With daylight fading and with the Marines still under fire, the "remaining extraction" of the marines became "a race against time."[346]

The Marines lost that race. In the near-chaos and deepening darkness of the extraction operations, three Marines were mistakenly abandoned on the island—anathema to the Marine Corps. The next morning, the USS *Wilson* returned to Koh Tang to search for the three men, but in vain. Further rescue attempts were called off. Although the Marines were initially listed as missing in action and then as killed in action, they were in fact captured by the Khmer Rouge and then executed, one on the island and the other two on the mainland.[347] (Ford doesn't count these three deaths among the total of *Mayaguez*-related fatalities he lists in his memoir *A Time to Heal.*) All in all, the first part of the three-part military plan was largely a debacle.

The second part was an air attack on the Cambodian mainland. Kissinger, Rockefeller, and Rumsfeld initially wanted to use B-52s stationed on Guam, and the president accordingly had them put on standby. But General Jones and Schlesinger disagreed, and Jones, Schlesinger, Ford, and eventually Kissinger realized that using attack aircraft on board the aircraft carrier USS *Coral Sea*, which had arrived late Wednesday (Washington time), would allow for more accurate targeting and less collateral damage, since the Navy aircraft operated at lower altitudes and were armed with precision-guided bombs. Minimizing collateral damage was desirable, since the White House recognized that the B-52s had become notorious among members of Congress, the press, and the American public.[348]

Ford clearly viewed the air strikes as an opportunity to display America's toughness. "We wanted to show them that we meant business," he writes in *A Time to Heal.* When told in the Tuesday late-night NSC meeting that there were two possible targets on the mainland, an airfield and a naval base about ten miles southeast of Kompong Som, he asked, "Why not hit both of them? There would be as many objections to hitting one as two of them."[349] And when Kissinger emphasized the next day that he wanted "a strong effort" from the military and to "take out the port," Ford agreed.[350]

Scowcroft's record on the air strikes is unclear. The minutes from the NSC meetings do not show Scowcroft calling for air attacks on the Cambodian mainland, possibly because they have been edited. Neither do they show him making any objections to the strikes.[351]

Between 7:00 and 11:30 A.M. local time on Thursday, May 15—the same morning as the ground assault on Koh Tang—F-4 Phantom II fighters, A-7 Corsair II attack aircraft, and A-6 Intruder aircraft, grouped in four waves of ten to twelve aircraft, attacked Kompong Som and the nearby Ream airfield and naval base. The first wave did not drop its ordnance, a failure that would become the source of contention after the crisis ended. (Scowcroft had initially relayed an order from Kissinger to the national military command center that the first wave was not to drop its ordnance until being notified by the president, but Ford then rescinded that order.)[352] However, the second and third waves of aircraft used strafing fire, cluster bombs, and five-hundred-pound bombs to hit the Ream airfield, the Ream naval base, oil storage facilities, a railroad yard, and the civilian port. The fourth wave was called off at 11:55, when the Joint Chiefs of Staff canceled all further offensive actions.[353]

The stunning feature of the air assault on the Cambodian mainland was that President Ford directed that the attack begin *before* he knew the location of the *Mayaguez* crew. On Tuesday evening, Scowcroft and the president talked about how the pilot of an Air Force A-7 had spotted three boats in the port:

> Scowcroft: Mr. President.
> Ford: Yes, Brent.
> Scowcroft: Three little boats have taken off toward the northeast. One boat has been sunk. The second has turned back and the third is continuing full speed. If they can't stop it any other way, we have no choice but to destroy it.
> Ford: I think we have no choice. . . . If we don't do it, it is an indication of some considerable weakness.
> Scowcroft: No question about it.
> Ford: I think we should just give it to them.
> Scowcroft: To show them we mean business.[354]

Soon thereafter, Scowcroft described the sighting of a boat with "a group of what looks like Caucasians huddled on the bow":

Scowcroft: The pilot thinks he can stop it without sinking it.

Ford: . . . Well, I don't think we have any choice.

Scowcroft: If they get the Americans to the mainland they have hostages and . . .

Ford: We have to predicate all these actions on the possibility of losing Americans.

Scowcroft: I will have them ask the pilot to do his best to stop it without sinking it.[355]

With no one in the Pentagon or White House knowing where the crew was and with Caucasians having been seen in the port, the attack on Kompong Son put the captured Americans at risk.[356] Ford nonetheless wanted to go ahead and strike the Cambodian facilities anyway, "whether or not we find the Americans" on the island.[357] He told Senate minority leader Mike Mansfield (D-Mont.), "We are not sure where they are," and when House Speaker Carl Albert (D-Okla.) asked if the crew was on the boats about to be attacked, Ford answered that there was "no way of knowing."[358] Ford later told Ron Nessen he had concerns that members of the ship's crew might be killed. And he warned his advisers that they should be prepared for the deaths of the *Mayaguez* crew: "I think we have to assume that the Americans were taken from the island and that some were killed. This is tragic, but I think we have to assume that it happened. Does anybody disagree?" No one disagreed.[359]

Still, some wondered whether they could avoid such a risk. In the Wednesday NSC meeting, Colby noted that the American crew "taken ashore may have been transported further inland by the Cambodians, and at present there is no way of telling where they may be."[360] And Ford's general counsel, Philip Buchen, cautioned, "You might hit Americans." Yet Ford decided to go ahead, irrespective of the risks: "I do not think we should delay. I think we should go on schedule. Then, whether or not we find the Americans [on the island], you can strike."

Once the decision had been made, Kissinger advised the president and the others at the meeting on how they could avoid being second-guessed:

I think it is essential in situations of this kind to make clear that it is we who define the hazards. We can argue that we are doing this to protect our operations. What we have to get across to other countries is that we will not confine ourselves to the areas in which they challenge us. So I think we should do the strikes at the same time of the operation. Then, if we have not found our people, we can mine or do other things. We can also issue an ultimatum. We can say that the 100 aircraft was a protective operation. Of course, we would have some difficulties with people on the Hill and with others.[361]

Late that evening, after a black-tie dinner with the Dutch prime minister, Ford was informed that the *Mayaguez* crew had been released and that they were all fine. They had been held at the Cambodian navy compound at Koh Rong Sam Lem, about ten miles from Kompong Sam. When Schlesinger called the president shortly thereafter to tell him that the *Mayaguez* crew had been spotted on a boat at sea, Ford roared with laughter. "Schlesinger didn't have a clue to what was going on. . . . He didn't even know the crew had already been recovered." Kissinger, Scowcroft, Rumsfeld, and others in the Oval Office then also "broke into loud laughter," reported Bud McFarlane, who also joined in. At that moment David Hume Kennerly took his famous photograph of President Ford and his top advisers all laughing and appearing to celebrate the news of the crew's release. Because the true story couldn't be told—that they were all laughing at Schlesinger's expense—the official description of the photograph was that it showed the happy reactions of the president and his aides upon learning of the crew's safe release, letting out "whoops of joy" after an extremely intense and trying four days.[362]

Scowcroft then quickly got back to business. "Is there any reason," he asked, "for the Pentagon not to disengage?"

"No," Kissinger answered, "but tell them to bomb the mainland. Let's look ferocious."[363] The president agreed, even though the third wave of attack aircraft had not yet reached its targets (and so could be called off), and even though the *Mayaguez* crew members had told Navy officers on the USS *Wilson* that "they promised [to the Khmer Rouge] air strikes would cease" upon their release. (Ford did order the Marines to halt the ground assault on Koh Tang.) So when General Burns checked with General Jones and Secretary Schlesinger to see whether he should continue on with the air strikes from the *Coral Sea*, they told him to proceed with the third strike. But there was no fourth strike, even though the White House hadn't countermanded its earlier orders. Indeed, the angriest the president became throughout the entire crisis was when he found out that neither the first nor fourth wave of aircraft had expended its ordnance over Cambodia. Ford recollected that he had said "to continue the strikes until I said to stop."

"That is my recollection," Scowcroft replied. "And you told Schlesinger."

The president, as a result, asked for "a detailed summary of the orders which went out and any changes which were made . . . including the time sequence of takeoffs and what happened."[364]

The third part of the White House's military plan was the recapture of the *Mayaguez*, timed to coincide with the assault on Koh Tang and the air attack. This turned out to be anticlimactic. Early Thursday morning, the USS *Holt*, which had arrived from Subic Bay, maneuvered alongside the *Mayaguez*, and forty-eight US Marines boarded the ship—the first ship-to-ship boarding by US Marines since 1836—only to find it abandoned. With the help of six merchant marine volunteers, the US marines got the ship's generator started and raised the American ensign over the stern. The ship's crew then got back on board; Captain Charles T. Miller took the helm and headed the *Mayaguez* to Singapore.[365]

In regard to the safety of the *Mayaguez*'s crew, the Ford administration got lucky. It's easy to imagine one or more of the crewmembers being accidentally killed, whether by their captors or by US ordnance. Fortunately, local commanders and pilots followed the president's orders to the letter and did not shoot on or sink any of the boats ferrying the *Mayaguez* crew to the mainland. Furthermore, although the ship's crew *was* taken to the mainland, just as the crew of the *Pueblo* had been, the Khmer Rouge did not exploit them for political purposes. In addition, the *Mayaguez* captain was "exceptional," able to keep the trust and loyalty of an independent-minded and potentially rebellious crew—one that included several former military men—over three and a half extraordinarily stressful days. Captain Miller succeeded at improvising in his negotiations with the Khmer Rouge and was able to convince them that if they were released, the US attacks would stop (seven Cambodian gunboats had been sunk over two days and, according to the account of one Cambodian official, a hundred of his countrymen had already been injured).[366]

But it was more than just luck. The president's quick decision making and the almost immediate mobilization of US armed forces created their own momentum, inducing the Cambodians, who were fearful of further military actions, to release the *Mayaguez* crew unharmed.[367] "Within forty-eight hours," Kissinger writes,

> an aircraft carrier, two destroyers, and one thousand Marines had already been deployed; an auxiliary carrier was scheduled to arrive a day later in a region where we had previously had no thought of taking any military action. B-52s were on alert, and tactical aircraft were blanketing the area. No

other country would have been capable of undertaking so rapid and relevant a deployment.[368]

But the quick decision making and fast deployment came at the expense of diplomacy. Ten hours elapsed between when the Ford administration learned of the *Mayaguez* seizure and when any official tried to contact the Cambodian government. On the evening of Wednesday, May 13, Ford and his top advisers essentially ignored a Cambodian radio broadcast indicating that the *Mayaguez*'s crew had been released. And the White House disregarded an undisclosed foreign government's communication fourteen hours before the assault on Koh Tang that it was intervening and soon expected the ship and its crew to be released.[369]

Nonetheless, with the ship's crew safely recovered and all in good health, most members of Congress, the press, and the American public regarded the *Mayaguez* incident as a great success. Even congressional Democrats agreed with the president's hard-nosed response and applauded the results. Editors and columnists praised the White House and Pentagon for saving the thirty-nine members of the *Mayaguez* crew and for restoring the reputation of the United States as the leader of the free world.

The Ford White House had successfully passed its three-part test. First, it had communicated to Cambodia, Korea, China, the Soviet Union, and other potential adversaries that the US government wouldn't hesitate to defend its citizens and its interests. Regardless of what had happened in Cambodia and Vietnam, the United States wasn't going to relinquish its role as the leader of the free world. Second, the administration had secured the safe release of the *Mayaguez* crew, with no one killed or injured. Third, the president had demonstrated his leadership. And while he also complied with the War Powers Act, he did so perfunctorily. He hardly "consulted" with the Democratic leadership, barely following the letter of the law by speaking with members of Congress late Wednesday, five minutes before the US Marines were to leave U-Tapao en route to Koh Tang. Ford himself acknowledged he didn't act according to the spirit of the law. When asked by Schlesinger at the Monday NSC meeting how he wanted to handle his authority as president and relation with Congress, Ford answered "There are two problems: First, the provisions of summer, 1973," and "Second, the war powers." He then told his associates, "I can assure you that, irrespective of Congress, we will move."[370] Just as he and his advisers had planned, they conceded as little as possible to Congress.

Unsurprisingly, a number of members of Congress were displeased at having been bypassed by the White House and asked the General

Accounting Office to audit the administration's actions.[371] The subsequent report, written without White House cooperation, was highly critical of the Ford administration for acting prematurely, before it exhausted diplomatic channels. The White House classified the report and only released a watered-down version in early 1976. Nonetheless, most members of Congress were "overwhelmingly positive" about the outcome of the crisis and didn't criticize him.[372] The *Mayaguez* incident boosted morale in the White House, within the military, and throughout the government, and the president's job approval ratings rose 11 percent.

The press helped secure this positive reaction. For four days following the release of the *Mayaguez* crew, the Pentagon maintained that there had been only one confirmed American death, some missing Marines, and several dozen injured. The White House and the Pentagon kept the news of the deaths in the Thailand helicopter crash "secret from the press for over a week," and the story of the final three Marines didn't emerge until much later. By the time the twenty-three deaths from the Thailand crash and the eighteen deaths on Koh Tang became known, the *Mayaguez* was old news. By then, the *New York Times*, the *Wall Street Journal*, and other influential papers had already featured leading stories celebrating President Ford's actions, newspapers nationwide had already run complimentary wire stories and syndicated columns—the nationally syndicated columnists Evans and Novak, for example, proclaimed the *Mayaguez* incident a "spectacular triumph"—and *Time*, *Newsweek*, *U.S. News and World Report*, and other magazines had run cover stories heralding Ford's success.

Of course, the public relations success shouldn't obscure the very real question of whether the Ford administration "deliberately withheld, delayed and falsified casualty figures in order to sustain as long as possible the general glow that followed the recovery of the ship and crew," as the *New Republic*'s John Osborne put it. Very simply: it did.[373]

BEHIND THE ADMINISTRATION'S apparent triumph lurked an unpleasant truth: the national security system didn't function nearly as well as it should have. There were repeated instances of communications being either delayed or transmitted incompletely, of poor or insufficient planning, and of flawed coordination within the military and across the government.

For example, the attack on Koh Tang, which was supposed to start at first light, didn't begin until sunrise—more than half an hour after nautical dawn—with the result that the attack was less of a surprise and provided less of a tactical advantage than it should have. Tactical aircraft weren't in contact with ground forces during the assault, so when the Air Force dropped a fifteen-thousand-pound daisy cutter on the island, the US Marines on the beach knew nothing of the bombing until the bomb actually went off. A more experienced Marine battalion based on Okinawa had been available but for some reason wasn't assigned to the rescue operation.[374] There were other problems as well.

President Ford was upset, as previously noted, to find out that on more than one occasion his orders hadn't been carried out. So at the Thursday NSC meeting he instructed Kissinger to let him know of any "observations or suggestions which you consider would contribute to the ability of the National Security Council machinery to deal effectively with crisis situations." Kissinger was to prepare a "consolidated evaluation report" for the president once State, Defense, and the CIA had finished their respective reports.[375]

Scowcroft and his NSC staff raised further questions. Why hadn't there been pre-attack strikes on Koh Tang directed against antiaircraft installations and other observed targets, which was standard procedure for ground assaults? Why had there been negligible support from air and naval gunfire once the Marines had landed on the island? Why had there been no plans for the Marines to be taken to the nearby USS *Coral Sea* or the *Henry E. Holt* once they had finished their mission, rather than being helicoptered all the way back to U-Tapao? (Some were in fact taken to the *Coral Sea*, the *Holt*, and the *Wilson* during the rushed evacuation, but not by predesign.)

Why were so few aircraft used in each of the attack waves directed at Kompong Som on the Cambodian mainland? The *Coral Sea* carried eighty-one airplanes, but only around half were deployed. Why were the intervals between those attack waves—ninety minutes—so lengthy?[376] And why weren't senior US government officials immediately informed of the capture of the *Mayaguez* when the national military command center first found out?

Scowcroft passed the president's and his staff's questions on to the relevant departments and agencies for answers. Three questions were of particular concern to him: Why did the Department of Defense not develop options for the president, as it had been directed to do in the Monday NSC meeting? Why did the United States' initial information about the ship's location prove to be so unreliable? And why did the first wave of *Coral Sea* aircraft not release its ordnance over Kompong Som?

Based on findings from the NSC staff, Kissinger drafted an "unusually long" memo to the president addressing many of the above questions.

Kissinger recommended specific changes in NSC procedures, and he requested Ford's authorization to send memoranda to Defense and the CIA
criticizing their performances in this crisis.[377] As one NSC staffer wrote in
an internal report sent to Scowcroft, "Defense was remiss in not insuring
that military commanders fully carried out several of the President's orders.
We have also concluded that both Defense and CIA did not provide as accurate information as was possible during the initial phase of the crisis."[378]

The US government's response to the *Mayaguez* seizure made two
things amply clear. One was the importance of coordinated action within
the administration, particularly in times of crisis. While President Ford was
ultimately in charge of managing the *Mayaguez* crisis, he could realistically
devote only some of his time to it. (During the four days, Ford conferred
with members of Congress on other matters, met with foreign delegations
and heads of state, and fulfilled other obligations).[379] The implementation of the president's policies therefore necessarily—and appropriately—
devolved to his senior foreign policy advisers, his military leaders, and their
respective staffs.

Here, the transcripts of the NSC meetings show that the Ford administration worked well as a team. The discussions were serious, intense, and
candid, and the records reveal no obvious rivalries or opposing coalitions.
Although Schlesinger, Kissinger, and Rumsfeld were known to oppose each
other on various policy issues—SALT II, for example—during the *Mayaguez* crisis they worked together effectively, trying to come up with sound
decisions under conditions of immense pressure.[380]

The NSC debates were remarkably professional and free-flowing, with
many of the principals and their deputies taking part, consistent with Ford's
preference for open debate—so much so that White House photographer
Kennerly at one point took the liberty to ask, "Has anyone considered that
this might be the act of a local Cambodian commander who has just taken
it into his hands to halt any ship that comes by? Has anyone considered
that he might not have gotten his orders from Phnom Penh?" (Kennerly's
participation—a clear breach of protocol—doesn't appear in the NSC
meeting transcripts, because the memoranda of conversations, according
to Scowcroft, were "edited and transcribed" for administrative purposes.)[381]

Only after the crisis had ended did the rivalry between State and Defense
reemerge. On Thursday, Pentagon spokesman Joseph Laitin publicized the
successful release of the *Mayaguez* crew without first informing the White
House and letting President Ford or the White House press office break
the good news. When presidential spokesman Ron Nessen was handed the

newswire bulletin announcing that the *Mayaguez* crew had been freed, he shouted, "That goddamn Laitin has already leaked the news!"[382]

So teamwork at the leadership level was not a major problem during the *Mayaguez* crisis. And this was largely because of Scowcroft. He was at the center of it all—orchestrating foreign policy, coordinating the military operations, handling press relations, and consistently doing the little things that held the US government together.[383] In fact, Scowcroft later described the *Mayaguez* rescue as a "beautifully done operation" that "went extremely well."[384]

Scowcroft arranged for the Monday morning NSC meeting. He briefed the NSC on where things stood during the critical Tuesday midnight NSC meeting. And he kept the meetings focused on what needed to be decided and made sure that crucial information surfaced. For example, Scowcroft (and Rumsfeld) made the important point that aircraft from the *Coral Sea* could arrive at the battle scene significantly in advance of the carrier itself, a fact Schlesinger and General Jones neglected to point out.[385] And Scowcroft reminded everyone of the diplomatic consequences of damaging US-Thai relations by using Thailand's bases in connection with US military operations and the *Mayaguez*.

Ron Nessen observed that Scowcroft did whatever was necessary to keep the government operating over the three and a half days of the crisis, even as he seemed ready at times to "collapse from stress and exhaustion."[386] Late on Wednesday, Kissinger wanted to let the Cambodians know that the United States was willing to stop attacking once it had reassurances that the *Mayaguez* crew would be released. But Nessen balked at the order; Kissinger wasn't his boss. So "Scowcroft, dressed in his tuxedo" for the state dinner with the Dutch prime minister, "burst into Nessen's office, grabbed Nessen by the arm, and literally pulled him to Kissinger's office." The White House then got the message out to the Cambodian government over the Associated Press wire: "As soon as you issue a statement that you are prepared to release the crew members you hold unconditionally and immediately, we will promptly cease military operations."[387]

Thanks to Scowcroft, the problems with the US response to the seizure of the *Mayaguez* were not so much those of teamwork. Rather, they involved deeper issues of what the president called the "mechanics of national security." This was the second revelation the *Mayaguez* crisis made apparent: the problems with the planning and execution of joint military operations.[388]

The crisis plan that turned out to be a political triumph was nearly a military disaster. As Bud McFarlane stated during the Senate's hearings on the restructuring of the Defense Department, the Pentagon's response to the *Mayaguez* seizure was "dysfunctional," and the dysfunction was "purely the consequence of service parochialism." The secretary of defense had been "too easily co-opted by the Air Force," in McFarlane's assessment. By patching together a rescue operation that combined a marine battalion with Air Force search-and-rescue helicopter crews, the Defense Department created a recipe for failure. Schlesinger showed "poor judgment" in his decisions on how to use the military and was "not really as knowledgeable as the crisis demanded."[389]

Scowcroft would get a chance to remake the NSC process in only a few months' time. The comprehensive reform of the military command system and of joint operations—integrally related to Ford's "mechanics of national security" and to the success of the NSC process—would not come until much later.

The *Mayaguez* became part of a cumulative history of botched joint military operations, extending from the "terrible problems in Vietnam in joint operations" and the ill-fated 1979 Iranian hostage rescue (Operation Eagle Claw) to the bombing of the US Marine barracks in Beirut on October 23, 1983, and the flawed invasion of Grenada in 1983 (Operation Urgent Fury). In the Grenada operation, for instance, the military services couldn't agree on which would control the island, so one-half of Grenada was controlled by the Army and the other by the Marines. As a result, Army helicopters weren't able to evacuate injured soldiers, because their pilots hadn't been trained to land on ships. And communication between the Army and Navy was so bad that an Army officer had to use an AT&T telephone card to call Fort Bragg, North Carolina, so he could connect with Navy officers. As one Pentagon official summarized, "Command and control, communications, [and] planning and operations" were all "just a disaster."[390]

Ultimately, this series of disasters led to the passage of the Goldwater-Nichols Act in 1986. Spearheading this effort to reform the US military's joint operations was General Jones, who later became chairman of the Joint Chiefs of Staff under President Carter.[391] And it was the *Mayaguez* crisis that convinced Jones "of the problems of the joint system." The Goldwater-Nichols Act concentrated military authority and promoted integration and collaboration among the services in order to make joint operations more effective. It strengthened the role of the chairman of the Joint Chiefs of Staff, making him the "principal military adviser to the President, the National Security Council, and the Secretary of Defense" and giving him authority over the service chiefs for military planning and the defense budget.[392] It also adjusted promotion requirements in each of the four services so as to foster the development of effective communication, command, and control of joint operations by military leaders. Officers were now required to have joint service experience before being promoted to general officer or flag officer. In addition, the Goldwater-Nichols Act sharpened the military chain of command so as to concentrate war-making responsibilities in the regional commanders (including CINCPAC, SOUTHCOM, and CENTCOM). These regional commanders were now directly answerable to the secretary of defense and given broad authority over military operations, joint service training, and the management of equipment and supplies.[393]

Although Scowcroft didn't play an official role in the wholesale reform of DOD practices, he "talked to the group that was running the operation many times." Not only did he strongly encourage the passage of the Goldwater-Nichols Act—unlike defense secretary Casper Weinberger, many high-ranking military officers, and many members of Congress, who opposed the bill—but Scowcroft's testimony before the Senate Armed Services Committee played an important role in shaping the ultimate legislation, according to James Locher's comprehensive account.[394]

SEVERAL WEEKS AFTER the *Mayaguez* crisis, the Department of Defense placed two letters in General Scowcroft's personnel file. The first, dated May 18, 1975, was from Henry A. Kissinger. "Dear Brent," Kissinger wrote, "Your extraordinary performance during the *Mayaguez* incident was no surprise to me, but it reminded me of the debt I and the President and the country owe you. You were the focal point of the effort. Your judgment and strength were a tremendous support. The successful outcome was your contribution as much as anyone's."[395]

The other letter, dated May 27, 1975, was signed "Jerry Ford." "During the *Mayaguez* incident your support to me was even more than your usual superb contribution," President Ford wrote. "Twenty-four hours a day, you were a pillar of strength. Your dedication and professional skill were in the highest tradition of service of the Armed Forces of the United States. I want you to know how much I appreciate it. Not only the crew of the *Mayaguez* and their families, but all Americans owe you a debt of gratitude."[396]

The *Mayaguez* incident was the last official battle of the Vietnam War; the names of the three Marines left behind on Koh Tang are the very last names engraved on Maya Lin's Vietnam Veterans Memorial. The United

States "had entered Indochina to save a country," Kissinger remarked, and it "ended by rescuing a ship."[397]

The irony of it all was that the seizure of the *Mayaguez* was wholly random. Local Khmer Rouge forces had been ordered to take the next ship coming along, and the *Mayaguez* happened to be in the wrong place at the wrong time. The young soldiers seizing the *Mayaguez* didn't even know the ship was American until they climbed aboard; the ship's crew hadn't hoisted the US ensign because the sea winds would have ripped it to shreds. In 1979 Sea-Land sold the *Mayaguez* for scrap steel.[398]

The Ford administration's response to the *Mayaguez* seizure was a bright spot in its history—but only a brief respite in the midst of more than two and a half very difficult years.

12

NATIONAL SECURITY ADVISOR

AMID THE CONTROVERSIES over intelligence, the fallout from the withdrawal in Vietnam, and the doubts in Congress, in the press, and among the public about the presidency as an institution, President Ford decided to take action to make it clear who was in charge. On Sunday, November 2, 1975, in what the press called the "Halloween Massacre," he announced his dismissal of several of President Nixon's top appointees, including CIA director William Colby, defense secretary James Schlesinger, treasury secretary William E. Simon, and agriculture secretary Earl Butz. He also removed Kissinger from his post as national security advisor, while keeping him on as secretary of state. At the same time, the White House leaked the news that Vice President Rockefeller wouldn't serve as Ford's running mate for the 1976 presidential campaign.

President Ford had various reasons for this array of personnel changes. On the foreign policy front, he'd been unhappy with Colby for his willingness to cooperate with Congress by handing over sensitive CIA records. Whatever the CIA's excesses, poor judgment, and egregious actions, the president and his top foreign policy advisers worried that additional disclosures by Colby or other agency employees would only make things worse. The White House no longer trusted Colby—and hadn't for some time.[399]

So at eight o'clock on the morning of Sunday November 2, Ford summoned Colby to the Oval Office and told him he was reorganizing the White House. He then asked the DCI if he wanted to be US ambassador to NATO. Colby said he'd think about it and left the office. Later that day, after talking things over with his wife, he called in and declined the president's offer.

After Colby left, the president called for Schlesinger, telling his deputy chief of staff, Dick Cheney, to "get that son-of-a-bitch in here so I can fire him." Cheney said it was the angriest he had ever seen Gerald Ford.[400]

Ford had been increasingly frustrated with Schlesinger, mostly because of the secretary of defense's attitude. During his weekly meetings with the president, Schlesinger would slouch in his armchair, wave his pipe around, and lecture Ford as though he were a none-too-bright student, not even bothering to button his shirt collar or tighten his tie. Schlesinger's behavior "just infuriated Ford," Scowcroft remarked, and over time Ford became less and less tolerant of his behavior. Scowcroft tried to intervene; he gently "tried to tell Schlesinger not to talk to him that way." It did no good.[401]

By contrast, Kissinger was savvy enough to defer to Ford and to show him respect in public, whereas the secretary of defense simply didn't bother. Reporters joked that "the difference between Kissinger and Schlesinger was Kissinger would come in to see the President and say, 'Mr. President, as you are well aware . . .' and then he would explain what was going on. Schlesinger would come in and say, 'Mr. President, you probably don't know this, but. . . .'"[402]

Ford did not like the constant clashes between Kissinger and Schlesinger, and their fractious relationship made his job and the process of policy making that much harder. His chief of staff, Rumsfeld, certainly had his own ambitions to become secretary of state and perhaps eventually run for president, and for months had been grooming Cheney to replace him as chief of staff.[403] He probably helped persuade Ford to make the change. Schlesinger further damaged his cause by making a series of public statements that contradicted official administration policy—revealing, for example, that secret agreements had accompanied the Paris peace accords. Schlesinger appeared to be a loose cannon, creating more problems for the White House than he was worth.

Schlesinger tried to dissuade the president from firing him and pleaded for his job. But Ford was adamant, and Schlesinger wanted no part of the job being offered him—directing the Import-Export Bank. Their ugly, hour-long conversation only reinforced in Ford's mind the correctness of his decision.[404] The dismissal would soon cause trouble, however. Schlesinger, a proud and accomplished man, did not take his dismissal lightly. He would try to retaliate.

Donald Rumsfeld was now named secretary of defense; he was replaced in his position as chief of staff by his thirty-four-year-old deputy, Dick Cheney. Ford's first choice for Colby's replacement as director of intelligence was his friend and confidant, the powerful Washington attorney Edward Bennett Williams. When Williams declined, Ford tapped George H. W. Bush.

Rumsfeld had started out as an Illinois congressman and was then appointed to a series of White House positions: counselor to the president under

Nixon, director of the economic stabilization program in the office of the vice president under Ford, US ambassador to NATO, and White House chief of staff (if not officially). He was smart, driven, a skilled bureaucratic operator, and immodest about his abilities. Nixon called him "a ruthless little bastard," meaning it as a compliment. Kissinger called Rumsfeld "a special Washington phenomenon: the skilled full-time politician-bureaucrat in whom ambition, ability, and substance fuse seamlessly." This might have also been meant as a compliment, except that Kissinger couldn't stand Rumsfeld.[405]

Almost everyone credits Rumsfeld with persuading Ford to reshuffle his cabinet—and many have commented about the personal political motives that may have been involved. Scowcroft, never one to cast aspersions on others without good reason, said that the entire reorganization was "Rumsfeld inspired," since moving Bush to the CIA "presumably [took him] out of the political arena." Rogers Morton, secretary of the interior under Presidents Nixon and Ford, told Bush, "I know damn well [the story is] true."[406]

Ford and Kissinger had both come to appreciate George Bush's talents. When Ford asked Kissinger about how Bush was doing as the United States' liaison to China, Kissinger replied, "Magnificently. I am very, very impressed with him." It was precisely because Rumsfeld viewed Bush as a fellow rising star within the Republican Party and a future presidential candidate that he wanted to isolate Bush in Langley, given how discredited the CIA was at the time. Rumsfeld was going to "bury the sonofabitch."[407]

Bush himself, perhaps because of his own good manners, expressed doubt that Rumsfeld was behind the appointment, but he did say that a lot of his friends advised him, "Don't do this, this will be the end of your political life." So he then "talked to Brent about it," and Scowcroft told him "Well, this is what the president wants you to do." Bush even suggested Scowcroft might have played a role in the cabinet reshuffling, saying, "If Scowcroft had a hand in this, I don't know."[408]

Bush accepted the position, of course, and the appointment did not end his political life. But he did have to agree—reluctantly—to a demand by Democratic senators as a condition of their approval that he not run for the vice presidency in 1976.[409]

Rumsfeld had his own ideas about who should replace Kissinger as the new national security advisor. His first choice was his friend Arthur Hartman, the assistant secretary of state for Europe. But Kissinger made a strong case on behalf of Scowcroft, "believing him to be best qualified and also the person most comfortable with existing procedures." Ford didn't have to think long and offered Scowcroft the position of national security advisor.[410]

Many Washington observers criticized Scowcroft's promotion, doubting that the change would actually reduce Kissinger's influence. Columnist George Will wrote that Scowcroft was Kissinger's "obedient servant." "To say that Scowcroft is independent," Sen. Henry Jackson commented, "is one of the [greatest] political fictions of all time." Scowcroft was "pliable" and wholly "unthreatening," according to Roger Morris, an NSC staff member in the Johnson and Nixon administrations, while a United Press International wire story described the switch of national security advisors as being merely "cosmetic." Many figured Scowcroft would continue to do Kissinger's bidding—assuming that that was what he had been doing all along—thereby leaving what they considered to be Kissinger's detrimental influence and flawed judgment in place. The eminent columnist Joseph Kraft characterized Scowcroft as "so much the loyal No. 2 that Dr. Kissinger's power will only be clipped slightly."[411] Kissinger would simply be making foreign policy from Foggy Bottom rather than the West Wing—and now without Schlesinger to serve as a counterweight.

Ford sought to correct the popular misperception that Scowcroft was "a Kissinger man," telling reporters his new national security advisor had "an independent mind." Other White House officials pointed out that Scowcroft had "too much moral integrity to become anyone's sycophant" and that he could scarcely be considered Kissinger's "tool." As one White House official explained, Scowcroft served "as a foil for the secretary" and as "a kind of alter ego."[412]

The president was right, and the critics were mistaken. Scowcroft was his own person, and his promotion would result in a significant decrease of Kissinger's authority. Part of the reason for Scowcroft's eclipse of Kissinger was that the latter had been tainted by his close ties to the disgraced Nixon presidency and by the subsequent revelations that he had his own White House taping system. By late 1975, as a result, Kissinger was not the formidable political figure he had once been, and he started to attract harsh criticism from right-wing Republicans—including some of Ford's own political advisers—as well as more criticism from Democrats.

Furthermore, Kissinger's loss of his position as national security advisor reduced his influence over the rest of the government, particularly the Defense Department and Treasury, since he wasn't any longer in a position to control the NSC process or NSC staff. He wasn't quite so indispensable now in forming and executing US foreign policy. However, he retained some of his influence on the NSC process by virtue of the fact that Scowcroft agreed that Kissinger could continue as chairman of the Washington

Study Action Group and the arms control Verification Panel; Scowcroft took over as chair of the 40 Committee in charge of covert activities (which would be renamed the Operations Advisory Group a few months later).[413]

Kissinger recognized the personnel shift as a blow to his authority, and he twice considered resigning after the Halloween Massacre. But Ford consistently reassured Kissinger that he couldn't do without him and asked him to stay on as secretary of state.

The day after the announcement, the White House telephone switchboard was jammed with calls. Kissinger told the president that the flood of phone calls was the work of Schlesinger, who'd "obviously been very active," and Al Haig said it revealed Schlesinger's presidential ambitions.[414]

Presidential ambitions were certainly involved in the Halloween Massacre—but they were those of Gerald R. Ford. The president was very much aware of the pressure building on the Republican right. He was sensitive to the widely held view that he was too deferential to and too dependent on his secretary of state, and his political advisers had been urging him to show the American public who was really running the country. Ford may have had other good reasons for removing and reassigning several of his top advisers, but the "best two," according to one anonymous White House official, were "New Hampshire and Florida, the first two Presidential primaries."[415]

But the reshuffling came as a great surprise, and some in the press condemned the president for the suddenness of the changes and the fact that the White House hadn't put up any trial balloons in advance of the announcement. Robert Hartmann commented, "The 'leaks' that give most Presidents so much pain serve a useful purpose by preparing people to accept sharp shifts in Presidential policies and dramatic personnel changes." Even the *New Republic*'s usually sympathetic John Osborne thought President Ford's decisions revealed him "to be intensely egoistic behind that humble façade of his . . . and desperately anxious to establish and prove himself as a national leader in his own right." Others disagreed. ABC News's David Brinkley said Ford "was in good shape," and the *New York Times*' James Reston wrote that "the shake-up didn't hurt" the president at all. But most commentators thought the shake-up made Ford look insecure and confused.[416]

Unfortunately for the Ford White House, Schlesinger was a friend of Senator Jackson's. Jackson thought of Schlesinger as a first-rate professional and a man of outstanding competence, courage, integrity, and honor. So he concluded that Ford, by firing Schlesinger, was manifesting his intolerance of differing points of view and lack of interest in receiving dispassionate, candid, and honest advice. Jackson further believed that with the dismissal of Schlesinger and Colby, Ford would be able to protect Kissinger's involvement in "a whole series of doubtful activities." He found risible the idea the president now had a new team of advisers: it was still the same old Kissinger-Scowcroft "machine." Scowcroft, for his part, was "a snake in the grass," in Jackson's description, someone who didn't explain his actions, who behaved in a cavalier manner, and who demonstrated a complete "lack of sincerity and credibility."[417] (Scowcroft attributed Jackson's comment to the pernicious influence of the senator's chief foreign policy aide, Richard Perle. Once Perle stopped working for Jackson in 1980, Scowcroft said, he found the senator to be "warm and friendly," notwithstanding their policy differences.)[418]

The only concrete effort to block Scowcroft's appointment was led by Representative Les Aspin, a young Democrat from Wisconsin. Aspin raised the point that according to Title 10 of the federal code, no military official could hold a civil office, and General Scowcroft's appointment as the president's assistant for national security affairs would make him the first military man to hold the position.[419] Yet Title 10 hadn't been much of an issue in the past. When President Harry Truman asked Gen. George Marshall to become secretary of state in 1948 and when Nixon selected Gen. Al Haig to be chief of staff in May 1973, Congress simply made exceptions. It would later do exactly the same with Lt. Col. Robert McFarlane, Adm. John Poindexter, and Gen. Colin Powell, each of whom was allowed to keep his military commission while serving as national security advisor.[420] (The legal restriction has since been repealed.)

Yet Scowcroft *agreed* with Title 10: he didn't think the national security advisor should be an active-duty military officer. For a senior White House official to retain a military commission would, he thought, divide his loyalty between his military superiors and the American president. Scowcroft was also concerned that members of Congress, the press, and the public might think that the national security advisor was providing the president with options and advice that favored the Air Force or the Department of Defense. With the precarious state of the presidency and the charged political environment of the mid-1970s, Scowcroft wanted to avoid any appearance of a conflict of interest. So he decided to retire from the Air Force effective December 1, 1975.[421]

Such conscientiousness was both highly unusual and unnecessary. Scowcroft could have fought to retain his commission, and had he chosen to do so, he almost certainly would have been able to keep his commission. In fact, toward the end of the administration, the president asked the national security advisor if he wanted to return to active duty; Scowcroft declined, telling Ford that it would smack of a political deal. Given his excellent reputation, any criticism and unwelcome attention would have in all likelihood dissipated quickly. Scowcroft would then have been able to receive a fourth star, as had Haig and as Powell later would—a fitting recognition of Scowcroft's public service. Scowcroft was giving up his rank, military salary, and future Air Force career for what could possibly turn out to be merely fifteen months in office. It was a "hell of a price," a White House official stated.[422]

The promotion barely altered Scowcroft's daily routine. He had been the acting national security advisor for all intents and purposes for over two years, ever since Kissinger had gone over to the State Department. So he simply kept doing his job: advising President Ford, managing the NSC staff, and working with Kissinger. Although some wanted Scowcroft to speak out more, since Kissinger was by then unpopular, the national security advisor sought the president's guidance. "Look, I work for you," Scowcroft said. "I'll do whatever you want." Ford said, "No, I want you to stay behind the scenes where you are now."[423]

Still, Scowcroft's promotion changed some things. Kissinger still played a major role in making US foreign policy and dominated the news accounts, but on key issues the president increasingly consulted with Scowcroft, whom he trusted not to have a personal agenda or ulterior motives. Quietly, Scowcroft "managed to have a prevailing influence," McFarlane observed.[424]

Scowcroft began to speak up more and took more initiative, especially on issues Kissinger didn't care much about.[425] For example, when Ford, Kissinger, and Scowcroft met in late 1976 to discuss how to handle wheat shipments to Israel, Scowcroft—who didn't want any formal agreement on wheat between the United States and Israel—suggested the White House release the news that Kissinger was preparing to offer a larger amount of foreign food aid in 1976. "Why don't we leak that?" he asked. Ford agreed.[426]

Scowcroft also began to talk to Kissinger as he would to a peer. After one of Kissinger's press conferences, for instance, he remarked, "You sure did slam the Soviets. Got a little too much, didn't you." It was an observation, not a question, to which Kissinger replied simply, "Yes, it was a little too much." As one former US ambassador who had formerly worked on the NSC staff told the author and foreign policy expert David Rothkopf, "Kissinger would expect Scowcroft to defer to him, and Scowcroft would very pleasantly say, you know, Henry, I don't think that's going to work."[427]

When Ford, Kissinger, and Scowcroft met in the summer of 1975 to discuss SALT, Kissinger said they didn't need a SALT meeting that week, whereupon Scowcroft replied quickly, "I think we should, just for the President to say he wants a SALT Treaty and expects everyone to focus on the national interest."[428] Ford held the meeting. In addition, meeting transcripts "may not reflect the whole story," as one White House military assistant remarked. Scowcroft "always [had] access to the President after a meeting," and Ford "undoubtedly asked him what he thought." The two "worked together." Scowcroft appreciated and respected the secretary of state, but by no means was he "overwhelmed" by Kissinger.[429]

With Scowcroft's increased confidence in his role and own judgment, he began to put into practice his ideas about how the national security advisor should behave and how the NSC's process should operate. He trimmed the NSC staff to about forty-five professionals (from about a hundred under Kissinger), reduced NSC expenses, added more women to his staff, and improved interagency coordination.

Scowcroft also changed the atmosphere of the NSC. Under Kissinger, the NSC process had been "a very shadowy operation." Kissinger liked to hold all the cards and limited the information he shared with his staff—Scowcroft included. He had also discouraged his NSC staff from contacting their counterparts in other departments and agencies and went so far as to deny them White House Mess privileges so they wouldn't fraternize with other presidential aides. The end result was rampant dissatisfaction and disillusionment among the NSC staff and a high turnover rate, despite the top-quality personnel Kissinger was able to attract.[430]

Although he'd never say so publicly, Scowcroft "strongly rejected Kissinger's model for running the NSC," one writer noted. Scowcroft sought to create a more open and friendly work environment.[431] He gave the members of his staff the opportunity to express their dissatisfaction and make requests, and he listened. When the NSC's chief of planning asked for better circulation and sharing of information, better feedback on decision papers forwarded by the staff, and a more open environment, Scowcroft largely complied. He shared the desire to make the NSC process more transparent.[432]

Scowcroft "was much more inclusive," said Lt. Gen. Daniel Christman, an NSC staff member who worked under both Kissinger and Scowcroft. Scowcroft reached "out to junior members on the staff, and just welcomed the give-and-take by creating an environment in which these differing views were elicited with very little tension. That's one of the reasons why I thought his model of dealing with complicated interagency topics was really very, very impressive." Added Christman, "It was Brent's ability to ensure that all thoughts were on the table, and to treat those who presented them respectfully."[433]

Scowcroft also began to delegate more, especially to his new deputy, William G. Hyland (who had been serving as the head of the State Department's Bureau of Intelligence and Research).[434] He began to hold more frequent meetings with the members of his NSC staff, he renewed their White House mess privileges, and he reduced the friction between the NSC and other departments and agencies. He reinstituted the position of NSC executive secretary to oversee the paper flow and provide institutional memory. And he leavened his directives and demands with humor and praise, believing he'd get much better work from his NSC staff through encouragement and empathy rather than by what he termed "whips" and "beatings."[435] Whereas Kissinger often got upset and screamed at his staff, Scowcroft stayed calm and under control, even—and perhaps especially—during crises. Almost never did he lose his temper, and rarely would he say anything stronger than "gosh." The NSC staff became a lot happier under Scowcroft.[436]

He also rearranged how the NSC handled press relations. Kissinger had effectively run his own press operation, causing friction between the White House press office and NSC staff. Had the coordination been better, Ron Nessen argued, they "could have averted a catastrophe such as the Solzhenitsyn problem." So when Scowcroft took over, he appointed a NSC press secretary, Margi Vanderhye, to work in tandem with Nessen and other press office officials, who, in turn, appreciated Scowcroft's willingness to trust them and grew comfortable working with him.[437]

Scowcroft continued Kissinger's practice of using background briefings. "I rarely do anything on the record," he explained to ABC News's Ann Compton. "I will talk to you on background or in some way that I can be more relaxed, and in which I can tell you more about what we both know is what you need to know."[438] What Scowcroft didn't tell Compton was that he was far less inclined to bad-mouth others, leak information, distort facts, or willingly mislead people than was his predecessor.

He took additional steps to make the NSC process more effective. Because he knew Ford liked to read and to have open discussions on issues, he reduced the length of NSC memoranda to "no more than three pages," in which he "summarized the issues to the extent I knew them, the views of the other senior advisers, and then my own judgments regarding the pros and cons of different opinions and recommendations." He then appended the original documents to the NSC summary so that the president could go over them if he wanted to.[439] These brief memos then became the basis for the larger policy discussions.

Most significantly, Scowcroft restored the NSC principals to their traditional status in the decision-making process. He reinstituted full meetings of the NSC as the primary venue for setting policy, thereby ensuring that "all the major agency heads got their say on key policy differences." He didn't take positions without first getting all the available facts on the table and letting all the principals give their positions. Rather than cutting Kissinger off from access to the president (as Kissinger had done to Secretary Rogers), Scowcroft made sure that all of the principals' views were fairly and equally represented. He also discontinued Kissinger's practice of drafting decision memoranda that predisposed the president to choose the option that Kissinger meant him to pick (it was always the second, or middle, option). Scowcroft himself acknowledged that he "was more solicitous of the need to try to co-opt people within the government in support of particular policies than Henry was, who was more inclined to move and let the chips fall where they may, and rely on the president to back him up."[440] The NSC process thereby became much more consensual and far less autocratic.

Contrary to the opinions of George Will, Henry Jackson, and others who'd believed that the locus of decision making would shift to the State Department, "the center of the interdepartmental policy-development process remained in the White House under President Ford and Scowcroft," three analysts of the Ford administration wrote. The administration's "handling of issues such as SALT, arms sales, economic development assistance, and of crises bears witness to this fact."[441] So even as Kissinger continued to strongly influence Ford's foreign policy and attracted the lion's share of media attention, Scowcroft, by virtue of his scholarship, honesty, and integrity, became that much "more valuable in shaping policy," McFarlane said.[442] But Scowcroft stayed very much behind the scenes, which both he and President Ford preferred.[443]

The president was comfortable working with Kissinger and Scowcroft both and appreciated their different contributions. "I used Henry for the primary purpose of executing and formulating foreign policy for my administration," he explained. "At the same time, Brent, as head of the NSC, would make comments and observations and consult directly with me on policy and the choices we faced." While Kissinger made the recommendations, Ford told David Rothkopf, he was the president and commander-in-chief. "And if I wanted additional background, I would turn to Brent."[444] Ford often wanted additional background.

As a result, Scowcroft played almost the opposite role as national security advisor that Kissinger had. He acted a mediator and conciliator of differences around the government. One of Kissinger's former NSC staff members said that, as a legacy of Kissinger's style, Scowcroft had to clean up after "all the breakage" his predecessor had caused in the State Department and other departments and agencies.[445] In contrast to Kissinger, Scowcroft was "a skillful manager of the bureaucracy," inclusive of the other principals, and respectful of others, one of his NSC assistants pointed out. Whereas power was "at the center" in Kissinger's NSC, according to NSC staff member David Gompert, Scowcroft didn't view the NSC "as sort of a platform from which to push a particular policy." Scowcroft thought "much more deeply in the consequences of things," McFarlane believed. This extended not just to international relations (where Kissinger himself was very capable) but to the rest of the national security bureaucracy, the Congress, and the press as well. In what was a "very, very difficult" period, Scowcroft was steadfast; he didn't "get rattled."[446]

Despite the changes Scowcroft introduced, Kissinger didn't resent his former deputy or object to his growing influence. Thanks to both Scowcroft's steadying influence and what Ford termed the "care and feeding of Henry Kissinger," Kissinger was content to go along with the NSC reforms. Scowcroft "gave Ford his independent judgment in dealing with foreign policy issues," Kissinger writes in *Years of Renewal*, "without ever giving me the feeling that he was competing with my responsibilities as secretary of state."[447] Kissinger "had total confidence" that his former deputy "would represent my views fairly to the president, the president's views accurately to me, and his own views precisely to both of us, whether we liked them or not." He was "the balance wheel of the national security process," Kissinger noted, "and he has remained a national asset and personal friend."[448]

Scowcroft recognized what he was doing. "I knew Henry very well. I knew how to get around the difficult side of him and appeal to the easy side of him." It was Scowcroft's emotional intelligence, coupled with his policy expertise and bureaucratic savvy, that allowed their role changes to go much more smoothly than might otherwise have been expected. "Henry Kissinger had worn two hats for a couple of years—that was a hard adjustment for him," Scowcroft told the political scientist John Burke, "*and I took account of that.*"[449]

Henry Kissinger remains the most influential national security advisor in American history. By centralizing information and the NSC process, Kissinger and Nixon—and, for a while, Kissinger and Ford—were able to control both the NSC process and the content of US foreign policy, with the result that they were able to act precisely and adroitly within the international system of states.[450]

But the drawback of this concentration of power was that when the cabinet-level appointees or sub-cabinet officials in the Department of Defense, the Joint Chiefs of Staff, the CIA, the FBI, and the Treasury Department didn't buy into the White House's policies, the result was serious news leaks, problems with policy coordination, and time-consuming and energy-draining bureaucratic battles. These divisions would then often pull Congress and the press into the fray, making matters yet worse.

The idea of an all-powerful Henry Kissinger, an image that prevails among many political writers, popular historians, and the American public, thus needs amending on several counts. Kissinger alone didn't make the Nixon and Ford administrations function. Nixon was very much his boss; it was predominantly *Nixon*'s foreign policy. And if Ford was more dependent on Kissinger than Nixon, especially at first, he also frequently overruled his secretary of state.

In addition, Kissinger's influence on Nixon and Ford would not have been possible without the assistance of Al Haig, Helmut Sonnenfeldt, Lawrence Eagleburger, Winston Lord, and others, none more than Scowcroft. Specifically, much of what Kissinger did—and therefore much of what Nixon and Ford accomplished—he achieved by virtue of Scowcroft's quiet abilities and complementary skills. "It would be difficult," as Richard Head, Frisco Short, and Robert McFarlane write in their study of presidential decision making, "to overstate Brent Scowcroft's contribution to both the substance and process of United States national security policy during his four years in the White House."[451]

The notion of an all-powerful Kissinger further ignores the fact that Kissinger's domineering and secretive style often alienated others within the government, leading to various forms of bureaucratic resistance—troubles exacerbated by Nixon's own suspicious and secretive personality. And his penchant for holding information close to the vest and refusing to share it with others who had a stake in US policies prevented Kissinger from making the best use of the contributions and talent of others in the White House and around the government.

"Secrecy may have enabled Nixon and Kissinger to obtain better results in negotiations with the Vietnamese, the Soviets, the Chinese, and within the Middle East," the writer and security analyst David Rothkopf pointed out, but it was hardly clear that the secrecy surrounding the Paris negotiations, the bombing in Indochina, the pacification program, and the covert efforts to upend the regime of Salvador Allende in Chile, among other initiatives, made those policies more effective. Kissinger's secret diplomacy may have fueled media interest, but it also made him that much more intent on controlling leaks, withholding information, and managing external perceptions.[452] That secrecy arguably caused the quality of US foreign policy to suffer, with the texts of the Strategic Arms Limitations Treaty in 1972 and the Paris Peace accords of 1973 as cases in point.[453]

Kissinger's management style exacted another cost. His attention to a few high-profile issues—the Soviet Union, China, Vietnam, and the Middle East, especially—deflected attention from other matters, which were left to lower-level officials in the relevant departments and agencies to sort out. Consequently, responses to these other issues were often not coordinated across the government. This was partly by design, a result of Nixon's memo of March 1970 that instructed Kissinger to focus on East-West issues and delegate the rest.[454] But with the concentration of power in two men with distinct, sometimes clashing personalities, Nixon and Kissinger often ended up worrying more about each other than about US foreign policy.

The opening to China and the triangulation of US-China and US-Soviet relations were foreign policy strokes of genius. Yet the concentration of power within the White House and the attendant secrecy ultimately made Nixon's foreign policy less successful than is commonly thought. Nixon's and Kissinger's new diplomatic ties helped little with Vietnam and Indochina—the chief reason for Nixon's overture, after all—and Nixon and Kissinger oversold détente and SALT to the American public. Kissinger's "failing was that he never really understood the American democracy," Eagleburger later remarked. "He never understood the fact that you had to have popular support—that was an issue that he didn't think much about."[455]

The consequence was the later demise of détente and the unhappy fate of SALT II, which disenchanted the public all the more. Americans had been led to believe that the rapprochement between the United States and the Soviet Union would greatly benefit them: détente would reduce military competition, lessen the US-Soviet rivalry, and result in more harmonious superpower relations. Kissinger similarly believed that détente "would spill over into other fields," as one NSC staffer put it. But Kissinger "was repeatedly disappointed"—as were those who hoped détente would lead to a better world.[456]

In short, the promises that Nixon and Kissinger held out to the American public—and, indeed, to the world—with respect to the Vietnam War and Indochina, the Arab-Israeli conflict and the Middle East, and SALT and arms control never materialized. Nixon and Kissinger's foreign policy failed to produce significant and lasting results, with the partial exception of China. Instead, as one scholar of US national security points out, "the to-ing and fro-ing concealed a lack of real achievement." Indicatively, the subsequent US-Soviet summits in San Clemente in 1973 and Moscow in 1974 produced only "minor understandings and protocols." Neither was Kissinger able to get the Department of Defense to agree to a mutually acceptable position on SALT II.[457] Nor would there be "peace at hand" in Vietnam, per Kissinger's announcement of October 26, 1972.

Meanwhile, the country became increasingly polarized, with Ronald Reagan and the Republican right on one side, and the Democrats and the left on the other. The Arab-Israeli conflict and other US foreign policy issues remained as difficult and seemingly intractable as ever, while the threat of nuclear war still hung over the world. Hence the backlash among the American public. Notwithstanding Kissinger's and Nixon's brilliance and the public acclaim bestowed on the two—*Time* proclaimed them its joint "Men of the Year" of 1972, and Kissinger shared the Nobel Peace Prize with Le Duc Tho in 1973—the Nixon presidency had to pay a steep price for its conduct of foreign policy.[458]

In contrast, Scowcroft never had to worry about his relationship with Gerald Ford, never lost sight of his goal of managing the NSC process as effectively as possible, and rarely ignored the lessons of history and the longer-term interests of the United States. And when he took over for Kissinger as national security advisor, he "surprised a lot of people" (as the editors of the *Chicago Tribune* later wrote) "by being very much his own man."[459]

=====

SCOWCROFT'S PERSONAL LIFE also changed over the course of the Nixon and Ford presidencies. Once he began working for Kissinger, he consistently put in extremely long hours, had very few off-days, even on weekends, and spent almost no time at home. Meanwhile, his daughter, with whom he talked every day—and he'd talk to her for hours on the telephone if there were things she wanted to discuss—finished high school in 1976, went off to college, and then law school.

More troublingly, Jackie, whose life revolved around Brent and Karen, had put on weight in the 1960s, following years of struggling with diets; although petite, she weighed over 200 pounds. She developed symptoms of type 2 diabetes in the 1960s, and her condition got worse in the 1970s. Very sweet but also somewhat shy, Jackie grew more and more self-conscious and agoraphobic. Although she had occasionally accompanied her husband to state dinners and other White House functions when he first began working in the White House, after the early 1970s Jackie didn't even venture outdoors unless she had to. And when Scowcroft came home after the 1972 trip to Moscow, he found that she "had nailed the doors and windows shut." President Nixon expressed concern for how many hours "the General" was working, and remarked to others in the White House that Scowcroft's wife was an invalid (a fact that Brent would never volunteer).[460]

Brent consequently had to take care of his wife every day of the week, except on the days he was traveling (in which case their housekeeper took over). He prepared all her meals, ran errands, did the chores, and helped her move around the house (which included lifting her). As her condition worsened over time, this meant doing her kidney dialysis at home twice each day, including before he went into work in the morning—a difficult task, but easier than getting her into a car and taking her to a dialysis treatment center.

Scowcroft breathed none of this to his White House colleagues or his friends. And no one, not even his closest associates—including Robert Gates, his deputy under George H. W. Bush and one of his closest friends— went inside his house, even when they had to speak with him in times of emergency or international crisis. The extreme compartmentalization of Scowcroft's life was yet another reflection of his intense self-discipline and dedication to duty—but one that suggests the enormous personal price he had to pay.

13

THE FIXER

THE MISTAKES AND missteps of the Ford administration drew brickbats from the Democratic Congress, White House correspondents, newspaper columnists and magazine commentators, and Republicans on the far right. In contrast, Scowcroft's quiet effectiveness as national security advisor received scarcely any attention.

Scowcroft played a critical role, in typically unpublicized fashion, in rescuing the British pound in the fall of 1976. It is no exaggeration to characterize Britain in the mid-1970s as a battlefield of class warfare being waged between the trade unions, which were seeking higher wages, and the leading businesses, which were resisting any concessions at a time when the British industrial economy was struggling. In response to the big budget deficits and large trade deficits Britain had run in 1974 and 1975 under the governments of Harold Wilson and James Callaghan, in 1976 the Treasury and the Bank of England made the decision to use a secret policy of controlled devaluation, embarking on limited periodic sales of the pound in the international markets, together with more public measures, such as restricting wage increases and reducing government expenditures to bring down the inflation rate.

The gambit succeeded at decreasing inflation, which fell from a 25 percent annual rate in mid-1975 to an 11.5 percent annual rate in June 1976. The expectation was that Britain would be able to regain the competitiveness for its exports which it had lost through rapid inflation without the use of the chosen alternative strategy: import controls. So far, so good—but in late 1976, things got worse. Trade Union Council (TUC) officials were upset about the new wage restrictions and cuts in public spending. They met with the Labour prime minister, Callaghan, to request that he reconsider government policies and switch to import controls as a means to boost the economy. Their demands carried weight, since the TUC had helped put Callaghan's government into office. A further run on the pound in the last quarter of 1976 increased the pressure on Callaghan to act—but he didn't want to yield to the TUC.[461]

Callaghan therefore began to talk with other heads of government about the prospect of putting together an IMF loan in the event that the falling pound sterling reduced British financial reserves to unstable levels. Any such loan would require International Monetary Fund approval, however, and since the United States played a dominant role in the IMF, Callaghan first had to secure the cooperation of the Ford administration.

Things got worse when news of the proposed rescue was leaked, possibly by union officials or their allies in the Labour government.[462] There were rumors of indiscreet hints by Callaghan's ministers, and the London managers of the volatile oil funds, who kept their balances in sterling, began to move them out, led by the Nigerians. The pound proceeded to plummet through the $2.00 level. But when the Bank of England continued to sell sterling, it was into a market that was already shedding the pound. With the run on the sterling and untenable budget deficits, Callaghan had no choice but to approach the United States.[463]

President Ford was strongly committed to helping Callaghan; in fact, Callaghan was his "biggest buddy" among all foreign leaders, as Robert Hormats, an economic adviser to Kissinger, later noted in an interview. But opinion in Washington was by no means unanimous. Many US officials, economists, and financial experts were highly critical of British policies and wanted to see the Labour government make much larger cuts in public spending and impose greater restrictions on wage increases before qualifying Britain for a loan. Treasury Secretary William Simon, Under Secretary Edwin Yeo, Federal Reserve chairman Arthur Burns, and Chairman Alan Greenspan of the Council of Economic Advisers were mostly unsympathetic to Britain's predicament. Furthermore, the financial markets had to perceive the British government's actions as both substantive and convincing if the rescue package was going to work. President Ford "knew that the British had to help themselves," and he said as much.[464]

A good solution had to be both economically plausible and politically viable, since a collapse of the Labour government would only trigger a further crisis of confidence.[465] So the question then turned on the conditions that the IMF would impose before approving a loan. How severely would the Labour government have to change its domestic programs?

This is where Scowcroft came in. The United States would have to coordinate any funding program with the other principal IMF member states. If the United States and the IMF pushed too hard, the Callaghan government would be in trouble and there could be "a very severe negative reaction," according to Hormats. But if Britain didn't respond to its plummeting currency and domestic situation, it could suffer an even bigger crisis.

So the United States and Britain began to engage in delicate international negotiations, along with the other leading IMF countries, Germany and France in particular. And with Kissinger at State and Simon over at Treasury at loggerheads, Scowcroft effectively took over.[466] Scowcroft was no banker, economist, or international finance specialist, but he was competent in economics and understood the ramifications of the falling pound. More important, he was able to collaborate with other members of the Ford administration and with the foreign ministers and other representatives of foreign nations. He also had help from his staff, especially Hormats, who was temporarily in the NSC, seconded from the Treasury Department, and who would later become a vice chairman at Goldman Sachs.

Scowcroft was committed to helping Britain. He regarded Britain as a bulwark of democracy at a time when communists and socialists were threatening to take power elsewhere in Europe, and as a stalwart ally of the United States with respect to NATO and the defense of Europe. As AFL-CIO president George Meany wrote President Ford in late September, "The collapse of the exchange value of the pound underscores and reflects the continuing economic and financial crisis faced by America's oldest and most steadfast friend in the world, Great Britain, and her people." For Meany, just as for Scowcroft, the United States' and Britain's fate were "irrevocably linked," and that the United States had to place its "'full faith and credit' behind the British people."[467]

So Scowcroft was greatly concerned about the larger geostrategic implications of a destabilized, crisis-stricken Britain and was worried that the whole situation could "come apart in quite a serious way." He said he spent more time on the sterling crisis "during those weeks than anything else. It was considered by us to be the greatest single threat to the Western world."[468] It is likely that for all these reasons he helped persuade President Ford early in the crisis to agree to help the Callaghan government.

However, Scowcroft had to proceed in such a way in order to prevent news leaks from those opposed to the president's efforts to help Britain. If the media and the financial markets discovered that the United States and the IMF were intervening to support the British pound, there would be even more currency speculation and the British pound's slide would accelerate. Scowcroft thus had to act very discreetly.[469]

Scowcroft set up an interagency process for handling the crisis, one that allowed Treasury officials to communicate their positions to the White House and coordinated US policy across the government. At the same time, Scowcroft and his staff had to convince Simon to remain quiet, prevent negative leaks, and, ultimately, agree to a favorable vote in the IMF. So, for instance, in late February 1976, when Alan Greenspan sought to comment publicly on British economic policy, Scowcroft advised him to couch his comments in a "positive framework" and suggested that he "avoid criticism of the British Government's past or present economic policies . . . Any such criticisms would most certainly be misunderstood and would have an adverse impact on US-British relations."[470]

Scowcroft also had to handle the delicate relationship with the British, and he was able to get the Treasury officials to listen to the British—and vice versa. Chancellor of the Exchequer Denis Healey visited the United States several times to plead his country's case and to clarify what his government could and could not do. Harold Lever, whose formal title was chancellor of the Duchy of Lancaster but who was essentially a minister without portfolio, also came to the United States. His visits were helpful, since Simon, Yeo, and others in the Treasury Department considered Healey a left-leaning big spender but regarded Lever, a former businessman, as more fiscally responsible.[471]

Throughout the process, Scowcroft, with the help of Hormats and Greenspan, proceeded quickly and quietly. Within a week he was able to orchestrate a favorable IMF vote for a $4 billion loan to the British government (more than $16 billion in 2012 dollars) and get the Callaghan government to agree to further fiscal restrictions as a condition, including cutting public spending drastically, being willing to transfer funds to investment, and accepting higher levels of unemployment. The British had to draft a seven-page "letter of intent" to be included as part of the paperwork for the IMF loan—the first time such a document had been required of an advanced industrialized nation. The "humiliating" letter (as one observer characterized it) expressed the Labour government's intention to pursue stable economic policies, such as spending less on roads, ending wage increases, raising taxes on lower-income wage earners, and setting aside more money for industrial investment—all bitter pills for Callaghan's Labour government to swallow. Sweetening the deal for Britain was a separate agreement by the United States to extend a $4 billion line of credit that would shore up the pound for a few years, up until the North Sea oil began producing significant revenue (in 1980).

With the British and US governments on board with this complicated compromise, Scowcroft was able to get other key IMF members, especially Germany, to agree to the proposed settlement. As a result, the pound stabilized and slowly regained some of its lost ground, and the crisis abated. But as Robert Hormats, Bud McFarlane, and others acknowledged, it was "a close-run thing."[472]

After the fact, some critics claimed that Callaghan and Lever had played Ford and Scowcroft by hinting at so-called end-of-democracy scenarios—such as the United Kingdom having to cut back its NATO forces on the Rhine and, by implication, therefore no longer being able to serve as the United States' reliable, constant partner in the Cold War.[473] The Treasury's Edwin Yeo, a conservative Pittsburgh banker by way of background, said that the British ambassador to the United States, Sir Peter Ramsbotham, presented the British side "with consummate skill" and "used to have Scowcroft practically in tears," Kathleen Burk and Alec Cairncross report in their book *Goodbye, Great Britain*.[474]

This is surely possible, if likely overstated. The British may well have presented the Ford administration with some worst-case scenarios, and such scenarios would have doubtless seized the full attention of Scowcroft, Kissinger, and the president. But the fact is that the financial situation in Britain was very real and very grave. Without the intervention of the United States and the IMF, there's no telling where it might have led.

"When the pound collapsed in the summer of 1976 and Callahan was forced to turn to the IMF for help, grimly swallowing £3bn in spending cuts in the next few years, he showed guts and leadership," the British historian Dominic Sandbrook writes. "It was one of the great unsung turning points of modern British history: the point at which the people at the top realized that only the strongest medicine would cure the nation's ills." For the British to have to go hat in hand to the United States and the IMF for a loan to shore up the pound was a huge loss in prestige for a country that had long been the world's supreme financial power. The collapse of the British pound and "the IMF crisis of 1976 was a turning point in another sense, too," Sandbrook observes. "It was the moment when the parochial, introspective assumptions of British politics were shattered for good." Britain could no longer remain an "economic island," and "Callaghan and Healey realised . . . that Britain was now inextricably locked into a vast global system."[475]

Although the crisis of the British pound may appear as a minor episode in the history of US foreign relations, it was no small thing for Britain, for the Ford administration, and, potentially, for European politics and economics during the Cold War. And Scowcroft was in the midst of it all. He served as a diplomat in managing US relations with Britain and other key IMF member states, as a geostrategist who had to consider the political and military repercussions of a failed Britain on Europe and on East-West relations, and as a banker concerned about the safety and security of taxpayers' and investors' funds. He was able to pull all the pieces together, get a divided Ford administration to agree on a single plan of action, win the cooperation of the United States' European allies and fellow IMF members, and broker an agreement that the Labour government, the US Treasury, and the IMF could all accept. All of this, too, without the media being alerted—suggestive of the trust that all the participants had in him and the process he put in place to handle the crisis.

———

MAKING THE INTERNATIONAL cooperation on the rescue of the British pound possible was the increased communication and diplomacy among the leading world economies, induced by the economic summits that began during the Ford presidency. While Scowcroft did not play a direct role in these summits, the NSC produced the advance briefing books for President Ford and had to help create a unified American policy on issues of East-West trade and investment, international finance, and other topics for the president to advocate and defend. Scowcroft attended the conferences along with a handful of other advisers and kept watch on developments.

It was French president Valéry Giscard d'Estaing who first proposed, in 1975, that the United States, Britain, Germany, and Japan meet to discuss global economic issues. Ford then asked that this Group of Five be increased to a Group of Six—the G-6—with the inclusion of Italy. The meeting was held at Rambouillet, an old castle thirty-five miles from Paris, the French equivalent of the country estate, Chequers, for the British prime minister. The results of the Rambouillet summit included a "controlled float" for international currency values (a compromise between the position advocated by the United States and that taken by France) and a deal limiting the use of trade quotas by the G-6 and other advanced industrial countries to protect their respective home industries.

In mid-April 1976, Ford approached German chancellor Helmut Schmidt about convening a follow-up economic summit to be held in San Juan, Puerto Rico.[476] Schmidt and then Giscard agreed, and Ford insisted that Canada be allowed to join, thereby creating the G-7. The heads of these seven economic powers duly met in Puerto Rico on June 27 and 28, when they discussed synchronizing their economies to mitigate the risk of inflation, talked about the energy crisis, and proposed areas where they could accept more free trade.[477]

We now take economic summits among the leaders of the world's largest economies for granted, but the Rambouillet and San Juan meetings were themselves extraordinary events, despite their paucity of concrete results. They brought together social democrats and conservatives alike. They got those who were opposed to the United States in Vietnam and uncertain about NATO policies (if not NATO itself) to talk to the American president and his advisers and to other leaders closely allied with the United States. And they enabled the several heads of government, many of them barely acquainted or even complete strangers, to get to know one another. What's more, the economic summits took place immediately following the oil shocks, a time when the Western leaders did "not fully understand the nature of the new types of problems they confront[ed]," as Hormats wrote to Kissinger. In addition, as Secretary Simon commented after the Puerto Rican summit, the informality of the meeting encouraged frank and honest dialogue. As significantly for the Ford administration, the president "was impressive and clearly gave others confidence in him as a leader of the Western World."[478]

The objective of the economic summits was to "achieve a better understanding" of common problems and to lead to "an improvement in public confidence"—and they largely succeeded on both fronts.[479] President Jimmy Carter continued the practice, participating in dozens of additional economic summits with the leaders of the other major advanced industrialized countries. Dozens more have been held over the decades since.

===

SCOWCROFT WAS MORE consistently and directly involved with respect to the Angola crisis. Once the crown jewel of Portugal's African possessions (in the words of President Ford), Angola won its independence in 1975.[480] Rich in oil reserves and mineral deposits, Angola had a transitional tripartite coalition government composed of the Popular Movement for the Liberation of Angola (MPLA), supported by the Soviet Union; the National Front for the Liberation of Angola (FNLA), supported by China and Zaire (and whose leader was on CIA retainer as an informant); and the National Union for the Total Independence of Angola (UNITA), supported by the United States. In January 1975, the 40 Committee and the Ford administration approved a grant of $300,000 for the FNLA. The FNLA quickly attacked the MPLA, and the Cubans and Soviets responded with arms and soldiers in support of the MPLA.[481] Angola was embroiled in a civil war.

President Ford, Kissinger, Scowcroft, and other advisers believed that the United States had no choice but to act, in light of the fact that the

Soviet Union was providing equipment and Cuba was sending fifteen thousand troops. Meanwhile, South Africa was assisting the FNLA and UNITA. Neither Ford nor Kissinger nor Scowcroft wanted another country to fall to communism on their watch. Angola thus became the site of a proxy war between the superpowers, with Ford and his foreign policy team again eager to demonstrate the ability of the United States to influence international developments.

In July, the administration approved $14 million in additional support for the FNLA and UNITA, to be supplemented by another $10.7 million in early September. Scowcroft followed this up with a request for a further $7 million, which Ford approved in November 1975. But the MPLA seized control of the capital city, Luanda, on November 11 and declared Angola independent.[482] That same day, Kissinger called for "a 40 Committee meeting on Angola to assess the situation." Scowcroft pointed out that the Soviets were sending in MiGs. But Kissinger optimistically told the president, "With a few arms and mercenaries, either side could win. We have done well with the weapons we sent. But it may turn with the new Soviet weapons going in."[483]

As national security advisor, Scowcroft was in charge of covert operations such as the Angola mission. Two weeks later, he unveiled four options the administration could take on Angola and scheduled a 40 Committee meeting on how they should proceed.[484] Scowcroft and the administration decided to inject another $25 million (on top of the $32 million they'd already spent) in support of the FNLA and UNITA.

All that spending couldn't remain secret—the CIA was running ads for mercenaries in *Soldier of Fortune* magazine, for instance—and the US Congress, extremely wary of CIA covert operations at this point, assigned oversight of the CIA to six different committees (later increased to eight). On December 20, 1975, it cracked down further, passing the Tunney Amendment, which cut off any additional covert aid to Angola.

Scowcroft thought Congress had behaved inexcusably. He charged that Congress, through its "explicit refusal to provide any assistance whatever to the 'pro-Western' forces" in Angola, had "clearly demonstrated [the United States'] general lack of interest in the political evolution of Africa. It is hardly surprising that this attitude was interpreted, rightly or wrongly, by the Soviet Union and its Cuban proxy as granting them virtually a free hand to serve as the sanctifiers of boundaries and of governments, at least in Africa."[485] And Scowcroft told representatives of the South African military that Congress was being "insane" on the issue of US military aid to southern Africa. "Even a loan is a problem," he complained.[486]

Ford agreed, saying in a newspaper interview that "Congress has done some things that interfered with the day-to-day execution of foreign policy. . . . In the case of Angola, I personally believe that if we had been able to put in the extra funds—no US military personnel—that UNITA and the FNLA would have been able to force a political settlement instead of having the MPLA take over and control Angola." The president continued, "Until Congress said 'No' the military situation was very fluid in Angola, but the minute Congress said 'No,' the Cuban intervention was doubled or tripled." And when "we couldn't provide our allies with what they needed," Ford said in another interview, "then the Soviet Union and Cuba won. It is just that simple."[487]

What also bothered Ford and his advisers during the prolonged Angolan crisis was the near-silence of conservatives in the House and Senate—those same members of Congress who vigorously denounced any sign that the administration was relenting in its waging of the Cold War. The presidential historian John Robert Greene has suggested that the passage of the Tunney Amendment may even have been the proximate cause for President Ford to issue his February 1976 executive order to overhaul the structure of the US intelligence community.[488]

On December 13, 1975, following Congress's ban on further assistance for Angola, Scowcroft called upon the secretary of state, the secretary of defense, the chairman of the Joint Chiefs of Staff, and the DCI to establish an ad hoc committee to review the situation in Angola and to present the president with options—due in three weeks' time. The administration's concern, according to Secretary of Defense Rumsfeld, was "to the extent that the Soviet Union improves its basing and airfields throughout the continent of Africa it [would be] able to project power to a considerably greater extent in that part of the world than previously."[489]

But Ford and Scowcroft refused to do in Angola what Kissinger wanted the president to do, what Nixon had done, and what Reagan and director of central intelligence William J. Casey would later do: to maneuver around Congress and find another way to secure US objectives. Instead, they allowed the MPLA to dominate in the Angolan civil war, and the Soviets and Cubans effectively prevailed. But as many Cold War hawks consequently asked themselves, what, then, was the use of détente?[490]

Scowcroft remained concerned about southern Africa, given the changes following the independence of Angola and Mozambique and the challenges possibly waiting in Rhodesia and Namibia. In April 1976 he therefore directed the State and Defense Departments and the DCI to review US policy in sub-Saharan Africa.[491]

In the years to come, resistance to the MPLA government in Angola would smolder, and the Reagan administration renewed US covert actions in support of UNITA and its leader, Jonas Savimbi, providing $15 million worth of antiaircraft and antitank missiles in 1986 and transferring another $15 million worth of Stingers and other weapons in 1987.[492]

Angola was just one of the foreign policy problems that Scowcroft was unable to fix. Another was a shift in the climate of American national politics toward a more morally driven and idealistic US foreign policy. Scowcroft joined Kissinger and Nelson Rockefeller in being outraged at Ronald Reagan's insistence on including a "morality in foreign policy" plank in the Republican Party's 1976 platform. The plank called for a foreign policy "in which secret agreements, hidden from our people, will have no part"; it praised Aleksandr Solzhenitsyn for his "human courage and bravery"; and it described the Helsinki agreement as "taking from those who do not have freedom the hope of one day getting it."

Scowcroft therefore wanted Ford to fight the Reagan plank, but Cheney, Ron Nessen, and campaign aide Stuart Spencer ultimately persuaded Ford that to do so would be to fall into a trap. The Reagan supporters wanted Ford to challenge them on this issue, they argued, and hoped to be able to bring it to a vote—one that Ford might then lose. So the president swallowed his pride and went along with the plank.[493]

Also beyond Scowcroft's control was the legacy of détente and its impact on the image of the United States. Scowcroft was convinced that for the United States to be able to play an effective role in the world, the "key element, again, is a perception of American strength and steadfastness," he wrote in the *Naval War College Review*. "On this point there is concern—beginning with Vietnam, the refusal to act in Angola, and on through the cumulative effects of a number of recent events. Confidence is a very fragile commodity in international politics," and "once erosion sets in, it is inordinately difficult to reverse."[494] He believed that among American and international audiences—especially the Soviets—the United States was no longer perceived as strong.

Scowcroft spoke of the "impressive growth of Soviet military power." And Scowcroft could

not recall a historical period when an unfavorable balance of power was not sooner or later translated into political advantage. . . . Equally important from a political standpoint is the impression of Soviet superiority. Should such an impression, accurately or inaccurately, gain currency, it can have a profound effect on the behavior not only of the Soviet Union but or our allies, the Third World, and even ourselves—an effect greatly to the detriment of the West. Such a perception could alter world political alignments, increase Soviet propensity toward adventurism and risk-taking, and add greatly to our burden of exerting effective leadership. *Our first and essential priority, then, must be to do whatever is necessary to prevent the reality, and the perception, of Soviet superiority.*

In 1978, Scowcroft would further note that, given that "the United States and the Soviet Union hold fundamentally antithetical views of world order, the organization of society, and man's place in it . . . [w]e must therefore gear ourselves to a long-term, steady, unremitting opposition to Soviet aggrandizement."[495]

In making these observations, Scowcroft was not so far away from Reagan's wisecrack that détente was what a farmer had with his turkey before Thanksgiving, or from the comment by British prime minister Margaret Thatcher after the Soviet invasion of Afghanistan that she had "long understood that *détente* had been ruthlessly used by the Soviets to exploit western weakness and disarray."[496] And in half a dozen years, the new Reagan administration would ask Scowcroft for his advice on how to base the MX missile and what kind of nuclear force structure the United States should have, on how to reform the NSC process in the aftermath of the Iran-Contra scandal, and on other issues—signs that Scowcroft's worldview and that of the Reagan administration were largely compatible.

Until then, Scowcroft had to find a new role for himself. Not only had he lost his job when Gerald Ford lost his 1976 bid to be elected US president in his own right, he was out of a career since he had retired from the Air Force upon accepting his appointment as national security advisor.

Ford's defeat may not have been surprising in view of the enormous difficulties Ford and his presidency had had to overcome. But he and his team were convinced they could have beaten Jimmy Carter.

— PART III —

The Carter and Reagan Years, 1977–1989

═══════

There is an almost eerie parallel between the situation today and that of the 1930s. Then there also were antiwar movements, movies designed to demonstrate the horrors of war, the Oxford movement in Britain and so on. The result was to encourage the major power in Europe—Hitler's Germany—to feel that it could embark upon aggression with impunity. In the end, of course, we had a world war.

—BRENT SCOWCROFT IN
U.S. NEWS & WORLD REPORT, DECEMBER 5, 1983

14

OUT ON THE STREET

SCOWCROFT CERTAINLY DIDN'T think Gerald Ford should have lost the 1976 election.[1] Ford was smarter and savvier than most politicians, journalists, and members of the public gave him credit for. Not only did he have a Yale law degree, but he was an expert on the federal budget, had considerable people skills, and understood national politics.

Former US trade representative Carla Hills, who would go on to work with presidents Ford, Reagan, and George H. W. Bush and advise George W. Bush, would recall that she found the Ford White House to be the most transparent she'd worked with and Ford himself to be uniquely decisive. "No other President I know has been [as] involved as Ford in calling the shots," she said. And no other president she knew of had such an "encyclopedic knowledge of our government and where the money is spent."[2]

Besides being very smart and decisive, Ford was energetic and positive. In less than two and a half years in office, he had more meetings with foreign heads of state (124) than any other US president, and in that brief period he was able to establish close personal relationships with British prime minister James Callaghan, French president Valéry Giscard d'Estaing, and German chancellor Helmut Schmidt, among others.

All in all, Ford turned out to be a good president—and arguably a very good president. Ford, Hills noted, "cared so much about the country and got so little credit."[3]

Scowcroft did what he could behind the scenes during the 1976 presidential campaign to see that Ford got elected in his own right. He helped draft position papers, write speeches, and prepare Ford for the election debates with Jimmy Carter.[4] But he was frustrated by the fact that Ford distanced himself from his own foreign policy. Under pressure from the right, Ford—or his leading political advisers—didn't feel he could run on his foreign policy record or that of Henry Kissinger, whom conservative Republicans were portraying as "cozying up" to the Soviet Union. So the president broke off further arms control talks with the Soviets and tried to distance himself from his famous secretary of state.[5]

Scowcroft wasn't entirely unsympathetic to some of this criticism. He disagreed with Kissinger's approach to détente as being an end in itself. Scowcroft feared the Soviet Union was "pulling the wool" over American policy makers' eyes, and he worried that Soviet leaders believed the United States' resolve was weakening.[6]

Thus, Scowcroft was somewhat ambivalent about the direction of US foreign policy in the mid-1970s. While he clearly supported the Ford presidency, he disagreed with how President Ford had backed away from his earlier support of SALT II, and he "deplored the killing of arms control." He wanted to see actual results from the US-Soviet détente, such as major agreements on nuclear and conventional weapons, not just rhetoric and symbolism. And he felt that by turning away from Nixon's and Kissinger's foreign policy during the campaign, Ford had put himself in a "very difficult position" in the Republican primary campaign against California Governor Ronald Reagan.[7]

Scowcroft played a crucial role in two significant events that occurred during the 1976 presidential campaign, one obscure and the other well known. The former was the "Korean tree crisis" (also known as the "Korean axe murder incident" or the "Panmunjom incident"), sparked by the killing of two US officers by North Korean soldiers in the demilitarized zone; the latter was Gerald Ford's infamous statement of October 6, made during his debate with Jimmy Carter, that the Soviet Union didn't dominate Eastern Europe.

The incident in the DMZ happened first. On the morning of August 18, North Korean officers and soldiers demanded that American and South Korean soldiers stop pruning a hundred-foot-tall poplar standing in the joint security area of the Korean demilitarized zone in the village of Panmunjom. The crew was accustomed to such harassments and to North Korean threats, and they continued their work. They had almost completed the pruning when Lt. Pak Chul of North Korea, the head of the North Korean troops in the joint security area, physically threatened the American-led crew if it didn't cease its work immediately. As the crew began to withdraw, Pak shouted out, "Kill" (or "Kill them all," depending on the translation), and the North Korean soldiers, who vastly outnumbered the American and South Korean work crew, began hitting them with axe handles as well as their hands and feet, using martial arts. Pak himself used an axe handle to bludgeon Capt. Arthur G. Bonifas to death, and other North Korean soldiers dragged 1st Lt. Mark T. Barrett a short distance away and took turns beating him to death.[8]

Although there had been constant friction and a steady stream of incidents along the DMZ, the murder of the two US military officers was unprecedented. It is possible that North Korean president Kim Il Sung wanted to provoke US and South Korean forces into a bloody reprisal, since any significant retaliation could have legitimated an invasion of South Korea. The North Korean army was more than double the size of the UN forces under US command in South Korea.

The Ford administration found itself in a tight spot. In the wake of the Vietnam War, the United States' support of the Indonesian government's invasion and annexation of East Timor, the US-supported coup against Chilean president Salvador Allende, and its support of Israel against the Palestinians, the United States had a poor reputation among nonaligned states. Several Third World countries expressed their approval of a proposed UN resolution that called for the United States to actually pull out of South Korea—a policy that was anathema to Scowcroft and others in the Ford administration. As Scowcroft explained in his 1979 article for the *Naval War College Review*, "We are here not simply dealing with the confrontation between two small powers on a remote peninsula. Korea is the point at which the interests of all the great powers in the Pacific area converge. . . . Any suggestion of US withdrawal or lessening interest is fraught with the profoundest implications, particularly if done at a time of the questioning at home of the moral validity of our commitment to South Korea's defense."[9] The secretive and mysterious nature of the North Korean regime complicated matters further. No one really knew what the North Korean leaders had in mind or how they would likely respond to any American actions.

When the news of the killings—and the US Army film footage of them—reached Washington later on August 18, military leaders and civilian officials within the administration were outraged. Scowcroft, who was then with Ford at the Republican National Convention in Kansas City, immediately set up a Washington Special Actions Group meeting for that afternoon (with William Hyland attending in his place). Although Ford was "extremely upset" at the killings, he pointed out that time wasn't of the essence in deciding how the United States should react, since there was no pending action the United States had to take by a specific date.[10]

In the WSAG meeting, Kissinger and State Department officials, officers from the Joint Chiefs of Staff, and officials with the International Security Affairs Directorate in the Defense Department explored a wide range of possible responses to the killings. One option was for the United States to retaliate militarily, whether by mining harbors, sinking a North Korean ship, or bombing North Korea. At the other extreme, the United States could choose not to respond and avoid any risk of escalating tensions in the DMZ. Or it could deploy additional equipment (such as an aircraft carrier) to the area or elevate the readiness level of the UN forces under US command in South Korea, with the goal of deterring the North from any further rash action and providing the president with additional military options should he later decide to respond with force.[11]

The WSAG participants recommended that the United States inform the UN Security Council and UN delegates of the North Korean attack and take a number of military steps, including increasing the alert status of US forces in the area, beefing up the number of American planes in South Korea with a squadron of F-4 fighters, another of F-111 fighter-bombers, and a number of B-52s sent from Guam, and having the aircraft carrier *Midway* (which was then in a Japanese port) sail to the area. As soon as the meeting ended, Kissinger called Ford and Scowcroft to fill them in, and Scowcroft agreed that the president should approve the WSAG's recommendations. Shortly thereafter, the State Department formed a Korean working group to address the crisis, including State Department officials and representatives from the NSC, the Joint Chiefs, the Office of the Secretary of Defense, and the CIA.

However, the next step taken by the United States was not proposed by any member of the WSAG's Korean working group. It came from Army Gen. Richard G. Stilwell, the head of the UN command in South Korea and commander of the US forces in Korea. Stilwell simply proposed that the UN command should reassert its rights in the DMZ by cutting down the poplar, since the tree obstructed sightlines in the sensitive area (which was why the work crew had been cutting it back), and by dismantling two illegal road gates that the North Koreans had erected in Panmunjom.

The WSAG met early on the morning of Thursday, August 19, and endorsed Stilwell's plan, named Operation Paul Bunyan. Kissinger then flew out to Kansas City to brief Ford and Scowcroft on the WSAG's recommendations. Kissinger spoke of his reservations about Stilwell's proposed action. The secretary of state wanted a stronger show of force, and he discounted the possibility that either North Korea or China would respond with military force.

Scowcroft disagreed. He believed there was a non-negligible risk of an armed response by North Korea, and he worried that an escalation of fighting in the DMZ would put the United States and South Korea at a severe disadvantage given the much larger North Korean military forces. Arguing that the United States' response should be commensurate with the original attack, he recommended that Ford endorse Operation Paul Bunyan.

After spending three-quarters of an hour reviewing the possible options with Kissinger and Scowcroft, the president decided on Stilwell's plan—with a few qualifications. He wanted additional US forces to be mobilized; he wanted the tree-cutting operation to be accompanied by extensive US air cover and US fleet maneuvers; and he wanted it executed without advance notice, to surprise the North Koreans and the rest of the world.

At 7:00 A.M. Korean time on Saturday, August 21—half an hour before the North Koreans were scheduled to man their guard stations—UN forces under US command moved into the DMZ and began cutting down the poplar with chainsaws and other equipment. The UN engineers quickly reduced the tree to a tall stump and removed the two illegal road barriers. With helicopters overhead, F-4s and F-111s flying over at a little distance from the joint security area, and B-52s flying toward North Korean airspace and then pulling off at the last minute, the North Koreans didn't interfere.

Less than an hour later, President Kim Il Sung issued a statement: "It is regretful that such an incident occurred in the joint security area." The North Korean leader hoped that "such incidents may not recur in the future" and urged that "both sides should make efforts." Interestingly, the message not only implicitly accepted at least partial North Korean responsibility for the situation—in stark contrast to the North Koreans' usual intransigence—but also expressed Kim's desire to put the crisis in the past and for both sides to proceed on a new basis.

This was not much of a concession, to be sure. Neither Kim Il Sung nor North Korean military leaders accepted responsibility for the murders or promised to punish those at fault, and General Stilwell and the State Department both initially rejected the North Korean statement. But the US officials in the interagency Korean working group were "amazed at the message," given the previous tenor of North Korean communication. So upon further deliberation, the State Department and the White House decided to accept the statement. It was "more than we expected," Kissinger said. In any event, it was enough to defuse the crisis. Kissinger released a statement indicating that the North Korean message represented "a positive step" and proposing that the military armistice commission convene so as to secure the safety of personnel in the demilitarized zone. President Ford was pleased by the strong signal the United States had sent to North Korea, the Soviet Union, and China by virtue of the quick, forceful response.[12]

Over the three days of the crisis, Scowcroft had had to devote most of his time to overseeing the US response as well as briefing and advising a very busy and preoccupied President Ford. Most important, he had persuaded Ford—and, implicitly, Kissinger—*not* to take more drastic action. He had also helped persuade Kissinger to accept the North Korean president's message as constituting a constructive step toward the stabilization of the DMZ.

Once the crisis blew over, the North Koreans and South Koreans agreed to jointly survey a new military demarcation line through the joint security area and to restrict all guard posts and military personnel to their respective sides. The overwhelming reaction in Washington, among foreign ministries, and in the American and foreign press was approval of both the content and the manner of the United States' response. And the nonaligned states quietly dropped any consideration of the proposed UN resolution calling for the United States' military withdrawal from the Korean peninsula.

Throughout the crisis, Scowcroft had exerted a stabilizing, tempering influence. In a situation in which the United States knew almost nothing about what motivated the North Korean leadership and how they would respond "to any kind of stimulus, either positive or negative," he had advised Ford "that more important than being tough is appearing steady [and] mature." In contrast to Kissinger, James Schlesinger (who had started working for Jimmy Carter), and others who advocated bombing North Korea, Scowcroft cautioned the president that the United States was "able to resolve a crisis in other ways" (as Robert McFarlane reported).[13] Events proved him right.

However, the quick defusing of the Korean tree crisis couldn't save the Ford presidency. By many accounts, a misstatement by the president in his second debate against Jimmy Carter played a central role in Ford's electoral defeat.

Ford was the first White House incumbent to debate a presidential challenger (there having been no incumbent in the Kennedy-Nixon debate, of course). In preparation, he trained hard, held mock debates with members of his staff, and rehearsed answers to the questions his staff expected. One such question was about the Soviet domination of Eastern Europe. The contents of Ford's debate briefing book show that the president was to deny that he or his administration accepted any such domination and to say that he "was totally opposed to so-called spheres of influence—or 'domination' of Eastern Europe—by any power."[14]

So when the *New York Times'* Max Frankel asked if the Soviets were getting "the better of us"—as they were bragging, presumably because of the Helsinki accords and other supposed gains—Ford was primed for an answer. But he was also, because of how the debate was evolving, on the defensive. And that was when the president got into trouble: "There is no Soviet domination of Eastern Europe and there never will be under a Ford administration," the president said. Neither the Yugoslavians nor the Romanians nor the Poles, he continued, "consider themselves dominated by the Soviet Union." On the contrary, "each of those countries is independent, autonomous. It has its own territorial integrity and the United States does not concede that those countries are under the domination of the Soviet Union."[15]

As soon Ford said these words—indefensible and absurd at face value—William Hyland let out a moan. Scowcroft, who was in a room near the stage in San Francisco, went white and told Stu Spencer, who was assisting the campaign, "You've got a problem." He then put his head in his hands.[16]

An hour after the debate, Scowcroft, Cheney, Michael Raoul-Duval, and Stu Spencer held a press conference to explain—or explain away—the president's comment. Scowcroft led off: "I think what the President was trying to say is that we do not recognize Soviet dominance of Europe and that he took his trip to Eastern Europe . . . to demonstrate, to symbolize their independence, and their freedom of maneuver." Scowcroft admitted that Ford made a "bad mistake" and emphasized that Ford didn't "concede the domination of Eastern Europe." But the clarification did little good. The press "damn near laughed us out of the room," campaign director James A. Baker III said, and he added that this had been an occasion "I will never forget as long as I live." (By contrast, Kissinger called Ford immediately after the debate and told him he had done a superb job; he didn't mention Poland or Eastern Europe.)[17]

Ford may have meant to use the word "dominion" instead, since to say "There is no Soviet *dominion* of Eastern Europe" makes more sense. Or he may have meant to say that the United States *did not accept* the Soviet domination of Eastern Europe (which was what Scowcroft repeatedly told the press).[18] In any case, if Ford had quickly conceded his misstatement, there almost certainly wouldn't have been much of a problem. Instead, he doggedly maintained that everyone knew what he meant and there was no need for a retraction—Ford was a "stubborn cuss," one White House observer remarked—and he refused to give in to Scowcroft's, Cheney's, and Nessen's entreaties to issue a correction. The national security advisor even pleaded with Ford to retract, but Ford refused: "I said what I said. I know what I said. I said what I meant, and I'm not going to change it."[19]

The press had a field day, and Jimmy Carter began to exploit Ford's comment in his own public statements. The result was that a debate the experts had scored as a narrow victory for Carter and that the public had considered a narrow win for Ford was transformed into a sharp defeat—a fifty-six-point swing, according to the White House's own poll.[20] Not until four days after the debate did the president finally offer a public apology. By then the damage had been done.

Of course, one debate gaffe, however serious, didn't decide the 1976 election. Ford had an uphill battle due to a series of challenges, many of them related to foreign policy. For example, there was Senator Jesse Helms's proposed plank for the Republican platform that called for a "moral foreign policy," directly targeting Secretary Kissinger's realpolitik approach. Scowcroft had urged Ford to oppose the plank, but Ford didn't feel he could do that, so he essentially ignored the whole platform.[21] Ford's narrow victory over Ronald Reagan in the most hotly contested Republican primary campaign since William Howard Taft defeated Theodore Roosevelt in 1912 divided the country and caused notable defections among Ford's supposed allies.

Former president Nixon didn't help matters. Ford and Kissinger both thought that Nixon wanted a primary stalemate between Ford and Reagan in hopes that John Connally, a former cabinet member and governor of Texas, could get the nomination (Connally had been Nixon's first choice for vice president after Spiro Agnew's resignation).[22] Just three days before the New Hampshire primary, Nixon stole the headlines—and reminded voters of Ford's unpopular pardon—by taking a well-publicized trip to China, possibly in protest of Ford's slowing of the normalization of US-China relations, as journalists Nancy Gibbs and Michael Duffy suggest in their book *The Presidents Club*. The private diplomacy appeared to do nothing to help US-China relations and indicated Nixon's lack of respect for his successor, since he had said when he resigned that he would not go to China. Ford was livid; even Scowcroft said, "Nixon is a shit."[23]

As the primary battle between Ford and Reagan raged, Kissinger tried to broker a deal with Reagan to get Ford on the ticket—at the bottom of the ticket, moreover—but did so a little too eagerly for Ford's taste. (The president didn't dismiss the idea out of hand, but soon discarded it as unworkable.) The secretary of state also attempted to woo the Republican right and ingratiate himself with Reagan's foreign policy advisers, but with little success: the Rockefellers, the mainstream media, and the financial establishment—his patrons and political allies—were all the bogeymen of the far right.[24]

All these maneuverings left Ford largely isolated in his own party and prevented him from using his foreign policy record as an asset in the general election campaign. Scowcroft considered Ford's response to the right-wing challenge a mistake. He believed that successful negotiation of a SALT II deal might have turned the 1976 election in Ford's favor. Instead, pushed by his political advisers and by Don Rumsfeld in particular, Ford backed off from SALT II, deemphasized the strategic arms limitations talks in Vladivostok, omitted the significance of the Helsinki accords, and downplayed foreign policy in general. Meanwhile, Rumsfeld was portraying the Soviet Union as a "dark menace" in his briefings to Congress, which made US-Soviet relations appear even worse.

On November 1, 1976, with the election still in doubt, President Ford wrote a letter to Scowcroft. "Dear Brent," Ford wrote, "I want to say, before the voters return their verdict, how deeply I have appreciated your loyalty and long hours of work throughout my Administration and especially during the demanding period of recent weeks. I have been greatly supported and sustained by the superb performance of my staff, and while you may have missed the excitement of the cheers and the crowds, you have my lasting gratitude for your continuing dedication to duty and the best interests of our country."[25]

Ford's praise of Scowcroft—he sent similar letters to other members of the NSC staff—was well deserved. He had performed admirably as national security advisor in the face of the huge challenges that confronted the Ford administration in the tumultuous mid-1970s—the hostile political climate fostered by Watergate, the ignominious end to the Vietnam War, the unraveling of détente, and a host of other foreign and domestic troubles. Amid these difficulties, Scowcroft was "the near-perfect national security advisor," in the words of Bud McFarlane.[26]

But with Watergate, Vietnam, the end of détente, the intelligence scandal, and the oil crisis, commodity price increases, and resulting inflation of the early 1970s, the Ford White House faced voters who now doubted the legitimacy of their government. Americans distrusted Washington and were ready to turn to a credible outsider. So despite the best efforts of Scowcroft and the rest of Ford's advisers—and contrary to the expectations of most people in and around the Ford White House—Jimmy Carter won the 1976 election.[27]

———

AFTER THE ELECTION, worried about the ascent of the Republican right, Scowcroft wanted Ford to "stay in the limelight and lead the party. Otherwise Reagan will take it over." Ford didn't follow Scowcroft's advice, however, and the Republican Party was indeed inherited by Reagan. Scowcroft and Kissinger also worried about US foreign policy under Carter. (Immediately after the election, Kissinger told Ford and Scowcroft, "Carter I think could easily be a one-term President.")[28] Zbigniew Brzezinski, Scowcroft's old acquaintance, became Carter's national security advisor.

As for Scowcroft, he joined one of the nation's capital's distinct subpopulations: the hundreds of policy experts, former government officials, and retired military, intelligence, and Foreign Service officers waiting for an opportunity to serve in the US government. In the meantime, they held a variety of positions—working at a DC-area think tank, teaching in a college or university, or working in a law firm, in the media, in business, or in another occupation.

Scowcroft left the White House in a cheery mood, ready for new challenges and new opportunities.[29] Neither was he "dying to go back." He signed up with a speakers agency and proceeded to go on the lecture circuit around the country, giving paid talks. The Air Force gave him an office and a desk in the Pentagon, which he used. He also helped friends with their transitions to civilian life, and "had good connections" and lots of friends, as Bill Gulley recalls.[30]

Instead of feeling despondent, Scowcroft felt relieved to be out of office, as though a great weight had been lifted off his shoulders after the intense, difficult, and frustrating four years of the Nixon and Ford administrations. "It was fun," he said about being out of office. No longer did he have to worry about negotiations with the Soviet Union. No longer was he responsible for nuclear weapons and the alignment of strategic forces. No longer did he have to work at all hours and, during crises, for all intents and purposes live in the White House. After a professional life devoted to the US Air Force, two US presidents, and the US government, he now had to answer only to himself, his family, his close friends, and others with whom he chose to associate.[31]

Despite his anger over Nixon's unauthorized trip to China late in the 1976 campaign, Scowcroft kept in touch with the former president after the election:

> I got very close [to Nixon] after he resigned. He asked me to come out after Ford's defeat to help him write *RN*. I stayed out in San Clemente a couple of weeks. After that we commuted when he came to New York, and I would go up and have dinner occasionally. He would call all the time during the Ford administration from San Clemente. With USSR, he'd call and I'd relay the messages to Bush. I had a great regard for him. In intellectual

sagacity he was very good and unusually close. He had a close relationship with Henry Kissinger, but I wasn't a threat so he would confide more.[32]

Scowcroft helped to write the foreign policy component of *RN*, Nixon's memoirs, with much of the work being done over the telephone, Gulley reports—all gratis. Scowcroft also said that the two of them would "have long, rambling conversations at this time when [Nixon] was relaxed." But as Scowcroft read draft chapters of *RN*, he found some occasions to say, "Mr. President, it really didn't happen this way." Nixon would say, "I'll show you, because my diary has it in it." It turned out that the president had a "Walter Mitty diary," one that captured how Nixon would have liked the day to end, not how the day actually ended. Sometimes the president would correct his chapters when Scowcroft showed him the records; other times he didn't.[33]

Although the two stayed in touch over the next decade and a half, it was never an especially close friendship—probably because Nixon was incapable of one. The transcripts of their telephone conversations show that the former president invariably maintained a certain distance from his former military assistant and often spoke to Scowcroft in a high-handed manner. Taken at face value, their conversations suggest that Nixon took Scowcroft for granted, apparently assuming that his former aide—despite being a retired three-star general with a doctorate in international relations—remained his loyal subordinate. Scowcroft, when asked, explained that Nixon's behavior was "somewhat his way," adding that Nixon's manner was "also a defense mechanism" since he was "so insecure." Even so, Nixon's friendship with Scowcroft may have been as close as the former president could get to anyone beyond his own family.[34]

Much of Scowcroft's energy during the next several years was focused on his new consulting business. He and five partners—four of them former White House officials, and three of them also former military officers—decided to form a company to specialize in opportunities in Oman and Iraq (but no business with the Pentagon). They called their company International Six Incorporated (ISI).[35]

Scowcroft and Bill Gulley first conceived of the partnership, and Nixon introduced the two of them to Omar Zawawi, a Harvard-trained MD, a wealthy owner of several Omani construction companies, and the brother of Oman's foreign minister. Zawawi put in $200,000 in start-up money. Charles Trout, a wealthy young entrepreneur from Ohio who had started and then sold a water purification company, also joined the company and put in his own money. Rounding out the six were Jack Brennan, a Marine

Corps colonel, military assistant, and Nixon's post–White House chief of staff, and Marvin Watson, President Lyndon Johnson's appointments secretary and the postmaster general.[36]

Scowcroft and his partners leased a four-thousand-square-foot double suite at 1875 K Street and hired a couple of secretaries. Just as he had in the White House, Scowcroft again had "stacks three feet high" on his desk ("but he knew where everything was," Gulley said). Brennan, whom Scowcroft called a "free spirit," soon dropped out of the company, as did Watson, although Watson stayed on as a consultant rather than as a partner. The remaining four agreed on an egalitarian business model: they'd divide their proceeds evenly, 25 percent each, after subtracting individual expenses and Gulley's salary. (Gulley thus received both a salary and a share in the company's net proceeds; the other partners each had independent sources of income.) The more typical partnership arrangement is for the founders of a company, which in this case would have been Scowcroft and Gulley, to receive larger shares of a partnership's profits or for the most prominent of the partners, who would have been Scowcroft, to receive a larger percentage of the proceeds.[37]

They hustled. Scowcroft and his associates devoted their biggest effort to getting a new Disney theme park built in Egypt outside Cairo—Zawawi had ties to Anwar El Sadat and Hosni Mubarak, who succeeded Sadat in October 1981—and they got a deal, but it never came to fruition. They sold Florida phosphate fertilizer to China through a French company, thanks to Chinese contacts that Nixon and Jack Brennan gave them. Even though they had established ISI to specialize in opportunities in Oman, Iraq, and the Middle East, they made most of their money from deals with China. They also pursued business in the United States, buying a company in California and property in Vail, Colorado, and brokering the sale of a large farm with an eight-bedroom farmhouse in upstate New York to members of the rock group the Eagles, among other deals.[38]

Scowcroft and Gulley would close up shop in late 1988, when George Bush asked Scowcroft to join his administration.[39] (When the FBI later questioned Scowcroft about ISI to clear him for work in the Bush White House, he declined to provide the FBI with any details about the company.) Gulley said that the company made only about $2 million over the course of its life.[40]

Meanwhile, and perhaps because of ISI's mixed success, Scowcroft embarked on another enterprise concurrently, joining with Kissinger in 1982 to establish Kissinger Associates, Inc., an international business consulting company. The two of them had talked about doing so for what Scowcroft called "a long time," without any single model in mind (though they had looked at Booz Allen). Kissinger, Scowcroft, and Lawrence Eagleburger, who came on board soon afterward, used their foreign policy expertise, government experience, and diplomatic connections to advise a small handful of US-based and foreign multinationals on joint ventures, strategic planning, risk assessment, and other matters. Scowcroft was vice chairman and Kissinger Associates' representative in Washington, DC. Among Kissinger Associates' clients in the early 1990s—some of which postdate Scowcroft's departure for the Bush White House—were American Express, AIG, Anheuser-Busch, the Atlantic Richfield Company, Chase Manhattan Bank, Coca-Cola, Daewoo, Ericsson, Fiat, Fluor, Goldman Sachs, GTE, Heinz, Merck, Midland Bank, Revlon, Union Carbide, and Volvo.[41]

Working with Kissinger was lucrative for Scowcroft; by one account, he earned $300,000 a year for his work with Kissinger Associates, while another researcher figured that in 1988 Scowcroft took in more than $500,000. Independently, Scowcroft also served as a private consultant to the Lockheed Corporation.[42]

Some have wondered whether Scowcroft's consulting work and his later assignments on behalf of the US government—for example, his chairmanship of the President's Commission on Strategic Forces, known as the Scowcroft Commission (discussed in Chapter 15)—expose him to accusations of conflicts of interest. Yet if anyone could pull off juggling these roles, it would be Scowcroft, with his capacity to wear different hats at the same time, his ability to compartmentalize, and his impeccable integrity. Nonetheless, Scowcroft's later service on the two Townes Boards that addressed missile-basing issues, the Scowcroft Commission, and the Defense Policy Review Board—all of which recommended policies affecting Lockheed and possibly other clients of Scowcroft and of Kissinger Associates—would cause some on both the left and the right to view his motives with suspicion.[43]

One specific episode—the so-called Iraqgate scandal—embroiled Kissinger Associates in controversy during the 1980s. Kissinger Associates did business with Banca Nazionale del Lavoro (BNL), an Italian bank with an office in Atlanta, which made $4 billion in unauthorized loans to Iraq. This appears to have been a way for the Reagan administration to covertly aid Iraq in its war against Iran. Critics also pointed out that from 1984 through 1986 Scowcroft was a member of the board of directors of Santa Fe International, a subsidiary of the Kuwait Petroleum Corporation, and was connected with several other firms that had a stake in the war between Iraq and Iran and, later, the Iraq-Kuwait dispute.[44]

It is not clear what if any role Scowcroft may have had in this, but for Scowcroft to help with US intelligence operations as part of his consulting work would be in character given his background in Air Force intelligence and his experience in the Nixon and Ford administrations.[45] No specific allegations of misconduct have ever been raised against Scowcroft in connection with his consulting work.

Despite their years of collaboration, Scowcroft and Kissinger gradually drifted apart. Kissinger lived and worked in New York City; Scowcroft lived in Bethesda and worked in Washington, DC. Scowcroft came up to New York only about once a month, and "didn't talk much on the telephone" with Kissinger and the New York company office. Eagleburger described the relationship between Kissinger and Scowcroft at the time as "less than close." According to Eagleburger, who was also living in New York, "Between Henry and him and between Brent and me . . . we were off doing things without a hell of a lot of conversation back and forth with Washington."[46]

Kissinger and Scowcroft also had different interests. Kissinger wanted to be wealthy—in 1988 he had annual earnings of $7.5 million—and he enjoyed socializing with those at the top of the New York financial, business, cultural, and social worlds, such as the investment banker Pete Peterson, who served as chairman and CEO of Lehman Brothers before cofounding the Blackstone Group in 1985. Scowcroft, for his part, wasn't particularly interested in high society or being a celebrity, and he didn't feel the need to adopt the lifestyle of the very rich or socialize with the extremely wealthy. As Gulley remarked, he wasn't one for spending a lot of money or ostentation.[47]

Rather, Scowcroft very much remained a student and analyst of US foreign policy and national interest. Even on the occasional weekend at the Palm Springs house he bought with Gulley, Jack Brennan, and two others in 1974, for instance—the house was sold in 1989—Scowcroft didn't sign up for tee times, sit around watching ballgames, or while away the hours drinking with his buddies (although Alan Greenspan and Dick Cheney would occasionally come down to visit, Gulley recalled). His attention was overwhelmingly devoted to national security as well as his business consulting.[48]

Scowcroft wrote a number of op-eds (many of them coauthored), contributed several scholarly articles and chapters in edited volumes, cochaired studies (four by the Atlantic Council, for which he coedited the subsequent pamphlets and books), and edited an American Assembly publication entitled *Military Service in the United States*.[49] Most of his writings focused on strategic issues; in some of his op-eds and (fewer) letters to the editor, he would make more pointed remarks, often in defense of the Nixon and Ford administrations' records. In his longer writings, Scowcroft typically took analytical and historical approaches to the United States' national security interests. As a cochairman of several Atlantic Council working groups and other commissions, he didn't do the drafting of the studies—a rapporteur did that—but he worked with others to create a consensus and closely edited the final drafts to ensure that they reflected his views and those of the group.

In a brief introduction to an edited volume on the all-volunteer army, for instance, Scowcroft and the volume's other contributors made it clear that in the period since the discontinuation of the draft in 1973, questions demanding debate had accumulated about the effectiveness and merits of the volunteer army. In the discussion of strategic deterrence, to give another example, Scowcroft and other members of the Atlantic Council working group expressed their fear of the growing dominance of the Soviet Union, noted their concerns about NATO and its challenges, and advocated higher levels of defense spending by Japan and the United States' European allies. In a study of oil and the Middle East, Scowcroft addressed the United States' dependence on oil imports from the Middle East, pointed out that the Soviet Union should be denied a larger presence in the region, and emphasized the importance of the Israeli-Palestinian relationship to the security and stability of the Middle East. He and his Atlantic Council colleagues commented that the United States could reduce its dependence on the Middle East's petroleum by both diversifying its energy supply and conserving more.

Scowcroft further engaged in US foreign policy and strategic issues through his participation in the Atlantic Council and the Aspen Strategy Group. The Atlantic Council had been founded in 1961 by Dean Rusk, Christian Herter, William L. Clayton, Theodore Achilles, and others as a nonpartisan, nonprofit institution formally united to support American-European cooperation under the Atlantic Treaty. "The essential elements in the ability of the United States to play an effective role in the world," Scowcroft wrote in an article published in January 1979, "are support and leadership for friends and allies and the capability and determination to react strongly and effectively to Soviet adventurism." And at the center of both those efforts was NATO. "NATO will remain the cornerstone of our national security posture," Scowcroft told officers at the Industrial College of the Armed Forces.[50] At the Atlantic Council, Scowcroft joined the security working group in 1977 and then the political committee, where he was with the NATO committee, and in 1978 he became cochair of the political committee's project on leadership in NATO. At the Atlantic Council's conferences, he worked with Gen. Andrew Goodpaster, Gen. John Vogt, and

Eugene Rostow—all members of the Committee on the Present Danger, with Rostow being one of the founders and Vogt also a member of the CIA's Team B exercise in 1976.

Scowcroft, like many other national security experts, was critical of how détente had played out by the end of the Ford administration. He believed in the deep conflict between the United States and the West, on the one hand, and the Soviet Union, Eastern Europe, and international communism, on the other hand, and he thought the United States should not only arm itself accordingly but also reach out to and educate the American public about the Soviet threat. In this sense he shared some positions with the first generation of neoconservatives. He would have little in common with the next generation of neoconservatives.

The Aspen Strategy Group was a smaller bipartisan group formed out of an annual conference on arms control and strategic weapons sponsored by MIT, Stanford, and Harvard, with about half of its funding coming from foundations (such as MacArthur and Carnegie), and half from individuals and corporate donors. Participants—and it was a mostly closed group, with about twenty-five to thirty members at the core, although about sixty to seventy people sat in on the weeklong summer seminars—would meet in Aspen each summer for five days for the purpose of rethinking perceptions about a single theme. The members would read serious papers on particular aspects of the topic, then open the floor to questions. The format was much like a news conference, only with everything on background; the information could be repeated, but not attributed to a particular person. It was a rigorous, intellectual atmosphere that involved policy makers, journalists, and experts from think tanks and the defense industry. The papers would then later be edited and published.

Among those participating in the late 1970s and 1980s were an "astounding" number of people who would become prominent in government, including William Perry, Dick Cheney, Al Gore, Strobe Talbott, and Joseph Nye. Scowcroft served as cochairman of the Aspen Strategy Group from 1983 until 1989. He typically said little during the meetings, contributing only when needed. What made him special, Aspen Strategy Group member and former NSC aide Jan Lodal said—Lodal had also been a president of the Atlantic Council—was that "he was always a stable rock that everyone leaned on." It wasn't that Scowcroft convinced everyone of his positions; rather, it was that "he was so respected for his fairness, his objectivity, and his lack of political agenda." And his stature only grew over time. What made him special among the members of the Aspen Strategy Group as well as with the Atlantic Council was—and is—the "incredible" amount of respect others have for him.[51]

═════

SCOWCROFT REMAINED OPEN to the possibility of returning to public service. As the 1980 presidential election neared, Ronald Reagan and his advisers were attracted to Scowcroft because of his expertise, his military and governmental experience, and his excellent reputation. Reagan invited Scowcroft to be one of his foreign policy advisers for the 1980 general election campaign, and Scowcroft received frequent mention in the press and in policy circles as a possible nominee as US ambassador to the Soviet Union. Once Reagan won the election, Scowcroft was again mentioned as a likely nominee for a top foreign policy position, particularly after Richard Allen resigned as national security advisor after only one year in office.

But Reagan and his advisers were somewhat suspicious of Scowcroft, and none of the appointments developed. Scowcroft later described the situation as if he was allowed to work in the yard, cutting the grass and trimming the flowers, but never allowed inside the house.[52] Some of Reagan's advisers viewed Brent as being too close to his discredited former boss, Henry Kissinger; others thought he simply wasn't a good fit in view of his realist positions, his pragmatism, and his lack of ideological fervor—views that clashed with the less nuanced and more ideological positions on US foreign policy taken by President Reagan and others on the Republican right. Indicatively, Alexander Haig kept his distance from Scowcroft and Kissinger when he served as Reagan's secretary of state, as did Allen.

Scowcroft never became a member of the Reagan White House. But with his work on the President's Commission on Strategic Forces (the Scowcroft Commission) and the Special Review Board (the Tower Commission), he was able to achieve things that may have been of greater importance than the work he might have done as an insider. One of these achievements was something that the Reagan administration was repeatedly unable to do itself—to find a solution to the vital MX-basing problem. The other was to acquire the power to inspect the Reagan White House and appraise its performance—a performance that he found sorely lacking on several levels.

15

THE SCOWCROFT COMMISSION

IN EARLY JANUARY 1983, editors at the *Los Angeles Times*, the *Chicago Tribune*, and other major newspapers expressed deep misgivings about the chances that the newly formed president's Commission on Strategic Forces would succeed in its mission. The *New York Times* called the task facing the commission "Missile Impossible."[53] Three times already, most recently in December 1982, Congress had voted down the Department of Defense's proposals on how to base the MX intercontinental ballistic missile, which was the Pentagon's planned replacement for the aging Minuteman III ICBM. As chairman of the new commission, Brent Scowcroft faced the challenge of getting the US Congress to approve the MX and to arrive on a consensus on the future force structure of US strategic weapons.

The Air Force had already invested billions of dollars on the MX ("Missile, Experimental," which President Reagan, as of November 22, 1982, began calling the "Peacekeeper"), and Lockheed, Boeing, Rockwell International, other major contractors, and thousands of subcontractors had already been lined up and were ready to go. But deciding where and how to base the MX was a more complicated matter. Between 1965 and 1982, the Pentagon had seriously considered more than thirty different missile basing schemes, including plans to put ICBMs in large Air Force cargo planes, on small submarines, in subterranean shelters, in shallow pools of colored water, and on movable rail platforms.[54] Most recently, two panels, both chaired by the Nobel Prize–winning physicist Charles Townes (and both, confusingly, called the Townes Committee), had failed to solve the puzzle.

The first Townes Committee, which convened in 1981 and included Scowcroft, Gen. Andrew Goodpaster, David Packard, Gen. Bernard Schriever, and James Woolsey (a former NSC staff member under Nixon and a Navy under secretary under Carter) among its eleven members, recommended a system based on multiple protective shelters (MPS). Two hundred MX missiles were to be dispersed among forty-six hundred separate missile shelters spread across Utah and Nevada. The premise of the MPS system was that the Soviet Union would never know which shelters housed the MX missiles. A majority of members of Congress supported the scheme, but politicians and residents in the Intermountain West protested. And President Reagan, in what Woolsey called a "most unwise decision," termed the basing mode a "Rube Goldberg scheme" and rejected it as being "unworkable."[55]

The second Townes panel, which met in early 1982 and again included Scowcroft, Goodpaster, Packard, Schriever, and Woolsey among its sixteen members, proposed a scheme of tightly clustered missile silos. The principle behind the so-called closely spaced basing plan (also known as dense pack) was that when an incoming Soviet ICBM exploded upon impact, it would commit "fratricide" against the other incoming Soviet ICBMs, while the American ICBMs, still tightly clustered in their hardened silos, would survive to serve as a counterforce.

However, the scientific logic supporting dense pack had never been tested, and the scheme attracted criticism and ridicule from members of Congress, military correspondents, and strategic weapons experts, including former defense secretary Harold Brown and John Deutch, dean of science at MIT and former director of research in the Department of Energy under President Jimmy Carter. Soviet officials also criticized the scheme, pointing out that MX deployment would violate Article IV of SALT II, which stated, "Each Party undertakes not to start construction of additional ICBM launchers"—an interpretation that many US arms control experts agreed with.

The result was that on December 7, 1982—perhaps fittingly, the anniversary of Pearl Harbor Day—the lame-duck Ninety-Seventh Congress voted not to fund the MX program, with 50 Republicans joining 195 House Democrats in opposition.[56]

The two Townes Committees had operated under serious handicaps. The panels were creations of the Defense Department, which had charged each panel to come up with a technical solution; neither board had been instructed to also look for a politically acceptable solution that would simultaneously appease the Democratic House, the Republican Senate, and the Reagan White House. (Democrats held a 242–192 majority in the House in the Ninety-Seventh Congress, from 1981 to 1983, and a 268–166 majority in the Ninety-Eighth Congress, from 1983 to 1985, while the Republicans controlled the Senate in both Congresses, 53–46 and 54–46, respectively.) And neither Townes Committee had the unequivocal public support of the Reagan administration.[57]

Scowcroft had become "quite well" acquainted with Charles Townes through his old mentor Gen. Richard Yudkin. He supported the first MPS scheme and agreed with Woolsey that the Reagan administration had been wrong to reject it, figuring that the Reagan administration had opposed the MPS system mainly because the program originated under the Carter administration.[58] For his part, John Deutch, then a member of the MIT's chemistry department, thought that "the Reagan Administration . . . placed domestic politics ahead of what was in the country's national security interests." By abandoning "the racetrack form of basing" proposed under Carter, Deutch said, Reagan had violated the "understandings which had been reached both with our Congress and with our allies."[59]

Making an agreement with Congress even more difficult was Defense Secretary Caspar "Cap" Weinberger's poor reputation among many on Capitol Hill. Weinberger, who had formerly been with the Office of Management and Budget and was a lawyer by training, didn't suffer fools gladly, viewed members of Congress with contempt, and made no effort to hide his feelings when he went before Congress to defend the Reagan administration's plans. Worse, Weinberger hadn't mastered his brief: he was unable to convince members of Congress how particular weapons systems fit the United States' strategic needs. As Bud McFarlane, who was again working on the NSC staff, put it, Weinberger couldn't "make the connection convincingly between the system and deterrence. He couldn't make the case intellectually."[60]

The hostility between the Democrats in Congress and the Reagan presidency was mutual, as was that between Congress and the Pentagon. (Many forget that the Reagan presidency wasn't very popular in the early 1980s, and that in 1982 Republicans lost twenty-seven seats in the House of Representatives.) After the defeat of dense pack, McFarlane went over to the Hill to talk to senators Sam Nunn, John Tower, and William Cohen. Cohen advised McFarlane to "put together a bipartisan team of respected analysts to study this issue for you." He also suggested that McFarlane establish the group "in the next two months" rather than later, "because if a new plan is sent up [to Congress] in March by Cap Weinberger, it will definitely fail."[61]

Both McFarlane and his boss, national security advisor William Clark, realized that Weinberger was a liability for the administration's congressional relations, and Clark approved of McFarlane's recommendation that Reagan establish a blue-ribbon commission to break the MX stalemate. McFarlane further suggested that the group be bipartisan and composed of strategic weapons experts who were in favor of the MX. He then consulted with his friend James Woolsey and with Thomas C. Reed, the special

assistant to President Reagan for national security policy and a former sec-
retary of the Air Force, and came up with the following list of commis-
sioners: William Perry, former New Jersey senator Nicholas Brady, John
Deutch, Alexander Haig, former director of central intelligence Richard
Helms, former deputy secretary of defense and Texas governor William
Clements, vice president of the AFL-CIO's subcommittee on defense John
Lyons, retired admiral Levering Smith, James Woolsey, and Thomas Reed
(who was officially the vice chairman of the commission, thereby giving the
White House its own representative).

But Reagan rejected McFarlane's initial choice as commission chairman,
Henry Kissinger. (The president's first national security advisor, Richard
Allen, despised Kissinger.) McFarlane then proposed Brent Scowcroft, and
Reagan agreed.[62]

To add to the commission's credibility and political heft—as well as to
avoid offending any key constituencies, as a student of presidential commission, Kenneth Kitts, points out—McFarlane, Reed, and the newly appointed chairman, Scowcroft, invited Harold Brown, former White House
counsel Lloyd Cutler, Henry Kissinger, Melvin Laird, Donald Rumsfeld,
former DCI John McCone, and James Schlesinger to become "senior counsels" to the commission. The seven new members all agreed on the need for
a strong national defense, had extensive political experience, and were committed to the MX. And despite the different origins of the new commissioners and despite the "senior counsel" title, all eighteen members effectively
functioned as a single body. McFarlane, Clark, and Reed had essentially put
the Office of the Secretary of Defense into receivership, in the characterization of the journalist Frances FitzGerald.[63]

The new commission was no mere tool of the Reagan White House.
Brown, Perry, Deutch, and Woolsey had served in the Carter administration. Schlesinger was a Republican critic of the administration, as was Haig
(who had been dismissed as secretary of state only months before, on July
5, 1982). Other members, such as Laird, Kissinger, Rumsfeld, and Scowcroft, were associated not with the Reagan White House but rather with
the Nixon or Ford presidencies. And while Reed was the commission's liaison to the White House, he attended meetings infrequently, sometimes
just sending a deputy, and he didn't participate on the commission in any
meaningful way. He was the "supervisor" of the commission, as Scowcroft
referred to him, in name only.[64]

Reagan officially established the president's commission on strategic
forces on January 3, 1983, under Executive Order 12400. It had until February 18, only six and a half weeks, to issue a report. Reed, for one, knew

the close deadline was unrealistic, but the Reagan administration sought the tight schedule so that the MX—assuming it was approved in some form—could be fitted into the upcoming federal budget.[65]

As chairman of the commission, Scowcroft's challenges were at once technical and political. The technical challenges were to decide how to base the seventy-one-foot tall, two-hundred-thousand-ton MX, determine how many new missiles to recommend building, and figure out how to modernize US strategic forces for the remainder of the twentieth century.

The political hurdles were tougher. First, Scowcroft had to come up with a single plan that all eighteen commissioners could agree upon. While Scowcroft had "learned a lot" from his experience on the two Townes Committees—especially with regard to technical matters—those panels had been "widely, widely split," in Scowcroft's description. As a result, the committee members had issued minority reports along with their majority reports. (In fact, a third of the members of the second committee, including Townes himself, supported a minority report that recommended that no MX missiles whatsoever be built.)[66] Scowcroft realized that a divided commission would almost certainly doom the chances of getting any agreement through Congress. So he had to achieve a consensus within the commission itself. Then he also had to obtain the support of the Democratic-controlled House of Representatives, get the Senate to agree, and have the Air Force, Joint Chiefs of Staff, secretary of defense, and White House sign off.

The commission had to "come up with a defensible new approach," the *Washington Post*'s Walter Pincus summarized, one that was "neither too much nor too little" for members of Congress and the community of strategic weapons experts.[67] The challenge was "to make [the MX] survivable" and "to make it something that was not supposedly a first-strike weapon," Scowcroft said. "Also, to make it big enough to carry a number of accurate warheads." And "to make it cheap enough that it could be deployed. All of those things."[68] The difficulty was finding a basing mode that was "simultaneously of low cost, [could] resist even the most determined Soviet attack, and [didn't] require any infringement on the public spaces of this country," Deutch noted. Such an objective, he conceded, could well prove to be "impossible" to attain.[69]

The larger political context of the Scowcroft Commission was inauspicious. In the early 1980s, the Cold War was arguably at its height. Ronald Reagan and his advisers had come into office believing that détente was fatally flawed and that the Nixon and Ford White Houses had compromised the strategic interests of the United States. So Reagan and his foreign policy team were determined to take a hard line against the Soviet Union and build up US defenses against the growing Soviet strength.[70]

Scowcroft acknowledged that US-Soviet relations in early 1983 were "not good," adding that it was "a substantial understatement" and that "they're bad."[71] Reagan gave his famous "Evil Empire" speech on March 8, 1983, describing what he and his administration regarded as the irreconcilability of US and Soviet interests. Korean Airlines flight 007 was shot down in September, and later that fall the United States and its NATO allies conducted large military exercises ("Able Archer") that the Soviets regarded as extremely threatening and highly belligerent.[72]

Members of Congress had their own concerns. Les Aspin, the chair of the House Foreign Relations Committee, and other congressional leaders felt that after two years in office, the Reagan administration "was not making any progress on arms control." The American people wanted action, according to Aspin and other Democrats, action that wasn't forthcoming: "Negotiators were not meeting . . . nothing was going on."[73] And while the weak economy bore some responsibility for President Reagan's low approval ratings and the Republicans' poor showing in the 1982 midterm elections, Americans were anxious about superpower relations and the dangers of nuclear war—especially when the president or other officials spoke of winning a nuclear war. Caspar Weinberger suggested precisely that in early 1982, when he signed a defense guidance calling for US nuclear forces to be able to "prevail and force the Soviet Union to seek earliest termination of hostilities on terms favorable to the United States . . . even under the condition of a prolonged war." It was, in Aspin's view, "a very unstable, dangerous situation."[74]

In response, many ordinary citizens had mobilized against the arms race and the threat of a nuclear Armageddon. The nuclear freeze movement peaked in the early 1980s, with millions of Americans, Europeans, and others around the world joining in protest against the danger, expense, and what they saw as the immorality of the nuclear arms race.[75] On June 12, 1982, between five hundred thousand and 1 million people, led by nuclear scientists, members of the clergy, and other public figures, had marched in New York City in support of a nuclear freeze.

As the chairman of the commission, Scowcroft was thrust into the midst of all of these issues. He strongly believed that the United States had to have a strong national defense in the face of the Soviet threat and that it had to be the resolute leader of the free world. And he took the arms race and the US-Soviet strategic balance very seriously, as we know, seeing it as the core of the United States' national security.

Such leadership was all the more necessary since the Soviet Union had only increased in military strength since the mid-1970s with its development of third-generation missiles such as the SS-20 mobile MIRVed missile, its new strategic submarines together with more accurate and MIRVed submarine-launched ballistic missiles (SLBMs), and its modernized tactical aircraft such as the Backfire bomber. Not only did the Soviet Union already have an advantage in conventional weapons, according to US intelligence estimates, but it was outspending the United States on weapons on both a relative basis and an absolute one.[76]

Neither were things getting any better, in Scowcroft's view. The United States' former advantages were now either compromised or matched asymmetrically with the Soviet Union's own advantages (such as the greater accuracy of US missiles as opposed to the heavier throw weight of Soviet missiles, or the US advantage in naval forces versus the Soviet edge in ground forces). Soviet leaders had a further advantage: unlike American leaders, they didn't have to worry what ranchers, farmers, environmentalists, other members of the public, and the press thought about where the military stationed its missiles.

What's more, Scowcroft believed that Soviet leaders did not even accept the validity of the assumption underlying deterrence, that of mutual assured destruction (MAD)—and never had. MAD ran "counter to all their developed and inherited attitudes about warfare," he wrote.[77] "The Soviet Union, as seen through its literature, force structure, and force employment, seems quite obviously to have a very conservative and traditionalist view of strategic military conflict," Scowcroft told one reporter. "That view is that if a nuclear conflict, for whatever reason, should occur, the Soviet plan is to do their utmost to 'win' it."[78] Not surprisingly, Scowcroft concluded that the Nixon administration had mishandled US-Soviet détente. Even as he supported détente, "we oversold it," he said. "It was a very sophisticated policy, and the American people got the wrong idea that the Soviet threat was over."[79]

Yet for all his wariness of the Soviet Union, Scowcroft held a nuanced view of the US-Soviet rivalry. As a student of geopolitics and Russian history, he acknowledged the Soviet leaders' very real fears of a potential conflict with China and of the possibility they might face a two-front war. He recognized the United States and NATO's nuclear dominance at the theater (regional) level. He understood that the United States enjoyed a technological superiority in strategic weapons. He knew that the NATO countries had a combined GNP four times that of the Soviet Union. He recognized, too, that the Soviet Union critically depended on the West for its petroleum, with 49 percent of its oil supplies at the time being shipped through the Straits of Hormuz.[80] And while he appreciated the fact that the Soviet Union was principally guided by geopolitics and history and not by ideology—as he had learned from his experience in Yugoslavia, from teaching Russian history at West Point, and from his graduate studies—none of these factors necessarily made the United States any safer.

Scowcroft firmly rejected the idea of a nuclear freeze. A freeze "might actually increase the risk of conflict," he explained. The solution to the threat of nuclear war was *not* to lock existing force imbalances into place, but to stabilize weapons research and development and to restrict the deployment of new weapons. What was needed, he emphasized, was to get the United States and the USSR to move away from their mutual reliance on nuclear weapons, to make the Soviet Union realize that there would be no advantage to using nuclear weapons, and to reduce the chance that either the United States or the Soviet Union would be motivated to use nuclear weapons, given the possibility that either side could miscalculate in the heat of a crisis.[81]

The United States therefore had to succeed at deterrence, based on the combination of US military capacity and Soviet leaders' perceptions of the United States' willingness to use that capacity. Here, the MX could help. "The MX would be very useful in stabilizing crisis situations, that in some crises, there's sort of a game of chicken," Scowcroft said. Only because Soviet leaders respected "strength and resolve," and "only on that basis," was it "possible [to] deal satisfactorily with them."[82]

The president, Congress, and the Pentagon accordingly had "to demonstrate US national will and cohesiveness," Scowcroft thought, since US officials couldn't hope to talk Soviet leaders out of their military ambitions. The United States had to build its own capacity by increasing its conventional military forces, by adding other strategic options—possibly a nuclear "quadrad" or "quintad" beyond the triad of strategic bombers, ICBMs, and submarine-launched ballistic missiles—and by involving NATO in matters beyond the borders of the NATO member states. Only "by strength" could the United States "convince the Soviet Union that its only recourse [was] to enter serious arms-control negotiations."[83] And the MX was a show of this strength. Scowcroft thought that "the MX had to be developed as a short-term deterrent to the Soviets, lest they think that their forces were capable of a first strike. That's what framed my thinking."[84]

If the Reagan administration and Congress could agree on the MX missile and future US strategic force structure, Scowcroft calculated, that might be enough to get the Soviets to come to the bargaining table and negotiate with the Americans so as to tamp down the spiraling arms race, lessen the dangers of a nuclear exchange, and ameliorate the worsening relations between the two superpowers.

Few national politicians, defense analysts, strategic weapons experts, or journalists expected anything to come out of the Scowcroft Commission. Former defense secretary Melvin Laird, who was one of the commissioners and who had "superb political antennae," observed that the commission was a hundred votes short—referring to how many Democratic votes any proposed legislation would need in order to make it through the House. He figured the commission was dead in the water, and he was by no means alone in thinking that. Even Scowcroft wondered what he'd gotten into. He admitted that he doubted "a solution to the problem could be found" and guessed he would be finding "a decent burial for the MX."[85]

Once the commission started its work, however, things began to look up. Scowcroft and Woolsey (the most junior member of the commission) quickly decided on a simple strategy for breaking the impasse: they would go ahead with the MX and at the same time introduce a smaller, mobile missile—the Midgetman, as the Air Force and the press would call it. And because they appreciated the seriousness of the deadlock between Congress and the White House, they immediately sought the support of Representative Les Aspin.[86]

Aspin was an old friend and tennis partner of Woolsey's, and he knew and respected Scowcroft from the Nixon and Ford administrations. Aspin realized there had to be "some kind of a political compromise" for any agreement to work. And because he had larger political aspirations—some thought he wanted to become secretary of defense—he had to demonstrate he could get a deal done. Given Congress's problem with Weinberger, the commission offered another route to a politically acceptable deal. So Aspin soon got "very heavily involved" in trying to work out a solution to the MX issue.[87]

Scowcroft, Woolsey, and Aspin came up with what amounted to a three-part package: to put the MX in existing silos in the near term; to build the smaller, mobile Midgetman over the longer term; and "to encourage both sides to move toward more survivable ICBMs" so as promote a possible future arms agreement. In a "purely political sense," Scowcroft observed, it was "a combination which got a variety of different coalitions together," since the three-part plan offered something for everyone.[88]

Keeping the MX would appeal to conservatives in Congress and the Pentagon, since the MX had multiple independently targeted reentry vehicles capable of hitting ten targets separately, with each warhead containing twenty times the destructive power of the Hiroshima bomb. With "their prompt, accurate military destruction potential," Deutch said, the MX missiles were critical "in the calculation of the Soviet general staff, in deterring them from considering a conventional or chemical or nuclear attack in Western Europe or on the flanks of NATO."[89]

On the other hand, Scowcroft and Woolsey "felt very strongly" that cancellation of the MX, "particularly after the Soviets had succeeded in . . . getting the neutron bomb cancelled," would deal an "absolutely crippling" blow "to NATO and to the notion of the American nuclear deterrent as part of NATO." The United States would then have no basis for asking its European allies "to deploy Pershing [IIs] and ground launch cruise missiles on their own territory when we would let the citizens of Utah and Nevada . . . essentially, effectively . . . stop all on-going US ICBM modernization."[90]

The Scowcroft-Woolsey-Aspin plan would appeal to those who didn't like the MX by introducing the Midgetman (later the MGM-134). The Midgetman, a thirty-eight-foot-long missile about one-seventh the size of the MX, was to be housed in large, armored tractor-trailers equipped with heavy protective skirts—nicknamed "armadillos"—to protect them from a nuclear blast. Because the huge trucks pulling the missiles could operate in the desert around Nellis Air Force Base outside Las Vegas, Nevada, and in other desert areas near existing Air Force bases, the Midgetman would be mobile and survivable.[91] The Midgetman would therefore please those members of Congress, the Reagan administration, military leaders, nuclear arms experts, and others who placed a premium on survivability.

Moreover, the less expensive Midgetman appealed to yet a third constituency—those who wanted US strategic weapons policy to go in a new direction. Since the Midgetman was to have only one thermonuclear warhead, it would be easier for the two superpowers to count ICBM warheads for the purposes of arms control. "Missile silos, submarines, and bombers were relatively easy to count and monitor" in order to verify compliance with the SALT I agreement, Scowcroft explained. But because the number of nuclear warheads on missiles was "considered to be beyond national capacity to verify," both sides were motivated "to multiply the number of individual weapons or warheads, to be installed in each launcher or silo." Developing a single-warhead missile would thereby induce predictability in the arms race, Scowcroft wrote, and serve to "integrate arms control . . . with the modernization of our strategic forces."[92]

Aspin told Scowcroft and Woolsey he would "run the traps" (a Wisconsin hunting term) by checking with his colleagues in Congress to gauge the likelihood of attracting the votes needed to pass the plan.[93] Meanwhile, Scowcroft faced the task of getting the commissioners on board. Since it made little sense to begin diving into the complex issues before the commissioners shared the same basic knowledge, Scowcroft took it upon himself to "review the history of US-Soviet strategic force relationships, of arms control, of previous attempts to solve this problem, and so on," including the relevant intelligence. He thereby managed to get his colleagues to understand relatively early in the process "why we were where we were" and to nudge them toward a common approach.[94]

He further helped his cause by how he handled the report-drafting process. The Air Force and the Office of the Secretary of Defense had personnel available for drafting the commission's report, but Scowcroft instead chose to make Woolsey his scribe and used the drafting process to bring the other commission members along. He had Woolsey, an accomplished writer, circulate a draft of the report, collect comments from the commissioners, compose a new draft (often staying up late at night to do so), and then at the next meeting (sometimes the next day) circulate another draft. And then he would then do it all again, "through days and days of drafting," Woolsey said. The process got the commissioners to buy into their mission and to dedicate themselves to solving the thorny MX issue.[95]

Once the commissioners were all in agreement, Nicholas Brady drew up a list of influential people they needed to talk to.[96] It was Brady's "idea to involve the Congress in a way and I thought it was brilliant," Scowcroft said. He and Brady assigned individual commissioners to meet with selected members of the House and Senate (mostly Democrats), White House officials, Pentagon officials, and presidential candidates (with the 1984 presidential election just around the corner) so as to persuade them of the merits of the MX-Midgetman deal.[97]

Scowcroft and his colleagues on the commission "systematically" reached out to "many, many individuals," Woolsey remarked, and "they had lunches and breakfasts and dinners, and private meetings with Congressmen."[98] In essence, they did a "sort of brokering," Deutch said, "going back and forth between the executive branch, the Defense Department, National Security Council staff, White House and the Congress, particularly key Democrats in the House such as Aspin and [Al] Gore and [Norman] Dicks and others."[99]

When it came to Congress, Aspin's help was critical. He met with younger House Democrats who were similarly conservative on defense but anxious about the nuclear arms race—Representative Dicks of Washington, Oklahoma's Dave McCurdy, South Carolina's John Spratt, and Tennessee's

Al Gore among them—to solicit their views. Not long afterward, in late January or early February, Aspin got back to Scowcroft and Woolsey and told them the deal "just might work."[100] Then Scowcroft and Woolsey began talking to members of Congress "likely to be highly influential in the decision." The two made repeated trips to the Rayburn and Cannon office buildings, working closely with Aspin and Dicks. They talked to senior Senate leaders, Scoop Jackson and other more hawkish Democrats in particular, and presented their arguments at Senate Armed Services Committee hearings chaired by Senator John Tower. Senate Democrats subjected Scowcroft and the others to intense questioning, but with Tower favorably disposed to the MX deal and with the Republicans in control of the Senate, the upper house posed less of a challenge for Scowcroft, Woolsey, and the other commissioners than the lower house. There were "a lot of meetings," Aspin recalled.[101]

Securing the cooperation of Al Gore, an up-and-coming Tennessee congressman, was critical to the commission's success. Scowcroft recalled that when he first proposed the joint MX-Midgetman package to Gore, the congressman told Scowcroft, "You're crazy," and "almost threw me out of his office." Gore was "an apostle of the small missile" who "hated the MX" and who strongly emphasized the arms control element of any modernization of US strategic forces. Together with Les Aspin, Charles Percy, Sam Nunn, William Cohen, and other members of Congress, Gore twice wrote letters to the president stating that they'd agree to the MX only on the condition of progress being made on arms control. In part because of Gore's insistence, Scowcroft was influenced to place more emphasis on progress toward nuclear arms control in his discussions with the White House and, eventually, in the commission's report. But Scowcroft succeeded in persuading Gore to support the MX, and by the time the commission finished its work, Gore had become one of the foremost advocates of the MX-Midgetman deal.[102]

All the work by Scowcroft, Woolsey, Deutch, the other commissioners, and Aspin began to pay off. A consensus started to develop among the commissioners, key members of Congress, White House officials, and the Pentagon. According to Woolsey, at one commission meeting, probably in early February, Melvin Laird came in and announced, "We're about fifty votes down in the House."

Woolsey immediately leaned over to Scowcroft and murmured, "We're going to win."

"How do you know?" Scowcroft replied.

"Mel Laird just changed from the second person plural to the first person plural," Woolsey replied.[103]

Scowcroft proceeded to undertake a full-court public relations campaign. Here, as with many of his actions as chairman of the commission, Woolsey and John Deutch were his closest associates.[104] He knew any proposed solution had to be approved by important opinion leaders, since the absence of such persuasive efforts had been one of the chief downfalls of the two preceding Townes Committees—and, indeed, of the Vietnam War. He and the other commissioners wrote op-ed pieces, granted numerous interviews, appeared in dozens of regional and national publications, and met with representatives of leading interest groups. Senator Jackson and Representative Aspin also spoke out on behalf of the commission. Scowcroft even had former president Jerry Ford telephone House Speaker Thomas "Tip" O'Neill Jr. to enlist his support.[105] Scowcroft himself talked to reporters from *Time*, *USA Today*, *U.S. News & World Report*, the *Washington Post*, the *Washington Times*, the *New York Times*, and other publications.[106]

Scowcroft took particular pains to address concerns over the "window of vulnerability." The idea, which had surfaced in the late 1970s in opposition to SALT II, mostly from critics on the right, was that the United States' nuclear forces were vulnerable to a Soviet first strike. Paul Nitze, one of Reagan's strategic weapons advisers, was largely responsible for disseminating the idea. Often working through the Committee on the Present Danger, Nitze had prepared charts purporting to demonstrate the vulnerability of the fixed-silo Minuteman ICBMs to incoming Soviet missiles. For critics of the United States' existing nuclear forces, substituting MXs for the Minuteman IIIs did nothing to solve this problem.[107]

Nitze wasn't alone in his concern about the vulnerability of the United States' silo-based ICBMs. The Townes Committee's 1981 report stated there was "no practical basing mode for missiles deployed on the land's surface available at this time that assure[d] an adequate number of surviving ICBM warheads." Indeed, Scowcroft's own views of Soviet capabilities implied that the United States' land-based ICBMs were vulnerable.[108]

Now, however, Scowcroft made a systematic effort in his public relations campaign to put the idea of a "window of vulnerability" to rest. It was just "a slogan," he told one reporter. "We didn't deny it. Nor did we accept it." He also did not think the Soviets were inclined "to risk everything on a single role of the dice" by attacking US ICBM silos with their own ICBMs, since there would be no guarantee that their missiles would all destroy their targets. The unrealistic assumption behind the vulnerability issue, a *Washington Post* editor wrote, was that the Soviets would risk their country "on an attack that had never been—and could never be—tested, and that would require the most stunning technological coordination and the perfect performance of hundreds of Soviet missiles." James Schlesinger, a commission member who publicly defended the MX deal, also noted that the "Soviets can never have a high degree of confidence that those accuracies would be achieved in a massive strike."[109]

The real risk in crisis situations, in Scowcroft's view, arose from the Soviets' own calculations of "the correlation of forces." If the Soviets were confident of their advantage, "critical dangers" could arise. In such cases, the antecedents to World War I were "much more illuminating" about how war might break out, Scowcroft explained, than was the buildup to World War II. He nevertheless conceded that "the vulnerability is growing and carries with it psychological, if not military, liabilities"—hence the need for the United States to build a smaller, accurate, and mobile ICBM.[110]

Besides attending to public relations, Scowcroft took Congress's legislative calendar into account. Although Scowcroft and Aspin had already lined up the votes they needed in the House, Scowcroft asked for, and received, a month's extension.[111] However, the delay wasn't because the commission needed more time (the public explanation that was offered). Rather, had the commission's report been released when originally scheduled, the release would have coincided with the debate in Congress over a nuclear freeze, a politically popular cause many moderate Democrats couldn't afford to ignore. Aspin also wanted to wait until after the upcoming budget vote, since many members of Congress were critical of the president's budget, as well as after the vote on Kenneth Adelman's nomination as the director of the Arms Control and Disarmament Agency.

Members of Congress already faced "three dove votes" (on the freeze resolution, the budget resolution to cut defense spending, and against the Adelman nomination), Aspin pointed out, and those votes were likely to make them "uncomfortable," causing them to wonder "if they've gone too far one way" and "start looking for a way to pop back the other way."[112] The delayed vote on the MX deal would allow them to do that, burnishing their Cold War credentials and balancing their voting records before the next election. Democratic representative Thomas Downey of New York, an opponent of the MX, said as much in his criticism of those House Democrats who went along with the administration's scheme: "Some of these people were for the freeze, and now they're for the MX. It's the same old game: everyone seeks the middle ground."

However, for Downey, Joseph Addabbo of New York, and other House and Senate Democrats, the middle ground was barren land. They thought the release of funds for the MX and Midgetman would be "a tragedy of the highest order." They and other critics also pointed out that the Scowcroft Commission was rigged, since none of the commissioners were opposed to the MX—which was, of course, what McFarlane had planned.[113]

For Scowcroft, the MX-Midgetman deal made obvious strategic sense. As for those House Democrats who attacked their colleagues, he thought they did so out of "partisan political heat" because their colleagues were "supporting the administration" rather than because of any "fundamental strategic differences."[114]

In the midst of the push to win support for the MX-Midgetman deal, President Reagan himself produced a giant distraction by unveiling the Strategic Defense Initiative (SDI), popularly known as "Star Wars."[115]

SDI would alter the US-Soviet superpower relationship, and today a missile defense system has been deployed over North America and much of Europe. In the early 1980s, however, SDI was little more than a gleam in President Reagan's eye—helped by Bud McFarlane, Adm. James Watkins, and Adm. John Poindexter[116]—an idea to invest research and development funds in the science and technology that could make an extended ballistic missile defense system possible.

The president had visited the North American Air Defense Command in Colorado Springs shortly after being elected president. Appalled by the horrific scenarios of what would happen were the United States to be hit by a nuclear attack, Reagan repeatedly declared his wish that the United States could "protect Americans from this scourge of nuclear annihilation."[117] So when the president learned of the possibility of building a shield against ballistic missile attack in a meeting on February 11, 1983, with JCS chairman Admiral Watkins, he encouraged the service chiefs to work on the issue. Three weeks later, they submitted a formal proposal, and on March 16, a week before the president was scheduled to make a televised speech on the defense budget, he decided to introduce the Strategic Defense Initiative to the American public. He told McFarlane to draft a section on SDI and include it in his address.[118]

Reagan kept SDI under wraps until the last possible moment. Neither the president, McFarlane, nor any other top advisers wanted weapons experts, journalists, politicians, or others to shoot down the concept before everyone learned of it. But the president did listen to McFarlane's concern about how his own Commission on Strategic Forces might react, so he had an aide inform Scowcroft shortly before the public address. Although Scowcroft warned McFarlane that the president shouldn't talk about missile defense publicly until the MX deployment was resolved, Reagan decided to go ahead. He just asked Scowcroft to keep an open mind.[119]

Scowcroft kept the president's news to himself, as Reagan had asked. So the other members of the Scowcroft Commission, like almost everyone else in Washington and around the country, were unprepared when Reagan announced the SDI program on March 23, seemingly out of the blue. They were "stunned," John Deutch remembered.[120] Scowcroft himself recalled that his commissioners "went berserk" when they "heard about the SDI speech." There was "real rage" at the commission's March 24 meeting, Deutch recalled. The commissioners "were uniformly surprised and uniformly . . . horrified" by the fact that "the President of the United States would make a major public address" that potentially transformed "the whole basis of strategy" from "deterrence to a new concept of strategic defense" without even consulting his "own commission charged with the responsibility of achieving a political solution to a very complicated subject." SDI "made their task, our task, a great deal more difficult," Deutch said, and "almost split [the commission] asunder."[121]

Even after things settled down, Scowcroft and his colleagues were left "scratching [their] heads" about the implications of Reagan's words and about how "it all fit together." They asked to speak with the president, who agreed to a meeting. "Why now?" Richard Helms asked. But Reagan "did *not* have a good answer," Deutch emphasized—especially since "no one thought" SDI was technically feasible.[122]

Since Scowcroft didn't see how SDI directly affected the commission's task, he "decided that the only way" to proceed was "to ignore it. Because it was only a speech. It had nothing behind it. We didn't understand the rationale or anything." It was "not practical at the present time, nor really in the time frame [the commission] looked at—the next ten to fifteen years." So "to focus on Star Wars was to in large measure confuse matters, whatever people thought of its desirability." The MX, in contrast, was a known quantity, and the technology for the Midgetman missiles was already developed and would only take a few years to build. Consequently, "we basically sort of shrugged and went on what we were doing," Woolsey said, since the commissioners "didn't know quite how to integrate [SDI] into what we were doing with the Scowcroft Commission." They "just plowed ahead."[123]

Scowcroft's own theory was that SDI was the product of Reagan's personal dilemma. He thought the president was psychologically torn between two mutually exclusive approaches to confronting the nuclear problem and his own place in history. One approach was the ideal: a comprehensive ballistic missile defense system. But SDI was "two or three" presidencies "down the road," and by then, Scowcroft noted, "he'll be dead." Scowcroft himself opposed SDI, he later explained. He didn't know how the technology would work, and he saw it as "severely destabilizing," since it upset the strategic balance that the United States and the Soviet Union were then working toward.[124]

Reagan's other approach, in Scowcroft's analysis, was the "more tentative arms control approach, which means two or maybe three smallish steps toward agreement" with the Soviets.[125] These were the talks that would result in START (the Strategic Arms Reduction Treaty), following in the path of SALT I and SALT II. And while START represented an important step in US-Soviet arms control agreements, it was ultimately a modest achievement for a president concerned about his legacy.

Scowcroft made his statement about Reagan's "split personality" in a WGBH interview on October 10, 1986. His remarks were remarkably prescient. On October 12, the second day of a historic US-Soviet summit meeting in Reykjavik, Iceland, the president found another way to reconcile the issue of nuclear weapons and his own place in history. He and Soviet leader Mikhail Gorbachev talked about ridding the world of intercontinental ballistic missiles over the next ten years, taking up an idea that had first been floated by Weinberger that June in response to Gorbachev's offer to eliminate all nuclear weapons.

Nothing came of Reagan's and Gorbachev's discussion, since Gorbachev wouldn't proceed without the United States halting work on SDI, and Reagan refused to do so. (The president said the United States would share the technology, but Gorbachev didn't find the offer credible.) Reykjavik nonetheless represented a "great moral breakthrough" in the US-Soviet superpower rivalry, according to Soviet Marshal Sergei Akhromeyev. Furthermore, it led to more serious bargaining between the United States and the Soviet Union on intermediate-range missiles and other strategic weapons issues, as the journalist Don Oberdorfer pointed out in his book *The Turn*.[126]

In the wake of Reagan's SDI bombshell, the Scowcroft Commission plowed ahead. On April 11, 1983, Scowcroft delivered the twenty-five-page "Report of the President's Commission on Strategic Forces" to President Reagan.[127] The report argued that the United States needed to balance the threat of mass destruction with the threat of aggressive totalitarianism, and that it could best do so by mitigating the first and containing the second. On the second issue, the United States couldn't ignore the Soviet Union's expansion of its military capability and political power, such as its development of the SS-18 and SS-19 missiles, which carried ten and six multiple warheads, respectively.[128] Rather, it had to make the Soviets believe that the United States and the West had the military strength and political will to resist aggression.

Successful deterrence depended on the United States' military strength, its political resolve, and its stable institutions—that is, on the Soviets' perception that they couldn't possibly gain from either a nuclear attack or, what was more likely, a conventional attack. The report accordingly recommended the further development of missile accuracy, silo hardening, missile mobility, antisubmarine war, and ballistic missile defense.

The report accepted and incorporated Reagan's SDI proposal, but it recommended that the United States needed the MX for the foreseeable future, since any missile defense system was years away. Besides recommending the installation of one hundred MX missiles in hardened Minuteman III silos, the commission report recommended developing the mobile, survivable Midgetman, as well as continuing with the Trident II submarine, airborne bombers (the B-1), and air-launched cruise missiles.[129] The commission noted that because no single component of national defense—whether the MX, the Midgetman, a ballistic missile defense, or other program—sufficed on its own, its recommendations had to be considered as integral components of a complete package. The report also reassured its readers that the Soviet threat to the United States' land-based missile sites was insufficient to worry about a window of vulnerability. The bonus was the fact that the combined estimated costs of the MX and Midgetman came out to less than the price of the dense pack or the multiple protective shelters basing mode.[130]

Scowcroft's unified approach on the MX issue succeeded in securing the unanimous approval of the other commissioners. On April 19, 1983, Reagan announced his approval of the report and forwarded the recommendations to Congress.

The commission's work wasn't complete. Aspin, Scowcroft, and his fellow commissioners continued to lobby members of Congress to see that the deal would go through. Some of their efforts were more complicated than they should have been. The evening before the House vote on the MX, the White House hosted a dinner for twenty-five moderate members of Congress and undecideds. The president opened with a short statement, followed by comments by Scowcroft and Secretary of State George P. Shultz. Unfortunately, according to another dinner guest, Shultz "demonstrated once again that he hadn't had time to master the issue." Worse, Reagan's own response to a question about reducing the numbers of MIRVed warheads was "less than convincing" and "confused."[131] As a result, Scow-croft and other commissioners at the dinner had to circulate around the tables and quietly reassure worried House members that things were well in hand and that they needn't "be concerned about Shultz's comments" or the president's lack of expertise.[132]

Aspin helped out by convincing Reagan officials and sympathetic members of Congress to downplay their enthusiasm for the Scowcroft Commission's solution. To ensure that the MX deal would be perceived as "middle ground" and not as a victory for the White House, he told Weinberger, "Don't crow when this comes out . . . we need you to grouse. Say this isn't very good, but, etc., etc.," the *New Yorker*'s Elizabeth Drew reported. And sure enough, when Weinberger publicly announced his support for the commission's package, the Pentagon showed "a lack of enthusiasm . . . about the development of the small missile." Aspin likewise downplayed his own enthusiasm for the commission's approach when he talked to his House colleagues about the MX, telling them, "This is as good a decision as you're going to get to a problem that has no good answer." This was essentially what the *New York Times* and other leading newspapers wrote in their editorials approving the MX deal.[133]

Some House members continued to express their intense disagreement. Some took the commission members to task for reversing their position on the issue of silo vulnerability (in November 1981, for instance, William Perry and Harold Brown had both argued that placing the MX in missile silos would put them at risk). Others criticized the commission's approach as representing a "cruel hoax" and suggested it was "preposterous" to think that the proposed solution would be able to induce any arms control negotiations between the Reagan White House and Soviet leaders.

Nonetheless, Congress approved the MX package, though with one change: Congress funded only fifty MX missiles, not the full one-hundred-missile complement recommended in the commission report.[134]

President Reagan and White House officials greatly appreciated the work of the commission and acknowledged the debt they owed Scowcroft and his colleagues. "The MX would have been 'completely lost' without the intervention of the panel," one congressional aide reported McFarlane saying. "Without the Scowcroft Commission, we'd never have the MX," the journalist Hugh Sidey wrote. "If Weinberger had said he wanted to put the MX in Minuteman silos he'd been laughed off the Hill." But since "virtually every top expert in strategic affairs had signed on," the "would-be doubters were instantly humbled."[135] Even Charles Townes, who might have resented

Scowcroft's success where his own efforts had failed, praised Scowcroft for being able to break the impasse between White House and Congress and for tackling "the whole batch [of issues] at once, both political and technical." The commission, he concluded, had done "a good job."[136]

Was the creation of the Scowcroft Commission merely a cynical White House ploy to get the MX, as some critics have suggested? The evidence doesn't support this claim. In fact, the White House didn't know in advance what the commission's solution would be, still less that it would get the support of a majority in the House and Senate. Furthermore, the administration did not get everything it wanted. Weinberger and the Department of Defense had to give in "on building the Midgetman," as Scowcroft pointed out (the Air Force much preferred the MX to the Midgetman); the White House had "to be more forthcoming on arms control"; and the administration had to integrate arms control more closely with the United States' strategic programs instead of treating arms control "rather as something one does off to the side."[137] As a result, while some in the administration were in favor of carrying out the commission's recommendations, others, Aspin pointed out, were not.[138]

On June 10, the president extended the life of the Scowcroft Commission for the duration of calendar 1983 so that the commissioners could oversee progress on the implementation of its recommendations as agreed upon by Congress. The commission (minus two of its members) met infrequently thereafter, with Scowcroft serving as the White House liaison.

One of the tasks Reagan asked the commission to undertake in the late spring of 1983 was an informal evaluation of the Strategic Defense Initiative. The commissioners' consensus was "quite negative" for "a lot of reasons," Scowcroft said. He advised the president to keep the findings quiet and not make them public, since, despite Scowcroft's own opposition to SDI, he "didn't take things public in those days." So the results "never saw the light of day."[139]

Because of the attention the Scowcroft Commission brought to arms control, Reagan in early June ordered Gen. Edward Rowny, the head of the US delegation in Geneva, to focus on restricting the number of warheads rather than on regulating the number of launchers. And while the Reagan administration's negotiations produced no immediate results, they managed to shift the conversation toward achieving an agreement on nuclear weapons reduction. They brought renewed attention to enhancing stability and deterrence, especially in times of crisis, and they eventually led to the signing of START under Reagan's successor, George H. W. Bush.[140]

In the short run, however, formal talks with the Soviets made little progress. With US-Soviet relations continuing to deteriorate over the rest of 1983, President Reagan invited Scowcroft to go to Moscow in March 1984 as part of the private Dartmouth Conference of US foreign policy experts. Once he arrived in Moscow, however, Scowcroft was unable to meet with Soviet party chairman Konstantin Chernenko because of Secretary Shultz's failure to follow up on Reagan's invitation. Although Shultz would have been kept wholly informed of Scowcroft's communications, he was loath to let US-Soviet diplomacy out of his control.[141]

After Reagan's reelection in 1984, White House officials considered appointing Scowcroft as its new arms control czar, but Secretary Shultz was again opposed; arms control negotiations were "his job" and he "would resign if need be" to protect his turf.[142]

Although the Scowcroft Commission didn't directly lead to any major breakthroughs in the arms race, it achieved its short-term objectives: it saved the MX, it moved the United States to a more diversified and more survivable ICBM system, and it provided for the updating and modernization of the United States' strategic force structure with the Trident II, the hardening of missile silos, and the continuation of the B-1 and B-2 bomber programs. Most important, it helped ensure the continuation of deterrence. The United States and the Soviet Union refrained from attacking each other despite the worsening political relations between the two superpowers, despite the insurrection in Afghanistan against the Soviet Union (with the rebels supported by clandestine US aid), and despite the situation in Nicaragua.

Most of the credit for the Scowcroft Commission's success goes to its chairman. Over the course of the dozens of commission meetings, Scowcroft was collegial, considerate, and accommodating. He was also clearly, if quietly, in charge. He had "a rare talent for persuasion," James Woolsey commented, and "for bringing out the reasonableness in others." "Scowcroft was great," Rumsfeld remarked. He wasn't ideological, didn't "trip over his own ego," and was "brilliant at working with hugely egotistical and hugely intelligent people," another commissioner observed.[143]

In meetings with Kissinger and Haig, the tables were now turned. "Scowcroft quietly dominate[d]," *Business Week* reported, and when Scowcroft and Haig went over to Capitol Hill to talk to senior members of Congress, "Haig deferred completely to Scowcroft and hardly said a word."[144] (Scowcroft attributed Haig's complaisance to the fact that he was his West Point classmate.) Notwithstanding the preeminence, political experience, and scientific expertise of Kissinger, Haig, and the other commissioners, they all bought into Scowcroft's proposed solutions and then worked to get the MX deal funded through Congress.

Scowcroft even got cooperation from the acerbic Weinberger, "a very powerful man" and a terrific "infighter" in Paul Nitze's words—and Nitze should know.[145] (On one occasion at least, the secretary of defense simply refused to carry out a presidential order. On November 16, 1983, Reagan ordered him to launch an aerial attack against the Iranian Revolutionary Guards stationed in the Lebanese town of Baalbek in retaliation for the bombing of the Marine barracks in Lebanon. But Weinberger didn't do anything, and Reagan, who was an old friend and hated confrontation, didn't have the stomach to call him on it.)[146] Weinberger thus could have caused serious difficulties, especially since the very existence of the commission was a testimony to Weinberger's failure as secretary of defense. Instead, Scowcroft and Weinberger met frequently, and their meetings "were always amicable," Scowcroft reported. Despite the fact that they didn't see eye to eye on the commission's proposed solution and despite the fact that Scowcroft worked closely with Democratic members of Congress who loathed Weinberger, the two got along. And in the end, Weinberger publicly approved of the commission's recommendations.[147]

As critical as journalist Elizabeth Drew was of the Reagan administration and of the Scowcroft Commission, she praised Scowcroft himself as "an honorable public servant, whose instinctive loyalty is to the Commander-in-Chief. He faithfully and competently gets the job done."[148] While this could be viewed as damning with faint praise—reinforcing the idea of Scowcroft as merely a highly capable civil servant, a "loyal staff officer," and a trustworthy "fixer"—the compliment has to be viewed in the context of the immense stakes and treacherous politics of the MX missile, and President Reagan's earlier decision to exclude Scowcroft from his foreign policy team. But when confronted with a seemingly intractable problem, "a problem this nation absolutely [had] to solve," Rumsfeld said, Reagan and his advisers "turned to Brent as the best man to solve the strategic weapons dilemma."[149]

Scowcroft accomplished something else: he helped shift the basis of congressional support for strategic weapons systems. Whereas defense and arms control policy in the House of Representatives were "normally seen to be the province of an older, longer tenured, more conservative element of the Democratic membership of the House"—senior southern Democrats, typically—Scowcroft formed a coalition for ICBM modernization and arms control among younger moderate Democrats.[150] He even won agreement for the MX deal from Scoop Jackson and Richard Perle, Jackson's former aide.[151] (Perle was then the assistant secretary of defense for international security policy, perhaps the administration's most hawkish member, and the intellectual leader of the Madison Group, an informal group of young hard-line conservatives who met regularly at the Madison Hotel.)[152]

Throughout the process, Scowcroft showed himself to be adept at navigating Washington politics on complex issues of high strategic salience, immense political stakes, and great financial importance. Scowcroft succeeded in getting his fellow commissioners, a majority in both houses of Congress, the Reagan administration, and the Defense Department to reach to a consensus on the United States' strategic force structure for the rest of the 1980s, the 1990s, and the early years of the twenty-first century. Four years after the commission issued its report, Scowcroft told a reporter he was "still very comfortable with the conclusions" and thought the commission's recommendations were "very sound." Such an accomplishment, he said in a moment of self-praise, was "hard to beat . . . in this field."[153]

———

NONETHELESS, THE SCOWCROFT Commission's policy recommendations would never fully go into effect. In early 1986, when Congress had approved only fifty of the proposed one hundred MX missiles and had not yet funded the Midgetman, Scowcroft, Deutch, and Woolsey wrote a critical op-ed urging Congress to implement the commission's recommendations.[154]

Scowcroft also found fault with the shifting arms policies of the Reagan administration. In June 1986, the same three writers expressed their disagreement with the administration's support of a comprehensive test ban treaty. And they criticized the wishful thinking on display in October 1986 at the Reykjavik summit. In a five-page *New York Times* magazine article, they defended the concept of nuclear deterrence and attacked Reagan's proposal that all ballistic missiles be banned in ten years' time. Not only would this cede to the Warsaw Pact its superiority in conventional weapons over NATO forces in Europe, they wrote, but the move would rashly eliminate two of the three legs—nuclear missiles and submarine-launched ballistic missiles—of the United States' strategic triad.[155]

The three likewise criticized the proposed "zero option" that would have the United States "dismantle its 572 warheads on Pershing II and cruise missiles" in Europe—eliminating a whole class of weapons, in effect—and the 810 warheads on 270 SS-20 missiles based in Europe. Without those

NATO intermediate-range nuclear forces, the Soviet Union would have the advantage with its more than five hundred shorter-range missiles, which in the three men's analysis would only augment the Soviets' superiority in conventional forces and eliminate the capacity of the United States and its NATO allies to employ a "flexible response" to any aggression by the Soviet Union. And the zero option would undermine US-European relations, since it would contradict the administration's previous push in 1983 to deploy the Pershing and cruise missiles in Europe.

Eliminating the intermediate-range nuclear forces would be a mistake, Scowcroft wrote in reply to Paul Nitze's editorial defending the zero option. A reduction in the number of nuclear weapons possessed by both sides did not ipso facto make for greater strategic stability. The zero option did not cohere conceptually, Scowcroft pointed out, and removing the NATO intermediate-range nuclear deterrent would not reassure the United States' European allies but in fact do the exact opposite.[156]

The Reagan administration's proposals to ban mobile ICBMs and put more nuclear warheads on the new Trident II submarines, Scowcroft, Deutch, and Woolsey wrote, would mean that the United States' fixed MX and Minuteman missiles, its strategic bombers, and its relatively few nuclear submarines (with only eight of the twelve being at sea at any one time) would be vulnerable to Soviet forces as time marched on and technology progressed. The United States couldn't rely on the Reagan administration's "childlike faith in strategic warning," they cautioned. Pearl Harbor on December 7, 1941, South Korea on June 25, 1950, and Israel on Yom Kippur in 1973 were lessons enough.[157]

In the end, only fifty MX missiles were ever deployed, and only a prototype of the Midgetman was ever built. "We won," said Michael Mawby, the political director of SANE, the antinuclear group that worked to stop deployment of the MX.[158] It's possible that the mere threat of the new missiles was sufficient for the purposes of deterrence and strategic balance during what turned out to be the final years of the Soviet empire.

Meanwhile, President Reagan was about to face the worst political crisis of his two terms in office—the Iran-Contra affair. And once again, Reagan and his advisers would turn to Brent Scowcroft for help.

16

A WATERGATE-TYPE PROBLEM

AFTER THE SUCCESS of the Scowcroft Commission, President Reagan invited Scowcroft to serve on the Commission on Defense Management (1985–1986)—also known as the Packard Commission—with the mandate to evaluate the Department of Defense's budget, monitor Pentagon procurement, and oversee the organizational and operational coordination of the military. Reagan also named Scowcroft to the Defense Policy Board, a standing commission charged with providing independent analysis and advice for the secretary of defense on long-range strategic planning and other topics.

Scowcroft served on these and other government boards, achieving results by virtue of his expertise on complex and sensitive matters as well as his analytical ability, common sense, interpersonal skills, and cordiality. Indicatively, Kissinger, Al Haig, and Zbigniew Brzezinski each served on fewer boards than did Scowcroft.

Of course, Scowcroft had his own reasons for agreeing to serve. One reason was that he enjoyed working on several tasks at the same time; at least since his days at West Point, Scowcroft had liked dealing with diverse challenges and difficult puzzles that involved significant issues—which is one reason the long hours spent writing his PhD dissertation and the days on end seated behind a desk in the Pentagon had held limited appeal.

Another was Scowcroft's extraordinary dedication to public service. Most retired military officers and former government officials—indeed, most Americans—are patriotic, but only a few are consistently willing to dedicate themselves to time-consuming, unpaid, and often sensitive projects on their nation's behalf. But Scowcroft invariably and unselfishly agreed to participate.

So on November 3, 1986, when the news broke that the Reagan administration had traded weapons to Iran for the release of American hostages, Scowcroft got a call.

The preceding five presidencies had all come to premature ends, whether because of assassination (Kennedy), the Vietnam War (Johnson), Watergate (Nixon), the Nixon pardon (Ford), and the Iranian hostages (Carter), as the *New York Times*' R. W. Apple Jr. wrote in his introduction to the Tower Commission's report. Now the news of the Iranian arms deal threatened to wreck the Reagan presidency, uncovering the "stumbling, short-sighted stewardship of the national trust from the President on down," Apple reported. It revealed a "National Security Council led by reckless cowboys, off on their own on a wild ride, taking direct operational control of matters that are the customary province of more sober agencies such as the CIA, the State Department and the Defense Department."[159]

The scandal had two components. The first, which first came to light in a story published in the Lebanese newspaper *Al-Shiraa*, was the news of an arms-for-hostages deal carried out by national security advisor Robert McFarlane assisted by David Kimche, Michael Ledeen, and other Israeli and American middlemen. In direct violation of the law, the White House had agreed to sell more than thirty-five hundred state-of-the-art TOW anti-tank weapons to Iran in exchange for the release of American hostages being held in Lebanon by the militant group Hezbollah. Reagan desperately wanted the seven captives freed and didn't care how it happened. As one senior government official who served under four Republican presidents said, "President Reagan imposed his will on issues that he cared about."[160]

The second part of the scandal was the secret transfer of funds from US weapons sales in the Middle East to the Nicaraguan Contra rebels for use in the fight against their country's socialist government. Leading this effort were Marine Corps Lt. Col. Oliver North and Vice Adm. John Poindexter. North, Poindexter, and several other middlemen—including Maj. Gen. Richard Secord, Secord's Iranian business partner Albert Hakim, Israeli counterterrorism expert Amiram Nir, Saudi moneyman Adnan Khashoggi, exiled Iranian arms dealer Manucher Ghorbanifar, and Maj. Gen. John K. Singlaub—had diverted the proceeds from the Iranian weapons sales to support the Contras. When attorney general Edwin Meese found out on November 25 that the funds from arms sales had been diverted to support the Contras, he had North fired, and Poindexter submitted his resignation.[161] Again, the president had wanted to help the Contras, and he didn't especially care how it was done.

The scandal revealed an NSC process that was out of control—at least out of the control of Secretary of State George Shultz and Secretary of Defense Caspar Weinberger. Reagan delegated operational control to his national security advisor and the NSC staff instead, thereby bypassing the State Department, the Defense Department, the CIA—although not DCI William J. Casey—and other departments and agencies. Since neither the national security advisor nor the NSC staff was subject to congressional oversight, the White House was able to hide its actions from Congress— which was important in this case, because Congress had earlier passed the Boland Amendments, which prohibited any US government agency from providing aid to the Nicaraguan Contras.

Members of Congress and journalists excoriated Reagan upon learn-ing the news. In substantive terms, both components of Iran-Contra were worse than the burglary of the Democratic National Party headquarters that launched the Watergate scandal. The arms-for-hostages deal also directly contradicted the president's own stated position during the 1980 campaign that the US government would never negotiate with kidnappers, terrorists, or any others who tried to hold the United States hostage. The criticism reached a crescendo immediately after Reagan's disastrous news conference of November 19, 1986, in which the president appeared "nervous [and] bumbling, got his facts wrong and contradicted information that had al-ready been acknowledged in the press," in Bud McFarlane's description, "but still refused to admit that a mistake had been made."[162]

The Iran-Contra scandal renewed talk about presidential impeachment, angered members of Congress on both sides of the aisle, brought the White House's legislative program to a standstill, and disillusioned the American public once again. The Reagan administration seemed to be turning back the clock to the early 1970s, to the dark days of Vietnam, Cambodia, and Watergate. Reagan's job approval rating dropped twenty-one points in just a month, the sharpest one-month decline in the history of presidential poll-ing dating back to 1936—even worse than the drop in President Ford's approval rating following the Nixon pardon.[163]

The Reagan administration had "a Watergate-type problem," said Don-ald Regan, White House chief of staff. But with polls in late 1986 showing that 59 percent of Americans still trusted the president and that fewer than one in ten respondents identified Iran-Contra as the United States' most important issue, Reagan's political advisers figured the best strategy was to put the scandal "beside" them, in the words of W. Dennis Thomas, the deputy chief of staff—they wanted to stay abreast of Iran-Contra, even if they couldn't get ahead of the problem. And the best way to do this was to go on the offensive.

So in late November, the White House set up an internal group for handling its strategy on Iran-Contra, with David Abshire, who was the president's special counselor, responsible for "all aspects of the Iran matter." The White House also coordinated its efforts with sympathetic members of Congress, fellow Republicans, and political allies across the country, asking them to speak out in support of the administration, talk to their members and constituents, and write op-eds for major news publications.[164]

Separately, the president tried to limit the damage by appointing Frank Carlucci as the new national security advisor in December 1986 (deputy national security advisor Alton G. Keel Jr., a former assistant secretary of the Air Force, had filled in as acting national security advisor between November 25 and December 2). William Webster then took over as DCI in January 1987, following Casey's death in December.

But the biggest step the president took to stanch the hemorrhaging was to sign executive order 12575 on December 1, 1986, creating the President's Special Review Board.[165]

At the press conference announcing the board, Reagan told the reporters he wanted "all the facts to come out."[166] However, that was not what the executive order specified. It actually defined the board's authority quite narrowly, to "conduct a comprehensive study of the future role and procedures of the National Security Council (NSC) staff in the development, coordination, oversight, and conduct of foreign and national security policy." In particular, it was to "review the NSC staff's proper role in operational activities, especially extremely sensitive diplomatic, military, and intelligence missions." The board was then to "provide recommendations to the President based upon its analysis of the manner in which foreign and national security policies established by the President have been implemented by the NSC staff." And this was what Chief of Staff Regan told the board's members: that he hoped they "would take particular care to look into the question of whether and under what circumstances the National Security Council staff was and should be directly involved in the operational aspects of sensitive diplomatic, military, or intelligence missions, such as the [terrorist hijackings of the cruise ship] *Achille Lauro* [and] TWA [flight 847], and Grenada and Iran."[167] The text of the executive order said nothing about assigning responsibility or taking legal action, and in his press conference announcing the formation of the board, President Reagan never elaborated on what he meant by having "all the facts come out." And he never said that the board was to determine legality or assign responsibility.[168]

Donald Regan wanted a commission with just three members, feeling this would facilitate quicker action and minimize the chance that the board would produce a divided report. Furthermore, since there were few prominent public figures who were at once familiar with the national security process, acceptable to key members of Congress, available on short notice, and perceived as being political responsible, it would be easier to find members for a small commission.[169]

Regan and his aides chose former Republican senator John Tower of Texas as the board's chairman. Tower, who had retired from the Senate in 1984, had been chairman of the Senate Armed Services Committee from 1981 to 1984 and had previously served under Reagan as an arms control negotiator. At the time, he was working as a defense consultant, serving on the boards of three defense industry companies, and teaching part-time. The White House also suggested former Democratic senator Edmund Muskie, who had been chairman of the Senate Budget Committee from 1973 to 1981, a vice presidential candidate in 1968, a presidential candidate in 1972, and (briefly) Jimmy Carter's secretary of state. Brent Scowcroft was to be the board's third member. Each member of the bipartisan group had extensive experience in different aspects of national security and brought different perspectives to the board. If the president was serious about "turning to outside advice" in order to regroup for his last two years in office, the *Washington Post* editorialized, then he had "the right men."[170]

Scowcroft admitted he wasn't very excited about being asked to serve on the Tower Commission (as it became known), considering the seriousness of the task and the amount of work that the group would face.[171] But the Iran-Contra scandal threatened to destroy the legitimacy of the national security advisor position and the whole NSC process, which struck a nerve with Scowcroft, and he was more than willing to help out on an issue of such central importance to him. Furthermore, Scowcroft believed he "knew as much about the NSC system as anyone" and had already developed his own positions on covert operations and the NSC process more generally. For example, he'd previously spoken out against the CIA's mining of Nicaraguan harbors and said that he thought the secret operations were "hurting the CIA." He also regarded the appointment as an honor.[172]

The fact that he would be put in a position to examine the actions of former colleagues and friends didn't bother him, he said, since "I had no idea what had happened." The prospect of investigating Bud McFarlane—a man to whom he had been a mentor, someone whom he liked and respected, and who had been a "tremendous asset" as his right-hand man during the Nixon and Ford administrations—didn't affect his decision.[173]

The two men had remained close throughout the Reagan years. McFarlane had recommended that Reagan replace Richard Allen as national security advisor with Scowcroft, and later urged his appointment as chair of the

President's Commission on Strategic Forces.[174] And when the Iran-Contra story first broke, Scowcroft had phoned McFarlane to warn him that Don Regan was suggesting to reporters that the whole affair was his doing. "Regan is hanging you out to dry," Scowcroft told his friend—something McFarlane, who called Regan his "nemesis," also suspected.[175]

Scowcroft was also close to Vice President George Bush, his former colleague and good friend.[176] But although Bush had picked intelligence as one of his areas of specialization and attended the White House NSC meetings as a matter of course, Scowcroft said he wasn't concerned about Bush's role.[177] Part of the reason was that it wasn't clear that the vice president was in a decision-making position or part of the operational chain of command. In any case, as of late 1986, few people had any idea of even the basic contours of the Iran-Contra affair—Scowcroft, Muskie, and Tower certainly didn't—and those who did know weren't telling.

So Scowcroft compartmentalized, just as he had done throughout his career, separating his personal relationships from his official duties on the Tower Commission.

The commission and its twenty-three-person staff began their investigation on December 1, 1986, borrowing a small suite of offices on the fifth floor of the New Executive Office Building, immediately west of the White House and on the other side of Seventeenth Street.

Tower, Muskie, and Scowcroft quickly decided to go beyond their explicit mandate and interpret their mission more broadly than stated in the president's executive order. They would "find out what had happened and why." And while they agreed that they weren't going to assign "blame or innocence," they did tell the members of their staff "to lay out *all* the facts."[178] The board therefore began to sort through the "shopping carts" full of documents brought over from the NSC offices and the White House and to interview those who were involved. Thanks to a tech-savvy staff member, the commission was also able to recover deleted e-mails in the NSC's mainframe computer. In the end, they would talk to more than fifty officials, including McFarlane, who by then was at Bethesda Naval Hospital recovering from a Valium overdose—an attempted suicide.

One set of interviews was with former national security advisors, former directors of central intelligence, and other former top officials—the "Wise Men," as Scowcroft called them. The goal was to glean lessons from past crises that might help reveal how the NSC process should best be organized for handling sensitive issues.[179] The other set of interviews was with individuals directly involved in Iran-Contra. Tower, Muskie, and Scowcroft therefore

interviewed President Reagan, Shultz, Weinberger, Bush, Regan, McFarlane, Richard Armitage, and others to find out exactly what had happened
and why. The Tower Commission's legal counsel, Clark McFadden, usually
led off the questioning, with Tower, Scowcroft, and Muskie participating
almost equally.[180]

Much of their time was spent simply trying to reconstruct a day-to-day
chronology of the confusing set of events, a harder task than it might seem
because of the many months that "The Enterprise"—Richard Secord's
name for the operation—was in operation, the several countries involved,
and the many participants. With four large file cabinets of documents to
sort through, Tower, Muskie, and Scowcroft divided their responsibilities.
Tower researched the political dynamics of the participants in the deals and
determined the cause-and-effect relationships. Muskie looked at the legal
implications of Iran-Contra. And Scowcroft analyzed the NSC process.

Making their job tougher still was the fact that there wasn't any previous
investigation of Iran-Contra to build upon. Although the FBI, the independent special prosecutor Lawrence Walsh, and David Abshire were each
conducting their own investigations, none of them would share what they
knew with the Tower Board.[181]

Notwithstanding the pressure on Tower, Scowcroft, Muskie, and
their staff and the intense workweeks, the board functioned remarkably
smoothly. Although they initially had some "sharp disagreements," Scowcroft said, and although Scowcroft experienced Muskie's "famous temper,"
the three developed a surprisingly collegial and cordial relationship. Tower
and Muskie were initially wary of each other, each believing the other to be
a strong partisan, but they soon came to have an easy relationship.

Neither man was worried about political bias on Scowcroft's part. Scowcroft had known Tower, a fellow Republican and conservative on defense
issues, from his work on the Scowcroft Commission and found him to be
a considerate chairman. He wasn't "impetuous or opinionated," Scowcroft
said, but "thoughtful and judicious" and an "upstanding human being."
He became a "good friend."[182] Scowcroft had more doubts about Muskie,
who'd been a member of the Democratic Congresses of the early 1970s. He
was concerned that the former Maine senator might be impetuous or opinionated, but he discovered that the opposite was the truth. Over the course
of their long hours spent working together, he found Muskie to be serious,
judicious, kind, and an "outstanding human being." The two men grew to
be quite close, helped by the fact Scowcroft gave Muskie a ride home each
day. Not once could Scowcroft recall an occasion when the three of them

couldn't reach an agreement on how to proceed or on what they should conclude.[183]

The fact that the members of the board worked well together didn't lessen their workload. Not only were there the file cabinets full of papers to sort through, but their inquiries were hindered by the fact that Oliver North, John Poindexter, Richard Secord, and several others refused to be interviewed. Unbeknownst to Scowcroft and Muskie, Tower, as chairman, came under particular stress. White House officials—Tower doesn't name names in his autobiography, although Don Regan or someone on his staff was probably involved—pressured Tower to ignore the president's initial statement of January 26, 1987, in which Reagan plainly and directly admitted that he had approved of the arms-for-hostages deal, warning Tower that the commission's findings would have both political and personal ramifications for him.[184]

Seeking to understand the historical role of the national security advisor and the NSC process, the three board members had outside experts draft case histories on the lessons learned from important events in the history of national security, such as the U-2 crisis of 1960, the 1961 Bay of Pigs debacle, the 1962 Cuban missile crisis, the secret bombing of Cambodia in 1969–1970, the seizure of the *Mayaguez* in 1975, and the fall of the shah of Iran in 1979.[185] They also questioned the Wise Men about their thoughts on the Iran-Contra affair, on the role of the national security advisor and the NSC in the national security policy process (including operations), on interagency relations, on institutional memory across presidential administrations, on secrecy, on congressional participation in national security policy, and on other topics. Because they were interested in practical experience, they didn't consult academic studies about the organization of national security or the presidency.[186]

The board and their staff worked seven days a week, including many "eighteen-and twenty-hour marathons" fueled by pizza, fast food, and Chinese carryout. Tower twice asked President Reagan for two-week extensions; both were granted. The board and the staff also moved into the Old Executive Office Building (now the Eisenhower Executive Office Building) so that Stephen Hadley and Nicholas Rostow, who were drafting most of the report, would have better locations in which to write. Hadley, an attorney by training, drafted the introduction, overview, conclusions, and recommendations; Rostow, also an attorney and the son of Eugene Rostow (an under secretary of state in the Johnson administration), composed the blow-by-blow chronological narrative.[187]

Tower, Muskie, and Scowcroft released the 550-page Tower Commission report on Thursday, February 26, 1987, eleven weeks after they'd started. Before releasing the report, Tower called Abshire and told him that the three of them wanted to brief the president personally before the report went public—without having to go through Chief of Staff Regan. So at 3:00 P.M. on Wednesday, February 25, Tower, Muskie, and Scowcroft went over to the White House, and Scowcroft explained to the president why the three of them had reached the conclusion that the White House had in fact been dealing arms for hostages. Reagan "appeared to have accepted the reality" of Iran-Contra, Scowcroft, Tower, and Abshire all agreed; they thought it had been a good meeting.[188]

A few days later, Tower secretly helped White House officials—along with Nancy Reagan—draft the president's national address of March 4, which was to be a response to the commission's report. Remarkably, it was Tower himself, journalist Lou Cannon reports, who convinced a reluctant Reagan to admit his wrongdoing. "A few months ago I told the American people I did not trade arms for hostages," the president said on national television. "My heart and my best intentions still tell me that's true, but the facts and the evidence tell me it is not. As the Tower Board reported, what began as a strategic opening to Iran deteriorated, in its implementation, into trading for hostages. This runs counter to my own beliefs," he admitted, "to administration policy, and to the original strategy we had in mind. There are reasons why it happened, but there are no excuses. It was a mistake."[189]

What Reagan did *not* include in the speech is also revealing. Shultz and Weinberger both requested that the president insert text in the speech challenging the Tower Commission's findings; they wanted Reagan to say that both officials "vigorously opposed the arms sales to Iran and they so advised me several times." But Howard Baker, the new chief of staff, and Vice President Bush strongly disagreed with inserting the proposed text, and Baker, along with Stu Spencer and others, persuaded Reagan to accept the commission's report unconditionally.

The speech was well received. "President Reagan gave the right speech last night," the *Washington Post* editorialized the next day.[190]

———

THE TOWER COMMISSION'S report was an indictment of the Reagan presidency. The commission determined that the president had agreed to secure the release of the American hostages being held in Lebanon and that he appeared "to have proceeded with a concept of the initiative that was not accurately reflected in the reality of the operation." Although the president's delegation of policy making was justified, he hadn't taken the critical step of ensuring accountability for what turned out to be a complex, "high stakes" operation, the board found. Neither had he conducted a critical performance review of the operations.

Nor had chief of staff Don Regan, national security advisors McFarlane and Poindexter, and other White House officials lived up to the president's trust. Worse yet, the two most senior and most important cabinet members, the secretary of state and the secretary of defense, knew what happening but looked the other way. Although both men expressed their opposition to the arms-for-hostages deal—and later the diversion of weapons sales to the Contras—they didn't go any further. After the December 7, 1985, meeting in which Reagan and his top advisers discussed the hostage situation in Lebanon, Weinberger said he thought that Shultz's and his arguments against the proposed operations had "strangled the baby in the cradle." But the two men didn't insist on discipline within the NSC process or on the accountability of national security policy, and they distanced themselves from the unfolding events. Instead, DCI William Casey, who played a "highly significant" role, encouraged Colonel North to take on "direct operational control," McFarlane reported.[191]

"What happened," Scowcroft told the press, was "that the system did not compensate for the management style of the President." Reagan "perhaps did not ask enough questions," he conceded, "but it was incumbent upon other participants in the system to insure that the president was absolutely clear about what was going on. There should have been bells ringing, lights flashing, and so on." The president, the board concluded, had been betrayed by his top advisers and his NSC staff—all of whom should have known better.[192]

Scowcroft himself drafted the section of the report that directly addressed the board's mandate. He found that the national security policy-making process had become dysfunctional. The Reagan administration had no set process in place for deciding and conducting national security policy, nor had the president and his several national security advisors coordinated the administration's foreign policy across the State Department, Defense Department, and other relevant departments and agencies.

Scowcroft then specifically addressed the role of the national security advisor and NSC staff in making US foreign policy. The essential quality of the national security process, in his analysis, was its fundamental dependence on the president. The role of the NSC, after all, is purely advisory;

the NSC principals meet as advisers to the president, not as representatives of their particular offices or departments or as advocates of particular policy or partisan positions. The president decides the role he wants the NSC to play in making US policy and how he wants to organize the NSC process.

The ability of the national security advisor to manage national security policy accordingly depends on his or her relationship with the president, on the other NSC principals, and on the departmental and agency heads involved in particular issues. The national security advisor does more than manage policy formation and oversee its implementation, however. He or she also has to advise the president on a regular basis. In this capacity, the national security advisor is in a unique position, since the occupant of the post is not subject to Senate confirmation and has no department or agency to defend. The national security advisor cannot overshadow the other foreign policy principals or exclude them from the policy-making process—but to be effective, he or she can't be subordinate to them, either.

Scowcroft recommended that NSC staff members be drawn from both within and outside the US government and that they reflect a balanced selection of officials from the various departments and agencies relevant to national security affairs, just so long as there are clear vertical lines of authority and individual staff members are held accountable. Scowcroft reasoned that the small size of the NSC staff allows it to be particularly flexible and therefore effective.

Thus, Scowcroft defended the latitude and discretion afforded by the NSC system, even as he strongly criticized the performance of the NSC process under President Reagan. He argued that to introduce new rules for the NSC system or rewrite the National Security Act would destroy the very flexibility that had served US presidents well from Eisenhower on.[193]

Scowcroft concluded that it was incumbent on presidents and national security advisors to make the NSC system work as it was supposed to. He proposed no changes to the National Security Act of 1947 and recommended that the national security advisor continue to be free of Senate confirmation. Other recommendations were that the national security advisor serve as chair of senior interagency committees, that the national security advisor formulate precise procedures for the handling of covert actions, that the role of the NSC's legal counsel be strengthened and enhanced, and that as little policy as possible be accomplished through intermediaries—whether private-sector contractors, other non-US-government personnel, or foreign nationals. Thus, neither Scowcroft nor the board used the Iran-Contra scandal as an occasion to criticize or amend the National Security Act of 1947. Instead, they reaffirmed the fundamental merits of the NSC system.

Although there had been other mishandled crises and botched operations in the recent history of the United States, the Tower Commission was the first government panel to undertake a comprehensive review of the institutions established under the National Security Act. Scowcroft's assessment of the NSC system amounted to a cautious and measured response to the Iran-Contra scandal.[194] For Stephen Hadley, the report was "Brent's view . . . of how the national security advisor should do it." And what the Tower board recommended was Scowcroft's interpretation of the role of the national security advisor and the NSC. "It's what he did for Ford," Hadley said, "and it's what he did for Bush 41. And I think it has become the starting point for every national security advisor. This really is how it ought to work. And if you're going to depart from this model, you better have a pretty good reason, because this is the one that works best."[195]

When he spoke to the Tower Commission, Kissinger essentially endorsed Scowcroft's vision of the role of the national security advisor: "While I cannot say I was overjoyed when President Ford decided to separate the two functions [of secretary of state and national security advisor], it was a good decision and it worked ideally. With Scowcroft as Security Advisor and me as Secretary of State we had what I consider the nearly ideal arrangement. A White House staff, NSC or otherwise, has an important choice," he said. "Do they want to utilize the psychology of the President or do they want to compensate for it? I think their duty is to compensate for it. If you know that here's a President who is given to flighty actions or intuitive actions, it is your duty to make him sit down and think about it. If he is an excessive worrier, then your duty is to show him the opportunities."[196]

These were Scowcroft's views as well. Scowcroft was "keenly focused" on saving the NSC system and on preserving the national security advisor position, Stephen Hadley commented in an interview.[197] He accomplished both goals.

The press liked the report. "Without question, the week's most gripping reading is the Tower commission's report on the National Security Council," the *Cleveland Plain-Dealer* editorialized. "A product of remarkable skill and objectivity, the document exposes the NSC and its staff as rogue policymakers." Other journalists and members of the public praised the commission's report for its comprehensiveness, straightforwardness, and well-stated criticisms of the national security advisors, the NSC system, and President Reagan. "Scowcroft and his colleagues have shown an admirable sense of contempt and outrage for an 'unprofessional' operation and a clumsy attempt to cover it up in the White House," the *Boston Globe* editorialized. "President Reagan was 'poorly served,'" it concluded. And yet "Scowcroft and former Sens. John Tower and Edmund Muskie . . . also conclude that President Reagan himself, through a policy of selling arms to Iran, poorly served the country." The *Globe* recommended that the American public, members of Congress, White House officials, foreign governments, and "especially . . . young military officers who might think of circumventing a chain of command through 'cowboy' antics" give the report "the closest study."[198]

But in some ways the Tower Commission was business as usual. It accomplished what Washington commissions are supposed to do: it provided cover for a besieged Reagan presidency. Some thought the report whitewashed the whole affair, since it held Reagan responsible only for his inattention to foreign policy and poor management of national security issues. The *Washington Post*'s Walter Pincus, a longtime Washington national security correspondent who was especially critical of the Reagan administration, thought the board's agenda was essentially to take a look, but not too close a look, at the scandal and to "protect the president at a time when nobody wanted to go down [the impeachment] path again. You had a president who was popular more because he looked and sounded like a president than he was a president and they didn't want to endanger that."[199]

Vice President George Bush escaped the focus of the Tower Commission—and of the other investigations, for that matter—despite the fact that he was at several of the key Iran-Contra meetings (those of August 6, 1985, and January 7, 1986, for instance), that he was copied on the key memos, and that he traveled to the Middle East on behalf of the president for the purpose of getting the hostages released. Even though Bush had not been at the December 7, 1985, meeting, he was clearly in the loop. And he presumably could have resigned or threatened to resign had he felt it was necessary to bring attention to the gravity of what going on.[200] But as Pincus pointed out, "Nobody stood up and said 'Don't do that.'"[201] And that failure certainly extended to Bush.

Still, it's important to remember that the Tower Commission was never in a position to perform a comprehensive and thorough investigation, given the serious constraints it was operating under. With their harsh criticism of the NSC process under Reagan, Tower, Muskie, and Scowcroft probably went as far as they could—perhaps further than we might expect—in view of their mandate merely to examine the operation of the NSC. "The sad, shared secret of the Reagan White House," the *Washington Post*'s Lou Cannon writes, "was that no one in the presidential entourage had confidence in the judgment or capacities of the president," with the result that the president's aides "did not hesitate to manipulate him."[202] The Tower report helped to show how that manipulation happened.

Another of the Tower board's constraints was its lack of authority to sub-poena witnesses and take sworn testimony (in contrast to the special pros-ecutor and the House and Senate committees investigating Iran-Contra). Tower, Muskie, and Scowcroft could only *request* interviews with people of interest. And if interviewees chose to lie—the president contradicted his statement of January 26, for instance, and McFarlane changed his story three times—the Tower group had no legal sanctions that it could impose. Neither would the president use his power as commander in chief to order Colonel North or Admiral Poindexter to testify before the board.[203]

A third constraint was the tight schedule. With only sixty days to issue its report—later extended by four weeks—the board didn't have much time considering the scale and intricacies of the Iran-Contra affair. By compari-son, the congressional investigation had almost a year to complete its study, and Lawrence Walsh had several years to conduct his investigation.[204] Un-der the circumstances, it's little wonder Tower, Muskie, Scowcroft, and their staff didn't uncover the whole story of the Iran-Contra affair, and that investigative journalists, historians, and other writers were later able to pro-duce more comprehensive analyses.

Scowcroft emphasized that the three of them and their staff had written an "honest report." But he said he doubted that the whole truth about the Iran-Contra affair would ever come out. Arthur Liman, the counsel for the Senate investigation of the Iran-Contra affair, also believed that "there was much the Tower Commission never found out" and that "great gaps re-mained in the story" because of the White House's lack of cooperation and the death of William Casey. "Still," Liman said, "within its limitations, the commission did a remarkable job of rescuing and putting together all the documents that had survived shredding by the NSC staff."[205]

Looking back, Scowcroft presumed that Reagan had given his approval of the NSC's rogue operations, but he, Tower, and Muskie couldn't find definitive proof of that. McFarlane's statements and Reagan's inconsistent and contradictory answers to the board's questions weren't enough. With-out testimony from multiple witnesses, an audio recording of Reagan's ap-proval, or a signed presidential finding, there was no smoking gun.[206]

In retrospect, however, there is no doubt President Reagan ordered and approved of the arms-for-hostages swap and the diversion of funds to the Contras, as Reagan admitted in his first interview with the Tower Commis-sion. In fact, the two actions were "intertwined" and constituted "a single continuum of cover foreign-policy actions," as journalists Murray Waas and Craig Unger observed. It is almost certain, too, that there *had* been a signed presidential finding authorizing the operations and that Poindexter had destroyed it. Tower, Muskie, and Scowcroft suspected as much, Nicholas Rostow reports, but they had no proof.[207] Without the irrefutable evidence and with the doubt caused by Reagan's apparently confused mind—very possibly a result of the early stages of Alzheimer's disease—Tower, Muskie, and Scowcroft had no real choice except to give the president the benefit of the doubt.

To Richard Secord, Michael Ledeen, and others, it understandably appeared as though the commission members went "easy" on Reagan.[208] Yet it's noteworthy that the longer and more comprehensive investigations by the House and Senate special committee and by the special prosecutor were also unable to definitively assign responsibility to Reagan.

Navy Cmdr. Paul B. Thompson, a lawyer on Reagan's NSC staff and an active participant in Iran-Contra—he told Rostow he was "the one person who represents the whole story"—had a different criticism. He characterized Tower, Muskie, and Scowcroft as focusing narrowly on the lack of professionalism of the president's advisers and believing merely that things had gone "too far." Thompson saw Scowcroft as a "plain vanilla bureaucrat," someone devoted simply to upholding the existing political system rather than probing its flaws.[209]

Scowcroft was never merely a "plain vanilla bureaucrat," of course, but it's certainly true that he *was* dedicated to upholding the 1947 National Security Act and to preserving presidential power. The Tower Commission's report didn't "ultimately question either the wisdom or the constitutionality of unrestrained executive discretion in national security affairs," as law professor Harold Hongju Koh writes in his critical overview of the Iran-Contra affair. On the contrary, the board reaffirmed the president's command of the national security process, as Koh points out, and sought to have the national security advisor play an even stronger, more definitive role in the making and implementation of US foreign policy.[210]

An incident recounted by former *Newsweek* reporter Robert Parry is suggestive of Scowcroft's position. On March 10, 1987, Parry attended a dinner party hosted by Evan Thomas, then *Newsweek*'s Washington bureau chief. During the dinner, "the soft-spoken" Scowcroft mused, "I probably shouldn't say this, but if I were advising Admiral Poindexter and he had told the President about the diversion [of funds from the Iranian weapons sales to the Contras], I would advise him to say that he hadn't." Parry was "startled" by Scowcroft's statement and inferred that he "really wasn't interested in the truth." He "stopped eating and asked Scowcroft if he understood the implication of his remark. 'General,' I said, 'you're not suggesting that the admiral should commit perjury, are you?' There was a brief silence around the table, as if I had committed some social faux pas." *Newsweek* editor Maynard Parker then loudly declared, "Sometimes, you have to do what's good for the country." After brief laughter, Parry writes, the awkwardness passed.[211]

It might seem surprising that one former national security advisor would advise another to lie. But Scowcroft would consider such surprise naive. He wasn't so much condoning perjury as advising that presidential aides act to uphold the institutions of government. According to this view, it would be disloyal for a national security advisor *not* to withhold the truth, if by so doing he or she could save the president from potential disaster. For Scowcroft, duty came first: duty to the president and to the government of the United States—especially at a time when there were calls for Reagan's impeachment and the possibility of another governmental and constitutional crisis. This was also Pincus's analysis: "The game was to protect the president."[212]

Poindexter would later admit that Reagan knew of the arms-for-hostages deal. "I can remember pretty clearly what [the president] said" at the December 7 meeting in the White House residence, Poindexter told the Senate Select Committee in the spring of 1987. The president "pulled up a stool. He was sitting there and very thoughtful. He said, 'Gentleman, I think we ought to go ahead. . . . As far as the hostages are concerned, I just couldn't sleep if we didn't pursue every possibility.' He—again, contrary to some of the reports—he clearly understood the sensitive public aspects of this." Poindexter recalled that Reagan then said words to the effect of "If we succeed in this, we will all be heroes; if we don't, it will be very difficult." But Poindexter would deny the president knew of the transfer of funds to the Contras and claim that he'd done everything on his own authority as national security advisor.[213]

The Tower Commission wasn't very successful at damage control. The House and Senate committees uncovered additional information, and the Walsh investigation continued throughout Bush's presidency. On December 24, 1992, less than two weeks before Caspar Weinberger was to testify at his own trial and fewer than four weeks before Bill Clinton assumed office, Bush pardoned Weinberger, McFarlane, Elliott Abrams, and three CIA officers, all of whom had been indicted for lying under oath to Congress in their Iran-Contra testimony. Defense secretary Dick Cheney, Vice President Dan Quayle, treasury secretary Nicholas Brady, and other advisers recommended that Bush issue the last-minute pardons; Scowcroft and Baker argued against the pardons. The pardons exonerated the very individuals who could have implicated Bush in the Iran-Contra affair. And because there would now be no trial, Bush's diaries wouldn't be made public, and neither would any other documentation that could have pointed to his involvement in Iran-Contra. The pardons triggered an onslaught of protests from members of Congress and political correspondents, with some charging that Bush had subverted justice.

The following summer, in August 1993, the special prosecutor issued his report on Iran-Contra. Walsh reported that McFarlane and North had been made scapegoats for their bosses within the administration and that Shultz and Weinberger had "lied or downplayed their roles and their awareness of the affair." Furthermore, General Colin Powell, Weinberger's assistant at the time—and one of those the Tower board didn't interview— almost certainly knew of the thirty to forty notepads on Iran-Contra that the defense secretary kept in his desk drawer. Powell also had to know of the arms-for-hostages deal and the diversion of profits from weapons sales to the Contras, since the TOW missiles being transferred to the CIA came from Army supply accounts.[214] Walsh wrote of President Reagan's and Vice President Bush's complicity in Iran-Contra, too, but he didn't charge either official with any criminal wrongdoing.[215]

The later investigations revealed aspects of Iran-Contra that the Tower Commission did not uncover, to be sure. But the board's purpose *wasn't* to be dispositive and put all the other investigations to rest, as the political scientist Kenneth Kitts points out. Rather, its purpose was to present the Reagan presidency and the Iran-Contra affair in as favorable a light as possible—to influence subsequent thinking about Iran-Contra and limit the damage.[216]

A "commission's job is to purge the system," Hadley observed. Hadley remembers John Tower saying at one point, "Look, our job is to give the President of the United States a punch in the stomach. And we're going to say it was arms for hostages, and you shouldn't have done it. It was wrong."[217] This is exactly what the Tower Commission concluded.

In the end, the president got off the hook. Vice President Bush would be able to run successfully for president, despite his knowledge of and apparent support for the Iran-Contra operations.[218] And—rightly or wrongly—the Reagan presidency would come to be perceived as one of the most popular and successful presidencies in American history, with the Iran-Contra affair regarded as merely a long, unsavory footnote to the Reagan legacy.

For Scowcroft, the investigation affirmed the central importance of the national security advisor's role as an "honest broker," someone who would centralize, organize, and coordinate information bearing on US foreign policy—not a policy entrepreneur or the president's personal agent, operating beyond the reach of the other foreign policy principals and congressional leaders. But Scowcroft still wanted the national security advisor to be able to serve as the president's special diplomatic agent and not be subject to Senate confirmation. Otherwise, he said, "the NSC becomes useless."[219]

One of the board's most troubling findings, in Scowcroft's view, was that the CIA appeared to have allowed its intelligence analysis to be influenced by the NSC's goals, thereby compromising the integrity of the NSC process. Tower, Muskie, and Scowcroft saw evidence that CIA officials had made intelligence analysis and policy recommendations, specifically "a revised Special National Intelligence Estimate on Iran in May 1985," in response to "pressure from members of the National Security Council." There had been "close coordination between the NSC and the writing of the revised estimate," Scowcroft told the *New York Times*. He added, "You don't want cooked intelligence," using a phrase that would later resonate in the debate over the 2003 invasion of Iraq. The head of the CIA's directorate of intelligence analysis at the time was none other than Robert Gates.[220]

Scowcroft's work on the President's Special Review Board had given him a practical opportunity to research and reflect on the role of the NSC and the national security director in the larger foreign policy process. He emerged from the assignment with a clear notion of how that process ought to work for the benefit of the president's administration and the nation. Twenty months later, beginning on January 20, 1989, Scowcroft would have the opportunity to put his ideas into practice.

Job Pingree (far right, no. 8), Brent Scowcroft's great-grandfather, in the Utah Penitentiary with fellow Mormons swept up in a "polyg hunt" organized by US marshals (August 12, 1885).

By 1920, the huge Scowcroft & Sons warehouse was the centerpiece of the largest dry goods and clothing wholesaler between St. Louis and San Francisco. COURTESY SPECIAL COLLECTIONS DEPARTMENT, STEWART LIBRARY, WEBER STATE UNIVERSITY

Scowcroft & Sons delivery trucks like this one delivered household wares to retailers throughout booming Ogden, Utah. OGDEN UNION STATION COLLECTION

Lucile Ballantyne Scowcroft, Brent's
mother COURTESY BRENT SCOWCROFT

Lancaster, the John Scowcroft family home,
built in 1893 COURTESY SPECIAL COLLECTIONS
DEPARTMENT, STEWART LIBRARY, WEBER STATE
UNIVERSITY

Undated photo of Brent Scowcroft as a boy
COURTESY BRENT SCOWCROFT

James Scowcroft, Brent's father, as a
young man COURTESY BRENT SCOWCROFT

Baseball, track meets, and Boy Scout expeditions like the one shown here were all part of young Brent Scowcroft's classic American boyhood. COURTESY BRENT SCOWCROFT

The aspiring pilot (seated second from left) with other members of the 82nd Squadron at Grenier Air Field (1948) COURTESY TOM HILDRETH, DAVE MCLAREN, AND LT. COL. O'DONNELL

Marian "Jackie" Horner, the pretty young nurse Brent Scowcroft met at Valley Forge Army Hospital—and later married. COURTESY BRENT SCOWCROFT

This near-fatal crash in a training flight in New Hampshire abruptly ended Scowcroft's career as a pilot. MANCHESTER *UNION LEADER*, JAN. 7, 1949, CITY EDITION, P. 2, OFFICIAL AIR FORCE PHOTO, COURTESY MANCHESTER *UNION LEADER* AND MANCHESTER CITY LIBRARY

Scowcroft's accident came as he piloted a P-51H fighter plane like this one, the fastest of the North American Aviation Mustangs. COURTESY TOM HILDRETH, DAVE MCLAREN, AND LT. COL. O'DONNELL

National security advisor: Scowcroft with President Ford, Henry Kissinger, William Simon, and Ron Nessen en route to the International Economic Summit in Rambouilllet, France, November 17, 1975 COURTESY GERALD R. FORD PRESIDENTIAL LIBRARY

Major General/Deputy Assistant to President Nixon
COURTESY RICHARD NIXON PRESIDENTIAL LIBRARY & MUSEUM

With CIA director William Colby and Vice President Nelson Rockefeller in the Cabinet Room at the White House (April 24, 1975) COURTESY GERALD R. FORD PRESIDENTIAL LIBRARY

With Kissinger, Donald Rumsfeld, and Jerald terHorst in the Scheduling and Advance Office COURTESY GERALD R. FORD PRESIDENTIAL LIBRARY

Scowcroft confers with Kissinger during a meeting on the seizure of the SS *Mayaguez* (May 14, 1975). COURTESY GERALD R. FORD PRESIDENTIAL LIBRARY

Dealing with refugees like those crowded on this boat was one of the major challenges Scowcroft took on while managing the American departure from Vietnam (April 3, 1975).
COURTESY GERALD R. FORD PRESIDENTIAL LIBRARY

At an NSC meeting on the Beirut, Lebanon crisis (June 17, 1976)
COURTESY GERALD R. FORD PRESIDENTIAL LIBRARY

With Chairman Deng Xiaoping at the Peking Capital Airport (December 5, 1975)
COURTESY GERALD R. FORD PRESIDENTIAL LIBRARY

Listening to President Ford
during a news conference at
the White House East Room
(November 3, 1975)
ASSOCIATED PRESS WIREPHOTO

With William G. Hyland,
deputy assistant for national
security affairs, in Scowcroft's
White House office (June 19,
1976) COURTESY GERALD R.
FORD PRESIDENTIAL LIBRARY

Meeting of the National Security Council on the Beirut crisis—
Ford, Kissinger, William Clements, George H. W. Bush, L. Dean
Brown, John Marsh, Richard Cheney, George Brown, and Scowcroft
(June 17, 1976) COURTESY GERALD R. FORD PRESIDENTIAL LIBRARY

Fishing with the first President Bush from the *Fidelity* off the coast of Kennebunkport, Maine (August 28, 1989) GEORGE BUSH PRESIDENTIAL LIBRARY AND MUSEUM

With President Bush and Secretary of Defense Dick Cheney in the Oval Office (April 19, 1989) GEORGE BUSH PRESIDENTIAL LIBRARY AND MUSEUM

The daily NSC briefing with President Bush at Walker's Point, Kennebunkport, Maine (August 25, 1990) GEORGE BUSH PRESIDENTIAL LIBRARY AND MUSEUM

President Bush and Scowcroft on the phone with Secretary of State James Baker from the Oval Office Study; Governor John Sununu looks on (January 16, 1991). GEORGE BUSH PRESIDENTIAL LIBRARY AND MUSEUM

President and Mrs. Bush share a laugh with Scowcroft, Robert Gates, and Marlin Fitzwater in the Diplomatic Reception Room (June 20, 1991). GEORGE BUSH PRESIDENTIAL LIBRARY AND MUSEUM

Elder statesman: at the Munich Security Conference (February 2, 2013) COURTESY KÖRBER-STIFTUNG/MARC DARCHINGER

— PART IV —

The Bush Administration, 1989–1993

═══

The fine gentlemen of the bourgeois countries will never overthrow the rule of the workers which has been established in the socialist countries. They will never return to what has gone. It is now becoming increasingly clear that the rule of capitalism is coming to an end in other countries, too, and that capitalism is an outmoded system which is doomed to inexorable death. The future is ours.

—NIKITA KHRUSHCHEV, NOVEMBER 4, 1958

Future historians will find it hard to understand why the United States, with the world at its feet, did not seize the opportunity it had itself created to install a new world order.

—CLAUDE MONNIER,
LE MATIN DIMANCHE (LAUSANNE), MAY 28, 1991[1]

17

ORGANIZING SECURITY

WHEN GEORGE HERBERT Walker Bush was inaugurated on January 20, 1989, as the forty-first president of the United States, many observers assumed that he would more or less continue the policies of the eight years of the Reagan administration. Instead, Bush and his advisers took office with a chip on their shoulder. They were determined not to be seen as mere stand-ins for a third-term Reagan presidency.

Like most presidents and vice presidents, Reagan and Bush had never been especially close. Bush wasn't one of Reagan's longtime California friends, and he was never invited to the presidential residence during their eight years together. Neither did Bush have the deepest respect for Reagan; according to one published account, Bush viewed Reagan as "kind of foolish and simplistic on many issues," and as someone "who needed to be watched." So the transition from President Reagan to his former vice president may have been a "friendly takeover," but it was a takeover nonetheless.[2]

The newly appointed national security advisor, Brent Scowcroft, went out of his way to make that point abundantly clear. He told Reagan's national security advisor, General Colin Powell, to let everyone on the NSC staff know they shouldn't plan on staying in office.[3] The same went for other incumbent Reagan appointees. Scowcroft was at pains to demonstrate in "every way [he] could," he said, that it was a new administration.

George H. W. Bush's troubles with the Republican right started here, the historian Russell Riley suggests, with Bush's dismissive treatment of Reagan's appointees.[4] The transition struck some as abrupt. Defense secretary Frank Carlucci and Secretary of State George Shultz, for instance, both thought they and their colleagues had been dismissed harshly and treated callously without proper recognition of their contributions, given that Carlucci and Powell had revived the NSC process after six years of neglect by Richard Allen and his successors.[5]

For his part, Scowcroft hadn't appreciated Shultz's handling of the MX ICBM deal. For these and other reasons, Scowcroft, Bush, and Baker treated Shultz with "remarkable frostiness" over their four years in office— and "frosty doesn't begin to describe it," Elliott Abrams commented. "They completely excluded Shultz," even though he had served as President Reagan's secretary of state for six and a half years.[6]

The Bush team wanted to reevaluate thoroughly what Shultz had done. Just as with other presidential transitions, even intraparty transitions like Kennedy-Johnson or Roosevelt-Truman, the new administration wanted to establish its own brand. So almost immediately after taking office, Scowcroft directed the Department of State, the Department of Defense, the CIA, and other relevant agencies to conduct thorough, independent reviews of US policies with respect to strategic weapons, arms control, conventional forces, economics, human rights, and areas such as South Asia, Arab-Israeli relations, the Persian Gulf, among others—especially the Soviet Union and the Cold War.

Little did anyone know that 1989 would turn out to be an extraordinary year in world history. If someone on the twentieth of January, 1989, had predicted that in just one year all of Eastern Europe would be liberated and the Warsaw Pact would be obsolete, Robert Gates later remarked, that "person would have been confined to a loony bin."[7] The fast-moving events in Poland, Hungary, and East Germany, the progress in arms control, and the growing economic and financial challenges facing the Soviet Union created their own momentum, culminating in the fall of the Berlin Wall on November 9, 1989. Germany reunited less than a year later, and by Christmas Day, 1991, the Soviet Union no longer existed. But these events were still in the unforeseeable future when George Bush and his team set about making plans for a fresh approach to foreign affairs during the 1988–1989 presidential interregnum.

Bush began by assembling a high-powered team. His first action as president-elect, announced on November 8, 1988, the day after his election, was to choose Thomas Pickering as the UN ambassador, thus signaling the value the new administration placed on the United Nations and career foreign service officers.[8]

At the same time, he named James A. Baker III his secretary of state. Baker had been a US Marine, was an extraordinarily able and successful attorney, had managed Ford's election campaign in 1976 and President Ronald Reagan's reelection campaign in 1984, and had served as the White House chief of staff and then as secretary of the treasury under Reagan. He'd been a close friend of George Bush's for thirty years, ever since Bush had moved from Midland to Houston. Baker had been Bush's campaign manager for his unsuccessful Senate bid in 1970, and Bush had been at Baker's side later when Baker's first wife died of cancer. Bush greatly appreciated Baker's toughness, determination, and competitiveness. Peter Rodman, an adviser to several presidents from Nixon to George W. Bush, called him the "most colorful" member of the Bush 41 administration and "the only larger than life personality in the cabinet."[9]

Bush and Baker had a relationship almost like that of brothers—including the competitiveness of brothers. When Baker became too self-assertive in the president's view, his friend would take him down a notch by asking, "If you're so smart, why aren't you president?"[10] The same sense of competitiveness may have underlain some of Bush's other appointments. He named John Sununu, a former governor of New Hampshire, as chief of staff, even though Craig L. Fuller had been the chief of staff on the 1988 presidential campaign and Baker had wanted him to have the job. The same logic may also help to explain why Bush chose Indiana senator J. Danforth Quayle, who wasn't among Baker's top choices, as his running mate.[11]

Dennis Ross, director of policy planning at the State Department, called Baker the best instinctive negotiator he'd ever known. "He also had that talent, as a negotiator, of knowing what counts for the interlocutor, what is the issue at the end, and why does it matter," Reginald Bartholomew, a top State Department official, said. "Baker commanded the issues, the essentials of the issues, he was dealing with." And although he wasn't a strategist in sense of a conceptualizer, he knew the importance of establishing priorities and setting strategy.[12] Robert Gates called Baker "a master craftsman of the persuasive and backroom arts at the peak of his powers," and although the two men would get cross-wise more than once, Gates "was glad [Baker] was on our side."[13]

Maureen Dowd and Thomas Friedman, who then covered the White House, offered a different perspective in an article in the *New York Times Magazine*:

> When you sit across from Baker, it is like looking at a length of black silk. There is stillness, as Baker holds you locked in his gaze and Southern Comfort voice, occasionally flashing a rather wintry smile. He controls the conversation with perfect sentences, perfect paragraphs and perfect pages. He shifts from on-the-record to off-the-record to background in a single thought. He has a compelling presence, but he is such a fox that you feel the impulse to check your wallet when you leave his office.[14]

Baker had "a deep fear of ridicule," Dowd and Friedman found. "[No] body got close to Baker," Lawrence Eagleburger said; there was part of him that was "not available, except perhaps to his wife." Bush, in contrast, was "willing to look a little foolish," would transparently reveal his annoyance or amusement, and was warm and spontaneous. Bush's wife, Barbara, did not especially take to Jim Baker.[15]

For his deputy secretary of state, Baker chose Eagleburger. Eagleburger would be the State Department's chief operating officer, the person responsible for managing day-to-day business and attending meetings if Baker were out of town. Eagleburger—who told the best jokes among Baker's top aides—also coordinated State Department operations with the White House and smoothed out any differences between the State Department and the NSC. Scowcroft recommended that Baker appoint Eagleburger, but he later said he was surprised Baker chose his close friend as his deputy, someone he regarded as Baker's equal on foreign policy issues.[16] That Baker would choose a career foreign service officer and a "Kissinger man" to this key position suggested the confidence Baker had in his own abilities and the trust he had in Scowcroft. Because of his relationship to Scowcroft, moreover, Eagleburger had a back channel to the president.

The Sunday after Thanksgiving, Bush asked Scowcroft to come down to the vice presidential residence for a morning cup of coffee with him and Baker. Bush then announced, "I'd like you to be my national security advisor." Although Scowcroft said at the time that he would have preferred to be secretary of defense—since he had already served as national security advisor and knew he didn't want to be the director of central intelligence—he readily agreed. Scowcroft later said he wasn't aware of all the "advantages" of being national security advisor, and that he subsequently came to appreciate how much influence he was able to have.[17]

Scowcroft had been doing a lot of thinking about the NSC process. During the first several years of the Reagan administration, the NSC had been riven by fierce turf battles and vicious personal politics—"a veritable nightmare," according to Brzezinski, or, as Baker described it, "a witches' brew of intrigue, elbows, egos, and separate agendas."[18] But once Frank Carlucci took over the national security advisor position from John M. Poindexter, the NSC process greatly improved. Carlucci removed the NSC staff members from operations, reduced their numbers by 60 percent, and restored the focus of foreign policy making to the State Department. Later, when Carlucci succeeded Caspar Weinberger as secretary of defense and Colin Powell took over as national security advisor, the two of them and secretary of state George Shultz started holding daily meetings at 7:00 A.M., without any aides or set agendas, so as to coordinate policy and crisis management.[19]

Powell and Scowcroft were in some ways very similar, in others very different. "Powell, like Carlucci and Brent Scowcroft, lived up to the classical model of the honest broker in that job," Peter Rodman observed. "Loyal first and foremost to his president, he conducted himself in a way that won the trust of the cabinet secretaries, who by law are the president's principal advisers. He pushed no personal agenda; rather, he ensured that all the cabinet views were accurately reflected in the president's deliberations," Rodman commented. Powell "showed an extraordinary political savvy (in the best sense), tact, and personal integrity," Rodman further noted, but he was powerless to break bureaucratic deadlocks if President Reagan was unwilling to do so—which was often frustrating for Shultz.[20]

Powell and Scowcroft worked well together during the Reagan and Bush administrations, although they didn't always see eye to eye on issues. Scowcroft, though, didn't put much stock in the NSC system that Carlucci and Powell had put in place, and he fundamentally disagreed with Powell on the role of the national security advisor. "In this administration," Powell writes in his memoirs, "Shultz was the single minister of foreign policy, and I made sure the NSC staff understood that and backed him all the way."[21]

That's not how Scowcroft understood the position. For him, the job had two chief functions. First, the national security advisor had to make the policy process work efficiently by providing the president with appropriate options for and perspectives on US foreign policy (and by taking as little of the president's time as possible while doing so). Second, he had to advise the president with views "unalloyed by department responsibilities and interests." Whereas the secretary of state and secretary of defense had to represent their own departments and couldn't stray too far or too often from their staff's strongly held views, Scowcroft had no client other than the president. Whatever biases he might have, they weren't institutional biases.

So Scowcroft couldn't share Powell's philosophy of deference to the secretary of state. If he was to be effective as an honest broker and the president's personal adviser, Scowcroft knew, he had to have at least equal standing with the other foreign policy principals.

George Bush agreed. He later observed that by appointing Scowcroft to be his national security advisor, he was sending a "signal to my cabinet and to outside observers that the NSC's function was to be critical in the decision-making process."[22] He appreciated the fact that Scowcroft would "give me his own experienced views on whatever problem might arise" by virtue of "his deep knowledge of foreign policy matters and his prior experience." He was "the perfect honest broker," Bush later wrote.[23]

What also made Scowcroft's ideal role possible was his close relationship with Bush. The two were almost exactly the same age (the president was ten months older), and both had been pilots (Bush with the Navy). They had known each other since the Nixon White House, when Bush was US ambassador to the United Nations (1971–1973). Scowcroft's first memory of George Bush was at a Nixon cabinet meeting in 1973 when Bush was about to leave his position as US ambassador to the UN to become the Republican National Committee chairman; Bush, Scowcroft recalled, was genial, warm, and extremely busy.[24] They later became friends during the Ford administration, when Bush served as US liaison to China (1974–1975) and Scowcroft served as "interlocutor"—the word Scowcroft used to describe their relationship—between Bush and the Ford White House. And the two worked together on a daily basis over the thirteen months when Bush was director of central intelligence (1976–1977). They stayed in touch when Bush was vice president because of Scowcroft's work with the Tower Commission, the Packard Commission, and the Scowcroft Commission.[25]

The two men shared the same worldview, one grounded in the history of World War II, the Cold War, and Vietnam. They believed that the United States had the responsibility to lead other states, that Europe was the United States' natural ally, that the United States should not appease aggressor states, and that when the United States used force it had to use it decisively. Both believed, too, in politics and diplomacy being best conducted through personal relationships, in the need for discretion in foreign relations, and in the indispensability of intelligence.

Both men also knew their ways around Washington and appreciated how things got done—how to give credit to others, how to avoid upsetting colleagues, and how to get others to cooperate. Neither one had patience for bureaucratic posturing, and both liked to figure out what needed to be done and then finding a way to do it.[26] They had found that it was imperative that Congress—or at least key members of Congress—be brought along by the White House. Bush and Scowcroft believed, too, in the importance of national service, honor, courtesy, and self-discipline. Both were also well mannered, unassuming, gracious, and cordial—behavior today many would label "old-fashioned."

Most important, Bush fully trusted Scowcroft, and everyone understood that Scowcroft spoke for the president. As Bush would repeatedly tell people, "Brent doesn't *want* anything." No one, with the exception of Barbara, had better access to the president—and Bush probably spent more time with Scowcroft than he did Barbara. Bush treated Scowcroft like "a beloved older brother," even though Bush was slightly older.[27]

Over the next few years Scowcroft would be "the short balding figure at Bush's side, on the golf course, on the speedboat, in the Oval Office, the ever-present adviser, the confidant," one reporter wrote. He was the president's "close and constant confidant." He was "the closest friend in all things," Bush told two scholars of the National Security Council—as close as one could be and not be related by blood.[28]

Bush and Scowcroft had a shared appreciation for the importance of personnel selection and of clearly defined administrative procedures; as Scowcroft emphasized repeatedly, the NSC process was principally about personalities.[29] So from late November 1988 until the inauguration, the two met nearly every day to work on personnel issues, often over long walks around the perimeter of Camp David. They discussed not only the NSC staff but also other appointments, such as ambassadorships. They also spent some of their time during the transition period mulling over their priorities and how they'd proceed once in office.[30] Bush "came in knowing the way," Scowcroft remarked, and he was "very explicit" about how he wanted to run the NSC process. There was little of the presidency or the US government that wasn't familiar to the president-elect, and he had clear ideas about how he wanted his administration to operate.[31]

Scowcroft had already seen firsthand instances where the NSC process didn't work. He had witnessed at close range the control Kissinger exercised on foreign policy, which had cut Secretary of State Rogers out of high-level decision making. He had lived through the rivalry between Kissinger and defense secretary James R. Schlesinger in the Ford administration; observed the clashes between national security advisor Zbigniew Brzezinski and secretary of state Cyrus Vance under President Jimmy Carter; and as a member of the Tower Commission, he had had to help clean up the damage done to the presidency by an out-of-control NSC process.[32] He knew that acrimonious rivalries among the foreign policy principals was a recipe for incoherent and poorly managed national security policy, something that Bush and Scowcroft both wanted to avoid.[33]

A potentially complicating factor in the NSC process, for Scowcroft, was Bush's exceptionally close friendship with Baker, who regarded his own position as being preeminent: "I had a great advantage as Secretary of State, because I'd been a thirty-five-year friend with the president. I was his political adviser. Nobody was going to get in between me and my President. And, when I would go out and speak, I could go out and speak with authority 'cause everybody knew how close I was to President Bush 41."[34]

Yet Scowcroft was every bit as secure in his relationship with the president, as the historian and former NSC staff member Philip Zelikow observes. Scowcroft's thinking "was, if anything, even closer than Baker's to the point that there were times at which I thought Bush and Scowcroft were almost like two dimensions of one person," Zelikow said. "He was almost a kind of doppelganger for Bush." Or as Elliott Abrams, a critic of the administration, remarked, it would "take thirty years to figure . . . out" the differences between Scowcroft and Bush and how much of the decision making can be attributed Bush and how much to Scowcroft.[35] Baker himself writes of the "enormous personal affection" Bush had for Scowcroft."[36]

Fortunately, Scowcroft and Baker had been acquainted since they worked on Ford's reelection campaign together in 1976, and they got along well. Scowcroft refused to take advantage of Baker's relative inexperience in foreign policy. Because Baker was "not deeply versed in foreign policy," Scowcroft observed, he was somewhat "ill at ease" when he first took office. But Scowcroft reassured Baker that there would be no repetition of the Kissinger-Rogers conflict or the Brzezinski-Vance history. He wouldn't speak to the press or go on television without letting Baker know beforehand. Neither would he nor any other NSC staff member meet with or visit foreign leaders without first notifying the secretary of state. Scowcroft also said he'd let Bush and Baker serve as the administration's principal spokespeople. "I bent over backwards not to appear to be repeating, frankly, what Henry Kissinger did," Scowcroft recalled. Three months into the administration, Baker simply "told Brent just to do what he thought correct."[37]

Baker, for his part, was careful not to exploit his access to the president. Arnold Kanter, who was on Scowcroft's NSC staff and served on several important committees, remarked that he couldn't recall any time Baker went to the president himself in order to air a disagreement with Scowcroft.[38] Instead, Baker kept to his regularly scheduled twice-weekly meetings with the president, which they usually used as occasions for catching up. They also talked on the telephone every day, often several times a day. It's also true that Baker, unlike Scowcroft, would sometimes take the initiative and act on his own authority without first checking with Bush. Nonetheless, despite what some people thought, Baker was far from the dominant partner in the Bush-Baker friendship. "Bush always had the upper hand," Vice President Dan Quayle notes, because "George and Barbara had consoled

Baker after the death of his first wife, and Bush had brought Baker around, not vice versa."[39]

Given these complex dynamics, although "Brent and Jim did get moderately crosswise," Bush later wrote, it happened "very rarely." And almost never did it play out in the press.[40] Because Baker and Scowcroft both wanted to avoid situations where Bush would have to choose between them, they worked hard at settling their differences so they didn't have to take them to the president and force Bush to choose between their positions. They found, moreover, that they were much more successful at resolving any differences than either of them expected.[41]

Scowcroft characterized their differences as follows: "I was primarily concerned with strategy, Baker was much more concerned with tactics. When, for example, we would discuss issues of arms control and what we should propose to the president, Baker would almost always home in on negotiability of what we wanted to do. And I didn't care much about that." On the contrary, "I was interested in what we could change and improve the balance. Our differences didn't go to the heart of things, not like Brzezinski and Vance with different philosophies about how to deal with Soviet Union."[42]

"Scowcroft himself was a tenacious in-fighter, very turf-conscious, and as the years went on he became closer than anyone else in the administration to the President," Quayle observes. "In fact, they eventually developed the best working relationship I have seen between any two people in all my years in politics. They saw each other constantly, and the advice that Scowcroft gave the President was unvarnished. Scowcroft knew how to win his battles with Jim Baker," Quayle adds. "He kept them from breaking out into the open, and he used his time with the President in a subtle way, moving Bush toward his own position and away from Baker's."[43] The vice president points out that "during the four years of the administration [Baker] lost most of his turf battles with Brent Scowcroft."[44] Scowcroft "was the quintessential inside bureaucrat who really knew the game." And if Scowcroft "didn't have confidence in someone he could cut him out real easily. Not that he would do it with the blessing of the President, but he could just cut you out."[45]

Quayle knew about that from firsthand experience. Soon after taking office, Scowcroft discovered that someone on the vice president's staff was leaking information to the press—chief of staff Carnes "Cary" Lord and William Kristol being the principal suspects—so he simply froze the Office of the Vice President out of the NSC process. Neither did Bush interfere.

But as soon as Quayle hired one of Scowcroft's assistants as his national security advisor, their relationship improved. Karl Jackson, who had headed the Asia desk, "had great interface with Brent and that whole team," and the relationship between the two offices "changed dramatically."[46]

The first step Scowcroft took to gain control of the NSC process was to hire Robert Gates as his deputy. Bob Gates had served in the Air Force, had followed the development of the Soviet Union's strategic weapons program, had worked under Scowcroft as a young NSC staffer in the Ford White House, and most recently had been deputy DCI under Reagan. Scowcroft knew Gates well, had followed his career, and thought he would make an ideal deputy. The fact that Gates had withdrawn his name as a nominee for DCI in 1987 revealed the quality of his character, in Scowcroft's view, since the act of taking himself out of consideration protected President Reagan and the White House from (further) public attacks and political embarrassment. (Baker, by contrast, considered Gates to be coming in as "damaged goods" by not having been approved as DCI.)[47]

As Scowcroft's right-hand man, "Gates was the executor" of Scowcroft's goal that everyone have an honest shot on policy, the national security advisor later said. Gates helped Scowcroft protect the president's time by seeing to it that memoranda were not only "clear" but also "concise." He had "been doing this [his] whole career," Gates said. Scowcroft and Gates also had their area directors read the cables going out from the State and Defense Departments so as to keep an eye on what was happening around the rest of the government, "because that's where policy is made." Otherwise, the actual policy on the ground could easily get out of sync with the president's decisions.[48] "Everybody tries to slip their stuff through without sharing it with anyone else," Gates noted; they all tried to play "games." What he and Scowcroft were able to do, then, was to "put a discipline in the process that after a few months . . . became less and less necessary because they understood it wasn't going through if it hadn't been properly coordinated." The staff thereby developed "a good sense of what [Scowcroft] wanted, and if preparing a letter or briefing book we knew the tone and substance of things. He was a great delegator and not a micromanager," as R. Nicholas Burns, who came to the NSC from the State Department, commented. "He was a big picture guy."[49]

By hiring Gates, Scowcroft had someone who could, when needed, step into his shoes for a meeting with the president or other chief policy makers. The two men essentially formed a partnership for running the NSC (not unlike Scowcroft's relationship with Kissinger from September 1973 through October 1975), and rarely did Scowcroft know something Gates didn't. "Gates had this fantastic capacity to process paper at a fairly high level of quality control," which complemented Scowcroft's strengths, Philip Zelikow noted, because "Brent was very much almost at the level of the president in terms of the breadth of vision he had to have and the things that were reaching him. And Brent also really felt the burden of decision." Gates helped ensure the quality of the NSC process, then, by knowing "which memos had to be acted on and which could wait" until Scowcroft got to them.[50] Further helping matters was Gates's rapport with Bush. They got along well personally and shared, with Scowcroft, a professional interest in the collection and assessment of intelligence as well as the oversight of CIA operations.[51]

"Gates and Scowcroft absolutely trusted each other, always watching each others' back," one of their NSC staff members noted. "They were complementary," the head of the international economics directorate, Timothy Deal, said, with their offices located just fifteen feet from each other—"and they were always in and out of each other's offices."[52] As Gates said, the national security advisor "could count on me to keep the trains running." (Scowcroft kept the same institutional arrangement when Adm. Jonathan Howe replaced Gates in 1991, although the latter two didn't have the same kind of relationship.)[53]

Making Gates virtually his equal was an unusual step for Scowcroft to take. "The first thing that Brent arranged that conveyed a different sort of status for me at the deputy assistant to the president level that was unique was that I would have portal-to-portal secure transportation," Gates remarked. A White House car picked Gates up in the morning and took him home at night—an unprecedented step for a deputy assistant.[54] Then, less than two months into the Bush presidency, Scowcroft appointed Gates "assistant to the president," thereby making Gates his equal in seniority. Gates now officially outranked all of the president's deputy assistants, special assistants, and most other White House officials. Gates could thus sit in the front of Air Force One with chief of staff John Sununu, for example, and be on hand should the president need him for any reason. "These little status things conveyed a message within the White House and throughout the government that this was a different sort of arrangement than had ever existed before," Gates commented.[55] The "little status things" weren't so little.

Gates's most important function was chairing the Deputies Committee, which included representatives from state (Under Secretary of State Robert Kimmitt or, less frequently, Director of Policy Planning Dennis Ross or Under Secretary of State for Arms Control and International Security Affairs Reginald Bartholomew); defense (Under Secretary of Defense Paul Wolfowitz); the Joint Chiefs of Staff (Air Force Gen. Robert Herres and later Adm. David Jeremiah); and the CIA (Richard Kerr and later William Studeman). Gates and Kimmitt had worked for the NSC under presidents Ford and Carter, and Kimmitt and Wolfowitz had been colleagues during the two terms of the Reagan administration. The result, Kimmitt said, was that the deputies committee was "highly collegial compared to past administration in which I worked where bureaucratic in-fighting between State, Defense, Intelligence, and the NSC was more serious."[56]

Previous administrations had relied on a Deputies Committee or an equivalent, but from October 1989 onward, the Deputies Committee developed into the Bush administration's workhorse for making national security policy—able to address issues and resolve problems before they reached the principals and, if need be, ultimately the president. If a problem needed further study, the deputies would create a working group to address that issue. Any member could call a meeting, and when meetings were called, nearly every member attended. Because of the committee's effectiveness and the implicit trust it enjoyed from the principals, full NSC meetings were infrequent after the administration's first few months (with the several held in the immediate aftermath of the Iraqi invasion of Kuwait being among the exceptions).

In the year 1990 alone, the committee met more than 150 times—often more than once in a day.[57] The cumulative effect of the frequent, intense meetings was to forge close, cordial ties among the members of the Deputies Committee. They got to know one another well and also socialized together with their spouses. And if they were at loggerheads, Gates simply had to say, "Well, let me talk to the President and see how things work out. You only had to do that once for people to understand how things ran."[58]

Scowcroft's second hire was Condoleezza Rice. Scowcroft had been Rice's mentor since he first met her in the spring of 1984 during a talk he gave at Stanford University and the dinner that followed. He found that Rice, only thirty years old at the time and the youngest at the dinner, was able to talk knowledgably about the MX missile, nuclear arms control, and the Soviet Union. Scowcroft said Rice asked "a brilliant question" about international law and "absolutely captivated" him.[59]

He also found her to be unemotional, analytical, and nonideological. A PhD student of Professor Josef Korbel—the father of Madeleine Albright, a future secretary of state—at the University of Denver, Rice was a realist in the tradition of Hans Morgenthau. He appreciated that she viewed the Soviet Union more in shades of gray rather than in black and white, and that she spoke Russian.[60] She was prepared, very articulate, self-confident, and impressive. Although she was a "slip of a girl," Scowcroft thought that she was "just outstanding." "She was charming and affable," he writes in *A World Transformed*, "but could be tough as nails when the situation required."[61]

Rice had grown up in Bull Connor's Birmingham, Alabama, had a school classmate killed by a bomb, and had great-grandparents who'd been slaves. As a young African American woman, a Republican, and a Sovietologist, she was a novelty, as Ivo Daalder points out: a black woman in the boys' club of security experts. As Rice's father himself remarked, "Blacks didn't do political science."[62]

She had a way of making a quick impression, and Scowcroft would not be the last to be taken with her.[63] He proceeded to help her career by introducing her to the larger national security community, inviting her to participate in and become a member the Aspen Strategy Group beginning in the summer of 1986, and then bringing her into the Bush 41 administration.[64] The fact that she held strong conservative positions on social and moral issues—she'd previously supported Ronald Reagan and would later be closely identified with George W. Bush—never came into play.

As for the others on the NSC staff, some Scowcroft and Gates personally knew, others they knew by reputation or came recommended. They wanted self-starters who didn't require much supervision. Significantly, none of their personnel decisions was based on party affiliation and none was made as a result of a personal request of President Bush. Scowcroft selected Bob Blackwill as the head of the European desk and Philip Zelikow, who was detailed from the State Department, as the director for European security affairs. Two areas were particularly sensitive: the Middle East, where Scowcroft chose Richard Haass, and defense policy and arms control, where he selected Arnold Kanter.

The resultant NSC staff was about 20 percent smaller than Reagan's NSC; more important, it required minimal supervision and caused few bureaucratic headaches for either Scowcroft or Gates.[65]

By virtue of the fact that Scowcroft hired very bright and strong-minded aides and because of his own self-effacing personality, those on the NSC—Gates included—often differed from Scowcroft on the issues. They would "forcefully debate policies" among themselves and argue "things out." Meanwhile, Scowcroft would take it all in. He "was a great listener," according to one of his staff members, R. Nicholas Burns. "He was a man of few words" and would soak up what people said without revealing a lot about his own position. "It was memorable and effective." The result was that Gates, Blackwill, Haass, Rice, Zelikow, and others on his staff were sometimes able to persuade him to adopt policies he otherwise wouldn't have.[66]

Staff members found Scowcroft supportive and felt motivated by his presence. He created an environment that kept their enthusiasm going. He didn't yell; Arnold Kanter said he never heard him raise his voice. He rarely got upset or angry at people, and when he did he was "very composed" and, at the same time, "demonstrative": "He let you know where things stood, and you needed to get things right." So when one staff member didn't fully communicate the Treasury Department's position on an issue, he was out of a job. And on the occasions when Scowcroft showed "flashes of anger," it was not about what was being said, but about "not being kept updated."[67]

Scowcroft also led through kindliness and consideration. When NSC staff member Ed A. Hewitt was diagnosed with cancer in February 1992 and died within the year, on January 15, 1993, "Brent handled this with great compassion," Burns remarked. He "was very solicitous of Ed's family, and held a memorial in the White House the day after Ed died. Ed's wife, his in-laws, and the staff were all there, and Brent gave a wonderful extemporaneous speech. He handled this difficult time as well as it could have been handled."[68]

The careful selection of personnel and attention to personal chemistry extended to two later additions to the Bush White House: Dick Cheney, who became secretary of defense two months into the administration, and Colin Powell, who succeeded Adm. William Crowe as chairman of the Joint Chiefs of Staff on September 30, 1989.

The president and vice president wanted to appoint former senator John Tower secretary of defense. Scowcroft wasn't quite so sure. He recognized Tower's knowledge of defense issues, appreciated the fact he was "very, very smart," and liked the fact that Tower had been "open and collegiate" as chairman of the special review board, "not dictatorial or dirigiste." Tower worked closely with military contractors—from 1986 to 1988 he earned over a million dollars as a defense-industry consultant—but he had also made remarks critical of SDI. More significantly for the purposes of his confirmation, Scowcroft knew that Tower's "imperious management of the Armed Services Committee" had created antagonisms and that nominating him might cause problems.[69] Though Tower had been "one of the most senior and powerful members of the Senate" before he retired in 1984, he was also "one of the least liked" and had a reputation for being high-handed and arrogant, according to treasury secretary Nicholas Brady, as well as "boorish" and "autocratic" in his handling of his Democratic colleagues.[70] Members of Congress and their staff wouldn't forget.

Scowcroft and Brady's concerns—shared by White House counsel Boyden Gray, Craig Fuller, and others—were borne out. Although Bush and Quayle put Tower's name forward, their nominee faced stiff resistance from many of his former Democratic colleagues and congressional staffers. Tower also became vulnerable to charges of excessive drinking, womanizing, and excessively close ties to military contractors. Senator Sam Nunn called Tower's drinking "a serious problem," and insisted it was the drinking, not the womanizing, that was at "the heart of the issue." And even Dick Cheney disagreed with the selection, according to CBS's Bob Schieffer. "We just want you to know that some of us on the other side of the aisle" think that denying Tower the nomination "is the right thing to do," Cheney told Senator Nunn (who then told Schieffer).[71] Meanwhile, former president Nixon spread the word that Tower was "bedding down" with "a beautiful and well-connected Chinese woman despite [Tower's] third marriage."[72]

Loyal to a fault, Bush stood by his nominee. The president and Barbara Bush thought the attacks were motivated by partisanship and that the rumors and innuendoes were a "disgrace," nothing more than "character assassination" achieved through unproven allegations.[73]

But the result was that for almost two months the administration was without a secretary of defense. Finally, on the morning of March 9—with the vote scheduled for that afternoon—Bush accepted the fact that Tower didn't have the votes to be approved (he would be defeated, 47–53). So the president met with Scowcroft and Sununu and the three of them decided to ask the House minority whip, Dick Cheney, to come to the White House at four o'clock that same afternoon.[74]

Scowcroft asked Cheney for his advice, and he suggested Don Rumsfeld as secretary of defense. Rumsfeld was a nonstarter, of course. He was Bush's old rival, had tried to undermine Kissinger during the Ford administration, and had endorsed Bush's rival, Senator Bob Dole, in the 1988 New Hampshire Republican primary. Scowcroft then asked Cheney if he'd be willing to serve, and Cheney accepted.

Although he hadn't chaired any important House committees dealing with national security issues, Cheney "had a reputation for integrity and for standing up to principles, and, at the same time, for getting along with people"; Bush thought him to be "strong, tough, and fair." Cheney was "the smartest guy in the room," in the description of one NSC staff member—and this wasn't to take anything away from Baker or Scowcroft. For his part, Cheney looked forward to working with Baker and Scowcroft, both of whom he regarded as "enormously talented individuals."[75] Cheney was quickly confirmed.

Scowcroft also had reservations about appointing Colin Powell as chairman of the Joint Chiefs. Not only had Powell had previously held Scowcroft's position of national security advisor, but while serving under President Reagan, had chosen to stay in the Army.[76] Too, Powell had leapfrogged over more than a dozen highly qualified, more senior general officers in the promotion process and hadn't had any true joint force experience, such as commanding a large-scale military operation (although he had commanded the US Army's V Corps in Germany) or serving as the NATO supreme commander. But both Bush and Cheney wanted Powell as chairman of the Joint Chiefs, and Scowcroft went along. "I need not have worried," he later remarked. "Powell was unfailingly imperturbable, even when the situation became tense. He managed brilliantly the sometimes awkward relationship between the secretary of defense and the chairman in NSC discussions with the president, serving as an NSC principal alongside his own immediate boss."[77] And when Scowcroft disagreed, Powell recalls, "Scowcroft would say, 'You know you got your head up your butt.' In front of the president of the United States!"[78] But this sort of ridicule was standard among those in Bush's inner circle.

The care with which Bush and Scowcroft selected personnel resulted in a foreign policy team of unusual loyalty, capability, and coherence. "Bush was probably the first president since Franklin Roosevelt or even before who was acquainted with all of the members of his cabinet before he named them," Bush's personnel director, Chase Untermeyer, remarked. "Various presidents, famously John F. Kennedy, or Bill Clinton, were given names of people who on paper looked good and either proved to be great winners, like McNamara was for Kennedy, or losers in more cases."[79]

———

PRESIDENT BUSH CARED about foreign policy. He liked reading intelligence briefings, enjoyed diplomacy, and personally knew many foreign officials and most heads of state and government. "It wasn't just the head of state" Bush was acquainted with, Vice President Quayle remarked. "He knew the Foreign Ministers, he knew Finance Ministers. He knew the Ambassadors because of his days at the United Nations. He knew all these people and he knew how to massage their egos, to work around them, and he was always, always in control." Bush knew "every foreign leader in the world," Sununu observed when they visited Tokyo in February 1989. "Not only did he know the Education Minister and the Economic Minister and he knew their . . . wives and children and what schools the children were in and what careers they were in or if somebody was in trouble with drugs or whatever, he knew it all. And he had a relationship."[80] Bush also knew well that many very small countries "have very influential representatives." As a former UN representative himself, the president understood that "when you needed votes," the size of a country "didn't matter." And the United States was particularly "effective, because we were the host country," UN Ambassador Thomas Pickering pointed out. "We had a special cachet, especially in New York."[81]

Bush was the "best-prepared president" ever to take the job, in Scowcroft's judgment. He had a warm disposition and was personally self-assured (unlike LBJ or Richard Nixon), and he had extensive experience in US foreign policy and international relations (unlike Ford, Reagan, Clinton, George W. Bush, or Obama). And if he was sometimes awkward in public, Bush was gregarious with his top advisers, other heads of state, members of Congress, and business leaders, as well as very effective in one-on-one meetings and small groups. He was patient and considerate of his foreign counterparts, moreover, as well as with members of Congress.[82] And he was relaxed in his dealings with the US armed forces and always happy to be with the troops. He "couldn't have been a better Commander in Chief," Cheney remarked, adding that Bush was "a hell of a boss."[83] Whereas Bush would sometimes "say 'I hadn't really thought about that'" with respect to domestic policy, Quayle pointed out that he "never heard [the president] say that in foreign policy. He always knew."[84]

Because of the priority Bush assigned to foreign policy and national security, he and Scowcroft agreed that either Gates or Scowcroft should be available at all times—the same policy Scowcroft had implemented in the Ford administration. So Scowcroft generally traveled with Bush when he went overseas, and Gates accompanied him on domestic trips.[85]

Scowcroft was also determined to avoid problems like those that had plagued past administrations. George Shultz, for example, had felt "burned" by the NSC as a result of the Iran-Contra affair and therefore had "wanted to reduce the NSC to an executive secretariat," according to defense secretary Frank Carlucci.[86] So now Scowcroft wanted to use his position as national security advisor to design an NSC system that could maximize the chances of success.[87]

The first thing that had to be established among principals, Scowcroft said, was trust. He and Bush were together able to establish that trust among the president's senior advisers.[88] There "was an element of trust that made it a delight to go to work every day," Cheney said. "You never had to worry that the Secretary of State or the NSC Advisor was going to take something you said, use it out of context, leak it to the press, or take advantage somehow in the bureaucratic wars. There was the concept that it was a team." Not only did the people at the subcabinet level know and like each other, Kimmitt remarked, they "worked very, very effectively to make our bosses successful."[89]

The Bush presidency was the most collegial of any of the four administrations in which Richard Haass had served; working there "was actually fun," he said. "It sounds bizarre, but it was by far the most enjoyable experience a lot of us had had before or since in government. There was a lot of camaraderie and kidding around . . . it was very relaxed." The principals "laughed a lot together," writer and analyst David Rothkopf observed. "Successful administrations, like successful baseball teams, are loose, relaxed." And with the "twelve- or fourteen-hour days, often six or seven days a week . . . humor [was] a critical ally."[90] The levity shared among the principals, their deputies, and assistant secretaries helped deflate tensions in times of crisis and eased the handling of the inevitable disagreements and conflicts.

The president himself liked practical jokes, such as subjecting his guests to exploding golf balls. He also liked dirty jokes (as long as women weren't present) and Baker's bawdy limericks. One of his favorite games was to bestow the "Scowcroft award" on any official who could fall asleep and then awaken without missing a beat. This was a talent Scowcroft himself had perfected. "He can fall asleep anywhere from the Oval Office to state dinners, cleverly masking the respite by striking the pose of 'The Thinker,' with chin in hand and eyes downcast," White House correspondent Maureen Dowd reported. "But he always wakes up before he topples off the couch and in good time to answer a query from the President."[91]

Despite his playfulness—or perhaps because of it—Bush could be secretive. Part of this was tactical: he wanted to surprise the Soviets, the Congress, and the press so as to gain a positional advantage. But he also delighted in misleading the press and confounding expectations—which could include surprising those in the administration who were not in his inner circle.[92]

Relations among the members of that inner circle were largely collegial and positive. Though some in the administration had trouble with Chief of Staff Sununu, Scowcroft and he generally worked together, and the two men even enjoyed playfully insulting each other. Sununu respected Scow-croft's knowledge of foreign policy and was happy to leave foreign policy to Bush, Baker, and Scowcroft, while he and budget director Richard Darman ran domestic policy. The one time Sununu trod on the secretary of state's turf, Baker exploded in anger and chewed him out—with President Bush and Gates taking it all in, embarrassed.[93]

Scowcroft didn't worry about being upstaged. He "did not feel the need to promote himself in meetings," one of his staff observed; instead, he dele-gated. "There was a sense that he didn't need to prove himself, that he was supremely confident of himself and his role with President Bush," Nicholas Burns said. "He would ask questions and let you speak, which is not always the norm in Washington. He impressed by his personality."[94]

In contrast to Brzezinski, who "had no hesitancy saying things critical of other cabinet members" and writing memos against other cabinet members, "that would never happen with Brent Scowcroft," Timothy Deal noted. "If he disagreed he would say it in person to the president and not in writing."[95]

Scowcroft had explicitly spelled out the role of the national security advi-sor in part five of the Tower Commission report (the section he had drafted). The national security advisor's responsibility, he wrote, was to "ensure that matters submitted for consideration by the [National Security] Council cov-ered the full range of issues on which review was required; that those issues were fully analyzed; that a full range of options was considered; that the prospects and risks of each were examined; that all relevant intelligence and other information was available to the principals; that legal considerations were addressed; and that difficulties in implementation were confronted."

Scowcroft appreciated that it was of critical importance that he not guide the president's thinking by how he structured the decision-making process, because a "lot of times you can get the answer you want by the way you ask the question." This, he believed, was how the Iran-Contra affair had developed. He also realized he could steer Bush's thinking by how he interpreted the president's guidance. If he had any doubt after a meeting as to what Bush had decided, he'd write down his understanding of the conversation and take it back to the Oval Office to ensure "that this [was] exactly what [the president] had in mind." He found miscommunication to be surprisingly common. It was "like that game of telephone with kids in a room," he said; frequently after NSC meetings "he would write up the decision and others would say, no that's not what happened."[96]

Scowcroft also had to be able to serve as a check on and as an extra resource for the president. As a practical matter, this meant that he might have to supplement the advice of the other foreign policy principals by questioning the options that Baker, Cheney, or Powell (earlier, Admiral Crowe) offered the president. Or he might have to persuade Bush to consider the long-term implications of policies being recommended by other administration officials. His job thus went beyond brokering; he had to be responsible for the quality of the political choices and policy options being given to the president.[97]

With his cordial and self-effacing manner, Scowcroft made things easy. He was "as abrasive as a silk scarf," in the words of Fred McClure, Bush's assistant for congressional relations.[98] He was thereby able to at once create an efficient, informal, and remarkably cordial atmosphere within the NSC and to get the other chief foreign policy advisers—Baker, Cheney, Powell, and others, such as US trade representative Carla Hills and DCI William Webster—to accept his vision of how the NSC process was to be managed. In 1987, just after Poindexter was replaced by Carlucci, the NSC was voted the "worst agency in the U.S. government" by the Retired Federal Employees Association; two years later, it was voted the best.[99]

Scowcroft also recognized the need to cultivate good relationships with key members of Congress and members of the news media, including individual reporters, columnists, and news analysts. He had already applied some of these lessons as chairman of the Scowcroft Commission and then as a member of the Tower Commission, and he would continue to apply them as Bush's national security advisor.

Scowcroft brought in Roman Popadiuk to assist with his and the NSC's media relations (although he stationed Popadiuk in the White House press office, along with two domestic policy press officers). He had Popadiuk (and his successor, Walter Kansteiner) sit in on NSC meetings so each was fully informed about NSC policy and could brief the press accurately and appropriately.[100] Scowcroft also gave regular backgrounders to small groups of reporters.

It helped that Scowcroft had no ambition to steal the spotlight. Since the national security advisor wasn't subject to Senate confirmation or being called to testify before Congress, Scowcroft didn't think it was appropriate for him to be the face of the administration. Happily, the "passion for anonymity" Scowcroft recommended in the Tower Commission report suited his own disposition, so he typically worked with reporters and other media personnel on background. Whenever possible, he deflected attention to Baker, Cheney, Powell, or others, such as CENTCOM commander Gen. Norman Schwarzkopf.

Working with reporters and columnists didn't come naturally for him; Scowcroft admitted he "had a psychological aversion to the press." He found he had "to be very careful" around reporters and that they "could just bring trouble."[101] Part of this was that he felt he'd been burned by Bob Woodward and Carl Bernstein in *The Final Days* (their book on Watergate and the Nixon presidency). "What [Woodward] does is all basically gossip," Scowcroft said, and write "his [own] story of personal relationships." So he didn't want to speak to Woodward for the reporter's book on the Bush administration's military policies, which would turn into *The Commanders*.[102]

Scowcroft didn't like doing television interviews, calling television "too personal" a medium. And while in office, he didn't have the time to write op-ed pieces, so a speechwriter would draft the op-ed pieces going out under his name (as with Bush's other senior advisers). Scowcroft nonetheless excelled at press relations. He was very good at briefing newspaper and magazine reporters, at providing background, and at doing prerecorded video in advance of the president's trips abroad. He had a "special relationship" with Maureen Dowd, the press secretary reported. He also worked closely with the *New York Times'* Michael Gordon (who would sometimes call him at home in the evening), Ken Walsh of *U.S. News & World Report*, Gerald Seib of the *Wall Street Journal*, and a handful of other leading reporters.[103]

Scowcroft deliberately kept discussions and decisions close to the vest, an attitude that press secretary Marlin Fitzwater attributed to the serious nature of national security policy and to Scowcroft's belief in the "loose lips sink ships" mentality of the World War II generation. But it also fit the president's own approach to policymaking. NSC staff member Robert Blackwill described the Bush 41 administration as "the most secretive since Nixon."[104] Bush himself had a "deep animosity" toward the press, Fitzwater later explained. Not only did he regard reporters as untrustworthy and indiscreet, but the president took "everything personally." And with all the ridicule that George Bush suffered in the press, it is little surprise he wanted to keep the media at bay.[105]

But those outside the White House's inner circles found the withholding of information and compartmentalizing frustrating. Nicholas Rostow, who was the NSC's legal counsel, said he felt as though he were "the kid with his nose pressed up against the candy store window a lot of the time." It was also true, however, that Scowcroft and Gates had little use for lawyers when making policy—Rostow and White House counsel Boyden Gray both—and that Scowcroft was "a very good, a pretty good international lawyer on his own," Rostow observed.[106]

BUSH, BAKER, SCOWCROFT and other senior administration officials were able to establish relationships based on trust. "One of the reasons why the system worked was that Baker and Cheney totally trusted Brent to keep them informed and to fairly represent their views to the president," Gates said. "He was the only national security advisor in my view that was ever so trusted by the other two principals"—and Gates had served under six US presidents at the time he wrote the above, before his time as defense secretary under George W. Bush and Barack Obama.

Scowcroft's management of the NSC process also worked well because of his creation of other interagency groups to expedite decision making. One of his key innovations (retained by subsequent presidential administrations) was the formation of the Principals Committee, which included the vice president, the secretary of state, the secretary of defense, the director of central intelligence, the chairman of the Joint Chiefs of Staff, the White House chief of staff, and the national security advisor—all meeting without the president.

Scowcroft had noticed that in President Reagan's NSC meetings, a lot of time had been wasted on debates over issues that did not involve presidential-level decisions. He therefore wanted to establish a smaller decision-making body that would provide a forum in which to discuss issues and clarify positions with the other foreign policy principals without taking up the president's time. Although a Principals Committee had been set up in the Reagan administration under national security advisor Colin Powell, it had never convened because Secretary of State George Schultz refused to attend any meeting of principals chaired by the national security advisor.[107] It was therefore "with temerity" that Scowcroft proposed the idea to Secretary Baker, who was well aware of Shultz's well-defined views on the matter. But Baker said, "Fine, let's do it."[108]

The Principals Committee made it possible for Scowcroft to present Bush with "crisp positions" about any significant policy matter. The president, for his part, appreciated Scowcroft's ability to "knock heads" so as to resolve disagreements "before he let them in my door." As a practical matter, the Principals Committee meetings quickly became unnecessary in areas other than arms control, Robert Kimmitt said. "When the president learned his senior advisers were meeting just down hall without him, he made clear to Brent Scowcroft that he wanted to be involved in such discussions."[109] However, Scowcroft himself regarded the Principals Committee (which met dozens of time during the administration) and the Deputies Committee (which met hundreds of times) as his two most important innovations.

In March 1989 Scowcroft created another decision-making body—the Core Group, which consisted of the foreign policy principals plus the president—essentially the National Security Council as originally designed in 1947 with the addition of the national security advisor. It originated during policy reviews for reappraising US foreign relations, especially those with respect to Europe and the Soviet Union. Scowcroft decided to convene an open session among the principals so as to promote candid discussion. The meeting, which took place without notes, without debriefings, and without any prepared remarks, was highly productive. Afterward Bush said, "Gee, I liked that," and the format stuck.[110]

The advantage of the Core Group setting was that each official could have his say, uninhibited by the presence of hangers-on (regular NSC meetings might number as many as thirty participants) who might constrain open discussion, leak self-serving information, or provoke a backlash by later telling someone, "Oh boy, you should have heard what X said" (as Scowcroft put it). Exemplifying the effectiveness of the Core Group was a series of three meetings held in January 1990 to discuss the INF treaty and troop reductions in Europe. The Defense and State Departments opposed the troop reductions and worried about how the United States' European allies would respond, while Scowcroft and others supported both the treaty and the force reductions (which were Scowcroft's idea). With the principals at an impasse, Scowcroft proposed that they simply ask the Europeans. The Europeans agreed to the reductions, which were then implemented.[111]

Other small, informal meetings also proved to be particularly productive. During weekly lunches, Scowcroft talked things over with the president and the secretary of state, and in their Wednesday breakfast meetings Scowcroft sorted things out with Baker and Cheney (and sometimes Powell) in his West Wing corner office. Because of these weekly meetings, relatively few issues—"four or five," Baker reports—had to be taken up to the president for his resolution. Instead, they "work[ed] them out in Brent's office." In Cheney's description, "The three of us could talk about virtually anything and know that your colleague wasn't going to go out and dump a load in the *Washington Post* the next day based on what you said. . . . I might show up with eight or ten issues that needed to be resolved, and it became a very efficient and very effective way to coordinate policy."[112] Other administrations had used other informal meetings to make decisions, to be sure—such as LBJ's Tuesday lunches with Walt Rostow—but what distinguished those of the Bush administration was the degree to which the informal meetings succeeded at settling interagency differences.

Scowcroft also continued to employ several lower-level NSC policy co-ordinating committees for the purpose of sharing information and coordinating action in particular regions of the world (e.g., Europe, Latin America, and East Asia) and in different functional areas (e.g., defense, international economics, and arms control).

Of course, other decisions were made by Bush and Scowcroft themselves. There was nothing Bush did in foreign policy, and little in domestic matters, that he did without first talking to Brent. Defense secretary Dick Cheney describes President Bush's style of decision making during crises, such as the Persian Gulf War:

> Much decision making took place around the fireplace in the Oval Office, might be upstairs in his residence, in his office up there. He was comfortable in that kind of a setting. It was not a formal sort of arrangement. It would involve Baker and me, Powell and Scowcroft, Quayle, Sununu usually. Sometimes Bill Webster, Bob Gates—Bob Gates would be usually involved. That's where a lot of the management of a crisis would actually take place. . . . Separate, apart from that, if you move off that to more normal peacetime operation, he did an awful lot in the diplomatic arena and the State Department arena, between himself and Jim and Brent, that I wouldn't be directly involved and didn't need to be directly involved [in].[113]

These informal decision-making processes allowed for close, sustained, and confidential interactions among the principals on sensitive and important issues. This is why it is often possible to write about the thinking of "Scowcroft, Bush, and Baker" or "Scowcroft and Bush" without distinguishing among the president, the secretary of state, and the national security advisor.

The NSC organizations and processes established by Scowcroft and approved by the president were designed to facilitate flexibility and creativity. The NSC staff consisted of about forty-five people divided into ten directorates, with four or five people in each. It was thus a very flat and compact organization (compared to the two hundred people or so the NSC had as of 2009), and they all met once a month for informational exchanges. Tellingly, the structural organization of the NSC process established under Scowcroft and Bush 41 has been used by every succeeding presidential administration.[114]

But the NSC process crucially depended on there being only one message coming from the White House, notwithstanding the inevitability of internal divisions within the administration. On military issues, discussions with the chairman of the Joint Chiefs of Staff first had to be cleared with the secretary of defense—just as Scowcroft had insisted during the Ford administration. Scowcroft was similarly careful about meeting independently with foreign ambassadors. Whereas "Shultz forbade it" and "Kissinger did it all the time," Scowcroft "only did it when," in his mind, "it served a larger purpose." Here, Lawrence Eagleburger's joint role as Baker's right-hand man and as Scowcroft's friend and political ally made him invaluable.[115]

Message discipline was strictly enforced. When one of the members of Scowcroft's NSC staff was found to be the source of a news leak, he was out of a job. Similarly, when Cheney in early 1989 publicly stated that "Gorbachev's going to fail," Baker called his friend, and the president "cut the ground out from Dick quicker than you can imagine," Baker said.[116] And when Gen. Michael Dugan, the Air Force chief of staff, made unapproved statements in September 1990 about the Pentagon's plans for its air war against Iraq, Cheney immediately asked for his resignation.

With examples such as these, other officials were loath to make statements or release information without being cleared to do so. Leaks on national security issues were, as a result, relatively few.

Scowcroft's normal routine was to get into the office before seven, read the *Washington Post*, government-based news, and intelligence reports while at his desk, and then meet with the president and Bob Gates for the daily intelligence briefing at 7:30 A.M. At the briefing, Scowcroft and Gates "would often disagree with the pieces" and grill the intelligence officer on his report, asking questions like, "Why do you think that? Do you have any evidence for that?" (Gates noted it must have been little daunting for the GS-14 or GS-15 intelligence analyst to come to the White House and have to brief a former deputy director of central intelligence, the national security advisor to two presidents, and a former DCI who happened to be the president.)[117]

After the intelligence briefing, the president and Scowcroft would go over the day's agenda, and the rest of Scowcroft's day was typically spent in meetings. Unlike most narratives of important foreign policy crises, in which presidents and their advisers focus on a single issue, Scowcroft and his NSC staff were always juggling several balls at once. Scowcroft's day was therefore chock-full of meetings with foreign visitors, ambassadors, businesspeople (especially from the defense industry), other interest-group representatives, and members of his own staff and others in the White House. He also had direct secure telephone lines to his counterparts in London,

Paris, and Bonn. And most days he'd drop in on the president three or four times.[118]

Rarely would a day go by without a telephone call or a meeting with one or more members of Congress on military affairs, foreign policy issue, or other matters. Scowcroft often invited important congressional leaders to his office for breakfast or lunch, one-on-one, to chat over key issues. For Scowcroft, these meetings with members of Congress were a "very important part" part of his job and a "very important part" of his responsibilities as national security advisor. He appointed Virginia Lampley as the NSC's congressional liaison.[119]

Once the business day ended at about 6:00 P.M., Scowcroft would catch up on paperwork. He'd then go home at around 9:30 or 10:00 P.M. He was "unbelievably hardworking," in the words of one of the members of his NSC staff.[120] And he expected his staff to work equally hard. Whereas Carlucci and Powell believed in the national security advisor and NSC staff taking evenings and weekends off (barring a crisis), Scowcroft thought that the seriousness of the national security advisor position demanded that he give the job everything he had. Working in the NSC was "a horrible job, long hours," as Gates characterized it, involving "lots of game playing and intrigue, a lot of bureaucratic problems and sorting things through." But Gates realized that he and Scowcroft would have to keep on top of "all of the backbiting and interagency rivalries and everything and all of that" if they were "to make things happen."[121]

Florence Gantt, who had worked with Scowcroft when he was a deputy under Kissinger, when he was national security advisor, and when he returned as national security advisor under Bush, spoke of "doing everything" for him: running his calendar, moving paper, traveling with him, handling his correspondence, making his schedule, "anything." But even though she "ran his life," Gantt said, "he never relaxed." He never slept in, not even on Sundays. And he didn't have any recreation or outside interests aside from occasionally watching a ballgame on television.[122]

Despite the brutal work schedule and his preference for doing business verbally Scowcroft was usually well behind on his paperwork. Gates described how his boss handled the paper:

> Scowcroft, when he left at the end of the Ford administration there were two file drawers of action items in his safe, all marked "urgent action." Some of them were two years old which is an object lesson of its own, in terms of the way government perceives urgency and how some of these situations

unfolded. Let's just say that managing paper flow was not one of Brent's strengths. And so, it fell to me. The stuff would come through me. A lot of stuff I would sign off on myself. And then the policy-oriented papers, a lot of the more important decision papers, I would send on to Brent. Then, what I would usually do at the end of the day is to go into his office, rifle his in-box, pull out the stuff that had to be acted on, make him sit down and sign them, or read them. One deputy national security advisor that I worked for referred to this process as the Strasbourg Goose Process, as I shoved this stuff down his throat.[123]

Behind his back, the NSC staff would joke about how "notoriously slow" Scowcroft was at moving paper, Nicholas Rostow reported. "You know, when [Scowcroft] leaves," he quipped, "I'll find something from 1975."[124]

Nonetheless, Scowcroft's apprenticeships in the Nixon and Ford administrations, along with the research, analysis, and reflection occasioned by his work on the Scowcroft and Tower Commissions, had equipped him exceedingly well for his role as national security advisor for the Bush White House. That proved to be very fortunate, since the next few years would be among the most unpredictable and consequential in the history of American foreign policy.

18

THE PAUSE
Preparing for Change

GALE-FORCE WINDS, pummeling rain, and fifteen-to-twenty-foot seas buffeted the American naval cruiser anchored in Marsaxlokk Harbour in Malta. President George Bush, James Baker, Brent Scowcroft, and other administration officials had flown into Valletta and taken the USS *Belknap* down the coast to meet with President Mikhail Gorbachev, foreign minister Eduard Shevardnadze, Marshal Sergei Akhromeyev, former ambassador Anatoly Dobrynin, and other Soviet advisers. But with the miserable weather—the worst in a decade, locals said—the seasickness-prone Gorbachev decided to remain on the cruise ship *Maxim Gorkiy*, moored at the dock, rather than transferring to a Soviet naval cruiser anchored out at sea as originally planned. So the Americans had to make the wet, uncomfortable trip by a small launch from the *Belknap* to the *Maxim Gorkiy.* Their shipboard meetings were to be reminiscent of Franklin Roosevelt's August 1941 meeting at sea with Winston Churchill off Newfoundland.[125]

The summit, scheduled for December 2 and 3, 1989, had been slow in coming. Two weeks after Bush's inauguration, on February 3, 1989, the US ambassador to the Soviet Union, Jack F. Matlock, had cabled a long memorandum to the White House that described the Soviet economy and the Communist Party government as physically and intellectually bankrupt and saddled with an unsustainable military burden. Matlock explained that Gorbachev's announced reforms reflected the fact that he was under great internal pressure from a society and an economy near collapse.

We now know that Matlock was right. But at the time, many in the Bush administration—especially Dick Cheney, Dan Quayle, and Bob Gates—had grave doubts about Matlock's assessment as well as about Gorbachev's and Shevarnadze's proposals for across-the-board arms reductions, including the withdrawal of five hundred tactical nuclear weapons from Eastern Europe.[126] So, too, did many intelligence officers and Pentagon analysts, who in their reports suggested that the idea of Gorbachev "being so embattled" was "a figment of the imagination." They thought there was little chance that Soviet military leaders and other top party officials would accept Gorbachev's reforms, and they didn't put much stock in Gorbachev's staying power. Cheney essentially called Gorbachev a fraud and imposter; Press Secretary Marlin Fitzwater famously called him a "drugstore cowboy."[127]

By contrast, James Baker and many of his colleagues in the State Department, as well as others in the CIA and the foreign policy community, agreed with Matlock that the Soviet Union had no choice but to alter its politics, society, and economy, and they were more sanguine about the prospects for glasnost and perestroika and about the future of US-Soviet relations. Accordingly, they believed that the United States needed to rethink its foreign policy.

Brent Scowcroft and Lawrence Eagleburger were somewhere in the middle, although more skeptical than optimistic. President Bush himself was not sure what to think. He was probably closest to Scowcroft's position, though he leaned at times toward Baker's more optimistic view.

But since Bush and Scowcroft couldn't be certain of Gorbachev, they were wary of taking the Soviet leader's statements and political overtures at face value.[128] Gorbachev's attempts to reform Soviet society might represent a genuine ambition to dismantle totalitarianism, but they might also represent efforts to stimulate the economy, enhance worker productivity, boost the Soviet Union's legitimacy both at home and in the West, and ultimately strengthen the Soviet empire without fundamentally altering its character.

Bush and Scowcroft understood that the administration had to establish its own firm position from which they could embark on any diplomatic initiatives. And the president and his top advisers unanimously agreed that any East-West initiatives they launched should be "bold ones." None of them liked being put in the position of having to react to Gorbachev and his favorable press coverage. They wanted to get out ahead of the Soviet leader.[129] But how should they do this, and what larger strategic goals should shape the specific tactics that the Bush administration would employ in dealing with the Soviet Union? The answers to these questions were far from obvious.

Most outside observers had expected that the newly inaugurated George H. W. Bush would continue the foreign policies of the Reagan administration. So it came as a surprise when Bush's newly appointed national security advisor, Brent Scowcroft, went on ABC's *World News Tonight Sunday* and declared that the Cold War wasn't over. Gorbachev was "interested in making trouble within the Western alliance," Scowcroft proclaimed.

And while there might be light at the end of the tunnel, he said, he wasn't sure if it was "the sun or an incoming locomotive."[130]

Scowcroft's over-the-air comments marked a retrenchment from the optimism of President Reagan and Secretary of State George Shultz. At a time when American and European leaders were unilaterally dismantling their Cold War defenses, Scowcroft feared that Gorbachev was in fact restructuring the Soviet economy and that the United States might wake up one day to find a rejuvenated Soviet Union and a West in shambles.[131]

Thus, Scowcroft was wary of the warm relations Reagan and Shultz had established with the Soviet Union in their last years in office, and he was particularly critical of the Reykjavik summit, held in early October 1986, when Reagan and Gorbachev had proposed to get rid of nuclear weapons entirely.

Scowcroft recalled that episode vividly. He and Bush had been having dinner together at the vice president's residence during the Reykjavik meetings, "watching television, eating," when he saw "Shultz—with tears in his eyes—saying how close we had come to something." He said he had the opposite feeling: relief. "We dodged a bullet," he told Bush, who replied, "What do you mean?" Scowcroft told him, "That would have been a classic disaster. Because there was no counter plan or anything else to support Europe and defend against the Soviet Union if they chose this path."[132]

James Woolsey, Scowcroft's partner in the Scowcroft Commission and frequent op-ed coauthor, agreed. Reykjavik was "one of the worse performances in foreign policy by an administration that this country has seen in the nuclear age," he said. It held up "for the world a completely unrealistic view of the possibility of doing away on the one hand with all ballistic missiles or on the other with all nuclear weapons," Woolsey said.[133]

Scowcroft had also spoken out against the White House's proposed ban on intermediate-range nuclear forces, which he viewed as "the wrong treaty" because it eroded Europe's nuclear and thus military defense and left it vulnerable to the Soviets' existing long-range nuclear weapons and to the Warsaw Pact's superior conventional forces. He thought the Reagan administration had put its plans for strategic weapons on the table for negotiations with the Soviet Union before those plans had been vetted by the Joint Chiefs of Staff and the Department of Defense.[134] Shultz and Reagan were both being naive, in his judgment, and overly credulous. He thought they'd been "snowed," acting as if they were living in a make-believe world.[135]

Listening to Gorbachev's calls for reform, Scowcroft felt as if he had seen it all before. Scowcroft had repeatedly warned of "the cyclical oscillations between euphoria and alarm which have been the hallmark of the American reaction to United States-Soviet relations in the past." The United States, he wrote in 1979, couldn't afford the "complacency" that accompanied the giddy optimism of "the spirit of Glassboro [New Jersey, 1967], the spirit of Camp David, and other euphoric manifestations." He didn't explicitly refer to the 1972 Moscow summit, SALT and détente in his warnings, but they were the obvious referents.[136] And now, American policy makers, the press, and the public were again succumbing to the false muse and counterproductive euphoria of Gorbachev—what some were labeling "Gorbymania." Just because Gorbachev was changing the Marxist-Leninist foundations of Soviet society through glasnost and perestroika, Scowcroft told the German newsmagazine *Der Spiegel* in October 1988, it didn't mean that he would change "the historical Russia, a major power with historical claims to the world." Moreover, Bush's national security advisor doubted "Gorbachev's use of the word 'democracy' matches up with the West's."[137]

In Scowcroft's view, Reagan and his advisers were warming up to the Soviet Union in the absence of any clearly defined strategic plan. For all of the seeming promise of the late 1980s thaw in US-Soviet relations, the Soviet empire was still very much in place when President Bush took office. It was still in command of the sixteen Soviet republics and Eastern Europe. It continued to have a one-party communist leadership in charge of a police state and a command economy. It still controlled a formidable arsenal of nuclear and conventional weapons that threatened the United States, Europe, and US allies around the world. It still was helping communist regimes and allied governments in Cuba, Angola, Afghanistan, and Nicaragua. It had neither renounced Marxism-Leninism and the belief in class conflict nor retracted its hope for the triumph of the workers and the defeat of capitalism.

The only thing that had changed, as far as Scowcroft could tell, was Soviet rhetoric. And he had had enough experience of dissembling by Soviet leaders to distrust Gorbachev's lofty pronouncements—at least not without concrete actions to back up his speech.

Worse yet, Reagan had been going about things the wrong way. His famous "Mr. Gorbachev, tear down this wall!" was a "lousy statement," in Scowcroft's judgment. The phrase itself didn't "advance anything," since the Berlin Wall remained standing. Not only did the United States have no way to enforce Reagan's declaration, but the statement was counterproductive, he pointed out—both belligerent and disrespectful. "It was presumptive and arrogant to tell another head of state how to act." Simple psychology suggested that by making such a blunt demand, Reagan "made it less likely that Gorbachev would tear down the wall," Scowcroft noted.[138] President Bush wholly agreed. "Every chief of state and head of government has pride in his country and should be treated with dignity and respect," he remarked on a separate occasion, "and that must include consulting with them."[139]

Rather than demanding that the Soviet Union take down the Berlin Wall, Scowcroft wanted a different approach, one that would make the wall "no longer necessary" by creating the underlying conditions that would cause it to be torn down. For the Bush administration to chart a new course, he believed the president first had to repair the damage done to both the substance and processes of national security policy. He had already seen the Reagan administration's 180-degree swing from being too harsh at the outset (calling the Soviet Union an "evil empire") to becoming "too embracing." He thus had reason to question Reagan and Shultz's handling of the US-Soviet strategic relationship. Where was the steady course? What was the overarching vision? What was the end game?

Scowcroft's understanding of the need for a comprehensive new strategy for dealing with the Soviet Union lay behind his call, in the first few weeks of the Bush administration, for strategic reviews of US foreign policy and of US-Soviet relations in particular—which was "obviously our first priority."[140]

Unfortunately, the review of US-Soviet policy turned out to be "very bureaucratic" and "very unimaginative," in Scowcroft's description (in large part because the political appointees in the State Department were carryovers from the Reagan administration who remained in office until the Senate approved their successors). So Scowcroft had Condoleezza Rice redraft the analysis based on a very productive and very positive talk the two of them had had in December 1988 about "getting ahead of the ferment in Eastern Europe." Rice's subsequent thirty-page memo outlined a process whereby the Bush administration would encourage change in Eastern Europe and try to get the Soviet Union to pull its troops out of Eastern Europe without provoking Gorbachev "to clamp down" or inducing "a hostile reaction against him." The United States should seek to "institutionalize" Gorbachev's reforms and then proceed to "move them in the direction we want."[141]

Getting the US-Soviet relationship right was the key to everything else, in Scowcroft's view, and the key to getting the US-Soviet relationship right "was Eastern Europe and changing things there." This meant building on what was happening in Poland and Hungary so that the administration could help the countries of Eastern Europe reform their own societies. But it also meant the United States would be reversing one of its Cold War policies: instead of encouraging those satellite countries that pushed back against

Soviet authority, such as Romania under the Ceausescus and Yugoslavia un-der Tito, it needed to support East European leaders who were already em-barking on internal reforms—even if such reforms coincided with the very policies Gorbachev was himself advocating. So Romania, "one of the most Stalinist of states," went "to the bottom of the list" under this logic, Scow-croft noted, while the Eastern Bloc states that were making most progress on political and economic reforms rose to the top of the list.[142]

Baker and Scowcroft delayed setting up any personal meetings between Bush and Gorbachev until they were sure of the direction they wanted to go. In July, Bush made a four-day trip to Poland and Hungary and attended the G-7 summit in Paris; he met with Gen. Wojciech Jaruzelski and Lech Walesa, and was enthusiastically received in Hungary. Only after this did Bush sit down on Air Force One, flying back from Paris, and write Gor-bachev a note inviting him to meet in person in advance of their planned formal summit in Washington in 1990. Had Bush called for a meeting any earlier than this, Gates said, "Gorbachev would not have had to face real-ity."[143] Bush and Gorbachev scheduled the summit for December 2–3 at the island of Malta in the central Mediterranean.

Before then, on September 22, the administration signaled a fundamen-tal shift in US-Soviet relations. National Security Directive 23 proclaimed that after forty years of containment, "a new era may be now upon us." Because the Soviet military still posed a threat, however, NSD 23 directed Cabinet members and agency leaders to promote "fundamental alterations in the Soviet military force structure, institutions, and practices" that, once started, "could only be reversed at great cost." The alterations would em-phasize verifiable arms control negotiations on reductions in force levels, transparency and confidence-building measures, and nonproliferation. They would further include economic, political, and cultural cooperation between the two superpowers so as to integrate the Soviet Union into the interna-tional system.[144]

Given the ten months that elapsed between Bush's inauguration and the Malta summit, a period that saw fast-moving events in Poland, Hungary, and East Germany, the Bush administration came under criticism for its "pause"—what the critics regarded as the administration's unneeded delay at working toward an end to the Cold War and its squandering of the pos-itive US-Soviet relations achieved by President Reagan and Shultz in their last years in office. Not only did Ambassador Matlock disagree with the pause, so, too, did Margaret Thatcher. Others were yet more critical. The White House had "no philosophy" and was "drifting," the Polish activist

Adam Michnik said. It was "sleepwalking through history." The *Washington Post*'s Don Oberdorfer similarly wrote of the "fledgling Bush administration['s] . . . painfully slow pace." The *Washington Post*'s David E. Hoffman was equally critical of what he considered to be the needless delay and, following Soviet official Anatoly Chernayev, called 1989 a "lost year." And on May 20, the *New York Times* editorialized: "Imagine that an alien spaceship approached earth and sent the message: 'Take me to your leader.' Who would that be? Without doubt, Mikhail Sergeyevich Gorbachev."[145]

Of course, it is impossible to know what would have happened had an earlier summit been held. But the subsequent success of the Bush administration in achieving its ultimate ends—culminating in the almost entirely peaceful end of the Cold War and the collapse of the Soviet empire—suggests that the critics were mistaken.

"You have to remember that this was a very amorphous time," the NSC director of Soviet affairs, Nicholas Burns, commented. "We were looking into the future and couldn't see clearly. The Warsaw Pact was falling apart; Eastern bloc states were expecting independence; [Boris] Yeltsin and Gorbachev were competing for power. [It was a] lot to handle."[146] And with the immense political, economical, and military stakes in play, Bush, Baker, and Scowcroft wanted to proceed cautiously and very deliberately.

Some on the NSC staff disagreed with Scowcroft's caution. "We saw this huge opportunity to change the Soviet Union," Burns noted, but Scowcroft "was very worried about all that could go wrong. Brent would bring us back to what could go wrong. Will it break up violently? Will we have warlords? What if it breaks up, if there are ethnic rebellions? It was a very, very prudent view, and got us to look at both sides of the equation," Burns commented. "But he was very much focused on this, and wanted to see change come peacefully."[147] Notwithstanding his deep-seated caution, Scowcroft was willing to be persuaded by new evidence and of new points of view. "Despite the fact that his experience and depth far exceeded ours," Burns added, "he listened to us."[148]

"We didn't know the depth of [the] forces" in play, Scowcroft conceded, and any number of outcomes were possible. It was "a matter of guiding and managing forces. Part of our goal was to keep things from moving too fast, and not have revolutions in Eastern Europe."[149] The transitions to new governments in Eastern Europe had to be handled very delicately, given the complexity of the situation there, the possibility of crackdowns and bloodshed by the ruling Soviet-backed communist governments, and the immensity of the stakes. Polish independence, the liberalization of East-West economic relations, and any other major changes in Eastern Europe could only occur peacefully if the Soviet Union allowed them.

Scowcroft and others in the administration wanted to encourage Gorbachev "in his moves to increase productivity, cut absenteeism, drinking, corruption," he explained, even though by doing so the Soviet leader "was pulling apart the sinews that held the system together." By encouraging reform and "trying to cultivate . . . 'little Gorbachevs' who would have popular support," Gorbachev was himself, oddly, acting the part of a US ally, Scowcroft observed. But what Gorbachev's pro-reform rhetoric ignored, he pointed out, was the fact that the communist regimes in Eastern European would likely be overthrown at the first opportunity, since their governments had been imposed from the outside, by the Soviet Union.[150]

It clearly wasn't in the United States' interest to incite "the military, KGB, or Party officials opposed to [Gorbachev's] reforms [to] energize enough to throw him out or to force him to turn and back away." Neither did the Bush administration want to leave a defeated Soviet Union feeling embittered and betrayed, as Germany had been after the Treaty of Versailles.[151] Scowcroft and the administration thus wanted to move slowly so as to coordinate changes in East-West relations with other developments on the balance of conventional weapons and nuclear forces, trade and finance, and political liberalization. The delayed response to Gorbachev's overtures and the quickly unfolding developments in Eastern Europe masked the care with which Bush and Scowcroft and Baker were orchestrating US policy.[152]

The administration wanted to move on several fronts. As soon as Bush, Baker, and Scowcroft were "confident about [their] purposes and agenda," they planned to communicate their intentions to the American public and international audiences. The White House needed to signal its commitment to the security of the United States' European allies, to the credibility of the NATO nuclear deterrence, and to making progress on arms control. It needed to take advantage of the "potential weak link" of Eastern Europe, where the best lever the United States and its allies had was economic aid. And it had to move "aggressively to promote regional stability" in the Middle East, Afghanistan and Central Asia, Indochina, Central America, and elsewhere.[153]

The administration proceeded according to the principles spelled out in Rice's memo of March 1989. President Bush would deliver a series of foreign policy addresses, while the administration simultaneously took additional steps.

They took up European security first. Following up on their conversations from the transition period, Scowcroft proposed to Bush that the United

States and Soviet Union each withdraw their ground forces from Central Europe, with the Soviets pulling back their troops into the USSR and the Americans pulling their forces back across the Atlantic. Scowcroft's logic was that the "NATO minus US and [the] Warsaw Pact minus USSR" would be to the United States' net advantage, and thought it was precisely the sort of bold initiative the administration needed to be making. After all, it was the presence of Soviet soldiers that allowed the Soviet Union to dominate its satellite countries, so it made sense for the administration to see if Gorbachev was actually willing to pull his conventional forces out of Eastern Europe in his stated effort to improve East-West tension and renunciation of repression.

The proposal generated a firestorm. "Many people thought it was a terrible idea," Scowcroft reported, and "Cheney about had a heart attack." In any event, the "idea got people thinking."[154] Bush decided to go ahead, but he did agree to scale back the plan, calling for each side to withdraw thirty thousand troops (instead of Scowcroft's larger number). The plan exemplified the dual basis by which Bush, Baker, and Scowcroft wanted to proceed: they would be proactive and look for real opportunities with the Soviet Union, on one hand, but also test the Soviets, on the other.

Scowcroft recognized that in the reductions in conventional force levels in the European theater were inevitably linked the numbers of nuclear weapons, especially with respect to short-range nuclear forces, whether nuclear missiles, nuclear artillery shells, or other nuclear weapons (SNF). And because he wanted to avoid a split in NATO—a majority of Germans opposed SNF—any change in strategic weapons had to be considered in conjunction with changes in the balance of conventional forces. Furthermore, any adjustment in the numbers of nuclear weapons placed in Germany had to be coordinated with other NATO members, especially Great Britain and France.

This promised difficult negotiations. The Bush administration wanted to keep its short-range nuclear missiles in Germany (the mobile-launched Lance missile) so as to have a credible deterrent, given the Warsaw Pact's great advantage in conventional forces. Scowcroft saw the short-range missiles as indispensable to German and European security. (In fact, Scowcroft had wanted to keep the INF and get rid of SNF, but the Reagan administration had already eliminated the INF.) However, a broad coalition of Germans wanted to eliminate the short-range missiles as well from German soil and, if possible, to denuclearize Europe. As one Bundestag member said of the Lance, "The shorter the range, the 'deader' the Germans."[155] Making things worse for Scowcroft and the Bush administration, the Soviets were openly encouraging West Germany to remove the Lance missiles.

The resulting controversy made the resolution of the Lance issue and the setting of conventional force levels in Europe exceedingly difficult, which was why Scowcroft called the administration's first six months "agony."[156] "What we needed to do, if we were to use nuclear weapons short of ICBMs," Scowcroft said, "was to get behind the front lines and be able to interdict Soviet reinforcements coming up to the battle line. Those are the INF forces," he pointed out. "They're not the short ones." Scowcroft continued:

I thought we gave ourselves two problems with INF. We removed our ability to do the kinds of strikes that they were useful for, what we really needed to stop a Soviet assault. It left us with weapons [the SNF forces] that were increasingly difficult politically to maintain, and to have acceptable in Germany. Actually, when the Cold War began to collapse in 1989 and things started to break down, it created a tremendous problem for us, especially with German unification coming up. Those weapons would all go off in Germany.[157]

Fortunately, the compromise on the conventional force reduction and Lance that Scowcroft and the administration would come up with made Bush look like a hero.[158]

With a possible summit meeting still months away, the administration wanted to provide a context for future negotiations with the Soviets. The president thus agreed to deliver a series of speeches to communicate the administration's views of US foreign policy to the Congress, the public, US allies, and, especially, East European and Soviet audiences.

The historic changes brewing in Poland—including the legalization of Solidarity on April 5, 1989, the creation of the position of president of Poland, the establishment of a one-hundred-seat senate, and the promise of democratic elections—gave the White House an excellent opportunity to present its message. If the Polish elections were held as scheduled, it would mark the beginning of the end of communist rule in Poland and set a stunning precedent for the rest of Eastern Europe.[159]

The administration planned its first speech for April 17 in a Polish American enclave near Detroit by the name of Hamtramck. In the speech, which Scowcroft described as the administration's "first major step on Eastern Europe," Bush spoke of the passing of totalitarianism, the spread of freedom, the right of self-determination for Poles and other East Europeans, and the need for an end to Soviet domination. He emphasized the United States' desire for a prosperous, free, and peaceful Poland and Eastern Europe, and said that the United States was willing to extend its economic support to those goals. The White House came up with a symbolic $100 million (Poland had requested $10 billion) and agreed to reschedule the Polish debt, conditional upon its adoption of market reforms, support of human rights, promotion of cultural openness, and opposition to international terror. There could be no progress without "significant political and economic liberalization," Bush stated, but should Poland undertake political and market reforms, US and Western assistance would be forthcoming.[160]

Although the speech received little coverage domestically—the mind-set of American reporters seemed to be that nothing of importance could possibly be announced in a small Polish community in the Detroit metropolitan area—Bush's address attracted careful attention from audiences in Poland, Eastern Europe, the Soviet Union, and Western Europe.[161]

However, the Hamtramck speech revealed two chronic problems besetting Scowcroft and his NSC staff. One was that Scowcroft and his staff rarely had as much control over the speechwriting as they would have liked—"a major irritant," in Scowcroft's words. Sununu ran the speechwriting out of the White House Office of Communications, and he tended to side with the speechwriters and their wish for "more dramatic rhetoric" rather than with the members of the NSC staff. Unfortunately, the snappy prose and the built-in applause lines didn't always match the seriousness of the foreign policy being proposed or the president's personality—to say nothing of Scowcroft's own sensibilities and those of his aides. In particular, Scowcroft complained of the "choppy political-campaign style" of the text, "hardly befitting a serious discussion of important policy issues." (Bush conceded that the problems were partly his own fault for not spending enough time with his speechwriters before giving an address.)

The second problem was money. The United States needed to encourage the changes happening in Poland, Scowcroft argued, and financial aid was one of the chief instruments available to the administration. The secretary of the treasury disagreed. Brady's argument in a NSC meeting of April 4 was that the United States had previously poured funds into Poland, but, without economic reforms in place, Poland ended up heavily in debt and no better off. He said, in effect, "Look, Poland squandered the money we gave them in 1976—let's wait." The president himself was torn; he recognized that the administration needed to be able to offer some financial assistance, but he would have preferred the program to be self-funding.

Scowcroft said this fight between the NSC and the Treasury Department was never settled, and so the administration ended up allocating "pathetically small amounts" of aid. Not only did this situation last throughout 1989, with the administration offering only $25 million to support Hungary, but it prevailed throughout the Bush administration's four years in office.[162] The Commerce Department wasn't much help, either, with officials worried that any changes in the United States' trade laws would create problems with its existing trade partners. Remarkably, Scowcroft found that Congress was more prepared to allocate money than was the administration. Where the government was willing to spend billions of dollars to fight wars, Scowcroft noted with irony, it wasn't willing to spend much to help its former adversaries adjust to their new democratic societies and market economies.[163]

The next opportunity for the president to present a fuller view of the administration's new policies came less than a month later, on May 12, at the Texas A&M commencement. This time, Scowcroft drafted most of the speech.[164]

"Containment worked," Bush told his College Station audience. The United States and the world were now "approaching the conclusion of an historic postwar struggle between two visions: one of tyranny and conflict and one of democracy and freedom." The United States therefore wanted US-Soviet relations to move "beyond containment" and integrate "the Soviet Union into the community of nations." But the United States had to be cautious, Bush warned, in consideration of the Soviet Union's "awesome military capabilities." He insisted that the Soviet Union stop aiding Cuba and Nicaragua, retract its ties with Libya and other terrorist states, respect the integrity of Chinese territory, and return Japan's northern territories.

Bush further exhorted the Soviet Union to reduce the numbers of tanks and military personnel stationed in Eastern Europe, to support the self-determination of East European states, to cease its support of Afghanistan and Angola, to expand its political freedoms at home, and to join the United States in combating global problems such as the drug trade and environmental destruction. If the Soviet Union sincerely wanted to establish a new relationship with the West, as Gorbachev said it did, then that relationship had to be earned and manifested through the Soviet Union's own actions; "promises," Bush stated, "are never enough." Still, "we are ready to extend our hand" and "are ready for a hand in return." He held out the carrots of increased trade with the United States and the West, greater foreign investment, and more financial aid should the Soviet Union reform its economy.[165]

The president provided further detail on his vision for Europe on May 21 at the Boston University commencement. He spoke of NATO as the centerpiece and, for forty years, the guarantor of European security. He emphasized the importance of the Atlantic alliance's flexible response—that is, the array of conventional and nuclear forces at NATO's disposal—and he warned of Western complacency. The Warsaw Pact still maintained a twelve-to-one advantage over NATO forces in short-range missiles and rocket launchers capable of delivering nuclear weapons and a two-to-one edge in battle tanks, for example. The United States sought "a real peace . . . of shared optimism," Bush declared, "not a peace of armed camps."[166]

Three days later, on May 24, Bush spoke at the US Coast Guard Academy. Unfortunately, the speech as drafted was "bombastic, hard-line, and full of 'macho' Cold War expressions," in Scowcroft's description. Luckily, Scowcroft was able to pull the draft, and he worked through the night to get it into shape.[167]

The final draft struck a balance between firmness and openness. On one hand, Bush called communism a "failed system" that was unable "to deliver the goods," and he warned of the "misguided notions of economic nationalism." He spoke of the commitment and resolve on the part of the United States and its allies, who were "strong, stronger really than at any point in the postwar period." The president also affirmed that US policy was to "defend American interests in light of the enduring reality of Soviet military power," and pointed out the indispensable role that nuclear deterrence had played in the United States' Cold War strategy. He also noted the United States' commitment to the Strategic Defense Initiative.[168]

Bush was careful to match his strong words with gentler ones, inviting the Soviet Union to join the world of democracies. So, on the other hand, he favorably referred to the "voices" in Tiananmen Square "speaking the language of democracy and freedom" (although two weeks later Chinese authorities would squash those very voices). He offered the prospect of Western aid should the Soviet Union "embrace free market reforms," and he invited Gorbachev to cooperate with him on creating a Europe where war was no longer an option and on establishing "a better, more stable relationship" with the United States.[169] As with the three previous speeches Scowcroft had helped draft, the New London address was at once plainspoken, hard-nosed, and optimistic.

With the NATO summit in Brussels coming up at the end of May, the Bush administration settled on a proposal for levels of conventional forces in Europe. In order to avoid having the proposal derailed by NATO's normal bureaucratic processes, Bush, Scowcroft, and Baker quietly presented it only to key allies such as British prime minister Margaret Thatcher and West German chancellor Helmut Kohl prior to the meeting. Their back-channel diplomacy paid off. At the Brussels meetings, the president and the European heads of state agreed to reduce the numbers of tanks, armored personnel carriers, and artillery as agreed upon by the Warsaw Pact nations, to cut existing NATO levels of combat aircraft and helicopters 15 percent below current levels, and put a ceiling of 275,000 on the numbers of US and Soviet soldiers in Europe—which meant the Soviets had to withdraw 325,000 troops, and the United States only 7,500, or 20 percent—and to a "partial reduction" of short-range nuclear weapons (not their total removal, as Germany wanted). All these measures were to go into effect by 1993.

Gorbachev welcomed the proposal as "a serious and specific response," and even Britain's hawkish prime minister, Margaret Thatcher, received the proposal warmly. As French president François Mitterrand said, "We need innovation. The President of the United States has displayed imagination—indeed, intellectual audacity of the rarest kind." Scowcroft called the NATO summit "a resounding success."[170] Kohl and other European leaders had looked to Bush to provide leadership and direction, and Bush, Scowcroft, Baker, and their staffs provided it.

Bush and his foreign policy team then accompanied Kohl to Mainz, Germany, where Bush delivered the fifth, capstone address in the administration's planned unveiling of its strategic vision for US-European and US-Soviet relations.[171] He spoke for the first time of "a Europe whole and free," in view of the fact that Poland was "taking the first steps toward real election, so long promised, so long deferred, and in Hungary, at last we see a chance for multiparty competition at the ballot box." The United States sought "self-determination for all of Germany and for all of Eastern Europe," he said. (Scowcroft struck out an explicit mention of "German reunification" from the final version of the speech, anxious not to unnecessarily stimulate German nationalism and foreign concerns by raising the "sensitive" topic.) The president voiced his support for a broadening of the Helsinki process, proposed that the United States work with Germany and other European nations on environmental issues, and called for an end to the arms race—especially in Europe, "the most heavily armed continent in the world." He wanted a continent with "borders open to people, commerce, and ideas."

Bush assured the Soviets that "our goal is not to undermine their legitimate security interests." Rather, the United States' "goal is to convince them, step-by-step, that their definition of security is obsolete, that their deepest fears are unfounded." Real security isn't based on "tanks, troops, or barbed wire," Bush declared. "It is built on shared values and agreements that link free peoples." After forty years, NATO's original mission was almost complete.[172]

But the ultimate challenge was Berlin. What would happen with respect to East and West Germany, beyond the transformations already afoot in Poland, Hungary, Czechoslovakia, and Bulgaria?[173]

═══

THROUGHOUT THE REVOLUTIONARY changes that occurred as the Cold War moved toward its end—such as the election of a non-Communist government in Poland in early April and the cutting of the barbed wire on the Austria-Hungary border in late June—Scowcroft managed US policy with a light hand, trusting his staff and coordinating policy with the State and Defense Departments as well as other relevant agencies. The national security advisor delegated extensively and saw to it that the president's speeches, diplomatic and military negotiations, intelligence, and other aspects of US national policy were consistent with the administration's objectives and coordinated across the government.

Scowcroft also participated as a policy maker in his own right, though because he did so behind the scenes, few outside the White House recognized his influence.

Part of this influence took the form of restraint: policy making through inaction. In this respect, Scowcroft's conservative and cautious attitudes in most cases coincided with those of George Bush.

The administration advocated a deliberate pace for self-determination in Poland, given that events were happening at a "stunning speed," and it avoided "rhetoric or the appearance of interference, which could only rankle the Soviets at a time when we hoped they would acquiesce in the positive evolution they had helped foster."[174] And when General Jaruzelski, who lacked the support needed to elect his own candidate as prime minister, asked Solidarity to form a government—with Walesa agreeing, in turn, to keep Poland in the Warsaw Pact and to name Communist Party members as the ministers of defense and interior—Scowcroft and others in the White House were overjoyed. But because the administration "did not want to embarrass the Soviets with Polish freedom at stake," its "public posture was therefore very restrained," with press secretary Marlin Fitzwater saying only that Bush "would encourage" the establishment of a noncommunist government.[175]

Later, the two men agreed there would be no celebrating after Hungary and Czechoslovakia renounced and overthrew their Communist governments and "no jumping on the wall" after the Berlin Wall fell. For the president, going to Berlin and making a triumphant speech, as some were urging, was "the last thing" he wanted to do because he still wanted "to be able to work with Gorbachev. We've got a big agenda out there, and if I do that I will have lost him because he will have been humiliated in his own context."[176]

Scowcroft sought to exert restraint in other ways—not always with success. When Gates planned to give a hard-line speech at Georgetown, Secretary of State James Baker objected and Scowcroft toned down the phrasing. Later, when Baker refused to let Gates give the softer address, Scowcroft didn't contest Baker's decision, and Gates wrote Baker a note of apology. Worse, Baker or one of his aides then leaked the story of Gates's squelched speech—that is, of the deputy national security advisor losing a turf battle to the secretary of state. While the leak enhanced recognition of Baker's clout within the administration, it undermined the administration's determination to present a united front in support of Gorbachev's reforms since it brought attention to Gates' (and others') pessimism on the prospects for Gorbachev and the Soviet Union.[177]

———

THE PRESIDENT'S NINE-DAY trip in July to Poland and Hungary met with resounding acclaim from both Polish and Hungarian leaders and their public audiences. Afterward, Bush, Scowcroft, and Baker traveled to the G-7 summit held in Paris on July 14–16. The meeting went smoothly and finished earlier than expected, with the United States managing to avoid establishing a general policy with respect to North-South economic issues, preferring to proceed bilaterally. The United States and the other six economic powers were able to establish a unified policy with respect to Poland's and Hungary's debt and to a program of foreign aid for them both—an accomplishment that Scowcroft credited Baker with achieving, in view of how little the United States had to contribute.[178]

But the US delegation did not appreciate Gorbachev's interruption of the meetings, in effect, to demand, via a letter he asked chairman François Mitterrand to read, that the Soviet Union be allowed to participate in the promotion of worldwide growth and the mitigation of the Third World debt. Gorbachev was effectively seeking to join the exclusive G-7 fraternity. "Perestroika," the Soviet leader wrote, "is inseparable from a policy aimed at our full participation in the world economy." Upon hearing Gorbachev's message, Baker exclaimed, "He's trying to hijack the summit! He's butting in, screwing up what we want to accomplish here." Scowcroft called the Soviet leader's actions "pure grandstanding!"[179]

Meanwhile, the growing popularity of the Russian democrat and populist leader Boris Yeltsin presented a separate problem. Cheney, the Department of Defense, and some in the intelligence community wanted the administration to be more aggressive with respect to US relations with the Soviet republics, and Gates and Condoleezza Rice doubted that Gorbachev would remain party secretary for long. For these reasons, they wanted Bush to meet with Yeltsin and other reformers in the Soviet Union. Gates remembered what had happened with the Ford administration not inviting Aleksandr Solzhenitsyn to the White House, and he thought it was dangerous for the president to pin everything on one leader, especially when that person was walking a political tightrope.

Scowcroft and Bush and Baker, for their part, were more protective of Gorbachev. Bush and Scowcroft were wary of a White House meeting with Yeltsin—who seemed to be a boor and drank too much—and they didn't want to undermine their relationship with the Soviet leader or assist his opposition in any way. Baker, especially, had developed a good relationship with Soviet foreign minister Shevardnadze and didn't want to jeopardize their relationship. It was only after what Gates called a "huge fight" that he and Rice had with Scowcroft that the national security advisor agreed to arrange a visit with Yeltsin. In order to deflect attention from the press and reduce expectations, they decided to have Yeltsin come to a side entrance to the White House to meet with Scowcroft in his own office, then have the president intentionally "drop by."[180]

Yeltsin wasn't pleased with the plan. It was only after some difficult persuasion and intense effort that Rice managed to override Yeltsin's objections, take hold of his elbow, and march him up to Scowcroft's corner office. Worse, once Yeltsin started reviewing at length the many ways the United States could help the Soviet economy, Scowcroft nodded off; fortunately, Yeltsin didn't appear to notice. Even better, his mood improved markedly ("chameleon like," Gates said), and Scowcroft woke up once the president arrived. Bush and Yeltsin then had a productive talk, notwithstanding Bush's affirmation of his support for Gorbachev.[181] Afterward, Yeltsin held a press conference outside the West Wing, telling reporters that he had presented the president and vice president a ten-point plan to save perestroika. Scowcroft didn't like his grandstanding, complaining that "Yeltsin was 'devious' and a 'two-bit headline grabber.'"[182]

Ten months later, on June 12, 1990, Yeltsin would be elected president of Russia.

———

ON SEPTEMBER 11, 1989, at 12:01 A.M., the gates between Hungary and Austria lifted and an unbroken stream of East German cars, carrying about ten thousand people in all, fled from behind the Iron Curtain. Less than a month later, on October 7, 1989, the Hungarian Communist Party dissolved, replaced by the Hungarian Socialist Party. In Czechoslovakia, the Communist Party in fell on December 5, replaced by an elected government, and on December 29 playwright Vaclev Havel was elected president. After the changes in Poland and now Hungary, East German leader Erich Honecker came under increasing pressure for reform.

Scowcroft watched Gorbachev carefully: with Honecker on the edge, would the Soviet leader "swallow his principles" to support his own Soviet empire, or would he distance himself from an unsympathetic Honecker? In fact, Honecker had met with the deputy prime minister of China, sympathized with his plight, and hinted that the East Germans could face the same violent response as the protesters in Beijing. Ambassador Matlock, too, warned the White House that the Soviet Union might intervene.[183]

Fortunately, it never came to that. On October 18 Honecker resigned, replaced as prime minister by Egon Krenz. Two weeks later, on November 1, half a million East Germans took to the streets in protest. Although Egon Krenz was no more successful at quelling the East German crowds, he reassured Gorbachev that he didn't want to fire on the demonstrators.[184] Less than a week later, on November 7, the whole East German cabinet resigned.

The influx of East Germans was making life difficult in West Berlin and for Helmut Kohl, who estimated that West Germany would have 150,000 refugees by Christmas.[185] Scowcroft worried that East Germany "would collapse into violent chaos" and then draw in West Germany and perhaps the Soviet Union, given East Germany's location on the front line of the Cold War and its prominence as the wealthiest and most successful Warsaw Pact state.

The fast-moving events culminated in the fall of the Berlin Wall on November 9, 1989. Upon hearing at about three o'clock in the afternoon that the Wall had opened, Scowcroft went into the Oval Office and told the president, where they were soon joined by Marlin Fitzwater. The three of them went into the small study off the Oval Office and watched live television images of the joyful crowds. Scowcroft then said he didn't know what was going on, and he urged rhetorical restraint. It was no time to declare, "We won, we have a victory." It wasn't the time to gloat over what most would see as a defeat for Gorbachev and the Soviet Union, he said. The only thing they knew for sure was that people were going through the checkpoints without hindrance. Both he and Bush wanted "to anticipate Gorbachev's reaction—and that of his opposition" within the Soviet Union, they later wrote.[186] It might take years for the situation in Germany to become clear, they thought.

The president did invite the White House press pool into the Oval Office. It was then that CBS correspondent Lesley Stahl said, "You don't seem very happy about this. Isn't this the fundamental breakthrough in the Cold War?"

"Well, I'm not an excitable kind of guy," Bush replied. He didn't want to say too much, especially things that might later be contradicted. His "mind kept racing over a possible Soviet crackdown, turning all the happiness to tragedy." He had been to the Wall and seen "where young East Germans had been shot as they tried to cross to freedom in the West." He knew that the process had to continue, and didn't want a false step to "destroy the joy" felt in Berlin and East Germany. But in being so reticent, he was blamed for being uncaring.[187]

Gorbachev reacted immediately to the news of the Berlin Wall. He cabled Bush, exhorting him not to overreact, and warned Kohl not to talk about reunification. Nevertheless, "overnight, the most important symbol of the Iron Curtain had been struck down," Scowcroft remarked. More than 250,000 East Germans had already left for West Berlin, and the "frontiers are absolutely open," Kohl told Bush over the telephone.[188]

Anatoly Chernyaev, Gorbachev's adviser, didn't miss the significance of what had happened: "The Berlin Wall has collapsed. This entire era in the history of the socialist system is over. . . . For it has to do not only with socialism, but with the shift in the world balance of forces. This is the end of Yalta . . . the Stalinist legacy and the 'defeat of Hitlerite Germany.'"[189] And within weeks, the Communist governments in Bulgaria and Czechoslovakia also fell.

As the December summit in Malta approached, one of Scowcroft's concerns was that Gorbachev might have a "surprise" for President Bush—a bold gambit for which they weren't prepared. Baker suggested the reverse: that Bush seize the initiative by proposing seventeen different initiatives. Scowcroft didn't like Baker's presentation, though, which he called "unprofessional at best and corny at worst." Rather, he wanted the president to offer a "big picture" of US-Soviet relations, so as to review "the perils and opportunities before us."[190]

But Bush decided to use Baker's plan. First, however, Bush reworked the initiatives, going over "every one of them" on the plane over to Malta. He took out the conditions and caveats the State Department and Pentagon had put on what he was prepared to give the Soviet Union and instead made the US offers harder and stronger while simultaneously including more opportunities for the Soviet Union.[191]

As revised by the president, Baker's plan worked. Bush presented Gorbachev with a long list of proposals: the renewal of strategic arms reduction talks (START); the expansion of trade and possibly bestowing most-favored-nation status on the Soviet Union (thus waiving the Jackson-Vanik restrictions); the further emigration of Russian Jews; the establishment of a detailed protocol for the conduct of on-site inspection of nuclear weapons; the determination of the terms of German reunification; a plan for cooperation in Latin America; and other initiatives. Each proposal was matched by a US concession. Hearing the points, Marlin Fitzwater reported that "Gorbachev's face lit up like sunshine"; the moment "defined a new relationship" and "set a whole new course for the East-West relationship."[192]

Scowcroft described the atmosphere on the *Maxim Gorkiy* as "friendly" although "not relaxed," even though he and Bush knew every member of the Soviet delegation. He recognized that Baker's gambit had worked: Bush "had obviously upset" whatever Gorbachev had planned, Scowcroft later wrote in *A World Transformed*. The Soviet leader "appeared nonplussed after having been buried in an avalanche of US proposals." On all fronts, the Bush administration had hoped to push the Soviets—and it succeeded in doing so.[193]

Following the opening plenary session, Bush met with Gorbachev privately for four and half hours, accompanied only by Scowcroft, adviser Anatoly Chernyaev, and their interpreters. Afterward, the US delegation barely managed to get back on board the USS *Belknap* because of the roughness of the seas, which meant that the Americans had to eat their dinner alone since it would have been impossible for a boat or helicopter to bring Gorbachev to their ship. For a brief time, the president and his staff were "truly isolated" from the outside world.

Though the weather improved a little by the next morning, Gorbachev still didn't want to budge from his ship. In the second day's meetings on the Soviet cruise ship, President Bush stressed that he "couldn't disapprove of German reunification" and that both sides were aware of the Helsinki Accords' position on national and German borders. Bush also emphasized the significance of the Baltics, notwithstanding Gorbachev's point that they had large Russian populations and had coexisted with the Soviet Union for fifty years. Scowcroft believed that Gorbachev signaled he would "restrict himself to non-coercive measures."[194] The two sides couldn't cover all of the points that Bush initially raised, since the weather had forced the cancellation of one of the sessions; Bush agreed that Baker and Shevardnadze would work on the remaining items.

In Bush and Scowcroft's judgment, the summit had been a great success. The president thought he had established a rapport with Gorbachev. Scowcroft thought the meeting had gone better than planned, since it renewed the impetus for further US-Soviet negotiations on conventional forces, START, chemical weapons, Cuba, Nicaragua, and other issues. (Gorbachev, in response, asked Bush why the United States was then able to intervene in Panama, Colombia, and most recently, the Philippines.)[195] For Scowcroft, "the key accomplishment was the exchange on almost every topic of mutual interest." Scowcroft further appreciated the fact that his fears hadn't been realized: Gorbachev did not try to use the concluding joint press conference to one-up Bush, score points, or distort the contents of the talks.[196]

As important, perhaps, Bush and Scowcroft began to get a feel for Gorbachev over the course of the meetings. They begin to like the Soviet president and empathize with his predicament in trying to reform an economically struggling Soviet Union, especially with a powerful, resistant military establishment lurking in the background. Although Scowcroft and Bush had been more cautious initially, Baker reports that by Malta, they all "came to the conclusion that these guys were genuine reformers, that we should work with them, that we could work with them, and that we hoped that they would succeed in the *perestroika* and *glasnost*."[197] Gorbachev also viewed the summit as a "clear success" and as allowing for a rapport to develop between him and Bush as well as between their two foreign ministers.[198]

If the Malta summit went as well as could be hoped by preparing the way for reductions in conventional and nuclear forces, the banning of chemical weapons, establishing further economic relations, and creating a rapport between the American and Soviet leaders ("Scowcroft said his conversation with General Akhromayev was the best he had ever had with a Soviet official," Bush reported), some issues remained unresolved.[199] Bush and Gorbachev could not agree on Cuba (that the American president open a dialogue with Fidel Castro), on US intervention in Panama and the

Philippines (where the United States acted unilaterally in both countries), and on Afghanistan (where the administration would not recognize the Najibullah government, even though Gorbachev claimed that "his position is stronger and many commanders and tribal authorities are cooperating with him").[200]

However, the Malta summit started a process of positive engagement, accompanied by diplomatic exchanges and punctuated by further meetings. In the face of Gorbachev's deteriorating political condition within the Soviet Union, Bush, Baker, and Scowcroft were able to offer the Soviet leader a consistent agenda and political structure within which to respond. In practical terms, this meant that the president, Baker, and Scowcroft avoided threatening the integrity of the Soviet Union or challenging it directly. Wary of the sensitivity and continued power of the Soviet military and Communist Party hard-liners, they didn't want to give Soviet conservatives anything to seize upon.

Meanwhile, the situation on the ground in central Europe—particularly in Germany—was changing fast, all too fast. The Bush administration's existing theories of geopolitics would require rethinking in dealing with this volatile new world.[201]

19

GARDENING IN A TEMPEST

GEORGE BUSH AND Brent Scowcroft had a better relationship and more experience with China than had any other US president and national security advisor with the exception of Richard Nixon and Henry Kissinger. It's understandable that they expected to be able to improve US-China relations following the difficulties of the Carter and Reagan years. But despite their optimistic outlook on US-China relations, they had even more serious difficulties than had the two previous presidencies. In many ways, the history of US-China relations during the Bush presidency was the history of four deaths—one in January, one in April, and two in December 1989—and the long shadows they cast.

But Bush and Scowcroft persevered. By the end of their administration, China would be engaged in the global economy, poised to prosper, and on the verge of becoming, at last, a superpower.

The first of those deaths was that of Emperor Hirohito of Japan on January 7, 1989. Hirohito's state funeral provided an opportunity for President Bush to engage in one-on-one talks in Tokyo with many heads of state and to make short visits afterward to Beijing and Seoul.[202]

The second death was that of former Chinese party secretary and political reformer Hu Yaobang on April 15. Two days after Hu's death, university students in Beijing donned black armbands and put up posters protesting his 1987 ouster and ongoing corruption within the Chinese Communist Party leadership. On April 22, fifty thousand students, workers, and city residents assembled in Tiananmen Square to present petitions for reform and democratization. The demonstrations grew in size until May 20, when the Chinese politburo—its ruling committee—declared martial law.[203] In the early morning hours of June 4, soldiers arrived in Tiananmen Square and opened fire on crowds of unarmed civilians. The killing continued for days, with the total number of deaths estimated at between 1,000 and 2,600.[204]

Tiananmen Square would become a byword for Chinese government repression and pose a huge obstacle to good relations between the United States and China—an obstacle that Bush and Scowcroft somehow had to overcome.

The third and fourth deaths were those of Nicolae and Elena Ceausescu, executed at almost exactly the same instant on Christmas Day, 1989, by a Romanian paratrooper firing squad. The Ceausescus had fled Bucharest after their country's December 21 revolution, only to be captured and, following a two-hour trial, placed against a wall and shot. Ceausescu's Romania had been a longtime ally of China, and the executions, which the Chinese leaders saw on videotape, darkly underscored the dangers of the developments in Eastern Europe. If the Tiananmen Square massacre made the elderly members of the ruling committee defensive, the deaths of the Ceausescus, coming on the heels of the peaceful revolutions in East Germany, Poland, Hungary, and Czechoslovakia earlier that year, spooked them. They understood that the same might happen to them.[205]

So Hirohito's death presented President Bush with an opportunity to reach out to China's leaders—but the other three deaths focused attention on the challenges those leaders faced in a world where the communist system was rapidly collapsing. The response of the Chinese party leaders was to clamp down. Not until early 1992 would the Chinese government start to make economic development its top priority, embrace entrepreneurship, accept business growth as desirable, encourage wealth, and open up to international trade and foreign investment. This slow turn toward capitalism and gradual return to Confucianism and Chinese tradition marked a departure from communist principles—though not from the rule of China's Communist Party leadership.[206]

The steadfast handling of China by Brent Scowcroft and the rest of the Bush administration throughout these tumultuous years amounted to a kind of "gardening": a careful attention to dialogue, diplomacy, and the cultivation of relationships even during difficult times when a clear agenda was lacking and the potential for results seemed scanty. It meant listening and waiting patiently until the time was ripe for moving forward.

However fallow US-China relations may have seemed for the years 1989 through 1992—the "worst" period in US-China diplomacy since before 1972, the NSC's Douglas Paal said in an interview[207]—the cultivation of US-China relations by Bush, Scowcroft, and their aides prepared the ground for future growth and blossoming. Their thoughtful engagement enabled US-China relations to morph after 1992 into the complicated, often mutually beneficial, and not always consistent mix of political, economic, and military policies connecting the two countries today.

———

SCOWCROFT HAD SUGGESTED to Bush that they contact Chinese leaders soon after the inauguration. Both men believed in the fundamental importance of US-China relations. What's more, Soviet leader Gorbachev was scheduled to visit China in May 1989, and Bush and Scowcroft wanted to talk to the Chinese leaders before he did. They "were frankly worried" about Gorbachev's skill. He had mesmerized Europe already, and they feared he would be able to charm the Chinese, holding out the promise of a better relationship and an end to conflict on their borders, which had been such a troublesome issue for both of them for a couple of decades.[208]

Emperor Hirohito's state funeral, scheduled for February 24, "gave us a great opportunity," Scowcroft said. State funerals can be windfalls in the world of international diplomacy. They allow national leaders to become acquainted, or reacquainted, with one another despite their extraordinarily busy schedules. Heads of state, foreign ministers, and other state representatives can conduct business free of the usual political constraints, and issues can be broached with foreign counterparts. The death of Hirohito would enable the onetime chief of the US liaison office in China—now the president—to confer with his old friends about Gorbachev, the Soviet Union, and the US-China relationship.[209] It would mark the first time in American history that a US president had traveled to the Far East before Europe upon taking office.

Barely a week after the presidential inauguration, Scowcroft met with Chinese ambassador Han Xu to plan Bush's visit. Bush would have meetings with Deng Xiaoping as well as president Yang Shangkun, premier Li Peng, and party general secretary Zhao Ziyang.[210] As the capstone to the trip, Bush was to host a banquet the Sunday after he arrived in Beijing. The dinner, to be held at the Sheraton Great Wall Hotel, would honor Chinese president Yang Shangkun and reciprocate for President Yang's dinner honoring President Bush the evening before. The meal was going to be Texas barbecue, complete with checkered tablecloths, country music, bandana-wearing waiters, and other Texas-themed decorations.

Five hundred guests were invited, a little more than half of them Chinese. The American embassy invited top party leaders and dozens of other prominent Chinese as well as important Americans residing in China. The list, compiled by ambassador Winston Lord and his staff, included a handful of political dissidents—foremost among them the astrophysicist Fang Lizhi.[211]

Fang Lizhi, fifty-three years old, was a brilliant astrophysicist, an outspoken dissenter, and immensely self-confident. Intensely committed to reform and courageous in pursuit of his ideals, Fang was a long-standing advocate of democracy and a fervent critic of Marxism. Chinese authorities had sent Fang to labor in a coal mine and a brick factory for a year as part of a reeducation campaign during the Cultural Revolution, and in January 1987 they expelled Fang from the Communist Party and banned all of his political writings. In January 1989, only a month before President Bush's visit, Fang had called for an amnesty for political prisoners and for the release of Wei Jingsheng, another prominent dissident.[212] Fang represented what Deng Xiaoping found most upsetting: the refusal of people to understand that China could develop only if there was political stability. To tolerate Fang would be to tolerate instability, and this, for Deng and the leaders around him, was impossible.

On February 10, the embassy sent the final guest list to the White House, with a cover letter in which the names of the dissidents, their identities, and the reasons for inviting them were highlighted. When the embassy received no response from the White House, it resent the list, once more flagging the names of the dissidents and highlighting Fang Lizhi's name.[213]

For American diplomats to invite political dissidents to US-hosted events in foreign countries wasn't unusual. It was important for the United States to acknowledge its commitment to human rights and political freedoms, sending a message both to American observers and to reformers and dissidents in China and elsewhere around the world.[214] During the Reagan years, US officials had contacted dissidents when they'd visited the Soviet Union, for instance. So in inviting Fang Lizhi to the Bush dinner, State Department officials believed they were simply carrying on the practices of the Reagan administration.[215]

However, the week before the banquet, Chinese officials learned that Fang Lizhi had been invited, and they complained to the US embassy that Fang's attendance would be unacceptable. State Department officials sought clarification of the seriousness of the objection, and a few days later, the Chinese vice minister for foreign affairs responded: President Yang Shangkun and other Chinese leaders would refuse to go to the banquet if Fang was there.[216] Ambassador Lord said he would inform President Bush.

Twenty hours before the president's arrival, scheduled for Saturday, February 24, the Chinese further stiffened their position in a particularly ugly meeting with the ambassador and other State Department officials. But not until four hours before Air Force One was to land in China did it become fully apparent that the Chinese leaders wouldn't attend the banquet. A very worried Lord flashed a cable to Bush to warn him of the deteriorating situation.[217] When Bush received the message, he shouted at his aides, "Who *is* Fang Lizhi?"[218]

The president was understandably upset. If the Chinese party leaders skipped the banquet, it would defeat the purpose of the evening and cast a grim shadow over the entire visit. Bush and Scowcroft were furious with Lord and the embassy. Feeling sandbagged, they gave Lord the cold shoulder upon arriving in Beijing.[219] Scowcroft and J. Stapleton Roy, the deputy assistant secretary of state, thereupon immediately began intense, secret negotiations with Chinese officials to see if they could resolve the problem.

Neither side could easily back down, for fear of international embarrassment if the story got out. Scowcroft, Roy, and their Chinese counterparts argued for hours, with no progress.[220] Scowcroft refused to rescind the invitation, despite the Chinese insistence that the United States do so, and the Chinese refused to accept the president's invitation if Fang were to attend the banquet, so the stalemate dragged on. The breakthrough came at around three o'clock in the morning, when the Chinese asked Scowcroft, "What if Fang doesn't come?" That, Scowcroft replied, would be Fang's business. (When asked about the statement later, he explained—a bit disingenuously—that he didn't think the Chinese would interpret it to mean they could forcibly prevent Fang from attending the banquet.)[221]

Meanwhile, President Bush met with party chairman Deng Xiaoping at the Great Hall of the People, with Li Peng, and then with President Yang. The Chinese welcomed Bush and his entourage with "wonderful red and white banners" strung across the road, and they even put the US president on live television—the first time any American had been so featured. Bush gave Deng Xiaoping a pair of handmade leather boots, and the Chinese leader gave Bush a bicycle in recognition of the bicycling he'd done around Beijing while serving as US liaison officer. It was George Bush's fifth return to Beijing since his time as China liaison, and, as Barbara Bush remarked, "It was great to be back."[222]

Bush and the Chinese leaders then talked about the Soviet Union and its "encirclement" of China, Gorbachev's upcoming visit, and other issues, including Taiwan, North and South Korea, Vietnam and Cambodia, the

Middle East, Afghanistan, and nuclear proliferation. President Bush was very much encouraged by the meetings, and his press secretary described the session with Li Peng as "remarkable."[223]

Later that Sunday, the US embassy received a note saying that the Chinese party leaders would be attending the banquet after all. Lord received the news with immense relief, and he made sure that Fang's table wouldn't be in the direct line of sight of the head table, where the Chinese leaders, President Bush, Baker, Scowcroft, and he would be sitting. The ambassador assumed everything was settled.[224]

That evening, however, Beijing police intercepted Fang and his wife, Li Shuxian, on their way to the Sheraton Great Wall Hotel. Over the next four and a half hours, security forces repeatedly blocked Fang's attempts to get to the banquet, whether by car, by taxi, by bus, or on foot. Meanwhile, at the banquet, neither President Bush nor Ambassador Lord realized Fang wasn't in attendance, and the dinner went on as planned, to great success.[225]

Fang Lizhi refused to be silenced; he called a press conference, announcing what had happened to him. President Bush responded with only a mild statement of regret concerning how the Chinese had treated Fang. Combined with the fact that Bush hadn't earlier brought up human rights issues in his meetings with Chinese leaders, Bush's weak response to the Fang Lizhi incident provoked a furor. The human rights group Asia Watch, for instance, called Bush's silence on the treatment of Chinese political prisoners "deafening."[226] Political commentators and politicians accused the president of ignoring human rights and of kowtowing to the Chinese. The result was that the visit ended up being a "disaster," in the description of Ambassador Lord and the NSC's Paal.[227] It was an inauspicious start for the administration's conduct of foreign policy.

Back in Washington, Scowcroft gave a background briefing to the press on the administration's actions. He hadn't paid attention to Fang's name on the guest roster, he said, and President Bush hadn't even known of the invitation. (Henry Kissinger later told Deng Xiaoping and the other Chinese leaders the same thing, that President Bush hadn't known about the embassy's invitation to Fang Lizhi.)[228] Scowcroft's words implied that since the US embassy had invited Fang, the embassy was responsible for what had happened. He then wryly conceded to reporters that since Fang's name had slipped through the White House's screening process, they clearly could have handled things better.[229]

Ambassador Lord, members of his embassy staff, and State Department officials became upset when they learned what Scowcroft had told the press, feeling they'd been scapegoated for a problem that was not of their making.

Stapleton Roy, who would later become US ambassador in Beijing, assured the press the White House *had* seen the guest list—a list that included Fang Lizhi's name and those of the other invited dissidents—and that no one in the Bush White House had made any objections.[230]

Roy was right. Bush and Scowcroft *had* known that Fang was going to be at the banquet. Before leaving for Tokyo on February 20, Bush, Baker, and Scowcroft had met for several hours with several China and Asian experts at Camp David, and Fang's name had come up at the meeting.[231] In a press briefing the day before Bush, Scowcroft, and their staff were to depart, a reporter asked Scowcroft whether Fang Lizhi had been invited to the banquet and he answered, "Yes, yes." And Fang been discussed on Air Force One before the Americans landed in Beijing.[232]

So Scowcroft had known that Fang had been invited—he just hadn't foreseen how much trouble it would cause. "I was confronted with a problem I didn't know existed," he said. That's why he and Bush blamed Lord and the Beijing embassy: the ambassador and his staff had failed to anticipate the vehemence with which the Chinese party leaders would react to Fang's presence at the banquet. (Of course, no one in Washington had anticipated it, either.)

Reflecting back on the incident, Karl Jackson, the head of the East Asia directorate, said that Scowcroft and Bush didn't want a "hot potato in their laps" and thought "Win Lord showed bad judgment in not knowing that it was his responsibility to know the mind of the Chinese leadership." This is why Bush and Scowcroft were so upset at what Barbara Bush called an "amazing . . . gaffe."[233]

With the controversy, Fang Lizhi became the focal point of the difficulties in US-Chinese relations in the latter half of 1989. He became what ambassador James Lilley (who had worked with Bush in the US liaison office and would succeed Winston Lord) referred to as "a living symbol of our conflict with China over human rights."[234]

Two days later, once the dust had settled, Lord sent Scowcroft a carefully drafted back-channel message (one he'd rewritten about ten times, Lord recalled) in an effort to clear the air with a man he both liked and respected. Lord had the letter (which he copied to Secretary Baker) sent to the White House via the CIA. In the correspondence, Lord emphasized how important it was for the US government to signal to Chinese citizens, as well as to American and global audiences, its support for human rights and the democratic values of speech and political freedom. To retreat before the Chinese—as he considered Scowcroft and Bush to have done—was to appear weak to both the Chinese and fellow Americans.[235]

Scowcroft said he did not remember getting Lord's message, though Lord said that the CIA station chief had assured him that the cable had been handed personally to Scowcroft. The *New York Times'* Patrick Tyler reported that an NSC or White House official also distinctly remembered Scowcroft receiving the cable, and that Scowcroft became infuriated when he read it and called Lord a "bum."[236]

Lord thought Scowcroft's failure to acknowledge or respond to the cable was graceless. The ambassador believed he'd been unjustly blamed for something that wasn't his fault, and he called the incident the worst experience of his entire career.[237]

Lord left Beijing two months later, on April 23, 1989, embittered. Back in the States, he began to publicize his disagreements with the Bush administration and to speak out on behalf of a tougher and more ethical US-China policy. Lord subsequently published his criticism in *Foreign Affairs* and in a scathing op-ed in the *Washington Post*.[238] Lord later supported Clinton in the 1992 election, with the Clinton campaign making US-China relations one of its issues, and then served in the Clinton State Department as assistant secretary for East Asian and Pacific affairs.[239] Lord and Scowcroft remained estranged for twenty-two years. Not until June 2011 did the two reconcile.[240]

Bush and Scowcroft omit the incident in *A World Transformed*. It also goes unmentioned in two notable books, James Lilley's *China Hands* and Ezra F. Vogel's biography *Deng Xiaoping*.[241] Yet the controversy points to the profound differences that mark US-China relations and reveals Bush's and Scowcroft's foremost priority: protecting the US-China relationship, even at the expense of alienating the US ambassador in Beijing, his embassy staff, and others in the State Department.[242] If this meant appearing less than zealous about defending the human rights of Chinese dissidents, so be it.

Bush wasn't naive. While serving as the head of the Liaison Office and living in Beijing, during what had in many ways been a difficult and frustrating year, he had seen the harsh aspects of Chinese rule firsthand. He also knew of the brutal history of Chinese communism under Mao. But he nonetheless believed the best way to advance US interests was to cultivate friendly ties with Chinese officials and improve relations gradually, step by step.[243] Neither did Deng Xiaoping want any surprises. "With regard to the problems confronting China," he told Bush on February 26, "let me say to you that the overwhelming need is to maintain stability. Without stability, everything will be gone, even accomplishments will be ruined. We hope our friends abroad can understand this point."[244]

The contrasting perspectives of Bush and Scowcroft, on one hand, and of Lord and other critics of the administration, on the other hand, reflected both differing personal experiences and the deep-rooted philosophical disagreements those experiences helped to produce.

Bush had gotten to know Deng Xiaoping when he lived in Beijing in 1974–1975—a period after diplomatic relations had been established but before the People's Republic of China was the official "China" for the purposes of US diplomacy. Bush considered Deng a friend. When Barbara Bush later took a trip to China, she personally told Deng of her husband's intention to run for president.[245] So in 1989, with Bush having been elected president and with Deng having risen to be first among equals—with authority over the Army by virtue of his position as Chairman of the Party's Military Commission, although not a member of the Chinese politburo— Bush had no desire to upset or alienate him.

By contrast, Scowcroft viewed Ambassador Lord and, later, Ambassador Lilley as "more political, more emotional, more democratic," and he viewed Lord and his wife, the writer Bette Bao Lord, as overly sympathetic to the victims of the Chinese government.[246] Lord had visited with and received Chinese political dissidents at the US embassy, and he recognized full well that his wife and he "were pushing the envelope in terms of political freedoms in China, seeing semi or outright dissidents." Barbara Bush had little patience with either the ambassador or Mrs. Lord, and it must have showed, because after one of her visits to Beijing, Lord called Mrs. Bush's treatment of his wife "unbelievably rude."[247]

Bush and Scowcroft appreciated how far the US-China relationship had progressed since the early 1970s. They knew about China's historic sensitivity to foreign intervention, dating back to its conquest by European powers. They remembered the horrors of Mao's Cultural Revolution and appreciated how strained US-China relations had once been. And they recognized China's strategic significance in the Cold War and could readily imagine the significant benefits that might result from friendly US-China relations, whether commercially or in strategic terms in relation to the Soviet Union.[248]

At the same time, they feared that the hard-won improvements in US-China relations could unravel quickly. No one could rule out the possibility that Chinese domestic affairs might revert to a newer version of the Cultural Revolution. And they believed the United States could do little to change China's internal policies. Aggressive diplomacy could easily provoke a political backlash. Rather than indulging in feel-good gestures such as openly criticizing the Chinese or penalizing them for their human rights record, a sounder policy would be for the United States to promote China's economic growth and further engagement in global society, which would inevitably lead to political liberalization. "Broadening and deepening the [US-China] relationship was in the national interest," Scowcroft said.[249]

Ambassador Lord and many critics disagreed. Not only were Bush and Scowcroft's reactions "supine," in Lord's description, but their actions ran contrary to sound US foreign policy; the Chinese respected strength, Lord emphasized, not solicitude.[250] He denied it was a matter of isolation versus engagement, as Bush administration officials often claimed. One didn't have to be "soft" on China to remain engaged; one could also have hard-nosed engagement, just as the United States had had with the Soviet Union, Syria, the Palestine Liberation Organization, and other governments and organizations that acted contrary to American values.[251] Lord himself advocated that the United States take a tougher position against Chinese political repression, and during the Clinton administration, Lord supported holding the issue of China's most-favored-nation trade status hostage to the human rights program.[252]

Others on the political right also criticized the Bush administration's China policy. Many neocons believed it was "possible to have a working relationship with a totalitarian communist power and a terrible human rights abuser and negotiate with them constantly," in the words of Elliott Abrams, "and yet be fairly clear on your condemnation of their system." The Chinese themselves were struggling to determine Chinese traditions and to define themselves, Abrams argued, and while the United States couldn't tell the Chinese how to be, the one thing it could do "is to just make our own position clear on the nature of Chinese-ness and how it doesn't necessarily include a Communist Party and a totalitarian government and doesn't necessarily exclude republican democracy and denounce human rights violations." Even if reform in China were to take decades, "clarity," he said, "is important."[253]

The tightrope challenge of engaging China while standing up for American values would soon become even more difficult for Scowcroft and the rest of the Bush foreign policy team.

=====

ON APRIL 15, less than two months after President's Bush controversial visit, the second crucial death of 1989 occurred when Chinese leader Hu Yaobang died of a heart attack at the age of seventy-three.

Hu had been a colorful politician, liberal in his views on Tibet, outspoken in his support of political and economic reforms, and renowned for his incorruptibility. At one time Deng Xiaoping's heir apparent, Hu had been held responsible for the student unrest in December 1986, and Deng was uncomfortable with Hu's message and style. So in early 1987 he removed Hu as party secretary.[254]

Hu's death thereby became a symbol for students, reformers, and others with grievances. Within forty-eight hours, people began to gather in Tiananmen Square, at the main entrance to the Forbidden City in central Beijing—just as people had assembled in the square in early 1976 after the death of long-term premier Zhou Enlai. More and more students as well as others massed in protest against Deng Xiaoping's ouster of Hu as general secretary and then, increasingly, in protest against other problems, including corruption, censorship, inflation, the condition of the universities, nepotism, and the abuse of power by the children of top party officials.

The White House began to become concerned. Douglas Paal wrote to Scowcroft that with Hu's death and the student demonstrations, China was entering "a prolonged period of extreme sensitivity" and that Hu's funeral was "likely to mark the end of the period of tolerance we have witnessed this week in Beijing's response to student demonstrations." Paal expressed concern over the divisions among the Chinese party leaders and over how the ongoing, spreading, and organized demonstrations "will work uniformly against the reformers," with Zhao's position "shaky" and Deng's "in growing disrepute." He recommended that any statements by US officials be kept "to the absolute minimum" and that the administration avoid entangling the United States "in Chinese internal politics" or giving the Chinese "reason to show Gorbachev extra warmth as a rebuke to the U.S."[255]

By April 24, a hundred thousand people had assembled in Tiananmen Square. With the upcoming seventieth anniversary of the May Fourth Movement, which protested how China had been betrayed by the Treaty of Versailles, there were further expectations of additional protests.[256]

At first, the Chinese leaders took no action. General secretary Zhao Ziyang, Wan Li, and other politburo members wanted to reduce tensions peaceably. Zhao and other more reform-and liberal-minded party leaders wanted to hear the students out and then let the demonstrations run their course. More conservative politburo members, such as Li Peng, and Beijing Mayor Chen Xitong, considered the student unrest and mass protests to be hostile to the party government and potentially dangerous. For them, the best course of action would be to squash the protesters.[257]

But with the party leaders unable to reach a consensus on how to handle the mass protests and with "enormous sympathy" for the demonstrators within the Chinese bureaucracy and among the residents of Beijing, the struggle between the reformers and hardliners persisted, paralyzing the Chinese leadership for the weeks leading up to Gorbachev's scheduled visit.[258] Shortly after Hu Yaobang's funeral on April 22, Deng Xiaoping sided with the hard-liners.

On April 25 Deng issued a warning that the Chinese media broadcasted and reprinted the next day in the *People's Daily*. He said that the extraordinary illegal protests caused turmoil and constituted incorrect behavior: "Their purpose was to sow dissension among the people, plunge the whole country into chaos and sabotage the political situation of stability and unity," he said. "This is planned conspiracy and a disturbance. Its essence is to, once and for all, negate the leadership of the Communist Party of China and the socialist system." Deng warned that it might be impossible to prevent bloodshed. He and Li Peng hoped to intimidate the protesters and get them to back down.[259]

Instead, feeling that any chance for a dialogue had now vanished, the protesters dug in their heels. Zhao himself tried to convince the students not to demonstrate during the upcoming Sino-Soviet summit. So, too, did a handful of well-known Chinese commentators and writers, who attempted to mediate the dispute so that the square could be cleared before Gorbachev's visit; more vigorous protests, they feared, would only play into the hands of Li Peng and other conservative party leaders. Chinese authorities even made a final plea for the protesters to clear the square. But to no avail.[260]

On May 13, tens of thousands of students from more than twenty universities escalated their protests against the Chinese government by launching hunger strikes. They hoped to use Gorbachev's visit, from May 15 to May 18, to capture the attention of the global media. Civil servants, journalists, academics, workers, and other Beijing residents joined the protests, with about 1.2 million gathering in the square on May 18. The international press noticed.[261]

On May 17 Deng Xiaoping and the other members of the politburo met with Zhao Ziyang, and Deng said that troops would be needed to restore order; Li Peng and other hard-liners agreed. So Zhao, who was the last holdout on the Politburo to advocate letting the demonstrations run their course, prepared his letter of resignation.[262]

Gorbachev left Beijing on May 18, and Zhao personally appealed to the students to stop their hunger strikes. But the protesters were too far committed, the party leaders had decided on a course of action, and Zhao himself was now out of power. It would be his last public appearance; on May 19, Zhao left office.[263]

Operating under the authority of martial law, Deng sent in fifty thousand People's Liberation Army (PLA) troops who had been stationed on the outskirts of Beijing, ordering them to disperse the protesters. Remarkably, the soldiers didn't get far. They were met by hundreds of thousands of protestors who used their numbers to block the roads, trains, and subways leading into Beijing. The soldiers were unable to move, and they'd been instructed by their commanding officers not to open fire. Worse for the Chinese party leaders, the troops appeared to be sympathetic to the protesters and were seen fraternizing with them. So on May 22, the PLA forces were instructed to withdraw from the city. Some wits called it a "partial martial."[264]

The ridicule didn't last long.

On May 22, Ambassador Lilley sent a cable to the White House and the State Department warning that the Chinese government was on the verge of violently suppressing the Tiananmen Square protesters and predicting the use of force within the next several days.[265] President Bush consequently sent a short letter to Deng Xiaoping in a last-ditch effort to avoid a catastrophe. He wrote of his "hope that there would be no outcome with respect to the student demonstrations which would interfere with my ability to pursue the kinds of policies which would promote the goals we seek in our relationship. Specifically it would be my hope that any solution you decide upon would avoid violence, repression and bloodshed."[266]

By May 24, Beijing was emptied of soldiers. A week went by before Deng Xiaoping and the other party elders decided to bring in the PLA once more. This time they wanted to be sure to clear Tiananmen Square of protesters.

The next day, all hell broke loose.

20

COLD WAR RELICS

Upheaval in Panama, Trouble in Afghanistan

ON MONDAY EVENING, December 19, 1989, while the president and dozens of guests were listening to the US Army chorus sing carols at a White House Christmas party, Brent Scowcroft slipped away to join Bob Gates in his West Wing corner office. The United States was about to launch Operation Just Cause for the overthrow of General Manuel Noriega. Earlier that day, Scowcroft had handed out assignments to the relatively few White House officials who knew of the planned invasion of Panama. The White House didn't even inform members of Congress until 10:00 P.M., just three hours before the operation was to get under way.[267]

US forces found the Panamanian leader on December 24, hiding in the Vatican's embassy in Panama City. General Noriega surrendered two weeks later and was immediately taken to Miami, allowing the United States to install a new government. The American public approved: Bush's job performance rating rose to 80 percent, according to a Gallup poll taken in early January 1990. It was a graceful recovery from the White House's earlier mishandling of an attempted coup against Noriega on October 3, 1989—a failure that led the White House to make critical refinements in the NSC process, paving the way for the success of the later Panama invasion.[268]

Manuel Antonio Noriega Moreno had been in contact with US officials since the Eisenhower administration; he became a paid CIA informer in the early 1960s. Although he was off the US payroll during the Carter administration, by the early 1980s he was receiving between $100,000 and $200,000 a year from the CIA. The relationship permanently soured after 1986, when Noriega's role in the torture and assassination of Panamanian opposition leader Hugo Spadafora was publicized by Seymour Hersh in the *New York Times*. It was also revealed that Noriega was dealing drugs and colluding with the Medellín cartel, and in 1988 he became the subject of a US Justice Department investigation for drug trafficking. Yet the Justice,

State, and Defense Departments couldn't agree on a course of action, and President Reagan didn't make a final decision as to how to proceed. Noriega was therefore still in power when George Bush took office.[269]

President Bush had met Noriega on several occasions and had passed messages to the Panamanian leader. Despite their "dubious relationship," once he got into office Bush requested a criminal indictment of Noriega and his exile from Panama. He wanted him gone, and issued a presidential finding that endorsed covert action against Noriega. The White House also began to expand its political and psychological efforts to unseat Noriega, carried out under the auspices of the US Southern Command (SOUTHCOM). The president and his advisers even discussed the possibility of kidnapping Noriega should he leave Panama.[270]

US-Panamanian relations dramatically worsened after the May 1989 election was stolen from Guillermo Endara by Noriega through corruption, fraud, and violence (the opposing vice presidential candidate, Guillermo "Billy" Ford, was badly beaten by Noriega supporters, for instance). Once Noriega realized that the election was "going very badly," he "stopped the vote count and seized the ballots," as Scowcroft described it. International election watchers attested to the fraud, and former president Jimmy Carter, who was among the election monitors, told President Bush "how awful it was." Even Scowcroft—who is not one to exaggerate and wasn't in favor of interfering in Panama's affairs—characterized the election as being "hijacked in the most outrageous, confrontational way" and recognized that it "fundamentally changed our attitude toward Panama."[271]

The Bush administration refused to recognize the Panamanian government as long as Noriega remained in power, and it encouraged other governments to do the same. The United States also pressured the Panamanian government by holding its assets in escrow.[272] Bush ordered the US military to leave Panama, and when SOUTHCOM's commander, Gen. Frederick Woerner, delayed (at one point blaming the delay on a shortage of cardboard boxes), Baker, Cheney, and Scowcroft unanimously recommended that he be replaced. The president agreed, and on September 30, 1989, Gen. Maxwell "Mad Max" Thurman took over command of SOUTHCOM.[273]

The coup attempt began just two days later. Maj. Moisés Giroldi Vega of the Panamanian Defense Forces (PDF) and a group of accomplices killed Noriega's bodyguards, captured the Panamanian leader at gunpoint, and held him at the PDF headquarters. Unfortunately for Major Giroldi, Noriega was able to place a telephone call before Giroldi and his collaborators could take full control. A few hours later, two loyal elite PDF battalions arrived and rescued Noriega. The whole coup attempt lasted just five hours.

The thirty-eight-year-old Giroldi had had the opportunity to shoot "the Maximum Leader of the Panamanian Revolution" but didn't. Giroldi had been close to Noriega, who was the godfather of one of his children, and he was unable to shoot his friend in cold blood. Noriega had fewer qualms; he had Giroldi tortured and killed. Over the next few weeks back in power, Noriega had hundreds of other PDF officers arrested and executed.

By all accounts, the Bush administration's response to the coup attempt was confused. President Bush's press secretary, Marlin Fitzwater, was astounded to learn of the coup from CNN on the morning of October 3 while it was under way, rather than from official White House channels. Scowcroft reached the Pentagon by phone, trying to sort things out. Scowcroft found out that the United States had A-37s (small fighter jets) and helicopters available for surveillance and little else; he didn't know where Noriega was, and neither did anyone else in the government. Scowcroft had no idea what Giroldi's motivations were, and expectations for the US forces stationed just outside Panama City were also unclear.[274]

As the coup continued, Bush and Scowcroft kept to their daily schedule. The president visited with Mexican president Carlos Salinas, attended a farewell ceremony for the outgoing chairman of the Joint Chiefs, Adm. William Crowe, and then had lunch with senior US government administrators. At 1:30 P.M., Bush and Scowcroft met with Defense Secretary Dick Cheney, who conceded that he also knew little about the coup, according to Fitzwater, although the Panamanian press was reporting that Noriega had been ousted and that Major Giroldi was heading a five-man provisional government. The president had Cheney order General Thurman to invite the rebels to ask for US support, which would allow the American military to engage (although Scowcroft did worry about how other Latin American leaders would react).[275]

Things didn't get that far. A little after 2:30 P.M., Bush, Scowcroft, Baker, Gates, Fitzwater, and others in the administration learned the coup was over. So they informed the press that the rebellion had been suppressed (after having previously told reporters that, while the coup was not a US operation, the administration remained "in very close touch" with the rebels).[276]

When reporters and members of Congress discovered the Bush administration had missed an opportunity to oust the Panamanian leader, they were outraged. With all the attention the Bush White House had focused on Noriega's political corruption, brutality, and drug trafficking, they expected a stronger follow-through. "Amateur Hour" was the headline of a *Newsweek* story; "The Gang That Wouldn't Shoot" was the title of a *U.S. News & World Report* article; and several influential editorial columnists, including Richard Cohen, Mary McGrory, and William Safire, castigated the president for his undue caution and passivity. Senator Jesse Helms called Bush and his top advisers a bunch of Keystone Kops, and Senator Sam Nunn criticized the administration for not being better prepared to support an attempted coup—since this was exactly what the administration had encouraged.[277]

Senator David Boren, the chairman of the Select Committee on Intelligence and a friend of the administration as a rule, was especially angered at the White House's inaction. Boren had been able to follow the whole coup proceedings thanks to his aide George Tenet, who had access to the US government's cable traffic, and he was appalled by how the events had played out. So when he and Scowcroft were asked to appear on national television to debate the coup, they "got into a heated argument" in the green room at the ABC studios, Boren recalled, almost coming to blows. Once he was on the air, Boren declared, "I don't think it's right" for the United States, as "a great country, to go out and encourage people to take action, to put their lives on the line, to imply by encouraging them to take action that we're going to help and not be there when we need them."[278] Scowcroft responded that the senator's statements left him "astonished."[279]

But Boren was just getting started. A few days later, he proclaimed that the administration had "blood on its hands for the lack of courage to reach out to the officers who were doing what they thought America wanted." When the president heard Boren's statement, he called the senator, who was then in Chicago for a fund-raiser, and chewed him out. Bush was "furious" and "uncharacteristically ill-tempered," in Boren's description, and told him, "I want your ass back here." Because it was too late in the day for commercial flights, Bush had the military fly Boren to Washington for a meeting the following morning.[280]

When Senator Boren entered the Oval Office, the president, the vice president, Powell, and Cheney were already there. Bush's face was "red" and "contorted with rage," Boren recalled. Powell looked "very uncomfortable," and Cheney was squirming in his chair. The president then asked how the senator could say he had "blood on [his] hands." So Boren went over what had gone wrong; he reviewed what he'd learned from the cable traffic and he explained why it would have been easy for the United States to act and help Major Giroldi. After hearing him out, Bush's whole demeanor changed. He apologized to Boren for making him come down to Washington, and then escorted him from the Oval Office, telling the senator, "These gentleman and I have something to discuss."[281]

What the gentlemen had to discuss was how poorly the whole affair had been handled—beginning with internal communications. The Tuesday of the coup, Gates told Marlin Fitzwater that neither Scowcroft nor he knew of the planned coup (although it had been mentioned in the CIA's daily briefing to the president). So Fitzwater told the press that President Bush, Scowcroft, Cheney, Gates, and others had had no foreknowledge of the coup. But this wasn't true; Bush, Scowcroft, Cheney, Baker, and the Joint Chiefs had known of the planned coup for a full two days, thanks to an advance warning from General Thurman.

On Sunday, October 1, Major Giroldi's wife, Adela Giroldi, had told the CIA station chief of the plans for the coup. Giroldi met with CIA officials the next day to confirm that the coup was on, and he requested that US forces block the roads to the PDF headquarters, where Noriega was to be held under guard, and keep the airspace clear of Panamanian aircraft.

Giroldi's news was passed on to General Thurman and his staff in Panama City, and Thurman in turn informed Powell. Powell called Cheney at 2:30 A.M., and Cheney then called Scowcroft. But Thurman discounted Giroldi's credentials and doubted the soundness of his plans, and Powell relied on Thurman's judgment. However, SOUTHCOM never informed Giroldi that they *wouldn't* support his coup; instead, they simply did nothing. In his book *The Commanders*, Bob Woodward attributes the inaction to Powell's directive that US forces were not to intervene.[282]

So Bush's senior advisers had known of the coup, although they didn't fully commit to supporting it. Yet the coup could have easily succeeded, just as Boren later stated. The US military could have supported Giroldi and prevented the two battalions loyal to Noriega from reaching PDF headquarters by controlling the air space and blocking roads. But Thurman didn't want to proceed without approval from Washington, Powell and Cheney were unwilling to commit US forces without better information, and Scowcroft and Bush simply didn't know enough to overrule the chairman of the Joint Chiefs of Staff and the commander of SOUTHCOM.

The result was an embarrassment—the squandering of a golden opportunity to rid Panama of Noriega. Making matters worse, Bush's advisers tried to cover up their indecision, dissembled, and offered contradictory excuses for the administration's inaction.[283] One explanation was that the coup might be a trap set by Noriega (it wasn't). Another was that this was an intra-PDF dispute, with one strongman merely replacing another (though Giroldi was not seeking political office for himself). Yet another was that the United States didn't know if Giroldi was committed to democratic government (he did want to see a popular government installed in Panama). And still another was that Giroldi had refused to hand Noriega over to US forces (he had refused at first, but later reversed himself). Scowcroft himself blamed interference by the Senate Intelligence Committee and by Congress more generally for preventing the White House and Pentagon from taking action (also inaccurate).[284]

These excuses were just that, excuses. The underlying problem was that the intelligence on the coup hadn't been clearly relayed up the chain of command or integrated across the government. What the State Department, CIA, Defense Intelligence Agency, and SOUTHCOM each knew wasn't aggregated within the government and shared with the relevant personnel across departments and agencies. Thus timidity and caution carried the day. "We did not act very decisively," Scowcroft said with characteristic understatement.[285]

The military's caution was no doubt an aftereffect of the Vietnam War, but other factors also played their parts. After the Iran-Contra affair, the Bush administration was wary of being overzealous and courting needless clashes with Congress. William Webster was now running the CIA, not the swashbuckling Bill Casey, and Generals Thurman and Powell were both new on the job and wanted to proceed cautiously. Furthermore, the NSC's Latin American specialist, Everett Briggs, had resigned just two days before the coup attempt.[286]

Whatever the reasons for the failure, Scowcroft took it hard. After the failed coup, he "sat slouched and dejected in his West Wing office," his press secretary, Roman Popadiuk, recalled. "Stoically and without comment, he read the reports of what State Department officials were telling the press"—and how they were passing the blame, as Popadiuk observed. "In particular, Scowcroft was being fingered for the lack of coordination of the administration's effort." Scowcroft conceded the administration "didn't do particularly well" in handling the crisis, and the misadventure gave him and his colleagues "a great sense of unease." "We *were* sort of Keystone Kops," Scowcroft admitted ruefully.[287] "You shouldn't minimize October 3," Scowcroft later said, adding, "It was probably my fault."[288]

But the president didn't blame Scowcroft. At a news conference a few days after the coup attempt, Bush told the press he hadn't "lost any confidence in our top people that are handling these matters, including—and I want to repeat it here—our military officers in Panama. None at all. And certainly not General Powell." But Powell "knew full well that such a sentiment was articulated when it was in question," as Bob Woodward points out. "The decisive factor at 10 to 11 A.M. on the day for the coup," one SOUTHCOM officer well recognized, "was US inaction." In vain, he and other his fellow officers stationed in Panama waited for instructions from Washington.[289] Scowcroft vowed the administration wouldn't "make that same mistake again."[290]

The NSC convened a few days later to conduct a brief postmortem of what had gone wrong. It also reviewed the new contingency plans and discussed further options, such as having constant visible tracking of Noriega and prohibiting the entry of Panamanian-flagged vessels into US ports. Cheney and Powell also tightened up the chain of command so as to ensure that military communications would flow better up and down the hierarchy. "All of us," Baker notes, "vowed never to let another such opportunity pass."[291]

Bush, Baker, Cheney, Scowcroft, and Powell soon began planning for a full-scale military operation against Noriega and Panama. This would become Operation Blue Spoon, later renamed Operation Just Cause.[292]

Perhaps the chief innovation to come out of the fiasco was Scowcroft's decision to rely more on the Deputies Committee in order to coordinate executive action in foreign policy and handle crises. Scowcroft found "that the State Department had its intelligence sources, Defense did, JCS did, CIA did, but all of these intelligence reports were going straight up to their principals and there was no cross communication." As a result, everyone at the Monday NSC meeting had "had a very different idea about what was going on in Panama, which is not too surprising, because it was extremely confused."[293]

Although the Deputies Committee had met before the coup attempt, it had been "catch as catch can," in Gates's description, when it came to handling crises. Now it was to have more decision-making responsibility, handle day-to-day crisis management, and clear decisions before forwarding them to Baker, Cheney, and Scowcroft or to the NSC. Gates "never went into a Deputies Committee meeting" thereafter "without knowing where we wanted it to come out. And Brent and I would figure out how to make it happen," Gates said. Scowcroft "diagnosed the problem and reimposed order," Powell writes.[294]

Much of the credit for the effectiveness of the Deputies Committee meetings goes to Gates. Daniel Poneman, who was on Scowcroft's NSC staff, recalled that Gates would "grind through" stacks of folders before he'd call a meeting, and each folder "of itself represented a huge complex rats' nest of an issue." He wanted each meeting to produce a decision and not to last more than sixty minutes. At the pre-briefing, he'd say, in effect "Okay,

I think there's basically three issues: This. This. And this. State is going to say this. Defense is going to say that. I want to turn to activator and say this, and if I do it this way, I'm going to get this result. What have I missed? And you would say, 'Could you go over that again a little more slowly this time?'" Gates, Poneman said, was "unbelievable."[295]

The lessons from Panama enabled the Bush White House to handle the attempted coup on Philippine president Corazon Aquino better than it might have otherwise. The coup began on December 1, 1989, when President Bush, Baker, and Scowcroft were on their way to Malta, and Quayle immediately convened the NSC, with Robert Kimmitt (and later Lawrence Eagleburger) representing Baker and with Gates representing Scowcroft. (Cheney, who disagreed with Quayle chairing the meeting, called in sick.) Scowcroft followed the discussion with a telephone in each ear, thirty-five thousand feet over the Atlantic Ocean. The group agreed to a solution proposed by Powell: US aircraft would fly a "cap . . . over the airport" rather than bombing the airport or shooting down aircraft hostile to President Aquino's government. They figured that just the threat of military action would deter hostile aircraft from taking off. Scowcroft was pleased that the administration had been able to come to a clear decision—although he had to awaken a sleeping President Bush to get his approval.[296] The strategy worked: the two F-4s flying above the palace spoke volumes about the US presence, and the coup failed.

Two and a half months later, a new crisis redirected the focus toward Panama. A small group of PDF soldiers shot two US soldiers, assaulted a Marine lieutenant, groped his wife, and threatened her with rape. President Bush decided the time had come to put Operation Just Cause into action.[297]

Scowcroft disagreed, thinking it made little sense for the United States to indict foreign officials over whom it had no jurisdiction. Nor did he believe that invading Panama and seizing Noriega would be sound strategically or enhance US relations with other Latin American states. Baker, too, thought the president was making a mistake, as did Cheney and Powell. But once the president had made it "abundantly clear" what he wanted to do, his advisers fell into line.[298]

In any event, Operation Just Cause was "extremely" successful. More than twenty-five thousand troops, including fourteen thousand assembled in just twenty-four hours, began by hitting twenty-seven targets simultaneously. By starting the invasion in the dead of night, the US military was able to use its technological advantages to move quickly and take few casualties. As the head of US Special Operations Command, Gen. Carl W. Stiner, boasted, "We own the night."[299]

The president had skillfully preempted negative responses from other Latin American leaders by repeatedly talking with them over the preceding summer and fall, "a minimum of a half dozen times about Panama, about Nicaragua, about Salvador, on and on and on," by Scowcroft's account. Bush continued his personal diplomacy once the invasion was under way, spending the small hours of Tuesday, December 20, calling foreign leaders such as Colombian president Virgilio Barco, Mexican president Carlos Salinas, Venezuelan president Carlos Pérez, Canadian prime minister Brian Mulroney, French president François Mitterrand, Spanish prime minister Felipe González, and British prime minister Margaret Thatcher. In the phone calls, Bush explained—sometimes through interpreters—why he'd finally lost patience with Noriega and why the United States had to act. Thanks to Bush's efforts, there was little more than a pro forma protest by the Latin American leaders; as Scowcroft put it, things "quieted down amazingly well."[300]

Not so quiet was Powell's reaction to what he considered Scowcroft's undue interference, what he regarded as micromanaging. He disagreed with Scowcroft's orders that the Panamanian government's broadcast tower "had to go," for instance, seeing little point in destroying a structure that the newly instated president, Guillermo Endara, would soon be needing. Both General Thurman, the commander of the US invasion of Panama, and General Stiner were "mad as hell at being over-managed from the sidelines," he later reported, "and for being ordered to take a pointless objective."[301] Powell attributed Scowcroft's action to public pressure—the "press heat" presumably becoming "too great" for the president and the national security advisor to resist.[302]

However, Scowcroft wasn't alone in his judgment. The State Department also wanted the tower taken down, and, Baker reports, "Powell and Cheney readily agreed" to the decision, even if "some in the Pentagon had different ideas."[303]

Powell also disagreed with Scowcroft's insistence that the military rescue "several correspondents . . . trapped in the Marriott Hotel in Panama City. 'We've got to put troops in to rescue them,' Brent said." Powell, though, didn't think so:

> "They're in no danger," I pointed out. "I've checked. . . . They're safe in the basement of the hotel. The fighting will soon sweep right past them."
>
> I thought I had convinced Brent until I got a second call. He was taking terrific pressure from bureau chiefs and network executives in New York. "We've got to do something," he said.

"We shouldn't do anything," I reiterated. "We've got a perfectly competent commander on the ground. He's got a plan, and it's working." Were kibitzers supposed to direct the fighting in Panama from executive suites in Manhattan? I reminded Brent that there were 35,000 other American citizens in Panama, and we were trying to ensure the safety of all of them. Only a few minutes passed before Cheney called. There was no discussion. Do it, he said. No more arguments.

Again I reluctantly called Thurman and Stiner. "I hate to tell you this. . . . But get those reporters out, and I'll try to keep Washington off your backs in the future."[304]

After the mission, Powell complained to Cheney, telling him he didn't want to have to pass along any more such orders in the future. "If the press has to cover a war," he said, "there's no way we can eliminate the risks of war." He then requested that the secretary of defense ask Scowcroft to refrain from issuing "any more orders from the sidelines."[305]

Powell remarked that Scowcroft had "an irritating edge" to his manner, one "that took getting used to."[306] Powell's prickly reaction may be explained in part by the fact that he was Scowcroft's immediate predecessor as national security advisor and a four-star general with considerable command experience. At the same time, Powell recognized Scowcroft's ability, his "obvious intelligence," and his "admirable" intentions. He appreciated the fact that Scowcroft didn't sugarcoat the possibility of American deaths when reviewing the plans for Operation Just Cause with President Bush, for example, and that he rightly held the chairman of the Joint Chiefs accountable for the soundness of the military's plans and for the anticipated number of US casualties.[307] He also recognized what one of Scowcroft's colleagues called "the ribbon of steel" that lay underneath his cordiality, poise, and expertise. "Brent has a temper," Powell acknowledged, and he argues his positions "forcefully" and "can get mad."[308]

The tensions between the two men derived in large part from their different responsibilities. Scowcroft had to navigate between the State and Defense Departments, coordinate intelligence, and ensure that military operations were being conducted with long-term foreign policy objectives in mind—all while taking Congress, the media, and the American public into account. Powell, by contrast, was responsible solely for military affairs. Given these different roles, it is no wonder they sometimes clashed.

The president's decision to forcibly remove Noriega from office met with widespread approval, but it exacted a price, claiming the lives of twenty-three American soldiers and costing hundreds of millions of dollars. Meanwhile, five hundred Panamanians lost their lives and the widespread destruction in Panama City residential areas displaced tens of thousands of people from their homes. The successful invasion, coming on the heels of the 1983 invasion of Grenada, also set a precedent—rightly or wrongly—for Somalia in 1992 and Kosovo in 1994.[309]

US-Panama relations during the Bush administration must also be seen as part of the broader story of US policy in Latin America. Baker and Scowcroft felt that President Reagan and his advisers had made a mistake battling Congress over Latin American policy. So they sought to remove Nicaragua and the rest of Latin America as points of controversy and to "try to co-opt Congress" instead.

Their efforts were largely successful. "Today, for the first time in many years," Bush announced on March 24, 1989, "the President and Congress, the Democratic and Republican leadership in the House and Senate, are speaking with one voice about Central America." The United States, the text of the Bipartisan Accord on Central America read, was now committed to democratization for Nicaragua, "an end to subversion and destabilization of its neighbors," and "an end to Soviet bloc military ties that threaten U.S. and regional security." Furthermore, Republicans and Democrats in both houses of Congress and both branches of government were "united on a policy to achieve those goals."[310]

In practice, the policy wasn't easy to follow "because people kept jumping out of positions," Scowcroft remarked, with "the El Salvador assassinations of the nuns" and Nicaraguan president Daniel Ortega saying he wasn't "going to continue with the cease-fire, etc." The Bush administration nonetheless managed to remove Nicaragua and Latin America as points of contention with Congress—helped by Violeta Chamorro's victory over Ortega in the February 1989 election (with help from the Contras and, more quietly, the United States). The new US policies allowed the administration to use Latin America as "a barometer of the Soviet Union and its changes," Scowcroft said, to see how Soviet actions matched their rhetoric.[311] Ten years later, on December 31, 1999, the United States handed the Panama Canal over to the Panamanian government, according to the terms of the 1977 Panama Canal Treaty—a successful transition to a new and better relationship between the two countries.

———

A BREAK FROM the past wouldn't be as easy with another difficult issue confronted by the Bush administration upon taking office: Afghanistan.

The United States had a three-part agenda with respect to the Soviet Union: conventional and nuclear arms control; US-Soviet bilateral issues; and a set of regional issues, where the Bush administration wanted to stop the Soviet Union's support of Afghanistan, Cuba's support of communist governments in Angola and Mozambique, East Germany's aid to Eritrea, Cuba's activities in Central America, and Vietnam's occupation of Cambodia. By the end of the administration, the Soviet Union had stopped its aid to Afghanistan and Cuba, Cuban forces had withdrawn from sub-Saharan Africa (a necessary condition for the end of apartheid in South Africa and the transition to the presidency of Nelson Mandela), East Germany no longer existed, and Vietnam was out of Cambodia (UN Security Council resolution 668, passed in September 1990).[312] Nonetheless, the situation in Afghanistan would remain a troublesome one for the United States.

Sandwiched between Iran and Pakistan, Afghanistan is located in a highly strategic region at the cultural and religious crossroads of the Middle East, Central Asia, and South Asia.[313] Notwithstanding its diverse and mountainous terrain—the result of British-made boundaries—it has been subject to numerous invasions over the centuries. And its inhabitants—which numbered 11 million or so as of 1990, with almost 6 million more refugees in Pakistan, Iran, and the West as a result of the Soviet occupation—are members of several ethnic groups living in areas that straddle national borders. The Pashtuns, for example, who constitute about 40 to 50 percent of the Afghan population, are also the second-largest ethnic group in Pakistan. Likewise, the Tajiks, who make up about one-quarter of the Afghan population, make up about two-thirds of the population of Tajikistan; the Uzbeks, almost 10 percent of the population, are also about 80 percent of the population of Uzbekistan; and the Turkmen, a minute proportion of the Afghan population, constitute about 85 percent of the population of Turkmenistan. These ethnic groups are, in turn, divided into tribes and further subgroups.[314]

The United States' covert war against the Soviet-allied government of Afghanistan had begun in 1980 under Zbigniew Brzezinski and the Carter administration and then escalated under President Reagan. The Reagan administration and the CIA wanted to aid the Afghan mujahedin leaders based in Peshawar, Pakistan, in their fight against the Soviet military and communist regime in Kabul, but they wanted to do so discreetly and indirectly. DCI Bill Casey therefore channeled money and weapons through the Pakistani intelligence agency, the Inter-Services Intelligence (ISI).

The 1986 introduction of Stinger surface-to-air missiles, which were deadly against Soviet helicopters and ground-support aircraft, shifted the balance in Afghanistan in favor of the mujahedin. And with the Soviet Union having suffered more than thirteen thousand military fatalities in Afghanistan and more than thirty-five thousand soldiers seriously injured, Gorbachev didn't want to up the ante.[315] He began looking for a way out.

The way out was the Geneva Accords, signed under UN auspices in April 1988. The agreement, which provided cover for the Soviets to withdraw, set the groundwork for a policy of noninterference between Afghanistan and Pakistan, with the Soviet Union and the United States to act as the agreement's guarantors; none of the Afghan mujahedin groups were a party to the Geneva Accords. The Soviet withdrawal on February 15, 1989, represented what many considered to be the United States' most impressive Cold War victory while simultaneously leading Polish, Czech, and other East European leaders to doubt the fortitude of the Soviet leadership.[316]

Almost everyone in the intelligence and diplomatic communities in Washington and in the large US mission in Islamabad thought it would just be a matter of weeks before the government of President Mohammad Najibullah Ahmadzai went down. Meanwhile, with the Afghan economy already in shambles, US officials, UN personnel, and NGO staff in the region braced themselves for a flood of Afghan refugees and other possible humanitarian crises.[317]

Three years later, Najibullah was still in power. Not until April 1992, following the Peshawar Accord, was the Kabul government replaced by a coalition of Afghan mujahedin, who proved unable to form a viable government.[318] Consequently, Afghanistan was divided into dozens of semiautonomous provinces under the command of old mujahedin and new warlords, many of whom turned to taxes, extortion, smuggling, opium production, and heroin trafficking—or some combination thereof—for income.[319] The city of Kabul, which had survived the Soviet occupation and the Najibullah government, was largely destroyed by the 1992 civil war among the mujahedin. Furthermore, the mujahedin as a group were not representative of the Afghanistan population: most professionals, many women, and many of those who were more educated didn't identify with the politics, ideologies, or religious extremism of most of the mujahedin.

The Bush administration did almost nothing to address these dangerous developments in Afghanistan. During the 1989–1992 period, the attention of Bush and his senior advisers was almost always directed elsewhere. And once the Najibullah government fell and the mujahedin took over, the Bush administration simply walked away from Afghanistan, eager to be done with what they regarded as a relic of the Cold War. Meanwhile, in the provinces, young radical Muslims were arriving from around the world, having been recruited for religious education and military training for future wars against the infidels of the West.

The bill for the Bush administration's neglect came due in the years that followed. Less than a week after the Bush administration left office, on January 25, 1993, a young Pakistani killed two CIA officials outside CIA headquarters in Langley and injured three others. A month later, on February 23, 1993, came the first World Trade Center attack. The Taliban (meaning "students") emerged in 1994, and in September 1996 the Taliban seized Kabul, captured and hanged Najibullah—who had been staying in the UN compound—and gave sanctuary to a Wahhabi extremist named Osama bin Laden. Five years later, the blowback from the United States' aid to radical Muslims culminated in the terrorist attacks of September 11, 2001.

How did the Bush administration stumble so badly in Afghanistan? It's a complex story of foreign-policy inertia and of what today would be called "limited bandwidth"—the inability of the Bush administration to process information and make decisions on policies in an area that Scowcroft, Bush, Baker, and their top aides considered to be of secondary importance once the Cold War wound down.

In early 1989, with the Soviet occupation of Afghanistan nearing an end, Scowcroft tasked a policy coordinating committee with reviewing the country's political and economic prospects, its internal and external politics, the Soviet Union's continuing interests in the region, and the likely behavior of Pakistan, Iran, and Saudi Arabia following the withdrawal. He also wanted to know what the United States' options were, what tools were at its disposal, which resources it should deploy, and which Afghan factions it should support.[320]

The review, drafted by Richard Haass, was released on February 7, 1989, but broke no new ground. According to the US ambassador to Pakistan, Robert Oakley, the Bush administration planned simply to continue to assist the Pakistani-based Afghan mujahedin against the Soviet-installed Najibullah regime.[321] For a time, there was hope that the United States and the Soviet Union would simultaneously reduce their commitments to the Afghan resistance and the Najibullah regime, but several meetings among the five permanent members of the UN security council failed to produce a working plan for what US officials called "negative symmetry." (UN ambassador Thomas Pickering blamed the Soviets, who, he said, had no interest in solving Afghanistan.)[322]

From mid-1989 through most of 1991, State Department officials worked repeatedly on finding a peaceful resolution of some kind for

Afghanistan. Under Secretary of State Robert Kimmitt headed what Peter Tomsen, then the US special envoy to Afghanistan, termed the Kimmitt Group, which was to sort out how to deal with Afghanistan. Kimmitt allowed that the United States wouldn't be opposed if Najibullah wanted to run for office against other Afghan leaders to form a post-Soviet government.[323] But the efforts of the State Department and the United Nations were handicapped by the Bush administration's refusal to negotiate with Najibullah. When the Soviet Union proposed convening a UN conference on Afghanistan, the United States and Pakistan rejected the idea. Neither did the administration pursue an international settlement with much vigor, since to do so would have antagonized Pakistan.[324]

So the Soviet Union kept reinforcing the Kabul government with arms, fuel, funds, grain, equipment, and other resources (totaling $4 billion annually), and the CIA, via Pakistan and the ISI, kept supplying the mujahedin.

The Kabul government lasted much longer than expected not only because of Soviet aid but also because Najibullah helped his own cause by abandoning communism, cultivating broader popular support, and using money and other incentives to attract the support of several of the Afghanistan warlords and local militias.[325] Notwithstanding these changes in the Najibullah regime, the Bush administration refused to recognize the Kabul government. Najibullah had been installed and was now being maintained by the Soviet Union, and he and his regime remained anathema to Washington and the Afghan mujahedin; too much brutality had taken place, too many Afghans had been slaughtered, and too many villages had been "cleansed."

For the United States to recognize and negotiate with Najibullah would have betrayed the mujahedin, who for all intents and purposes had been allies of the United States since 1980. Neither would several important members of Congress, including New Hampshire senator Gordon Humphrey and Texas representative Charles Nesbitt "Charlie" Wilson, approve of recognizing the Najibullah government. (Hence the nickname "Charlie Wilson's War" for the American program of support to the mujahedin.) Others in the Bush administration remembered the fall of the shah of Iran in 1979 and feared they might lose Iran's neighbor, Afghanistan, to Shi'a radicalism.[326]

Also adamantly opposing any recognition of the Kabul government were Pakistan's leaders, who wanted an Afghanistan they could dominate— the idea of so-called strategic depth for Pakistan in Afghanistan. "We have earned the right" to have in Afghanistan a "very friendly" power, President Mohammed Zia-ul-Haq said in 1986, and "we will not permit a return to the prewar situation. . . . The new power will be a real Islamic state, part of a pan-Islamic revival, that will one day win over the Muslims in the Soviet Union." With Pakistan's seven-to-one population advantage over Afghanistan and with what Pakistanis viewed as their greater sophistication and cultural superiority, Zia thought they could establish an allied government in Kabul.[327]

President Zia didn't live to see the fruits of Pakistan's efforts. Zia, along with his army chief of staff Gen. Akhtar Abdur Rahman, the US ambassador to Pakistan Arnold Raphel, and other Pakistani and US political advisers and military aides died on August 17, 1988, when their airplane crashed on a return flight to Islamabad. Although India, Iran, the Soviet Union, and other states—including Israel and the United States—all had reasons to want one or more of the airplane's passengers dead, neither Pakistani nor US investigators ever found a probable cause for the crash of the normally reliable C-130 Hercules.

According to UN special envoy Diego Cordovez, Zia had been willing to consider a proposal for Najibullah to step down in favor of a transition government for Afghanistan, and it is possible that Zia might have been able to get the mujahedin, the Soviets, and the Americans to go along. But with Zia's death, the chances of reaching such a settlement quickly worsened.[328]

Throughout 1989, 1990, and 1991, the White House repeatedly ignored overtures from President Najibullah and his representatives to normalize relations. When Najibullah wrote President Bush on March 10, 1989, reporting infiltrations from Pakistan of heavily armed Afghan groups, the deployment of the Pakistani army in border areas, and plans under way for "wide scale armed attacks on a number of eastern frontier cities of Afghanistan . . . with the direct participation of Pakistan," the White House didn't bother to respond.[329] The "major impediment" to "a rational, democratic, and just solution to the Afghan crisis," Scowcroft wrote, was "the current illegitimate government in Kabul." Only when it was gone could "an independent government . . . based on self-determination" be established.[330] For Bush and Scowcroft, Najibullah "was the symbol of what was wrong in Afghanistan." Furthermore, "the US-backed Mujahedin had made clear that they would not stop fighting until he was gone."[331]

But the administration didn't invest in alternative plans for Afghanistan, either. Consumed by other issues, Bush, Baker and Scowcroft spent negligible time on central Asia. Only 7 of the 461 Deputies Committee meetings and 2 of the 77 NSC meetings held during the Bush presidency had Afghanistan as their topic. Indicatively, the NSC met several times to discuss what the CIA's Bruce Riedel identified as the "greatest problem"

Washington thought it had in Afghanistan: the appearance of Stinger missiles on the international black market. (The administration consequently authorized a CIA program to buy the Stingers back.)[332] In the words of the *Washington Post*'s Steve Coll, Afghanistan was a "third-tier" foreign policy issue for the Bush administration.[333] This inattention to the region is mirrored in Bush and Scowcroft's *A World Transformed*, Baker's *The Politics of Diplomacy*, Quayle's *Standing Firm*, and other accounts of US foreign policy during Bush's years in office. All mention Afghanistan and Pakistan very briefly, if at all.[334]

Meanwhile, the CIA continued to provide covert assistance to the mujahedin, under the assumption the Afghan rebels would force Najibullah from office and be able to reclaim their homeland. This marked the continuation of "Charlie Wilson's War" under DCI Casey, President Reagan, and a handful of members of Congress.

In late 1989, the White House and congressional conservatives persuaded the Senate Select Committee on Intelligence to fund $280 million in secret aid to Afghanistan. The covert aid continued in 1990 ($250 million) and 1991 ($200 million) and was supplemented by Saudi matching funds. After the Gulf War, the administration had the CIA transfer $30 million worth of captured Soviet-made weapons to the mujahedin. And even after US aid stopped as of the end of 1991—over the opposition of the CIA—Saudi Arabia and private sources in the Gulf continued to furnish about $400 million a year (total Saudi aid to the ISI and the mujahedin in 1989 and 1990 exceeded aid by the United States).[335]

The CIA quietly assisted the mujahedin with planning the attacks against the Najibullah government, provided them with sophisticated radio equipment and Toyota four-wheel-drive trucks, and helped them with clandestine operations to disable or destroy Najibullah's supply lines from the Soviet Union.[336] For years, the CIA let the ISI handle the funding and distribution of weapons, funds, and other supplies, despite the fact that the ISI, the Pakistani army, and Saudi Arabia's Prince Turki heavily favored the religiously extreme and ethnic Pashtun warlords. Only after the Soviet departure did the CIA begin to question the ISI and Pakistan's imbalanced allocation of aid and in secret began to provide separate, extra payments to Ahmed Shah Massoud ("the Lion of Panjshir" and the foremost military leader among the mujahedin)—$200,000 a month in cash as well as military supplies—to counterbalance the larger amounts the ISI and Saudi Arabia were channeling to radical Sunni mujahedin such as Gulbuddin Hekmatyar.[337]

The practical effect was that between February 1989 and April 1992 the Bush administration operated at cross-purposes. The CIA's aid to the mujahedin subverted diplomatic attempts to resolve the situation in Afghanistan. It's not clear to what extent Scowcroft or Baker challenged the CIA-led initiative, despite the detrimental effects of the United States' support for the Afghan resistance on US-Soviet relations and on the prospects for peace and a stable government in Afghanistan.[338] Perhaps indicatively, on September 23, 1991, Bush, Baker, Scowcroft, UN Ambassador Pickering, and others met with UN Secretary General Javier Pérez de Cuéllar and his aides at the United Nations, with Pérez de Cuéllar stating that he had met with the presidents of Iran and Pakistan and King Fahd of Saudi Arabia. "Recent US-USSR statements have been extremely good," the secretary-general said. "The Soviets are now saying that Najibullah is prepared to step down during a transition process. . . . I am preparing to call a meeting in Geneva of all Afghan factions." Baker reassured Pérez de Cuéllar that the United States was trying to persuade the Pakistanis to support the UN's effort, but nothing came of the initiative.[339]

Bush, Scowcroft, and other US officials regarded Pakistan as their ally and didn't want to deviate from their Cold War strategies—including continued support for the mujahedin. Yet Pakistan's interests didn't necessarily mesh with those of the United States. General Zia and General Akhtar, the head of ISI, both vigorously promoted Sunni fundamentalism by establishing up to eight thousand official religious schools (madrassas) and another twenty-five thousand unofficial ones.[340] Militant Muslims from around the world flocked to Afghanistan and Pakistan, volunteering their services in the CIA-supported jihad. "The Afghan conflict proved to be a training ground for the Islamic militias, which received comprehensive training in the ISI centres that gave them the skills in sabotage, assassination, endurance and other techniques of guerrilla warfare," one Pakistani scholar summarizes. And the ISI imparted these skills "under the guidance of US CIA, US Special Forces from the famous Green Berets, the British SAS and Chinese weapons instructors."[341]

By early 1989, the State Department's Edmund McWilliams, then serving as the US special envoy to the Afghan mujahedin, concluded that the United States was assisting "a ruthless anti-American cabal of Islamists and Pakistani intelligence officers determined to impose their will on Afghanistan." McWilliams pointed out that Pakistan's best interests were not Afghanistan's, and he recommended that the United States fund the more moderate mujahedin leaders instead of Hekmatyar. McWilliams's analysis wasn't well received by Ambassador Robert Oakley, however, or by the CIA station chief in Pakistan or CIA officials in Langley, and it would soon get him transferred. But for others in the State Department and CIA, McWilliams's analysis struck a chord.[342]

Oakley would eventually come to agree with McWilliams. But although Oakley and the State Department recommended that the administration not fund the mujahedin in fiscal 1991, the CIA was divided on the issue, and Representative Wilson and others in Congress insisted on a continued effort. The House, the Senate, and the administration went along, hiding the $200 million in a $298 billion defense bill. Almost single-handedly, Wilson managed to save the CIA's covert aid program for another year.[343]

US policy in the region was at cross-purposes in a second sense. During the 1980s, Pakistan had received more US foreign aid than any country in the world outside of Israel and Egypt. Yet at the very same time, many in Congress and the US government wanted to curtail Pakistan's nuclear weapons program. The 1985 Pressler Amendment tried to reconcile conflicting goals by prohibiting any further US economic and military assistance to Pakistan if US officials determined that Pakistan possessed "a nuclear explosive device." But this set a very high bar on Pakistan's nuclear weapons development. As long as the last turn hadn't been made on the last screw, as the saying went, the United States could certify that Pakistan didn't possess nuclear weapons. And from 1986 through 1989 the Reagan and Bush administrations did precisely that—even though Pakistan may have had a crude atomic device as early as 1984 and certainly by 1987.

Reagan and Bush were willing to look the other way, given their dependence on Pakistan. But a number of US officials and influential members of Congress remained concerned about the Pakistani nuclear program.[344]

"Pakistan [stands] very close to the line," Scowcroft warned Pakistan's chief of army, Gen. Mirza Aslam Beg, in early 1989. Separately, Scowcroft and Powell each told Beg—general to general—that the administration knew of Pakistan's nuclear program, and they insisted it had to be curtailed. "You have to realize that the administration's hands are tied on the nuclear issue," Scowcroft said. "President Bush [will] certify as long as he [can] under the Pressler amendment, but he [will] not lie." Scowcroft told General Beg he had enough material to make two more nuclear weapons—what Beg said constituted a sufficient deterrent—and proposed the following deal: the US would grant Pakistan its wish list of military aid as long as Pakistan limited its nuclear program. Beg agreed that it was in Pakistan's best interests to impose a freeze on its nuclear program, thereby allowing US military aid to continue.[345]

When President Bush met Prime Minister Benazir Bhutto in Washington on June 6, 1989, he reinforced the administration's call for restraint on the nuclear front.[346]

But US-Pakistan relations quickly went sour. In April 1990, Pakistan and India nearly went to war as a result of Pakistan's support of Kashmiri insurgents, and US officials held Pakistan responsible for the conflict. Because of concerns over a possible war with India, General Beg and President Ghulam Ishaq Khan decided to reactivate the nuclear program—a fact subsequently confirmed by US intelligence sources. The conflict induced a trip by Bob Gates to both Pakistan and India, and when Gates visited Islamabad in May, he and Oakley privately told President Khan that Pakistan had to stop its nuclear program. Over the next several months Oakley met repeatedly with the president, General Beg, and Prime Minister Bhutto, telling them that they had to "cease and desist." But none of them appeared to be listening.

That fall, US intelligence officials all concluded that Pakistan was proceeding with its nuclear weapons program.[347] Meanwhile, the strategic calculus had shifted. With the Soviet empire collapsing, the United States no longer needed Pakistan to play a role in its Cold War rivalry. In addition to Oakley, others in the State Department, and some in the CIA were becoming increasingly frustrated with Pakistan's support for the most radical and anti-Western elements among the militia.[348] Pakistan was also aiding opium production and heroin trafficking. Making matters worse, American favorite Benazir Bhutto had been forced out of office in August 1990, replaced by Prime Minister Nawaz Sharif. The delicate partnership between the United States and Pakistan was looking less and less sustainable.

The hammer fell. The Bush administration decided that as of October 1990 it was no longer willing to certify that Pakistan didn't possess a nuclear device. According to the Pressler Amendment, the US government therefore had to cut off *all* aid—which amounted to $564 million in fiscal 1990—and cancel all existing US-Pakistan military contracts. The United States stopped delivery on some of the forty F-16 fighter jets that Pakistan had already paid for—and, adding insult to injury, Pakistan then had to pay for the storage of those aircraft on a US Air Force base.[349]

Not surprisingly, the Pakistanis reacted with shock and anger. They felt that after years and years of a special US-Pakistan relationship, the United States was discarding them like a piece of used tissue paper.[350] Yet Pakistan's leaders—President Khan and General Beg—had brought this on themselves in large part by resuming their nuclear weapons program. Furthermore, the ISI, the Pakistani army, and Saudi Arabia had been double-crossing the

Bush administration, in effect, by using the US fixation on the Cold War to manipulate the CIA so as to support Muslim fundamentalists such as Abdul Yusef Mustafa Azzam and Osama bin Laden and thereby influence US-Afghanistan policy.[351]

After the Persian Gulf War, the Bush administration lost what little interest it had in the area. In September 1991, Under Secretary Kimmitt became US ambassador to Germany, and that same month Baker and Soviet foreign minister Eduard Shevardnadze both agreed to stop supplying military equipment to Afghanistan, effective January 1, 1992. Afghanistan proceeded to vanish from the United States' radar screen. And while Pakistan, with its 1990 population of 111 million, couldn't completely stay out of view, no longer was it an American ally—at least not in the short term.[352]

After years in the thick of the superpower rivalry, Afghanistan and Pakistan were now mere relics of the Cold War. That Afghanistan in 1992 would be taken over by a band of thugs—which was how many viewed the fractious mujahedin—didn't matter; the $2 billion the United States had devoted to the Afghan mujahedin over the 1980s in the form of money, weapons, and other goods had paid off. After about 1 million Afghans killed as of 1990 (estimating conservatively), 100,000 resistance fighters dead, 500,000 disabled war veterans, and nearly 750 million widows and orphans resulting from the war, President Bush, Secretary Baker, and Scowcroft simply withdrew from the region. They saw little reason to invest more resources in establishing a viable government in Afghanistan, despite the fact that Baker warned Bush that local rivalries and tribal differences would likely result in a "fragmented and violent" future for Afghanistan.[353] Neither did the Clinton administration pick up the ball; it, too, showed a "genuine lack of interest" in the area.[354]

When later asked about US policy in Afghanistan, Scowcroft said he wasn't aware "we were at cross-purposes," although he admitted the idea "wouldn't surprise me." He also agreed that "we had overdone our aid" to Pakistan and the mujahedin, and both he and Gates later acknowledged they had been insufficiently attentive to the problem.[355] Scowcroft and his staff didn't give Afghanistan the attention it required or think they had to reconcile the serious interagency differences on Afghanistan and Pakistan—although this was presumably the purpose of the Deputies Committee and interagency review process. Scowcroft conceded the administration hadn't managed Afghanistan "particularly well"—thus implicitly blaming himself. And Gates admitted to the Senate Armed Services Committee that the administration had "abandoned" Afghanistan, "only to see it descend into Taliban hands."[356]

Scowcroft subsequently acknowledged that the administration had no use for the mujahedin once the Soviets left and that he, the president, and their other top advisers "sort of gave up" on Afghanistan. But that wasn't quite true, as we know: the Bush administration *did* continue to use the mujahedin. What was true, though, is that the Bush administration had other priorities once the Soviets pulled out of Afghanistan, and so it showed little further interest in the region.[357] The United States "is only interested in the withdrawal of Soviet troops," General Zia remarked presciently in 1986, and "doesn't care what happens to the Afghans afterwards."[358]

Within a few short years, Afghanistan would be taken over by the Taliban. Not until January 2002—after the United States went into Afghanistan to overthrow the Taliban, find Osama bin Laden, and set up a new government—did Afghanistan again have a US ambassador. In the intervening thirteen years, there was no US embassy in Kabul and thus no Foreign Service officers, no intelligence personnel, no military attachés, and no one else to represent American interests, evaluate political developments, or furnish information for Washington officials and policy makers.

To some extent, the Bush administration's inattention with respect to Afghanistan and Pakistan was understandable. There were signs of growing Islamic fundamentalism in the early 1990s, but the Taliban of 1992 was not the Taliban of 1996. And in the early 1990s Osama bin Laden was known simply as an influential and extremely wealthy man from a family in the construction business. He was not exiled from Saudi Arabia until 1990 and did not permanently move to Jalalabad until 1996. (Bin Laden had previously lived in Afghanistan when he fought against the Soviets in the early 1980s and later resided in Peshawar for part of 1986.)

Neither did the United States have much influence on many key developments in the region. Benazir Bhutto's difficulties as prime minister (from 1988 to 1990 and from 1993 to 1996) arose partly from the fact that she had no effective control over the Pakistan military and its Afghanistan policy, an arrangement she agreed upon before becoming prime minister and later tried to alter. She was also authoritarian and vindictive (not unlike her father) and, together with her husband, corrupt beyond "acceptable" levels.[359] Had she governed differently, the situation in Pakistan and Afghanistan might well have played out differently.

Nor did the United States have much leverage over Saudi Arabia's support for Sunni fundamentalism in Pakistan and Afghanistan. Although the United States had worked with the Saudis for many years to enhance the ability of Pakistan and the Afghan mujahedin to fight against the Soviet Union and to contain Iran's influence and the spread of Shi'a Islam in the

Middle East and southwest Asia, US and Saudi interests now diverged. The Saudis continued to favor the "fundamentalist" Sunni and Pashtun mujahedin, fearing the influence of Iran and the moderate mujahedin of the north, while the United States viewed the fundamentalists as extreme and potentially dangerous.[360]

Most important, the United States could not control the rivalries between the mujahedin (especially the blood rivalry between Gulbuddin Hekmatyar and Ahmad Shah Massoud, who would be assassinated on September 9, 2001) or the enmity between the fundamentalists and the more moderate mujahedin. What had united the mujahedin, as the political scientist Olivier Roy points out, had been the war against the Soviets. Once the jihad against non-Muslims ended, regional and factional disputes reemerged. In the absence of a single compelling leader, the mujahedin were too distrustful and too jealous of each other, and the ethnic, regional, and religious differences among them were too strong for them to cooperate in the formation of a new government.

Even in the best of conditions it would have been hard to establish a stable confederation in Afghanistan. To a large degree, the history of Afghanistan during the Bush presidency was the history of the failure of the "much-romanticized Afghan Jihad" following withdrawal of Soviet forces, as former ambassador Riaz Mohammed Khan writes in his book *Afghanistan and Pakistan*.[361]

But the United States could have done better. Richard Haass admitted that the Bush administration—including his Middle East desk—mishandled the situation in Afghanistan. Haass likewise conceded that "Panama was a problem," one they also didn't handle "terribly well." And Yugoslavia "clearly didn't work out well."[362] All these countries that had once been the focus of Cold War rivalries had fallen way down on the Bush administration's priority list—and they all suffered as a result. And with Afghanistan not being a priority, policy reverted to the existing players and existing trajectories. In an oral history interview, Haass spoke of the Bush administration's inertia in Afghanistan: "I found it very frustrating because the CIA was so tied to various characters, and I thought they were extremely slow to transition from the anti-Soviet basis for policy to a post-Soviet basis."[363]

By contrast, China was a high priority for the Bush administration and the focus of intensive, highly disciplined analysis and strategic planning by the president and his national security advisor—although the results here, too, were far from an unequivocal success.

21

BLOOD ON THE STONES

ON THE EVENING of June 3, 1989, more than 180,000 troops stationed in and around Beijing and drawn from three separate regions of China simultaneously converged on Tiananmen Square, mobilizing trucks, armored personnel carriers (APCs), tanks, and other vehicles from the equivalent of ten army divisions. In response, thousands of students, workers, professionals, bureaucrats, and other protesters went out to barricade the main streets and avenues leading into the heart of the city. Despite an evening news broadcast warning everyone to stay at home and keep away from Tiananmen Square, the protesters weren't particularly afraid. Seven weeks had already elapsed, almost entirely without violence, since they'd begun their protests. The PLA had been unsuccessful in its previous attempt at removing them, and the protesters' sheer numbers gave them confidence.[364]

This time it was different, however. This time the PLA soldiers didn't hesitate to use their AK-47s, machine guns, and other weapons on the crowds of students, workers, and others. The civilians only had improvised weapons such as bricks, stones, and Molotov cocktails to fight back with. The protesters managed to set a number of trucks, tanks, personnel carriers, and buses on fire, and they killed several soldiers. But the PLA forces easily made it through the makeshift barricades and hostile crowds.

What happened next is still a matter of some controversy. Regime sources insist the demonstrators were allowed to depart Tiananmen Square without interference. Other sources, based on eyewitnesses' reports, paint a very different picture. According to the US Department of State, by 4:30 on the morning of June 4:

SOME 10,000 TROOPS IN THE SQUARE FORMED CONCENTRIC RINGS, ONE FACING INWARD TOWARD SOME 3,000 REMAINING DEMONSTRATORS, AND THE OTHER FACING OUTWARD. AT 0530 A COLUMN OF ABOUT 50 APCS, TANKS,

350

AND TRUCKS ENTERED TIANANMEN SQUARE FROM THE
EAST. DEMOSTRATORS SHOUTED ANGRILY AT THE CON-
VOY AND PLA TROOPS IN TIANANMEN OPENED A BARRAGE
OF RIFLE AND MACHINE GUN FIRE. WHEN THIS GUNFIRE
ENDED AT 0545, A NUMBER OF CASUALTIES REMAINED LYING
ON THE GROUND. AT 0620, A SECOND COLUMN OF ABOUT
40 APCS AND TRUCKS ENTERED TIANANMEN SQUARE BY
THE SAME ROUTE AND THE STUDENTS AGAIN MOVED INTO
THE ROAD. PLA TROOPS IN TIANANMEN AGAIN OPENED FIRE
WITH RIFLES AND MACHINE GUNS, ONCE MORE CAUSING A
LARGE NUMBER OF CASUALTIES.[365]

Others described some soldiers using flamethrowers and witnessed at
least one tank plowed into a crowd, killing and injuring dozens of people.
PLA troops smashed the Goddess of Democracy—the ten-meter-high
plaster, Styrofoam, and metal statue that the protesters had erected—into
small pieces. Then, according to eyewitnesses, they proceeded to detain an
unspecified number of protesters, many of whom were tortured and then
systematically executed with knives or by blows from rifle butts. The State
Department reported the next day "the severity of the assault on Tiananmen Square is clear. Troops shot indiscriminately into crowds of unarmed
civilians, including women and children. In one case students attempting
to parlay with troops were gunned down." The State Department's source
added that foreign journalists saw "fleeing protesters shot in the back,"
whereupon the enraged demonstrators "burned personnel carriers and
killed some security personnel." James Baker called Tiananmen Square a
killing field.[366]

The killing continued on June 5 and 6. On June 7, PLA soldiers sprayed
dozens of bullets into the diplomatic residencies overlooking Tiananmen
Square, which included ten US embassy apartments. Ambassador James
Lilley, who writes about the massacre in his memoirs, believed the PLA was
trying to drive away the international news teams, which had been using
some of the residencies to film the massacre. James Baker and the State Department quietly issued orders for the voluntary evacuation of all embassy
dependents and other Americans in Beijing and China (about six thousand
left out of a total of over eight thousand).[367]

Because army, medical, and Chinese governmental records have been
destroyed or made inaccessible, the exact number of deaths and injuries
and their exact causes will most likely never be known. Although Chinese

officials later admitted arresting six thousand people (Amnesty International put the figure at more than ten thousand), many others were imprisoned and executed over the succeeding weeks, without announcement or recognition. China had its own "disappeared."[368]

The fact that the Chinese leadership wanted to clear the square of protesters shouldn't be surprising, as Henry Kissinger writes in *On China*. Similarly, Scowcroft argued that if the blocks around Times Square in New York City were occupied by tens of thousands or hundreds of thousands of protesters over several weeks' time, US authorities would surely take action.[369] But why was the Chinese repression so violent? The contrast with the methods later used by US authorities to evict the participants in the Occupy Wall Street protests, for instance, is obvious—and shocking.

Deng Xiaoping, Li Peng, Yang Shangkun, and other Chinese leaders had been doubly embarrassed by Mikhail Gorbachev's state visit. They had resented the popular acclaim Gorbachev received because of the reforms he had instituted in the Soviet Union, and they had felt humiliated by the ongoing public protests against their own government. Because of the noise of the crowds, the welcoming ceremony for the Soviet leader couldn't be held at the Great Hall of the People on Tiananmen Square, but had to be conducted at the airport.[370] It was right after Gorbachev's departure, on May 20, that Chinese officials publicly declared martial law.

By this point, the demonstrations had long been a source of anxiety for Chinese party leaders. The hundreds of thousands of students, workers, bureaucrats, professionals, journalists, and other residents of Beijing who showed up in support of the protesters signaled that the Chinese rulers had lost the support of countless citizens. The demonstrations were spreading to other cities, with protests in Nanjing, Xian, Changsha, Wuhan, and elsewhere, thereby revealing just how fed up the Chinese people were.[371] The top Communist Party officials may have feared that a revolution was in the offing and that their own physical safety might be threatened.[372]

Once the frightened party leaders decided to treat the occupation of Tiananmen Square as a military operation rather than a civilian disturbance, several factors narrowed the timing to early June.

One was the challenge posed to the Chinese rulers and the powerful mayor of Beijing on May 28 by the arrival of thousands of sleeping bags and articles of clothing for the protesters, along with other goods and a significant amount of cash that had been raised at a charity concert in Hong Kong. The new resources lifted the protesters' spirits and enabled them to prolong the occupation.[373]

Another was the appearance on May 30 of the "Goddess of Democracy," modeled on the Statue of Liberty—"obviously designed for American television," as Scowcroft said. Chinese leaders called it an insult to the nation.[374]

A third factor was Deng Xiaoping's concern over succession in the Communist Party. He had already selected Jiang Zemin to succeed Zhou Ziyang, and he wanted the new party secretary to be able to take office as soon as there was a consensus for him to do so—and the protests presented an obstacle.[375]

In addition, the evening of June 3 was a new moon, the darkest day of the lunar cycle, and therefore well suited to military operations. The unsuccessful advance of the PLA on May 22, by contrast, had taken place during a full moon, when the ample moonlight had helped the demonstrators resist the incoming troops.[376]

So some kind of military action against the protestors early in June may have been all but inevitable. Less explicable is why Deng and other Chinese leaders sanctioned an attack that even former president Richard Nixon—a hard-nosed policy maker and a longtime friend of China—called "brutal and stupid."[377]

One reason is that Deng and his politburo colleagues wanted to send an unequivocal message to the protesters and Chinese people: what had happened in Romania and Eastern Europe wasn't going to happen in China. So instead of issuing water hoses, tear gas, and rubber bullets to the PLA troops—equipment normally used to handle public disturbances—authorities equipped the soldiers with live ammunition for their AK-47s and their APC-mounted machine guns and sent them out with flamethrowers and other deadly ordnance. Thus when Deng Xiaoping ordered the 150,000 to 200,000 PLA soldiers into action on the evening of June 3, he and his fellow politburo members knew exactly what they were getting.[378]

What they were getting was terror. But the scale of bloodletting appears to have gone beyond what the Chinese leaders anticipated. One cause may have simply been poor management. A few military units got lost within Beijing as they made their way to Tiananmen Square, for instance. Soldiers didn't help their fallen fellow soldiers or come to the rescue of those whose safety was being endangered by civilians. On the contrary, some units of the PLA attacked other units, perhaps by accident or perhaps not—since there were reports of internal conflicts within the PLA—and more than a hundred soldiers were killed in action, a very high number under the circumstances (since they were fighting unarmed adversaries, essentially).[379] One possible explanation is that the PLA casualties came from friendly fire, with tens of thousands of troops pulled in from different armies from around China using their AK-47s, which had a half-mile range, and APC-mounted machine guns, with an even longer range, in almost total darkness.[380]

Further consistent with the idea that the massacre was the result of a botched military operation is the fact that after the massacre, Beijing streets were filled with burned-out vehicles, including a thousand trucks and hundreds of armored personnel carriers, police vans, buses, and tanks. Although protesters set some of them alight, several eyewitnesses reported seeing soldiers themselves setting their own army vehicles on fire.[381] It is possible the Chinese soldiers were ordered to destroy equipment to make the conflict seem more serious militarily than it actually was.

Consistent with this scenario, Chinese officials repeatedly low-balled the number of civilian casualties—Deng Xiaoping told Scowcroft when he visited in July that there were only 310 deaths—while emphasizing the relatively large number of soldier casualties and destroyed vehicles.[382] And in the following months, numerous soldiers, officers, and commanders from the army units involved were disciplined, relieved of command, or executed. By the end of 1989, 111 officers and 1,400 enlisted men had been subjected to some form of disciplinary action.[383]

The evidence points to a profound lack of coordination within the PLA as well as a glaring absence of effective centralized military command. Scowcroft said that his own worst fear was that the PLA was not following its orders and that the Communist Party wasn't in control of the military. And we still don't know the Chinese side of the story, he observed. "If you actually analyze that period of a little over a month," he said in an oral history interview, "it becomes much more complex with many more forces at work. Did we understand them? No. Not even close."[384]

Whatever its causes, the massacre pushed back the clock on years of progress in Chinese civil rights and undermined the country's record of political and economic reforms in the 1980s. For Bette Bao Lord, who remained in Beijing to report for CBS News, "the legitimacy of the Chinese government" had "been destroyed." (Deng Xiaoping thought the opposite, claiming "Westerners would forget.")[385] But the immediate impact was enormous. Televisions worldwide broadcast searing images of the atrocities, and newspapers printed graphic photographs of the injured and dead—especially those of a lone protester facing down a column of tanks the following day.[386] The news shocked Chinese communities in Hong Kong, Taiwan, Malaysia, Canada, and elsewhere. In the United States, outraged members of Congress, reporters and commentators, human rights advocates, Hollywood celebrities, and others—Chinese students especially—condemned the massacre.

The Tiananmen Square tragedy seriously damaged China's foreign relations and international reputation, and it set back US-China relations almost to their pre-1972 status. It also made things extraordinarily difficult for Bush, Scowcroft, the Beijing embassy, and the State Department.[387] They now had to find a new course of action that could both respond to the horrors of the massacre and somehow put US-China relations back on track.

The president was under no illusions about the reality of the Chinese government, as his China diaries show. But he wanted to penalize the Chinese military and not the Chinese people. So after issuing a muted response only hours after the killing, he made a stronger statement two days later. Although his inclination as a former professional diplomat and a conservative was to be unsympathetic to the Chinese protesters, his advisers on China policy from across the government, guided by the interagency process managed by the national security advisor, convinced him that he needed to do more. So he halted weapons sales to China, stopped the exchange of senior-level officials between the two countries, cut off joint military R&D with China, and denied the issue of new multilateral loans. There would be no more business as usual.

Scowcroft wondered whether everything they had worked for was "going down the drain."[388] But many members of Congress, media commentators, and Chinese students in the United States cried out for further sanctions. All notable Chinese scholars but one, Michel Oksenberg, abandoned the administration. And other politicians, policy experts, and pundits, meanwhile, questioned the very purpose of US-China relations, wondering whether the two countries were simply too different culturally, politically, and ideologically to get along.[389] President Bush later remarked that "a lot of people wanted to cut China off," including some members of Congress, and that "in the beginning," the administration "had no support" for its moderate tone.[390] Whereas public opinion had been 69 percent favorable toward China in mid-February 1989, by mid-June only 16 percent of Americans had a favorable opinion of China; 78 percent had an unfavorable opinion.[391]

But Bush's "gut instinct"—one Scowcroft fully agreed with—was that however deplorably the Chinese had behaved, "the relationship with China was a crucial relationship and we shouldn't let it flounder on [their] one mistake." The United States "had too much invested in the China situation to throw it away in one stroke."[392] Former president Nixon agreed. Early in the morning of June 5, he called the White House precisely because he feared that if the United States responded with harsher measures, it would unravel years of careful diplomacy and inflict lasting damage on US-China ties. The former president wanted to be sure Bush didn't panic, since, in his analysis, from a "long range strategic standpoint, the United States has no choice but to strengthen its relationship with China."[393]

In fact, it seems that the Chinese may have viewed US-China relations in much the same way, as bleak as their relationship seemed. As one State Department analyst wrote to Secretary Baker on July 1, 1989, "Chinese leaders have consistently signaled their desire to minimize damage to US-Sino relations in the wake of the Tiananmen crackdown. Public statements have been carefully formulated to present China's position on the Fang Lizhi issue without committing Beijing to respond in any particular way." Scowcroft, too, was surprised that the Chinese didn't try to stop the cooperative intelligence program on the Soviet Union.[394]

Nonetheless, the pressures on the administration remained intense. Further straining US-China relations was the dissident Fang Lizhi, who'd secretly taken refuge in the US embassy. Initially—and mistakenly—Fang was refused asylum. But a savvy State Department official alerted Washington, and the embassy was ordered to grant Fang asylum. Ambassador Lilley then hid Fang and his wife in the nurses' station, a small outbuilding in the compound with blacked-out windows, where the couple had to reside twenty-four hours a day with only minimal outside contact. They stayed there for almost a year, with only Lilley and a handful of others knowing where they were. As "China's leading dissident," Fang was "with us as constant reminder of our connection to 'bourgeois liberalism' and puts us at odds with the regime here," Lilley said. "He is a living symbol of our conflict with China over human rights."[395]

But Fang's presence at the embassy made things that much more difficult for administration, and Lilley, Scowcroft, and Bush were furious at the imposition—especially since Fang had been outspoken in his condemnation of the president and the United States after having been prevented from attending the hotel banquet.[396]

Chinese officials soon discovered Fang was at the US embassy, and they responded angrily, insisting that the United States was interfering in China's internal affairs. But since Fang was on a list of people who were to be arrested, the US embassy had little choice. If the embassy had released Fang, he would have been picked up quickly by Chinese authorities and imprisoned, at minimum. Chinese officials stationed guards armed with automatic weapons around the perimeter of the embassy grounds in order to prevent the Americans from smuggling him out.[397]

The Chinese made things difficult for the Bush administration in other ways. They continued the crackdown against dissidents and arrested thousands, ferreting out those in the universities and the bureaucracy who had supported the demonstrations. They pressured citizens to inform on one another, to admit to their own errors, and to declare their support for the repression. They purged the media of individuals who had expressed support for the protesters. They inflamed the Chinese public by publishing and televising news stories blaming the massacre on the United States and warning of the evils of "bourgeois liberalism." They also talked of shutting down the intelligence facilities that China and the United States had been jointly using to monitor Soviet missile and nuclear tests.[398]

Throughout this period, information about what was actually happening in China was murky. Scowcroft himself conceded that the Bush administration knew little about the structure, goals, and organization of the demonstrators and that it did not understand the forces at work resulting in the Tiananmen Square massacre.[399] Sometimes Deng Xiaoping appeared in charge, at other times he was wholly absent. Elderly members of the politburo acted indecisively or seemed out of touch. And for a while no one even knew the whereabouts of Deng Xiaoping and Li Peng. Rumors swirled that the Chinese leaders were ready to flee.[400]

The day after he learned of the massacre, President Bush repeatedly tried to telephone Deng Xiaoping—against the advice of his NSC staff—but he couldn't get through. Chinese leaders were unaccustomed to doing business over the telephone and uncomfortable doing so. So Bush drafted a private message for Deng Xiaoping in which he expressed his respect for Deng and China and spoke of his hope that Deng would show "clemency" toward the students. When Chinese officials responded with a bland admonition that the United States had to stop taking sides, Scowcroft went over to the Chinese embassy on June 21 to meet the ambassador, Han Xu, a friend of his since 1971. Scowcroft explained that President Bush wanted to discuss US-China relations and to send over a special envoy from the administration to deliver Bush's letter. Deng replied on June 24, agreeing to receive Bush's envoy.[401]

The president considered sending Nixon or Kissinger, but after thinking how famous each of them was and how much attention each would receive, he decided on a less conspicuous alternative. He would send Brent Scowcroft, who knew Deng Xiaoping better than anyone in the White House except Bush himself.[402] Secretary Baker asked that someone from the State Department accompany Scowcroft, and Bush chose Scowcroft's colleague and close friend Lawrence Eagleburger. President Bush said the idea was "mainly mine, but it was strongly supported by Scowcroft" as well as "to some degree Jim Baker."[403]

While Bush and Scowcroft were planning the trip, Secretary Baker announced the suspension of high-level contacts with China. He meant to refer only to commerce secretary Robert Mosbacher's trip scheduled for later that month, but his statement inadvertently implied that all high-level visits were off. With the politics of the time, neither President Bush nor Baker was in a position to issue a correction.[404]

At five o'clock in the morning of June 30, barely three weeks after the massacre and under conditions of extreme secrecy, Scowcroft, Eagleburger, a small support staff, and an Air Force crew took off from Andrews Air Force Base. They traveled in a converted C-141 Starlifter military transport, disguised as a commercial carrier, that contained special voice and data communications equipment so Scowcroft and Eagleburger wouldn't have to rely on the State Department's communications system. In order to further safeguard the mission's secrecy, the aircraft was refueled in the air over Seattle/Tacoma. Even Ambassador Lilley wasn't briefed on Scowcroft's secret mission until after the national security advisor arrived back in Washington. Neither did Colin Powell, Robert Kimmitt, nor other senior administration officials know of the trip.[405] And the NSC staff was told that Scowcroft was off to visit his sister in Utah. China's foreign minister, Qian Qichen, observed that Scowcroft's visit was even more secretive than Kissinger's trip of October 1971, because at least the US ambassador in Pakistan had known of Kissinger's trip.[406]

Scowcroft reports in *A World Transformed* that Chinese air defense officials spotted an unidentified aircraft penetrating Chinese airspace. It was a moment fraught with potential for a disastrous misunderstanding. Fortunately, Chinese officials checked with President Yang Shangkun before taking any action, and the plane was allowed to proceed unimpeded. An hour later, at 1:00 P.M. on July 1, Scowcroft and Eagleburger landed in Beijing and began their quiet one-day visit—a stay conspicuous for the absence of any ceremony or public display of American flags on cars, on the walls of their hotel, or in the streets.[407]

Scowcroft and Eagleburger met with Deng Xiaoping the next day, and then talked with Li Peng and Qian Qichen. Scowcroft described Deng's reception as very warm and very friendly, as though he were greeting an old friend. Yet Deng's message was anything but friendly (although he said that President Bush had been "wise and cool-headed" to send Scowcroft). He refused to make any concessions whatsoever on the Tiananmen Square massacre, which he described as the suppression of a "counterrevolutionary rebellion"; it was an internal Chinese affair, he emphasized, and no one else's problem. Deng said that China didn't fear the United States and it wasn't going to back down now—not after the Communist Party had already proven its mettle in its twenty-two-year war for the establishment of the People's Republic of China. China had no choice but to punish the instigators of the Tiananmen Square demonstrations, he continued, and under no circumstances would China tolerate outside interference. The United States, and not China, was at fault for endangering US-China ties.[408]

Scowcroft replied that George Bush was an old friend of China's who was doing all he could to resist attempts by Congress to adopt harsher anti-China policies. Unfortunately, the Chinese government's actions had left President Bush and the United States with little choice except to impose sanctions.

Deng replied that while he considered Bush a friend and while he hoped that the two of them could treat each other as friends, he didn't agree with what was being said. He then left the room.[409]

Scowcroft remembered being struck by Deng's insistence that he wasn't going to be the chief policy maker any longer, even though he was still in charge and appeared in good health.[410]

In Scowcroft's meeting with Li Peng and Qian Qichen, Li denied the reports concerning the Tiananmen casualties in the Western press, saying that only 310 people had died—just thirty-six of them students—and maintained that Chinese authorities had been restrained in their actions. Scowcroft explained again that, while he accepted that the Chinese government's action was a "wholly internal affair," China's actions created grave problems for President Bush and threatened the US-China relationship.[411] He pointed out that as long as China continued to impose martial law, repress its citizens, and publicly and stridently criticize the United States and American values, nothing could happen, as much as the Bush administration hoped to preserve the security ties between the countries and continue US-China military and commercial relations. He further explained that the president could do only so much, the US Congress had a key role in setting in US-China policy, and Bush also had an obligation to consider the views of the American public. The Tiananmen Square incident had effectively become a joint problem for China and the United States, Scowcroft pointed out; both states needed to work at overcoming what had happened.[412]

Scowcroft's meetings with Deng Xiaoping, Li Peng, and Qian Qichen were less about the content of US-China relations than about the principles underlying their ties. The goals were to let each country know where the other stood and restart a dialogue while signaling President Bush's good intentions toward Deng Xiaoping, his fellow party leaders, and China itself. In this limited sense, the visit, as tense and strained as it was, paid off. At a minimum, the trip helped keep the administration's relationship with China from deteriorating further.[413]

Scowcroft and Eagleburger returned to Washington as secretly as they had left. (Months later, the Pentagon found out about the secret visit after being given an invoice from the Chinese government for refueling the C-141, journalist James Mann reports in his book *About Face*.)[414] Scowcroft and Eagleburger downplayed what they'd been able to achieve in their subsequent conversations with President Bush and Secretary Baker, and they made no claims that the Chinese had since relaxed their political repression or become more favorably disposed toward the United States.

Ambassador Lilley was similarly equivocal about the prospects of US-China relations. "Today the Chinese are engaged in a massive campaign to discredit U.S. influence to the Chinese people. At the same time China wants our trade our technology and enough of a security connection so that it does not end up facing the Soviet Union alone," he cabled on July 9. "China now confronts a severe erosion of popular trust and confidence in the leadership, the probability of economic stagflation and possibly recession, and a shattered image to the outside world. The overall prospects are grim and the techniques China uses to deal with its crises are backwards and conservative but still occasionally cunning," he wrote. "Hardliners dominate temporarily, but there are constant signs of a leadership struggle between forces representing an outward orientation and those that prefer to turn inward."[415]

A few weeks later, Bush wrote Deng, thanking him for hosting the visit and assuring him he was doing everything he could to preserve their friendship. But the president stressed that it took two to make the relationship work—the Chinese had to help.

In his reply, Deng expressed his frustration with the United States and again scolded Bush for the United States' interference in China's internal affairs. Deng and Bush each thought the other had "tied the knot"—that his counterpart was hindering progress in their relationship—and each therefore believed his counterpart had the responsibility to untie the knot and fix the relationship.[416] Yet as Scowcroft rightly observed, it was President Bush who was going the extra mile to revive the US-China relationship, not the Chinese party leaders.[417]

A CIA analysis of China's attitudes toward the United States "in the wake of the Tiananmen crackdown" suggested that Chinese leaders were "preoccupied . . . with the daunting task of shoring up regime legitimacy and restoring bureaucratic discipline," and officials "consistently have held out the olive branch, stressing China's desire for friendly relations with all countries." The report found that "Beijing has deliberately avoided the appearance of a crisis in US-China relations" and did not publicize the news "that China would reciprocate for the US halt in military contacts and cooperation." Instead, "the vast majority of press articles mentioning outside support for democracy activists, including articles attacking VOA [Voice of America] and maligning Fang Lizhi and his wife and student leaders with US ties, have been aimed at an internal audience. Their primary aim is not to send threatening messages to the US . . . but to justify Chinese government actions" and to discredit "alternative (negative) assessments and sources of information." In sum, "the more difficulty the regime has in efforts to shore up its legitimacy, the greater the temptation to 'prove' that outsiders with evil anti-China intentions are behind regime critics."[418]

As for the attacks on the foreign media, "especially the American media and the VOA," Lilley attributed these to the Chinese desire to avoid the negative coverage associated with controversial human rights policies. "They realistically understand that continuing public violence against their own people risks foreign support," Lilley said. "This was the lesson for them of media coverage of Tiananmen."[419]

Since official visits between the two countries were temporarily discontinued, Bush and Scowcroft used separate private visits by Nixon and Kissinger to learn more about the Chinese thinking and to keep the dialogue open.[420]

Nixon's visit had been planned for some time, then delayed until October 1989 because of Tiananmen Square. (According to Kissinger biographer Walter Isaacson, when Kissinger communicated with him about coordinating their travels, Nixon deliberately chose not to respond with his travel dates to ensure that his visit would come first.)[421] Because of the high regard with which he was held in China, Nixon received "remarkable access" to Chinese leaders and was received by Deng Xiaoping, Li Peng, Jiang Zemin, Yang Shangkun, Qian Qichen, and Zhu Rongji (mayor of Shanghai at the time), among others.

In his meeting with Deng Xiaoping, Nixon forcefully explained how the massacre had immobilized the United States and how it was in the mutual interests of the United States and China to move their relationship forward.

Deng insisted that the United States was in the stronger position and China in the weaker one; it was therefore up to the Americans to take the initiative. Nixon was able to secure one concession, however: he got the Chinese authorities to stop posting armed guards around the perimeter of the US embassy grounds.[422]

After receiving Nixon's report in early November and having him for dinner in the residence, Bush wrote Deng Xiaoping once more, this time to express his interest in sending another envoy for the ostensible purpose of updating Deng on the talks scheduled with Gorbachev the first week of December. In the letter, Bush reassured Deng that the Malta summit would not adversely affect US-China relations and that he still valued the US-China bilateral relationship. Deng replied—via a letter that the Chinese ambassador handed to Scowcroft on November 15—that he, too, wanted an improved relationship and that he would welcome another visit.[423]

Kissinger's early November visit to China, his fifteenth overall, combined commerce and politics. He was accompanied by Maurice Greenberg, the chairman of the multinational insurance giant AIG, and by Judith Hope, a prominent Washington lawyer and member of the Harvard Corporation and of the Union Pacific board of directors. Kissinger, still a celebrity, was one of the few statesmen who could straddle the political, business, and cultural worlds. In honor of his arrival, the US embassy hosted a gala reception, with many of China's business, cultural, and political leaders in attendance.[424]

Kissinger met with Deng Xiaoping, Li Peng, and the new party general secretary, Jiang Zemin. He spoke of his support for Bush's message and conveyed the administration's interests (and his interests) in seeing US-China relations flourish. Kissinger also tried to help out on the most contentious issue dividing the two governments, the Fang Lizhi situation, which Bush himself had called "a real stick in the eye to the Chinese."[425] Deng proposed a package deal: he would allow Fang to leave China if the United States promised not to exploit the dissident for political purposes, agreed to resume economic cooperation with China (that is, to continue with business deals, loans, and military sales that had all been put on hold), and consented to host a visit by Jiang Zemin.[426]

The Nixon and Kissinger visits reaffirmed the fact that the Chinese leaders were interested in renewed dialogue with the United States and confirmed to the Chinese rulers the importance that President Bush and national security advisor Scowcroft assigned to nurturing their ties with China. The two trips thus prepared the ground for Scowcroft's second visit to Beijing in December, 1989, shortly after the US-Soviet summit in Malta.

With his role in the Nixon and Ford presidencies, his subsequent private visits to China in the late 1970s and 1980s, his focus on the United States' long-term strategic interests, and his very close relationship with President Bush, Scowcroft was perfectly positioned to serve as the point man for US-China relations from 1989 to 1993. In this area, Secretary Baker took a backseat, especially after the Tiananmen Square massacre.[427]

But controversy was to surround Scowcroft's second China trip. On November 30, shortly before the president, Baker, and Scowcroft were to leave for Malta, Representative Nancy Pelosi's Emergency Chinese Immigration Relief Act had landed on Bush's desk for his signature. (It was the first time Pelosi's name would become familiar to any significant numbers of Americans outside her own California congressional district.) The bill would allow Chinese students to stay in the United States when applying for a change in their visa status, rather having to return to China before applying (which had been the normal practice). Scowcroft feared that if the bill passed, China would stop allowing students to come to the United States for study. And given that the Chinese government also opposed the bill, neither Scowcroft nor Bush wanted to put any more barriers in the way of a recovery of US-China relations.

For these reasons, Bush wanted to veto the bill, but it did not appear he had the votes in Congress to prevent an override, given the veto-proof margins by which Congress had passed the bill (by 403–0 in the House, and a voice vote in the Senate). Bush decided to preempt Congress by issuing an executive order to virtually the same effect, thereby achieving unilaterally what Congress wanted to do through law, but with the advantage that the executive order allowed him to retain his executive authority and to later rescind the waiver if he so chose. So on November 30, Bush vetoed the Pelosi bill, stating that it constituted "congressional micromanagement of foreign policy."[428] Soon thereafter, he departed for Malta.

The issue did not die there. Now the challenge was to find the votes needed to sustain the veto in the Democratic-controlled Senate. (There was no chance of sustaining the veto in the House.) Scowcroft and others in the administration worked ceaselessly in the attempt to prevent the override. They contacted individual US senators, discussed at length with them the condition of and the prospects for US-China relations, and consulted with their political allies and acquaintances in the press so as to further promote the administration's position. Scowcroft said he'd never worked so hard in his life.[429]

The efforts paid off. On January 25, the Senate sustained the president's veto by a vote of 62 to 37.

Meanwhile, the Bush administration were continuing to push ahead on the diplomatic front. On December 9, Scowcroft and Eagleburger arrived in Beijing, accompanied by Ambassador Lilley as well by Douglas Paal and Chase Untermeyer, the president's director of personnel and a longtime aide. Untermeyer explained that for him to go along with Scowcroft and Eagleburger on the trip—an unusual decision by the president—indicated to the Chinese just how committed Bush was to the relationship.[430] The inclusion of Lilley and Paal likewise showed that both the NSC and the State Department were strongly invested in the US-China relationship. The central goal of the trip was to establish a road map for improving US-China relations.[431]

But Scowcroft and Bush miscalculated how the American media would react to news of this trip. With the US-Soviet summit just concluded and with the level of anti-Chinese sentiment around the country at the time, there was no good moment to announce the upcoming trip, which was to be low profile though not secret. As a result, the White House delayed announcing the trip as long as it could and didn't release the news until Scowcroft and Eagleburger were already en route to Beijing. With the two envoys arriving in the middle of the night in the United States and with the news breaking on a weekend, the press, members of Congress, and the public were immediately suspicious of the Bush administration's motives and its apparent pro-China agenda.[432]

Scowcroft first debriefed the Chinese leaders on the Malta summit, with the discussion centering on the development and implications of Soviet Union's weakened condition. He found that the Chinese had been surprised at Gorbachev's request for financial assistance during the May summit in Beijing; Qian Qichen went so far as to predict the collapse of the Soviet economy, since he didn't see the Soviet Union undertaking any meaningful economic reforms to address its serious underlying problems.[433] Scowcroft then raised the topic of Fang Lizhi, mentioned some of the unresolved military and commercial issues the United States had with China, and talked about the specific steps the two governments might take to improve their relationship. Deng restated his offer of a package deal for Fang's release. He also asked that China be allowed to launch three Hughes Corporation satellites for its Australian and Hong Kong corporate clients, and that the suspended World Bank and Japanese loans be resumed.

For his part, Scowcroft requested that martial law be lifted, that the Chinese stop jamming the popular Voice of America—listened to by tens of millions in China—and that China halt its sale of M-9 (Silkworm) missiles to the Middle East.[434] Although the status of Fang Lizhi remained the largest sticking point in the normalization of US-China relations, Scowcroft refused the package deal tying Fang's freedom to specific US actions. He argued that the resolution of Fang's situation and the lifting of the economic sanctions should be disconnected; he wanted the United States and China to proceed on separate timetables, with each side doing what it could to improve the relationship gradually rather than moving in unison.[435]

The release of Fang Lizhi did happen on its own schedule, as Scowcroft planned, without being explicitly linked to the lifting of economic sanctions. And on the same day as the US invasion of Panama, the administration announced the authorization of the satellite launch (Paal joked, "we invaded Panama in order to launch the satellite").

Scowcroft would be the last foreign visitor to be received by Deng, who retired from public life soon after the visit (with the important exception of his southern tour in early 1992) and became increasingly reclusive until his death in 1997.[436]

Scowcroft's second trip to Beijing became notorious for the toast he gave his Chinese hosts. At a banquet held on December 9, his first evening in China, Scowcroft was about to toast foreign minister Qian Qichen and the other Chinese leaders when, to his "total surprise," several photojournalists entered the hall. The sudden presence of the cameras forced Scowcroft to make a difficult decision. He could go ahead and make the toast with the likely outcome that excerpts from the speech would be replayed to millions of Americans under headlines to the effect of "Bush's National Security Advisor Toasts the Butchers of Tiananmen Square." Or he could decline to give the toast and dishonor his hosts, but thereby spare the Bush administration a public relations disaster.[437]

He "swallowed his pride," he said, and made the toast. In the speech, drafted by Lilley and Paal and not intended for either American or international audiences, Scowcroft spoke of trying to overcome the difficulties in the bilateral relationship. He acknowledged the different values and distinct ideologies separating the two countries, saying, "Speaking as a friend, I would not be honest if I did not acknowledge that we have profound areas of disagreement—on the events at Tiananmen [and] on the sweeping changes in Eastern Europe." But he went on to assert China's central importance to the United States and to recognize the need for both countries to protect the other's "face." He reminded his hosts of the good-faith efforts that Bush had already made—restarting the Peace Pearl project (upgrading the electronics on China's F-8s), defeating the congressional sanctions bill, and vetoing the Pelosi bill. The United States and China could either revert to the personal exchanges and ping-pong diplomacy of the 1970s or move forward with a new strategic and economic partnership.[438]

A CNN news crew photographed Scowcroft and Qian beaming at each other after the toast and clinking their glasses. The news footage stunned the American public and audiences worldwide. Members of Congress of both parties, journalists, and other opinion leaders vilified Scowcroft and Bush for conducting an amoral foreign policy and sanctioning tyranny. One member of Congress called the toast "obscene." Another called Scowcroft and Eagleburger's trip "embarrassing" and said it was a slap in the face to freedom-loving people. Senator Mitch McConnell called the visit "the wrong message at the wrong time."[439]

News commentators said the trip contradicted the administration's own ban on high-level meetings between the countries and claimed Chinese officials were reveling in the attention. The *Washington Post*'s Mary McGrory compared Scowcroft and Eagleburger's "inexplicable and indefensible" mission to Robert McFarlane and Oliver North's ill-considered trip to Iran. The *New York Times*' A. M. Rosenthal reminded readers that Scowcroft and Eagleburger were both former associates of Henry Kissinger, first in the Nixon and Ford administrations and then with Kissinger Associates, and described them as essentially kissing Deng Xiaoping's bloodied hand. Similar criticisms reverberated in the US heartland: the *St. Louis Post-Dispatch*, for example, editorialized that the Bush administration was kowtowing to the Chinese and discarding human rights as a concern of US foreign policy. The White House was disgracing American ideals, the *Post-Dispatch*'s editors concluded.[440]

Scowcroft himself felt "sandbagged." He had previously come to an understanding with his Chinese hosts that the American media weren't supposed to be at the dinner. And he knew the camera crews could have entered the banquet hall only with official permission. However, he refused to speculate on the motives of the Chinese for reneging on their understanding.[441]

Fang Lizhi had no such reticence. The "obvious objective" of Chinese leaders was to document Scowcroft's words as proof of the United States' endorsement of China's Communist Party and to show the Chinese people and the world that US-China relations were again on track.[442]

Nine days after the news broke of Scowcroft's trip to Beijing and his infamous toast, Scowcroft and Eagleburger's secret July visit became public knowledge, pouring more oil on the flames. Former ambassador Winston Lord, who'd turned "very hostile" to the Chinese government after the Tiananmen Square massacre, condemned the Scowcroft trips as "pilgrimages" and called the Bush administration's China policy weak-minded and misguided. He also repeated the charge that the administration was practicing a double standard on human rights, treating China one way and Eastern Europe and the Soviet Union another.[443]

For George Bush, a seasoned politician and a national figure for fifteen years, the criticism from members of Congress and in the press was nothing new; if he was bothered by the attacks, he never let on. But Scowcroft wasn't a politician; he was a consummate foreign policy professional, a dedicated public servant, and occasionally the president's personal agent. The fierce condemnations were new for him.[444] While he was more than willing to stand up for President Bush's—and his—China policy and accept the consequences, the public attacks stung.

At almost the same time, however, Scowcroft and the Bush administration were succeeding on another foreign policy front.

22

ONE GERMANY

IN EARLY 1989, it would have been hard to find a single prominent journalist or political leader who favored the creation of a single, united Germany. "Neither West nor East has an interest in German reunification," the *International Herald Tribune* foreign affairs columnist William Pfaff wrote in February 1989. "This is a fact of international life." And indeed, French president François Mitterrand, British prime minister Margaret Thatcher, Soviet president Mikhail Gorbachev, and other European heads of state, East and West alike, were all uncomfortable with the idea of a reunited Germany in view of that country's unhappy twentieth-century history and its potentially vast political and economic clout.

Policy makers close to Brent Scowcroft were also deeply skeptical of a reunified Germany. Former president Nixon wrote Bush soon after the Berlin Wall came down, "I would strongly urge that you indicate that you are *not* going to negotiate German unification or the future of NATO with Gorbachev. The recent loose talk about the 'inevitability' of German unification," Nixon commented, "is irresponsible."[445] Henry Kissinger, too, opposed reunification and called for "the peoples of Eastern Europe to choose their own political future."[446]

But German chancellor Helmut Kohl made it happen. He envisioned a reunited Germany, staked his political future on that vision, and persevered. He had one indispensable ally: the president of the United States. Unlike Kohl's fellow European heads of state, Bush fully supported Kohl's efforts. "I'd love to see Germany reunited," Bush said in the *Washington Times* on May 16, 1989. A single Germany was "fine," he said, as long as it could be achieved "on a proper basis." At a press conference in Helena, Montana, four months later, the president announced that German reunification was for the two Germanys to decide. "I believe that Germany has earned the right to be accepted as a full democratic partner," Bush declared on September 18.[447] And on October 25, in a front-page story in the *New*

York Times based on an interview with Bush, R. W. Apple Jr. reiterated that the president didn't fear German reunification, warning only that it would take "prudent evolution" and a lot of work for the two German governments. Chancellor Kohl and others in the German government took heart from the self-confidence and ease with which President Bush stated his acceptance of German reunification within NATO.[448]

The president was ahead of everyone in his administration—including Baker and Scowcroft. So when Gates called the national security advisor from Helena, telling him of Bush's statement, Scowcroft exclaimed, "Oh shit."[449] The national security advisor recognized the thorny issues reunification would raise, from short-range nuclear weapons and conventional force levels in Europe to the future of the NATO and Warsaw Pact alliances.

Scowcroft wanted to proceed deliberately. He understood that the fate of German reunification would depend on how the Soviet Union, with its thousands of tanks and hundreds of thousands of soldiers on the ground, reacted. And neither Scowcroft nor anyone else in the administration could be sure of Gorbachev's hold on power or of how far his reforms could go. Soviet shipments of weapons and ammunition to guerrillas in El Salvador and of MiG-29s to Cuba made Scowcroft wonder whether "we were still facing a Brezhnev system with a humanitarian paint job."[450] In fact, when Vernon Walters, the new ambassador to Germany, gave a speech soon after arriving in Bonn, in which he said he believed that Germany would unite while he was ambassador, Scowcroft telephoned Walters and "reamed" him for his premature statement.[451]

So when Chancellor Kohl, two days before the Malta summit, proposed an ambitious ten-point plan for the reunification of Germany, Scowcroft wanted to move slowly. However, President Bush promptly telephoned Kohl, expressing his support. In the meantime, the NSC combined Kohl's proposal with its own ten-page strategy paper it had forwarded to Scowcroft on November 20 that explored how the United States could best achieve reunification notwithstanding the range of possibilities and the fast-moving, uncertain dynamics.[452] They came up with a gradual, step-by-step approach that wouldn't alarm Paris, London, or other European capitals, on one hand, or an anxious Moscow, on the other.

Bush then raised the issue at Malta, telling the Soviet leader, "We cannot be asked to disapprove of German reunification," adding, "I realize this is a highly sensitive subject and we have tried to conduct ourselves with restraint."[453] But knowing of Gorbachev's and his advisers' views of the matter, Bush and his senior advisers never presented Gorbachev with anything that he could reject. Since the Soviets themselves didn't appear to know exactly what was going on, as Philip Zelikow and Condoleezza Rice point out in their book *Germany Unified and Europe Transformed*, the administration didn't want "to force them to declare a bottom line."[454] They played it brilliantly.

Immediately after the summit, Bush headed to Brussels for a NATO meeting. The evening before it started, he had dinner with Kohl. During that dinner, the president told Kohl, "Go ahead, I'm with you completely." After that, Scowcroft and Baker never "so much as hesitated" in their support of a reunited Germany. President Bush "didn't change," Scowcroft said, "I did."[455]

Bush then debriefed the European leaders and secured their agreement on a gradual plan that endorsed self-determination, supported German reunification within NATO and the European Community, and respected European borders according to the principles established in the Helsinki Final Act.

But events on the ground were moving quickly. The continued demonstrations, the flight of East Germans to the West, and the instability of the East German government under Hans Modrow provided clear evidence that the forty-year-old system of two Germanys was dysfunctional. One million East Germans flooded over the border in the three days after the Berlin Wall came down (most for temporary visits). With the turmoil and political uncertainty, Kohl did not want to work further on German reunification with the Modrow regime until a stable government could be reestablished in East Germany—which meant after the parliamentary elections scheduled for May. The outcome of those elections would determine whether or not East Germany would join West Germany.

But Kohl and Modrow both realized that the East German government couldn't hold on, so they moved the elections up to March 18, 1990.[456] Kohl had additional reasons for advocating the earlier date: he wanted to move before West Germans became fully aware of the hardships being imposed by the influx of East Germans and the high cost of reunification.

Bush and Scowcroft, however, worried that the change would help the Social Democrats or Communists gain votes, since the earlier date gave the Christian Democrats and their partners less time to mobilize. Scowcroft and his staff also worried that West Germany might try "to go it alone," given Kohl's determination and his political commitment to German reunification.[457] "We had great faith in Kohl," Scowcroft noted, "but Gorbachev might try to push hard. We could not rule out the possibility that Gorbachev could tempt—or threaten—him." Gorbachev might follow his adviser Valentin Falin's advice to offer "very attractive" proposals to the two Germanys, lure French support, and thereby shut the United States out of the reunification process. In Kohl's rush toward reunification, NATO itself might be negotiable.[458]

For a moment, the Americans' fears seemed to be realized. On January 31, 1990, West German foreign minister Hans-Dietrich Genscher proposed that a reunified Germany be part of a trans-European security arrangement uniting NATO and the Warsaw Pact in combination with the Conference for Security and Cooperation in Europe (CSCE) and the European Community (EC). Scowcroft commented, "There was no way we could accept [the CSCE] absorbing NATO and its functions." But the proposal carried no official weight: Genscher hadn't let Kohl know of his proposal, it turned out—just as Kohl hadn't informed Genscher of the ten-point plan he'd earlier presented to the Bush administration.[459]

Neither did Scowcroft and NSC staff want a "Helsinki II"—another CSCE conference—for settling Germany's future, given the difficulty of achieving consensus among all thirty-five members, including the Soviet Union. For Bob Blackwill and Scowcroft, this could develop into "an open-ended negotiation about the future of Europe in about the worst multilateral setting one can imagine." The consensus structure of the CSCE "allowed any country uneasy with the prospect of a large Germany much greater potential stall or delay," Scowcroft wrote. He feared a "CSCE summit to ratify the reunification agreement" could reopen "old wounds and unresolved disputes." Scowcroft was especially dismayed at Thatcher's interest in using the CSCE to handle German reunification.[460]

The administration did support institutionalizing the CSCE, however, and strengthening its ability to handle political issues and mediate disputes—just so long as it didn't conflict with NATO or interfere with the CFE negotiations.[461] Although Baker, too, was skeptical of the CSCE, calling it an "extreme unwieldy and frustrating organization," he understood its importance for Europe. So Baker and other US officials participated in CSCE meetings in Copenhagen (June 1990), Moscow (October 1991), and Helsinki (July 1992), among others. As Scowcroft wrote Bush in July 1992 in advance of the Helsinki summit, the administration had three main objectives: "not want CSCE to turn into a pan-European security system that would reduce NATO's role or effectiveness"; "not want CSCE to become a rigid, legalistic structure" that would be "too fragile" to deal with the "messy realities of political conflict"; and "wanted to reform the way CSCE works" so it could effectively avert conflicts and settle disputes."[462]

Scowcroft also opposed the idea of a separate conference among the Four Powers that had occupied Germany after the Second World War, an idea proposed by Gorbachev and supported by Britain and France. The Four Powers actually did convene on December 11, 1989—the Bush administration making a concession to the Soviet Union as well as France and Britain—but the administration restricted its agenda so as to *exclude* the German question and refused to agree to a follow-up Four Powers meeting.[463]

NATO was the cornerstone of German reunification for Bush and Scowcroft. Among other advantages, keeping Germany in NATO would ensure the United States' continuing military presence in Europe "despite the absence of an enemy," as the French historian Frédéric Bozo points—an important bulwark against the cost-cutting and "very strong isolationist pressure" in Congress. So the best way to manage reunification, Scowcroft later told Jacques Attali, one of Mitterrand's top advisers, was to use NATO.[464]

Some on the NSC staff wanted to slow reunification, which would presumably allow the United States to better control the process and make the situation more predictable, but Scowcroft disagreed: the best possible route for reunification would be the fastest and most direct, minimizing the chance that external factors or questions of process or procedure could interfere.[465] It was a logical conclusion, but it meant that the administration's step-by-step, controlled process for the liberalization of Eastern Europe and German reunification was now obsolete, along with Kohl's measured ten-point program.

Scowcroft wanted East and West Germany to come up with their own plan for reunification and then let them proceed—a process that presumably would give the Bush administration inside influence and squeeze out the Soviet Union, France, and the United Kingdom. The State Department, sensitive to US diplomatic relations with those three powers, recommended a different route: to have the two Germanys themselves control the internal aspects of reunification, while the postwar occupying powers would decide the external aspects (such as borders, military alliances, and foreign troop levels).[466] This was the "Two-Plus-Four" approach. Bush accepted it, after first making sure that Kohl was supportive.

Scowcroft opposed the Two-Plus-Four plan. "I'm not sure this is a good idea," he told Baker when he first learned of it. He thought the administration was ceding too much control over the process and believed Baker had presented the president with Two-Plus-Four as a fait accompli. Baker and his top staff, for their part, believed that Scowcroft was the one slowing down reunification. Fortunately, none of this hostility and mutual suspicion between members of the NSC and the State Department—what Philip Zelikow described as "real acrimony"—made it into the press.[467]

In fact, the supposed antagonism between the State Department and the NSC was overblown: Scowcroft and Baker both wanted to accelerate German reunification, and both thought their counterparts and their staffs were being unduly cautious. Baker didn't want the six powers to make decisions; he and his top aides wanted to limit discussion of external security issues, while leaving decisions to Germany (and, if relevant, the sixteen members of NATO). The real purpose of Two-Plus-Four was to bring the Soviets along while preventing separate German-Soviet deals. Most important, as Zelikow and Rice point out, Baker had not committed the administration to formalizing the Two-Plus-Four plan, or even to making it an unofficial decision-making process.[468]

Indeed, only two days after Genscher announced his plan, Baker got him to agree to the Two-Plus-Four concept.

Scowcroft had some of his concerns over Two-Plus-Four allayed by virtue of the strong relationship he was able to establish with Horst Teltschik, Kohl's national security advisor. Teltschik agreed that the CSCE was no place for negotiations on the future of Germany and that neutrality was not an option for a united Germany. He reassured Scowcroft that the United States and Germany would be working toward the same outcome and that Kohl would communicate this position to Gorbachev. Interestingly, Scowcroft had a direct telephone line to Teltschik, as well as lines to Charles Powell and Adm. Jacques Lanxade, his British and French counterparts, respectively—secure lines originally established by Henry Kissinger.[469]

Meanwhile, East Germany was becoming, in Kohl's description in late February, "a basket case." East German troops were showing up at West German barracks and asking for jobs with the Bundeswehr (the West German army), while Soviet soldiers in East Germany "were demoralized, hungry, and selling weaponry for cash." Even Gorbachev realized the East German government under Hans Modrow was doomed. Scowcroft, who had considered East Germany "the powerhouse of the Warsaw Pact," "at the forefront of espionage, training terrorists, pouring arms into the hands of left-wing and anti-US regimes," and crucial in its financial support of other communist states, now realized that the United States intelligence about East Germany had been "far off the mark."[470]

West European, East European, and Soviet leaders formally approved the Two-Plus-Four framework on February 13, in Ottawa, on the occasion of the Open Skies ministerial conference. Nonetheless, there was little unanimity among the national leaders. The NATO ministers other than those from France and Britain reacted with understandable anger and resentment at being excluded from the plan, and John Major (who had replaced Thatcher as British prime minister on November 28, 1990), François Mitterrand, and Mikhail Gorbachev each disliked the prospect of a unified Germany within NATO. These tensions worried Scowcroft, as did his belief that the Social Democratic Party seemed likely to win the upcoming March election in East Germany.[471]

Yet Scowcroft guessed wrong on the East German election outcomes. The Christian Democratic Party and its coalition partners won a surprising 48 percent of the East German vote, and the two main left-of-center parties, the Social Democratic Party and the Party of Democratic Socialism, receiving only 22 and 16 percent, respectively. These results greatly increased the momentum toward reunification. Thatcher and Mitterrand, seeing where things were heading, agreed to limit the scope of the Two-Plus-Four negotiations so as to constrain the ability of the Soviet Union—now the odd man out—to expand the agenda.[472]

But the Soviet Union still wielded veto power among the Four Powers over Germany's external relations, and the issue of German membership in NATO remained to be settled. As Scowcroft wrote the president in mid-February, if Moscow was to be credible and allow Germany reunify in a manner consistent with perestroika, "Moscow must find some way to prevent the unification of Germany on wholly Western terms. This places us on a probable collision course with the Soviets on the question of the continued full membership of a united Germany in NATO."[473] Furthermore, a resolution of the NATO issue depended on the quantity and types of conventional and nuclear forces in the European theater and how NATO was to be defined in the transformed Europe.

But the membership of reunited Germany in NATO was non-negotiable for Bush and Scowcroft. As Bush had told the *New York Times*' R. W. Apple on October 24, 1989, "German unification has been a goal of the NATO alliance for forty years, and if Germany unifies within NATO, the United States is 100 percent in support."[474]

There were good reasons for this insistence. West Germany had been a reliable NATO partner throughout the Cold War, providing the alliance's single largest manpower contribution and the second-highest financial contribution, and it was centrally located on the European continent. Even more important, membership in NATO would "keep Germany in check," thereby reassuring its neighbors in both Western and Eastern Europe, especially the Soviet Union.

Furthermore, fully 80 percent of American troops in Europe were based in Germany. Their continued presence depended on Germany's fate. "If Germany is out of the integrated NATO structure," NATO secretary general Manfred Woerner cautioned, "the United States will be out of Europe. This will lead to great destabilization in Europe." For this reason, every European head of state wanted the United States to stay in Europe.[475] "Having troops on the ground in Europe was the best kind of security for preserving the Atlantic alliance," Scowcroft said. Or as Bush put it, continued German membership in NATO would allow the United States to remain "a European power."[476] And with the United States and Germany insistent on this point, they ensured that neither Thatcher nor Mitterrand felt they had any room to maneuver.[477]

Still, it was clear that NATO had to change, since its traditional focus on the Soviet threat made no sense with the end of the Cold War. In late April, Bush called for a NATO conference to determine the Atlantic alliance's new role. Specifically, Bush, Baker, and Scowcroft wanted to settle (1) what the West needed in conventional forces and its goals for negotiations on Soviet forces in Europe, (2) NATO's objectives in nuclear arms talks with the Soviets, (3) the role of the CSCE in relation to that of NATO, and (4) the timetable for a treaty on conventional forces and on modernizing short-range nuclear forces. The NATO summit was scheduled for early July 1990.

That meeting, however, would be preceded by a critical US-Soviet summit scheduled for May 31 to June 2 in Washington. The Soviets were pushing hard against the idea of a reunited Germany joining NATO. So Kohl told Bush, "Irrespective of developments, we will stand side by side. And one sign of this cooperation are the links between us by the future membership of a united Germany in NATO without any limitations. You should make this clear to [Gorbachev]. . . . There should be no doubt about that." But Kohl also wanted to offer the Soviet leader incentives to agree. "We can help find a sensible economic arrangement with him," he told Bush. "He needs help very much."[478]

Bush told Kohl that didn't expect any breakthroughs in Washington with respect to the "German question." But late in the afternoon of the first day of the summit, the logjam broke. Scowcroft describes what happened:

When the Summit meeting with Gorbachev started, there had been no progress on the issue of German membership in NATO. The first plenary session we had deal with this issue, with the delegations of each—it was a room full of people. The President tried different approaches and wasn't really getting anywhere. I was about to send him a note saying, "Look, it's hopeless. Let's move on to other subjects," when he happened to say to Gorbachev, "Do you agree that the Helsinki Accords give every country the right to choose its own alliances?"

He said yes, and the room suddenly got very, very still. I can't remember who it was, maybe Bob Blackwill, who passed him a little note and said, "Get him to say that again." So the President did, and he repeated it. The President pressed the point. I can't remember the exact dialogue, but Gorbachev essentially said, "Yes, if Germany wants to be in NATO, they have a right to be. If they don't want to be in NATO, they have a right to be."

At this time Gorbachev's delegation was just beside themselves, and there were visibly nasty comments being passed back and forth between them. Finally, Gorbachev, who certainly saw this, asked [Valentin] Falin to make a presentation . . . on why a Germany in NATO was not the right thing to do. He engaged in a backdoor discussion with Marshal [Sergei] Akhromeyev and a couple of his other advisors.

Well, this was an unbelievable scene. When they finished their little conversation and he came back in the discussion, he tried to backpedal.[479]

It was too late. "Gorbachev had taken a step from which there was no retreat," Scowcroft said. "Once he acknowledged that countries had the right to select their own alliances, he had cut the ground out from the Soviet position."

Bush was astonished and mystified by Gorbachev's "amazing performance." He and Scowcroft guessed that Gorbachev might have come to realize that the American and German position would prevail, especially since Baker, Mitterrand, and Canadian prime minister Brian Mulroney had each separately made the same argument to Gorbachev in meetings running up to the Washington summit. Indeed, the Soviet leader had suggested as much in a meeting with Kohl in Moscow just weeks before the summit. Gorbachev's actions may have been the best way for him to manage his own military and foreign policy advisers. But it was obvious the move hadn't been scripted.[480]

Anatoly Chernyaev identified Gorbachev's statement as the moment when the Soviet Union conceded German reunification within NATO; Teltschik called the concession a "sensation."[481]

The next day, June 1, the president, who, with Scowcroft, was aware of how important an economic deal was for Gorbachev, signed a pending agreement on grain and trade with his Russian counterpart. The Soviet

leader later wrote he regarded the economic agreement as the tangible manifestation of the United States' support for perestroika and saw it as a "turning point" in US-Soviet relations. The two then signed multiple agreements
that banned chemical weapons, limited nuclear testing, and addressed additional topics. Bush also offered the Soviet Union nine assurances with
respect to German reunification.[482]

They all then flew out to Camp David for the third day of the conference, where Bush and Gorbachev were able to relax and to get to know
each other better. (Gorbachev scored a ringer at horseshoes on his very
first throw.) Most surprising was that Gorbachev and the Soviet delegation
didn't back away from their concession over NATO. In fact, on the last day
of the summit, there was not a murmur of protest from the Soviet delegation on the United States' draft of their joint press statement, which stated
that "the matter of alliance membership—in accordance with the Helsinki
Final Act—is a matter for the Germans to decide."[483]

Gorbachev's acceptance of the Helsinki principle in regard to alliances
underscored yet again the long-term value of the much maligned and politically sensitive Helsinki Final Act. Helsinki had changed expectations and
inspired reforms. It led to the creation of "Helsinki Groups" in support of
the rights of political dissidents throughout Eastern Europe, even in the
Soviet Union. It helped turn the tide toward liberalization and reform behind the Iron Curtain, as noted by leaders from Czechoslovakia's Alexander
Dubcek to Soviet diplomat Yuri Kashlev.[484] And now the Helsinki Final
Act had paved the way for the reunification of Germany within NATO by
providing a basis for honoring the principle of self-determination.

When editing the president's speeches, Scowcroft had been routinely
crossing out references to the end of the Cold War. But after the June summit, he decided he could leave them in. "Why? Because the fundamental
building of the Cold War focused on Germany, on the division of Germany, [and] the subsequent division of Europe. And nothing could be more
symbolic of the end of that period of history than the unification of Germany inside NATO." The Washington summit marked a turning point in
world history, Scowcroft thought. It demarcated the end of the Cold War,
or what some on his staff called "VE-Day 2."[485]

———

A LOT OF work remained to be done. The United States and Soviet Union
needed to finalize the details of the accelerated conventional arms talks, set

the specific levels of Bundeswehr forces in a united Germany, and define the exact terms of German reunification. Soviet foreign minister Shevard-nadze indicated that the negotiations over these details would be tough and contentious.

In order to handle the multifaceted negotiations with the Soviets, the Germans, the British, and the French, Scowcroft set up the European Strategy Steering Group, also known as the Gates Group. It included four deputies from the State Department, two from the NSC, and a handful from the other departments and agencies represented in the Deputies Committee, and was chaired by Gates. But Robert Zoellick, Bob Blackwill, Philip Zelikow, Dennis Ross, and Condoleezza Rice did the heavy lifting, Gates reported. This small and collegial group met regularly in the situation room from June 4 through early July, allowing Scowcroft and Baker "to bypass the US bureaucracy."[486]

Some of the most difficult issues were addressed at a series of mid-July meetings between West German and Soviet officials. In their discussions, Gorbachev agreed with Kohl that the US military would remain in Germany, given that a reunified Germany could choose the security alliance that it wanted, which was NATO. He further agreed to terminate the rights of the Soviet Union as one of the Four Powers. Kohl, in turn, agreed to provide $3 billion in credit to Moscow, to assume all of East Germany's foreign obligations, to pay the costs of Soviet troops in East Germany during the three-to-four-year transition period, and to keep only German NATO troops in East Germany once the Soviets left. "Never in my life have I had to work so hard," Kohl later said, and "never in my life have I also been so happy."[487]

For Scowcroft, the "gut issue" remained the long-term mission of NATO, he told the president and other senior advisers at a pre-NATO summit briefing in Kennebunkport.[488] As Scowcroft wrote Horst Teltschik in a letter of June 30, "Above all, we are pleased that you agree that we need a strong political document with new ideas for the transformation of the alliance. Our most difficult task in London will be to convince our colleagues that this will not be just another NATO communiqué that is watered down like all the rest." In order to control the content of the communiqué, Scowcroft and Bush expressed "a strong preference" for having "the NATO and the Warsaw Pact countries reciprocally give declarations of non-violence, instead of trying to negotiate a joint document."[489]

Bypassing the normal NATO bureaucracy, Scowcroft, Horst Teltschik, and their staffs—with the support of NATO secretary general Woerner—drafted a communiqué on NATO's new role. It made twenty-three points, four of which Bush considered essential. First, it reaffirmed that NATO was a defensive alliance and would not be the first to use force. Second, it proposed a new military doctrine for NATO that involved cutting back conventional forces further and introducing additional measures to reduce offensive capabilities. Third, it shifted NATO's military strategy from one of "flexible response" to one in which nuclear weapons would now be "truly weapons of last resort." NATO would therefore eliminate its short-range nuclear forces, meaning that the United States would not only forgo modernizing the Lance but also remove all of its eighty-eight short-range missiles from Europe. Fourth, it stated NATO's commitment to strengthen the CSCE process so as to bring all of Europe together for the purpose of promoting political development through elections, the rule of law, economic liberty, and environmental cooperation.

Bush emphasized that the communiqué would show Gorbachev that NATO was a purely defensive alliance. He recognized that the Soviets viewed NATO through the lens "of the fact that they lost 20 to 27 million lives" during World War II, but they should see NATO "not as a threat to their borders or to their people." Moreover, the changes would make German reunification within NATO more acceptable to Gorbachev as well as his domestic political opponents. Indeed, this was how Gorbachev saw the NATO declaration (which also invited the Soviet Union to participate, although not as a full member): he called it "very important" and said that the London conference brought about "very positive steps" that made further talks with Kohl possible.[490]

The key was getting Thatcher and Mitterrand to sign off. Thatcher passionately opposed the idea of nuclear weapons being used only as a "last resort" and wondered why the Warsaw Pact countries, dire enemies until very recently, should be invited "so close to the innermost councils of our defense and preparedness." So when Bush and Kohl unveiled their bold proposals at the NATO meeting in Paris, Thatcher got Bush to tone down the language, although the NATO communiqué essentially survived intact.

Mitterrand, for his part, thought the United States would be leaving Europe one day (as Scowcroft later told the Norwegian Prime Minister), yet the "the biggest problem" of the French, according to NATO Secretary-General Manfred Woerner, was "that they themselves do not know what they want." They feared a too-strong America in Europe, and they feared the United States would leave Europe.[491] Indicatively, the French minister, Roland Dumas, "objected to almost everything," consistent with Mitterrand's position against the reorientation of NATO. But in the end, Mitterrand agreed to the communiqué. Even though the French president was more positive than Thatcher was toward the NATO proposal, he, too, was opposed to the idea of NATO having liaisons to the Warsaw Pact countries. He preferred that NATO keep to security issues and let the CSCE take over political relations between NATO members and those of the Warsaw Pact.[492]

Conversely, Scowcroft, Baker, and Bush sought to carefully limit the role of the CSCE. Fortunately, they had an ally in the Kohl government. "The attitudes of our two governments concerning the CSCE are very closely aligned," Scowcroft wrote Teltschik just before the July NATO summit. "We want the text of our declaration and your ideas not to be discussed at the political level until July 5 in London. Our biggest challenge," he stated, "will be to preserve the significant initiatives which are now in the declaration, and to avoid attempts to recoin the declaration in well-known rhetoric." The last thing the administration wanted was to give the Soviets an opportunity with the CSCE summit to turn it into another peace conference on Germany.[493]

The result of what Baker called "radical initiatives" was that NATO became stronger than ever. Had the administration gone along with a greatly reduced role for NATO and a greater security role for the CSCE, or another pan-European security arrangement that included the East European countries as well as the Soviet Union, the United States would have put its influence in Europe, eastern Eurasia, and the Mediterranean region at grave risk. President Bush, Scowcroft, and Baker thus worked closely with NATO Secretary-General Woerner on articulating NATO's mission and on unveiling initiatives for the upcoming NATO Summit in Rome, scheduled for November 1991. They also tried to arrange it so that Gorbachev wouldn't attend. "His attendance makes our argument that we need a strong NATO much weaker," Bush said, "He'll come to the G-7. . . . But he won't get any money from us. I don't want him to use the G-7 as a springboard to go to the NATO Summit."[494]

For Scowcroft, NATO was more than just a military alliance or a political organization; it was a cultural institution that represented a community of peoples with shared beliefs about the relationship between individuals and the state and similar values about government, individuals, and society. This is why he consistently opposed the eastward expansion of NATO. Scowcroft didn't mind if Eastern European countries were included in the EC or a new European Union. But NATO needed to be reserved for the inheritors of Western values and traditions. Because of these shared values and traditions, the NATO members were usually able to act in concert when circumstances demanded—as they did during the Persian Gulf War, passing a resolution in support of evicting Iraq from Kuwait and serving as the coordinator for aid from European allies in addition to Middle Eastern countries and a handful of others around the world.[495]

However, despite Scowcroft's doubts, subsequent history shows that NATO has continued to take strong positions even after its expansion east into Hungary, Poland, and the Czech Republic in 1999, north to the Baltics and east to Slovenia, Romania, and Bulgaria in 2004, and southeast to Croatia and Albania in 2009. NATO intervened in Bosnia and Herzegovina in 1995, Kosovo in 1999, Afghanistan in 2001, Somalia in 2009 and subsequent years, and Libya in 2010. All these actions confirm Scowcroft's vision of NATO's central role in guaranteeing stability in Europe, southwestern Asia, and northern Africa.

Having agreed on the evolving status of NATO, the foreign ministers of the six powers met on September 12 in Moscow to sign the treaty on German reunification. The Germans renounced aggression, agreed to ban nuclear, biological, and chemical weapons, and ceded German claims to prewar territory east of the Oder-Neisse line (which had remained a sticking point on account of domestic German politics).[496] They also limited the Bundeswehr to 370,000 troops, a number Genscher and Kohl had agreed upon en route to their meeting with Gorbachev in Moscow. To make the transformation more palatable, the changes were to take place gradually, with the Soviets withdrawing their forces from the former East Germany by the end of 1994, for instance. Finally, the four powers relinquished any further responsibilities and rights over Germany.[497]

German reunification officially took place on October 3, 1990, with West Germany simply absorbing East Germany's five *Länder* under Article 23 of the German constitution. It was a takeover, not a merger. East Germany would adopt West German institutions and Western values—open government, market economics, and personal freedoms. As in many corporate takeovers, there was a financial inducement (if one downplayed by German and Soviet leaders alike); Kohl ended up granting the Soviet Union a total of 100 billion Deutschemarks by 1994 (about $62 billion) including grants, loans, credits, and DM15 billion more in funds for the housing and then relocation of the Soviet Western Group of Forces—a sum that could be considered either a purchase of or a compensation for the loss of the German Democratic Republic.[498]

THE UNITED STATES had prevailed in what John J. McCloy had called "The Big Game": the determination of the postwar political geography of Europe.[499] Even so, the peaceful end of the Cold War and the reunification of Germany were far from preordained. Some have suggested that Bush and his advisers misjudged the Soviet Union and mishandled US-Soviet relations over this critical period. But until the actual breach of the Wall, Bush and his top advisers couldn't be wholly sure *what* would happen in Eastern Europe and East Germany. For all of Gorbachev's reassurances, Bush, Scowcroft, and others in the administration couldn't know how the Soviet Union would respond to the popular uprisings throughout the region. It was entirely possible that Soviet and Eastern European military forces, with the support of party rulers, could have taken matters into their own hands and reined in reform, believing that the Soviet cession of East Germany would mean that the millions who had died in the Second World War had died in vain.[500]

Fortunately, in the immediate aftermath of the fall of the Berlin wall, on November 11, East German spokesman Günter Schabowski stated, "There will be no Tiananmen Square solution here." And the next day, the Soviet ambassador spoke with Baker and didn't disagree with him when the secretary of state said there would be "no turning" back, that the process had to be "peaceful," and that "free elections" were essential.[501]

As President Bush conceded, events could have broken in many other ways.[502] Authorities in East Germany and Czechoslovakia came very close to initiating massive military crackdowns in Leipzig on October 9, 1989, and in Prague between November 17 and 28. And in late December 1989, the Ceausescu regime did massacre demonstrators in Timisoara.[503]

What's more, Gorbachev could have almost certainly driven a harder bargain on German reunification by enlisting other European leaders in a plan for a "common European home," by insisting on Soviet inclusion in pan-European political and economic structures, or by putting a firm limit on NATO's expansion eastward as the price of Soviet approval of German reunification within the Atlantic alliance.[504]

Philip Zelikow and Condoleezza Rice, for their part, point out the importance of timing in their comprehensive account of German reunification. What if the administration had stalled for another year before meeting Gorbachev and the Soviet leaders? On December 20, 1990, Eduard Shevardnadze resigned as foreign minister; without his desire for reform and his good rapport with James Baker, the resulting talks might have gone far worse. What if Chancellor Kohl had been less motivated, less committed to

NATO, less media-savvy, and less responsive to the historic opening that had suddenly appeared thanks to the revolutions in Poland and other parts of Eastern Europe?[505] What if President Bush had decided to claim victory by "dancing on the Wall" and attempting to solidify the United States' advantage vis-à-vis the Soviets as definitively and rapidly as possible, rather than gradually and gently coaxing Gorbachev to allow the Soviet empire to dissolve?

President Bush deserves credit for his hands-on foreign policy and his interpersonal diplomacy. Reflecting on the administration's success, White House chief of staff John Sununu used a fishing metaphor. "George Bush's handling put just enough tension on the line. You know, it's like catching a 10-pound bass on a 3-lb line. You've got to keep the tension so if there's a pull the line doesn't snap—as it will if it's slack. Bush handled it exactly right," he said. "That was the art at the time: to give them encouragement, to drag them along slowly, but not to pull too hard because you can break the line. It was really an artful, artful dance. And everybody's convinced it would have happened anyway." Sununu didn't "believe it" for a second, not "at all" that the end of the Cold War was foreordained. As German Foreign Minister Hans-Dietrich Genscher later said, "If America had so much as hesitated . . . we could have stood on our heads" and gotten nowhere.[506]

Even the administration's critics agree that George Bush, James Baker, and Brent Scowcroft conducted their foreign policy masterfully and that the administration achieved almost all of its foreign policy objectives.[507] The fact that so much of their policy making was done by the seat of their pants, by virtue of the incredible pace at which events in Europe were unfolding, makes their accomplishments that much more impressive.[508] And it puts the effectiveness of the NSC process managed by Brent Scowcroft front and center.

Scowcroft himself acknowledged that the policies of the Reagan administration had helped. "In the latter half of the 1970s," he told the German weekly *Der Spiegel*, "the Soviets had come to believe that the United States was a world power in decline. That calculus proved wrong, and the reversal of American policy in the eighties led to these new Soviet considerations."[509] Of course, he had done much to shape the United States policies on strategic forces in the 1980s, during the Reagan era.

To paraphrase the Roman philosopher-statesman Seneca, luck is the result of preparation coupled with opportunity. Bush, Baker, and Scowcroft had prepared for the reforms in Eastern Europe and were already starting on the process they'd developed for handling the Soviet Union and the

Soviet bloc. So when confronted with an unexpectedly accelerated timetable, Bush and his advisers were to able to navigate the sudden turmoil skillfully. They convinced France, the United Kingdom, and the Soviet Union to accept the Two-Plus-Four framework in early 1990, they united Western Europe behind Germany's membership within NATO, and they used a combination of persuasion, guarantees, inducements, and negotiation to get Gorbachev to accept a reunified Germany within NATO.[510] If, as Robert Gates has said, "we shot the rapids of history, and without a life jacket," the president, the secretary of state, the national security advisor, and their staffs had the experience, insight, knowledge, and skill that allowed them to navigate the white water successfully.[511]

23

ON-RAMP

AT 8:20 P.M. on Wednesday, August 1, 1990, Brent Scowcroft informed President Bush that Iraqi troops were on the verge of invading Kuwait. He had been paged at a nearby restaurant, called the White House, and heard the news from Acting Secretary of State Kimmitt.[512] About an hour later, US intelligence sources confirmed the story. Within just six hours, the Iraqi army had seized all of Kuwait, an area slightly smaller than the state of New Jersey with a population of 1.8 million (although over 1 million subsequently fled).[513]

Scowcroft's "very instinctive" and "visceral reaction," he told one of his NSC staff members late that night, was that Saddam Hussein would get away with it.[514]

He wouldn't, of course. And it was Scowcroft who was largely responsible.[515] Almost single-handedly, he determined what the United States' response to the Iraqi invasion of Kuwait was going to be. But there were many steps along the way, none of them preordained.

In times of crisis, power flows to the national security advisor and the NSC, a fact that was particularly evident in the first few days after the invasion. Scowcroft was involved with "setting up the president's schedules, staying at Mr. Bush's side as he met with allies, receiving foreign officials himself, writing inserts on the Middle East crisis for the president's speeches, [and] helping set up talking points for phone calls to world leaders," as Maureen Dowd, then the *New York Times*' White House correspondent, reported. He had "an uncommonly high profile role" during the crisis, Dowd noted, especially since none of the president's other foreign policy advisers took the invasion as seriously as he did. "If I'm not here, talk to Brent Scowcroft," as Bush himself told King Hussein of Jordan shortly after the invasion.[516]

The night of the invasion, Scowcroft scheduled an NSC meeting for early the next day. Bush declined to take Dan Quayle's advice to call an emergency NSC meeting that same evening, a decision the vice president attributed to

Scowcroft.[517] Instead, Scowcroft first wanted to convene a Deputies Committee meeting. After Scowcroft made a quick trip home to check in on Jackie,
he, Kimmitt, Wolfowitz, Kerr, and Jeremiah met over secure video (with
Scowcroft acting as chair, since Robert Gates was on vacation). Over the next
three hours, until "well after two" in the morning, by Scowcroft's account,
the deputies reviewed the situation and Iraq's behavior. They decided that
the United States should freeze Iraqi and Kuwaiti assets and that the administration should ask the UN Security Council to demand Iraq's immediate and
unconditional withdrawal from Kuwait. (Later that day, the UN Security
Council unanimously approved Resolution 660, which unequivocally condemned the invasion, directed Iraq to remove its armed forces from Kuwait,
and called for the two countries to hold negotiations over the issues dividing
them.) The deputies also agreed to move a squadron of F-15s into forward
positions, pending Saudi approval.[518]

Afterward, Scowcroft and White House counsel Boyden Gray worked
together on editing the executive orders that had been drafted by Treasury
officials to impose economic sanctions on Iraq and freeze Iraqi and Kuwaiti
assets in the United States. At 4:30 A.M., the national security advisor went
over to the presidential residence, briefed the president on the overnight developments, and had him sign the two executive orders. (The two men were
relieved to find that Iraq hadn't withdrawn its financial assets from Western
banks overnight.) At 6:00 A.M., Scowcroft called UN ambassador Thomas
Pickering about the NSC meeting, and shortly after 8:00 A.M. the full National Security Council—the foreign policy principals, their deputies, and a
handful of others—convened in the cabinet room.[519]

After DCI William Webster reported that Iraq's army of a hundred
thousand was now in control of Kuwait and outmanned Saudi Arabia's
seventy-thousand-person army, the conversation turned toward international diplomacy and the steps that the United States and other states had
taken. The attendees then held a lengthy discussion of the world's oil reserves. Scowcroft said little at the meeting, making only one comment on
the possibility of shutting off Iraqi oil exports.

Bush himself seemed uncertain as to whether the United States should
try to force Iraq from Kuwait. Just before the meeting, he told the senior
UPI correspondent, Helen Thomas, "We're not discussing intervention,"
adding, "Even if we'd agreed upon [the use of force], I would not discuss
any military options." (Scowcroft said that Bush's words, if "not felicitous,"
only meant that the NSC was meeting simply to discuss the situation and
review the United States' options, not to make any final decisions.)[520]

Privately, however, Scowcroft was appalled by how mildly his colleagues were reacting to the invasion. He agreed with Richard Haass that the meeting was "unfocused and a sharp disappointment," and described it (with his typical understatement) as being "a bit chaotic." He sensed that the other members of Bush's foreign policy team had already accepted the invasion of Kuwait as a fait accompli and were conceding Iraq's conquest of the country—just so long as the Iraqi military didn't cross over into Saudi Arabia. Gates had the same impression.[521]

Scowcroft considered this unacceptable. After the meeting, he took the president aside and argued forcefully that the Iraqi invasion shouldn't be tolerated. "This was a case of naked aggression," as Scowcroft later said, "as clear as you could find."[522] There was too much at stake in the Middle East, especially with the Saudi oilfields lying just to the south. Iraq already possessed 20 percent of the world's oil, and if it took Saudi Arabia it would control fully half the world's oil supply.[523] Furthermore, for the United States to leave the invasion unchallenged would set exactly the wrong kind of precedent in the new post–Cold War era. The United States should accept nothing less than the complete withdrawal of Iraqi forces, he argued.

Scowcroft wanted to convene another NSC meeting as soon as possible once the president returned from a planned trip to Colorado, where, ironically, Bush was scheduled to talk about plans Scowcroft had drawn up for restructuring the military—and cutting it by 25 percent.[524] "I would like to start out the meeting and lay out why Kuwait is important," he said. That was "something that I usually didn't do," he admitted later. Bush volunteered to make the case for intervention himself: "Why don't I do it?" But Scowcroft demurred, saying that if the president led things off, "the discussion would quickly be over. . . . If I run the meeting, then we will see how others think." Before leaving for Aspen with the president, he asked Haass to draft a memorandum making the case.[525]

The next day, Bush, Scowcroft, and John Sununu were the only passengers aboard the eight-passenger G-20 Gulfstream (also known by the air traffic control call sign Air Force One, which applies to any Air Force aircraft the president is traveling on). The president telephoned King Hussein of Jordan, President Hosni Mubarak of Egypt, and President Ali Abdullah Saleh of Yemen to solicit their views and to inform them that the new status quo "was unacceptable to the United States." King Hussein and Mubarak each promised to talk to Saddam Hussein. Scowcroft, meanwhile, worked feverishly to modify the president's Aspen speech in light of the Iraqi invasion of Kuwait.[526]

In Aspen, Bush met with Margaret Thatcher at the home of the US ambassador to Britain, Henry E. Catto Jr. He discovered that he and Thatcher "saw the situation in remarkably similar ways." Neither of them was willing to accept the Iraqi takeover of Kuwait, and both recognized that the cooperation of Saudi Arabia was absolutely critical.[527] It was during the discussion with Thatcher, Scowcroft later told the BBC, that the full significance of Iraq's actions hit them. If Iraq continued to grow in power, it could easily become a serious threat over the next ten to twenty years, with the potential to dominate the Middle East and OPEC oil supplies and to threaten Israel and Saudi Arabia.[528]

President Bush and Scowcroft arrived back in Washington late that evening, and the NSC met at 9:10 Friday morning. In the meantime, Scowcroft gave the president the memo he'd had Richard Haass draft. "I am aware as you are of just how costly and risky such a conflict would prove to be," it read. "But so too would be accepting this new status quo. We would be setting a terrible precedent—one that would only accelerate violent centrifugal tendencies—in this emerging 'post Cold War' era. We could be encouraging a dangerous adversary in the Gulf at a time when the United States has provided a de facto commitment to Gulf stability—a commitment reinforced by our statements and military movements—that also raises the issue of US reliability in a most serious way."[529]

Bush was on board.

The president began the meeting by reporting that he and Thatcher were "seeing eye to eye." Scowcroft chaired the remainder of the sixty-five-minute meeting. He began by making the argument that the Iraqi invasion of Kuwait could not be accepted. Unless the United States opposed the Iraqi invasion, Iraq "would dominate OPEC policies, Palestinian politics and the PLO, and lead the Arab world to the detriment of the United States, and the great stakes we have in the Middle East and Israel."[530]

Deputy Secretary of State Lawrence Eagleburger spoke next, carefully distinguishing his views from those of Secretary of State Baker (who was in Moscow meeting with Shevardnadze and Gorbachev). "I couldn't agree more," Eagleburger said, pounding the table. "This is the first test of the postwar system," one in which "Saddam Hussein has great flexibility. . . . If he succeeds, others may try the same thing." Cheney remarked that Saddam's forces were only "40 kilometers from Saudi Arabia." Even if Iraq didn't take the Saudi oilfields, it was now in a position "to dominate OPEC, the Gulf and the Arab world." They "should not underestimate the U.S. military forces we would need to be prepared for a major conflict," he warned.

Scowcroft then interjected, saying, "This should be kept in this room. The press has already indicated interest in this."[531]

The conversation turned to the impact of Iraq's action on oil supplies, to the United Nations and US diplomacy more generally, and to what might happen afterward. What caused those at the NSC meeting special concern was the fact that "in 72 hours," Cheney pointed out, Iraqi troops "could take the eastern province" of Saudi Arabia. Saudi Arabia was highly vulnerable, and if Iraq chose to invade, there wouldn't be much the United States would be able to do.[532]

Colin Powell, however, was concerned and a bit incredulous. Even before Thursday's NSC meeting, Powell had told CENTCOM commander Gen. Norman Schwarzkopf he thought the administration would go to war over Saudi Arabia, but said he doubted it would "go to war over Kuwait." As he told Cheney, Wolfowitz, and others in the secretary of defense's office, "Wait a minute, it's Kuwait. Does anybody really care about Kuwait?"[533] (Robert Gates, too, noted that "the honest analysis is that there was not a lot of sympathy for the Kuwaitis, either in Washington or the Arab world.")[534] Powell had lived through Vietnam and the Lebanon disaster of 1983, and at the NSC meeting he sought to be sure that the president and the others were clear on their ultimate objectives—especially when the opponent would be a battle-hardened Iraqi military.

Yet Powell's cautionary remarks came across as though he were lecturing the president and his top aides. A chill came over the room, Powell himself reports. Although they were all too polite to say anything at the time, Cheney thought it was out of place for Powell to be telling his civilian superiors how to conduct US national security policy—and later that day, at the Pentagon, he told Powell precisely that.[535]

The consensus was that Iraq's international aggression couldn't go unchallenged. "Naked aggression against an unoffending country" was bad enough and sufficient justification for a response, Scowcroft said on the PBS show *Frontline*. "But what gave enormous urgency to it was the issue of oil."[536]

The administration's views became unmistakably public two days later. As the president was making his way across the lawn from the Marine Corps One helicopter to the White House that Sunday, returning from Camp David, reporters repeatedly asked whether he was going to take military action. Finally Bush's "face hardened." Visibly upset, he "began stabbing the air with his finger. '*This will not stand*, this will not stand,' he said, 'this aggression against Kuwait.'"[537]

When Powell heard the news, he was stunned. It was "as if the president had six-shooters in both hand and was blazing away," he said, according to Bob Woodward in *The Commanders*.[538] Yet Powell either had not been paying attention or was being disingenuous. He surely was smart enough to realize that Scowcroft, Eagleburger, and Cheney would not have spoken in favor of intervention at the August 3 NSC meeting if they didn't know the president's mind. He surely must have seen reports of Bush and Thatcher's joint news conference in Aspen, where both called for Iraq's withdrawal from Kuwait. And he surely must have realized, just as Haass and others at the Friday meeting did, that "the future direction of US policy"—of not "allowing Saddam to keep Kuwait"—"was there for all to see."[539]

President Bush said that Powell "may have known beforehand," but he conceded that his declaration on the White House lawn "was an unscripted moment" and that "some were surprised, including Colin Powell."[540] Powell, for his part, described important meetings with the president as being too jovial and too informal. He blamed Scowcroft for the inappropriate atmosphere, telling Woodward that while the national security advisor "had become the First Companion and all-purpose playmate to the president on golf, fishing and weekend outings," he "was regularly failing in his larger duty to ensure that policy was carefully debated and formulated," Powell later told Woodward, and he "seemed unable, or unwilling, to coordinate and make sense of all the components of Gulf policy, military, diplomatic, public affairs, economic, [and] the United Nations."[541]

Despite Powell's misgivings, ousting Saddam from Kuwait was now the administration's official policy. Brent Scowcroft set about implementing it.

The first thing the Bush administration had to do was to convince Saudi Arabia to allow foreign military forces on its soil—no small feat, given Muslim customs, American culture, and the reluctance of the Saudi ruling family to alienate Saddam Hussein, a fellow Arab head of state and Sunni Muslim. Neither did King Fahd and others in the Saudi ruling family trust the United States fully after an emergency shipment of jet fighters in 1979 (following the fall of the shah of Iran) had been delivered by the Carter administration unarmed and after the sudden withdrawal of US military forces from Lebanon following the 1983 bombing of the Marine barracks.

Later that day, Scowcroft met with Prince Bandar, Saudi Arabia's ambassador in Washington, to ask for his country's cooperation. The president wanted to send a small US delegation to talk to King Fahd, and Bandar asked Scowcroft if he would go. But when Scowcroft contacted Cheney, the secretary of defense said he himself should go. Scowcroft agreed, but only if

Saudi Arabia agreed to be defended by the United States. Bandar thereupon called King Fahd, who gave his approval. Helping to persuade Fahd was an arms package for the kingdom, consisting of F-15s and other equipment able to address Saudi Arabia's "immediate and short term crisis related needs."[542]

On Sunday, August 5, Cheney, General Schwarzkopf, Gates, and Wolfowitz flew to Saudi Arabia. The US delegation met with King Fahd on Monday evening and, after a two-hour presentation, Fahd agreed to the United States' intervention plans. The delegation then visited Egypt and Morocco, to get permission for the aircraft carrier USS *Eisenhower* to pass through the Suez Canal, and to enlist the support of Morocco's King Hassan for the United States' intervention.[543]

That same day, Bush signed National Security Directive 45, drafted by Scowcroft and his NSC staff. NSD 45 stated that the United States had "vital" interests in the Persian Gulf, including "access to oil and the security and stability of key friendly states in the region"—reiterating Jimmy Carter's Presidential Directive 68 of 1979, which established the Persian Gulf as a vital national security interest—and that the United States would defend its national security interests "through the use of U.S. military force if necessary and appropriate" against any hostile power. NSD 45 also declared that the administration wanted "the immediate, complete, and unconditional withdrawal of all Iraqi forces from Kuwait," and "the restoration of Kuwait's legitimate government." NSD 45 further directed the United States to work with other countries, the UN Security Council, and other international organizations in pursuit of its diplomatic, economic, and military objectives—among them the formation of a multinational military force and adjustments in the global supply and demand of oil so as to compensate for the loss of 4.3 million barrels a day from Kuwait and Iraq.[544]

Scowcroft and Haass stayed up until 3:00 A.M. Monday drafting a speech for the president to deliver to the American public and a global audience, explaining why the invasion wouldn't be tolerated. Bush spoke of the threat posed by Iraq, given the United States' dependence on Middle East oil, and compared Saddam Hussein's invasion of Kuwait to Hitler's conquests of Poland and the Rhineland. The Iraqi invasion of Kuwait was more than a Saudi, American, European, or Middle Eastern problem, the president stated. It was a world problem.[545]

The president's resolve was clear, but the precise nature of the United States' commitment was not. Scowcroft began working on a series of tasks dedicated to assembling the resources needed to reverse the invasion of Kuwait.[546]

One was improving the functioning of the NSC process. Scowcroft created a small decision-making group that became known as the "Gang of Eight." Essentially an expanded Principals Committee, it consisted of the president, Quayle, Baker, Cheney, Powell, Gates, Sununu, and Scowcroft. (Press secretary Marlin Fitzwater also attended regularly, although he rarely spoke.) Scowcroft was the only principal who had a deputy. Neither Quayle, Cheney, nor Sununu had a deputy present. Others, such as Nicholas Brady, Schwarzkopf, Eagleburger, Haass, Jeremiah, Webster, and USMC Gen. Paul Kelley, as well as others, would attend the meetings if need be. Baker described them as "frank, honest discussions that went on for hours," with issues debated openly and trustingly.[547]

Of further importance was the establishment of the "small group" consisting of Gates, Haass, Jeremiah, Kerr, Kimmitt, and Wolfowitz. The six men met before the Gang of Eight, and Gates would then take their recommendations to the Gang of Eight. The small group would convene after the Gang of Eight meetings to see to the implementation of the policies that were agreed upon. It met several times a week and "at the peak of the crisis, several times a day," with the result that they often worked late into the night and missed weekends. After the war, Bush said, "the contribution made by the 'small group' to our success in the Gulf was really nothing short of monumental," and awarded each of the six, along with Eagleburger and Deputy Secretary of Defense Donald Atwood, a Presidential Citizen's Medal.[548]

Less formally, Scowcroft, Haass, and Gates began to gather on Saturday mornings in the national security advisor's office. "Brent would be lying down on his couch, and . . . say, Okay, what do we do now?" Haass reports. "What do we do next? What aren't we thinking about? And we just institutionalized it. Every Saturday morning, the two or three of us would spend time taking a step back, saying okay, here's my list. Here's everything we're working on. What are we comfortable with? What could happen that we're not thinking of? And we just tried to do that, to stay one step ahead of events."[549]

Scowcroft further contributed by making sure that the Pentagon's positions and plans were consistent with those of the president and the White House. So when Air Force chief Gen. Michael Dugan on Sunday, September 16, 1990, was quoted by the *Washington Post* as saying that the Joint Chiefs had concluded that airpower was the "only effective option to force Iraqi forces from Kuwait if war erupts," Scowcroft was "aghast," according to Woodward, and Powell and Cheney were furious. Cheney called Scowcroft, and on CBS's *Face the Nation* that same Sunday, Scowcroft emphasized that

General Dugan didn't speak for the Bush administration. Cheney fired Dugan the next day—contrary to Powell's advice.[550]

Three weeks later, when General Schwarzkopf's chief of staff presented Bush and his advisers with the Pentagon's combat plans on October 11, Scowcroft questioned why the US military should go "force on force" and not instead "go around and come in from the side." He also took Powell to task, snapping at him for presenting an unimaginative plan that made a direct assault on Iraqi forces—what Haass termed the "hi diddle-diddle, up the middle" football rushing scheme. Scowcroft persuaded Bush to reject the Joint Chiefs' plans. He thought the plans had been "prepared by people who didn't want to do it and it just didn't make sense, so I resisted," he said.[551]

Members of Cheney's staff came up with the scheme that was eventually adopted: a combination of the US Marines' landing on the coast of northern Kuwait, which was to serve as a feint so as to lure the attention of Iraqi forces, and the famous "left hook" plan whereby allied armored forces would sweep far to the west so as to outflank the Iraqi forces dug in north of the Saudi border.[552] Cheney's staff then handed over the plans to the Pentagon for further development.

On October 30, the Joint Chiefs met the president to present him with the revised plans. This is Gates's account:

> Briefer says, you'll need Seventh Corps out of Germany, heart of NATO's defense. Six carrier groups, a week before mid-term elections, and "Oh, and you'll have to activate both the National Guard and the Reserves." In other words, you're going to reach into every community in America and take people away from their homes and their jobs. To the day I die I'll never forget, Bush pushed his chair back, stood up, looked at Cheney and said, "You got it, let me know if you need more," and walked out of the room.
>
> Cheney's jaw dropped. Powell's jaw dropped. Cheney looked at Scowcroft and says, "Does he know what he just authorized?" And Brent smiled and he said, "He knows perfectly well what he authorized."[553]

Scowcroft wondered whether the joint chiefs had made their force requirements "so large" because "they were set forth by a command hoping their size would change [the president's] mind about pursuing a military option." Haass thought that the military was simply erring on the side of caution with its demands, and he pointed out that he'd rather have the military be reluctant to commit US forces than have it promise and commit to more than it could deliver.[554]

The administration consequently doubled the number of US troops in the Gulf. But it didn't announce the move until November 8, two days after the midterm elections. One of Baker's top aides, Janet Mullins, noted that Baker, who was out of town, was furious with Scowcroft and Haass for not informing him of the decision. Neither did they inform Congress. "Sam Nunn went bananas," Mullins reported. "Les Aspin went bananas. The leadership went bananas. Finally, they knew what it meant. Oh! This is really serious." And at a bipartisan leadership meeting at the White House once Baker returned to Washington, "[House Speaker Thomas S.] Foley and [Senate majority leader George] Mitchell and [Senator Sam] Nunn were apoplectic that [the president] had obviously made this decision and not just on his own but really [not] given them any kind of warning whatsoever. It was the closest we came to losing these guys on this issue."[555]

A less heralded but nonetheless critical contribution was Scowcroft's work with the press. He realized the administration had to make Americans *care* about Kuwait and support the legitimacy of and logic of the planned military action. The whole White House communications operation, Director of Public Affairs Dave Carney recalled, was "extremely well run," with Gates, Rice, Haass, Roman Popadiuk, and the NSC being "very engaged" in the White House public relations' efforts. "Brent was very sensitive to the process," NSC staff member Walter Kansteiner noted, "so he completely understood the role of the press and was very comfortable with it all."[556]

Scowcroft regularly met with individual journalists one-on-one, gave telephone interviews, and spoke weekly with small groups of newspaper, newsmagazine, and network television reporters so they could get color and context for the people and events featured in their news stories. Scowcroft excelled at these background briefings.[557] While he didn't take over a room through the sheer force of his personality and presence in the way that Kissinger, Powell, Bill Clinton, or, for a period, Rumsfeld could, he was nonetheless very effective because of his precise and deliberate diction, his nuanced understanding of foreign policy, his command of the facts, and his ability to contextualize events within the broader picture of national security, military affairs, international politics, and world history. Words left "his mouth slowly, with long pauses between phrases," one reporter observed, "each carefully weighed to ensure that they contain not a gram more of information than their author wishes to convey."[558] And thanks to his teaching experience at West Point and the Air Force Academy and his years of Pentagon briefings, he was well experienced at explaining complex situations in clear and accessible terms. He didn't bullshit.

Scowcroft also worked with the White House communications office and the White House press office to orchestrate the administration's public relations campaign. Scowcroft and his NSC staff helped with the president's speeches, prepared Bush's talking points for conversations with members of Congress, foreign leaders, and press conferences, and coordinated the timing and substance of what administration officials would say to the media. Ten days after the invasion of Kuwait, for example, Scowcroft went over the themes for the Sunday television talk shows and Sunday newspapers along with Baker, Cheney, and Wolfowitz. Scowcroft also appeared on television talk shows himself, from CNN's *Newsmaker Saturday* to ABC's *This Week with David Brinkley*.[559]

Shortly after the invasion, Kuwaiti leaders contacted Hill & Knowlton to form Citizens for a Free Kuwait, an organization to manage its public relations campaign—that is, to conduct focus groups, commission polls, and work with the media to promote the interests of the exiled Kuwait government. Heading Hill & Knowlton's Washington office was Craig Fuller, who had been Bush's chief of staff during his vice presidency and the director of the 1988–1989 presidential transition team.

Fuller "was in frequent contact with National Security Council members and staff, with whom he exchanged information about the situation in Kuwait," a Hill & Knowlton associate told the *Washington Post*. Fuller attended "a lot of the meetings" with White House personnel; after all, the Bush administration and Hill & Knowlton "had the exact same mission, which was to liberate Kuwait," as one official noted. Indicatively, when President Bush hosted a lunch for many of his trusted political advisers to discuss how to shore up a "'softening' of public support for military intervention in the Gulf," for instance, not only did Quayle and Sununu attend, but so did Fuller and a half dozen others, including Fred Malek (who had worked in the Nixon administration, served with the Carlyle Group, and would later serve as the president's 1992 campaign manager) and Haley Barbour (a prominent Washington lobbyist who had worked for Reagan and on Bush's 1988 presidential campaign). With "119 Hill & Knowlton executives in twelve offices around the U.S. . . . working on the Kuwait account," Fuller and his colleagues were well placed to be supportive.[560]

The plight of Kuwait in the aftermath of the invasion was one of the factors that heightened the president's eagerness to act. He had met with the Kuwait ambassador, who told Bush of billions in gold bullion that had been taken from Kuwaiti vaults and of widespread plundering, pillaging, and rape. "I thought we should try to get the word out about Iraq's brutality," Bush remarked, "but despite these reports, the world did not seem to be really aware of what was happening in Kuwait, and this deeply disturbed me."[561]

Hill & Knowlton subsequently put out more than thirty "video news releases" of atrocities and other human rights violations that were then run by CNN and other broadcasters, often without attribution. It provided photographs for use by news organizations. And it used focus groups and polling data to perfect the messages of its video news releases, calibrate the content of its communications with Congress, and select witnesses who would attract the best press coverage.[562] By law, Hill & Knowlton—as well as the Rendon Group and Neill & Co., which were also being paid by Kuwait—should have been subject to the Foreign Agents Registration Act, but the Justice Department chose not to enforce the law in this case.[563]

Fuller realized he was on treacherous moral ground, at one point asking rhetorically, "Is it right to help a foreign government build popular support for an American war effort?" The answer was "a complicated one. But it is not easy for someone raised in Kuwait City to explain his case to the national news media," he said, "and it was important that the case be accurately portrayed."[564] In the end, Fuller believed there was no contradiction between his duties as an American and his work on behalf of Kuwait. "By helping the Kuwaiti citizens," Fuller said, "it was clear we would be helping the Bush administration." And Bush, Scowcroft, and others in the White House just as clearly agreed.

Yet by late October the president realized that there was "incredible fuzziness" among Americans about "what the hell we were doing in the Gulf," despite Hill & Knowlton's efforts, and that the administration had to be sharper with its message. Bush contacted his chief of staff, and Sununu called Scowcroft, telling him there was "a big problem." Scowcroft had Gates meet with Sununu and David Demarest. In the meeting, Demarest said the administration had to have a coordinated communications strategy and that he would be happy to lead the effort. Sununu and Scowcroft agreed, and officials in the White House Office of Communications, Office of Political Affairs, and other offices began constructing a "communications plan" for "getting the message out" about Operation Desert Shield.[565]

Leading the effort was the Gulf Working Group (officially, the White House Communications Working Group on the Persian Gulf), similar to the ad hoc groups the White House had previously set up for getting China's most-favored-nation trade status approved in the Senate and for handling the supreme court nomination of David Souter.[566] With the Office of Public Liaison (which handled the interface between interest groups and the presidency) and the Legislative Affairs Office both reporting to him, and with about "four or five deputies and four or five special assistants," Demarest said, he "had more authority and clarity about my role and my mission than at any other time in the four years" at the White House.[567]

Five days later, Demarest came up with a communications plan. "Ultimately," it said, "our goal is broad, grass-roots support for the President's initiative." The plan noted that "as time passes, the President's critics will become more vocal. The message that the President has gone to historic lengths to avoid war (economic embargo and ten UN resolutions) and garnered unprecedented international support should be a fundamental component of all outreach activity." It went on to observe that the administration should immediately "offer up key administration spokesmen (Sununu, Cheney, Baker, Powell) for satellite interviews on Thursday. Radio interviews as well." Plans were crafted for op-ed articles and guest editorials to be distributed to leading newspapers.[568]

The Gulf Working Group developed and implemented these and other tactics in the period between mid-November and the end of the year. These tactics involved scheduling new activities, floating ideas for the future, and regularly updating Scowcroft and Sununu on developments. It was the job of one of the members of the Gulf Working Group, NSC executive secretary Bill Sittmann, to keep Scowcroft "completely up to speed" on their progress.[569]

On December 5, for instance, Deb Amend (now Deb Gullet), who was with the Office of Public Liaison, reported that the group had "about 45 non-cabinet level presidential surrogates on the road," most of whom had "scheduled local press interviews and editorial board meetings." Her goal was "100 for next week." She reported she now "had a three-tier surrogate program," one that "makes all kinds of sense and will help us track people and events more efficiently than [she] ever imagined." (As for finding surrogates, Demarest said that was easy: he used the president's fat Rolodex.) "In the new ideas department, [the Office of Public Liaison] has suggested we target young college age people with a 'not another Vietnam' theme. We all thought this made tremendous sense. A subgroup is developing a plan."[570]

For its planning, the Gulf Working Group relied on the NSC staff for briefing materials and other communications. The NSC had "extraordinary expertise," Amend noted. The NSC employees were "committed to advance the president's agenda" and were "good at providing background material and talking points." They were "always easy" and "unbelievably pleasant to work with" whenever the communications team needed something, too—especially since this was "in an environment with a lot of intensity."[571]

On December 11, "an inventory of ideas we've proposed and projects in the works" included:

- Former hostages welcomed home by President.
- Weekly mailing for opinion leaders—content this week?
- Presidential meeting with all the ambassadors from countries (26 militarily, 50 financially) united against Iraq.
- Status of the President visiting a large military base or hosting an event with military families at the White House during the Christmas season.
- On December 22, convene military chaplains from commands that have deployed soldiers, sailors, airmen, and marines at the US Naval Academy. President Bush and Mrs. Bush attend an ecumenical service and ask the attendees to carry the Bush's best wishes to troops, families, etc.
- Inviting all four of the living past Presidents to the WH for a briefing with the President. President Ford was briefed by DOD, Bob Gates is meeting with Presidents Reagan and Carter this week.
- Surrogates on radio interviews (All members received lists of target stations).
- NSC/State Department Statement on Christmas services in the Gulf. Pending discussions with the Saudis.
- Target potential witnesses and favorable MC's with information before Congressional committees such as House Foreign Affairs and Senate Armed Services convene. Cheney and Powell testify this week.
- Schedule both Roosevelt Room and room 450 briefings for a variety of constituent groups. Need report—these were to include:
  - Top CEOs from across the country
  - Religio[u]s Leaders/Minority Groups
  - Foreign Policy Groups/Veterans Groups
  - Business Leaders/oil executives
  - Labor leaders/Educators/Ethnic Groups[572]

Other proposed projects included a *New York Times* op-ed by Ann Lewis, the former political director of the Democratic National Committee, a *New Republic* article by Representative Stephen Solarz, an op-ed column by former UN ambassador Jeane Kirkpatrick, and an op-ed by Senator Howard Baker. At one point in *A World Transformed* Bush describes these activities, but he doesn't suggest that the cooperation of the administration's supporters was anything but voluntary and serendipitous.[573]

Scowcroft played his part in the public relations campaign. Scowcroft went on *Face the Nation* on December 2, for instance, and spoke of UN Security Council Resolution 678, which authorized the use of force, as showing "Saddam Hussein the strength of the world coalition against him, the fact that there's no temporizing, that there's no negotiating, that he has to get out." He emphasized that Iraq couldn't just hope to delay and thereby slowly cause the dismantling of the twenty-eight-nation coalition. On the contrary, Saddam Hussein had to withdraw or "face the consequences." The following weekend Scowcroft went on CNN's *Newsmaker Saturday* and NBC's *Meet the Press*, where he stated that Saddam Hussein had to realize that his "options [were] very limited" if he did not "get out," given the fact that the United States and an international coalition were "determined to enforce" the UN Resolution. Iraq had reached "the moment of truth."[574]

The White House's campaign was distinct from Hill & Knowlton's, partly because Hill & Knowlton had Democrats in prominent leadership positions—for example, the head of the Citizens for a Free Kuwait account, Lauri J. Fitz-Pegado, and the vice chairman, Frank Mankiewicz, had worked for Robert F. Kennedy and George McGovern.[575] Furthermore, for White House officials to work closely with a private public relations company would have "not only not fit the president's personality," Demarest said, but would have "start[ed] bumping up against anti-lobbying laws." He didn't want to go "to jail for anybody."[576]

But neither was this an arm's-length arrangement, precisely. While the degree to which the White House and Hill & Knowlton coordinated their efforts isn't exactly clear, a five-person subgroup of the Iraq Working Group headed by Dave Carney *did* meet "with Craig Fuller of Hill and Knowlton to discuss grassroots [communications efforts] with the Kuwaitis since they were having some difficulties in this area."[577] Too, the White House used polling data from the Wirthlin Group commissioned by Hill & Knowlton, and Fuller was himself in frequent contact with the White House. And in New York City, the Kuwaitis and Hill & Knowlton worked closely with Ambassador Pickering of the US mission to the United Nations so as to persuade the UN Security Council.[578]

Significantly, Hill & Knowlton arranged for the remarkable congressional testimony in October 1990 by a young Kuwaiti woman claiming to have "seen Iraqi soldiers killing children by unplugging and stealing incubators from a neonatal intensive care unit" in a Kuwait City hospital; she wasn't identified at the time, allegedly for her own protection. The president himself referred to incident, of fifteen babies being removed from their incubators, six times over the next four weeks, and for weeks the story dominated the news. Furthermore, seven US senators referred to the story in speeches supporting the January 12, 1991, resolution to authorize military action. But not only had Hill & Knowlton arranged for the hearings, the company's employees had coached the girl on her testimony—and she turned out to be the daughter of the Kuwaiti ambassador.[579]

Fuller defended his actions, saying that "to debate the degree of atrocity is useful, but I'm not sure how useful. It had to be a horrifying place to be, and that was the message we were trying to get out." Yet the planted baby-incubator story amounted to what *Time* would later describe as a "ruthless deception."[580] By effectively claiming that the ends justified the means, however, Fuller was conceding the incubator-baby story to be a fraud.

Interestingly, Bush and Scowcroft omit any mention of Craig Fuller, Hill & Knowlton, or the incubator-baby story in their extended account of the Persian Gulf War in *A World Transformed*. Woodward, too, neglects to bring up Fuller's connection to Hill & Knowlton in *The Commanders*.[581] Yet the members of the press, Bob Schieffer pointed out, were "always aware" of the administration's communications and outreach efforts.[582]

This outreach was particularly important during the debate in Congress over the possible war. Senator Sam Nunn opened the hearings on November 30, 1990, and invited several prominent policy makers to testify. Paul Nitze, James Schlesinger, Gen. David Jones, and Adm. William Crowe (Crowe was the former chairman of the Joint Chiefs of Staff under President Bush) all spoke out against the war; they variously questioned the readiness of the military, wanted to see stronger American popular support, criticized the White House's process and its lack of consultation with Congress on doubling US troops in the Gulf, and wanted to give sanctions more time. Henry Kissinger, in contrast, argued in favor of the war, saying that the sanctions would take too long and that the longer the situation persisted, the harder it would be to hold the coalition together. President Bush thought the Democratic-controlled Senate had stacked the witness list.[583]

At the same time, the administration was engaging in public diplomacy to build international support for intervention.[584] President Bush was an emotional man who believed in the importance of personal connections. In the first ten days of the Iraq-Kuwait crisis, for instance, Bush had thirty-four telephone conversations with foreign heads of state; he originated all but two of them.[585] This personal contact, in turn, made it easier for him to form coalitions and reconcile differences—as with German reunification—and he was often on the phone with other world leaders. This personal diplomacy was instrumental to forming the twenty-nine-member coalition against Iraq, getting the positive votes in the UN Security Council, and, with the help of Baker, Brady, and Kimmitt, in getting Germany, Japan, South Korea, Saudi Arabia, Kuwait, and the United Arab Emirates to contribute over $60 billion toward defraying the cost of the war effort (in lieu of providing troops or matériel). Separately, two dozen countries contributed over $50 billion in economic assistance to Egypt, Turkey, and Jordan—the states most economically affected by cut-off of trade to Iraq— via the Gulf Crisis Coordination Group, headed by David Mulford in the Treasury Department.[586]

Bush's personal approach to international relations also had its drawbacks. When other heads of state behaved unacceptably or acted in ways Bush viewed as immoral—which was how he saw Saddam Hussein—Bush lost his normal affability and became angry, even vengeful, and was not above humiliating or ridiculing those he considered his antagonists. By invading Kuwait, mistreating its people, and deceiving the world, Saddam had violated Bush's moral code. The president now considered him a personal enemy. So he deliberately mispronounced Saddam Hussein's first name, for instance—the emphasis should be on the second syllable—thereby not only disrespecting and insulting the Iraqi president, but also changing the meaning of his name.[587] As a result, the same genuine emotion that induced Bush's comparison of Hussein to Hitler and enabled the president to rally public opinion against Iraq also clouded his judgment and potentially interfered with a dispassionate interpretation of US interests and objective analysis of foreign policy.

Scowcroft consequently had to ask the president to tone down his rhetoric on occasion, as with the Hitler analogy—an occasion where Powell, Gates, and Haass very much agreed with the national security advisor. Conversely, Scowcroft also helped sharpen the president's speeches, as with his first address of September 9 and then the president's address to a joint session of Congress two days later.[588]

Bush and Scowcroft shared the concern that US relations with the Soviet Union on Iraq and Kuwait had to be handled carefully. Since Baker had been traveling with Soviet foreign minister Shevardnadze in Irkutsk when Iraq invaded Kuwait, the secretary of state was able to persuade Shevardnadze that the two of them should issue a joint statement condemning the action. (The fact that Saddam had lied to the Soviets and not informed them of the invasion in advance made it easier for Shevardnadze and the Soviets to break with him.) The president and his advisers wanted to maximize the size of the US-led coalition against Iraq, and having the Soviets on their side would be a tremendous coup, given that the Soviets had been patrons of Iraq for three decades and that many Soviet military officers and diplomatic officials had previously worked with and lived in Iraq. They also needed the Soviets to vote with them in the UN Security Council—or at least to refrain from vetoing any US-led action (just as the United States needed China's cooperation).[589]

So when Bush and Gorbachev met in Helsinki on September 9, Bush told him that American and Soviet cooperation in response to the Gulf crisis could lay the foundation for a new world order of collective security. The president further told the Soviet leader that he would be happy if sanctions worked, but if Saddam Hussein "does not withdraw, he must know that the status quo is unacceptable." With the two superpowers working together, Bush thought that he and Gorbachev would be able to "close the book on the Cold War and offer [the American people] the vision of this new world order in which we will cooperate." Gorbachev agreed, saying that the Soviets accepted the UN position and "condemned Iraqi aggression."[590]

Scowcroft described the meeting as a historic moment, "a new era in international affairs." For Scowcroft, the Helsinki meeting came to "nothing short of the complete acceptance, implementation of the Security Council resolutions," and if the first steps weren't sufficient, "then further steps will be considered," he said to one historian.[591]

But collaboration with the Soviets came with its own problems. Neither Bush, Scowcroft, nor any other senior adviser wanted the other members of the coalition to constrain the United States' diplomatic initiatives or military actions. And if the Soviet Union became a near-equal partner in the coalition, it would be in a prime position to do so.[592] In fact, the national security advisor thought the administration had dodged a bullet. "We had worked for decades to keep Soviet forces out of the Middle East," Scowcroft said. So when Baker's "spur of the moment" invitation on August 4 to Shevardnadze that the Soviets participate with the United States on its multinational force, Scowcroft was relieved that the Soviets declined to send troops and only later had a few of their naval vessels help monitor the blockade against Iraq.[593]

Scowcroft was also worried that Gorbachev would try "to straddle: stand strong by the United States, but work diligently behind the scenes to protect Saddam and the Soviet investment" in Iraq. He and Bush were further concerned that Gorbachev and Shevardnadze would want to link Israel's occupied territories with the occupation of Kuwait, thereby bringing Israel's Shamir government into the mix and jeopardizing the Gulf coalition.

So they were very much against the Soviet proposal to have an international peace conference on the Middle East that September.[594]

Britain, by contrast, was the United States' foremost ally. When Thatcher exhorted that Bush "not go wobbly," it was in reference to stopping an Iraqi oil tanker in the Gulf. ("The common wisdom is that she stiffened my spine" with respect to opposing the Iraqi invasion of Kuwait, Bush said, "pisses me off.")[595] Thatcher, along with Cheney, Powell, Scowcroft, and Gates, thought the United States should stop the Iraqi vessel from going any further, thereby enforcing a trade embargo in advance of the approval of a resolution that the UN Security Council sanctions would be upheld through force. However, Baker, Sununu, and Eagleburger, as well as the French, argued that the United States should wait for UN authorization instead—which also meant Soviet agreement—so that any interdiction of shipping by the United States would have sanction in international law.

The president decided to wait, and later, with Baker's assistance, he was able to get the Soviets to agree to a UN resolution giving the United States the right to enforce the trade embargo against Iraq—if necessary, by stopping and boarding cargo ships and oil tankers. Scowcroft subsequently acknowledged Bush had made the right choice.[596]

Over time, Bush, Baker, Scowcroft, and other administration officials (such as UN ambassador Pickering and Under Secretary Kimmitt) succeeded in building an extensive multinational coalition that included France, Turkey, and a total of ten Arab states as well as more likely allies such as Canada, Australia, New Zealand, Norway, and the Netherlands. Cooperating heads of state, such as Turkish president Turgut Özal, helped the administration by giving interviews on American television and in US newspapers during the full-court press to bring Congress on board.[597]

What truly infuriated Scowcroft and Bush, though, was learning from Canadian prime minister Brian Mulroney that former president Jimmy Carter had been taking diplomatic initiatives behind their backs. They found out that in mid-November Carter had written personal letters to the heads of the countries on the UN Security Council, requesting they that negotiate separately with Saddam Hussein. The former president then secretly sent a dozen additional letters out to other heads of state in the hope that these other countries would pressure the four permanent members of the UN Security Council to drop out of the US-led coalition, Nancy Gibbs and Michael Duffy report in their book *The Presidents Club*. Not only was Carter's behavior in clear violation of the Logan Act, which bars private individuals from lobbying foreign states and conducting diplomacy for objectives contrary to those of the US government, but Carter's actions could have had the effect of undermining the cohesion of the international coalition and weakening its resolve.[598]

Scowcroft, via a third party, told Carter to "cease and desist." Yet only a few days before the deadline for Iraqi to withdraw from Kuwait, Carter again sent private letters to President Mubarak, King Fahd, and Syrian president Hafez al-Assad, requesting they "call publicly for a delay in the use of force while Arab leaders seek a peaceful solution to the crisis"; he assured each that they'd find the Soviets and French receptive.[599]

Even though Bush and Scowcroft were again outraged, the president declined to publicize Carter's actions and asked Scowcroft to drop the matter. But the administration quietly began to exclude the former president from all foreign policy matters—contrary to the courtesies normally afforded ex-presidents—and withdrew any further cooperation with or assistance to Carter by the State Department or other US department or agency.[600]

While the anti-Iraq coalition was being built, efforts to negotiate a peaceful solution continued. On November 30, at an early morning meeting with Baker and Scowcroft, the president said he wanted to meet with Saddam Hussein. Baker wrote that Bush thought the meeting could well avert war, help the administration domestically, and further the unity of the allied coalition. Scowcroft, though, was nervous that the Iraqi leader would exploit the meeting and force the administration into a difficult position if he offered most of what United States wanted. Bush nevertheless offered to send Baker to Baghdad on the week of December 10.[601]

Although the visit never happened, Baker's last-minute peace attempt caused headaches. Saudi Ambassador Bandar, King Fahd, and the Kuwaiti leaders were very concerned that Iraq would pull its military out of Kuwait but leave its forces intact, poised to attack later on. And while the British were quietly informed of the proposed visit, other US allies were not at all pleased at not being consulted in advance. Scowcroft described the last-minute initiative as having "shaken the coalition to the core."[602]

But the idea—that the secretary of state should try to meet with Iraqi leaders one last time and that the United States should make every effort to avert war—persisted. On New Year's Day 1991, Bush, Gates, Cheney, and Powell met over dinner at the White House residence and agreed that Baker should try to negotiate with Iraq one last time. Over the next two days, they worked out that Baker would meet Tariq Aziz, one of Saddam's top advisers, in Geneva.[603] Scowcroft, however, worried that last-minute negotiations would send the wrong signals to the members of the Arab coalition about the president's and the United States' resolve. He suspected, too, that Baker might like nothing better than to come out with a deal—even a less-than-desirable one.[604] (Of course, practicing diplomacy was central to the job of secretary of state; as Cheney remarked, "If he's not going flat out" to make a deal, he wasn't "doing his job.") Together with other hawks in the administration and the US-led coalition, Scowcroft was "very apprehensive" some kind of a deal might be cut that would save face for Saddam Hussein and leave him with something in his pocket after the invasion. He worried that Iraq would be receiving an award, in effect, for withdrawing its forces:[605]

> I could think of any number of deceptively attractive, purposely vague proposals and ploys Saddam could put forth which could result in severe strains on the coalition and accentuate divisions within the Unites States. There was absolutely no doubt that Jim Baker was a brilliant negotiator. But I also had no doubt that he would do everything possible to attain our demands by persuasion rather than force. The unhappy reality of the situation . . . was that an Iraqi withdrawal would leave us in a most difficult position. Saddam could pull his forces back just north of the border and leave them there, poised for attack. US forces, on the other hand, could not long remain in place. The force exceeded our capacity to rotate it and, in any event, it would not be tolerable for the Saudis to have such a large foreign force indefinitely on their territory.[606]

Scowcroft therefore feared "that there would be a settlement with Tariq Aziz," he told Cheney. Instead, he "wanted [the] Iraq situation solved as decisively as possible."[607]

At the same time, Scowcroft realized "there was strong logic to the argument that the stakes were so high that a serious effort at direct discussion was important." It was Scowcroft who in a January 3 meeting with congressional leaders recommended that a vote on a joint resolution authorizing the use of force be delayed until after a final attempt at negotiations was made.[608] If Bush and Baker could in good faith say they made every effort and if the overture to Iraq gave the president peace of mind, he was happy to help. So he and Baker had Haass and Kimmitt draft a tough statement for President Bush to deliver to Saddam Hussein via Tariq Aziz.

But there was ultimately little need for Scowcroft's concern about any promised Iraqi deal; as the Baker-Aziz meeting of January 8 dragged on hour after hour, it became apparent that neither Aziz nor Saddam expected anything to come of the negotiation. Aziz claimed the letter—which had been altered slightly at Mitterrand's suggestion beforehand to make it less explicit—contained "nothing but threats" and said the Iraqis "were insulted." He refused even to deliver the letter to Saddam Hussein.[609]

Having gone the extra mile and with the international community almost unanimously in agreement—and this was one of the rare occasions where there was a palpable "international community," thanks in large part to Bush's incessant personal diplomacy—the White House began its full-court press to achieve the support for the US armed forces to engage in military operations from a majority in the House and the Senate.

Scowcroft mildly opposed having the administration seek Congress's approval for its plans. Under the terms of the UN Charter, which gives member states the right to come to the aid of other states' self-defense, and given the Carter Doctrine—Presidential Directive 63 of 1979—that established the Persian Gulf as a region of US vital interest, the United States had the authority to act under UN Security Council resolution 678 and respond to Kuwait's request for assistance, so long as it abided by the terms of the War Powers Resolution (requiring that the administration inform Congress within forty-eight hours of committing US forces to military action and disallowing actions beyond sixty days without a formal determination by Congress).

Congress had the constitutional authority to declare war, but President Bush was the commander in chief. Since the division of power between the two institutions was ambiguous and "not a black and white issue," he didn't think the administration had to ask Congress for the authority to go to war. Neither did he want to concede anything to the Democratic-controlled Congress, since it might later turn on the administration. Would the White House then have to recall the half a million troops in Saudi Arabia before they had a chance to evict Iraqi forces from Kuwait?[610]

The president nonetheless decided he wanted to secure congressional support before proceeding. Certainly, many in Congress (including Senator Bob Dole and other leading Republicans), in the press, and among the public strongly preferred that any US military engagement have the express support of Congress. Among Democrats, Senator Sam Nunn was among those upset they had never been consulted on the decision to double the number of troops in the Gulf; Nunn and other members of Congress certainly wanted to be able to have a say on a possible war. There was thus considerable risk in Bush's plan to consult with Congress. If Congress didn't grant its approval and if the military then got bogged down or faced unexpected setbacks, it might bring impeachment charges against him. Bush understood these risks and decided to go ahead anyway.[611]

Scowcroft became the administration's point man. He lobbied individual members of Congress, talked to members of the press, and otherwise assisted the administration in any way possible. He didn't engage in horse-trading: Scowcroft didn't cut deals with members on Congress on behalf of the administration, but simply argued on the merits.

In the final week, Scowcroft—who Mullins described as carrying water for the administration—"and the President were lobbying one on one themselves on the phone."[612]

Bush and Scowcroft report the debate being "passionate," although "not bitter." Senator Nunn questioned the "rush to war," as did Paul Nitze, who argued in an op-ed that sanctions coupled with air strikes might possibly be enough.[613] Many on the Hill sided with the administration. Representative Stephen Solarz emphasized that this was a bipartisan issue, and Senator Arlen Specter of Pennsylvania argued that if Congress rebuked President Bush and repudiated the UN Security Council resolution, "the credibility of the United States will be diminished . . . [and] we will be incapacitating the president as an institution in the future."[614]

Interestingly, the only member of the Senate who cast a purely political vote, according to James Baker's aide Janet Mullins and others, was Al Gore. "And he just . . . calculated it start to finish, and had some outrageous conversations with Brent in the process, and made a purely political calculation." So Gore would say he was leaning one way and then he'd lean the other way. He would tell Senator Mitchell he was "going to vote against and Brent he was going to vote for the war resolution," Mullins said.[615]

In the end, the administration was able to secure Congress's approval. The outcome in the vote in the House of Representatives, 250–183, was never seriously in question, and the White House saw to it that the House voted first so as to provide momentum for a positive vote in Senate. On January 12, the administration got ten Senate Democrats on its side, with a final Senate vote of 52–47. Senator Nunn later told Dick Cheney that voting against the Gulf War resolution was "biggest mistake he ever made."[616] The Democrats did get one symbolic victory, though: Bush asked for congressional *support* for the administration, but the joint resolution stated that Congress *authorized* the administration's use of force. Bush later admitted he would have gone ahead anyway under his authority as commander in chief, but he hoped to have Congress's approval.

Bush and Scowcroft knew they wanted to force the issue. They had become increasingly impatient with the sanctions and were more and more pessimistic that they would work. In fact, Scowcroft and Bush never held an NSC meeting to explicitly discuss whether or not to give the sanctions time to work; they knew they wanted to force the issue. As Senator Nunn observed, there was no way the administration was going to put out a force of this size, with no rotation, for a year or two. The president was committed to action unless Iraq unconditionally withdrew its forces from Kuwait. Without a complete withdrawal by Iraq, the administration's deployment decision of October 30 was tantamount to a decision to go to war.[617]

As Scowcroft explains in *A World Transformed*, he wanted "to reduce Saddam's military might so that he would no longer pose a threat to the region." He said, "Our Arab allies were convinced, and we began to assume, that dealing Saddam another battlefield defeat would shatter what support he had within the military, which probably would topple him. Hitting the Republican Guard went to the heart of the problem." In his view, "the best solution was to do as much damage as we could to his military, and wait for the Ba'ath regime to collapse."[618] He was worried, too, about any significant delay in taking action, since the large numbers of US troops couldn't be rotated out easily (thus constraining how long the American soldiers could remain in the region). Moreover, a postponement of military operations would conflict with the Muslim holy month of Ramadan, the *hajj* to Mecca, and the later onset of unbearably hot weather.

Scowcroft was also troubled by Iraq's progress on acquiring nuclear capacity (justifiably, as was later confirmed), and on November 25 he warned on national television that if the United States relied solely on an economic embargo, it risked facing a nuclear-armed Iraq, whether "in months" or "as much as ten years." (Defense secretary Dick Cheney appeared on a separate news show and issued the same warning.) And in early December, Scowcroft went on NBC News's *Meet the Press* to advocate that Iraq's weapons of mass destruction, Saddam's "nuclear, biological, and chemical programs," be placed "under strict international supervision so that he cannot develop that kind of capability."[619]

Every bit as much as Bush, and possibly more, Scowcroft wanted war. One member of the NSC staff described Scowcroft's thinking as being "we need to have this war . . . we need to do something to him. . . . We need to mess [Saddam Hussein] up."[620] Another senior member of the administration, who asked to remain anonymous, likewise reported that Scowcroft would have been disappointed by a diplomatic solution. Had Scowcroft ever actually been in combat and "had young kids die in [his] arms," this official remarked, "he would have thought differently about going to war." And an eyewitness separately reported that Cheney and Scowcroft exulted upon learning there had been no progress in Geneva. (If things hadn't later gone so well in the aerial and ground phases of the Gulf War, this official noted, "we could have lost a lot more kids. Unfortunately," he added, "there wasn't a single person in that room except for George Bush who had ever seen a shot fired in anger. That is Cheney, [Prince] Bandar, Scowcroft, [and] Gates. The toughest battle Scowcroft was ever in [was in] the social science department of West Point.")

The day after the Senate vote, the president and his senior foreign policy and military advisers met in the residence, where they decided that the time of attack would be 3:00 A.M. Gulf time on January 17 (7:00 P.M. on January 16, Eastern Standard Time). They further determined the aircraft and missile flight paths, and they selected which infrastructure targets (power stations, refineries, highways, and so on) they would hit, and in which order.[621]

On January 15, the president signed NSC 54, which authorized the use of military force. And on January 16, Bush announced to the nation and the world that the United States and its coalition partners were about to begin air strikes against Iraq. The United States had exhausted all of its alternatives, he said, and any further delay would serve no purpose other than to "reward aggression" and continue to harm the international economy. The war would not be another Vietnam, Bush promised. "We will not fail."[622]

Then the United States and its coalition allies began their attack.

24

WAR IN THE GULF

THE AIR WAR began on January 16, 1991, at 7:00 P.M. sharp in Washington—3:00 A.M. on January 17 in Iraq. It seemed at first that Navy and Air Force had blown the timing. At 6:35 P.M., CNN showed the Baghdad night sky being lit up by tracers; Bush, Quayle, Scowcroft, Sununu, and Marlin Fitzwater, who were all in the national security advisor's West Wing office, couldn't account for why the Iraqis were firing before the attack.[623] But at 7:00 P.M. sharp, the president and his senior advisers heard a large boom on the television. Scowcroft, Bush, and the others watched the aerial assault in real time. The first bombs hit the power grid, Iraq's air defenses, its airplanes and airports, and its telecommunications—though not the oil refineries or civilian targets. With an itemized schedule of the United States' air war plans in his lap, it was if Scowcroft could read a movie script while that same movie was being screened in front of him.[624]

But once wars are under way, they have a way of departing from their scripts. Later that same day, Iraqi-launched SCUD missiles—Iraqi versions of the Soviet R-17, ballistic missiles that have a range of 100–180 miles—landed in Israel, four on Tel Aviv and three in Haifa, killing and injuring Israeli civilians and spreading fear and panic.[625] Other SCUDs landed in Riyadh, but without casualties; about half the SCUDs launched by Iraq were targeted at Saudi Arabia, half at Israel. Making things even more intense and raising the stakes higher still were reports that some of the SCUDs were carrying nerve gas.

Upon hearing the news of the missile attacks, Baker, Quayle, Eagleburger, Haass, Sununu, Richard Darman, and deputy chief of staff Andy Card crowded into Scowcroft's office, with the secretary of defense on speakerphone. Scowcroft was able to get them all to agree that they would try to delay the Israelis from retaliating. "But it is hard to talk the Israelis out of responding," Scowcroft said on January 18, "even though the situation looks all right for today."[626] Baker proceeded to telephone Israeli prime

410

minister Yitzhak Shamir, who agreed to withhold any Israeli actions for the time being. But Cheney and others in the Department of Defense were "furious" the White House didn't approve of Israel's participation in the air attacks once the SCUDs began hitting Israeli civilian targets. Cheney believed that Israel had a right to defend itself against the SCUDs, which were terrifyingly unpredictable because of their poor accuracy.[627]

Scowcroft disagreed. Including Israel in the allied coalition would be unacceptable to most of the Arab states. Furthermore, any attack by Israeli forces would require Israel Defense Forces (IDF) aircraft to fly over Saudi Arabia, Jordan, or Syria to reach Iraq. None of those countries was likely to grant Israeli aircraft permission to do so, and their own air forces would try to intercept any Israeli aircraft. The exclusion of the Israelis from the multinational coalition meant that IDF aircraft wouldn't have friend-or-foe identification codes, placing the IDF aircraft in grave danger of being shot down by US and other coalition aircraft.[628] So any retaliation by the Israelis for the SCUD attacks risked setting off a larger Arab-Israeli conflict and wrecking the international coalition the administration had worked so hard to create. Bush told King Fahd that Saddam Hussein was deliberately trying "to draw Israel into this conflict" so as to split the coalition. No one in the Gang of Eight other than Cheney thought it made sense for the Israelis to join the coalition forces.[629]

Further exacerbating Arab-Israeli relations was the news earlier that on October 8 Israeli security forces had killed twenty-one Palestinians on the Temple Mount. In response, even the United States voted in favor of a UN resolution condemning Israel's excessive use of force (No. 672 of October 12, 1990)—but only after diluting its language.[630]

Fortunately, the reports that the SCUDs contained nerve gas were mistaken. But the SCUD attacks were nonetheless terrifying to the Israelis, and when another missile killed three people in Tel Aviv on January 22, Scowcroft proposed that Deputy Secretary of State Eagleburger and Under Secretary of Defense Wolfowitz travel to Israel to meet with Prime Minister Shamir and his aides, accompanying an overnight shipment of Patriot missiles and their specialist military operators. In the meantime, the United States deployed F-15s based in Turkey as well as other aircraft to search for and destroy the SCUD launching sites—fixed or mobile—in Iraq.[631] Nonetheless, additional SCUD attacks killed one more Israeli and injured an additional forty-two. As President Bush told Gorbachev, "The attack on Israel . . . [adds] a whole new dimension."[632]

Despite the immense pressure building up on Shamir, the Israeli prime minister overruled his defense minister, Moshe Arens, and others in his cabinet by letting the terrorist missile attacks go unpunished. He also kept quiet the fact that the Patriot missiles didn't actually work very well, which helped prevent any domestic outcry and discouraged Iraq from further SCUD attacks on Israeli targets. The United States had helped with $3 billion in military and economic aid to Israel in 1990, with 56 percent of the aid consisting of foreign military sales (and some of the economic aid going to pay off military debts).[633]

What was remarkable about the US-Israeli cooperation was the fact that Bush, Baker, and Scowcroft weren't as close to Israel as most US presidents and their top advisers. Bush found the Israeli prime minister to be cold and arrogant (although the two were always polite and civil) and the two never had an easy friendship, unlike Bush's relationships with so many other heads of state.[634] Nonetheless, when Shamir visited Washington on December 11, Bush reassured him that the United States was avoiding a linkage between the Iraqi conflict and the Middle East peace process at all costs. And the two countries set up a secure hotline in case US satellites detected any missiles being launched.[635] Bush, Baker, and Scowcroft well understood the importance of the US-Israel relationship and the need to work with Jewish-American leaders, and they were at pains to separate the Israeli-Palestinian issue from the Iraqi invasion of Kuwait. After the war, they could get to work, beginning with the subsequent Madrid peace process.[636]

The air war evoked another issue that Bush, Baker, and Scowcroft had to handle delicately. This was the peace initiative for resolving the Iraqi occupation offered by Gorbachev and Yevgeny Primakov, Gorbachev's special envoy to Iraq. Scowcroft and others in the administration suspected that right-wing military leaders and party officials were behind Gorbachev's initiative. Iraq was a former ally of the Soviet Union, and the Soviet leaders didn't want to see the United States get a "big victory" or embarrass the Soviet Union by revealing how poorly the Soviet equipment matched up against American matériel. Yet the Soviet proposal was too little, too late; it set no time limit on when Iraqi forces would withdraw after a cease-fire, made no mention of POWs, and had no reference to reparations, for instance. Bush and his advisers were extremely wary of *any* cease-fire proposal, given the difficulty of keeping the hundreds of thousands of troops in the Gulf and holding the coalition together. Baker said he regarded Primakov's plan as a disaster. And "unconditional" meant unconditional.[637]

Five weeks later, on February 21 and 22, Gorbachev again tried to broker a peace deal with Iraq, just days before the ground war was to begin. Again, it was to no avail, with President Bush charging Saddam with "stalling and ducking and sending Jordan and the PLO and Yemen to stall and give his side." Bush thought the Iraqi president was taking advantage of Gorbachev's good faith effort, and he found no way to bridge the "profound differences" the two of them had on the matter.[638]

Still, it was uncomfortable for President Bush to have to repeatedly reject the proposals offered by the Soviets, especially since Bush had formed a personal relationship with Gorbachev. Too, he was sensitive to the Soviet leader's pride as well as internal Soviet politics. So when Bush had to dissuade Gorbachev from making an attempt to broker a deal on January 18, for example—an effort that came just after the United States began the air attack—he repeatedly talked to the Soviet leader, who, as journalists Thomas Friedman and Patrick Tyler pointed out, was trying to address his own domestic concerns but was also unwilling to break with the United States. And when Bush finally had to say no, he delivered the news considerably over the course of an hour-long phone call.[639] One other scare for Scowcroft came during Bush's State of the Union address on January 29, when Scowcroft learned that Baker and Soviet foreign minister Alexander Bessmertnykh had agreed "that a cessation of hostilities would be possible if Iraq would make an unequivocal commitment to withdraw from Kuwait." The two ministers also agreed that "dealing with the cause of instability and the sources of conflict, including the Arab-Israeli conflict, will be especially important" and that "without a meaningful peace process—one that promotes a just peace . . . for Israel, Arab states, and Palestinians—it will not be possible" to achieve peace and stability. Furthermore, they "agreed that in the aftermath of the crisis in the Persian Gulf," the United States and the Soviet Union, along with "other parties in the region," would facilitate efforts to establish peace and stability.[640] The joint statement's use of the word "commitment," its linkage of the Gulf crisis with an Arab-Israeli settlement, and its involvement of the Soviet Union in a settlement after the Gulf War contradicted the administration's policies, and Baker later conceded he had erred.

With the success of the ongoing air war and the delay in starting the ground war, Scowcroft and Gates became increasingly frustrated over what they saw as General Schwarzkopf's undue caution. "Brent and I began making references to McClellan and military after the air war began, and how he delayed," Gates recalls, "while Schwarzkopf kept saying he needed more time to prepare ground war." (President Lincoln had found Gen. George McClellan notoriously reluctant to move against the Confederate forces during the Civil War.) Gates said, "McClellan lives," and Scowcroft and Cheney also spoke of "our reluctant generals."[641] But when some in the military learned of the White House's reactions to Schwarzkopf and Powell's foot-dragging, it was pointed out that none of Bush's four most hawkish advisers—Cheney, Scowcroft, Gates, and Quayle—had themselves ever served in combat. Some in the military accused Scowcroft of attempting to fight a war from his West Wing office.[642]

Part of the problem was a discrepancy in intelligence. Schwarzkopf wanted to delay launching the ground attack until at least seventeen hundred Iraqi tanks (40 percent of the total) had been destroyed. Using pilot reports, CENTCOM estimated that this had been achieved by mid-February. But the CIA was unable to confirm the military's numbers. When the president asked Scowcroft to resolve the uncertainty, Scowcroft sided with CENTCOM. But postwar analysis showed that the military had overestimated the actual number of destroyed tanks by a factor of two, while the CIA had used more accurate satellite images that employed thermal imaging.[643]

Scowcroft was becoming increasingly impatient with the Pentagon's deliberateness and Gorbachev and Primakov's repeated efforts to intervene and go to the United Nations. "We no longer have the luxury of time to resolve our differences w/in the UN and then gain Saddam's acceptance" he jotted down in his notes at a Camp David meeting on February 23. "We must act now, especially in view of his disgusting scorched earth attack on Kuwait. Time is precious."[644]

On February 25, 1991, five weeks after the start of the air war, the coalition forces began the ground war against Iraq, led by the US Marines and the US Army. The Air Force and the Navy had more than proven their capacity with their aerial bombardment and cruise missiles and their repeated attacks on many of the key Iraqi targets, such as its binary chemical weapons facilities, other weapons sites, and communications centers.[645]

The Marines and Army likewise exceeded expectations. The war was over remarkably quickly. Employing the strategy first proposed by Scowcroft and Cheney—a western sweep of coalition forces into Saudi Arabia and then Iraq in combination with the publicized shore landing by the Marines in Kuwait—American and allied forces succeeding in defeating the Iraqi military and taking Kuwait in just one hundred hours of fighting. For all of the dire predictions of thousands of American deaths—the Pentagon ordered some sixteen thousand body bags—only 383 US casualties resulted directly from the war, according to the US Department of Veterans Affairs, 148 caused in battle and 235 by accidents, friendly fire, and other causes.[646]

With the world glimpsing photographs and videos of Iraqis fleeing Kuwait via the so-called highway of death and heading to Basra, where columns of troops and equipment were being destroyed by US forces—and with American pilots talking of a "turkey shoot"—Powell went to the Oval Office to propose that the United States end the war. Gates says that Powell was bothered more than anyone else by what seemed to be a mass slaughter of Iraqi soldiers, but Scowcroft also mentioned that the images of the highway of death were a "significant aspect of the decision." The president and his advisers "did not want to look like butchers who were bent on revenge by slaughtering people."[647]

Scowcroft therefore joined Powell in recommending the United States stop the attack. Baker also worried about the world reaction if the US military continued its strikes on the retreating Iraqi columns: it would have been like "piling on in football," he said, producing a counterproductive political effect in the eyes of the world. Cheney, too, argued that the coalition's goals had been accomplished. There was also the fear that the Soviet Union, opposed to the ground war, might call for a UN Security Council meeting. In the end, the key leaders all agreed—General Schwarzkopf, Admiral Jeremiah, and President Bush included—on ending the war and not pursuing the retreating army further into Iraq. Bush said it wasn't the American tradition to shoot people in the back.[648]

The decision was also shaped by the agreed purpose of the intervention. CENTCOM was operating under a UN resolution mandating the expulsion of Iraq from Kuwait, not the removal of Saddam Hussein. It was precisely for that purpose that the administration had built an international coalition among Arab states, European allies, and other countries worldwide. Those who had voted in favor of the UN resolutions against Iraq and the members of the U.S.-led coalition had not agreed to an invasion of a sovereign Arab state or the overthrow of its president, and there would have been significantly less agreement on continuing to invade Iraq, much less to shifting the coalition's objectives to include deposing Saddam Hussein.

Here, for Scowcroft, the Korean War set a useful precedent. His analysis of what happened in Korea suggested that it would be a mistake for the United States to change its objectives in midstream, no matter the revised circumstances (as the United States had done in Korea by pushing all the way to the Chinese border after the success of General Douglas MacArthur's landing at Inchon, rather than stopping at the already-established 38th parallel).[649]

"At the time [going to Baghdad] was not an option," Cheney said, "and the whole way in which we had built the coalition, devised the policy, conducted the campaign was as a coalition. . . . I don't know what the hell we would have done if we'd captured him. What do you do, shoot him?"[650] As

Gates also pointed out, Noriega had a half dozen residences in Panama and large number of "hidey holes"—and he was less paranoid than Hussein. The likelihood "of being able to find Saddam we thought was almost impossible and it was based primarily on our experience in Panama."[651]

Besides not knowing what they would do once they invaded Iraq and captured Saddam, Scowcroft warned that "Iraq could fall apart" were the Iraqi leader removed from power. He and Haass both wanted to preserve "sufficient military capability, to prevent Iraq from becoming a power vacuum (unable to deter or prevent dismemberment by one of its neighbors)." The administration didn't want the United States drawn into an internal Iraqi conflict. No one in the administration wanted a partition of Iraq, either, since an intact and secular Iraq functioned as a regional balance to the religious, Shi'a-dominated Iran.[652]

What's more, no one in the administration figured that Saddam would survive his embarrassing defeat. Rather, Bush and Scowcroft, along with others, believed there was a strong chance that the Iraq leader would be "overthrown by his own people for the death and destruction he brought down on them," as Powell described the White House thinking.[653]

All the same, the US-led coalition could have affected the odds of Saddam Hussein being overthrown and weakened his military capacity had the Bush administration let the military finish its encirclement of the Republican Guards. In fact, several US generals in Kuwait opposed the timing of the decision to halt the war, Michael Gordon and Bernard Trainor report. However, those consulted chose not to answer Schwarzkopf's request for objections to ending the war (the same language and phrasing that Powell had used with the CENTCOM commander). By ending the war when it did, however, the US-led military enabled half of the Republican Guard equipment to escape destruction and 70 percent of the Republican Guards to survive. Hundreds of Iraqi tanks—842 according to a postwar analysis—and 1,412 armored vehicles were able to flee to Basra. Furthermore, almost 130 of Iraq's best military aircraft were flown to safety in Iran in January and February 1991, notwithstanding the eight-year Iran-Iraq War; some aircraft were simply stationed in Iran for safekeeping, while others may have been used as reparations.[654] But with so much of Saddam's forces intact, the Iraqi president was not only hugely relieved but also able to present himself as a victor to the Iraqi people.[655]

Many Americans didn't understand why Saddam Hussein was allowed to stay in power. If he were the equivalent to Hitler, as the president had claimed, then the Iraqi president should at the very least be removed from power and be tried for war crimes.[656] And if he was so dangerous, critics wondered, why the president and his military advisers—Schwarzkopf, Powell, Cheney, and Scowcroft, in particular—didn't build on the coalition's overwhelming victory and the superiority of US forces to insist on seizing the advantage and destroying more of Iraq's military?

Notwithstanding the fact that an important share of the Iraqi military survived unscathed, the overall damage to Iraq was "near apocalyptic," according to a March 1991 UN report. Another study estimated the damage to Iraq at $100 billion, with Iraq's energy-generating capacity and water purification systems degraded to the point of being insufficient to meet foreseeable demand. Roads, highways, bridges, railroads, and telecommunications were also badly damaged. The CIA's own estimate of the destruction in Iraq came to $30 billion. Then there was the immense environmental damage done by the 650 oil wells ignited by Iraqi forces on their retreat from Kuwait (and only two hundred of them capped as of August 1991). The Kuwait government figured its oil loss alone at $12 billion.[657]

Critics specifically questioned the decision by Schwarzkopf—and therefore by the Bush administration—to allow the Iraqi army to keep its helicopter gunships following Iraq's surrender. The Iraqi government argued they were necessary for transport to remote areas, and Schwarzkopf had been given no special instructions for handling the surrender, after which UN forces were to supervise the terms of the peace agreement. Later, the administration learned to its horror that the Iraqi military was using its helicopters to kill thousands of Kurds in northern Iraq and Shi'a in southern Iraq. Although Scowcroft had opposed letting Saddam keep the helicopters, "I lost that argument," he said to his staff. He wanted CENTCOM to intervene to stop the Iraqi helicopters from making any further attacks, but others in the administration feared that if the president issued this order, it would undermine Schwarzkopf's authority. Scowcroft didn't press the case.[658] But neither the president, the defense secretary, nor the national security advisor wanted to interfere with the judgment of the uniformed military this time around.[659] Once the attacks began, the administration didn't want to be drawn into an internal Iraqi conflict, and so US forces stationed nearby were explicitly ordered *not* to intervene.[660]

Scowcroft said he wasn't proud of the action and recognized the cold-bloodedness of the administration's behavior with "more than a hundred thousand people" dying as a result.[661] What made United States' abandonment of the Kurds and Shi'a in Iraq especially troubling was the fact that the administration had encouraged the Iraqi people to rebel, with the CIA distributing leaflets over Iraq calling for Saddam Hussein's overthrow.[662] And because Bush and his advisers assumed Saddam would be toppled soon after Iraq's devastating defeat, Scowcroft, Cheney, and Powell hadn't given much thought to what would happen once Iraq was defeated and hadn't made the necessary contingency plans. The administration "could have done a better job of thinking through the more classic war termination issues," Robert Kimmitt noted. If it had, the helicopter fiasco might well have been avoided.[663]

The names Operation Desert Shield and Operation Desert Storm are themselves somewhat confusing. Desert Shield was the name for the military defense of Saudi Arabia and its oil installations by the United States and the multinational coalition following Iraq's invasion of Kuwait, and Desert Storm was the air and ground war against Iraq. So they are viewed sequentially, with the air and then the ground war following on the heels of the buildup of forces in Saudi Arabia, and with CENTCOM launching an offensive only once it succeeded in deterring Iraq from an invasion of Saudi Arabia.

What is confusing about the two terms is that Scowcroft and Bush *always* had offensive plans under serious consideration. The administration's decision in late October to massively increase the numbers of US troops in Saudi Arabia merely manifested its commitment to use force, given the Pentagon's requests, the fact that Iraq wasn't relinquishing Kuwait, and that the effects of the sanctions were occurring too slowly to suit Bush and Scowcroft. They didn't want to let Saddam off the hook or enable him to profit in any way possible from the invasion—and any kind of a compromise or last-minute face-saving deal would have done precisely that.

For all of the impressiveness of the United States' victory in the Persian Gulf War, the Bush administration "displayed shockingly poor foresight about what it would mean to leave Saddam Hussein in power in Iraq afterward," one critic later writes. For leaving Saddam in power—where he would ultimately remain longer than either President Bush or Prime Minister Thatcher—and for destroying only about a third of his military forces, the Bush administration came under serious fire from conservative Republicans, military strategists, and media commentators. Not only did the neoconservatives such as William Kristol criticize the Bush administration, but so, too, did other Republicans and Democrats.[664] As one of Bill Clinton's 1992 presidential campaign bumper stickers read, "Saddam Hussein still has his job. Do you?"

Over the next few years, the Bush administration and then the Clinton administration would have to grapple with Saddam over no-fly zones, weapons inspections, and the enforcement of economic sanctions.

There were other criticisms of the administration's—and therefore of Scowcroft's—handling of the Gulf crisis. One was that, prior to the invasion of Kuwait, President Bush and his foreign policy advisers, especially the US ambassador to Iraq, April Glaspie, were too close to Iraq, and that the administration falsely encouraged Saddam in his dispute with Kuwait and failed to discourage the invasion. Another was that the war was all about the United States protecting its oil supplies, and that the arguments in support of the war on the basis of international law and humanitarian concerns were mere rhetorical subterfuges.

Both arguments contain some truth, yet both are somewhat misleading.

As Michael Gordon and Bernard Trainor point out in *The Generals' War*, the Gulf War represented the utter failure of deterrence.[665] Had Bush, Scowcroft, Baker, and their aides not misperceived the situation, the war might have been avoided. This was a likely legacy of the fact that the Reagan administration—of which Bush was a key member—had quietly helped Saddam Hussein in his fight against Iran by providing Iraq with funds, military equipment, and agricultural credits.

The new Bush administration kept working with Iraq upon first taking office. According to the National Security Directive 26 (October 1989), "Normal relations between the United States and Iraq would serve [the United States'] longer-term interests and promote stability both in the Gulf and the Middle East. The United States should propose economic and political incentives for Iraq to moderate its behavior and to increase our influence."[666] On November 6, 1989, the administration granted Iraq $1 billion in credits, with $500 million as the first tranche, and the Export-Import Bank gave Iraq almost $200 million in agricultural credits for grain purchases. The Deputies Committee also recommended a continuation of the Reagan administration's policies, even though the Bush administration's internal review found Iraq's human rights record to be "abysmal." And in July 1990 the White House blocked Congress's attempt to deny Iraqi loan guarantees on the basis of its human rights record.[667]

The Bush administration's benign diplomacy vis-à-vis Iraq may thus have caused the president and his senior advisers to misperceive Saddam Hussein's intentions. And Saddam, upon receiving this kid-glove treatment and observing how the White House responded to China after Tiananmen Square, may have thought the administration wouldn't respond to an invasion of Kuwait.[668]

So even as the Defense Intelligence Agency and the CIA gathered evidence from satellite photos and other intelligence of the movement of Iraqi military vehicles and troops, the administration didn't act. On July 25, the CIA estimated the probability of an Iraqi attack on Kuwait to be 60 percent, but Bush and his top advisers were reassured by Prince Bandar of Saudi Arabia, King Hussein of Jordan, and Egypt's Mubarak, all of whom maintained that Saddam Hussein was bluffing. Iraqi ministers were also engaged in talks in Jeddah with representatives from Kuwait over their differences.[669] This was a regional matter that many argued the Gulf states could sort out themselves. Neither did either Soviet or Israeli intelligence predict the Iraqi invasion of Kuwait.

Nor was the Bush White House wholly unsympathetic to Iraq's complaints about excessive levels of Kuwaiti oil production, which had the effect of depressing world oil prices, and about its diagonal drilling under Iraqi soil. On July 24, 1990, Margaret Tutwiler, Secretary Baker's spokesperson, told a reporter, "We do not have any defense treaties with Kuwait, and there are no special defense or security commitments to Kuwait." The very next day, July 25, Ambassador Glaspie met with President Hussein and infamously declared that the demarcation of the Iraq-Kuwait border wasn't the United States' concern. And she said nothing to Saddam to deter him from invading Kuwait.[670] But the White House had a chance to follow up with a personal message from the president, and here, too, the message—one drafted by Richard Haass, Gordon and Trainor report, and then cabled to Glaspie for her to deliver personally before July 30—was conciliatory and reassuring.[671]

However, the US-Iraq relationship had already begun to show signs of strain. In early 1990, the Israelis and Americans found out that Iraq was trying to buy a "supergun" from the Canadian artillery engineer Gerald Bull that could launch shells up to four hundred miles away through a barrel hundreds of feet long. In April 1990, Saddam Hussein threatened Israel with "incineration" if it appeared that Israeli forces would again attack Iraq, and he denounced the immigration of Soviet Jews to Israel. In response to these threats, the NSC Deputies Committee came up with two dozen options, ranging "from the largely symbolic to a virtually total economic embargo and political break with Iraq." Scowcroft decided there was no need to change policy. However, in May, the administration decided to cancel the second half of its $1 billion credit for wheat purchases, other agricultural products, and farm equipment (such as dual-use trucks); as it turned out, the Senate defeated the administration's proposal.[672]

Michael Gordon of the *New York Times* argues that the Bush administration should have taken further precautionary measures against an Iraqi conquest of Kuwait, such as deploying an aircraft carrier in the North Arabian Sea, moving a squadron of F-15s to the region, or sending B-52 bombers to

Diego Garcia. Some US officials, including Dennis Ross and Paul Wolfowitz, had earlier drafted a report on handling precisely this sort of Middle East contingency, Gordon points out. Yet the administration was uninterested in seeming belligerent and had little wish to upset friendly Arab states or assume the worst of Iraq.[673]

Given the mixed evidence and the reassurances the president was receiving from his Middle East counterparts, Bush, Baker, Scowcroft, and other top officials gave Iraq the benefit of the doubt. It appears that the president and Scowcroft would have been prepared to accept some Kuwaiti loss of territory. They just didn't think Iraq would take all of Kuwait. Two days before Iraq's invasion, the assistant secretary of state for Near Eastern affairs, John Kelly, told members of Congress that the "United States has no commitment to defend Kuwait and the US has no intention of defending Kuwait if it is attacked by Iraq." And immediately after the invasion, Glaspie told a reporter that she "didn't think, and nobody else did, that the Iraqis were going to take all of Kuwait." As Gates later said, "My guess is that if Saddam had just taken the Rumalia Oilfield, he would still be there. There would have been no war."[674]

Ambassador Glaspie became the scapegoat for the Bush administration's misjudgment—that of Scowcroft and Haass in the NSC, Baker, Ross, and others in the State Department, the CIA and military intelligence, and the president himself. She dropped out of sight for several months, and later, in April 1991, testified about the incident before the Senate. Glaspie was subsequently assigned as the US consul general in Cape Town, South Africa, and in 2002 retired from the US Foreign Service and State Department.

The administration did ultimately draw a line in the sand—but not until after Iraq had already ventured well past that line and threatened to cross another line, the Saudi border. Indeed, Scowcroft later admitted he had made the wrong call on the Iraqi invasion. As Gates said of Saddam, "Nobody thought he'd be that crazy."[675]

As for the charge that the Gulf War was essentially about oil, it's certainly true that the president's economic advisers were deeply concerned about the supply shortages and higher oil and gas prices that were expected to result from the loss of Kuwaiti and Iraqi oil.[676] And the one trigger for the United States to depose Saddam Hussein was if Iraq destroyed the Kuwaiti oil infrastructure, in which case NSD 54 mandated that "it shall become an explicit objective of the United States to replace the current leadership of Iraq."

Yet there was more at stake than Kuwait's oil. There was Iraq's (and Kuwait's) location and the implications for regional stability and the near-term safety of Saudi Arabia—and, of course, its oil. Iraq possessed binary chemical weapons, sophisticated military technology, and nuclear weapons materials, which posed a regional threat as well as possibly endangering Israel. Then, too, there was the ruthless and arrogant nature of Iraq's action, not unlike Argentina's conquest of the Falklands eight years earlier. And there was the timing of Iraq's invasion of Kuwait at the beginning of a new, undefined post–Cold War era.

———

ONE OF THE most positive results of the Gulf War was the Madrid peace conference, where Israelis and Palestinians met face-to-face for the first time. Without Madrid, there would have been no Oslo agreements in August 1993. Madrid occurred because Baker wanted to build on the momentum from the Gulf War and give the peace process a try. Scowcroft was skeptical, but the president supported the secretary of state, and Baker's effort paid off—a separate story that Baker tells in *The Politics of Diplomacy*. One of the casualties of the single-term Bush presidency was that Baker and others in the administration were unable to leverage what happened in Madrid into an agreement toward a lasting peace between the Israelis and Palestinians. The Oslo accords were of only limited effect, despite the renunciation of violence by the PLO and prime minister Yitzhak Rabin's formal recognition of the PLO. The agreements on curtailing the construction of new settlements, on allowing for limited Palestinian sovereignty, and on other issues quickly lost their momentum following the assassination of Rabin in November 1995, with the Israelis and Palestinians both violating the agreements and being deeply split over the merits of the accords.

Yet what happened on the West Bank and Gaza affected Arabs (and Jews) around the world. Abdul Rasul Sayyaf, an Afghan military commander, who was affiliated with the Sunni, pro-Saudi, and Pashtun mujahedin, noted that Osama bin Laden, besides being "more anti-American than our leaders," was "deeply concerned about other Islamic causes," such as the Arab-Israeli conflict. "He was always telling us, 'Behind every rock and mountain, there is the shadow of Palestine.' And when we beat the Russians, he said, 'We should go to Palestine.'"[677]

The statement suggests the potentially huge payoff that might have accompanied a settlement of the Arab-Israeli conflict. Had the Bush administration been able to defuse the Palestinian issue, the course of world history might have been dramatically altered.

Less positive was the situation in Iraq, where more than a quarter of a million people, mostly women and children and overwhelmingly Kurds, fled the northern part of the country, accumulating on the Turkish border. Secretary of State Baker visited the region, the United States, France, Britain, and other countries airlifted in food and medical assistance, and the United Nations and other NGOs stepped in. The United States also enforced what was in effect a safe haven or enclave north of the 36th parallel, where Iraq was not to use military force. In Mitterrand's words, not to act would have ruined the moral credit that the United States and the coalition earned by their victory in the Persian Gulf.[678]

Despite this mixed historical record, the consensus is that the Gulf War was a triumph for the Bush-Scowcroft foreign policy team. The war is celebrated as a "war of necessity" in Richard Haass's description, rather than a "war of choice." It is regarded as an American victory and considered to be a "good war." For Ambassador Ryan Crocker, who was the director of the Iraq-Kuwait Task Force at the time, it ranks "among the finest moments of American diplomatic and military achievement."[679]

Yet this striking success was far from inevitable. Many of the critical components of Desert Shield and Desert Storm involved extremely hard work, difficult negotiations, and an element of the unpredictable.

Saddam Hussein himself was responsible for some of the unpredictable events that helped ensure international support for the war. His use of hostages, his treatment of prisoners, the SCUD attacks against Israel, and the widespread environmental destruction caused by setting fire to almost all of the Kuwaiti oil fields—including wells and storage tanks and distribution facilities—were among the unnecessary "horrible things" that antagonized the international community.[680]

Buoyed by the worldwide revulsion against Saddam, the Bush administration was able to create an international coalition of almost thirty states aligned against Iraq. It was able to have twelve UN Security Council resolutions passed that supported and ultimately led to the coercive eviction of Iraq from Kuwait (ten were passed before the war, in the summer and fall of 1990, and two afterward). It succeeded in deploying hundreds of thousands of American troops on Saudi Arabian soil. It enjoyed overwhelming success in the US military's air and ground attacks on Iraqi targets. It was able to elicit large contributions from its allies to the cover the costs of Desert Shield and Desert Storm. And it was able to persuade the Israel Defense Forces not to retaliate after SCUD missiles hit Jerusalem and Tel Aviv.

Bush, Scowcroft, and others in the administration took all the necessary steps to secure a dominant military victory. The White House successfully mobilized policy experts, opinion leaders, and American public and international opinion toward the objective of restoring the Middle East to the status quo ante, and it was able to muster and transport more than half a million troops to the Middle East (most of which were to be based in Saudi Arabia), get the UN Security Council to support its proposed policies, and persuade a majority in both houses of Congress to authorize the use of force against Iraq. For all these reasons, the Gulf War is considered to be one of George Bush's major achievements as president. Heads of state from around the world almost unanimously praised the American president for his handling of the crisis and his strong leadership.[681]

"People underestimated George Bush's determination to make good on what he said [on August 4], that this 'will not stand,'" Philip Zelikow remarks. Zelikow credits Bush with leading the United States and the world in reversing the Iraqi conquest of Kuwait. The president "doesn't want Saddam to have a graceful retreat. He doesn't want him to be able to go back into Kuwait in six months. He doesn't want a compromise solution. He doesn't want Saddam Hussein to save face. Bush wants to win."[682] To Zelikow it was obvious from "the very start, within the first 24 hours," that "Bush was going to act . . . [and that] Brent thought the same way."[683]

Phillip D. Brady, the president's staff secretary, likewise observed that his boss was an extraordinarily disciplined man during Desert Shield and Desert Storm and that his attention was, "understandably, very much focused" on the crisis. In particular, his "focus was more on those things that Brent wanted to get done and had to get done, and those sort of communications," Brady said—confirming Zelikow's observation that Bush and Scowcroft operated in tandem.[684] The president ran with the ball that Scowcroft handed him. Zelikow identified Bush as the "chief hawk," as have most other historians and journalists, but it was Scowcroft who at the very outset persuaded Bush to become that chief hawk.

So the credit that outside observers accord President Bush for his determination at seeing through the defeat of Iraq results from the fact that Bush quickly accepted Scowcroft's logic and then acted rapidly to lead the United States in Desert Shield and Desert Storm. Scowcroft himself has helped to obscure this reality, since he has "loyally insist[ed]" to reporters "that the President arrived at his decision alone," journalist Jeffrey Goldberg writes. But as Goldberg corroborates, "several of Scowcroft's former colleagues said that it was Scowcroft's firmness, along with Thatcher's prodding, that strengthened Bush's resolve to confront Saddam."[685]

In late February, one day before Desert Storm was to end, White House officials told the *New York Times* that it was Scowcroft's presentation at the Friday morning NSC meeting of August 3 "that made clear what the stakes were, crystallized people's thinking and galvanized support for a very strong response." And Bush himself, David Schmitz points out in his biography of Scowcroft, "gave the lion's share of the credit to Scowcroft for conceiving the rationale for the war" and then putting it into practice.[686]

The Gulf War made the bond between Bush and Scowcroft even stronger. The "President just loved him," NSC staffer Deb Amend recalled. "He really, really adored him. . . . A number of times I went by the Oval Office and outside I'd see Cheney, Powell, Sununu, by themselves or with others waiting. And Scowcroft would be in there, talking to the President. He was valued by the President above all others [and] Scowcroft would see him before anyone else." And Bush, thanks to the NSC process he and Scowcroft had put in place, gave Scowcroft and his staff "a lot of control."[687]

Gates, too, writes of how "Scowcroft's loyalty toward and affection for Bush was reciprocated." Indeed, in his 1996 book, Gates writes that he didn't think that any president and national security advisor had ever had a closer personal bond. "With all the game-playing and maneuvering that goes on in every White House, no one would have dared utter a criticism of Brent to George Bush—substantive issues apart. And his friendship with Barbara Bush was equally strong."[688]

Notwithstanding his friendship with Bush, Scowcroft "was fair, intellectually open, and did not use his close relationship . . . to undermine others or prevent them from making their case," Haass said. "Indeed, he would often make it for them just to make sure [the president] knew what everyone was thinking."[689]

The president himself appreciated that Scowcroft had "a great propensity for friendship. By that I mean someone I can depend on to tell me what I need to know and not just what I want to hear, and at the same time he is someone on whom I know I always can rely and trust implicitly." He was the opposite of "a blowhard,'" Bush told one writer.[690] Indeed, after "intelligence confirmed that Iraq had swept into Kuwait with a large number of troops," Bush wrote in *A World Transformed*, Brent would play "a critical, and often overlooked, role" in the coming months. "Much of the subsequent original planning and careful thought was done with him at my side, probably more than history will ever know."[691]

The huge role played by Scowcroft in the successful prosecution of the war is even more extraordinary in light of the personal pressures he was under at the time.

Throughout the months of crisis, Scowcroft's wife, Jackie, was very ill—an invalid, in effect—and Brent would accompany the president only on overseas trips, because when he left town he had to hire a full-time nurse and arrange for twenty-four-hour-a-day care for his wife. When Margaret Thatcher found out about Jackie, she cabled a personal message to "DEAR BRENT," telling him she was "SORRY TO HEAR THAT YOUR WIFE IS ILL AND IN HOSPITAL . . . AND DON'T LET IT GET YOU DOWN. WE ALL OF US, FROM THE PRESIDENT DOWN DEPEND ON YOU VERY MUCH. YOU ARE AN ABSOLUTE TOWER OF STRENGTH."[692]

Jackie's condition was most likely the chief reason President Bush was never offended when Brent dozed off in meetings: he knew that his national security advisor had to go home to care for his wife after spending fifteen or sixteen hours at the White House. At home, he'd have to "do the laundry, the cleaning, he'd go to the grocery store, he'd do all these things."[693] And as "Brent's wife became sicker, the President and I would conspire against Brent," Gates reported, "and I would find a way to let the President know that Jackie was in the hospital again and so the President would call Brent, maybe at 4:30 or 5:00 in the afternoon, and tell him that he was going over to the residence, that he was done for the day. Then Brent would come back to the office and we'd do a couple more hours' work. It was a very close feeling among all of us and I think it made a big difference on substance."[694]

Gates and Bush had no choice but to intervene, given that Scowcroft was virtually living in White House office during those months, often "sleeping on his couch" to grab a few minutes of rest when he wasn't working.[695] He had "almost no social life," a former colleague commented; rather, he was "always thinking, always working." As another White House official observed, "he was there all the time."[696]

Writing in *A World Transformed*, Bush acknowledged the contributions of his "superb team," particularly Powell, Schwarzkopf, Cheney, and Baker. His final accolade was for the national security advisor and his beloved friend, Brent Scowcroft, who lifted the "burden off the president, task[ed] the bureaucracy, spott[ed] out the differences and never with credit for himself." He was "always quiet but always there and always dependable."[697]

On Wednesday, July 3, 1991, four months after Desert Storm, President Bush assembled staff and guests for a White House ceremony. He bestowed Presidential Medals of Freedom on James Baker and Dick Cheney. He then announced a final Medal of Freedom:

> The ideal of a statesman, a quiet yet passionate defender of the American interests, Brent Scowcroft's sound counsel has enhanced our national security

and advanced American foreign policy and the cause of freedom around the world. In the Gulf, General Scowcroft never wavered in pursuit of this nation's goal of reversing Iraq's aggression against Kuwait. He superbly coordinated the national security system in the development of recommendations for the President, enabling the United States to conduct an effective and united foreign policy and a victorious military campaign. America honors an outstanding general, a true patriot, and a wise statesman.[698]

The honor came as a complete surprise. Of all the awards and the prizes Scowcroft has received over the years, he told his close friend and colleague, Virginia Mulberger, it is the one of which he is most proud.[699]

25

END OF EMPIRE

MIKHAIL GORBACHEV LOOKED down on the Maryland countryside from Marine Corps One. The Soviet party secretary was flying with President George Bush and their respective advisers on their way out to Camp David and couldn't quite grasp what he was seeing. "He seemed so surprised about the real estate that was there, the size of some of the houses, the tracts that had a house on every end and the agriculture that he saw out the window," White House chief of staff John Sununu later recalled. "And he started talking to the President about it, about how real estate is bought and sold in the U.S., who decides what they plant and what they don't plant, the marketing of the stuff, how do they make money," and other topics.

> And I'm absolutely convinced . . . that [this] convinced Gorbachev that this was a losing battle. I really mean it. It [was] the way he was looking out the window. Not just the questions. Not just what he saw. It was like somebody who had been taught to say that you have just put on this show for me, and in his heart he knows you can't be putting on that show. And you know the landscape from Washington to Camp David, it's got very attractive real estate, very attractive farms. Anyway, he became very interested in the way things were done in the U.S. and would always ask these kinds of questions.[700]

While there's no evidence for Sununu's conviction—Gorbachev had conceded to Germany's reunification within NATO under the principles established by the Helsinki Final Act two days earlier—his observation underscores one of the great contradictions of the Cold War: the fact that the Soviet Union and United States, who had implacably opposed each other around the world for forty years, had roughly equivalent military capabilities economies and societies that were utterly different.

Gorbachev reflected on another irony on that same flight. "Near President Bush sat a military aide with the nuclear codes enabling him to destroy

428

the Soviet Union. Near me sat my military aide with the codes required to destroy the United States. Yet President Bush and I sat together on that small helicopter talking about peace," Gorbachev remarked. "Neither of us planned to ever use the awesome power we each possessed. Yet we possessed it. And we both knew how ordinary and fallible we both were."[701] In just a few months, Gorbachev and Bush would jointly condemn the Iraqi invasion of Kuwait, marking the first time the United States and Soviet Union had been on the same side of an international dispute. And in little over a year and a half, there would be no more Soviet Union.

Gorbachev knew he was in the hot seat. With the Warsaw Pact shattering—it would be officially dissolved on February 25, 1991—pressure from hard-line party members and military leaders for the Soviet Union to maintain its power, and the growing threat of Russian and other nationalist movements, Gorbachev had few policy options and fewer resources. "There is no alternative to perestroika," Soviet foreign minister Eduard Shevardnadze had told Bush, Baker, Scowcroft, and others in the Oval Office on September 21, 1989. To that end, Shevardnadze said, the Soviet Union was "creating a new political culture." He and Gorbachev wanted to work with the United States on banning chemical weapons, limiting conventional forces, eliminating short-range nuclear forces, and reopening negotiations on START (the Strategic Arms Reduction Treaty, discussions for which had been initiated during the Reagan administration).[702] All would come to pass.

Unlike Margaret Thatcher, Vaclev Havel, or Deng Xiaoping, who, as John Lewis Gaddis points out, embarked on their political reforms with specific goals in mind, Gorbachev undertook to change the Soviet system without a clear destination.[703] With the country's rising foreign debt, the decline in world oil prices, the increasing cost of imports, and its rising military expenses, the Soviet Union had no choice but to reform its economy. But as suggested by Gorbachev's reaction to his glimpses of the Maryland countryside, the international market system was a world he didn't understand. As Canadian prime minister Brian Mulroney later said in reference to the 1991 G-7 Summit, were Gorbachev to attend, "he wouldn't have a clue what we were talking about."[704] (He did attend, in fact.) So even as Gorbachev recognized that the dysfunctional Soviet system had to reform, he didn't know "how on God's good earth to hold this thing together," Scowcroft's press secretary, Roman Popadiuk, commented. And once Gorbachev started the reform process, "the whole thing got away from him."[705]

Gorbachev's chief hope for political success and economic recovery was through his foreign policy, where the United States and the West held most of the cards. Here the Bush administration used its advantage to push Gorbachev and the Kremlin as hard as it could while offering inducements to secure Gorbachev's cooperation. The strategy worked. As James Goldgeier and Michael McFaul summarize in their book *Power and Purpose*, Gorbachev and Shevardnadze ended up agreeing "to almost every major policy preference of the Bush administration."[706] At the same time, Bush, Baker, and Scowcroft expressed their support for Gorbachev's reforms, worked with him on economic and financial issues, moved forward on conventional and nuclear arms control talks, and—just as important—treated him and his senior advisers with respect. "Whatever the course, however long the process took, and whatever its outcome," Bush said, "I wanted to see stable, and above all peaceful, change." Despite the revolutionary nature of the changes that occurred, that's almost exactly how they unfolded—thanks in large part to the guiding efforts of Brent Scowcroft. "We were not bucking a tide," Scowcroft later said of the collapse of the Soviet empire. "We were trying to mold and guide it into channels that would produce the right outcome and be peaceful."[707]

During these months of change, Bush and Scowcroft were focused on two main issues: the military and strategic relationship between the United States and the Soviet Union (and later Russia and the other newly independent republics) and the reform of the Soviet and then Russian political economy. The United States largely remained aloof from the internal politics of the Soviet Union and its successor governments, although these political matters and the two main issues of concern to the Bush administration were deeply intertwined.

On the military front, Scowcroft's chief concern, as it had been throughout his career, was to reduce the chances of an actual conflict and especially a nuclear exchange between the United States and the Soviet Union. Thus, he wanted to reduce both the opportunities and the motives for either superpower to make a first strike. But the balance of conventional forces complicated matters. Given the Warsaw Pact's dominance in conventional forces, the US and NATO had always relied on a doctrine of "flexible response" in the European theater, with the understanding that NATO might have to resort to intermediate- or short-range nuclear weapons in the event that the Soviet military overwhelmed NATO forces. However, the unpopularity of the presence of the intermediate- and short-range nuclear weapons on German soil, indicated by the controversy over the short-range missile intended to follow the Lance, showed just how politically sensitive, and therefore potentially unsustainable, NATO's reliance on these weapons was.

The signing, after protracted negotiations, of the Conventional Armed Forces in Europe (CFE) Treaty on November 19, 1990, alleviated many of the administration's and NATO's concerns. The agreement eliminated the Soviet Union's overwhelming advantages in conventional weapons by imposing equal limits for NATO and Warsaw Pact countries on the numbers of tanks (20,000), armored combat vehicles (30,000), heavy artillery pieces (20,000), attack helicopters (2,000), and combat aircraft (6,800). It also contained special provisions for allowing on-site inspections and preventing any single country from having more than a third of the total amount of equipment—thus restricting the possible massing of conventional forces on Europe's northern or southern flanks. (The limits on the Soviet Union's conventional forces would later be allocated among eight of its successor states.)[708]

Nine months later, another breakthrough treaty was signed. On July 31, 1991, after ten years of negotiation, the United States and the Soviet Union agreed on START at the US-Soviet summit in Moscow. The agreement placed aggregate limits on the numbers of warheads (6,000) and delivery vehicles (1,600), and ceilings on the number of ICBM and SLBM warheads (4,900). It also limited two forms of weaponry possessed only by the Soviet Union—heavy ICBM warheads (1,540) and mobile ICBM warheads—in exchange for US agreement to give up on the deployment of the Midgetman missile, among other restrictions. Just as important, START contained extensive provisions for verification, such as allowing for on-site inspections and mandating the exchange of telemetry data from test launches. START represented a 35 percent reduction in the Soviet arsenal and a 25 percent cut in the US stockpiles.[709]

Although both treaties represented triumphs for the administration, the Soviet Union did not always comply with their terms. In fact, the Soviets immediately began fudging the CFE treaty, putting infantry into naval forces and then saying that naval forces didn't count. Later, US officials learned that the Soviet Union had also secretly retained hundreds of SS-20 intermediate-range ballistic missiles following the 1987 INF treaty, after all 654 missiles were supposed to have been destroyed.[710] Nonetheless, the two treaties significantly reduced the threat of war and made military affairs much more stable and predictable for both the United States and Soviet Union.

Meanwhile, Gorbachev's position at home was becoming increasingly unstable because of the underperforming Soviet economy, the polarizing domestic effects of Gorbachev's reforms, and the rise of nationalist movements. In mid-June, 1991, even as START was nearing completion, Gorbachev survived an attempted "constitutional coup" at the hands of his prime minister, Valentin Pavlov.[711]

The seismic shifts threatening Gorbachev's future and that of the empire he headed soon embroiled American leadership. On August 1, 1991, the Bush administration's triumph in the Moscow summit was overshadowed by the reception of a speech delivered by President Bush to the Ukrainian parliament in Kiev. Drafted by Scowcroft and the NSC staff, the speech was intended to encourage the leaders of the Ukrainian republic to negotiate with the Soviet Union rather than make a unilateral break. Bush stated that the United States would "not support those who seek independence in order to replace a far-off tyranny with a local despotism," and mentioned Babi Yar—a ravine near Kiev where the Nazis slaughtered a hundred thousand Jews in 1941 and which he had visited earlier that day. The president distinguished between independence and liberty, and then made the basic—and fundamentally sound—point that the new countries arising from the ashes of old empires wouldn't necessarily be liberal democracies. Bush received a standing ovation.[712]

Other Ukrainians who heard the speech took Bush's comments to mean that he didn't sympathize with Ukrainian self-determination and that he supported the Soviet Union rather than Ukrainian independence. For many American commentators who were mindful of the tremendous toll exacted by Soviet tyranny, Bush's remarks came across as heartless, patronizing, and tone-deaf. In his nationally syndicated column, the *New York Times'* William Safire cruelly called the speech "Chicken Kiev." Other correspondents quickly took up Safire's phrase, and the label stuck.[713]

Afterward, Scowcroft noted, "Ukraine was the only spot outside Russia where the issue was relevant since the ethnic composition of Ukraine contained the potential for national strife."[714] But the speech could have made the point more subtly, expressed more support for Ukrainian nationalism, and voiced more hope for Ukraine's future. Bush never forgave Safire, and he never spoke to him again.[715]

Less than three weeks later, at eleven thirty in the evening of August 18, Scowcroft was in bed at the Nonantum Hotel in Kennebunkport, Maine, reading cables and watching CNN, when he learned that Gorbachev had taken ill and was being replaced by former vice president Gennady Yanayev. Scowcroft thought that sounded suspicious, and he checked in with his deputy, Gates. He then called President Bush and spent the rest of the night trying to find out more from the situation room so that the president would be able to explain the shocking news to the American public at a press conference the next morning.

At 5:30 A.M. Scowcroft called Bush, and the two of them talked over how they wanted to proceed. The coup posed a diplomatic challenge. On the one hand, it was dispiriting for those hoping for the continued reform of the Soviet Union and for a new era in US-Soviet relations. On the other hand, Bush might have to deal with the new Soviet leadership, and so he couldn't simply condemn the coup by calling it "illegitimate" or "illegal." Scowcroft reminded him that coups led by important officials "usually succeed," so the president's first public statements had to be carefully nuanced so as not "to burn our bridges with them." To that end, Scowcroft came up with the term "extra-constitutional." Bush then "milled his way" through the press conference and "came as close as he could—thought he could—or [Scowcroft] would let him—to denouncing the coup. But he didn't come right out to it." He did say that "coups can fail"—in contrast to some foreign leaders who were already accommodating themselves to what they considered the new reality.[716]

Bush then got on the telephone with his foreign counterparts to find out what they knew about the coup and to see if they could coordinate their responses. He and Scowcroft quickly left Walker Point to return to Washington, sent Baker over to Brussels for an emergency NATO ministerial meeting, and continued to make phone calls. And as he learned more about what was going on—thanks to an encouraging message from populist Russian leader Boris Yeltsin and a report from the deputy director of the CIA, both indicating that the coup had gone off half-cocked—Bush hardened the United States' position against the coup with Gates and Scowcroft inserting the word "condemn" in remarks the president made about the coup later that day.[717]

The coup soon ended with Yeltsin emerging as the popular hero of a democratic Russia. It became clear the coup had been undertaken in great haste, perhaps to prevent the signing of the Union Treaty (Gorbachev's proposal for a new constitutional basis for the USSR) or to preempt Gorbachev's planned dismissal of some of his top officials. Whatever the reasons for the coup, Scowcroft pointed out that if it had been better organized—or had it been attempted a year or two earlier—the outcome and thus the resulting course of world history "could have been quite different."[718]

With his newfound stature, Yeltsin had Gorbachev stripped of his position as party secretary and forced the Soviet president to accept a ban on further Communist Party activities. (Myopically, Gorbachev thought that things could go back to how they had been before the coup and that his own reforms had prevented the coup from succeeding.) Within a week, Ukraine, Belarus, and five other Soviet republics announced their independence. Lithuania had declared its independence in late 1989, and reaffirmed it after the coup.

Scowcroft and Bush didn't want the United States to humiliate Gorbachev by recognizing the three Baltic countries before the Soviet Union did so voluntarily, and Bush also asked other countries to delay their recognition. However, under continued public pressure to act, the president publicly recognized the Baltics on September 2, 1991.[719] (The United States wouldn't recognize the other republics as long as the Soviet Union still existed: the Baltics merited an exception since the United States had never formally recognized their absorption by the USSR in the first place.)

Even as the condition of the Soviet Union deteriorated over the latter half of 1991, the administration sought to distance itself from internal Soviet politics. "We will support those in the center and the Republics who pursue freedom, democracy, and economic liberty," Bush said in Kiev. "We will determine our support not on the basis of personalities but on the basis of principles. We cannot tell you how to reform your society. We will not try to pick winners and losers in political competitions between Republics or between Republics and the center. That is your business; that's not the business of the United States of America." Bush later told Yeltsin much the same thing shortly before the dissolution of the Soviet Union: "The republics and the center must decide on how things evolve." Bush made it a point to talk to Yeltsin if he spoke with Gorbachev and vice versa, so that neither felt slighted in any way. "The U.S. will not make statements saying that anybody should be kicked out."[720] Neither did Scowcroft want the United States to be seen as advocating the dismantling of another superpower by supporting Ukrainian independence.[721]

The administration was eager to avoid taking any risky steps that might cause an "explosion in Moscow," Scowcroft noted, "much less a global conflagration."[722] This is why the administration hadn't jumped on the Yeltsin bandwagon, why it proceeded so cautiously in the months before and after the breakup of the Soviet Union, and why it would resist the temptation to push the Russians hard on economic and political reforms.

The administration's noncommittal position was harder for it to maintain vis-à-vis Ukraine. With the 2012 election just eleven months away, candidate Bill Clinton was criticizing Bush for being slow to recognize the independence of the Soviet republics. So the White House agreed to recognize Ukraine following its December 1 referendum on secession (which, as expected, passed overwhelmingly). This violated Bush's own position and effectively sealed the fate of the Soviet Union, embittering Gorbachev. Scowcroft considered it bad policy, saying, "I think we've signaled a more forward-leaning policy than we had in mind," and he worried that the administration's action might cause difficulties between Kiev and Moscow.[723]

Yet the administration's policies effectively favored Gorbachev, because they were predicated on dealing with the Soviet Union as it was and, therefore, with its standing president. Bush and his senior advisers found it easier to work with a single person and were wary that by embracing the independence of the Soviet republics, they might be opening up a Pandora's box of nationalist leaders, some of whom might be democrats, some not. As Bush told Chancellor Kohl in early November, he supported Gorbachev and "the Center." "Otherwise we could have anarchy."[724]

The personal rapport that Bush had with Gorbachev may also have played a role in shaping the administration's approach. The two leaders were comfortable enough with each other to engage in playful banter. At a luncheon in the Soviet embassy on October 29 where Bush, Gorbachev, and their advisers were present, Bush told Gorbachev it had been "stupid to try to overthrow you," whereupon Gorbachev pointed at Scowcroft and joked, "This is what generals do sometimes." Bush replied, "If Brent Scowcroft wants my job, or Baker's for that matter, he can have them."[725]

By contrast, Scowcroft didn't particularly care for Boris Yeltsin. He found him bumptious and boorish. He especially did not like how Yeltsin had forced him to wait during the Moscow summit in late July. In private conversations with British prime minister John Major and Major's aides in Kennebunkport later in August 1991, Scowcroft "referred to the Russian president as an egoist, a demagogue, an opportunist, and a grandstander who had never resisted the chance to use his meetings or phone calls with Bush to upstage Gorbachev," Michael Beschloss and Strobe Talbott report. Even in remarks published in the press, which were barely disguised as coming from "a senior administration official," Scowcroft spoke of Yeltsin's "instinct for the demagogic," commented on how he pandered to the Russian public, and questioned "to what end" Yeltsin would govern. Ambassador Jack Matlock had to cable the White House, letting Bush know that the attacks served no purpose and didn't help.[726]

But Bush, Scowcroft, Baker, and the State Department, with their focus on stability, would stay with Gorbachev as long as he was the leader of the Soviet Union. This is despite the fact that Scowcroft would tell the president, upon watching Yeltsin humiliate Gorbachev in a public meeting on August 23, "It's all over"; Gorbachev was no longer an independent actor, the national security advisor pointed out, and didn't even grasp what was happening.[727]

Scowcroft was particularly concerned about the possibility of bloodshed, about how any new borders would be established, and about command and control of the Soviet nuclear arsenal. In hopes of averting violence, maintaining order, and protecting property, Baker and the State Department came up with five principles for the Soviet Union and the several republics to follow: "self-determination through democratic methods; respect for existing borders, with any changes made through negotiation; respect of democracy and the rule of law; human rights; and adherence to international law and the USSR's existing treaty obligations."[728] The United States and its Western allies were to use these principles as criteria by which to evaluate the merits of any economic proposals emanating from the Soviet Union.

Secretary Cheney and others in the Defense Department saw the situation differently, especially after the July coup attempt. In a vigorous NSC meeting on September 5, Cheney called the postcoup period "a great opportunity for the United States" and said he hoped the president would press the United States' advantage by encouraging independence among the Soviet republics and establishing diplomatic relations with them as soon as possible. After the decades of intense rivalry and the frustrations of the arms race, many Pentagon officials as well as others in the government reacted with "a steady glee," Popadiuk observed; they wanted to pick winners.[729]

In the end, of course, the Soviet Union did dissolve, to be sure, and Gorbachev more than anyone else was responsible for its demise. But Yeltsin forced the issue. In a speech to Russian judges on October 17, Yeltsin stated that "his task was to help the remnants of the center to collapse in the near future" and to take over Soviet institutions such as the KGB.[730] He was able to do precisely that. By pushing for independence for Russia, Ukraine, Belarus, and Kazakhstan, which between them controlled 90 percent of the Soviet Union's economic production, and by aggressively challenging Gorbachev at almost every turn, Yeltsin led the way to the formation of the Commonwealth of Independent States (CIS) on December 8, 1991. Russia, Ukraine, Belarus, and Kazakhstan served as the core members of the CIS, which would have a united military command and cooperate for international security, peace, arms control, and defense expenditures.

By mid-December, Scowcroft told the president that it "really is the end" and described Gorbachev as "kind of a pathetic figure at this point."[731] On December 21 in Alma-Ata, capital of Kazakhstan, all of the republics except for Georgia and the Baltics agreed to become part of the CIS, thereby marking the end of the Soviet Union.[732] Four days later, on Christmas Day 1991, Gorbachev resigned as president of the Soviet Union. Bush immediately recognized Russia, Ukraine, Kazakhstan, Belarus, Armenia, Kyrgyzstan, and Moldova, and declared that the United States would establish formal diplomatic relations with the other former Soviet republics on a case-by-case basis.

As the Soviet Union proceeded to disintegrate, a number of important issues remained to be resolved, especially with respect to strategic weapons. Scowcroft himself had raised the biggest hurdle to the 1991 START agreement by calling for strict terms on the conversion of MIRVed ICBMs to single-warhead missiles. But he had been opposed by Soviet military leaders, who wanted more leeway on how many of their three kinds of missiles they could "download" (that is, convert from a MIRVed warhead to a single warhead), as well as by civilians in the US Department of Defense, who wanted to retain the United States' nuclear arsenal, and by Secretary Baker, who wanted to complete the agreement (Scowcroft believed Baker sought to finalize the treaty almost irrespective of its substance). Bush took Baker's and Cheney's advice and decided to accept more relaxed terms for the Soviet downloading.[733]

After the START agreement, Scowcroft continued to push for further arms control across the board and, especially, for the elimination of MIRVed missiles from both the US and Soviet nuclear arsenals. With up to ten independent warheads, the MIRVed missiles at once made missile attacks that much more attractive and, conversely, made preemptive strikes that much more appealing—just as Scowcroft had argued as chairman of the Scowcroft Commission eight years previously. De-MIRVing ICBMs lowered the stakes of nuclear confrontation by eliminating the logic of "use them or lose them." As Senator Sam Nunn has remarked, it was not in the United States' interest to have Russia think itself vulnerable to a first strike. Scowcroft's ideas became the foundation for the next round of arms control talks, culminating in START II.[734]

Doing much of the groundwork for the START negotiations and coordinating the important and technical issues of strategic weapons and arms control among the multiple agencies involved was the "Un-Group," an interagency group set up by Scowcroft and Gates in mid-1990. Arnold Kanter and Bob Blackwill had the idea to create an informal group that would meet in Kanter's office or the White House situation room to handle the very delicate and vital issues surrounding nuclear arms control. By including members at different levels of seniority who were senior enough to hold sway in their agencies (and get their principals' buy-ins) and, at the same time, junior enough to have strategic weapons and arms control as their sole or dominant portfolio, the Un-Group broke with established administration hierarchies and government protocol.[735] Hence its name.

Scowcroft appointed Kanter, his senior director for arms control and defense policy, as its chairman (later replaced by Col. John A. Gordon when Kanter was promoted to under secretary of state for political affairs in October 1991). The other members were Under Secretary of State for International Security Affairs Reginald Bartholomew, Assistant Secretary of Defense Stephen Hadley, the CIA's Douglas MacEachin, the NSC's John Gordon, Lt. Gen. Howard Graves, assistant to the chairman of the Joint Chiefs of Staff (succeeded by Gen. John Shalikashvili), and the head of the now-defunct Arms Control and Disarmament Agency, Ron Lehman. Kanter met regularly with the other Un-Group members and would then discuss matters with Scowcroft.[736]

Kanter described the Un-Group as having "all of the attributes of what you would want an interagency process to be." The absence of bureaucratic games and turf battles in the Un-Group meshed with the nonideological and pragmatic perspectives of Bush and Scowcroft, both of whom had "no patience for bureaucratic posturing."[737] The Un-Group subsequently helped negotiate the START agreements with the Soviet Union, helped forge the agreements on chemical and biological weapons and assisted with the agreements on the Open Skies Agreement (signed on March 22, 1992, in Helsinki) and on conventional force levels in Europe.

With the collapse of the Soviet Union, the Un-Group under John Gordon then laid the groundwork for Secretary Baker to get Ukraine, Belarus, and Kazakhstan to sign the Lisbon protocol and sign letters toward the surrender of nuclear weapons—thousands of strategic nuclear weapons and tens of thousands of tactical nuclear weapons—an objective sought by Baker and completed under the Clinton administration. It also dealt with the threat of loose nuclear weapons, the serious danger of nuclear proliferation, and the fate of top Soviet scientists and engineers.[738]

In addition, the Un-Group, along with the deputies committee and other US government organizations and agencies, began to monitor the growing number of private trading groups formed by scientists, military and government officials, and laboratory managers to sell special alloys, electro-optics, imagery enhancement, power systems, and other technologies on the private market.[739] The Bush administration began a program to buy Russia's highly enriched uranium and recycle it for use in domestic US power plants (an agreement to this effect was signed in February 1993, and implementation began after that). The Un-Group continued its work through the end of the administration, with the submission of the Chemical Weapons Convention to the UN General Assembly in September 1992 and then its approval on November 30, 1990, and then with the signing of START II on January 3, 1993, and its subsequent submission to the US Senate.[740]

Several officials identified the Un-Group as possibly the "single most successful interagency group" of the Bush presidency. While it is by no means clear that it was more effective than the "small group" convened during Desert Shield and Desert Storm or the Deputies Committee, which was the workhorse for the administration, the Un-Group was no doubt among the most effective of the administration's interagency groups.[741]

Giving impetus to the administration's management of the problems of potential nuclear proliferation and the possible sale of enriched uranium to third parties was the Nunn-Lugar Act, also known as the Soviet Nuclear Threat Reduction Act of 1991. The Nunn-Lugar Act, which Bush signed on December 12, 1991, authorized $400 million for the Defense Department's use. It dedicated $10 million in February 1992 to help with many scientists, engineers, and laboratory managers who were now without funding. And it brought about the elimination and destruction of thousands of warheads and hundreds of missiles and launch vehicles over the two decades since its inception.[742] "We didn't think of it before [Sen. Sam] Nunn and [Sen. Richard] Lugar did," Scowcroft conceded. While it might seem astonishing that Scowcroft, with his focus on strategic weapons and a whole career dedicated to reducing the risk of a nuclear exchange, would not have proposed the legislation himself, there wasn't any enthusiasm for it from Cheney and the Department of Defense. The Pentagon wanted to spend more money on SDI, not take money from the Defense budget and its existing programs to help another country dispose of its own nuclear weapons, and Scowcroft may not have wanted to force the issue.[743]

There are other reasons, though, why Scowcroft wasn't more proactive on the matter of loose weapons, leaving Congress to take the initiative. For one, many programs were already underway, as described above. As early as September 1989, Scowcroft and Gates had established an interagency group under Rice (with Ross at State, Wolfowitz from Defense, Robert Blackwell from the CIA, and two others) for the purpose of commissioning CIA studies in the event that the Soviet Union should "go bad in a hurry."[744]

Early on, Secretary Baker was more concerned than Scowcroft (or the Department of Defense) about "loose nukes." "That didn't bother me, because there would be that many fewer [missiles] aimed at us," Scowcroft said. The administration "didn't really come to an agreement" on unified command and control of the Soviet nuclear weapons, Scowcroft said, so he and other US officials just "let the process play out." The republics "were not run by nuts," he observed. "They were all sensible people. To me it was not a big issue" (although he described the secretary of state as being "frantic" on the issue). But as the breakup of the Soviet Union loomed over the course of 1991, especially after the attempted coup, Scowcroft became more concerned about instability and the fate of the former Soviet nuclear weapons establishment.[745]

Beginning in November 1991, the Deputies Committee under the new chairmanship of Jonathan Howe coordinated the administration's efforts with respect to incentives and controls for individual scientists, engineers, and organizations within the former Soviet military complex—which demanded comprehensive and overarching policy as well as close-run programs on the ground.[746]

Yet another interagency group formed because of the Soviet transformation was the successor to the European Strategy Steering Group, which was to consider potential US responses to specific Soviet contingencies such as rebellion or insurrection in the armed forces, escalating ethnic conflict, a dramatic acceleration of economic disintegration, a hemorrhage in military industrial exports, a loss of control of nuclear weapons, Gorbachev's death, resignation or removal from office, Yeltsin's death, resignation, or removal from office, and major industrial or natural disasters.[747]

Scowcroft and the Bush administration *had* been minding the shop, not that everything was wholly under control.

Most significantly, Scowcroft and Bush had proceeded with their own arms-control breakthroughs. After the failed coup of July 1991, Scowcroft realized the United States had the opportunity to press for major arms-control breakthroughs. After Bush and Scowcroft talked over the idea over Labor Day weekend at Walker Point, they went ahead. Scowcroft called for the US bomber force be taken off alert status for the first time since 1955, recommended that the United States remove and destroy all tactical nuclear weapons from US naval vessels except for submarines, and proposed that all ground-launched tactical nuclear weapons, both artillery rounds and Lance SNF missiles, be removed from Europe and destroyed. Perhaps surprisingly, Powell was fully supportive of the initiative, and he and Cheney then worked out the policy specifics. The secretary of defense qualified Scowcroft and Bush's initiative by insisting that half of the naval tactical nuclear weapons be kept in storage rather than destroyed and that the United States explicitly "challenge" Gorbachev and the Soviet Union to match its unilateral actions with specific weapons cuts of its own.

Gorbachev responded almost immediately, announcing the Soviet Union's own set of extensive arms reductions. Although he proposed measures the United States couldn't accept—such as no first use and withdrawal of all nuclear forces from Europe—the Soviet leader agreed to eliminate all SNF and nuclear artillery, to remove all tactical nuclear weapons from naval aircraft, surface ships, and submarines, to remove the alert status on hundreds of ICBMS, and to confine the rail-launched ICBMs to garrison, among other steps.[748]

The Presidential Nuclear Initiative of 1991 (as it became known) was then followed by a second initiative of early 1992, where Bush canceled the silo-based small ICBM (the Midgetman), ended production of the MX, capped production of B-2 strategic bombers at twenty aircraft, and stopped procurement of additional advanced cruise missiles. Most important—and once more following Scowcroft's lead—the Presidential Nuclear Initiative of 1992, which Bush presented in public in his State of the Union Address of January 28, provided that the United States "would eliminate all Peace-keeper ICBMs, download all Minuteman ICBMs to one warhead, reduce deployed SLBM warheads by 'about one-third,' and 'convert a substantial proportion of our strategic bombers to primarily conventional use [contingent on the Russians eliminating all of their MIRVed missiles].'" These measures, the NSC's Susan Koch points out, became "the core of what became the START II Treaty."[749]

Yeltsin and Russian officials followed with their own reductions, as had Gorbachev, by going further with respect to eliminating and destroying tactical nuclear weapons; halting production on strategic bombers, air-launched cruise missiles (ALCMs) and sea-launched cruised missiles (SLCMs); and limiting the size of military exercises. Yeltsin and the Russians sought deeper cuts in strategic forces than the US Department of Defense preferred, however. They sought a reduction to 2,000 to 2,500 warheads, to eliminate all MIRVed missiles, which Yeltsin called "the root of evil" (seemingly echoing Scowcroft). This included SLBMs, a key leg of the US strategic triad and nuclear deterrent. They also proposed ideas the United States wouldn't accept: a ban on antisatellite weapons and further limits on nuclear testing.[750] In subsequent negotiations, Russian Foreign Minister Andrei Kozyrev agreed to exclude SLBMs from the calculus. But the Pentagon considered 2,500 ICBMs to be too few, to the frustration of Baker, who was doing much of the negotiation, even though the Russians would have to de-MIRV 80 percent of their ICBMs and even though both sides were working toward a final target close to the Bush administration's goal of zero MIRVed ICBMs without eliminating MIRVed SLBMs.[751]

The Russians finally proposed a range of 3,800 to 4,250 total warheads in the first phase (through the year 2000) and between 3,000 and 3,500 in the second phase (up to 2003). Bush agreed, declaring "the nuclear nightmare recedes more and more for ourselves, for our children, and for our grandchildren." The agreement eliminated land-based ICBMs and set the lowest overall level of ICBMs since 1969. START II was signed on January 3, 1993—only one and a half years after START. But it was not ratified by the Senate until January 1996 and, conditionally, by the Russian Duma in 2000, and never fully went into effect.[752]

With START, the administration's unilateral initiatives—hoping for the Soviet Union and then Russia to reciprocate—and START II, President Bush and his top advisers did much to greatly reduce, if not eliminate, the chance of a nuclear Armageddon—the world portrayed by Nevil Shute in *On the Beach*, ABC in *The Day After*, and other novelists and screenwriters.

The end of the Cold War and the reductions in conventional and nuclear force levels called for a variety of adjustments for the United States and the Soviet Union (and then Russia). For the Soviet Union, demilitarization was "more a social problem than a military one," Treasury Secretary Brady observed. "Seventy percent of their industrial base connected to the military and the workers are the elite and highly paid. The Soviets cannot just shut these plants."[753] Most of the conversion of the Soviet military-industrial base would happen after Bill Clinton took office.

Meanwhile, the United States was embarking on its own post–Cold War conversion in light of the collapse of the Soviet Union, Americans' demands for a peace dividend, and the sluggish US economy. The United States had given up the use of tactical nuclear weapons. It revised the Single Integrated Operation Plan (SIOP), which was finally eliminated in 2003. It cut back its forces in Europe to 150,000 troops. It closed military bases following the recommendations of the Base Re-Alignment and Closure Commission, and the Navy reduced President Reagan's 600-ship fleet to approximately 450 vessels. Scowcroft also began shutting down covert activities against the former Soviet Union, program by program.[754]

SDI (or missile defense) occupied marginal ground as a component of US strategic forces. SDI was kept out of the START I and START II negotiations, even as it remained in the background. By the late 1980s, the missile defense program had acquired a constituency within the Department of Defense, large defense contractors such as Motorola and Raytheon, scientists and universities, and individual lawmakers. Helped by the apparent success of the Patriot missiles used in the Persian Gulf War, moreover—under the mistaken assumption by many that the relatively simple Patriot missile technology was equivalent to a functioning missile defense system—the Missile Defense Act of 1991 passed in midyear.

But given the technical hurdles faced by a missile defense system and the fact that neither Scowcroft, Cheney, nor Bush had the emotional connection with SDI that Reagan and his aides did—Vice President Quayle was an exception—the Bush administration scaled back funding for SDI to about $3 to $4 billion a year. Halfway through the administration, the emphasis evolved from research toward a complete nuclear shield to a system that could target a handful of incoming missiles—the Global Protection Against Limited Strikes, which the Pentagon announced in February 1991. Despite the fact that Scowcroft had never been much of a supporter of a missile defense system (and had previously said so in his report to President Reagan on the MX and US strategic forces), he kept his own counsel and didn't speak out against SDI, notwithstanding its cost and the opposition of the Soviets and the Russians.[755]

Even more important to the Soviet and Russian leaders than nuclear weapons were their economic problems. Had Gorbachev adhered to a clear plan of economic reform, the Soviet Union may well have been able to develop a more efficient market system and attract more investment. (Yeltsin in 1992 created hundreds of thousands of privately owned farms, for instance.) Instead, Gorbachev knew little about economics, and now, as the leader of the losing side in the Cold War, he wanted assistance from the victors. Consequently, the feelings of triumph and relief among Bush administration officials upon witnessing the Soviet Union's progressive deterioration were mixed with those of consternation and puzzlement.

Yet the demise of the Soviet empire opened up a range of hopeful possibilities. "I believe we in the West—especially the members of this Alliance—must act in concert now for we face an historic opportunity to turn the demise of communism into victory for democracy and economic freedom," Baker explained to other foreign ministers at a NATO meeting on December 19, 1991. "Were the democrats in Russia, Ukraine, Belarus, and elsewhere to fail, we would all suffer." The secretary of state warned of the "grave dangers posed by anarchy or authoritarian reversal in the former Soviet Union" and spelled out several particular challenges facing the United States and the West: the collapse of central control and the devolution of power to the republics; the absence of "anything concrete" to replace the Soviet Union and the need to prevent "further disintegration and the chaos that that disintegration could bring"; the command and control of nuclear weapons; the deteriorating economic situation with "very long" food lines and an "extremely anxious" Russian public with the winter ahead; and the lack of consensus among the leaders of the several republics on what they were going to do next.[756]

Yet by speaking of the challenges facing the United States and the West, Baker's statement somewhat misrepresented the situation. The United States did not have an unlimited capacity to help or hinder Soviet and Russian reforms.

Over the course of the Bush administration, the imbalance between the superpowers became ever more obvious, as epitomized by the several long telephone conversations Bush had with Gorbachev to gently tell him that the United States was going to proceed with the ground war against Iraq, notwithstanding the Soviet Union's efforts to bring about a last-minute peace settlement. Yet Bush, Baker, and Scowcroft continued to be considerate of Gorbachev, Shevardnadze, and other Soviet leaders. "I don't think we're dealing in terms of victory and defeat," Bush told reporters after the July 1990 NATO summit. He viewed those "kinds of rhetoric" as "counterproductive." "We're dealing in terms of how do we stabilize and guarantee the peace and security of Europe."[757] Not until the 1992 State of the Union address, with Gorbachev no longer in office, with the Soviet Union dissolved, and with the 1992 election campaign underway, did the president begin to boast about the administration's accomplishments in bringing the Cold War to a peaceful end.

The administration set clear limits to its willingness to help the Soviet Union economically. "Gorbachev must understand the political context in which we all operate," Scowcroft wrote in June 1991. As long as Soviet leaders continued to devote "at least one-fifth, and probably more, of its GNP to defense," to provide "financial support to regimes such as that in Cuba and Afghanistan," to refuse "to extend 'New Thinking' to the Asia-Pacific region," and to allow "tensions to continue in the Baltics," he stated, the United States couldn't help. The United States and the West shouldn't be "throwing money at a problem," Scowcroft advised the president in advance of the 1991 G-7 meeting in London. He didn't think the Soviet Union should reschedule its debt, since it "would greatly curtail the Soviet Union's future access to external credit." Neither was he "prepared to break Bush's attempts to balance the budget." Rather, the United States should "offer strong support without large scale financial assistance" by focusing on procedural issues.[758]

Some, including Blackwill, Baker and his aides (Dennis Ross in particular), former president Nixon, and others suggested the United States and the West put together a large aid package—a new "Marshall Plan"—for assisting the Soviet Union. Scowcroft was sympathetic, but he pointed out that war-ravaged Western Europe had had the educational and legal structures for rebuilding in place and only lacked capital, whereas the Soviet Union and Warsaw Pact countries lacked the necessary political and social institutions. Instead, Scowcroft was prepared to offer a generous package of measures to "normalize our economic relations with the USSR," including a trade bill, the granting of most-favored-nation (MFN) trade status, repealing congressional restrictions on Export-Import financing and the Overseas Private Investment Corporation (OPIC), and special associate status at the IMF and World Bank, conditional on "Soviet adherence to and implementation of a truly wide-ranging economic reform program." But the "absence of conditionality would result in wasted resources and do nothing to encourage the transition to a market economy," he said.[759]

Scowcroft was skeptical of the Soviet efforts at economic restructuring. He opposed the notion of a "grand bargain," proposed in May 1991 by the American political scientist Graham Allison and the Ukrainian economist and politician Grigori Yavlinsky: that the administration give generously to the Soviet Union so that it could import badly needed goods and pay off its debts. Not only was there some internal resistance among Soviet officials who wanted to avoid being supplicants to the United States or be seen as dependent on American patrons, there was also no guarantee to US officials that the money wouldn't be squandered.[760] Neither the public nor Congress nor the Bush team were eager to funnel money toward the Russians under the circumstances, and the Treasury Department firmly resisted any Marshall Plan–type program. "We didn't give them economic aid because we just couldn't see how to do it without putting money down a rat hole," Scowcroft later said.[761]

The administration further believed that any foreign aid money should go to the countries of Eastern Europe, given their grave economic problems, rather than to Russia, whose reform efforts appeared to be flagging. Scowcroft wrote his colleagues in late May that "the economic situation among Europe's new democracies is getting worse, as noncompetitive industries are feeling the full brunt of transformation." He warned that "any shift of resources—or even apparent shift of attention—away from helping Central and Eastern Europe could have adverse economic, political, and even security consequences." Whereas the Eastern European countries had already undertaken many of the difficult steps toward the structural and political reform of their economies, the Soviet Union had not. "Reform is a desperate attempt to prevent collapse," he commented about Gorbachev's plans earlier that month at Camp David, "not an attempt at reform."[762]

The administration was unwilling to provide significant economic assistance until the Soviet Union was "committed to a market economy," Scowcroft stated in May 1991. "When Gorbachev rejected the 500-day plan," he "also undermined any hope of significant financial assistance tied directly to reforms." (The 500-day plan was to free prices and wages, privatize agriculture and industry, cut subsidies to agriculture and industry, restructure the banking and tax systems, and liberalize foreign trade, including making the ruble convertible.) While the national security advisor recognized that "Soviet laws have taken an increasingly radical tone, legalizing private property, commercial banks, foreign exchange markets, and 100% foreign-owned enterprises," it was still "clear that Soviet leaders hold strongly to the notion that administrative measures are the only way to stabilize the economy and get to markets."[763] Indeed, at the London G-7 summit on July 17, 1991—the summit that Mulroney had previously not wanted Gorbachev to attend—the "leaders of the G-7 were left shaking their heads sadly" at how poorly Gorbachev made his case for economic assistance. "It's almost as though he doesn't recognize the severity of the problems," Scowcroft said to Bush afterward, "which might explain why he doesn't acknowledge the need for really drastic solutions."[764]

This was why Bush was embarrassed when Gorbachev asked him over lunch what kind of a Soviet Union the American president wanted. Gorbachev later described Bush as grimacing, though he evidently didn't understand why. The reason was that Bush wasn't able help him achieve the kind of democratic and market-oriented Soviet Union both leaders favored; he couldn't tell Gorbachev—a man he respected and had come to like—how to run his own country.[765]

There was one area in which the United States did exercise considerable influence on Russia's fate. The administration took a hard line on the Soviet Union's debt, estimated at between $65 and $100 billion in November 1991 (whereas it forgave some of the Polish foreign debt). In fact, Scowcroft said that the Treasury Department's number-one priority in the fall of 1991 was to ensure that the former Soviet republics would assume the USSR's foreign debt, and it insisted that Russia put up half of the Soviet Union's gold reserves as security.[766]

"The stand of the Group of Seven was extremely tough," Yegor T. Gaidar, deputy premier for economic policy in the Russian Federation, said. "'Either you accept our conditions without any reservations,' they said, 'or we stop the negotiations and thus stop all credits, including food credits.'" The Treasury under secretary for international affairs, David Mulford, didn't disagree: "The alternative that the Soviets faced," he told reporters, "was simply catastrophic"—default on debt repayment, an immediate and near-complete halt to their foreign trade, and the collapse of their financial system. But as one State Department official noted, the debt "locked them in."[767]

The United States did help with $1.5 billion for Gorbachev in late 1991 (the Soviet leader asked for $10 to $15 billion) and provided food aid to help with the dire shortages. In 1992, Air Force cargo planes flew sixty-five sorties as part of Operation of Provide Hope, fifty-four in February alone, and delivered $189 million and thousands of tons of food and medical supplies. (James Goldgeier and Michael McFaul report that these deliveries also had an ulterior motive: the Department of Defense chose cities in which to drop off supplies so US officials could look at the targets of their planned strategic attacks).[768]

Russia's economic troubles, its potential conflict with Ukraine, and the threat of internal chaos, including a possible military coup, confronted Boris Yeltsin with enormous difficulties. Scowcroft himself was pessimistic about Yeltsin's chances, as he told Bush in a memo written in advance of a February 1, 1992, meeting. Scowcroft viewed Yeltsin's commitment to markets to be "somewhat idealist," noting "there is more courage than coherence to what Yeltsin is actually doing. He put his economic reforms in the hands of a brilliant, but inexperienced team of young economists, who have plunged ahead with explosive price increases without sequencing them properly with other reforms." In addition, there were "unbelievable levels of infighting and intrigue within his government," and Yeltsin's inexperience made it "very difficult for the U.S. and other countries to deal with Russia on small or big issues." Even worse, this "scene of disorganization and chaos" threatened the military stability of the former Soviet Union. Still, Scowcroft hoped Yeltsin would succeed as the president of the Russian Federation and believed this would be in the United States' interest. He recommended that Bush provide Russia with bilateral humanitarian and technical assistance (including an additional $645 million in economic aid) and provide assistance in improving the defense and military relationships between the states.[769]

Former president Nixon weighed in with a long memo to the national security advisor and other key Washington official and opinion leaders, strongly arguing that the United States needed to do much more to help Yeltsin, "the most pro-Western leader of Russia in history." Later, Scowcroft said in an interview that he dismissed Nixon's advice and described the former president as "annoying" and as having "no impact on what we did."[770] (The national security advisor listened to Nixon on other issues, though, as with Nixon's visit to China after the Tiananmen Square massacre. Scowcroft read the former president's long letters, occasionally met with him in person at the White House or elsewhere, and frequently talked with him over the telephone.)[771]

In March 1992, the administration came up with an aid package to complement billions in IMF money and G-7 multilateral deals, with much of the initiative coming from Secretary Baker and his staff. The Freedom Support Act, which passed Congress in October and was signed by Bush on October 24, provided for $410 million in bilateral assistance, a $12 billion increase in the United States' share of the IMF, humanitarian assistance, agricultural credits, resources, and personnel to "destroy nuclear and other weapons, and to convert to peaceful purposes the facilities that produced these weapons," and it offered "support for trade and investment activities of US companies to help lay the economic and commercial foundations upon which the new democracies will rest."[772]

The Bush team also tried to help Russia by encouraging free-market investments. The administration introduced Party officials and Soviet industry leaders to American industrialists and financiers during the 1990 Houston Summit, for example, and at the Moscow summit in late July 1991 the White House brokered a deal for Chevron.[773] As one of Scowcroft's staffers wrote in a report on the "Role of the American Private Sector in the Economic and Democratic Development of the Soviet Union and Its Constituent Republics," the United States "should accord a high priority to the role of the American private sector." It was "American and Western private-sector investment," the report argued, that would bring the Soviet Union the large amounts of capital needed for job creation and sustained economic growth. Accordingly, the "U.S. Government must do everything it can to ensure that the Soviet Union provides a level playing field and an attractive place for American investment."[774]

The Freedom Support Act itself contained numerous provisions meant to further US business opportunities, help small business, and otherwise advance commerce in Russia and the other former Soviet Republics (except Azerbaijan)—despite the fact that these newly opening markets were vulnerable to all kinds of opportunism, cronyism, and corruption. As of July 1992, Yeltsin "had a long way to go," President Bush said to the gathered G-7 heads of state in Munich. "This is a challenge of political economy, not just technology. He needs to establish the fundamentals. He needs a political base through a middle class of property holders; to get retail shops into private hands, as Central and Eastern Europe did; [and] to allow farmers to buy, sell, and mortgage land." Bush further called for the Russian president "to give trucks to soldiers, which will earn them a living and provide competition," and "to break up monopolies." Bush noted that "Yeltsin talks as if he understands, but I'm not sure he does."[775]

The terms of the Freedom Support Act, the nonforgiveness of the Soviet debt—almost $71 billion in external debt as of June 1992—and the priority given to US support of Eastern European countries thus partially belie Scowcroft's statement that the administration was "not at all able to impose its will on the post-Soviet world" and that it was "almost completely unsuccessful in steering the transformation of the Soviet Union." US assistance policies could have an impact on Russia's prospects, but the scope of the assistance was limited. It was not simply because of American impotence but also because of the administration's (and Congress's) decisions not to invest heavily in aid to the Soviet Union and then Russia.[776]

"We're a nation of investors," Bush had told Gorbachev when they met in December 1988 on Governor's Island, "and an investor wants to know what conditions are like today. But an investor is even more interested in the prospective situation." And for most in the administration, the Soviet Union's and then Russia's prospects looked both unstable and unpromising.[777]

Although there is no guarantee that a massive assistance package would have dramatically altered Russia's prospects, a large, structured aid program combined with debt forgiveness might have done an immense amount of good—especially in Russia's crucial first year of independence, with 50 percent of its population below the poverty line. Germany, Canada, and Japan gave far more to Russia than the United States in per capita terms, for instance. But the result was that the Bush administration didn't give Yeltsin and Russia a fighting chance, as Goldgeier and McFaul and others point out.[778]

Despite the Bush administration's preference for Gorbachev and the status quo and despite the slowness of its turn to Yeltsin, the "mistake" of staying too long with Gorbachev appears not to have produced negative consequences. Yeltsin showed no sign of harboring any lasting resentment against the administration for its lukewarm response to him, Baker observed. On the contrary, in a tour the secretary of state made in Russia, Kyrgyzstan, Kazakhstan, and Ukraine in mid-December 1991, he was impressed by a single theme he repeatedly encountered in his travels and discussions with local leaders: "the intense desire to satisfy the United States."[779]

Scowcroft's initial reaction to the end of the Soviet Union was a combination of numbness, disbelief, incomprehension, and pride in what the administration had accomplished after all the years of effort by Bush and his advisers and their staffs. He recognized that the "key actor in the final scenes was most certainly Gorbachev." But the Soviet leader had a fatal flaw, Scowcroft remarked: his vacillation; he didn't make a decision and then follow through. Had Gorbachev had the willpower of Stalin, the national security advisor remarked, "we might still be facing a Soviet Union." Instead, Gorbachev's inconstancy helped clear the way for "the end of an era of enormous and unrelenting hostility," all of which was accomplished "without a single shot being fired." In the blink of an eye, "we were suddenly in a unique position," Scowcroft said, where they were "without experience, without precedent, and standing alone at the height of power."[780]

The national security advisor, like others in the administration, had little sense of what would be in store for them. Even in early 1991, when Condoleezza Rice returned to her faculty position at Stanford, she told the students, "The Soviet Union is still going to be there, the Soviet Union is going to be around for a long time to come." President Bush himself said he had no ambition to end the Cold War, he just "wanted to manage it a little bit better."[781]

For all of the administration's inability to anticipate the fast-changing events, the breakup of the Soviet empire ended up being a remarkably orderly process. Given the scale of the Soviet conventional and nuclear forces, the Communist Party's and the Soviet military's stakes in the status quo, and the centrifugal forces of rising nationalism, the loss of Eastern Europe and the internal instability in the Soviet Union could well have led to military intervention, a civil war, or other kinds of turmoil. Instead, and primarily because of Gorbachev's leadership, the Soviet Union disintegrated with minimal bloodshed, without a war in central Europe and without the use of nuclear weapons. The collapse of the Soviet empire was "one of the most fundamental changes in world history," Scowcroft observed, "and the fact that it took place at all, and so rapidly, and almost literally without a shot being fired is an incredible epic."[782]

But the national security advisor recognized that this was uncharted ground. "My notion about the world that I was entering intellectually as I got deeper and deeper into foreign policy did not really include a world without a U.S.-Soviet confrontation," Scowcroft told interviewers. "Did I think that at some point it would end? Yes. Did I know how it would end? No. I thought that eventually the Soviet Union would change," but that "eventuality was outside the policy framework in which I thought."[783] Little wonder, then, that he expressed "a sense of amazement through the whole administration" at the end of the Cold War and the collapse of the Soviet Union.[784]

In terms of pursuing and achieving the United States' own interests, it's hard to see how Bush, Baker, Scowcroft, and the rest of the administration's team could have handled the end of the Soviet Union much better. They crafted a set of objectives and moved systematically toward achieving them. The pause in US-Soviet diplomacy during 1989 gave Bush's foreign policy team the time it needed to prepare and allowed it to set the terms of engagement, while the changes in Eastern Europe, the Gulf War, and the Soviet economic struggles gave the administration additional leverage, leverage that Bush, Baker, Scowcroft, and their aides used to channel Gorbachev down a path where he would ultimately have very little room to maneuver.

WITH THE END of the Soviet empire, what came next were post–Cold War growing pains—not just with the Iraqi invasion of Kuwait, but also in such widely scattered trouble spots as Yugoslavia, Somalia, Cambodia, Chechnya, Haiti, and Rwanda. The Balkans posed a particularly difficult challenge and ultimately left a black mark on the administration's record, as well as on the records of the United Nations, NATO, and the European Community.

When Tito was in power, it was said that "Yugoslavia had six republics, five nations, four languages, three religions, two alphabets, and one party." With Tito's death in 1980, the fall of the Berlin Wall, and the transformation of Eastern Europe, however, the central government of Yugoslavia under prime minister Ante Markovic came under pressure from growing nationalist movements. And Markovic's new party, which was to reform the Yugoslavian federation, was unable to keep the six republics, five nations, four languages, and three religions from spinning apart and then coming into conflict.

In particular, Slovenia and Croatia, the two northernmost and wealthiest republics, had long resented being controlled by the Serbian-dominated government in Belgrade. There was also deep unrest in Kosovo, a semiautonomous region that had a 90 percent Albanian majority and was of vital cultural significance to Serbia, as well as a strong desire for independence in Macedonia. Meanwhile, Slobodan Milosevic, who had designs for an imperial Serbia, succeeded in undermining Markovic's economic program and securing the loyalty of the Yugoslavian army, the JNA.[785]

The Bush administration had long been aware of the explosive nature of the situation. In October 1990 the CIA predicted, "Yugoslavia will cease to function as a federal state within one year, and will probably dissolve within two." It further warned that "intractable and bitter . . . large-scale ethnic violence" were near-certainties, and that efforts to keep Yugoslavia whole would be "contradictory to advocacy of democracy and self determination."[786]

Scowcroft disagreed with the CIA's analysis. It didn't make sense for Yugoslavia to break up, he thought; it had held together throughout the Cold War and in the years since Tito's death, and it should be able to muddle through again. Eagleburger, who had spent four years in Yugoslavia as a

Foreign Service officer and had been ambassador from 1977 to 1981, agreed with Scowcroft. Both men had lived in Belgrade—not in Pristina, Zagreb, or Sarajevo—and neither wished nor expected to see Yugoslavia disintegrate. Guided largely by Scowcroft and Eagleburger, the administration had no interest in backing either the seceding republics or the Serbian government.

Extremely shrewd and very charming if he wanted to be, Slobodan Milosevic was also duplicitous and ruthless. A former New York investment banker, Milosevic spoke fluent English and knew what buttons to push. After US officials spoke with Milosevic, they would describe Yugoslavia using the same terms and with the same images as those used by the Serbian leader—that it had taken six German divisions to hold the Balkans during the Second World War, for example, or that Yugoslavia ran the risk of turning into another Vietnam. But Milosevic attempted to undo democratic institutions at every turn, made direct appeals to racial hatred, used both the JNA and Serbian civilians to achieve his ends, and capably manipulated the international community to discourage outside interference.[787]

Croatian president Franjo Tudjman, for his part, was anti-Serbian as well as anti-Semitic. The hatred between Roman Catholic Croatia and Eastern Orthodox Serbia was such that of the 1.7 million Yugoslav deaths in World War II, approximately half were at the hands of their fellow countrymen.[788] Meanwhile, Bosnia and Herzegovina had a near-majority of Muslim residents, and it wasn't obvious to the Bush administration how secular an independent Bosnia would be.

When Tudjman visited Scowcroft in Washington in September 1990, begging him to support the establishment of a Yugoslav confederation of sovereign states, Scowcroft told him he supported the unity of Yugoslavia "at any cost."[789]

The following summer at the Berlin CSCE meeting of June 19 and 20, 1991, Baker informed the Slovenian and Croatian representatives that the United States strongly disapproved of "preemptive unilateral actions" and that the administration wanted to see the Yugoslavian situation resolved peacefully. Later, Baker traveled to Yugoslavia, where he held extensive talks with republican leaders. But they wouldn't budge from their demands for independence, with one Croat leader complaining that the "owner of the biggest ranch in Wyoming" couldn't escape "the American tradition of demonizing secession."[790]

At a White House meeting on June 25, NATO Secretary-General Manfred Woerner said he didn't think there was any role for NATO in the crisis. Bush then responded, "We're not doing contingency planning. We're not thinking of intervening." Baker cautioned, however, "Once the shooting starts, and I think it will, it'll be a mess." The secretary of state predicted "the equal danger of various gangs starting to shoot at each other. The Yugoslavs will use their army. NATO will not get involved. The emergency mechanism of CSCE will likely be used." "And do what?" Scowcroft asked. "Nothing," Baker replied. Even though the CSCE had just passed "a strong resolution" at the Berlin meeting, the secretary of state feared the "political demands in Yugoslavia are so great, that we may be unable to stop the crisis."[791]

Although it's not clear whether Milosevic deliberately chose to misinterpret Baker's message as an implicit endorsement of the use of force to prevent a breakup of Yugoslavia, Milosevic was intent on using force to secure Serbian areas. Thus when Slovenia and Croatia declared independence on June 26, just three days after Baker's meetings, the JNA moved to seize border positions in Slovenia. The well-organized and well-prepared Slovenian army held off the JNA with few casualties, and the European Community succeeded in negotiating a cease-fire. But with few ethnic Serbs residing in Slovenia, neither did Milosevic very much care if Slovenia seceded.

The issue of Croatia, with a considerably larger population of Serbs, wouldn't be resolved so easily. The Serbian minority resisted and the JNA moved into action when Croatia announced its independence; Serbian forces succeeded in seizing about a third of Croatian territory in fighting that lasted from July through December 1991. Although the members of the European Community voted unanimously not to recognize Slovenia and Croatia should they declare independence, the EC was actually divided, with some members (including France and Britain) favoring a united Yugoslavia, and others (including Austria, Italy, and Germany) supporting the self-determination of Slovenia and Croatia.[792] Meanwhile, the fighting in Croatia, which included the shelling of the old coastal city of Dubrovnik, an assault on Vukovar, mass executions, and systematic atrocities, resulted in an estimated ten thousand deaths, thirty thousand wounded, and one hundred thousand refugees.[793]

Germany proceeded to recognize Croatia and Slovenia on December 23, 1991, notwithstanding Scowcroft's admonition to Kohl in early November that "if we extend recognition to Yugoslav republics that can't defend themselves, and then don't defend them, this will be a disaster."[794]

The Bush administration went back and forth about whether to get involved in first Croatia and then Bosnia when the latter declared its independence in April 1992. But for Scowcroft, just as for Eagleburger, Baker, Cheney, Powell, and the president, the key point was that the Yugoslavian conflict did not merit deploying US forces and risking American lives. Yugoslavia may have played an important role during the Cold War, but that was then. Who now wanted to die for Sarajevo?

The NSC's Arnold Kanter noted that this was the "shared view at the top" as well as a widespread attitude across the government, although it frustrated him as well as others on the second or third tiers of government.[795] Yet it may have reflected something more: the disadvantage of the Deputies Committee was that however effective it was, it "just sucked the life out of the Assistant Secretary level of government," Robert Kimmitt—himself one of the deputies—pointed out. The deputies' workload caused them to burn out faster, narrowed the range and quality of input from the lower levels of government, and discouraged up-and-coming career officials in State, Defense, and the other departments and agencies.[796]

Furthermore, Scowcroft, Eagleburger (who became acting secretary of state in August 1992), and Bush's other advisers perceived—and certainly portrayed—the Balkans as a region of ancient hatreds and timeworn hostilities that outsiders couldn't hope to quell.[797] While this was an exaggerated trope, there wasn't much appetite among the public, members of Congress, and the press for American casualties in a remote corner of the world where US interests weren't obviously at stake. Neither did the administration want to set a precedent of the United States as the global policeman, intervening throughout the world when things went grossly wrong and then having to pick up the tab afterward.[798]

Yugoslavia was a "problem from Hell," one administration official remarked. Not only was the administration worn out from all that they had already accomplished, it was an election year, where the incumbent was being perceived as too absorbed by foreign policy. With 78 percent of Americans in early 1992 thinking the country was on the "wrong track," Bush and his advisers didn't want to descend into Hades.[799]

Scowcroft and Eagleburger considered using NATO air strikes on Serbian forces in Bosnia to drive Milosevic to the bargaining table, and Scowcroft questioned US ambassador Warren Zimmermann extensively about the possibilities. But it was clear that aerial attacks might not be decisive, and no one in the administration was interested in a ground war.

Bush and his senior advisers succeeded in getting a UN resolution passed to deliver relief aid to Sarajevo for a short while in early July 1992.[800] It was impossible to pass any stronger UN resolutions, though, because the Russians wouldn't agree to concerted international actions against Serbia. So Baker and the administration wanted to leave Yugoslavia to Western Europe. Yet the

European countries wanted to minimize their involvement as well. A corps of UN Protection Forces (UNPROFOR) had been established on February 11, 1992, and assigned to protect the lives of the Bosnians. But the lightly armed UN soldiers were ill-equipped to stop the aggressive, heavily armed Serbian irregulars or the JNA, and they were ineffective as neutral third parties.

Too little too late, the UN forces in Croatia and then Bosnia constituted little more than a cover for international inaction. In fact, they effectively served as hostages for Serbian purposes, guaranteeing against any NATO-led air attack. The international response to Croatia and Bosnia was what one writer called "collective spinelessness."[801] By letting Europe take the lead, moreover, the administration contradicted and undermined the new post–Cold War role it had planned for NATO—one in which it would presumably tackle missions precisely such as that in Yugoslavia.

Unfettered by international force, Milosevic proceeded with the "ethnic cleansing" of Bosnians in the summer of 1992. (The term "ethnic cleansing" had been coined in July 1991 in reference to the forced deportations, concentration camps, mass executions, and other routinized horrors being conducted by the Serbs in Croatia, since neither the Americans nor Europeans wanted to use the more honest term "genocide.")[802]

Still, there was a line Scowcroft wouldn't allow Milosevic to cross: a Serbian invasion of Kosovo. The national security advisor's nightmare scenario was that a Serbian attack on Kosovo would cause Kosovars to flee into Macedonia and then further south, into Greece. In that case, Turkey and Albania might come to the aid of Kosovo, and Greece would then decide it had to come to the aid of Serbia, its longtime ally. Not only would this scenario drive a wedge between Greece and Turkey, Scowcroft feared, but a shooting war might break out between the two NATO members. A Serbian invasion of Kosovo could, in this scenario, bring about the end of the Atlantic Alliance.[803]

Bush took Scowcroft's worries to heart. Having received intelligence suggesting a new Serbian deployment in the province, possibly for the purpose of ethnic cleansing, and worried that Milosevic might choose to take advantage of the US presidential transition period to move into Kosovo, Bush sent the Serbian leader a "Christmas warning" on December 25, 1992. Delivered verbatim by the US chargé d'affaires in Belgrade, Bush's message warned Milosevic about violating the UN no-fly zone in Bosnia, attacking UN forces, or interfering with UN relief efforts. It then added a fourth warning: "In the event of conflict in Kosovo caused by Serbian action, the US will be prepared to employ military force against Serbians in Kosovo and in Serbia proper."[804]

Milosevic was puzzled. Why would the United States now, for the first time, threaten to use force in the Balkans? And why did Bush think Serbia was planning to attack Kosovo? (In fact, neither the US embassy nor the Russians had picked up any indication of Serbian operations against Kosovo.)[805]

Some members of the Bush administration were confused as well, if for different reasons. Why hadn't the administration previously drawn a red line in Bosnia, given the Serbian atrocities? And why hadn't the Christmas warning been subject to the same sort of interagency scrutiny that other administration decisions on Yugoslavia received? Dick Cheney, for one, didn't think the United States had any business intervening in Kosovo and, along with others, thought Scowcroft's end-of-NATO scenario was highly improbable.[806]

In the end, the Bush administration left the remnants of Yugoslavia for Bill Clinton's foreign policy team to handle. Subsequent US and NATO intervention, including aerial bombing, the deployment of Navy and Air Force cruise missiles, the use of Army helicopters, refugee resettlement, and reconstruction, would cost the United States more than $50 billion—not to mention the terrible costs borne by Croatians, Bosnians, Kosovars, Serbians, and others. Only after a hundred thousand deaths, millions of refugees, and years of effort by the Clinton administration and the George W. Bush administration would the situation in the Balkans stabilize in 2001, following the war in Macedonia.

If it is an overstatement to call Yugoslavia "the greatest collective failure of the West since the 1930s," as Richard Holbrooke did, it was surely a serious failure. American and European leaders, the United Nations, NATO, the EC, and the CSCE all failed to act in concert in the face of the horrible Serbian atrocities so as to protect their larger, longer-term interests. As some observers have pointed out, the new NATO, the CSCE, and the Western European Union were all put to the test before they were operational.[807] Despite the fact that the Bush administration had insisted to Congress that 150,000 US troops were needed in Europe so as to ensure European stability and peace—indeed, the Rome summit in late 1991 revised NATO strategy to emphasize force projection in lieu of territorial defense—the Bush administration and its chief European allies did not press for NATO intervention.[808]

In addition, the United States actually did have several strategic interests in what happened in Yugoslavia, Ambassador Zimmermann pointed out. It had a geopolitical interest in southeastern Europe, from Italy to Greece to Turkey (as Scowcroft's nightmare scenario made clear). Furthermore, the breakup of Yugoslavia posed a global test of the United States' and the West's post–Cold War leadership. Most significantly, the situation in Croatia and then Bosnia arguably constituted a moral challenge for the United States as both the sole remaining superpower and the standard-bearer of multiethnic societies: was the United States willing to accede to the suppression of pluralism in multicultural societies?[809]

Reflecting back on Yugoslavia, Scowcroft conceded he wished he had handled the situation differently.[810]

———

EVENTS IN THE Horn of Africa would pose the next major post–Cold War challenge faced by the Bush administration.

Following the overthrow of Somali leader Siad Barre in January 1991 and the disbanding of the national army, a civil war had broken out between rival warlords in the impoverished, famine-stricken East African country. The battling warlords stockpiled food as a measure of their power, employed it as a bargaining chip, and used access to food as a weapon against rival clans. By mid-1992 a thousand Somalis a week were dying from starvation. With many more on the verge of starving to death, hundreds of thousands of Somalis fled to Kenya and (in smaller numbers) Ethiopia. In the meantime, gruesome images of gaunt and emaciated children, women, and men were being published and broadcast around the world.

The UN Security Council first became involved in April 1992, trying to see to it that relief organizations could distribute the badly needed food. But the warlords and other groups terrorized the NGOs by stealing the food, seizing relief supplies from airlift landing sites in the countryside, and killing those who refused to pay protection money.[811] Then, in August 1992, the UN Security Council endorsed UN secretary general Boutros Boutros-Ghali's plan for an emergency airlift to deliver relief supplies to the worst-hit areas in southern Somalia and to deploy 550 lightly armed Pakistani UN troops to serve as a peacekeeping mission.

The United States also got involved. In response to the widespread news coverage of starvation in Somalia and Bill Clinton's campaign criticism of US inaction, President Bush met with Baker, Cheney, and Scowcroft on August 12 and decided to supplement the UN effort with Operation Provide Relief, which was to deliver food and medical supplies to Somalia by helicopter airlift from Mombasa and other Kenyan sites. From August 1992 through February 1993, US aircraft made nearly twenty-five hundred sorties and delivered almost thirty thousand metric tons of relief supplies. Yet with the increase in aid came a pervasive sense for many in Somalia that everyone—everyone who had the wherewithal, that is—could take what he wanted. As a result, the actual amount of food reaching those Somalis in need fell by 40 percent over the course of the fall of 1992 as a result of increased looting and hoarding by the warlords.[812]

As the weeks went by, pressure to act increased on the United States. Yet there were also strong arguments against doing anything. Bush's advisers were concerned about opposition from members of Congress, political commentators, and the public to undertaking a significant relief mission in the absence of a US vital interest in Somalia (to be distinguished from a compelling humanitarian interest). The US military was already providing relief in northern Iraq, helping with the cleanup in Florida from Hurricane Andrew, and housing Haitian refugees in Guantanamo Bay. In addition, Stephen Hadley and other Defense Department officials warned that should US forces be deployed, they would become the object of guerrilla attacks and would have a difficult time getting out once they were in. As the US ambassador to Kenya Smith Hempstone quipped, "If you liked Beirut, you'll love Mogadishu."[813]

The drumbeat of bad news continued. The International Red Cross estimated that between 1.5 million and 2 million Somalis, or about one-third of the population, were in danger of dying from starvation if nothing was done. In response, the 102nd Congress (1991–1992) held more hearings and passed more bills, resolutions, and floor statements having to do with Somalia than it had for any other country. With the "CNN effect" and the grim reality of the Somali situation, the White House consensus shifted.[814] "Isn't there something we can do?" the president started asking.

Scowcroft (and Gates) argued that the international community would have to commit to a long-term intervention in Somalia if it were to be successful, and they wanted to deploy the US military and provide the leadership that the world needed with the end of the Cold War. Other Bush aides agreed; they thought that by acting, the president could leave office by acting decisively—an antidote to the depression his electoral defeat had brought on.[815]

The NSC Deputies Committee met several times in mid- and late November in an attempt to hash out a policy on Somalia, but the deputies were unable to reach any kind of consensus. The State Department, with the US Agency for International Development and the Office of Foreign Disaster Assistance, wanted to establish "points of security" or "zones of tranquility" so as to be able to deliver relief supplies, but didn't recommend deploying

US troops. The Defense Department thought that significant numbers of troops would be needed if the relief effort was to be effective—something along the lines of Operation Provide Comfort in northern Iraq after the Gulf War—but the Joint Chiefs resisted sending ground troops.

Not until November 21 did the vice chairman of the Joint Chiefs of Staff, Admiral Jeremiah, break the gridlock, stunning the other deputies in the process, by proposing that the United States deploy ground forces.[816]

For the Pentagon to volunteer to send troops into action was highly unusual, as we saw with Desert Shield and with Yugoslavia. But Jeremiah and Powell had visited Somalia in October and been shocked at what they saw. Too, the Joint Chiefs wanted to establish that the military could do the job if need be—and they considered the relatively flat terrain of Somalia to be more favorable for military action than rugged and wooded Bosnia. The Joint Chiefs were impatient with questions about the US military's capability and will to fight. They saw the issue in Somalia *not* as one of the US military's capability and will, but as a policy decision.[817] It may be, too, that Jeremiah was aware of Scowcroft's and Gates's position on Somalia: they wanted the United States to act decisively.

Meeting on November 23 and 24, the Monday and Tuesday before Thanksgiving, the Deputies Committee drafted three options to present to the National Security Council, scheduled to meet Wednesday morning. Option 1 was for the continuation of Operation Provide Relief in support of the United Nations. Option 2 was for the United States to organize a multinational force under UN command and to provide airlift, sealift, logistical support, and communications—though not ground troops. Option 3 called for the deployment of US forces, ground troops included, with the United States retaining command and control rather than ceding them to the UN; the Pentagon would then be able to direct operations and determine the size of the force, as Powell and the Joint Chiefs wanted.[818] That same Tuesday, the UN secretary general wrote President Bush, asking him for assistance (letters he also sent to the other members of the UN Security Council).

The president began the Wednesday NSC meeting by saying, "We want to do something about Somalia." Moved by the searing images from Somalia and wishing to spare President-elect Clinton from having to immediately confront a messy problem needing military action, Bush chose the third option, to send in two infantry divisions—the 1st Marine Division and the Army's 10th Mountain Division to lead Operation Restore Hope—in order to accomplish what the UN was unable to do. The president also chose Robert Oakley as the administration's special envoy to Somalia.

The president and Scowcroft emphasized that the operation would be a limited one, and insisted the troops be out by January 20, 1993, leaving the long-term control of the mission to the UN. But Cheney and Powell warned Bush and Scowcroft that getting out in less than two months' time was almost certainly unattainable; the chairman of the Joint Chiefs also expressed concern about the later transition to UN control.[819]

That afternoon, Bush sent Eagleburger up to New York City to inform a happily surprised Boutros-Ghali of the US decision. And on December 3, the UN Security Council unanimously passed Resolution 784, which allowed a UN member to "create a secure environment." Given the amount of force needed to disarm the warlords and ensure the safe distribution of food and other relief supplies, the US mission didn't exactly fit the practice and principles of UN peacekeeping. So the UN agreed to endorse the US effort, allowing a US commander to carry out UN resolutions (as with Korea in 1950 and Iraq in 1991). However, Resolution 784 did not spell out the precise relationship between the US initiative and official UN operations, nor did it explain how the mission would resolve Somalia's chronic problems.[820]

President Bush proceeded to telephone other foreign leaders to ask for their assistance. All major allies except Britain quickly agreed to assist with the relief effort; twelve countries offered 13,659 troops to serve with the United States in the mission to "disarm, as necessary, forces which interfere with humanitarian relief operations," and a total of twenty-three nations (including Britain) eventually contributed troops or equipment.[821]

The first US troops landed in Somalia on December 9, 1992. The US-led effort, known as the Unified Task Force under CENTCOM's commander in chief, Gen. Joseph Hoar—who replaced Schwarzkopf at the head of CENTCOM—soon achieved some success. Over the next several weeks, UNITAF succeeded in destroying many of the "technicals" (trucks mounted with heavy machine guns, light cannons, or mortars) and much of the extensive arms caches of the warlords. It opened the port of Mogadishu and succeeded in getting food and other supplies distributed. In fact, two days after the landing of US Marines in Somalia, on December 11, Oakley got the two chief rival warlords, Mohammed Farrah Aidid and Ali Mahdi Mohammed, to sign a cease-fire. Bush even had fifteen hundred troops withdrawn by January 20, 1993.[822] But the balance of the twenty-eight thousand US soldiers and coalition troops remained in Somalia, since even with the immense amount of aid the United States was delivering, the looting continued and most food was still not reaching its intended beneficiaries.

In the period before Clinton's inauguration, Scowcroft briefed the president-elect daily on the developments in Somalia. Once in office, the new

Clinton administration took a longer view of the Somalia crisis. It strongly supported a nation-building effort in the country, since if the Somalia situation was to be remedied, political solutions, including the removal of Aidid, would be necessary. So the relief operation continued, and on March 26, 1993, UN Security Council Resolution 814 gave the UN a nation-building mission and set up a new UN command (UNOSOM II) under an American force commander, Admiral Howe—Scowcroft's former deputy.[823]

Later that year, in early October 1993, came "Black Hawk Down" (or the Battle of Mogadishu), when two US Black Hawk helicopters were shot down, eighteen Americans were killed, and about eighty were wounded. The United States continued to participate in the UN mission, helping Howe and UNOSOM, until it finally threw in the towel—an image Howe used—in March 1994.

Despite the limited success of UNITAF in 1992 and early 1993, the larger lesson of Somalia was that the UN Security Council's stated ambitions didn't match what UN forces, even under a US commander, could realistically accomplish. Not so much an out-and-out failure, the Somalia mission manifested the disconnect between rhetorical ends and operational means. President Clinton and his advisers did not want to commit the forces necessary for either the Unified Task Force or, beginning on March 26, the UN mission to succeed at further disarming, better distribution, and nation building. Complicating matters for the UN was the personal animosity between UN secretary general Boutros Boutros-Ghali, an Egyptian, and the Somali warlord Mohammed Farrah Aidid.[824]

The Somalia case also points to a second lesson: the inability of the United Nations to work effectively without either NATO or a single major power having the will and dominant capacity to support the UN mission (as was the case with Desert Storm). "You can't have thirty different hands on the tiller," Howe said in February 1994, looking back on the frustrating experience of dealing with UNOSOM contributors who were "either unresponsive or working at cross purposes." As a result, UNOSOM constituted an incoherent force and turned the force commander into little more than a figurehead.[825]

Somalia signified a new kind of engagement for the United States and the United Nations in the post–Cold War era: a mission that was neither precisely a peacekeeping operation nor precisely a military operation and that involved armed intervention without prior approval by the existing political authorities in the affected area.[826] It didn't put the United States in the role of the global policeman, but rather reflected the concept of shared international responsibility for undertaking limited measures to address serious humanitarian crises.

On balance, Scowcroft believed, American intervention in Somalia was appropriate, given the country's sensitive location, the scale of the humanitarian crisis, and the military and logistical capacity of the United States and other UN member states. But in other circumstances, such as with Haiti in 1994 and Syria in 2013, he believed such intervention would be unwarranted.

The mixed success of the Somalia mission suggested that there are no easy solutions to the human tragedies that can arise when ethnic and political hatreds combine with such age-old human traits as greed and lust for power—worldly realities that the passing of the Cold War had done little to change.

26

CHINA RISING AND
THE INTERNATIONAL ECONOMY

IN THE TUMULT of 1989, Romania had been the only East European country to attempt a Chinese-style solution to mass public unrest. Nicolae Ceausescu ordered the army to attack protestors in Romania's capital city, Bucharest. But the Romanian leader was unable to prevent the military from joining the rebels, and when he and his wife tried to escape into the countryside, they were soon captured and then shot.[827]

As noted earlier, the executions traumatized the Chinese Party leaders, especially since Romania had been China's staunchest ally in Eastern Europe. Jiang Zemin, Deng's handpicked new party secretary, had spent part of his career in Bucharest and even spoke some Romanian. And Scowcroft recalled that, shortly after the Tiananmen Square massacre, the Chinese had commented on the strength of the Romanian government.[828] Thus the downfall of the Romanian government badly scared the Chinese ruling class. Within a week, the Chinese leaders held several sessions of the politburo's standing committee and convened a plenary meeting with all of the politburo members and another with the first secretaries from the provinces and the autonomous regions.[829]

Deng Xiaoping repeatedly emphasized the paramount importance of the continuity of the Chinese state. The lesson from Romania was that the leadership had to be ruthless in the suppression of protests so as to ensure stability—albeit preferably out of public view, as quietly and unobtrusively as possible. "Close the door," as the Chinese saying once quoted by Ambassador Lilley went, "to beat the dog."[830]

The death of the Ceausescus ended the momentum toward the improvement of US-China relations following the Nixon, Kissinger, and Scowcroft visits in the aftermath of the Tiananmen Square massacre. It "froze everything" and reversed the progress of US-China relations. China continued to jam the Voice of America, and the Chinese media kept attacking American values and policies. And in April 1990, as will be discussed later in this chapter, the Chinese cancelled the Peace Pearl project.[831]

American attitudes toward China shifted in response. Vice President Quayle, for instance, judged Scowcroft's two visits as essentially failures, having produced intense controversy but few results. Like many other conservatives and human rights advocates, Quayle essentially gave up on China, believing that Chinese leaders were blind to the inevitable victory of freedom and democracy.[832]

For a time, positive steps in US-China relations were few and relatively insignificant. On December 19, 1989, a few days before the Ceausescus were shot, President Bush allowed the Export-Import Bank to lend money for the construction of the Shanghai subway system (a project that included several American subcontractors). On January 11, 1990, Chinese leaders lifted martial law in Beijing. On June 25, the Bush administration agreed to proceed with the sale of $2 billion worth of Boeing 757 jets. On the same day, Ambassador Lilley finally arranged for Fang Lizhi's release after many months of negotiations, ostensibly for reasons of health (a heart murmur): Chinese officials agreed to allow Fang to leave London (he would eventually go to the United States), while the US government agreed not to use Fang for political purposes. And at the G-7 summit in Houston in July, 1990, Bush and Scowcroft agreed to the resumption of suspended loans to China from the World Bank ($1.6 billion) and Japan ($5.6 billion).[833]

More complicated was the administration's effort to renew China's most-favored-nation (MFN) trade status, which encountered heated opposition from Congress and involved intense lobbying by the Congressional Liaison Office, Scowcroft, and others. The White House solicited the participation of "special interests," such as Boeing, grain producers, and wood product manufacturers, and asked former presidents Nixon and Ford to contact members of the Senate on behalf of China's MFN status. And Baker pointed out to US senators that since Scowcroft and Eagleburger had been to Beijing, China hadn't sent M-9 missiles to Syria or medium range missiles to the Middle East, nine hundred political prisoners had been released, and martial law had been lifted.[834]

The renewal was passed conditionally on May 24, 1990, which gave the United States leverage over China during the international maneuverings after the Iraqi invasion of Kuwait. Not wanting to alienate itself from the United States or from nonaligned states—where China had formerly been the head of the nonaligned movement—China abstained from the vote on the UN Security Council resolution of November 29, 1990, which authorized the use of all necessary means against the Iraqi occupation of Kuwait, rather than vetoing the resolution.

But China's nonveto didn't come about easily. As Robert Suettinger reports in his book, *Beyond Tiananmen*, Qian Qichen, the Chinese foreign minister, refused to disclose to Secretary Baker how he would vote—and this after he accepted Baker's invitation to come to Washington. Baker was outraged at Qian's refusal to commit to a decision, and when he then told the Chinese foreign minister that President Bush couldn't fit him on his schedule—Qian had assumed a visit with the president would be part of his visit to Washington—Qian was, in turn, outraged. The Chinese ambassador in Washington then called Scowcroft at 3:00 A.M. to see if Bush would see Qian.[835]

Scowcroft agreed to accommodate Qian. The administration did not need an international crisis on its hands after its success with the UN Security Council vote, he later explained, so he set up the meeting. The Chinese got their photographs of Qian and the president—despite White House efforts to the contrary—which were then reproduced in all the major Chinese newspapers.[836]

But Baker got the last word. President Bush's talking points prioritized human rights, missile proliferation, and intellectual property rights—all sore points with China. Afterward, both sides tried to put the best face on what had happened, but Congress, influential voices in the American press, and some in the administration—Baker especially—were ever less tolerant of what they viewed as a politically repressive and religiously intolerant government that dumped low-cost or pirated good in the United States and sold weapons and military technology to unstable Third World states.[837]

Almost one year later, on November 15, 1991, Baker made the first Cabinet official to visit to China since the Tiananmen Square massacre (although Under Secretary of State Kimmitt had visited on May 1991). Attuned to public relations, Baker avoided Scowcroft's mistakes. He made sure that there was only a working dinner during the negotiations—with no state dinner, no official banquet, and no diplomatic toasts that could be photographed. By doing so, however, he denied Chinese authorities the domestic publicity they wanted and thereby sowed the seeds for a difficult set of meetings. Baker and Qian proceeded to engage in tough, protracted negotiations over missile sales, arms proliferation, economic cooperation, and human rights issues, with Qian conceding nothing. Baker then met with Li Peng the next day in a bitter, antagonistic round of talks, what Douglas Paal called the "worst meeting he had been to in his life." Baker ended up delaying his departure from Beijing no fewer than seven times during the visit, but the unpleasant sessions had a payoff. Qian persuaded his colleagues to make concessions on missile sales, to reiterate China's support for the Nuclear Non-Proliferation Treaty, and to negotiate further with the United States with respect to trade in goods made by prison labor and intellectual property rights. And Baker pledged the United States' support of China's bid to join GATT and to cancel its ban on China's satellite exports.[838]

That same month, in November 1991, Deng Xiaoping began to lay the foundations for the liberalization and reform of China's economy. He and Jiang Zemin foiled an attempt by hard-liners to arrest their economic reforms, Deng called on party officials and the media to mute their criticism of the United States and the West, and he began to plan what became known as his "southern tour"—an extensive trip through southeastern China designed to herald his plans for a more robust, capitalist-style Chinese economy.

For Deng, Jiang Zemin, Zhu Rongji, and other allies, economic reform was necessary for China's future success, and Deng was willing to take calculated chances—revolutionary steps, even—to realize that success. He and his allies, especially local party leaders in southeast China, believed that unless China wanted to be swept downstream and left behind in a world of ever more interconnected markets, the party had to be willing to experiment with stock markets and to accept the private accumulation of wealth.[839]

It's difficult to overstate how revolutionary these steps were. Though China in the early 1990s was far more affluent than it had been two decades earlier—the department stores stocked merchandise, hotels and homes were furnished in stylish décor, and the women and children were now dressed in bright colors—its economy had scarcely begun its transition to capitalism.[840] While there were twenty banks and more than seven hundred trust and investment companies by 1988 (as compared to the single bank that had existed as late as 1978), all of the banks were affiliated with party offices. When five state-owned enterprises in Shenzhen (near Hong Kong) issued initial public offerings in 1988, they were only 50 percent subscribed.[841] And when Bush visited in February 1989, fewer than one hundred thousand businesses were in private hands. Not until July 1991 would the Shanghai stock exchange open its doors.[842] So Deng Xiaoping's call for experimentation with capitalism and for the creation of special economic districts was a novel and unprecedented move.

At first, Deng's message remained hidden, since Li Peng and other conservatives still controlled the Chinese media. For forty days following Deng's southern tour, there was no public report about his message of economic reform. Word got out nonetheless. Then, on March 11, Deng went public over radio, proclaiming that China "should be more daring in opening and reform." Later that month, the Chinese politburo ratified Deng and Jiang's initiatives. Even Li Peng, who was aware of the political currents, had little choice but to endorse Deng's proposals, while another hard-liner, the seventy-four-year-old Yao Yilin, resigned.[843]

The party leaders were now in agreement, committed to taking a chance on reform. China would become a developmental autocracy as Singapore, South Korea, Taiwan, and Malaysia were previously, with economic and social freedoms coexisting with authoritarian politics and controls on information.

In support of this initiative, the Bush administration negotiated the 1992 Market Access Memorandum of Understanding, whereby China began a rolling five-year tariff reduction on some ten thousand trade items, beginning on December 31, 1992. This was accompanied by the 1992 Intellectual Property Memorandum of Understanding. The two agreements were the most significant of those made between the United States and China and, in the judgment of a former US International Trade Commission official, "contributed significantly to China's economic success."[844]

Capitalist China took off. Jiang Zemin proposed that China should be called a "socialist market economy"—and the next year it was.[845] A Chinese company placed an initial public offering (IPO) on the New York Stock Exchange on October 7, 1992, for the first time ever, and raised $80 million. Over the rest of the 1990s and through the first decade of the twenty-first century, Chinese companies started issuing successively larger IPOs, and the market valuation of Chinese firms soared accordingly. The overall Chinese economy grew by 13 percent in 1992, and foreign investment soared by 66 percent. Comparably rapid growth continued into the 2000s.

The rise of China's special form of capitalism dovetailed with US interests, particularly those of American investment banks and financial firms, manufacturing and trading companies, and consumers.[846] The strength of these interests caused President Clinton, who had run for the White House by linking human rights to economic policy and attacking Bush for coddling the "butchers of Beijing," to reverse his course once in office. Indeed, the boom in US-China commerce ended up profiting Clinton politically, while George Bush, with his fifteen-year history of constructive diplomacy with China, had struggled with US-China relations throughout his presidency.[847]

Toward the end of Bush's term in office, one more serious hitch in the US-China relationship arose. It began when Bush agreed to sell 150 F-16s to Taiwan to replace the Taiwanese air force's fleet of older (and notoriously unsafe) Lockheed F-104 Starfighters.

Domestic politics played a role in the decision. In early 1992, General Dynamics had announced fifty-four hundred planned layoffs at its Fort Worth plant. The US economy was in a slump, and Bush was trailing Clinton badly in the polls. A big armaments deal would give a boost to business and presumably enhance Bush's reelection prospects.

The defense needs of Taiwan also strengthened the case for the deal. China had bought twenty-four SU-27s—known as the "Flanker" to NATO—from the Soviet Union in late 1991. Since China now had longer-range, more potent fighters that it could match up against Taiwan's twenty-year-old aircraft, Taiwan purchased sixty Mirage 2000-5s from France and was prepared to buy even more. But Taiwan and the Bush administration both preferred to have the Taiwanese air force buy the F-16s rather than more Mirages. It was "a compelling case," according to the US Department of Defense.[848]

Baker and Cheney favored the Taiwan deal, though Scowcroft did not. However, once the president decided to go ahead, it fell to Scowcroft to break the news to the Chinese. The Chinese public reaction was one of "controlled fury," especially since only two weeks before the announcement of the F-16 decision the Office of the US Trade Representative had declared $3.9 billion in punitive tariffs as a result of China's market restrictions. The Chinese retaliated by breaking off bilateral discussions on human rights, attacking American "lies and deceit" in the press, announcing the sale of a nuclear power reactor to Iran, and beginning a campaign to contest any change in US-Taiwan relations. But once Bush didn't get reelected—the Chinese had still preferred Bush to Clinton—China sold its M-11 missiles to Pakistan—filling in where the United States had left a vacuum.[849]

The F-16 sale in many ways marked Taiwan's coming of age. Since Taiwan's transformation into a democracy, US officials had in effect moved away from the one-China policy to an undeclared dual-China system. Indicatively, during the presidential transition period before Clinton took office, trade representative Carla Hills visited Taiwan, the first high-level US official to do so since 1979.[850]

———

THE YEAR 1989 had ushered in the most difficult phase of US-China relations since 1972. The most obvious cause was the headline events of that year—the Fang Lizhi incident, the Tiananmen Square massacre, the collapse of the Soviet bloc, and the execution of the Ceausescus. But a more subtle reason was the disappearance of the dominant factor behind the growth of the US-China relationship: the Cold War.

The fact that the United States and China had a shared fear of and enmity toward the Soviet Union was a key factor in the rapprochement between the two powers. This was why the United States had sold avionics and radar equipment, ammunition manufacturing facilities, torpedoes, and other military technology to China during the Carter and Reagan administrations.[851] It was also why the Soviet Union was the chief topic during Bush's meetings in February 1989 with Chinese leaders, and why US Navy ships sailed to Shanghai to show off US-China military cooperation and upstage the Soviet president during Gorbachev's visit to Beijing in May 1989.[852] The collapse of Soviet communism thereby severely undermined the rationale for US-China cooperation.

The impact can be seen in the fate of the so-called Peace Pearl project, a secret $502 million project to upgrade the avionics on Chinese F-8 Crusaders being done at Grumman facilities on Long Island and Wright-Patterson Air Force Base in Dayton. After the Tiananmen Square massacre, the project was suspended for four months; forty Chinese technicians at the Grumman plant were furloughed, along with two Chinese officers stationed at Wright-Patterson AFB. Neither the United States nor China wanted to cancel the project, a Pentagon spokesman noted—but that's exactly what happened just two years later.[853]

So as the Soviet empire deteriorated further with each passing month, so, too, did the geostrategic basis for the US-China relationship further erode. As the Cold War subsided in significance, then, the differences between the two countries came into greater relief—differences over institutions and values that became glaringly obvious after Tiananmen Square. The US-China relationship therefore had to be rebuilt on a new foundation.

One piece of this new foundation was China's quest for economic prosperity. With the thawing of the Cold War, international trade and finance loomed relatively larger in US strategy, and in this area the interests of the two countries converged. China needed access to foreign capital, new technology, and overseas markets; US policy makers and business leaders, for their part, sought access to the vast and growing Chinese domestic market, hoped to be able to invest in new or growing Chinese companies, and wanted to harness China's productive and low-cost labor force. And if American companies didn't get their foot in the door, European companies would.

Another basis for a constructive new US-China relationship was the shared desire to prevent another Cold War. Many feared China would simply supplant the Soviet Union as the new rival superpower—a fear that is widespread in the United States to this day. Scowcroft believed that the way to avoid such a development was to embed China in the global economy and international institutions. A China folded into the world community would be far less likely to become a geopolitical archenemy lurking behind a bamboo curtain. In view of what Scowcroft saw as China's "enormous potential for good or ill," it was very much in the United States' interests to reach out.[854] Too, Chinese leaders shared the desire of American leaders to avoid the expense and dangers of a new Cold War. They appreciated the fact that the United States had (and has) an overwhelming edge in military technology, dominant air power, and a blue-water fleet capable of shutting down the trade and shipping lanes that keep the Chinese economy afloat. Deng Xiaoping had little desire to mount a military challenge to the United States, and he listed military development fourth among China's four points for modernization.[855]

US and Chinese interests also converged in the desire for internal stability within China. Bush administration officials worried about the possibility of a return to Maoism, particularly if the Chinese hard-liners were empowered after a popular uprising or a military coup. So Bush and Scowcroft were eager to defuse tensions in China and to dispel any idea that the United States was trying to take advantage of internal dissension and the instability it might cause.[856]

For all these reasons, Bush and Scowcroft wanted to advance policies that encouraged the development of a more prosperous, more politically stable, and less belligerent China. (During the Clinton administration, in January 1994, Bush and Scowcroft did exactly this; the two visited Beijing on behalf of the Clinton administration so as to give a private presentation and analysis to the Chinese leadership on the politics of the Clinton White House.)[857]

Was the Bush administration being "morally obtuse" with its business-as-usual attitude toward China following the Tiananmen Square massacre, as charged by Col. Andrew Bacevich, an international relations scholar and retired Army officer? As noted by Bao Tong, the former general secretary of the Communist Party, an aide to Zhao Ziyang, and the most senior leader jailed after the Tiananmen Square massacre, "There are miniature Tiananmens in China every day, in counties and villages where people try to show their discontent.[858] And were Bush and Scowcroft being unduly deferential to the Chinese leadership, as Winston Lord has said?[859]

Bush and Scowcroft would say no. The United States imposed more severe sanctions after Tiananmen Square than any other country. But further reactions would only make China's leaders feel less secure and more besieged. "Our efforts may [have looked] one-sided, and maybe objectively they could be considered one-sided," Scowcroft recognized. "But it was a context of a very difficult period for Chinese leaders. They were in a panic."

The Communist Party leaders "perhaps realized they'd made a terrible mistake in the way they had handled Tiananmen Square," he said, but the rulers had "no way to admit that, since that, in a sense, would be acknowledging that they were somehow inferior, and outsiders had a better concept of how the Chinese should manage their affairs than did the Chinese."[860] In Scowcroft's judgment, the adoption of harsher measures against China might have mollified American domestic audiences but would actually have done nothing to lessen political censorship, alleviate repression, promote further political liberalization, or better guarantee human rights. Rather than improving political conditions within China, they would have worsened US-China relations.

After leaving office, Scowcroft wrote that human rights should not be "at the apex of our policy priorities" with China. "Human rights will be best served over time by encouraging the evolution of a market-oriented and more democratic China with ties to the West. Equally, we need to avoid being so mesmerized by the Chinese market (and our fear of losing access to it) that we ignore our other interests," which include "strategic as well as political and economic concerns"—"the Korean peninsula, non-proliferation, and Taiwan" in particular.[861]

Scowcroft recognized that the US-China relationship would "never be warm and cozy," and he appreciated that there were many ways for it to go sour, as with the controversy with Google in China in 2012 or with respect to Chinese military hackers. But he didn't see any reason why there necessarily had to be confrontation. Although China was building antisatellite weapons and submarines (developments that were consistent with the lessons it had learned from the 1995 confrontation in the Straits of Taiwan, Scowcroft pointed out) he recognized that China was "way, way behind" the United States and was becoming increasingly dependent on foreign oil—oil that had to travel on ocean routes that the United States, with its worldwide naval fleet, controlled.[862]

The Bush administration's policy of economic engagement with China combined with (only) mild pressure on human rights has remained essentially in place ever since. "I would say that the most successful foreign policy of the United States has been China policy," Scowcroft declared. "All of the presidents [take different positions in their election campaigns] and are always ending up with a remarkable continuity of policy."[863]

President Clinton is an example. Not long after he took office, he found he had to scale back his demands on the Chinese and accept the fact that neither Congress nor the US business community wanted linkage between economic policy and human rights. China's initial worry about Washington dissipated by 1994.[864] George W. Bush did the same following his anti-China and pro-Taiwan presidential campaign. Both presidential administrations had to adopt more pragmatic—and more realist—China policies as soon as campaigning gave way to governing.

In Scowcroft's view, the administration's "gardening" in China paid off in two chief respects. First, China refrained from challenging the United States at crucial moments—it abstained from voting against the UN Security Council resolution for the removal of Iraqi forces from Kuwait, and it muted its reaction to the sale of F-16s to Taiwan, for example. "China remembered the terrible savaging Bush took for them," Ambassador Lilley said. "And when it came time to collect the fee for that, he could do it."[865]

The other payoff was that, over time, Chinese Communist Party leaders eventually agreed to many of the objectives sought by the Bush administration. They consummated most of the commercial and military deals postponed by the Tiananmen Square massacre; they released Fang Lizhi; they agreed to the UN resolution to end the Vietnamese occupation of Cambodia; and they opened the Chinese economy to the world, encouraging international trade and foreign investment, establishing capital markets within China, and joining the General Agreement on Trade and Tariffs.[866]

These initiatives helped China, to be sure, but they also helped American businesses and inculcated deeper commercial and cultural ties between the United States and China. By virtue of its large trade surplus with the United States and amassed dollars, China has become the leading foreign investor in US Treasury securities and has begun taking significant stakes in US companies and other American assets. China has also achieved faster economic growth than even the "Four Tigers" of the 1980s and early 1990s (South Korea, Taiwan, Singapore, and Hong Kong) and become a much wealthier society, with a middle class numbering in the hundreds of millions. As President Bush told General Secretary Zhao Ziyang when they met in February 1989, after Emperor Hirohito's funeral, "Let me first talk about the trade and investment climate between our two countries. This is an area where we can move forward. . . . Our policy is designed to allow U.S. companies to make the greatest possible contribution to your development."[867]

Most significantly, China's political center has held. For all of the censorship and corruption, there has not been a repetition of the great famine experienced under the Cultural Revolution, much less a civil war. And there's been relatively little violence in recent decades between China and its neighboring states—the occasional rattling of sabers at Taiwan, the disputes over the Senkaku or Diaoyu Islands beginning in 2010, and the computer

hacking in 2013 excepted. Scowcroft and most of the Washington establishment have been comfortable with these trade-offs.

The United States over the decades has tried hard to work with China,
rather than against it, and that "started with Nixon," Scowcroft points out.
He realizes full well, though, that the relationship is still open to debate and
that it remains undetermined with respect to "military issues, human and
political rights, Taiwan, and internal disruption."[868]

As for the notion that the United States was practicing a double standard with respect to China vis-à-vis Eastern Europe and the former Soviet
Union, Scowcroft rejected the premise that there are, or should be, universal
standards applicable to peoples and states. For Scowcroft, China's modest
progress on human rights and political freedoms over the past two decades
had to be weighed against the great advantage of having a stable government
and an orderly society in the face of the centrifugal forces bearing on Communist Party leaders. Things could be worse—much worse.

The administration actually spent about the same amount of time on
Japan as it did on China, but Scowcroft played a much smaller role in US-
Japan relations, since they predominantly involved economic issues, trade in
particular. And in the late 1980s and early 1990s, those issues attracted significant public attention. At the time, the Japanese economy was perceived
as a juggernaut. With Japanese companies buying American factories, prime
real estate, and Hollywood movie studios, American politicians and pundits
dredged up American fears of the "yellow peril"—harking back to World
War II and to Asian immigration in the mid- and late nineteenth century.

Yet for Bush and Scowcroft, the competition posed by Toyota, Hitachi,
Nissan, Sony, Honda, Mitsubishi, and other Japanese companies was of
secondary concern. What mattered to the national security advisor and the
president was Japanese cooperation on military issues, intelligence collection, and East Asian regional security. And on national security issues, Japan
was a strong ally. Other administration officials took their cue from Bush
and Scowcroft and thus likewise didn't heed the anti-Japan hysteria of the
period.[869]

Scowcroft nonetheless conceded that Japan "was probably the most difficult country we had to deal with. I don't think we understood the Japanese
and I don't think the Japanese understood us." His explanation was the two
countries' very different decision-making models: one direct and often confrontational, the other consensual and highly indirect.[870]

Still, the US-Japan relationship was never fundamentally in doubt.
Despite missteps such as the trip in January 1992, when President Bush

famously threw up on the Japanese prime minister's lap, Scowcroft has said he always felt secure about the United States' military and strategic relationship with Japan, never worried about their economic relations, and therefore was willing to delegate almost all of US-Japan policy.

———

THE OPENING OF China to the global economy was a chief component of a larger whole—the Bush administration's push for the expansion and deepening of market economies around the world.

As national security advisor, Scowcroft played a secondary but important role in this economic strategy. He recognized that the national economy constituted a "deep underlying aspect" of the United States' national defense—that economic health constituted the foundation of national security—and he understood the importance of economics as foreign policy.[871] As national security advisor, he oversaw negotiations at the July 1989 Paris economic summit among the G-7 states, helped with the preparation for the Houston economic summit of July 1990, and advised the president on the Uruguay Round of GATT talks and in other G-7 meetings. Although US trade representative Carla Hills, treasury secretary Nicholas Brady, Council of Economic Advisers chairman Michael Boskin, Bob Zoellick at the State department, and commerce secretary Robert Mosbacher generally took the lead on trade policy, Scowcroft "spoke regularly to Bush about economic issues," since economics, politics, and strategy all intermeshed and eventually had to be coordinated. Because the president's briefing books and talking points for his G-7 meetings with foreign heads of state were prepared by the NSC, for example, everything had to go through Scowcroft, Gates, and the NSC staff. And it fell to Scowcroft to judge the soundness of economic policy in relation to national security. As with many other areas of foreign policy, Scowcroft "kept tabs" on what was going on, as Hills put it.[872]

The crowning achievement and chief economic legacy of the Bush administration was its negotiation of the North American Free Trade Agreement (NAFTA), building on and greatly extending the 1988 US-Canada free trade agreement. With NAFTA, President Bush, together with Mexican president Carlos Salinas and Canadian prime minister Brian Mulroney, managed to create a single North American market for industrial goods, to open the service sector after allowing for a transition period, and to protect investors. By the time the Bush administration left office, representatives of the Mexican and Canadian governments had already signed the agreement and the only thing left for the new president to do—no easy thing, to be sure—was to get Congress to endorse it.

The idea for NAFTA arose early in the Bush administration in an informal 1989 conversation between Bush and President Salinas. It was formalized in early 1990 in a series of memos from Salinas and then a meeting in Davos, Switzerland. Scowcroft helped orchestrate the discussions. "Brent was not hands-on," one of his economic experts noted. "But his touch on getting high-level political approval, getting 'all the agencies' on board," and getting the free-trade agreement to be the "subject of negotiations and the ministries of three countries" was indispensable, those close to the trade negotiations attested.[873]

On June 10, 1990, Bush and Salinas agreed on the idea of a comprehensive free trade agreement and began to hash out the details. Canada then notified the Bush administration and the Salinas government that it wanted in, and on May 1, 1991, the United States, Mexico, and Canada committed to the broad outlines of an agreement. Negotiations were completed thirteen months later, on August 12, 1992. They reflected a great deal of careful diplomatic work given the many separate and complex relations involved: finding ways that the three countries could integrate their agricultural and industrial sectors, determining the terms of road and rail connections within North America, and settling on investment and property rules for the three countries, among other issues. Scowcroft made sure that NAFTA was put on a "fast track"—without Congress being allowed to add its own amendments to the tripartite agreement—so that the agreement between the United States, Mexico, and Canada could be signed quickly, and ideally before the 1992 presidential election. The agreement was signed, and later approved by Congress after the Clinton administration took office.

Bush's vision of the global significance of free trade and an open, vibrant international economy was also reflected in US-Soviet relations. It is no accident that the first six proposals Bush and Scowcroft put forward at the US-Soviet summit in the waters off Malta involved economics and commercial relations. Besides calling for the Soviet Union to be granted MFN status and observer status in the next round of GATT meetings, Bush and Scowcroft wanted to expand US-Soviet economic cooperation in agriculture, finance, and small business development, develop a joint anti-monopoly policy, sign a bilateral investment treaty to protect American and other foreign investors, and improve ties between the Soviet Union and the Organization for Economic Cooperation and Development. Following the Malta summit, Bush and Scowcroft then worked to iron out policy differences across the

US government regarding the proposed economic initiatives and asked that the State Department and the Treasury develop legislative and public liaison strategies for removing restrictions on export credits and guarantees.

Later, after the collapse of the Soviet Union, the administration used economic assistance to encourage further free market reform in Russia and to better integrate Russia into the global economy. The Bush administration pushed for more private involvement in agriculture and food distribution, oil, gas, and nuclear power, telecommunications, and other sectors of the Russian economy.

Scowcroft was instrumental in implementing these policies. He had his staff provide briefing materials for conferences, dinners, and other meetings between Russian officials and individual American businesspeople and trade associations. He and his economic advisers worked on reforming Russian statutes with respect to taxes, property, contracts, intellectual property, and barriers to further trade and investment. Thanks to the drastic reforms enacted under Boris Yeltsin and economic reformer Yegor Gaidar, US support helped bring Russia and the sixteen other former states of the Soviet Union into the international economy.

Scowcroft considered international economics the most difficult issue he had to deal with because almost all agencies had some stake in it. For example, when dealing with an issues such as import protections on steel, oil pipes, semiconductors, textiles, machine tools, and other products, the attorney general's office, the Department of the Treasury, the Commerce Department, and sometimes the Environmental Protection Agency (EPA) and the Department of Labor would all get involved. In consequence, the existing organizations, such as the National Security Council or the Principals Committee, rarely handled international economics directly; instead, the administration had to use ad hoc arrangements that involved many top officials from numerous US departments and agencies. (The Clinton administration tried to address this issue by creating the National Economics Council, chaired by treasury secretary Robert Rubin, as a formal organization to integrate international economics policy, in parallel to the NSC.[874])

In contrast to NAFTA, the administration was somewhat less successful with the Uruguay Round of GATT talks, where it came within "a gnat's eyebrow" of completing negotiations before leaving office. However, Europe, and particularly France, could not be brought along in agricultural policy (where the Uruguay Round was the first round of trade talks to include agriculture).[875]

Agricultural policy was the most intractable aspect of international economics for Bush and his senior advisers. US rice growers, sugar producers, and other commodity interests pushed hard for protection of their markets, forcing the administration to grant exceptions on trade policies for some domestic producers and to continue farm subsidies for the wealthy, despite the administration's general practice of preferring open trade.[876]

Dealing with European agricultural interests was especially difficult, since Europe paid more for farmers to grow crops or raise livestock than did the United States and since it provided support to its producers at significantly higher levels. So the Europeans often dumped their crops, given that their costs were higher than the prices their goods could fetch on the international market.

For the Uruguay Round of GATT negotiations, Scowcroft came up with an approach for dealing with three aspects of the issue: domestic price supports, export subsidies, and improved access to European markets. Although the three-part Blair House Agreement concluded between the Bush administration and the European Community—the European Union as of November 1993—didn't go into effect for two years after the administration left office, it became the basis for the final deal of the Uruguay Round.

Economics may not have been Brent Scowcroft's main interest or his chief area of expertise, but with the end of the Cold War, the death of Soviet communism, and the opening of China to capitalism, it had become a central stage for international competition and cooperation—and Scowcroft played a strong supporting role in guiding the Bush administration's efforts to navigate these complex channels. With respect to international economics, in fact, White House officials assumed without question the main tenets of neoliberal economics and the Reagan administration: that markets worked efficiently, that labor issues and environmental problems were of secondary concern, and that regulations as a rule interfered with market efficiency.

But they also believed that there had to be coordination and communication for markets, and worked to create the institutions that would allow US firms to flourish. To that end, the administration established the Asia-Pacific Economic Cooperation forum (APEC) so as to further trade and business relations and cooperation among ministers from twelve (now almost two dozen) states bordering the Pacific Ocean, from North and South America to those on the Pacific Rim. It created the European-American Business Council (EABC, formerly the European Community Chamber of Commerce), which became the TransAtlantic Business Dialogue (TABD), consisting of public and private officials meeting for the discussion of trade and investment issues. And, beginning in 1993, it set up annual summits between US and EU officials.[877]

The environment was a significantly smaller focus, especially for a Republican administration stocked with conservative politicians unsympathetic to environmental causes, most prominently Chief of Staff John Sununu, Vice President Quayle, and agricultural secretary Clayton Yeutter. Scowcroft, though, "had an appreciation of the issue," the NSC's Eric Melby noted, and tried to ease the "tensions between the EPA and the White House." On several occasions, the national security advisor was the only one of Bush's principal advisers to join EPA administrator William Reilly in supporting environmental initiatives. The two of them were the only senior advisers to agree to a ten-year commitment to carbon emission limits, for instance. In the lead-up to the Gulf War, Scowcroft was incredulous that the administration wasn't planning for an energy tax to support the war, Reilly said, and that the United States was doing nothing to inhibit its oil and gas dependency.[878]

Most prominently, Scowcroft thought President Bush "couldn't avoid going to the UN conference" on the environment held in Rio de Janeiro in January 1992, even though the president had initially decided he wouldn't go. But he was persuaded by Scowcroft and Reilly that it was important that the president of the United States be there and "that his absence would be more noticed than his presence," despite the dominant sentiment within the administration.[879] Although the United States' positions didn't change as a result of Bush's presence in Rio de Janeiro—the administration had already committed to doing very little—the president was able to sit down and talk with NGO leaders and heads of foreign states, and eased at least some of the tension through his "natural rapport talking to people."[880]

It was important that Bush, Scowcroft, Reilly, and others represent the United States and that the administration commit morally and rhetorically to pro-environment objectives (even if it didn't bind itself legally). Even so, with the partial exception of the Clean Air Act, environmental policy cannot be regarded as an area of notable achievement by the Bush administration.

27

A NEW WORLD ORDER—OR
THE RESUMPTION OF HISTORY?

ON THURSDAY MORNING, August 23, 1990, Scowcroft and George Bush went fishing on the waters off Kennebunkport. The two had been out for several hours on Bush's cigarette speedboat, *Fidelity III*, and while waiting for the bluefish to bite—they didn't—the men talked about the state of the world following the Iraqi invasion of Kuwait.

It was then that Scowcroft thought up the phrase "new world order."[881] (Soviet premier Mikhail Gorbachev had actually used the phrase in his speech before the UN General Assembly on December 7, 1988, but Bush and Scowcroft do not seem to have been aware of this earlier usage.)

Almost as soon as Scowcroft, his NSC staff, and the Bush foreign policy team took office, they started "casting about" for words and expressions to describe their understanding of the changing world, Scowcroft said. But none of the new phrases they had earlier come up with for the president's speeches, such as "commonwealth of free nations, commonwealth of freedom," or "Europe, whole and free," had caught on. After the Iraqi invasion of Kuwait, however, the need for a new phrase became acute, one that could unite the United States and Soviet Union in their joint effort to repel Saddam Hussein's aggression and uphold the rule of law.

Scowcroft introduced the phrase to the public later that Thursday when he told a reporter, "We believe we are creating the beginning of a new world order coming out of the collapse of US-Soviet antagonisms." He went on, "We want to use the crisis to build support around the world that the behavior of Saddam and the Iraqis is unacceptable. If we can do that, it could be very, very important as we look to the future. . . . We're trying to build an order beyond this crisis."[882] Then, on September 11, 1990, the president used "new world order" in a speech to Congress. And during the rest of 1990 and the first half of 1991, Bush, Scowcroft, and other administration officials made repeated references to the "new world order." By mid-July

1991, the president and top White House officials had spoken of or written about a "new world order" on 325 separate occasions.[883]

Yet even before the Gulf War ended on February 28, 1991, President Bush began to shy away from referring to a "new world order." Although the president and other White House officials continued to speak and write of a new world order for months after the defeat of Iraq, the use of "new world order" as a phrase or caption for the administration's foreign policy faded away. Scowcroft used his own position as national security advisor to slowly suffocate the very concept he had originally launched.

The evolution and early demise of the "new world order" reveals some important truths about the weaknesses and strengths of the Bush-Scowcroft approach to foreign policy.

The "new world order" concept itself always remained fuzzy, since there was no single speech or document in which President Bush explained it clearly and thoroughly. The president consistently emphasized his dedication to the traditional goals of US foreign policy: global peace, freedom from terror, and a more just, prosperous, and harmonious world. Perhaps the chief new element in Bush's quest for these goals was his desire to renew the promise of the United Nations, long stymied by the Cold War rivalry between the United States and the Soviet Union and the consequent paralysis of the UN Security Council. ("United Nations" had in fact been the name for the group of states allied against Germany, Italy, and Japan during the Second World War.) Bush had been US ambassador to the United Nations, of course, and in the 1980s Scowcroft had chaired the United Nations Association of the United States and been very active in meeting with the Soviets on a nongovernmental basis. In that role, Scowcroft had been quite effective in discussions over force reductions, SDI and strategic force balances, and how the United States and the Soviet Union could build up more trust.[884]

Bush and Scowcroft now believed that the end of the ideological and military rivalry between the two superpowers offered the prospect that the United Nations could, for the first time, work as an effective international institution.[885] As NSC counsel Nicholas Rostow noted, "The collapse of international communism and military victory in the Gulf have aroused growing interest in the President's vision of New World Order."[886] The UN would be supported in this work by other international institutions, including NATO, the CSCE, and the European Community, as well as economic organizations such as the World Bank, the IMF, and GATT—all largely guided by the world's preeminent power, the United States. If the "new world order" meant anything, it referred to this general vision—a vision of a "world where the United Nations, freed from cold war stalemate, [was] poised to fulfill the historic vision of its founders," as President Bush told a joint session of Congress in early 1991, one "in which freedom and respect for human rights [could] find a home among all nations."[887]

But the vague concept of the "new world order" swiftly began to draw criticism from both internal and external sources. One NSC staff member wrote a long memo sharply critical of the concept on theoretical grounds, a memo that got wide circulation within the White House. Neither did Gates like the idea; he considered it to be a hollow phrase and joked that the new world order was what happened when Bush and Scowcroft went out fishing and the fish weren't biting.[888]

Henry Kissinger wrote an op-ed arguing that the Gulf War was a one-of-a-kind achievement and opining that, in a world where the United States had "few permanent enemies and few permanent friends," the idea of a new world order didn't make much sense.[889] Some objected that the concept of a new world order placed too great a burden on the United States to play the role of global enforcer of a pax Americana.[890] Critics said that European countries were too self-absorbed, too stingy, and too unconcerned with the rest of the world to provide the funds, matériel, or troops for distant engagements or wars. And the fact that the United States got other countries to pay for the Gulf War was an exceptional occurrence in international relations that portended a worse implication: that the US military was becoming a mercenary force.[891]

Others said that the concept was too idealistic, too Wilsonian. To successfully lead international action, as it had in the Gulf War, the United States would have to depend heavily on the cooperation of an unreliable Europe, an unsteady Middle East, and a UN Security Council and General Assembly that had many undemocratic and illiberal states among its members. On most issues of international consequence, these critics contended, cooperation would prove chimerical.[892] And still others pointed out that the concept assumed the preeminence of Western liberal values: individual human rights, political freedoms, and private property. Where did civil wars, sub-state ethnic rivalries, and other intrastate conflicts (Hindus versus Muslims, Hutus versus Tutsis, Shi'ites versus Sunnis) fit in?[893] And if US-Soviet cooperation was to be the linchpin of the new world order and anchor the UN Security Council, critics further pointed out, the Soviet Union was an unreliable and defective partner, too weak institutionally and too undemocratic to be a genuine partner.[894]

The new world order constituted a bundle of contradictions, other skeptics pointed out. It wasn't "new," since it had been preceded by Woodrow Wilson's Eighteen Points, Franklin Delano Roosevelt's Four Freedoms, and the UN Charter; it wasn't about the "world," since it applied only to those rare circumstances where regional and international consensuses were simultaneously possible; and it didn't provide for "order," since the Gulf War merely restored the status quo ante in Kuwait. The successful liberation of Kuwait hardly provided a reliable precedent.[895]

China posed a particular difficulty. In a February 1991 speech the president gave to the Economic Club of New York City, Bush conceded he had "left China out of the equation" in his discussions of a new world order. He said he "ought not to [have done] that."[896] But Bush, Scowcroft, Kissinger, Nixon, and others were keenly aware there was no chance of any improvement in US-China relations if the United States insisted on the rule of law, on promoting democracy, or on guaranteeing minimum human rights.

It's not known which, if any, of these specific objections appeared compelling to Bush and Scowcroft, but in any case by mid-February 1991 Scowcroft directed Bush's speechwriters to bury the idea. The new world order was not a "full, comprehensive plan," he later explained, but rather "a limited vision of the world and of threat posed by interstate aggression." With the considerable pressure the administration was under in the Desert Storm phase, however, the concept "never found its feet." He and his staff were simply "trying to keep up with things" and come up with a "comprehensive strategy for a world that we were moving to at a rapid rate."[897]

Scowcroft complained that the new world order had become burdened with "grandiose meanings beyond anything he or Bush originally conceived." In fact, he was "openly embarrassed about all the attention and different interpretations of the phrase."[898] So he "persuaded Bush to back off gently" from the vision of a new world order, according to one unnamed NSC official, and got the president to drop plans to develop in early April 1991 a series of four speeches that would "explain conceptually and concretely what we mean by a new world order." Though at the moment the country could capitalize on its strong political and international position, the United States of 1991 was in a period of strategic adjustment—not unlike the way it had been in 1918 and 1945. President Bush spoke of a new world order in an April 13 speech at the Air Force War College, but did not then bring it up in his later speeches.[899]

Scowcroft accepted responsibility for the idea's demise. The administration let it "drift," he conceded, and "never invest[ed] in a new program." The phrase became used "for all kinds of pernicious things, mostly turning the United States over to the UN," he remarked. "You know, if you come from Utah like I do, where every helicopter you hear overhead at night is the UN, you . . . have second thoughts."[900] Yet he also recognized that

Americans have native suspicions "about international organizations taking our freedom" even as the idea of the United Nations is part of Americans' idealism; we "want it in a perfect world," but we are "deeply conflicted as a nation."[901]

A second concept proposed by Scowcroft and Bush in their efforts to accentuate their foreign policy strategy emerged from an implicit dialogue with scholar Francis Fukuyama's description of "the end of history"—the idea that, with the end of the Cold War, global battles over ideology had now been put to rest. In a speech before the Council on Foreign Relations on September 11, 1991, Scowcroft spoke instead of "the resumption of history." He argued that the rise of international communism and the bipolar rivalry that resulted had interrupted the course of history. Now the world could get back on track. He pointed to the renewed desires of people everywhere for economic opportunities, political liberties, and self-determination, and to the great challenges facing the United States with respect to Russia and the former Soviet Union, Eastern Europe, China, and resurgent nationalisms. There was going be a new world order, regardless of what the Bush administration did. The real questions were what kind of an international order would there be? And what role would the United States play in this transformed world?

Less than two weeks later, President Bush spoke of the resumption of history in an address before the United Nations General Assembly. "Communism held history captive for years," Bush said on September 23, 1991. "It suspended ancient disputes; and it suppressed ethnic rivalries, nationalist aspirations, and old prejudices. As it has dissolved, suspended hatreds have sprung to life. People who for years have been denied their pasts have begun searching for their own identities—often through peaceful and constructive means, occasionally through factionalism and bloodshed." For Bush, the "revival of history"—the world of today—ushered in an era "teeming with opportunities and perils."[902] However, like the "new world order," the "resumption of history" was doomed to quickly fade from the world's consciousness, as neither Bush nor his team invested further in the concept or tried to use it in articulating an overarching vision.

The fact is that the Bush administration "didn't have any great ideas about how the world was going to go," Scowcroft admitted. "We were sort of batting around all the ideas: What was the world going to be like? Would we be able to cooperate with the Soviet Union? What was going to happen in China? Was China falling apart? There was a really wide-ranging discussion about what the future might look like. . . . It's all fuzzy other than the New World Order, which I wish I had never thought of."[903]

In truth, the Bush administration wasn't enthusiastic about initiating new ideas and institutions. President Bush himself wasn't an abstract thinker or "enamored with great concepts," and when he had larger visions of American society or international relations, he "didn't like to articulate them," Richard Haass pointed out. And while Secretary Baker was a tactician par excellence, he wasn't a strategist. The upshot was that the three architects of US foreign policy in the early 1990s—Bush, Scowcroft, and Baker—were never able to present the American public and the rest of the world with a picture of what a post–Cold War international system might look like and of what the United States' role in this new international community might be. Nor was there anyone else in the White House who was able to pick up on the idea of the new world order and run with it.[904]

This lack of enthusiasm for abstract global thinking and messaging weakened the administration politically. If President Bush wasn't prepared to gloat, neither was he able to establish rapport with the American people and win their trust. He didn't articulate their joy over the liberation of Eastern Europe and the end of the Soviet Union, he didn't communicate their outrage over the Tiananmen Square massacre, and he didn't give voice to their hopes of a better, more peaceful world. For all of his charm and persuasiveness as a diplomat and politician in one-on-one meetings or in small groups, Bush didn't have the common touch.

Neither did his secretary of state. James Baker was "incapable of expressing passion," Dowd and Freidman report. "Passion, symbols, bread and circuses—those [were] for political campaigns, not for governing." Scowcroft was similarly disciplined and careful in his language. But the result, Dowd and Friedman note, was that the Bush foreign policy had "no voice, no music and no poetry." The administration's message on US foreign policy was "a perfectly acted silent movie for an audience that likes to sing along."[905]

What's more, by 1991, the members of the Bush foreign policy team were exhausted from "victory fatigue." Success can be as demanding as failure, and with so much that had already happened—Eastern Europe, China and Tiananmen Square, Panama, Germany, the Gulf War, the coup attempt on Gorbachev, and the rise of Boris Yeltsin—Bush and his advisers weren't ready to make major new policy innovations.[906] They weren't prepared to address the challenge posed by the breakup of Yugoslavia. They didn't try to intervene in Somalia until late in their term, during the lame duck presidency. And Congress, with the Nunn-Lugar Cooperative Threat Reduction Program, assisted them with the handling, destroying, and disposing of Russia's excess nuclear, chemical, and biological weapons.

Still others, Scowcroft and Fitzwater included, point to President Bush's thyroid problem, which caused him to collapse on May 4, 1991, while out jogging. After the collapse, the result of Graves' disease, Bush was "not himself." His energy, stamina, and "aggressiveness," Scowcroft said, were off. The president was lethargic, in a striking contrast to his usual "manic energy." Not until after leaving office was his medication calibrated properly.[907] Suggestive of the drop in Bush's energy level is the fact that after May 1991 there was a significant reduction in the number of Bush's telephone conversations and personal meetings with foreign leaders—even though more than a third of the presidential term lay ahead.[908]

In addition, the Bush White House began to be preoccupied with the reelection campaign and sought to avoid appearing fixated on international relations when the economy and other issues called. And if Bush wanted to have any hope of winning, he had to appeal to his party's conservative base, which traditionally favored a strong defense and meager levels of foreign aid. Since the administration was already seen as too skewed toward foreign policy and too distant from domestic concerns, Bush and his political advisers had no stomach for undertaking an overhaul of the United States' national security policy later in their time and thereby possibly taking on formidable domestic interests, both public and private, with strong stakes in the status quo.

Scowcroft, too, was extremely conscious of what could go wrong. He saw the risks inherent in initiating new policies and the possibility of unintended consequences. Scowcroft was superb at analyzing issues, managing operations, fixing problems, and handling crises—at working with existing pieces and placing them in such a way as to best protect US interests and values. But even more, thanks to his knowledge of world history, he looked out for the potential pitfalls that could accompany significant departures from existing policies and established institutions—not to mention radical changes. He could envision the downsides to proposed actions more clearly than he could discern new patterns or see new potential arrangements of the puzzle pieces in this new, transformed world. And he admitted that while he "always thought that the NSC . . . ought to have a long-range planning function," it never worked. "Either nobody had time to pay attention to it or you had to grab them when a fire broke out. That was one of the most frustrating things to me."[909]

Yet there was a distinct vision of the United States in the world that did survive the Bush administration—albeit one that Scowcroft opposed. This was the Defense Planning Guidance drafted by Paul Wolfowitz, I. Lewis

"Scooter" Libby, and Zalmay Khalilzad in late 1992, all in the Office of the Secretary of Defense. The document spelled out how the United States should behave if it wanted to dominate the rest of the world. It specified that the United States needed to be prepared to proceed independently in case its European allies, other partners, and international organizations were unwilling to go along with its initiatives, and it argued that no other country should be allowed to match the United States militarily, economically, or politically, and that none should be encouraged to try. This idea—that the United States was to be the indispensable nation, one capable of shaping the world in its image—not only would turn out to constitute the foundation for the Clinton administration's foreign policy but also, for all intents and purposes, would subsequently serve as the basis of George W. Bush's foreign policy.[910]

Scowcroft, however, "thought it was arrogant" and emphasized that this never became the national strategy for the Bush 41 team. It was the "wrong approach," in his judgment, and had Bush been reelected, the Defense Planning Guidance would have been "a subject of strong debate." Bush wasn't, of course, and so "it wasn't." Instead, it was leaked to the press, to Scowcroft's regret; as an internal administration document, it should have stayed under wraps.[911]

A few years later, in *A World Transformed*, Scowcroft described his own view of US grand strategy: the United States was obligated to lead the world, as it had done with Iraq, and "should attempt to pursue our national interests, wherever possible, within a framework of concert with our friends and the international community." Not only should the United States lead, but it should use international institutions *wherever possible*. The implication was that there might be occasions when the United States would have to act alone if its interests didn't coincide with those of other nations. Scowcroft also implied that there might be occasions when the United States shouldn't attempt to pursue or uphold the universal principles expressed in the new world order if they conflicted with the United States' own strategic interests.[912]

The differences between Scowcroft's vision and that of the Defense Planning Guide were thus ones of degree, of the assertiveness of American values and ideology, and of the importance of process—that is, whether the United States should consult with and rely on international institutions and multilateral coalitions. Their differences were not necessarily those of the United States' international hegemony or of the role of the US government in the promotion of American interests.

Despite these various efforts to articulate an overarching national security policy, the end result was that at the apex of the American century—a moment in world history when the United States had by far the most dominant military, economy, political, and cultural influence—the United States failed to develop a grand vision commensurate with its potential. For all the deftness that the Bush team displayed in dealing with the Soviet Union, disarming Central Europe, helping to reunify Germany, expelling Iraq from Kuwait, and laying the ground for a larger and more interconnected global market, it was unable to offer Americans a vision of a transformed world. There is thus more than a germ of truth to Representative Les Aspin's comment that the Bush White House did an exemplary job of winning wars and reaching its immediate goals but didn't win the peace.[913]

=====

ANY JUDGMENT OF the Bush administration's failure to outline an overarching vision of US grand strategy needs to be tempered by the fact of just how fast everything happened. It's easy to forget the vastness of the perceived political, economic, and ideological gulf that separated the United States and Soviet Union and the fear and suspicion both sides felt about each other. "You know, the Cold War so profoundly affected all of us," Scowcroft said. "It infused every part of our lives. It was a pattern of thinking. It was the world that we knew." The end of the Soviet empire represented a historic shift "at least as dramatic as Columbus discovering the new world that changed the whole shape of the globe. It was literally outside our frame of reference, and it remained so to me."[914]

Scowcroft acknowledged that the sheer pace of events could be overwhelming. The Bush White House did all it could simply to keep on top of things. Scowcroft conceded that the administration "didn't have a comprehensive strategy" for the world that was developing all too quickly. There was a lot to digest, with events happening with amazing rapidity, Scowcroft commented, "too soon." He, the president, the NSC staff, and the others didn't have the time to "find our feet, we were just trying to keep up with things."[915]

Under the circumstances, it might have been unrealistic to expect the US government to be able to absorb all that had happened over such a short period, much less to formulate, agree upon, and mobilize behind a new grand strategy. Indeed, Scowcroft himself described the administration as being in "limbo" until after the president's (anticipated) reelection. By way of comparison, eight years elapsed between the end of the Revolutionary War and the ratification of the Constitution (1781–1789), and nearly five years passed between the end of World War II and the emergence of a US policy consensus on the nature of the Soviet threat and need to contain global communism (as articulated in NSC 68 in April 1950).[916] The one-term Bush presidency was probably too brief a period to fully assess how the United States would reorient itself in a transformed world.

Given the realities of what American policy makers were facing in the late 1980s and early 1990s, Brent Scowcroft's prudence, sobriety, knowledge of history, and dedication to public service almost perfectly suited the times. In an era of amazing turmoil and complexity, Scowcroft worked indefatigably to coordinate, manage, and execute George H. W. Bush's foreign policy across and among the State Department, Defense Department, Treasury Department, and other departments and agencies.

"I love his style," Bush said of Scowcroft. "I respect his intellect. I respect his knowledge of world affairs. He's the ideal, the perfect national security advisor. He's an honest broker, yet he has strong opinions of his own. And he would present the opinions of the principals, the unvarnished truth, just the way they would have said it, and then I'd say, 'Well, Brent, what's your idea?' and he'd tell me."[917] As another White House official said, "When he would speak, it would be dead silence . . . he just had a lot of respect and there was just no question about it." Scowcroft was "revered," Bush's director of public affairs, Dave Carney, remarked, and "no one" in the administration "ever really criticized him." Even outside the White House and the government, people didn't criticize Scowcroft "in the sort of a combative way" that people would criticize Darman, Sununu, and others in the administration. Scowcroft knew "he could make a difference, and he has."[918]

"In my twenty years of working in the US government," Nicholas Burns remarked, "Brent provided the best example of leadership and management I saw. How he used the staff, and had it act in its primary role: as the direct foreign policy staff for the US president, and to coordinate information and policy, and to bring out the best out of the rest of the government. He encouraged us to work closely with the Defense Department, with the intelligence community, and with others." For Dick Cheney, Scowcroft was the best he'd seen "as a guy who could take a very difficult, complex policy area and run it on behalf of the president, coordinate it with big egos in the Cabinet, and manage that whole process." And Cheney made these comments in 2009, well after he and Scowcroft had fallen out.[919]

Baker, too, allowed that Scowcroft was "the perfect national security advisor—low key, low profile, and we never had [any major disagreements]— except maybe that time when I got in the way of the State of the Union, and that was my fault." The former secretary of state added, "He was a terrific NSC advisor, and he, too, knew how it should work."[920] "It comes back to

Brent Scowcroft," said former State Department and NSC official David Gompert. An NSC process "like this will only work if you've got strength at the center. But it's not the kind of strength that threatens anyone, that crowds anyone, that has an agenda other than the agenda of the whole," Gompert continued. "And Brent believed so strongly in those principles that it was possible to be effective with a strong center, to be able to hold meetings and make things happen without any one of the principals, or their bureaucracies, or their immediate staffs feeling in the least bit threatened."[921]

He was an honest broker, to be sure, but not just an "aggregator" tallying up and apportioning points of view from around the government (what Richard Haass identified as an "honest balancer").[922] Rather, he checked the viability of the proposed options and filled gaps in the range of issues being considered—and proposed additional policy options if need be. This quality control was manifested in the attention Scowcroft paid to the NSC process, specifically his careful selection of personnel and his establishment of the venues for making national security policy—as with his reintroduction of the Deputies Committee and his creation of the Principals Committee, the Core Group, and other ad hoc decision-making bodies. Furthermore, if he had strong views he wasn't above expressing them forcefully, as the president, Baker, Cheney, and Powell all experienced. Good people and sound processes don't automatically lead to wise decisions, of course, but it's almost impossible to make good decisions with any consistency or to avoid serious mistakes *without* quality personnel and a sound policy process—and Scowcroft ensured both.

Scowcroft went beyond being an honest broker in a further sense. Not only did he faithfully present the views of others and give his own opinion when solicited, he also occasionally acted as the president's assistant or personal agent in sensitive matters, as with his secret visit to Beijing in July 1989, his backchannel diplomacy with Charles Powell, Horst Teltschik, and Jacques Lanxade, and his quiet meetings with other officials, whether in Washington or overseas. Baker was very much aware of Scowcroft's backchannel contacts. (By contrast, Carter and Reagan did not rely on such contacts to the same degree.)[923] Scowcroft almost always stayed in the background, moreover—unlike Kissinger, Brzezinski, and Rice, who as national security advisors were often in the news—and, accordingly, was able to act with great discretion. The fact that Stephen Hadley (the national security advisor in George W. Bush's second term) and Thomas Donilon (the national security advisor spanning Barack Obama's first and second terms) have more closely matched Scowcroft's "passion for anonymity" testifies, perhaps, to the wisdom of the approach and the benefits it brings to policymaking.

Further testimony to Scowcroft's knowledge of "how it should work"—that is, his sense of organizational politics—is the fact that the model of the national security advisor and the NSC process he set up is essentially what has continued under presidents Clinton, George W. Bush, and Obama. For the national security advisor, the model is that of a "counselor." And for the NSC process, the model is that of a Principals Committee chaired by the national security advisor, a Deputies Committee, and an assortment of policy-specific working groups (called interagency policy committees under President Obama).

But Scowcroft's sense of organizational politics, his willingness to act as the president's agent, the control he exercised on the quality of the NSC process, and his respect for the views of others in government had, in combination, that much more effect because his actions were infused by his ability as a strategist: his ability to discern the people and organizations in play, to understand their backgrounds and origins, and to see how they interacted and what the likely consequences would be in relation to the desired objectives of US policy. The *New York Times'* Leslie Gelb, who served as an assistant secretary of state in the Carter administration, called Scowcroft the best national security advisor he had ever worked with.[924]

"The Tiffany, the 'gold standard' if you will, of foreign policy interaction and deliberation and consensus building really was President George Herbert Walker Bush's administration," said NBC's Andrea Mitchell, "and that has to be credited to General Scowcroft." Mitchell pointed out that the later Bush 43 presidency showed a very different side of Powell, Cheney, and Baker—one that led to far less positive results for the administration and the nation. The individuals in question didn't change dramatically in the intervening years, Mitchell said; the real difference was that "General Scowcroft was the common denominator that welded them into a well-functioning team."[925]

It may be true that Bush, Scowcroft, and the other members of the foreign policy team never hammered out a grand vision of global policy to guide the thinking of future generations. But it's equally true that, in a time of extraordinary change and widely varied dangers, they managed to handle a remarkable range of immediate challenges with exceptional skill and intelligence—among other accomplishments, helping to guide the unforeseen and almost completely nonviolent dissolution of one of the world's great empires. It was a feat of statecraft without parallel, and one of which Bush and Scowcroft—and those they served—can be justly proud.

— PART V —

Citizen-Statesman

———

But while Sept. 11 and the invasion of Kuwait are poles apart in most ways, there is one critical aspect in which they are strikingly similar: The war on terrorism will be, if anything, even more dependent on coalition building than was the Gulf War.

—BRENT SCOWCROFT,
THE WASHINGTON POST, OCTOBER 16, 2001[1]

28

AN INDEPENDENT VOICE

WITH BILL CLINTON'S election as the United States' forty-second president, Scowcroft was again wrenched from his position as national security advisor. Once more, he did not expect to be out of a job. And like almost all other White House officials, he did not actually believe Bush would lose his reelection bid. Even the president couldn't fathom the election results. "I just never thought they'd elect him" Bush told Colin Powell.[2]

Scowcroft had "played a minor role in the campaign," although at Lee Atwater's request he spoke to Republican groups on foreign policy and at fund-raisers for House Republicans. Otherwise, Scowcroft didn't have a relationship with Bush's campaign advisers—except when on behalf of the president he had to ask Baker to leave his position as secretary of state and take over the reelection campaign. Bush couldn't ask his friend directly—he'd then be conceding he needed Jim's help. Baker agreed, and he quickly stopped the self-destructive infighting that had been damaging the campaign. But the change came too late to salvage Bush's reelection.[3]

The president was handicapped by not having "Jim Baker and Brent Scowcroft running his domestic policy," said Dave Carney, a political consultant with the Bush campaign. Bush's domestic policy team did not operate "as smoothly" as his foreign policy team and was "not as focused, not as unified, and . . . not as media-savvy."[4] Worse yet, the campaign staff "decided that foreign policy was a negative," Scowcroft said, and they chose to stay "away from foreign policy through the whole of 1992." Scowcroft thought—as he had during the Ford campaign—that it was "ill-advised" for them "to run away from what [Bush] had done at a very crucial period in U.S. and world history."[5] He found it immensely frustrating that the campaign didn't play to Bush's strong suit and didn't do a good job of reminding the American people what President Bush and his administration had accomplished; they never really explained to the American people, in no uncertain terms, why the president deserved reelection.[6]

Even so, without the third-party candidacy of Ross Perot, who received 19 percent of the popular vote, Bush might have been reelected. Scowcroft, by his own account, had to devote a "huge amount" of his time to handling Perot, who was obsessed with Vietnam POWs and MIAs, and the subsequent investigation by Massachusetts senator John Kerry and Senator Robert Smith of New Hampshire into the missing US servicemen.[7] To Scowcroft, it seemed that Perot was "just dredging up issues" nearly twenty years after US troops had been fighting in Vietnam. He thought there was little to gain through further investigation, and he regarded Perot's inquiries as "much ado about nothing." He believed Perot was just demogoguing the issue, trying to "make hay" at Bush's expense and, in the process, going "way off the reservation."[8]

Perot clearly had it in for Bush, who, in turn, regarded Perot with undisguised hostility; Bush perceived Perot as erratic and unreliable, and assumed he'd sooner or later self-destruct. Their falling-out dated from when Perot had said to Vice President Bush, "This world is full of lions and tigers and rabbits. And you're a rabbit." From then on, Herbert Parmet reports, Bush was "in Perot's crosshairs." Perot continued to go around "talking about Bush as 'weak' and a 'wimp.'"[9] It's not surprising Bush didn't try very hard to placate Perot, then. Perot's very presence in the campaign exemplified one of Bush's vulnerabilities as a politician, however: his tendency to take insults and disagreements personally.[10]

Further damaging to Bush's bid for reelection was the last-minute news of Friday, October 30 that special prosecutor Lawrence Walsh had indicted former defense secretary Caspar Weinberger in the Iran-Contra scandal. Played up by the major television networks' anchors, the news once again raised questions about Bush's role in Iran-Contra and resulted in an almost overnight reversal in public opinion polls as to whether Americans could "trust" the president. With Election Day on Tuesday, moreover, there was no time for the administration to respond or otherwise reverse the swing in the public's confidence in George Bush.[11]

But if Walsh had not released the news when he did, if Bush had originally had a better campaign team in place, if there been an earlier or stronger rebound in the American economy, or if there been a less capable opponent, Bush could well have won reelection, regardless of Perot.

This time around, it was easier for Scowcroft to be out of a government job. Not only had he accomplished a great deal over the past four years as national security advisor, he had his consulting experience with Kissinger Associates and International Six behind him. Yet he said he didn't want to go back to work with Kissinger and didn't want to be doing something he had already done. Instead, he and his colleagues and friends on the NSC staff wanted to do something that would allow them to work together.[12]

Scowcroft planned to form a different kind of think tank. He brainstormed with Arnold Kanter, Virginia Mulberger, Stephen Hadley, and Richard Haass, and they came up with the idea to establish a nonprofit company, to be called the Forum for International Policy. It would be a brain trust whose principals would use "Op-Eds, articles, Issue Briefs, media interviews, and informal meetings with decision makers to provide cogent and practical perspectives on current international issues and forecast developments not yet in the public eye" and thereby able to provide "practical, real-world policy options designed to further U.S. national interests in the new international environment." The premise for establishing the think tank was Scowcroft's concern that with the Cold War over, the United States would withdraw from its international commitments, turn inward, and pull back from global leadership—that as Kanter put it, policy makers would think that "we can go home and tend our garden."[13]

By setting up a small, quick-responding organization able to turn out short, relevant pieces on the issues of the day, Scowcroft and his partners—Haass ended up not joining—would be offering a different product than other Washington think tanks. The latter usually commissioned lengthy, in-depth studies, with the result that some were already dated by the time they were released. Scowcroft and his colleagues further agreed they wouldn't do any Monday-morning quarterbacking; they wouldn't second-guess presidential actions or revisit decisions that had already been made or get in the business of assigning blame for past mistakes.

By January 20, 1993, the day of President Clinton's inauguration, Scowcroft, Mulberger, and Kanter were already settled in two vacant law offices loaned to them by Fred Fielding, an attorney friend of Scowcroft's who had been Reagan's White House counsel (Fielding later served as President George W. Bush's White House counsel). They worked on rented desks and fished out the files they needed from cardboard boxes stacked in their offices. A few months later, they moved to new space on Farragut Square—the present offices of the Scowcroft Group—in downtown Washington.[14]

The Forum for International Policy started with just Scowcroft, Mulberger, and Scowcroft's personal assistant, Florence Gantt. Kanter also had a position at RAND, where he spent much of his time, and Hadley was an attorney with Shea & Gardner (since merged with Goodwin Procter). Their initial funding came from a $30,000 loan from Scowcroft himself, and then he and Mulberger began fund-raising, receiving contributions from former president Bush, George W. Bush, and other friends and former associates; in the late 1990s and early 2000s, annual contributions totaled in the low six figures. They soon realized they wanted the Forum to be self-financing, though, and so they soon began plans to establish a consulting business.[15]

Once in office, the Clinton administration quickly moved away from Bush and Scowcroft's deliberate, realist policies. The change of direction, coupled with the near-absence of any alternative vision of the United States' role in the world, gave Scowcroft and his coauthors multiple opportunities for writing op-eds. Scowcroft wrote or coauthored eight op-eds in the Forum for International Policy's first two years, 1993 and 1994, which he placed in the *New York Times* (three), *Washington Post* (two), *Newsweek*, and the *Washington Times*. He coauthored four others, separately, with Lawrence Eagleburger, Eric Melby, Kanter, and Haass. (Never did others ghost-write editorials for Scowcroft.)[16]

Over the two terms of the Clinton administration Scowcroft wrote about three dozen op-eds, which also appeared in the *Wall Street Journal*, *Los Angeles Times*, *Christian Science Monitor*, *Newsweek*, and *National Interest* as well as other newspapers and periodicals. The op-eds were often reprinted in other US and foreign newspapers, moreover, especially in the *International Herald Tribune*, the *Financial Times*, the *Asian Wall Street Journal*, and major Canadian and Australian newspapers.

The variety of Scowcroft's topics reflected the range of his interests and the intellectual diversity of the dozen friends and associates with whom he coauthored many of the op-eds. The op-eds reflected Scowcroft's abiding emphasis on the need for US leadership and constructive engagement in the post–Cold War world, whether with respect to trade, Russia, nuclear arms control, China and China-Taiwan relations, India-Pakistan relations, North Korea, Iran and nuclear proliferation, or the Middle East peace process. The United States, he wrote, now had "an opportunity to mold an international system more compatible with the values we have held for two centuries." Exiting the international system was no option; the United States thus needed to "maintain a global presence backed by credible forces."[17] But because of the United States' finite resources, it had little choice but to work as much as possible with international institutions such as NATO, the IMF, the UN Security Council, GATT, and the World Trade Organization—and to develop a full range of policy options, whether diplomacy, foreign aid, military intervention, or other actions. Scowcroft also emphasized that the president could not and should not tolerate interference with respect to his foreign policy responsibilities, and stated his opposition to a post–Cold War peace dividend.[18]

The Forum for International Policy became the victim of its own success. Virginia Mulberger (formerly Virginia Lampley) said "corporations started coming to us and saying, 'Would you help us with this problem and that problem?'" Motorola was the first, and was followed by others, such as Pennzoil (on whose board Scowcroft served).[19] And since Scowcroft and Mulberger were the only two raising money for their nonprofit, since neither particularly enjoyed fund-raising, and since the Forum for International Policy paid none of the principals' salaries (except for Mulberger's), they liked the idea of starting a for-profit international consulting firm, which would allow them to add Scowcroft's associates and friends as their partners. They would now have a source of livelihood, be able to cover their office overhead, and be able to keep writing op-eds.

Scowcroft, with the help of Kanter, Mulberger, Melby, and Hadley, therefore created the Scowcroft Group in June 1994 to advise US multinationals on risk assessment, foreign investment, and joint ventures in emerging markets in China, Russia and Eastern Europe, the Middle East, and Africa. Once they were on their feet financially, they brought in Walter Kansteiner and Daniel Poneman (both of whom had served on the NSC under George H. W. Bush); later they added a former US ambassador, a retired career Foreign Service officer, a former consultant to the energy and telecommunications industries, and a lawyer in defense and technology sector mergers and acquisitions. For the board of directors, Scowcroft and his partners asked Lawrence Eagleburger to be chairman, and invited Dwayne Andreas, David Boren, John Deutch, Robert Gates, Rita Hauser, John Hennessy, Carla Hills, Kenneth Lay, Harold Poling, and Robert Strauss—all of whom were committed to the United States' international engagement. Scowcroft was also on the board.[20]

The fact that Scowcroft and his associates formed the Scowcroft Group to capitalize on their expertise is hardly unusual; they all agreed it would be a good way to make a living. What does make it unusual was its genesis as the outgrowth of the Forum for International Policy and the fact that all of its partners were from the NSC (with some referring to the company as the "NSC in exile"). Also unusual was its very small size, with only eight or nine principals—smaller than almost any other similar firm with the exception of Kissinger Associates Inc., which J. Stapleton Roy called "really a boutique consulting firm."[21]

The reason for the company's small size, the company's managing partner says, is that they wanted to have an office where they liked coming in to work and could enjoy each other's company. Their concern with compatibility has been a hallmark of the firm, and only a few partners have left—Poneman went to the Department of Energy under President Obama, Kansteiner left to work for Exxon, and Kanter passed away.

With its small size, the Scowcroft Group, unlike most other consulting firms, doesn't have "people on the ground," doesn't provide weekly newsletters, and doesn't offer other targeted benefits, such as setting up schedules or preparing detailed planning documents. Neither, however, do Scowcroft and his partners "parachute in" to handle problems or crises; rather, when they took on a client they took a hands-on approach and would communicate with that client on a weekly basis.

Large multinationals have their own contacts in foreign governments, to be sure, but they usually don't have the personal ties with officials at the ministerial level. This is where a Brent Scowcroft, a Henry Kissinger, or a Madeleine Albright is indispensable—someone who knows how decisions get made, who has extensive experience with foreign governments, and who can't be replaced. Scowcroft and his staff are thereby in a position to work with their clients on sensitive and complex political and governmental issues, whether having to do with trade restrictions, tax laws, constraints on direct investments, licensing agreements, market strategies, closing particular deals, or assisting on other points of business transactions.

Yet it's not as though a Scowcroft, Kissinger, or Albright can simply meet with a foreign leader, raise a client's concerns with the host country, and resolve matters. Rather, the government officials—friends or acquaintances of the consultant—want something in return, usually a substantive discussion of issues, and if the consultant "abuses the access, he won't get the appointments anymore." So the consultant has to understand "how to walk those lines," Stapleton Roy said. The issue has to be approached in the right way if the consultant is to have a chance of moving it in the right direction. And if it is a big issue, the corporations need to be able "to turn to people who know how the government functions . . . if there's going to be any hope of moving an issue in the right direction," in former ambassador Stapleton Roy's analysis.[22]

Neither Scowcroft nor his partners wanted their company to become a lobbying firm or to work as a foreign agent.[23] "I would say that my passion is foreign policy and strategy," Scowcroft says, "so my business interests are as close to that [as I can] and make money."[24] He and his partners emphasize that the Scowcroft Group works only with companies that are committed to the highest ethical and legal standards. They believed that their business interests needed to coincide with the United States' strategic interests as much as possible. Scowcroft describes the "fairly simple" criteria they use for accepting clients:

Do I think this company behaves in a way that advances the interests of the United States and is someone I'd be proud to associate with? Do I think this company and country X is operating in a way and has the interest of that country, as well? It's just . . . kind of common sense, but I'm careful about that. I don't want to do lobbying; I don't want to represent foreign governments. So, it's my sense of being a part of the government for a long time now, that still is what makes me operate.[25]

In a situation where "what we proposed to do was contrary to US policy or our understanding of our interest, we won't do it," Arnold Kanter said. The firm works to serve "the interest of the United States, not just the interest of our clients." In this sense, the Scowcroft Group differed from other consulting firms. "There's an alignment between our personal beliefs and what we do," Kanter went on. And because most of the Scowcroft Group's clients are major US corporations, it is in the interest of both the Scowcroft Group and its clients to ensure that neither the firm's interests nor those of the United States would be damaged as a result of the actions of the client corporations. The integrity of his own name and of his firm is of paramount importance to him. Mulberger, the company's managing partner, explained that Scowcroft wanted nothing scandalous, questionable, or embarrassing to appear on the front page of the *Washington Post*—or anywhere else in the news. Because trust is the "scarcest, most precious commodity," she said, Scowcroft and the partners do what they can to create and retain this trust with their clients and foreign governments.[26]

There is a self-selection process, in short—Scowcroft and his partners are only interested in working with certain clients, and other potential clients are, for those same reasons, either inclined or not incline to retain the Scowcroft Group.[27]

Among the Scowcroft Group's early clients were Motorola, Pennzoil–Quaker State (now part of Shell), and SBC Communications (now AT&T). The company's website says that Scowcroft's "clients are industry leaders in the telecommunications, insurance, aeronautics, energy, and financial products sectors; foreign direct investors in the electronics, utilities, energy, and food industries; and investors in the fixed income, equity, and commodities markets around the world," including hedge funds—about one and a half to two dozen at a given time, according to one member of the Scowcroft Group.[28]

Neither is the Scowcroft Group's emphasis on integrity just talk. Even though Lockheed Martin was a client, for instance, Scowcroft had for years publicly opposed the development of Lockheed Martin's F-22 fighter plane. "So when he spoke for a client, he was very credible," Mulberger said. And with confidentiality agreements in place, the Scowcroft Group didn't release the names of its clients, and the clients didn't disclose they had retained Scowcroft's firm as a consultant.[29]

What further distinguishes the Scowcroft Group is its atypical compensation model. The Scowcroft Group's partners (it has only a "tiny" backbench of associates) receive equal remuneration from total revenues (after adjustments for the business they bring in and for their individual expenses). This distinctive pay structure—most companies compensate their chairpersons and leading partners more than the others—replicates how Scowcroft's first consulting firm, International Six, compensated its partners. (It is possible the Scowcroft Group's egalitarian business model was influenced by the examples of Mormon businesses, but Scowcroft denied any linkage. He says he simply wanted an association rather than a hierarchy and that "Ginny [Mulberger] was the prime mover.)[30]

Although law firms, investment banks, and public relations firms have long represented US clients internationally, just as they have represented foreign clients in Washington, strategic consulting firms are relatively recent phenomena. The archetype is probably Kissinger Associates, Inc. (although Alexander Haig, Richard Helms, William Colby, Richard V. Allen, and other former officials also went into business for themselves at about the same time, though with less success).[31] In 2001, former senator William Cohen formed the Cohen Group. That same year, Madeleine Albright, President Clinton's secretary of state, formed the Albright Group and Sandy Berger, Clinton's second national security advisor, separately established Stonebridge International. The two firms then merged in 2009 to create the Albright Stonebridge Group. Also in 2009, Condoleezza Rice and Stephen Hadley formed the RiceHadley consulting company (in partnership with APCO Worldwide) and in 2012 Rice and Hadley brought in former defense secretary Robert Gates as a third partner to form RiceHadleyGates. (It is not clear whether Scowcroft seriously considered inviting Gates to join the Scowcroft Group. In any case, Gates said he preferred to stay on the West Coast.)[32]

The Scowcroft Group's peers, including the Albright Stonebridge Group, the Cohen Group, and international law firms such as Akin Gump, Mayer Brown, and WilmerHale, vary in size, economics sectors in which they specialize, the range of services they offer, and the strategic alliances they have with other consulting companies, law firms, or strategic communications firms. While these and other companies are all ostensibly in the same business, each typically occupies a distinct economic niche and stakes out one or more particular geographic regions. The Cohen Group concentrates in the defense sector, for instance, while others focus on finance or strategic communications. The clients also tend to stay with their consulting firms, and vice versa, so there's little jumping ship or poaching of others' clients. The consulting firms' standard fee for major corporate clients is between $350,000 and $500,000 a year usually (as of 2013).[33]

The business model Kissinger and Scowcroft first developed with Kissinger Associates, Inc. has now proliferated, and consulting partnerships, virtually all of them privately held, have become a standard feature of the nation's capital. Yet these firms and their famous principals typically receive little attention, since they almost always work behind the scenes, often do business in foreign countries, and are hidden behind the confidentiality agreements signed by both parties. And as privately held companies, their transactions are not a matter of public record. At the same time, the consultants are often active in the Washington policy community, participate in advisory groups, and help draft think tank reports on issues of US foreign policy.[34]

The Scowcroft Group has provided well for Scowcroft and his partners. The firm reigns as one of the most prestigious international business consulting firms in the nation's capital, with some regarding it as the single most respected and influential firm. David Jeremiah, who also had investment banking experience, described the Scowcroft Group and Kissinger Associates, Inc. as the "granddaddies" or "patriarchs" of the international business consulting firms. Another former policy maker and businessman identified Kissinger Associates as being "at the top of the pyramid" and the Scowcroft Group "to some degree being its successor." The Scowcroft Group set the gold standard, though, according to Jeremiah and others in the DC area. It recruited "very good people" who were "very steady and well regarded." Another longtime Washington observer and prominent national security expert said that none of the other consulting firms "had the juice" of the Scowcroft Group.[35]

Scowcroft and his partners ran the Scowcroft Group and the Forum for International Policy side by side for about a dozen years. Few of the op-eds the Forum published identified Scowcroft as being affiliated with the Scowcroft Group, though, in part because the newspapers (or other publications) themselves determined how Scowcroft (and his coauthors) were to be identified. It was also because Scowcroft did not want to be identified that way, since he might then be seen as defending the interests of one or more of his clients or to be promoting his own business, with the result that his arguments would then be taken less seriously.

As the 1990s turned into the 2000s, however, more and more of Scowcroft's op-eds, letters to the editor, articles, and reports identified him as a former national security advisor rather than as the president of the Forum for International Policy. The last use of the "Forum for International Policy" by which to identify Scowcroft in the byline was in a *New York Times* op-ed of January 4, 2007. In 2012 he and his colleagues formally shut down their nonprofit.[36]

Besides writing op-eds and screening clients, Scowcroft's concern with national security manifested itself in other ways. He gave newspaper and magazine interviews or went on television so as to ensure that the perspective he wanted to present was being reflected in policy debates. More commonly, he quietly contacted the policy makers or officials involved in the policy in question, since many of the people in office during the Clinton and Bush presidencies were his acquaintances, former colleagues, or friends. White House advisers, too, have often sought him out for advice, notwithstanding any differences they might have on US policy toward Somalia, Haiti, Kosovo, or the expansion of NATO. "He knows a great deal," former national security advisor Sandy Berger told Jeffrey Goldberg; "I always found it useful to speak to him."[37]

***

SCOWCROFT ALSO SOUGHT to influence the thinking of public officials, business leaders, and policy experts on national security by using his role in and leadership of such groups as the Atlantic Council and the Aspen Strategy Group to educate others. In these venues he could speak directly on issues of national security and international relations, depending on the topic of the particular session or conference, and also indirectly shape the debate by virtue of his role in the choice conference topics, the decisions on who was to speak and be on the panels, and the selection of who was to be invited to attend and become new members. While these were rarely his decisions alone to make, his fundamental roles in both organizations gave him considerable influence.

The Atlantic Council was formed in 1961 as a nonpartisan and not-for-profit think tank to sponsor speakers, symposia, and research on directed topics—most of them on the North America–Europe relationship, although others involve Asia or other regions or have a global focus. Smaller and more specialized, it is less well known than the Council on Foreign Relations. In the early 1990s, after the Cold War, the Atlantic Council was at its most critical stage since its establishment according to its current president and CEO, Fred Kempe. It was underfunded, had lost some of its foundation money, and had diminished membership. This was when Scowcroft took over.

Scowcroft, with the assistance of Christopher Makins, a British diplomat, and former US ambassador to the United Kingdom, Henry Catto, "shook it up." Scowcroft and Makin introduced new leadership, revived the membership, and got the Atlantic Council on better financial grounds. Makins served as president until his death in 2005, and a year later Scowcroft recruited Fred Kempe from the *Wall Street Journal* to head the Council. Scowcroft himself served as chairman of the board of directors in 1998–1999, after which Catto was chairman until 2007. Scowcroft then asked Gen. James Jones to serve as chairman. When Jones was appointed Obama's national security advisor in 2009, Scowcroft asked former US senator Charles Hagel to take over. When Hagel left in 2013, to become secretary of defense, Scowcroft filled in until January 2014, when Jon Huntsman, former US ambassador to China, became chairman.[38]

One of Scowcroft's most important contributions was to create an international advisory board composed of prominent company executives and former policy makers of cabinet rank or above. Scowcroft chairs the international advisory board and recruited about two-thirds of its members.

Scowcroft also helped create the Young Atlanticist program for the purpose of bringing along the next generation of leaders, Kempe also pointed out.

Kempe, who administers the Atlantic Council on a daily basis, could unequivocally say that there was "no doubt" that over the past two decades Scowcroft was the Atlantic Council's most important person.[39] The former national security advisor was "instrumental" in saving the Atlantic Council, Kempe said—"more important than people know"—and in increasing its membership sevenfold in the last six years (to about five hundred as of 2013), recruiting new board members, and raising funds. The Council's funding comes principally from four sources—foundations (such as the Ford Foundation and the German Marshall Fund of the United States), corporations (such Boeing, Chevron, Daimler, General Dynamics, Goldman Sachs, Northrop Grumman, and Toyota), governments (the German government, the Air Force, Army, Navy, and Energy Departments, and the US Mission to NATO), and individuals. Scowcroft and Kempe are at pains to ensure that the Atlantic Council stays independent from its funders, however, so as to protect its credibility. For this reason, there are no "Atlantic Council positions" on particular issues.

In view of Scowcroft's central role in promoting the Atlantic Council, he agreed in 2012 to have the centerpiece of the Atlantic Council, the International Security Program, renamed the "Brent Scowcroft Center on International Security." Although Scowcroft didn't endow the center with his own money, putting his name on the center served as a way to emphasize the Atlantic Council's nonpartisan nature, and the stellar quality of his reputation assisted in development.

Scowcroft has also been deeply committed to the Aspen Strategy Group, which was established in the mid-1970s for holding serious bipartisan discussions about strategic warfare and nuclear arms control. Scowcroft calls it "nonpartisan" instead of "bipartisan," since when the members come to Aspen each August for up to five days, they are expected to leave ideology and personal agendas behind and to focus on the issues at hand. From its original focus on arms control, strategic warfare, and nuclear proliferation and its original membership of twenty to thirty people, it now has a broader mission, with an expanded scope of security-related seminar topics, including economics and finance. The membership, too, has steadily expanded to between fifty and sixty. Scowcroft and his cochair Joseph Nye, together with the director and deputy director, try to strike a balance in the membership in terms of age, partisanship, open-mindedness, government service, and business and economics. It is trigenerational, in effect, with Scowcroft and Nye representing the senior members, people such as Madeleine Albright, Philip Zelikow, and Condoleezza Rice occupying the middle tier, and a younger group of policy makers and experts in their late thirties and forties.[40] With the Aspen Strategy Group, too, Scowcroft has been intent on building the succeeding generations of leaders.

Scowcroft and Nye have been cochairs of the Aspen Strategy Group since the late 2000s; Scowcroft had previously been chairman from 1983 to 1989. Nicholas Burns serves as director, succeeding Philip Zelikow. Scowcroft and Nye, together with the director and deputy director, choose the annual topics to be discussed each summer.

Since genuine discussion on serious foreign policy and strategic issues confronting the United States is rare in Washington, the Aspen Strategy Group meeting is an oasis of relaxed and open exchange. The participants get to know each other not only through the multiple-day panels and discussions, but also more informally by taking hikes together, riding horses, going fishing, playing softball, and participating in other activities. Perhaps needless to say, the connections formed at the Aspen meetings are able to create valuable personal networks, they often lead to later collaboration, and they can help launch careers.[41]

Scowcroft was also consistently willing to chair or to serve on government and nongovernmental boards as a way of focusing attention on what he believed to be issues that affected US interests and those of the American people. He served on several government boards, just as he had in the 1980s and late 1990s, and did some troubleshooting for presidents George W. Bush and Barack Obama. He enjoyed working on different aspects of national security, as he had throughout his career, and almost always agreed to serve when asked. In 1996, for example, he and Zbigniew Brzezinski served as cochairs of a Council on Foreign Relations group to investigate US policy in the Persian Gulf (the study was triggered by Congress's passage of the Iran and Libya Sanctions Act of 1996). Scowcroft's and Brzezinski's 1997 report recommended that the United States be more flexible and more nuanced in its approaches to both Iran and Iraq. Since "strident" approaches weren't working and since the stability of the Persian Gulf was of paramount interest to the United States, the report stated, the United States should explore "creative trade-offs" with Iran and ways to facilitate mutual accommodation in the region.[42]

Scowcroft was also asked to serve on or advise other corporate and nonprofit boards after leaving the White House, and he served on the boards of Northrop-Grumman (1993–1997), Enron Global Power & Pipelines (1994–1997), Qualcomm, Inc. (1994–present), and the American-Turkish Council (2000–2010). He has also been on the boards of the Center for Strategic and International Studies, the National Defense University, Rand, the School of International and Public Affairs at Columbia University, the US Air Force Academy, and the George Bush Presidential Library Foundation (where he is also president).

Qualcomm, for instance, wanted a director with strong foreign policy experience, and George H. W. Bush recommended Scowcroft, who joined the board in December 1994. In 2000 CEO and founder Irwin Jacobs met Scowcroft in Beijing and after "lots of discussion" about Qualcomm's expectations for China and its state-guided economy with Prime Minister Zhu Rongji, Scowcroft and Jacobs helped get a license for Qualcomm to provide China Unicom, China's second-largest telecommunication company, with its proprietary CDMA cell phone technology. Only after things settled down following the bombing of the Chinese embassy in Belgrade and the Hainan Island incident and China sought to enter the WTO, however, was the deal struck for Qualcomm to enter the Chinese market.[43]

Scowcroft has been "exceedingly helpful" to the Qualcomm board over the years, Jacobs said, because of his ability to listen carefully and his broad understanding of organizations and business. It is his continued "very valuable" advice—a result of his historical and international perspective on issues and sound judgment as well as his Chinese contacts and close knowledge of China—that has kept Scowcroft on Qualcomm's board of directors for two decades.[44] (Interestingly, when Scowcroft traveled to China, whether on behalf of Qualcomm or another of the Scowcroft Group's clients, he sometimes carried messages from the White House.)[45]

Because of Scowcroft's long-standing role on the Qualcomm board and because of Qualcomm's continued commercial success, his stock options have made Scowcroft a very wealthy man. Scowcroft doesn't think of himself as being wealthy, perhaps because his circle of friends includes people worth considerably more, such as Henry Kissinger and the CEOs of IBM, Exxon, and other major corporations. Neither does he especially seem to care.[46] On the contrary, he lives unostentatiously even though he is able to do whatever he wants and travel wherever he wants. And he is still in his same modest house in Bethesda, the one he first bought in 1964.

One of Scowcroft's grandnephews lived with him for about a year in 1999 and 2000 and was astonished at the energy of the seventy-five-year-old Scowcroft. "Workaholic doesn't begin to describe it," said the young man, adding that he didn't "know how he keeps the pace he does." Scowcroft would doze off on the couch after work, "then revive, and sometimes go jogging around midnight, three to five times a week." Sometimes he never made it up to bed and just slept on the couch. Then he'd be "up at 5:30 A.M., ready to go again." Scowcroft's grandniece, who also lived with him for five months when she first moved to the Washington area, was similarly "shocked by how much he works." The twenty-four-year-old discovered she was "working less than her eighty-year-old great-uncle." Neither was Scowcroft an absentee landlord. He helped with the cooking—according to her, he "makes a nice salmon loaf" and "always had dessert." More importantly, when Scowcroft wasn't off to China, Saudi Arabia, California, or elsewhere and they were at home together, the two of them discussed serious issues as well as family matters. They talked about campaign finance, about the conflicts involved with raising money, and—to her mild surprise—about how he didn't think that women needed to change their names when they got married. She also revealed his favorite joke for starting off his public speeches: "Washington is the only city in the world where people walk down Lover's Lane holding their own hand."[47]

SCOWCROFT TOOK ON another commitment in the mid-1990s: working with George Bush on *A World Transformed*, Bush and Scowcroft's account of the Bush administration's foreign policy. Bush said he had no desire to write an autobiography—his collected letters and diary entries effectively served as substitutes. But when Scowcroft proposed writing a book together, Bush agreed. The book was to be about "the seven dramatic changes in the world during the four years of the Bush administration," according to Barbara Bush. But Bush was never wholly comfortable writing. When talking to Nixon about his and Scowcroft's idea, Bush complained, "Dick, *you* can write. I can't."[48]

Their chief assistant for the research and writing was James McCall. McCall would take notes of their conversations, which were taped and then transcribed. It was because Scowcroft couldn't very well pass longhand pages back and forth to Bush and McCall that he learned how to use a computer. Until then, he had always had secretaries type up what he wrote out longhand.

The origins of *A World Transformed* explain its unusual format, which consists of three interspersed and complementary texts: (1) a general history (set in boldface) that Bush and Scowcroft both agreed to, drafted by Scowcroft and McCall; (2) Bush's own accounts of events, which were his own responsibility and which he mostly drew from his diaries; and (3) Scowcroft's own descriptions and analyses, which he wrote himself.

A World Transformed reviews how Bush and Scowcroft planned the United States' international relations when they took office. It describes their initial wariness of Gorbachev and the Soviet Union, and the reasons for that caution. It addresses the events in Panama and the role of Manuel Noriega. It deals at length with the reunification of Germany and with the administration's reaction to the Tiananmen Square massacre. It explains how President Bush, Scowcroft, and others responded to the Iraqi invasion of Kuwait and then handled the Persian Gulf War. And it explores the rise of Boris Yeltsin, the fall of Mikhail Gorbachev, and the collapse of the Soviet Union. Because of this limited focus, the book skips over other aspects of Scowcroft and Bush's foreign policy with respect to Russia and the Commonwealth of Independent States, the Israeli-Palestinian peace process, NAFTA, Somalia, the Uruguay Round of GATT talks, the environment and global warming, Cambodia, Afghanistan, and other issue areas. Neither does the book focus on the budget, economic policy, the reelection campaign, or other hallmarks of the Bush administration, such as the Clean Air Act and the Americans with Disabilities Act.

That Bush coauthored *A World Transformed* with Brent Scowcroft, rather than James Baker, Nicholas Brady, Robert Mosbacher, Boyden Gray, or another longtime friend who served in his administration, speaks to how comfortable the two were with each other personally and how well matched they were with respect to how they viewed US foreign policy. (But they always remained "Mr. President" and "Brent," just as Scowcroft always called Gerald Ford, who also became a close friend, "Mr. President" when they were together after Ford left office).[49] And of Bush's friends, only Scowcroft bought a condominium near Bush's compound on Walker's Point in Kennebunkport after leaving office.

Despite Scowcroft's insider status in Washington and his connections in the national security community, and despite Scowcroft's occasional lunches with Clinton's national security advisors, first Anthony Lake and then Sandy Berger, the Clinton administration essentially viewed him as an outsider. The Clinton White House worked under different assumptions than the Bush presidency and proceeded in different directions. It reoriented the US mission in Somalia; it intervened militarily in Haiti; it expanded NATO eastward and initiated the extension of a missile defense system into Eastern Europe. And in 1994 it intervened in Bosnia and in 1999 in Kosovo.

———

ONLY TWO AND a half years after he left office, Scowcroft's world was darkened by Jackie's death on July 17, 1995, at the age of seventy-two, from complications from diabetes. Jackie and Brent had been married forty-three years.

Her health problems had begun in the 1970s and only got worse. Matters were not helped by the fact that despite a family history of type 2 diabetes, her condition was misdiagnosed for ten years. The fact that her blood sugar levels were only marginally higher than normal levels misled her doctors. Not until Brent took Jackie to the Mayo Clinic in the mid-1980s was the correct diagnosis finally made. During the intervening decade, she was subjected to numerous misdirected treatments and suffered needless complications. For example, to relieve the severe pain in her legs, she underwent several operations, including having her veins stripped and her back operated on.

Even when he was Bush's national security advisor, if Jackie was in the hospital, Scowcroft would leave the office at 5:00 P.M. to visit her; he would return to work later that evening. Scowcroft cared for her at home, and at one point got a hernia from lifting her and had to have surgery. So for a while he had to conduct business while lying down on his office couch.[50]

George Bush acknowledged he never got to know Jackie Scowcroft—a remarkable statement considering how close the two men were and how well Brent and Barbara Bush knew each other. "All the time [Scowcroft] was national security advisor he'd go home at night—he worked until eight or nine at night—go home at night, feed her, get prepared for bed, and then come back into the office. He was an indefatigable worker," Bush remarked. "He had this—I would say burden, and he would say love—that he had for his wife and daughter. But we didn't really get a chance to know her. She wouldn't come to receptions. . . . I know just know he was devoted to her." Robert Gates, too, who had known Brent since 1974, said, "Over those years, I never met her."[51]

Scowcroft's personal assistant said Brent's wife attended social events during the Nixon administration, but ceased doing so in the early 1970s. Lawrence Eagleburger said he met Jackie a couple of times in the early 1970s, but then "at some point she was bedridden" and remained so for many years . . . she was very heavy." Scowcroft "had to carry her from one place to another. He did all that without complaining [about it] to anyone I know," Eagleburger remarked. "If sainthood is deserving, he's one of them." Robert Strauss spoke of how devoted Brent was to her. When people asked about Jackie, "the only thing Scowcroft would say is 'she's okay,'" even though her problems continued "for a long time."[52]

Marian Horner Scowcroft was buried at Arlington National Cemetery two days after she died, complete with full military honors. A thirty-five-minute Catholic service in the large chapel, packed with friends and relatives, was followed by a graveside ceremony that lasted twelve or thirteen minutes. Three rifle volleys by seven soldiers were succeeded by a cannon salute and finally by a bugler playing taps.[53]

As hard as Jackie's death was for Brent, it also came as something of a relief. He had taken care of his wife for decades and almost always by himself, except when he was traveling. The stress had been almost constant and the sacrifice considerable. Now he could work, travel, and visit family members and friends without worry. Close friends noticed that after her death he seemed more open and relaxed.[54]

Jackie's death nonetheless left Scowcroft with a great hole in his life, and for weeks after the burial he visited Arlington Cemetery every afternoon to put fresh flowers on her grave. And for years afterward he couldn't eat chicken, since his routine had been to shop for the week's groceries each Sunday morning, boil a chicken, and then make enough chicken salad so that Jackie could have it every day for lunch.

Scowcroft dedicated *A World Transformed*, which was published three years after Jackie's death, to his wife. He never remarried.

29

THE BROKEN PROCESS

GEORGE W. BUSH'S election as the nation's forty-third president propelled Scowcroft back into national view.

George Walker Bush was determined not to repeat his father's mistakes. He wasn't going to raise taxes. He wasn't going to back down before Congress or break a campaign promise. He wasn't going to go to war and leave the job unfinished. He wasn't going to be a one-term president. And he certainly wasn't going to let others think of him as a wimp. "Bush 43 was highly resistant to being instructed by his father on how to deal with issues," one former US ambassador said. "There was a rebellious streak there." There was also family honor at stake: George H. W. Bush hadn't finished the race, as he wrote one of his brothers after the 1992 election. Now his eldest son would take over.[55]

When it came to foreign policy, the former Texas governor and managing partner of the Texas Rangers baseball team needed a tutor. He chose Condoleezza Rice. He initially became acquainted with Rice through her close friendship with his father and Brent Scowcroft, and they became better acquainted during her summer visits to the Bush family compound at Walker Point. Not only did he find her to be smart, articulate, and talented, they shared interests in staying fit and in sports—Rice had dated several football players—and both spoke using sports metaphors. They also shared a devout Christianity.

So when George W. Bush was readying his run for the presidency in 1999, he asked Rice to lead his foreign policy team. She formed a group of advisers to hammer out and then draft the campaign's foreign policy positions. The group included Richard Armitage, Bob Blackwill, Stephen Hadley, Richard Perle, Paul Wolfowitz, Dov Zakheim, and Bob Zoellick. Although Rice wasn't the most senior of the group—Rice named them the "Vulcans," after the Roman god of fire, Vulcan, whose statue towered over her hometown of Birmingham, Alabama—she called herself the quarter-back and was skilled at managing the group's different personalities.

Five days after the US Supreme Court awarded George W. Bush Florida and thus the national election, the president-elect announced that Rice would be his national security advisor, assuming the job that had previously been held by her mentor. Little wonder, then, that she said she wanted to model her role as national security advisor on Scowcroft's performance in office.

Like her former boss, she didn't believe the national security advisor should take an active policy-making role or upstage the secretary of state, the secretary of defense, the secretary of the treasury, the director of intelligence, or other foreign policy principals. She didn't follow the policy-making approach of Kissinger or Brzezinski, nor the adventurism of McFarlane or Poindexter. Rather, she saw her new role as that of a dedicated adviser and assistant to the president.[56]

Although George W. Bush appointed several other former members of his father's staff to positions in his presidency, including Blackwill, Hadley, Wolfowitz, and Zoellick, he declined to have either Baker or Scowcroft play a significant role. Neither would he ask Baker, Scowcroft, or his father for advice; that was why he had Rice, Cheney, Powell, and Rumsfeld. "You're not going to see any Jim Bakers around me when I'm in office," he told reporters early in his campaign.[57]

For all of President Bush's stated intentions of proceeding without the help of his father's two closest advisers, he wouldn't have become president without Baker, who was indispensable at securing Florida for the Bush campaign. And only a few months later, Bush had to call on Scowcroft to help with settling the Hainan Island incident of April 1, when a Chinese fighter jet collided with a Navy EP-3, an NSA spy plane, forcing the US aircraft to land on Hainan Island, where its crew was held captive and the airplane disassembled. After the incident, President Bush spoke out against Chinese aggression and, in reference to the Taiwan Relations Act, said the United States would do "whatever it takes" to help Taiwan to defend itself in the event that it was attacked. Because Bush in his comments did not explain the conditions of the United States' defense of Taiwan—the agreement didn't hold if Taiwan initiated conflict—Chinese leaders were upset and viewed the president's message as belligerent. In order to clarify the US position, mollify the Chinese, and "tamp this down," Rice advised Bush to ask for Scowcroft's help. Scowcroft quietly traveled to Beijing, met with the Chinese president, Jiang Zemin, and the foreign minister, Tang Jiaxuan, and explained that the United States remained committed to a one-China policy. He reassured them that the United States was under no obligation to act if Taiwan initiated hostilities. What had begun as a "very bad first year" for the Bush administration had improved, Scowcroft later told an audience at the US Institute for Peace—although he did not tell the audience that this was partly the result of his own intervention—since the administration was now viewing China "with more balance."[58]

Soon afterward, Bush, on the recommendation of DCI George Tenet and Rice, asked Scowcroft to advise him on restructuring the intelligence community. Bush had issued National Security Presidential Directive 5 (NSPD 5) on May 9, 2001, authorizing a ninety-day review of intelligence. The twelve-member committee and its twenty-five-person staff were to conduct an external review of the intelligence community, to be chaired by Scowcroft; a separate internal review, to be chaired by Joan Dempsey, would complement the external review. Both reviews, which shared the same staff, were tasked to reevaluate the organization and functioning of the US intelligence community, so as to "ensure that U.S. intelligence capabilities are honed to serve us on a wide range of critical challenges that face us now and in the future." According to a White House press statement, the reviews were to "challenge the status quo and explore new and innovative techniques, systems, practices and processes" of foreign intelligence.[59]

Although Tenet could select the members of both panels (Rice joined Tenet in appointing the members of the external board), the DCI was also wary of the possibility that an independent review board might report findings that would unduly upset the status quo and thereby potentially weaken the Agency and damage the DCI's authority. Neither was Dempsey enthusiastic about the internal review, according to a member of the external review board. But Scowcroft "took it very seriously." Not only did he do "whatever he was asked with his usual thoroughness," the *Wall Street Journal*'s Ron Suskind reports, he "dove into the task with a young man's energy."[60]

George W. Bush had initially gotten to know Scowcroft through Brent's close association with his father. The younger Bush had helped on his father's campaigns, had assisted the White House in the early 1990s, and had had the chance to get better acquainted with Scowcroft during his visits to Kennebunkport. Scowcroft admitted that he didn't know Bush's eldest son very well, though his impression of him as a college student was that he was "kind of a smart aleck and had a pretty sharp temper and didn't seem to me to be much like his father." Scowcroft liked the younger Bush's bipartisanship when he was governor of Texas, though, and he supported his campaign for the presidency. During the 2000 presidential campaign, the two men spent three hours together on a porch in President Mubarak's guesthouse in Cairo (the younger Bush was en route to Israel), where the two of them had a friendly, constructive visit. While Scowcroft was aware of the possibility that Bush 43 might hire Rice for his new administration, the newly elected president did not discuss it with him.[61]

The president gave Scowcroft further responsibility in August 2001, again following Rice's recommendation: Bush asked him to head the President's Foreign Intelligence Advisory Board (work related to, though separate from, his chairmanship of the intelligence external review board). PFIAB was established during the Eisenhower presidency as a nonpartisan board that could offer the president expert and impartial advice on the conduct of foreign intelligence. Yet the actual influence exerted by PFIAB depended both on whom the president appointed to the board and on how the president intended to use the sixteen-member board.

Scowcroft's work on the two boards revealed that the intelligence agencies had poor morale after years of cutbacks and underfunded budgets. Offices were equipped with outdated technology—not all of the offices had computers as of early 2001, for instance—and the huge National Security Agency was suffering brownouts because of the power demands of its massive computers. Virtually every agency in the intelligence community as of 2000 was "on the verge of collapse," according to one former senior intelligence official.[62] There was some support among managers in the CIA and related agencies for reform, then.

Scowcroft was in a position to make things happen. With his outstanding reputation, political skills, bureaucratic savvy, and knowledge of how Washington worked, he had a good chance of significantly reforming the intelligence community. Members of the intelligence community responded favorably to Scowcroft's appointment as the chairman of the NSPD 5 review board; they saw him as a knowledgeable, sympathetic supporter of the community. As national security advisor, he had sanctioned and overseen covert operations and the intelligence community more generally, so he understood what could be expected in the collection and analysis of intelligence. And while there are many demanding consumers of foreign intelligence in Washington, there are relatively few who are at once supportive, skeptical, pragmatic, and judicious.[63]

The members of the panel convened every two weeks in a secure space on K Street. At the board's first meeting on July 3, Scowcroft said that terrorism had to be the nation's highest national security priority, but that the United States had not yet come to grips with the matter. The commissioners then discussed the Federal Aviation Administration and talked "more broadly [of matters] outside of the normal intelligence community," including domestic intelligence, the board's chief of staff reported. There was a general recognition that "the whole concept of central intelligence had broken down. And largely because of budgetary reasons," because the Department of Defense "controls so much of the budget."[64]

A preliminary draft of the report was ready by August, and Scowcroft presented it to Vice President Dick Cheney, who "mostly listened, and seemed to agree," Suskind writes. "It was a cordial meeting."[65] So Scowcroft and the other board members went back to work to revise and polish their report.

Notwithstanding his seniority and reputation, Scowcroft ran things with a light touch, according to members of the commission, and delegated as much as he could—especially to David Jeremiah, who effectively served as the vice chairman (officially, there was no deputy or vice chairman). Scowcroft "was very down to earth, very easy to work with," said one of his staff members. Even when traveling across Washington in muggy summer weather, for example, he insisted on going by Metro rather than taking up a colleague's offer to let him use a government car.[66]

The panel's work was interrupted when terrorists destroyed the World Trade Towers and attacked the Pentagon. Scowcroft was in the Andrews Air Force Base departure lounge on the morning of Tuesday, September 11, 2001, waiting to fly out to Offutt Air Force Base. Offutt AFB, just south of Omaha, Nebraska, was the headquarters of the Strategic Command (STRATCOM), and Scowcroft was the chairman of a study commissioned by Defense Secretary Donald Rumsfeld. The purpose of the "end-to-end review," something that the Pentagon did every four years, was to systematically survey the entire complex of US nuclear weapons policy, from conceptualization to the laboratory to production, deployment, maintenance, and disposition of old nuclear weapons.[67]

In the days immediately before September 11, the Pentagon had been conducting a series of war games under the code names Vigilant Guardian, Northern Guardian, and Global Guardian. The aim of the war games was to test US defense capabilities against different kinds of hypothetical strategic attacks. Because of the exercises and because of Scowcroft's role as the chair of the quadrennial nuclear weapons study, he was going out to STRATCOM headquarters to monitor this "practice Armageddon." Scowcroft and those accompanying him were to fly out on one of STRATCOM's four E-4Bs so they could witness the operations of the United States' military defenses against airborne strategic attacks. (The E-4Bs are adapted Boeing 747-200s that house the National Emergency Airborne Command Post. Each aircraft is essentially a mobile Pentagon, and provides its personnel the capability to coordinate the actions of civilian authorities, issue military orders, and direct forces—command, control, and communications, or "C3." During the Cold War, the E-4Bs were called "doomsday planes," since their purpose was to allow the US government to keep functioning in the event of a nuclear exchange.)[68]

It was while Scowcroft was waiting at Andrews AFB to board the E-4B that he learned an airplane had crashed into the World Trade Center's North Tower. He assumed it was an accident, so he and the other passengers climbed aboard the aircraft and were already airborne when the second plane hit the South Tower. Scowcroft then realized that the two crashes were acts of terrorism, and his first thoughts were of the sheer enormity of the attacks and the immense tragedy.[69] (It was probably Scowcroft's large white E-4B, with its distinct hump behind the upper deck, that was the mystery airplane the television networks reported flying over Washington, DC, that morning, that people photographed, and that the counterterrorism expert Richard Clarke and others have written about.)[70]

Scowcroft's aircraft continued to Offutt, where he proceeded to STRATCOM headquarters, a fortified bunker sixty feet underground. There he spent the next several hours witnessing the Air Force's desperate scramble to identify and track the hundreds of aircraft over American skies. He headed back to Washington, DC, later that day, taking off from Offutt at about the same time President Bush was landing in Omaha (after having been airborne since leaving Florida earlier that day). While being driven back into Washington from Andrews AFB, Scowcroft saw the smoke rising from the Pentagon.[71]

Scowcroft considered the attacks to be the culmination of a logical progression dating back to the first attempt on the World Trade Center towers in 1993, followed by the US embassy bombings in Tanzania and Kenya in 1998 and the suicide attack on the USS *Cole* in October 2000. So he didn't think the attacks of September 11 changed the world; what had changed, he thought, was how the United States now related to the world.[72]

The nine-month-old Bush administration now had to manage that change. George W. Bush and his advisers needed to decide what the awful events signified and how the United States would respond.

The decision to go to war against Iraq in the aftermath of the successful campaign against the Taliban in Afghanistan manifested a fact common to politics everywhere: that it's much easier to achieve political agreement on the "what" of policy than on the "why." Agreement on the "what" is relatively straightforward: reaching a consensus on a particular policy. But agreement on the "why" demands a consensus on matters much less amenable to agreement: on the logic of cause-and-effect relationship, on the likely consequences that follow from actions, and on assumptions on ideology and ultimate beliefs.

It's not exactly clear what precise mix of motives led George W. Bush to make the decision he did. There was Iraq's alleged possession of weapons of mass destruction, as many in the Bush administration believed and most of the American public assumed. There were Iraq's supposed ties to Al Qaeda and its support of terrorism, as Dick Cheney, Doug Feith, and others claimed. There was the idea that a liberated Iraq could become a beacon of democracy in the Middle East, serving as a precursor to and harbinger of other such transformations in the region, as Paul Wolfowitz and others thought.[73] Iraq also had the second-largest oil reserves in the Middle East (and the world) as Alan Greenspan, Dick Cheney, and others pointed out.[74] Furthermore, overthrowing Saddam Hussein was in Israel's interest, influential neoconservatives believed, given Saddam Hussein's enmity toward Israel and anti-Semitic rhetoric.[75] And there was President Bush's wish to complete what his father had started—to rid the Middle East of Saddam and his Ba'ath government. As George W. Bush told Senate minority leader Tom Daschle in early 2003, "The sonofabitch tried to kill my father."[76]

Domestic politics played a role as well. While the 2004 election was predominantly Karl Rove's concern, it was of no minor interest to the president and others in the White House. George W. Bush could achieve what his father had not been able to. Scowcroft, too, speculated that reelection may have been the foremost reason for the Bush administration's decision to go to war against Iraq: "I'm not sure how much the President is driven by the [neoconservatives] and how much he is driven by wanting to be re-elected—maybe more than most Presidents do—because his father was defeated," he said. "And I think it's not impossible that, freed from that demand, he might behave somewhat differently."[77]

Neither is it clear if administration officials genuinely believed the various views they espoused. Some officials were probably sincere in their arguments, while others were very possibly being sophistic in theirs.

Removing Saddam from power had been discussed even before George W. Bush's administration took office. The Project for a New American Century had previously advocated Saddam's removal, and in September

1998 President Clinton signed the Iraq Liberation Act into law. "It should be the policy of the United States to support efforts to remove the regime headed by Saddam Hussein from power in Iraq," the act read, "and to promote the emergence of a democratic government to replace that regime." With Bush 43 in office, those hoping for Saddam's removal had their chance. The question was when. Revealingly, the administration's first NSC meeting, in January 2001, was on ridding Iraq of its president. And barely two weeks after the inauguration, on February 7, Rice chaired a Principals Committee meeting to discuss Iraq. At the meeting it was decided to establish an Iraq Operations Group within the CIA's Directorate of Operations, which was to plan for covert operations that might be part of a larger solution for regime change in Iraq.[78]

Within a few hours of the September 11 attacks, Richard Perle, Michael Ledeen, and other neoconservatives began calling for the removal of the Iraqi government, and a few days later the Bush White House began to develop plans for a possible war against Iraq.

With the focus of Washington suddenly on terrorism, Al Qaeda, Afghanistan, and Iraq, attention turned away from the reform of the intelligence community—especially since any comprehensive reform would have been contentious. Tenet "brought [the NSPD 5 review] to a halt. He said we're done." But Scowcroft and others on the board thought "it was a waste not to continue" their work. Scowcroft talked to Rice, and she prevailed on Tenet to allow the study to continue (although Dempsey's internal board was not revived). Rice and Tenet then redirected the external review "to think about how intelligence supports homeland security."[79]

The board members finished revisions on their twenty-page report, and Scowcroft himself carefully attended to the exact phrasing of the text. The report didn't differ much from their previous draft, interestingly, because the board had previously discussed the possibility of a horrific incident resulting from a threat that was "hard to monitor, hard to assess," in Jeremiah's words.[80] The report did criticize the organization and processing of intelligence—and, of course, failures in the handling of intelligence had enabled 9/11 to occur. In particular, the report condemned the imbalance within the intelligence community: the fact that the military controlled the overwhelming majority of the intelligence budget—about 85 percent—and the CIA only 10 percent (the remaining 5 percent being divided among the State, Treasury, and Energy Departments as well as several other departments and agencies).

The report recommended that the three large independent agencies controlled by the Department of Defense—the National Reconnaissance Office

(NRO), National Security Agency (NSA), and National Imagery and Mapping Office (NIMO)—come under the administration of a new director of intelligence with statutory responsibility over the whole intelligence community. Scowcroft also recommended the establishment of a "massive intelligence research library," where all data would be assembled and available to those with the proper levels of security clearance, since under the existing system the information that constitutes the raw material of intelligence was dispersed among more than a dozen different agencies. Before September 11, for example, US officials had to rely on at least nine different terrorist watch lists, so when the CIA lost track of two of the terrorists, the terrorists had already made it through US customs by the time the CIA released their names to other agencies. The FBI likewise had information on the terrorists in the months leading up to September 11, but hadn't shared its data with other federal agencies.[81]

With a draft of their report in hand, Scowcroft and Jeremiah made the rounds. They first briefed Cheney, and this time the vice president told them they were rearranging the deck chairs on the *Titanic*. So Scowcroft asked Cheney whether he and his fellow board members should bother to proceed. The vice president disingenuously told him to "go ahead" and brief Bush's other top advisers, knowing full well, just as Scowcroft surely did, that the secretary of defense, Donald Rumsfeld, was as dead set against any lessening of the Pentagon's control as he was.[82]

Scowcroft presented the board's findings to Secretary of State Colin Powell, FBI Director Robert Mueller, Rumsfeld, and Attorney General John Ashcroft. Powell wished them luck, although he told them he didn't think the proposal would go far. Rumsfeld, of course, was opposed; in fact, the Department of Defense had opposed a proposed reorganization of the intelligence community back in the mid-1990s. And when Scowcroft and Jeremiah spoke to Ashcroft, they "got our heads handed to [them] in a basket," because they'd talked to the FBI—a unit within the Department of Justice, of course—before meeting with the attorney general.[83]

There was nonetheless a general consensus among Bush administration officials on the need to centralize intelligence for the purposes of command and control. Opinions diverged over where that centralizing should occur, whether in the Pentagon (which is what Rumsfeld wanted) or in a new office, that of an independent director of national intelligence, which would oversee the CIA, the Defense Department's intelligence agencies, and the other agencies involved in intelligence (which is what Scowcroft wanted). As it was, however, the managerial responsibility over the intelligence community— the control over personnel, budgets, and organizational structure, in other words—was at odds with the responsibility for the intelligence itself, including how intelligence was collected, who or which offices were in possession of which information, how intelligence was to be analyzed, and where and how it was to be aggregated and dispersed.

However, Tenet and others in the intelligence community were not willing to agree to any significant changes in the immediate aftermath of September 11, 2001. And neither President Bush nor any of his advisers, including his national security advisor, were willing to lead a reform effort. What "fell by the wayside was community responsibility," the chief of staff for the external review board, Kevin Scheid, said. "You didn't have that cross-community intelligence integration necessary that would have helped us, given us a fighting chance before 9/11."[84] So when Scowcroft and Jeremiah presented the board's recommendations at an NSC meeting, Rumsfeld and Cheney both strongly opposed Scowcroft's proposed reorganization of the intelligence community, and their judgments carried the day. Neither man gave the report a fair chance in Scowcroft's view. He recalled telling Rumsfeld, "Don, you know if our positions were reversed you would be making this same suggestion to me."[85]

Scowcroft felt "he was being set up for failure or irrelevance," Unger reports.[86] Cheney's treatment of Scowcroft and the NSPD 5 report alienated Scowcroft from his White House partner in the Ford administration, his close colleague from the first Bush White House, and his erstwhile friend. The two were never again close. It was this event, in the view of two of Scowcroft's closet friends, Bill Gulley and Arnold Kanter, and not the later decision to go to war against Iraq, that caused the break between Scowcroft and Cheney.[87]

Equally disappointing to Scowcroft was Rice's passivity with respect to intelligence reform. The members of the panel had expected to be working closely with her, anticipating that as national security advisor she would be deeply involved with their efforts. Instead, she did not "show any particular interest" in what was going on, according to Jeremiah, and opted to stay on the sidelines.

The establishment of the Office of the Director of National Intelligence was the "one big idea" that carried over from the intelligence review board to the independent 9/11 Commission. The Homeland Security Act of November 2002 created the DNI position, a role above the CIA director and the heads of the other intelligence chiefs (including the new under secretary of defense for intelligence). The new DNI would henceforth report directly to the president, not unlike the chairman of the Joint Chiefs of Staff (who was elevated within the military as a result of the 1986 Goldwater-Nichols Act). But the new arrangement only added another layer of bureaucracy rather than imposing more effective control, since the DNI didn't exert centralized control of either the personnel or the budget of the intelligence community. Not only was the CIA still relatively autonomous, but four-fifths of the intelligence community budget, including the funding for the NRO, NSA, and NIMO remained in the hands of the Department of Defense.[88]

The Homeland Security Act did set up a national center for counterterrorism staffed with personnel from the FBI, CIA, NSA, and other intelligence agencies, just as the report by Scowcroft's intelligence review board had recommended and just as Scowcroft had discussed as chair of PFIAB. Philip Zelikow, Scowcroft's former NSC staff member, his colleague on PFIAB, and the chair of the 9/11 Commission, also encouraged the move. And though there are still issues with respect to the sharing of information among the different intelligence agencies and residual feelings that there is not enough "honest collaboration" among the agencies, the situation of the 2010s is "night and day" compared to that of the 1990s and early 2000s.[89]

Nonetheless, the intelligence community avoided serious reform. "After 9/11, Agency employees expected the axe of accountability to fall at any moment," one intelligence official, frustrated at the lack of change in CIA, reported. "The bureaucracy, a living, breathing creature, was in fear for its life. Employees at [Langley] expected the Agency's top managers to be fired. Talk at HQs was that the 'seventh floor,' where the CIA's top mandarins dwelt, would be swept clean." But nothing happened. "The days turned to weeks and still nothing happened." On the contrary, "Tenet stated that there had in fact been no intelligence failure."[90] And while eventually the DCI would be forced to resign, neither he nor the administration sought to reorganize or reorient the intelligence system.[91]

Once the commission drafted and presented its report, Scowcroft and his colleagues had fulfilled their mandate; the intelligence review was solely advisory, for internal government use only, and it was George W. Bush's prerogative not to accept the commission's recommendations. Neither Scowcroft nor any of the other commissioners and staff leaked the report. If some felt it had been "swept under the rug" or "deep-sixed" by Rumsfeld, that was the administration's business; the report was for the president and his advisers to use as they thought best, as Scowcroft saw it. And they used very little.[92]

With the terrorist attacks of September 11, the struggling Bush presidency had a clear purpose and an obvious mission. Cheney's grim views of the world now resonated throughout the US government and American society, and the vice president quickly became the most powerful person in the administration besides the president himself. In the characterization of journalists Evan Thomas and Richard Wolffe, Cheney was "Bush's unofficial prime minister"—at least for a while.[93]

With Bush's description in the 2002 State of the Union address of an "axis of evil," most government officials, most journalists, and many in Washington and around the country figured it was only a matter of time before the United States went to war against Iraq. George W. Bush and his top aides didn't want any advice from Bush 41, Baker, or Scowcroft. The president had no wish to have his administration's actions tied to the counsel of his father's hypercautious "wise men."[94] Even more astonishing is that the decision to go into Iraq never went through any formal decision-making process. Neither the president nor Rice convened an NSC meeting or other high-level meeting to explicitly address the question of whether the United States should invade Iraq and depose Saddam Hussein, and, if so, what the United States' objectives would be and how the administration should best pursue those ends.[95]

Scowcroft was reluctant for the United States to intervene in Iraq. With the administration heading to war seemingly without much forethought, he decided to take his case to the public. On August 4, 2002, he appeared on *Face the Nation*, where he explained to Bob Schieffer and millions of CBS viewers why he objected to the administration's planned invasion. Scowcroft conceded that Saddam might well be a despot and untrustworthy, but he noted that it wasn't because of terrorism that the Iraqi leader was a problem. He predicted that if the United States went in, it would turn the Middle East into a "cauldron." Given the United States' priorities and the costs and benefits of any invasion, he warned that an attack on Iraq would be "premature" and "counterproductive" in the absence of genuine progress on the Israeli-Palestinian issue and without the establishment of a UN inspection regime that could review Iraq's chemical and biological weapons systems. Saddam Hussein was "not a man who will risk everything on the roll of a dice," consistent with the fact that "during the Gulf War, he didn't do everything he could have done," Scowcroft noted, such as planting chemical weapons in New York or releasing nerve gas. Later that Sunday, the *CBS Evening News* showed clips of the interview, and a story in Monday's London *Times* repeated Scowcroft's arguments.[96]

Curiously, no one in the Bush White House responded to Scowcroft's comments (although on the evening of Monday, August 5, Powell had a long—and what he regarded as a very successful—conversation with the president at the Residence, Bob Woodward reports in *Plan of Attack*). Neither Rice nor any other White House official released any statements or tried to contact Scowcroft once the media picked up the story. Perhaps they thought the story would simply disappear. Scowcroft explained their inaction by pointing out that they already knew of his position, so there was no reason for them to contact him or respond to his criticisms.[97] (Hadley recalls that in early 2002 when he stopped by the Scowcroft Group's offices for lunch, Scowcroft joked that the deputy national security advisor was meeting with "the infidels."[98])

But the story didn't go away. A week later, on August 11, Juan Williams discussed Scowcroft's arguments on *Fox News Sunday*. That same Sunday, Senator Barbara Boxer spoke of Scowcroft's objections on *Late Edition with Wolf Blitzer*, and Senator Richard Lugar and CBS's Bob Schieffer both commented on his views on *Face the Nation*.[99] There were related news stories on PBS, MSNBC, and NPR. In the meantime, Arnold Kanter and Virginia Mulberger suggested to Scowcroft that he write up his *Face the Nation* remarks as an op-ed.

"I was watching [Scowcroft on] *Face the Nation*," Kanter recalled, and Brent gave "this strategic answer. And I sort of said, 'Well, shit, that's pretty good.' So the next morning I come in the office and I say, 'Brent, that was really good. You ought to write it in an op-ed.'" He agreed, using the TV transcript as the basis for the editorial. After he had finished writing, he sent the op-ed to the *Wall Street Journal*. (Kanter credited himself as being "somewhere between a nudge and an editor." He emphasized his name didn't belong on it, but said that Scowcroft "every so often" jokingly reminded Kanter that it was his idea to write the op-ed.)[100]

The op-ed wasn't the elder Bush's idea, then, contrary to what many assumed, and neither did the former president give his approval. Although Scowcroft talked to the former president almost every day, according to their mutual friend Robert Strauss, Scowcroft wasn't writing on behalf of his friend or for anyone else.[101] In fact, it would have been out of character for the former president to ask Scowcroft to write a dissenting op-ed, just as Bush was too respectful of the presidency and too diffident to presume to tell his son how to do his job—especially not in public.[102]

All the same, Bush and Scowcroft shared deep misgivings about the foreign policy direction being taken by his son, and the two of them, together with Barbara Bush and a handful of others, had been discreetly but unsuccessfully searching for ways to halt the momentum building for war on Iraq.[103] And each certainly knew the other's mind. "Do I know what the father thinks about most things? Yeah, I think so," Scowcroft told a reporter. "If I don't, I've been sleeping for 30 years, because we've been together a long, long time. We talk about a lot of things, and we talk about a lot of them very quietly. We have a wonderful relationship, and I have to be very careful about the appearance of speaking for him out of turn."[104]

When Scowcroft learned the *Wall Street Journal* would be running the op-ed, he faxed a copy to Kennebunkport, since he didn't want to put the elder Bush in the awkward position of learning about the editorial from reading the newspaper or finding out about it secondhand. Out of courtesy, Scowcroft also faxed a copy to Rice's personal secretary at the NSC; again, he heard nothing back.[105]

Reading the morning newspapers on August 15 out on his ranch in Crawford, Texas, President Bush was outraged to see Scowcroft's op-ed in the *Wall Street Journal.* He immediately called Rice, who was in Washington. "What is he doing?" he demanded. "Scowcroft has become a pain in the ass in his old age," he told her.[106]

Rice then called her one-time mentor, former boss, and dear friend and began yelling at him, telling him that both she and the president felt blindsided. She berated him for betraying the president, betraying the trust of his friends and former associates in the administration, and betraying the Republican Party. She wanted to know why Brent hadn't called her beforehand to let her know his position. Scowcroft mildly commented that the arguments in the op-ed were the same as those he'd made on national television two weeks earlier. "It's different when you put it in print," Rice responded. In Scowcroft's description, "I got taken to the woodshed."[107]

Rice hadn't been blindsided, though. Scowcroft's fax had gone through to her private office number, and she was aware of her mentor's other media statements. In fact, she'd spoken to him on the morning of Sunday, August 4, before he went on *Face the Nation.*[108]

Yet she could hardly admit these facts, given how embarrassing the op-ed was for her. Everyone believed she had considerable influence over Scowcroft, but it was now apparent she hadn't been able to prevent him from writing in the widely read *Wall Street Journal*—the editorial page of which amounts to the daily bulletin board for the Republican Party— notwithstanding their close relationship.[109]

The op-ed carried a further unpleasant implication: Rice hadn't protected her principal, the president of the United States, from public humiliation. By saying that she hadn't seen the op-ed, Rice was able to distance herself from both the op-ed and her mentor. She had good reason for distancing herself from Scowcroft, moreover, since she suspected that some might think he was arguing on *her* behalf (as she writes in her memoirs).[110] So she was at pains to let the president, her White House colleagues, her fellow Republicans, the press, and the public think she had been unaware of the op-ed, and that in any case it didn't express her views.

The op-ed also constituted a clear indictment of how Rice was running the NSC process. In his memoirs, George W. Bush writes that Scowcroft's op-ed made sense, but that he was "angry Brent had chosen to publish his advice in the newspaper instead of sharing it with me."[111] Yet if the president didn't know about Scowcroft's op-ed and his argument against an Iraqi war—and Eagleburger maintained that "it was obvious the president knew" of Brent's disapproval of his plans for war—then Bush had been poorly served by Rice, the NSC staff, and his other advisers, since it would then appear they hadn't informed him of what he described in his memoirs, *Decision Points*, as Scowcroft's "fair recommendation" on Iraq. Or if Bush *did* know, as Eagleburger believed, then Scowcroft's position should have been widely known and been debated within the administration, in which case the former national security advisor probably would not have felt that he had to go public. But his views hadn't been credibly and forcefully presented.[112]

The fact is that George W. Bush hadn't participated in a full and open discussion about the pros and cons of going to war against Iraq. Rice hadn't informed Bush of the full set of policy alternatives for countering terrorism and dealing with Iraq and hadn't insisted that the president consider the potential consequences of his actions. Perhaps "because she lacked Scowcroft's convictions" or perhaps because she agreed with Bush and rejected Scowcroft's analysis and assessment of the situation, the national security advisor "failed to frame Scowcroft's policies as an option for Bush to consider," Craig Unger writes.[113]

Powell was the one person in the administration whom the op-ed helped, at least in the near term. The secretary of state telephoned Scowcroft afterward, telling him, "You gave me some running room." The "initial reaction" of almost everyone else in the Bush administration, though, "was he's helping the bad guys," Powell said. Elliott Abrams conceded that few among them—himself included—appreciated the fact that Scowcroft "has a loyalty to the country that is great than his loyalty to the Republican Party."[114]

In any case, the die had already been cast. The day before Scowcroft's op-ed appeared, in fact, Rice chaired an NSC meeting for the purpose of drafting a strategy for war against Iraq and placed one of her NSC aides in charge of an interagency group, the Executive Steering Group, that was tasked to oversee and coordinate the many steps that had to be taken to support US military operations in the Gulf.[115] Left unquestioned was its premise: that the United States *should* invade Iraq.

═══

GEORGE W. REJECTED the possibility that his father wanted "to send him a message on Iraq." It "was ridiculous" to think that he was trying to communicate through Scowcroft, Bush writes. "Of all people, Dad understood the stakes," and "if he thought I was handling Iraq wrong, he damn sure would have told me himself."[116]

While the younger Bush was right to assert that his father wasn't sending him a message—with the implication that Scowcroft had written the op-ed independently—he was also being disingenuous: he knew his father would *not* "have told [him] himself." It wasn't Bush 41's style to impose his views on another US president, even his own son. The two of them weren't close, in fact, and when they got together they avoided discussing the presidency or the substance of foreign policy. Scowcroft himself describes the father-son issue as "huge." Former senator David Boren, who was a friend of Scowcroft and Bush 41, reports that there was a total breach of communication between father and son, and that the elder Bush wouldn't have shared his views on Iraq with his son.[117] George W. Bush also well knew that Scowcroft and his father agreed on virtually all foreign policy issues, including Iraq, and that Scowcroft's editorial would have dovetailed with his father's own thinking.

Indicatively, a few days after the op-ed appeared, the elder Bush and Robert Hormats, then a vice chairman of Goldman Sachs, had breakfast in Veracruz, Mexico. Hormats reported that George H. W. Bush had only the nicest things to say about Brent and was effusive in his praise. He "wouldn't have done this," Hormats said, "unless he felt comfortable with Brent."[118]

Rice, the NSC staff, and others in the administration officials simply miscalculated. They thought they could safely ignore Scowcroft, no doubt assuming that Scowcroft's dissent would stop with his remarks on television.

A few weeks after the publication of the op-ed, Rice and Scowcroft had dinner with some other friends at the restaurant 1789 in Georgetown, and the national security advisor told Scowcroft she wanted to bring democracy to Iraq. "Condi, it's just not going to happen," he remembered responding. "'You can't build democracy that way.' She said, 'Oh yes you can.'"

The conversation got heated, and Rice then declared, "The world's a mess and someone's got to clean it up." Scowcroft strongly disagreed with her position, but he was too fond of her and too much of a gentleman to argue further over dinner. But, as he later told friends, he was bewildered by her "evangelical tone."[119]

The Republicans were "intensely angry at him," Lee Hamilton remarked. They hated Scowcroft for the op-ed, and "some very strong language was used against Brent." The war against Iraq stood at the center of Bush's foreign policy—reforming the world "through our foreign policy and military action," in Hamilton's words—and now Scowcroft, a former national security advisor to two presidents and a Bush family friend, was rejecting Bush's plans. For Bush and his advisers, it was "You're either for us or against us." And because Scowcroft, a lifelong Republican, had the temerity to challenge them, he was seen as disloyal, a heretic.[120]

Scowcroft was associated "with everything we didn't like about the George H. W. Bush administration," Abrams said, "which was to say we viewed it as weak foreign policy." For Abrams, who was then on the NSC staff, the epitome of Bush 41 and his advisers' undue regard for the Soviets and preference for the status quo was the Chicken Kiev speech advocating the restraint of nationalist sentiments. He and other neoconservatives believed that it was Reagan, because of his increases in US defense spending, his pursuit of SDI, and his other bold initiatives, who had won the Cold War—not Bush 41, Baker, and Scowcroft. They had wanted to hear George H. W. Bush bluntly declaring to the Soviets and to the world: "We win, you lose."[121] They believed that the defeat of the Soviet Union marked the triumph of the United States and of American values, and they *wanted* to see Americans dancing on top of the Berlin Wall. And Scowcroft's excessive caution was now again in evidence.

Early the next month the administration pulled out all the stops. The White House reported that Iraq was developing nuclear weapons. "We don't want the smoking gun to be a mushroom cloud," Rice declared on national television (using speechwriter David Frum's words). And in a speech to the United Nations on September 12, President Bush made the administration's case to a global audience, affirming the United States' commitment to action against Iraq.[122]

Many members of the press and much of the public rallied behind the Bush White House. *Wall Street Journal* readers wrote letters condemning "Scowcroft's appeasement." The *New Republic*'s Fred Barnes said it was "absolutely shocking" that Scowcroft would write a piece "attacking the foreign policy not only of President Bush's son, George W. Bush, but attacking the foreign policy favored by his very own protégée, Condoleezza Rice, now the national security advisor in the Bush White House—the same job Scowcroft had in the [first Bush administration]."[123] William Kristol, writing in the *Weekly Standard*, called Scowcroft and Colin Powell "appeasers" who "hate[d] the idea of a morally grounded foreign policy" that "aggressively and unapologetically [sought] to advance American principles around the world," and he characterized Scowcroft's arguments as "laughably weak." John Podhoretz of the *New York Post* described Scowcroft and Bush 41's other advisers as being "among the most mediocre ever to staff an administration" and charged that they had "displayed shockingly poor foresight" by leaving Saddam in power. He also described the senior Bush as "the most unimaginative president of the second half of the 20th century."[124]

The *New York Times'* managing editor, Bill Keller, also weighed in. Keller cast aspersions on Scowcroft's motivations in a signed editorial, warning readers they should know the background of those criticizing the plans for war against Iraq. The former national security advisor "makes his living advising business clients," he pointed out, "some of who would be gravely inconvenienced by a war in the Middle East." Keller's criticisms applied to other skeptics of the war, moreover, such as Lawrence Eagleburger.[125] Still others commented that while they didn't know what Scowcroft's motives were, they knew he was wrong. "Scowcroft and his leave-Saddam-alone acolytes," William Safire wrote in his syndicated column, were resorting to "strategic, self-justifying, political, or pacifist grounds" in order to oppose "finishing the fight" against Saddam.[126]

Kissinger, too, disagreed with his friend and former deputy. "Brent [didn't] explain against what specific aspect of the war against terrorism [an attack against Iraq] distracts from," Kissinger said on CNBC's *Capital Report*. He thought the United States was right to act aggressively the Middle East, "the area in which terrorism grew up." The Bush administration should show "that to challenge the United States is simply too dangerous." And "an operation against Iraq, especially if it is imbedded in the proper political framework, would," in Kissinger's view, "help the war against terrorism."[127]

The *New York Times'* editorial board argued otherwise:

> Brent Scowcroft is a cautious, deliberate man accustomed to sharing his foreign policy views with Republican presidents in private, as he did as national security advisor to Gerald Ford and George H. W. Bush. That

Mr. Scowcroft would publicly question the current president on a matter as sensitive as Iraq is an extraordinary challenge to the Bush administration as it weighs whether to go to war to oust Saddam Hussein from power. Mr. Scowcroft's concerns about attacking Iraq, aired yesterday in an op-ed article in The Wall Street Journal, were the equivalent of a cannon shot across the White House lawn. The piece should erase any doubt about the need for a national debate on Iraq.[128]

Morton Kondracke of *Roll Call* also thought the op-ed served a valuable purpose. The Bush administration needed to go beyond claiming that Saddam Hussein was "a bad guy," Kondracke reasoned, and "go down the line and start answering Scowcroft's, Senator Carl Levin's, and others' objections."[129]

Scowcroft himself felt frustrated by all the attention and ultimately misused. His views were well known to Rice, Hadley, Cheney, Rumsfeld, and others in the administration—including the president, in all likelihood—as well as to Washington-area national security experts, and they had been for some time. In addition, the tone of the *Wall Street Journal*'s headline for the op-ed, "Don't Attack Saddam"—a title chosen by the editors, not by Scowcroft—was off-base. Scowcroft had never written that the United States *shouldn't* attack Iraq; he merely insisted that Bush and his advisers be certain that the attack was warranted and that they think through the consequences. The former national security advisor didn't want an attack on Iraq to divert the United States from the more important objective of the war on terror. The op-ed made an appeal for serious deliberation and caution, moreover; by no means was it a command to the Bush administration. It would have been wholly out of character for Scowcroft to use the imperative to address an American president.

The effect of Scowcroft's guest editorial was to estrange him from his former friends and associates, however. He essentially became *persona non grata* for George W. Bush and others in his administration. Even Robert Gates, the president of Texas A&M University at the time, writes that he was "dismayed when my closest friend and mentor, Brent Scowcroft," publicly disputed "the administration over his opposition to going to war in Iraq."[130] Also, because Scowcroft was chairman of PFIAB, his dissent "changed what PFIAB was able to do," one intelligence official observed, and it altered "the relationship between the White House and the intelligence community." In fact, Scowcroft's op-ed may have been the reason PFIAB was moved from "its offices next to the White House and stuck in a less desirable office building a few blocks away." (Scowcroft, perhaps charitably, attributed the relocation to renovations, not retribution).[131]

Although he never regretted writing the op-ed, Scowcroft scarcely imagined the hostility it would provoke. It caused him considerable personal discomfort and anguish, a longtime friend and associate noted. A reserved and private person by nature, Scowcroft hardly enjoyed being vilified by his former friends and colleagues, by commentators in the press, and by his fellow Republicans.[132]

WITH BUSH'S REELECTION in 2004, Scowcroft asked each member of PFIAB to submit his resignation. The president accepted Scowcroft's and that of most of the other PFIAB members. With that, George W. Bush "unceremoniously . . . dumped Brent Scowcroft," without having any private conversation with him or making any public acknowledgment of his government service.[133]

Scowcroft, in turn, was greatly disappointed with President Bush, Vice President Cheney, and Bush's other senior advisers. He was especially unsettled by Rice's behavior, according to the journalist Elizabeth Bumiller, confiding to a senior European diplomat, "I don't understand how my lady, my baby, my disciple, has changed so much."[134]

General Brent Scowcroft had made Condoleezza Rice. He had introduced her to others in government, industry, and the small world of foreign policy experts. In 1987 he had invited her to become a member of the Aspen Strategy Group. He introduced her to George H. W. Bush and his son, George W., and he appointed her to head the Soviet desk on his NSC staff. Not only did they become colleagues, they became close friends. And like most close friends, they shared common attributes. Rice, like Scowcroft, was well-spoken, fast on her feet, highly competent, a very quick study, public-spirited, and seemingly tireless. She was also poised under pressure, adept at working with people with strong personalities, and savvy at finding common ground among people with contending points of view. She was an outstanding teacher, too, one capable of making complex ideas accessible to those with less knowledge and experience.[135]

"We were just attracted to each other pretty early on," Rice said. "I adored him. I adore him now." The feeling was reciprocated.[136] Not only had Rice visited the senior President Bush and Scowcroft several times in Kennebunkport during the Bush 41 presidency, but in the mid-1990s she helped Bush and Scowcroft write *A World Transformed*, assisting on major portions of the manuscript addressing US-Soviet relations. The "most personally satisfying" part of working in the Bush 41 White House, she told one of her biographers, "was working with Brent Scowcroft."[137]

Notwithstanding Rice's stated intentions, her international realism, her past experience on the NSC staff, and their close friendship, their policy views didn't entirely coincide. Rice advocated the aggressive pursuit of a missile defense system, for instance, whereas Scowcroft remained a skeptic. She was much less willing to risk an open disagreement between the United States and Israel, and she didn't think an Israeli-Palestinian settlement was the United States' highest priority in its relations with Israel, much less in US policy toward the Middle East. Indicative of Rice's more pro-Israeli (and less pro-Saudi) foreign policy was the membership of the Vulcans. The group not only included conservatives who'd worked under Bush 41, such as Richard Armitage, Bob Blackwill, Robert Zoellick, and Stephen Hadley, it also included several neoconservatives: Richard Perle, Paul Wolfowitz, and Dov Zakheim (a former deputy under secretary of defense, a member of the Project for a New American Century, and the comptroller for the Department of Defense from 2001 to 2004).[138]

When Rice was working on the NSC staff with Scowcroft, their differences had little occasion to emerge, since neither SDI nor the Middle East was in Rice's portfolio. Rarely did her influence on national security policy extend beyond US-Soviet and East-West relations. So what Scowcroft may have perceived as her agreement on the goals and conduct of US foreign policy may have simply reflected Rice's limited role, her relatively junior status, and her ambition.

The attacks of September 11 made the differences between the two Bush presidencies increasingly apparent, however, differences that went well beyond content. They brought into relief more fundamental contrasts on how to run the NSC process. For one, Bush and Rice misjudged their top personnel choices. Whereas Bush 41 and Scowcroft paid extensive attention to how their top foreign policy appointees would interact—as well as they could anticipate such interaction from their past acquaintance—Bush 43 and Rice picked their top foreign policy advisers on the basis of talent and experience. The cost of not attending more to interpersonal chemistry was that policy making during Bush 43's first term was marked by a distinct absence of camaraderie and trust among several of the foreign policy principals.[139]

Powell, Rumsfeld, Cheney, and Rice simply didn't get along well together, as historians, journalists, and insider accounts have revealed. Cheney prevailed on Bush to select Rumsfeld as defense secretary. Once in office, Cheney and Rumsfeld proceeded to work in tandem to neutralize Powell's influence and undermine the State Department's voice in setting US foreign policy.

Powell's celebrity, outspokenness, charisma, and media savvy had begun to irritate Cheney and Rumsfeld, and the vice president "considered Powell an overreaching publicity hound, a man who spent too much time talking to Bob Woodward to be trusted," writes Victor Gold, a former aide to Barry Goldwater and longtime Republican. Powell, for his part, regarded "Cheney as a man who, not having experienced war, was given to grandiose military projects that played well in war games, but played hell in actual war."[140]

While this wasn't the first time that the secretary of state and secretary of defense were at odds with each other, as the histories of the Ford, Carter, and Reagan administrations show, it was the first time an extremely powerful vice president was part of the mix. Blackwill observed that "Powell and Rumsfeld, who sat next to each other" at White House meetings, might as well have been "on separate planets." At one NSC meeting in late August 2002, for instance, Blackwill was flabbergasted to see that neither Powell nor Rumsfeld was making any pretense of listening to the other; he realized there was "no engagement, no real discussion of military strategy or Iraq." Yet neither President Bush nor Rice forced the issue or insisted on a genuine dialogue. Absent such intervention, Rumsfeld and Cheney were able to marginalize the secretary of state.[141] In the words of one diplomat, Powell was "the Secretary of State who wasn't," and Kissinger joked that foreign policy makers looked upon the Department of State "as a small country that occasionally does business with the United States."[142]

Rumsfeld had similarly strained relations with the nation's military leaders and especially with the incumbent chairman of the Joint Chiefs of Staff, Gen. Hugh Shelton. In fact, former defense secretary William Perry found Rumsfeld's relationship with the Joint Chiefs—his direct subordinates under the 1986 Goldwater-Nichols Act—to be as broken as any he'd ever seen.[143] A few years later, many of those military leaders would be clamoring for Rumsfeld's resignation.

Neither did Rumsfeld or Cheney give Rice much respect. She was a generation younger; she had little bureaucratic experience (having previously spent only three years in Washington, one year as special assistant to the director of the Joint Chiefs, in 1986–1987, and two years as a member of Scowcroft's NSC staff); and she wasn't a conceptual thinker. They saw her as a lightweight, someone who deferred to them and didn't engage with them as equals—at least not during Bush's first term in office. "What Condi is really good at," the writer Nora Ephron observed, "is making nice." Like other women of her generation, Rice was brought up to smooth over differences and not to force issues. She kept her thoughts to herself, knowing that she could always get in a word with President Bush later, if need be, given how close she was to the president.[144]

When Rice gave "tasks and guidance to combatant commanders and the joint staff," for instance, Rumsfeld let her have it. "You and the NSC staff need to understand that you are not in the chain of command. Since you cannot seem to accept that fact, my only choices are to go to the President and ask him to tell you to stop or to tell anyone in DoD not to respond to you or the NSC staff," he told her. "I have decided to take the latter course. [If] it fails, I'll have to go to the President. One way or the other, it will stop, while I am Secretary of Defense." Taken aback, Rice didn't know what to say.[145]

When Rice convened meetings, moreover, Rumsfeld and Cheney sometimes neglected to do the necessary background reading, walked out of the meetings while they were still going on, or skipped them altogether—all without repercussions. One anonymous "very senior official" from the first Bush administration said he'd "never seen more high-level insubordination in the US government in almost thirty years" than with Rumsfeld and the Bush 43 presidency.[146]

As serious as Rumsfeld's insubordination may have been, more serious was the vice president's calculated circumvention of Rice and the NSC process.

Vice presidents normally don't have staffs large enough to allow them to participate in more than the one or two issue areas in which they choose to specialize, so as a practical matter they attend high-level policy meetings on only their chosen specialties and don't participate in others. Cheney broke this mold. He added fourteen staff members in national security alone to the Office of the Vice President and created a total staff of fifty to sixty people—about as large as the NSC staff of several postwar presidencies. As a result, the vice president had enough assistants to staff out issues and "work the paper"—that is, do the research, draft the memoranda for his and the president's consideration, and mark up and respond to the documents being received by the White House from others around the government.[147]

Cheney also set up his own sources of intelligence from within the government—including within the NSC staff—and from Iraq. Not only was he close to Donald Rumsfeld (although the exact quality of their relationship remains a mystery), he was on very good terms with the deputy secretary of defense, Paul Wolfowitz, the under secretary of defense, Douglas Feith, and the under secretary of state for arms control, John Bolton. He'd also been Hadley's boss during first Bush administration, and the deputy national security advisor routinely forwarded NSC communications to the Office of the Vice President. With the research and information that Cheney now had available thanks to these information stovepipes and his expanded staff, the vice president was able to engage in almost all high-level policy discussions. And because of his connections with Rumsfeld and others in the Department of Defense, he was able to circumvent Powell and the State Department and even Rice and her NSC staff.[148]

Making Cheney's operation even more effective was the fact that the vice president operated in secret. He worked with assistants that others in the White House didn't know about—and whose names he didn't share. He did business behind always-locked doors. He received clandestine visitors whose names were scrubbed from the White House's visitor logs.[149] And he promoted his chief of staff, Scooter Libby, to presidential assistant—just as Scowcroft had done with Gates under Bush 41—which gave Libby the same seniority and official rank as Rice and the chief of staff, Andy Card.[150]

Cheney thereby managed to subvert the policy-making process and transform how the office of the vice president had previously functioned. At first, he wanted to run the NSC meetings when Bush was out of town or couldn't attend, but when the president sided with the national security advisor, Cheney made an end run. He set up a shadow NSC in the Office of the Vice President in effect, thereby undermining the NSC process as it was supposed to function.[151] And like Rice, he had an office located in the White House's West Wing, close to the Oval Office, and a relatively small staff.

It was Cheney who Scowcroft in 2005 called "the real anomaly in the Administration"—not the president, Rice, or Hadley, each of whom also acted contrary to his expectations. Scowcroft had "consider[ed] Cheney a good friend—I've known him for thirty years. But Dick Cheney I don't know anymore," he told Jeffrey Goldberg for a profile in the *New Yorker*. Cheney responded to Scowcroft's statement by saying the chief reason his views had changed over time—as "happens to most of us"—was his continued fear "of a 9/11 with nukes or biological agents." He worried about "a handful of terrorists in the midst of our cities with far deadlier technology than they used on 9/11. And that fundamental fact led me to a set of conclusions about the kind of strategy we needed to pursue, how aggressively we needed to pursue it, if we were going to successfully defend the nation against follow-on attacks." "Brent," he went on, "is entitled to his view and his opinion." He then added: "Of course he wasn't in the White House bunker on 9/11. . . . I think his views might be very different if he'd gone through and had to deal with that set of issues we found ourselves having to deal with the morning after 9/11."[152]

But Scowcroft had not been talking about Cheney's fearful reaction to 9/11, his belief in US military supremacy, or his advocacy of executive privilege. What Scowcroft was objecting to, and the proximate cause for his remark, was Cheney's uncritical acceptance of the views of the Princeton historian Bernard Lewis, who the vice president consulted after September 11, 2001. "I believe that one of the things you've got to do to Arabs is hit them between the eyes with a big stick," Lewis had said. "They respect power."[153]

Scowcroft found it remarkable that Cheney would accept this simplistic, racist, and ultimately uninstructive analysis. Whereas Cheney had been previously willing to negotiate with Baker, Scowcroft, Powell, and President Bush over the issues and haggle with congressional Democrats, the vice president now seemed to have lost his reasonableness and respect for others. Scowcroft had seen this quality earlier, in Cheney's reaction to his report on intelligence reform, and he then witnessed it with Cheney's claim that Iraq had purchased yellowcake uranium from Niger, despite the dodgy intelligence, and his direct link between Saddam and Al Qaeda operatives, despite the lack of evidence for any significant connection. *This* was the anomaly for Scowcroft: that Cheney seemed to have lost his sober judgment and intellectual honesty—someone who Representative Martin Frost, a Democrat from Texas, called a "man of integrity."[154]

Some wondered, too—Scowcroft included—whether Cheney's several heart operations had altered his personality, since cardiac surgery may cause behavioral change.[155] Whatever the cause, many in Washington thought Cheney had changed, Lawrence Eagleburger among them. In 2009, Eagleburger said of his former White House colleague, "I wouldn't trust him with my dog across the street."[156]

═══

PRESIDENTIAL ADMINISTRATIONS ARE renowned for their fractious politics; the Lincoln, FDR, and Reagan presidencies are cases in point. Yet what distinguished the Bush 43 administration was that when confronted by crisis, the president and Rice were unable to forge a coherent NSC process. The clash of personalities in the administration of George W. Bush led to cata-strophic results.[157]

There were no NSC meetings to examine the underlying premise that the United States should go to war against Iraq. Neither were there meet-ings of the NSC, the Principals Committee, or any other organizational body to address what would be two critical, disastrous decisions made by L. Paul "Jerry" Bremer, the presidential envoy to Iraq: to expunge all thirty thousand Ba'ath Party members from the Iraqi government and to disband the half-million-member Iraqi army and its intelligence services.[158]

Yet Bremer's ill-advised actions—which had the effect of removing al-most all public officials from Iraq's government while under US occupa-tion, including government officials with critical expertise, Ba'ath-affiliated schoolteachers, and policemen on the street, as well as alienating potential allies of the United States within Iraq—were never run through an inter-agency process. Neither the Joint Chiefs, the CIA, nor the State Department had been consulted, even though the decisions ran contrary to the lessons of post–World War II Germany and Japan and contradicted the commonsense notion that foreign occupiers need the help of middle- and lower-tier gov-ernment authorities to maintain political order and to ensure the continuity of government. Without a substitute system ready to put in place after the invasion, and with the CIA and State Department often excluded from the decision process, the Defense Department took over handling of the US occupation of Iraq.[159]

In his memoirs, George W. Bush distances himself from these decisions by using the passive voice: "The Iraqi police force had collapsed when the regime fell," he writes. "The Iraqi army had melted away." Bremer may have acted on his own authority, which is what Scowcroft suspected; others credited Rumsfeld (Bremer himself said the policies came from Doug Feith, the under secretary of defense).[160] But the responsibility for vetting the soundness of national security policy decisions and for coordinating admin-istration policy lies with the national security advisor—and Rice failed to exercise that responsibility.

The result was that secretary of state Colin Powell, deputy secretary of state Richard Armitage, DCI George Tenet, and others in the government—especially in the State Department and CIA—were essentially made irrele-vant. And as Ivo Daalder and I. M. Destler point out, Rice, Hadley, and the NSC joined in to help make them feel as though "they were not on the team."[161]

The "National Security Council was dysfunctional," one of the mem-bers of the 9/11 Commission remarked—a view shared by all of the commissioners, according to this official.[162] Rice and the NSC "had failed in the principal job of resolving differences among the cabinet members," Armitage bluntly told Rice in July 2003. Elliott Abrams thought the foreign policy process had gone "off the rails."[163] Army Gen. Wesley Clark bluntly described the NSC process "out of whack."[164]

It would be "deeply unfair" to blame Rice, Robert Blackwill says. In Blackwill's view, it would have been nearly impossible for anyone to be able to simultaneously manage Powell, Cheney, and Rumsfeld. Even Kissinger and Scowcroft would have found the "class of egos and worldviews similarly difficult" to handle, he said. Robert Gates similarly remarked that "when you have two players who aren't willing to participate, no one could have made it work." Or, in the words of one of Scowcroft's former NSC staff members, Rice "didn't have a prayer."[165]

Blackwill and Gates were being generous. Kissinger and Scowcroft *would* have handled things very differently. Not only did Kissinger always have a highly privileged relationship with presidents Nixon and Ford, the secretary of state made sure the relationships stayed that way. When Kissinger thought things weren't going as they should, he would threaten to resign—a threat he made repeatedly. There's no doubt that Kissinger *would* have resigned had he felt he was being outmaneuvered, ignored, or otherwise cut out of the policy-making process. And he came close to doing so on several occasions. (When Kissinger said he was going to quit during Ford's reelection campaign, Tom Korologos, a political adviser to the president, quickly said, "Henry, for Christ's sake, if you're going to quit, do it now, we need the votes.")[166] It is impossible to imagine Kissinger letting a secretary of state, secretary of defense, or vice president marginalize his input on policy decisions.

Scowcroft likewise enjoyed very close relationships with presidents Nixon, Ford, and Bush 41, and exercised tight control over the NSC process. With his knowledge of the bureaucracy, his attention to personnel decisions, his expertise and command of the facts, and his strength of will, Scowcroft wouldn't have permitted the NSC process to deteriorate as it did under Bush 43. And while Scowcroft never threatened to resign, it is similarly impossible to imagine him letting a secretary of defense, vice president, or other senior official push him to the margins of the decision-making process. As Senator Sam Nunn pointed out, one of Brent's "rare" and "amazing" talents was his ability to handle "big egos."[167]

However effective Rice had been as head of the NSC's Soviet desk from 1989 to 1991—and she had been highly effective—she did not manage the NSC process as it needed to be managed. Yet she could have threatened to resign if that was what it would have taken to bring discipline to the NSC process, just as Kissinger had during the Nixon and Ford administrations and as Shultz did during the Reagan presidency. Instead, she preferred to be a confidante, close personal adviser, and friend to George W. Bush.[168]

Of course, how the government runs and how the national security advisor is used is the president's prerogative. "In the end it's the president's responsibility," Scowcroft observes.[169] Yet "at the outset of his administration," a new president "must put together a team of staff members even when he has only the dimmest notion of what his own job really is."[170] The president has little way to "know whether he is putting together a closely knit team or a bunch of people who will spend most of their time fighting each other rather than constructing and managing his policy."[171] The success of a president's foreign policy necessarily depends on the quality of those who coordinate decisions, then—the national security advisor and the White House chief of staff, in particular—and the quality of their interactions. He has to trust that his appointees don't prioritize their own ambitions or their particular policy, partisan, or ideological objectives when working with their fellow principals. This is especially true for the national security advisor, on whom the president has to rely to get the advice he needs in order to make the best possible choices.

Scowcroft described his own "approach to almost every question is to view it with informed skepticism," because "if it doesn't work, what happens?" It was "important that the national security advisor tell the president what you think he or she needs to know, not what he wants to hear. And that," he admitted, "can be tough."[172] If "all the advisers agree on a certain course of action," then things are relatively simple, he observed. But when "they disagree, it becomes more complicated, and the issue is how you deal with the disagreements." The "best way" to handle disagreements, he thought, was to convene a meeting of the president's senior advisers. He would "have each one of them explain their rationale, and then [he would] help the president decide among them."[173] Some presidents, like Nixon, preferred to do this on paper. Nixon would "study the different options and come back and decide." Others, such as Ford and George Bush, "liked to hear the discussion in person and hear the arguments back and forth as an aid to making decisions."[174]

Rice didn't see her role as that of a skeptic or as the enforcer of a rigorous NSC process, however. Neither she nor any of Bush 43's advisers insisted that the president see the information he needed to see. She left it up to others to propose ideas and suggest initiatives, Scowcroft told Marcus Mabry, one of her biographers. For all of her talents as a synthesizer and debater, he didn't view Rice as an innovator or particularly intellectual. Indeed, one of Rice's friends and a colleague at Stanford called her "the least reflective person" he knew.[175] Instead, she saw her role as helping the president fulfill his own preferences, reassuring him about his decisions, and protecting him. As she warned one foreign diplomat after she became secretary of state, "Don't upset him."[176]

Rice's preference for staying close to Bush—and she had more access to him in the presidential residence, at Camp David, and out on the ranch in Crawford than any other White House official—may explain why she was willing to tolerate a dysfunctional NSC process. Missing, though, was a cold-eyed, objective perspective on the United States' long-term interests, however much she may have agreed with the administration's causes and courses of action. What bothered Scowcroft more than Rice being upset with him, said a friend, "was the fact that here she is, the national security advisor, and she's not interested in what a former national security advisor had to say"—someone whom she had professed to respect and admire.[177]

Rice's stepmother mentioned another factor that may have led Rice to defer to Cheney and Rumsfeld and to accept their hijacking of both the substance of national security and the NSC process after September 11. "I just can't see [Condi] taking failure . . . just the thought of losing, I don't think that would go too well with her," Clara Rice said in reference to Rice's decision not to run in 1998 for Pete Wilson's open California senate seat. Or, as Victor Gold suggests, she may have been a "careerist with eyes fixed on the next rung up the political ladder." Scowcroft said as much: that he thought he had been "helpful and useful to her."[178]

Yet this ambition, however blind, meshed with another, pricklier reality. As a young, very bright, and attractive African American woman in the older, white, and male world of national security policy experts (and the Republican Party), Rice no doubt made her patrons feel good about themselves. Consistent with this role, she participated in George W. Bush's 2000 presidential campaign by giving speeches and otherwise serving as a symbol for African American women and of the Republican Party's inclusiveness.[179]

George W. Bush, to be sure, shoulders much of the responsibility for his hands-off decision making, which intersected in unfortunate ways with his overconfidence, his incuriosity, his lack of skepticism, and his zeal. Neither did he "encourage truth-telling or at least a full exploration of all that could go wrong," Evan Thomas and Richard Wolffe wrote in *Newsweek*. Scowcroft was more plain-spoken: he said Bush 43 was the worst foreign policy president he had known.[180]

Scowcroft also acknowledged the complicity of the president's advisers, however, and was "very disappointed with Condi Rice and Dick Cheney." Although neither Cheney nor Rumsfeld trusted Rice or wanted to let her run the NSC process it came "down to Condi Rice," as the national security advisor, to insist on having a structured decision-making process, a former intelligence official explained. This official called Rice "perhaps the worst national security advisor we've ever had." It is "utterly amazing" how "one person . . . can make all the difference in the world."[181]

Rice later conceded she had been in over her head. "No one told me Iraq would be so difficult," Rice told Scowcroft at a dinner party. "Yes, they did," he replied, "but you weren't listening."[182]

30

ELDER STATESMAN

THE FACT THAT the White House cut its ties with Brent Scowcroft after his controversial *Wall Street Journal* op-ed in August 2002 didn't dissuade him from remaining in touch with Rice, Hadley, and others in the White House. Even though he was hurt by Rice's harsh reaction to his dissenting op-ed, he didn't "want to break with the administration," he told her—and he didn't.[183] In August 2003, only a few months after the United States entered Iraq, Scowcroft wrote that the United States had "no choice but to succeed"—this just a year after his dissenting op-ed.[184] In fact, Scowcroft was seen visiting Rice not long after she became secretary of state in early 2005 and was in touch with the new national security advisor, Stephen Hadley. Two years later, in February 2007, Scowcroft spoke before the Senate in support of President Bush's proposed troop surge in Iraq.[185]

Yet the damage had been done. The US government would spend more than $1 trillion on the war in Iraq. Thousands of American soldiers would lose their lives, and tens of thousands more would suffer debilitating physical injuries and serious psychological damage. Hundreds of thousands of Iraqis and Kurds would be injured or killed, while millions more would be displaced. There were also many deaths and injuries among the United States' allies as well as among US-based and foreign military contractors.

As opinions in Congress, the press, and the public shifted against the Iraq war beginning in 2004, the administration itself changed tack at the beginning of Bush's second term. One manifestation of this new turn was the president's selection of Stephen Hadley as national security advisor. Hadley reinstated the role of the national security advisor as an honest broker, began to hold more regular meetings—formal and informal—and when there were strong disagreements among the principals, he didn't attempt to "dumb it down" or "reach a consensus" at all costs. Instead, he made sure that all had "their say" and that the NSC process functioned "in a transparent way." Not only was Hadley "comfortable" bringing issues before the president, he explicitly modeled his role on the model articulated in the Tower Commission report and Scowcroft's example. Like his former boss, business partner in the 1990s, and friend, he kept a low profile, exposed the president to more options, and gained Bush's confidence.[186]

Scowcroft's views on foreign policy gained further traction when after the 2006 midterm elections Bush appointed Scowcroft's former deputy and close friend Robert Gates as secretary of defense. Scowcroft was in touch with Gates at least once a week—and several times a week when Gates first got into office—and the two met regularly for lunch or dinner. They shared a fundamental commitment to the current and future security of the United States, held similar views on the United States' global responsibilities and on the need for international cooperation, and were equally cautious with respect to the use of force.[187]

Part of the reason Gates received such strong praise for his performance as defense secretary—and he is generally regarded as one of the best secretaries of defense in the postwar era—was his good working relationships with Secretary of State Rice, with whom he had worked under Scowcroft on the NSC, and with Hadley. Meanwhile, Cheney's influence over the president and the administration's policies waned over the course of Bush's second term.[188]

Gates joined the Bush administration under difficult conditions, however. Faced with the United States' lack of success in Iraq, the increasing cost, and the growing unpopularity of the occupation, Gates began to rethink the US role in Iraq and, with Rice, Hadley, and the president, began to consider various exit options. Victory wasn't a realistic outcome, at least not as conventionally defined, so unless the United States was prepared to occupy Iraq indefinitely, Gates had to find a way for the administration to be able to pull out US forces and leave Iraq with a viable elected government.

Gates, Rice, and Hadley also realized that they'd put themselves into a bind with respect to the Middle East. They knew the United States was in a poor position to attack Iran, despite the calls from neoconservatives, others on the right, and the vice president himself for just such an attack. The administration consequently began to reduce its belligerent rhetoric against Iran and opened up an avenue for dialogue with Iranian leaders. This, of course, had long also been Scowcroft's position. Just as important, the administration proceeded to jump-start talks between the Israelis and the Palestinians, appreciating that a resolution of the Israeli-Palestinian issue was critical to political stability in the Middle East.[189] In December

2007, Secretary Rice hosted a large summit in Annapolis, Maryland, to mark its new diplomatic course on the Middle East and to try to begin a dialogue. The summit no doubt came too late in the second term to have much impact, given all that had already happened, but it nonetheless signaled to domestic and international audiences alike that the administration was trying to repair the dismal situation in the Middle East.

It's hard to know just how influential Scowcroft was with respect to US Middle East policy and US foreign policy more generally during Bush's second term in office. Rice, Gates, and Hadley could hardly publicize the fact that they were receiving advice from Scowcroft, and Hadley gave Rice all the credit for progress on talks toward a Middle East peace settlement. Scowcroft, for his part, only says that he "stayed in touch with people, but quietly and carefully." We know that all three principals were in close touch with him, however, as was DCI Michael Hayden, and that they wanted to make changes. Scowcroft's successor as PFIAB chairman, James C. Langdon Jr.—an attorney with Akin Gump and close to President Bush—simply says that Scowcroft was "very, very instrumental to major decisions Bush made" after 2004.[190]

With his renewed visibility, enhanced reputation, and established experience, Scowcroft became a prime source for US and foreign correspondents writing on US national security, foreign policy, and military affairs. Paul Krugman wrote that Scowcroft was among the few who should be honored "for their wisdom and courage" in braving "political pressure and ridicule to oppose what Al Gore has rightly called 'the worst strategic mistake in the history of the United States.'"[191] Or, as a close observer of the intelligence community remarked, "There's nobody more respected, nobody up and down the line, who is more respected than Scowcroft." Others have said much the same.[192]

Scowcroft's informal advising during the last years of the Bush 43 White House and then the Obama administration—where he remained in touch with Gates—was one indicator of his stature as an elder statesman. Another was his participation in the mid-2000s and early 2010s on a number of important commissions—invitations that Scowcroft's ethic of public service made it hard for him to decline. He cochaired a 2004 study of the United Nations, a 2008 Council on Foreign Relations study on the control and reduction of nuclear weapons, a 2009 National Research Council study of export controls, US economy, and national security, and President Obama's 2011–2012 Blue Ribbon Commission on America's Nuclear Future, which studied the disposal of nuclear waste. (Its deliberations were hampered by the Fukushima disaster in March 2011; the Obama administration ultimately decided to bury the report.)[193]

Scowcroft's life in these more recent years remained full with public appearances, meetings, consulting work, travel, interviews, and other obligations. He continued to spend almost half of his time on Scowcroft Group business (and continued to arrive at the office by six in the morning on the weekdays so he could beat the traffic). Throughout, he continued to think about, give speeches on, and write of the larger issues at stake in US foreign relations and national security policy.

He wrote more than thirty op-eds over the two terms of the George W. Bush presidency, where the issues he addressed in those pieces were much like those he had emphasized in years past. He maintained that the United States had to be willing to act either bilaterally or multilaterally, since different issues called for alliances with different partners.[194] He insisted that the United States needed to persuade other states to cooperate, even states such as Russia, China, India, and Pakistan, if it wanted to reduce international instability. He exhorted policy makers to be willing to rely on international institutions such as the United Nations, NATO, or the European Union if doing so would help the United States achieve its objectives. Likewise, the United States had to agree to participate in, abide by, and, when required, renegotiate treaties and agreements such as the Non-Proliferation Treaty on nuclear weapons and the comprehensive agreements on chemical and biological weapons (the Chemical Weapons Convention and the Biological Weapons Convention).

He argued in 2002 that the United States should be prepared to use force in the 2002 unless Pyongyang stopped expanding its nuclear weapons capabilities. With respect to Iran, however, he recommended that the United States work with other nuclear powers and that Iran itself should commit to an international agreement that would make it unnecessary for it to continue with its nuclear weapons program—an approach that came to fruition in 2013.[195]

The Israeli-Palestinian issue likewise remained a prominent subject. Scowcroft repeatedly called for US officials to directly engage in defusing Arab-Israeli hostilities—a possibility made easier by Yasser Arafat's death in late 2004—and to take the lead in pursuit of a two-state solution, which he believed held the key to stability in the Middle East.[196] And he wrote on Colombia, Taiwan, or other topics when he felt US policy demanded a policy debate or deeper analysis. Only infrequently did he go on television.[197]

THE FACT THAT Scowcroft's active career extended into his eighties is to some extent the result of his disciplined attention to physical fitness. When in Washington he works out regularly with a personal trainer who mixes aerobic exercise with strength and resistance work; he also does calisthenics on his own at home. When hiking during the annual Aspen Strategy Group meetings in Colorado, Scowcroft in his seventies and early eighties could climb thirteen-to-fourteen-thousand-foot peaks faster than colleagues and friends in their fifties and sixties. (One of the standard hikes was nicknamed "Scowcroft's Bataan Death March" or simply "Scowcroft's Death March" by Aspen Strategy Group members, with some of the members contacting the Aspen Strategy Group staff before the five-day August meetings to find out what day the hike would be on, so they wouldn't miss it.)[198]

On one occasion, in the summer of 1991, his enjoyment of hiking and physical exertion got the better of his judgment. He and Jan Lodal—Lodal was one of McNamara's "whiz kids" who had been on Kissinger's NSC staff and was an active Aspen Strategy Group member from 1976 until 1994— didn't start their hike until two o'clock in the afternoon. But because they wanted to have lunch and had to drive to the base site before even starting to climb the fourteen-thousand-foot mountain, they didn't return before nightfall. Others naturally got worried, and DCI William Webster joked that he would use all of his powers to find them. The two finally got back at ten o'clock that night with some "fairly minor injuries" from stumbling in the dark.[199]

Notwithstanding Scowcroft's superb fitness, in the 2000s he began to be bothered by arthritis and bad knees, had to have hip replacement surgery, suffered outbreaks of bronchitis and shingles, and experienced more fluctuations in his energy than he had previously. On some days he felt "okay," "fine," or "pretty good," while on others he'd say self-disparagingly that he was "still vertical," "surviving," or doing "better than I deserve." On still other occasions he described himself as feeling "worse and worse" or as having "a horrible day."[200]

More than compensating for his slowly declining health was the birth of his granddaughter, Meghan, in 2008. She "made him absolutely euphoric," said one of his longtime friends. He was "so proud of her, and so excited to be with her." Perhaps because he spent a lot of time with his granddaughter and she was wearing him out, he began to sleep a little longer, take a little more time off in his busy schedule, and cut down on his travel. Most weekends he spent with his daughter and granddaughter, either in New York (he'd take the train up) or at home in Bethesda (they'd come down). In the summers they would often meet up at his condo in Kennebunkport.

Before Meghan was born, he spent every other summer weekend up in Maine, going up on Friday and taking the six o'clock air shuttle back on Monday morning. On vacations he would go skiing at various Utah resorts, often with his daughter, until his knees gave out. He also took trips with former president George H. W. Bush until that was no longer possible because of the former president's fading health. He also spent more time with his nieces, nephews, and other members of his extended family.[201]

Scowcroft also began to devote attention to his legacy. He wanted "to help people the way I would have liked to have been helped when I was in their position"—perhaps referring to times in his early career, such as after his crash and before his attendance at West Point, when he'd been largely on his own. Now, he said, he wanted to "give back in appreciation" what he'd "been lucky to get" at other points in his career, from mentors like Fox and Yudkin. Accordingly, he began to establish various programs to assist people who had ambitions similar to his own.[202]

He helped fund a scholarship for West Point cadets in 2000, the Government Internships Endowment. The money allowed West Point to underwrite a cultural and professional immersion program that gave thirty to fifty cadets the chance to spend three to eight weeks in the Department of Defense, the Department of Energy, the White House, and other departments and agencies of the US government in Washington. Separately, Scowcroft contributed to another fund, the Olmstead Scholars Program, that enabled young officers to spend time overseas and in the District of Columbia.[203] General Daniel Christman, the superintendent at West Point, said Scowcroft "felt so strongly about the necessity of young officers to have this identification with other religions, cultures, languages." And Scowcroft made a point of attending a reception that Senator Jack Reed of Rhode Island hosted every summer in Washington for cadets in the West Point programs.[204]

Scowcroft also funded the Arnold Kanter Chair at the Atlantic Council's Brent Scowcroft Center on International Security in 2006 and established a paid internship program at the Aspen Strategy Group. The highly competitive internship program allowed four outstanding college graduates interested in working on national security issues to spend a summer in Washington and part of August out in Aspen.[205]

When former president George H. W. Bush established the Bush Presidential Library and the Texas A&M regents created the Bush School of Government and Public Service, they also wanted to establish an affiliated research institute. When the former president asked his friend if he would like his name on it, Scowcroft said he would be honored. The Scowcroft Institute opened on November 10, 2007, and Scowcroft himself endowed it with funds for scholarships, administrative support, grants, a major annual conference, and a chaired faculty position. Just as important, he helped find other donors to get the Bush School off the ground. As a member of the Bush School advisory board, he goes to College Station at least once a year and uses the time to meet one-on-one with students, give a public address, and visit the former president.[206]

In 2009, he established and endowed the Brent Scowcroft Professorship in National Security Studies within the Eisenhower Center for Space and Defense Studies in the Department of Political Science at the US Air Force Academy. The chair was to be filled by a scholar of national reputation, someone with a distinguished military record as well as outstanding academic record.

He even set up an internship program at the Scowcroft Group. The program began when Scowcroft was president of the Forum for International Policy and Condoleezza Rice, who was back at Stanford University, asked him to host her teaching assistant one summer. He agreed, and ever since then, the Scowcroft Group has as a matter of routine had two interns at any one time. They work full-time in the summer and on a part-time basis during the academic year, since they are typically also taking graduate classes at DC-area universities while they are working at the Scowcroft Group. The interns are exposed to strategic issues and international business consulting during their internship, and every two weeks Scowcroft sits down with them and invites their questions in an off-the-record "stump-the-general" session. With just the three of them in this setting, Scowcroft can be "extremely candid"; the interns call him "Yoda."[207]

Neither could he say no when schoolchildren or students wanted to meet with him, his colleagues attest.

"Brent . . . feels a strong obligation to help the next generation of scholars, public servants, whatever," Kanter said. "He gives interviews, answers questions from graduate students and people working on their dissertations . . . [T]his or that group will ask him to give a speech" and he will do so, even though "he's not getting paid." When a friend and West Point classmate, Maj. Gen. Edwin Robertson, invited Scowcroft to give a talk to junior officers at the Chanute Tactical Training Center in southern Illinois, Robertson observed that for all his brilliance, "Brent . . . never talks down to anybody. And if you express an idea, he always interested in it, and he's just a delightful person to deal with."[208]

Scowcroft's attention to cultivating succeeding generations of public servants constitutes an implicit response to the lesson of Vietnam as captured by David Halberstam in *The Best and the Brightest*: that leadership by foreign policy elites failed. Scowcroft's answer is that with proper mentoring and more careful attention to personnel decisions—and here is where personal networks are critical—policymakers can make better choices. Institutions such as the Aspen Strategy Group, the Atlantic Council, the US Military Academy, and the National Defense University enable future public servants to be exposed to their peers and their seniors in the federal government, in Congress, in the military, in the media, in academia, and in the business world—that is, with those they will have to work and those whose views they will have to take into account.

⸻

IN EARLY 2008 Scowcroft and David Ignatius worked together on *America and the World*, in which he and Brzezinski offered their perspectives on the changes of the previous two decades, from the end of the Cold War to the late 2000s, and used the occasion to look both backward and forward in time. *America and the World* was the brainchild of Steve Clemons of the New America Foundation, and the project gave Scowcroft (and Brzezinski) the chance to expand on several of his many op-eds, provided him the opportunity to delve into the history of contemporary issues, and also allowed him to be more speculative.[209]

The first argument Scowcroft made in *America and the World* was to underscore that the end of the Cold War "marked a historical discontinuity." The Cold War conditioned "everything we did," for a single mistake could "blow up the planet"; anything not related to the Soviet-US relationship was "pinpricks," in Scowcroft's analysis. But then, "in the blink of any eye, that world came to an end," and now everything was pinpricks. The problem was that the US and global institutions and ideas that accompanied the Cold War had been developed and had evolved with the Cold War in mind. So even while American policy makers and opinion leaders understandably felt "enormous relief" with the passing of what Scowcroft considered to be the last of the great empires, the collapse of the Soviet Union also left US policy makers and opinion leaders "befuddled" and rudderless.[210]

Scowcroft recognized that the terrorist attacks of September 11, 2001, arrested the drift of US foreign policy. But the attacks weren't inevitable, just as the United States' war against Iraq didn't have to happen. The Bush administration's ill-advised decision to invade Iraq was, in Scowcroft's view, a failure of intelligence. He also observed that there seemed to be "a fundamental change in the attitude of the president after 9/11. A sort of religious fervor"—hinting at the selective perception and ideological zeal of the president, Cheney, Rumsfeld, Rice, and others, especially after 9/11.[211]

If the events of September 11 constituted one of the benchmarks of the contemporary world, others were the rise of China and India as centers of power and the rapid globalization arising from changes in information technology, public health, and the environment. In a world with more interdependent national economies and more liquid global finance (thanks in part to sovereign funds), the United States had no choice but to adjust its national security policy. Yet the United States' own institutions, whether the Defense Department, the CIA and intelligence community, the State Department, or other department and agencies, as of 2008 weren't suited to this new complexity. They hadn't been developed for today's interdependent, globalized, quickly changing world. The same held for international institutions such as the United Nations, which were likewise created for "a very different world" of separate nation-states.[212]

Scowcroft proposed that the worldwide effects of globalization were analogous to the effects that the industrial revolution had on regional economies and the formation of the nation-state. It was as if a new world, with its flood of instantaneous (and often unchecked) information, its near-immediate financial transactions, and its fast-moving trends, had been superimposed on the timeworn international structures of the old. What made things even more difficult was the fact that the United States of the late 2000s and foreseeable future was more negatively disposed to international organizations than it had ever been before.[213]

If there was nothing groundbreaking about Scowcroft's analyses in *America and the World*, what *was* striking about his comments was the comprehensiveness of his thinking, his command of the issues, his knowledge of the histories of individual countries and regions of the world, and his ability to connect the details of policy with a larger perspective on the United States' grand strategy.

There was another issue Scowcroft weighed in on shortly after the publication of *America and the World*. This was a widely heralded call for a world free of nuclear weapons written by George Shultz, William Perry, Henry Kissinger, and Sam Nunn in a *Wall Street Journal* op-ed on January 4, 2007. Using statements by Ronald Reagan, Mikhail Gorbachev, and Rajiv Gandhi advocating the abolition of nuclear weapons and the end to the possibility of a nuclear war as their points of departure, the four men outlined the concrete steps the United States could take so as to lead an international coalition of nuclear powers to realize their vision of a world free of the nuclear threat. These included increasing the warning time on nuclear weapons, reducing the size of nuclear forces, and ensuring the physical security of stockpiles of nuclear weapons, weapons-grade plutonium, and highly enriched uranium.[214]

While Scowcroft didn't disagree with the steps that Shultz, Perry, Kissinger, and Nunn were recommending, he had serious disagreement with the goal of "zero nukes." "The concept has several serious flaws," he told an interviewer. "First of all I think it's unlikely that we could ever achieve it. Even trying to achieve it, I think, may get in the way of doing some more practical things to improve the stability of the nuclear world and to achieve a goal which I think is perhaps possible, and therefore may be more desirable, and that is to insure that nuclear weapons are never used." And while he didn't think the United States and other nuclear powers "could ever get to zero, if we somehow did, and nothing else changed in the world, it could be a very perilous, unstable world." There was no way that "the knowledge of how to build nuclear weapons and, in a world of zero, just a few nuclear weapons could make a tremendous difference." It would leave the United States in "an extremely unstable world." The zero nukes idea was chimerical and it gave rise to false hopes to Americans and people around the world. For Scowcroft and Kanter, it was "unhelpful rhetoric."[215]

Instead, Scowcroft recommended finding ways to "make it most unlikely that there would ever be a resort to nuclear weapons in a crisis." One way to do this would be to alter "the character of the arsenals on each side" so as to make it "unlikely or impossible" that "he who strikes first can destroy enough of the opponents' weapons that he can survive a retaliatory strike."[216] But the most important thing, Scowcroft told Charles Ferguson, the president of the Federation of American Scientists and the project director for the Council of Foreign Relation's task force on US Nuclear Weapons Policy, was "the issue of crisis stability." No matter what the United States' policy was, "we have to make sure that we're not inadvertently creating an incentive for the first use of these weapons." Scowcroft wanted to minimize the chances that the use of nuclear weapons be a policy choice, even as he didn't renounce the "no first use" of nuclear weapons.[217]

Whether as the cochair and coeditor the Council of Foreign Relations' "US Nuclear Weapons Policy" report, the cochair of other task forces, such as "Colombia Task Force" of 2000 or the Blue Ribbon Commission on America's Nuclear Future of 2010–2011, Scowcroft took a broad, conceptual approach in his role. He insisted on using specific, forceful prose rather than the vague, general language that many reports use. He sought to make meaningful, practical recommendations. And he tried to achieve as much consensus as possible among the commission members by involving the other task force members in drafting the report from early on and by leading with a light touch—even though he usually had a very good sense of where he wanted to go. Thanks to Scowcroft's style, when task force members had differences with the final draft of the report, they expressed their views as "Alternative Views" rather than "Dissenting Views." Scowcroft said he couldn't remember any commission he chaired or cochaired issuing a "Minority Report."[218]

Besides serving on blue-ribbon commissions and engaging in his many other activities, Scowcroft began writing his memoirs in the early 2010s with the assistance of Charlotte McCall, who had assisted Scowcroft and George H. W. Bush with *A World Transformed*. He had started thinking about writing his memoirs once he reached his eighties, and his friends and colleagues had been pushing him to do so for some time. Not until 2012, however, when he began to realize his memory was starting to fade and he started to feel more palpably the other effects of age, did he commit to the project.

Notwithstanding Scowcroft's bipartisan foreign policy, the former national security advisor remained a loyal Republican. He consistently contributed to Republican candidates at the local, state, and national levels and in 2008 supported his old friend Senator John McCain, contributing to the campaign and offering foreign policy advice, despite his philosophical differences with McCain and the neoconservatives who dominated the campaign's foreign policy positions. Although some of the Democratic presidential hopefuls approached Scowcroft for his support in advance of the 2008 primary election and although the foreign policies being proposed by Senator Hillary Clinton and Senator Barack Obama came closer to Scowcroft's own positions than did McCain's, Scowcroft declined to endorse either campaign.

But once Obama was elected president, Susan Rice, who would become Obama's UN ambassador, talked to Scowcroft before she took office, as did the future secretary of state Hillary Clinton. Obama's first national security advisor, Marine Corps Gen. James Jones, was Scowcroft's friend as well as a former chairman of the Atlantic Council. Jones spent considerable time with Scowcroft before taking office, in fact, and periodically checked in with Scowcroft once in the job.[219] In fact, members of the Obama administration repeatedly talked to Scowcroft about foreign policy issues involving the Middle East, China, Russia, Europe, and global strategy (Latin America and

Africa not so much). And we know that Gates, an older hand who could guide the young administration feeling its way in foreign policy as James Mann points out, regularly stayed in touch with Scowcroft.[220]

In 2010 Scowcroft went so far as to describe himself as a Republican in name only—a RINO—in light of his general agreement with the Obama administration's early foreign policy and the bitterly partisan behavior of the Republican Party in Washington and nationwide.[221] Revealingly, Scowcroft didn't support Mitt Romney in 2012, notwithstanding the Republican nominee's international business background, his previous record as a pragmatic and moderate Republican when he was governor of Massachusetts, and his Mormonism. The problem for Scowcroft was that seventeen of twenty-four foreign policy advisers working on the Romney campaign were neoconservatives affiliated with George W. Bush.[222]

———

SCOWCROFT'S CAREER ACQUIRED another aspect as he aged: he started receiving prestigious awards. Many retired generals, admirals, statesmen, policy advisers, politicians, and diplomats receive awards in the latter stages of their lives, to be sure. What is extraordinary in Scowcroft's case, though, is the combination of the large number he has received, the prestige of the awards, and the variation among the bestowing organizations. The prizes manifest the almost universal respect others have for him and reflect the desire on the part of many people to recognize the scope and quality of Scowcroft's contributions to public service.

Scowcroft says that he is proudest of the Presidential Medal of Freedom he received after the Gulf War and then of the award of the insignia of an Honorary Knight of the British Empire (KBE) from Queen Elizabeth at Buckingham Palace in 1993. Yet these are only two of many. Others awards include the Eisenhower Institute's Eisenhower Leadership Prize from Gettysburg College (1992), the Hudson Institute's James H. Doolittle Award (1994), the Les Aspin Democracy Award from the Les Aspin Center for Government at Marquette University (2003), and the Association of the US Army's George Catlett Marshall Medal (2003).

Scowcroft also received the William Oliver Baker Award for service on behalf of the US intelligence community (2005), the Andrew Wellington Cordier Award for superior and distinguished public service from Columbia University (2005), the Andrew J. Goodpaster Award for his exemplary service to the nation (2008), the Distinguished Service Award of the

Military Order of the Carabao (2008), and the Grand Cross of the Order of Merit of the Federal Republic of Germany (2009). On March 13, 2013, Scowcroft was elected into the National Defense University's National Hall of Fame and received the National Defense University Foundation's first Lifetime International Statesman and Business Advocate award. And in April 2013, he received the Gerald R. Ford Foundation's Medal for Distinguished Public Service.

The many awards bear witness to Scowcroft's multiple spheres of achievement and the tremendous appreciation that former government officials, former elected officials, and prominent citizens have for him. The awards from Great Britain and Germany reflected Scowcroft's efforts on behalf of two of the United States' chief Atlantic partners. The William Oliver Baker award evidenced his commitment to the intelligence community. His prizes from the US Army Association, the Hudson Institute, and the National Defense University indicated his invaluable contributions to national security and the US armed forces, and his award from the National Defense University spoke to Scowcroft's contributions to global peace and international commerce. The Goodpaster and Carabao prizes reflected others' recognition of Scowcroft's selflessness in the cause of national service. And the Les Aspin and Gerald Ford awards pointed to his extraordinary character and remarkable commitment to the government of the United States.

Scowcroft joked that the prizes are "a pain," but added, "How could you not be pleased?" He was more than pleased in 2008 upon being inducted into the Hinckley Institute Hall of Fame at the University of Utah in Salt Lake City, however. He broke down, telling the audience the induction was "a vindication that my parents gave me all their love and work."[223]

The prizes further testify to the deep affection others have for him. He's "very endearing" says NBC News's Andrea Mitchell, a friend and longtime professional acquaintance. He has "a wonderful sense of humor" and "he's sort of mischievous," as though there were a "sort of a leprechaun quality to him at times." John Deutch, Robert Gates, and Gen. Joe Jordan each separately used the identical term to describe Scowcroft, calling him a "national treasure." And Eagleburger spoke of his colleague and friend as being "worth his weight in gold"—although finding that out, he added, "was a slow, gradual process."[224]

The honors indicate just how uncommonly devoted Scowcroft has been to the presidency and his country. Neither did he "have a false sense of his own importance," Gates remarks. Very simply, he has an encompassing dedication to national security, an extraordinary sense of duty, and no serious competing interests aside from his family. Even during relaxed moments together when Scowcroft was national security advisor and over the years since then, Gates says the two of them would "talk about foreign policy."[225] It's hard to imagine many people being more single-minded about US national security broadly conceived or being so dedicated without having their own personal, policy, or ideological ambitions getting in the way.

Even those with whom Scowcroft got crosswise respect him. George Shultz, who profoundly disagreed with Scowcroft and Bush on US-Soviet relations in the late 1980s, who as one of the "Four Horsemen" (as some called them) differed with him on "zero nukes," and who felt unfairly blamed by Scowcroft in the Tower Commission report, says "He's always been a person that you have to respect because he's thoughtful, informed, careful, and whatever his judgment is, it's worth listening to. You may agree with it or you may not agree with it, but . . . you respect it." Shultz even compliments the former national security advisor: "I thought the end game of the Cold War, they managed very well. I thought he must have had a lot to do with that." Neither do neoconservatives such as Bill Kristol or Elliott Abrams have anything negative to say about Scowcroft, despite their ideological differences and their substantive disagreements over US foreign policy.[226]

31

THE STRATEGIST

FOR NEARLY A half century Brent Scowcroft has kept his eyes on the big picture, observing events and developments around the world, anticipating how
domestic and international factors interrelate, and calculating the best way
for the United States to protect its national security and further its own interests. As a practical matter, this means engaging with foreign countries,
working within international institutions, and participating in multinational
coalitions—notwithstanding their problems, weaknesses and flaws. He ac-
cepts the world as it is, a world in which tyranny, corruption, ethnic hatreds,
and failed states persist. Consequently, he tolerates the moral failings of other
regimes. He has been willing to cooperate with Indonesia despite its brutal
repression of East Timor in the 1970s, for instance, with Iran under the shah,
and with China under Mao and then in the wake of Tiananmen Square.

Neither has he hesitated to advocate harsh measures if he thought they
were necessary, as with the Ford administration's response to the *Mayaguez*
incident, his insistence that Iraq leave Kuwait, and his call for air strikes
against Serbia in 1992.[227] Nor has he called for US intervention in humanitarian crises if he felt US interests weren't at stake, as with the Cambodian
genocide under Pol Pot and the Khmer Rouge after the fall of Phnom Penh
in 1975, the ethnic cleansing in Bosnia in 1992, and the Syrian government's brutal repression of rebel forces in 2013. In a world replete with
horror, US policymakers often have to make disciplined, hard-nosed, and
unpleasant choices. Scowcroft has been willing to make his share.

The seriousness with which Scowcroft studies US national security—the
possible result of the annealing effect that Pearl Harbor and the Second
World War had on him as a boy—leads Scowcroft to seek to minimize the
chances of near-term and future disasters and to preserve an acceptable status quo. In his view, it makes little sense for the United States to undertake
initiatives that risk going into uncharted territory where more horror and
worse demons may lie in wait.

In all these ways, Scowcroft exemplifies the realist approach to foreign policy. Yet Scowcroft differs from most realists in two respects. One is the thoughtful, independent manner by which he interprets American interests. Scowcroft has resisted being swayed by Congress, the press, or public opinion even when other policy makers and experts have not been immune. Whether with respect to the MX missile in 1983, Iraq in 1991 and 2001, the expansion of NATO in the 1990s (which he opposed) or the effort to forge a two-state solution in Israel, Scowcroft has called for distinct courses of action by US policymakers, often in the teeth of the preponderance of opinion within the foreign policy establishment.

He departs from most realists in a second way: he identifies himself more an "enlightened realist." Where classical realism assumes that international relations is a zero-sum game between foreign countries (or their leaders) and takes a skeptical attitude toward the possibility of international cooperation, Scowcroft sees US strategic interests as allowing for positive-sum exchanges among states—win-win solutions, in other words. Savvy policymakers can enhance US security and advance American interests as well as those of other states by engaging with foreign governments, working through international organizations, and participating in other institutions. In the United States' pursuit of many of its goals, whether the provision of a well-functioning international economy, the prevention of terrorism, the control of pandemics, or the protection of the environment, policy makers can be far more effective by seeking collective solutions, negotiated with other countries, rather than by acting on their own.

This is to say that Scowcroft believes in "global public goods," although it is not a term that he uses. Examples of other global public goods are the international agreements established by the United Nations on telecommunications, postal service, medicine, meteorology, maritime navigation, civil aviation, and other areas. These negotiated, collective agreements make international travel possible, facilitate global commerce, and provide for numerous other benefits in a world of interdependent states.[228]

However, some individual, organization, or government always has to initiate the action—to serve as a first mover. For Scowcroft, the natural catalyst is the United States. As the world's dominant power, the United States stands to benefit the most from international cooperation and a stable world order. But this requires that US presidents and other officials invest in and conduct the diplomacy that will enable organizations such as NATO, IMF, United Nations, and G-7 to resolve disputes, suppress conflicts, mitigate crises, and address other international issues. And because Scowcroft sees Americans and Europeans as sharing similar Western values, cultural assumptions, and, ultimately, philosophic and religious beliefs dating back to the seventeenth century, he considers the United States, Canada, and Western Europe to be natural allies and collaborators on addressing collective problems. (By contrast, after September 11, 2001, Vice President Cheney said he "just didn't have much time" and energy "for the international bureaucratic process." Neither did the George W. Bush administration accept other NATO members' willingness on September 12 to invoke Article 5, which provides for the collective defense of NATO members: if a NATO ally is a victim of an armed attack, the attack is regarded as an attack on all members.[229])

Scowcroft has both the tough-mindedness and military mind-set of the hawk and the dove's willingness to make contacts, negotiate, and improve political ties with other countries, organizations, and foreign leaders. Guided by this enlightened realism, Scowcroft has been extraordinarily successful in his handling of the complex and often hostile world of US foreign relations and national security, whether as an Air Force officer, a presidential adviser, or a business consultant. It's a world that demands decisive leadership, secrecy, and sometimes violence; it's one that also calls for a long-term perspective and a patient adherence to national goals. At the same time, he has been remarkably effective as a policy adviser in a second dimension—the fact that the United States is a democracy governed by its citizens acting through their elected representatives and informed by a free press. In his several public roles, Scowcroft has had to answer to Congress—if unofficially, since he has never held a position subject to Senate confirmation—been subject to scrutiny in the press, and been called upon to help win public support for controversial policies. It's a world that values consultation, calls for open debate, demands due process, and requires consensus building. At the same time, it is dominated by short-term considerations, especially the prospects for the next round of elections.

Scowcroft has operated where these two spheres coincide—and often collide—and he has been usually good at managing to reconcile the two. When he felt it was necessary, he resisted investigations into the intelligence community, wanted to closely hold information, stonewalled Congress, and zealously guarded the confidentiality of his clients. Scowcroft is "quick to purse [his lips] tightly shut," the *Los Angeles Times'* David Lauter observes, even as he is also quick to break into a smile.[230] At other times, however, Scowcroft has made a point of being available to Congress, other public officials, and members of the press. Indeed, many in Congress, across the departments and agencies of the government, in the press, and in business view him as more reliable and straightforward than other prominent officials and foreign policy experts.[231]

His effectiveness at handling these intersecting and sometimes clashing realms derives from the combined effect of his single-minded dedication to national security, his integrity and trustworthiness, and his selflessness and modesty. In a competitive world where everyone "wants to toot his horn," Scowcroft, his friend Bill Gulley observed, is "the last guy" to do that. "To understand Brent Scowcroft, you have to understand his humanity," says Daniel Poneman, an NSC colleague, a former partner in the Scowcroft Group, and a personal friend. "Not just his intellect. Not even just his judgment. But his humanity. It's a genuine humanity that respects other individuals as individuals. He knows exactly who he is and he is very comfortable with who he is. He feels fortunate to have had things happen to him that he never could have dreamed of as a kid growing up in Utah, as one of his friends and colleagues said. And he's never forgotten that kid from Ogden."[232]

Eagleburger described Scowcroft as indelibly Mormon (even though Scowcroft hasn't been an observant member of the church since his days at West Point—what is known as a "Jack Mormon").[233] His Mormon upbringing is reflected in the way "he does good as he can, without worrying about others," Jan Lodal remarks, adding, "He doesn't motivate anger and ill will, and he never shows it." He stays "even-keeled and authentic," even when others underestimate or misunderstand him—which, in Scowcroft's mind, is simply an inevitable consequence of leadership responsibility.[234]

Unsurprisingly, Scowcroft's dry-eyed, long-term view of US national security has its critics. Like most realists, he has been accused by those on both the right and the left of being indifferent to human rights.

Although he has not stated so explicitly, Scowcroft believes in an indirect pursuit of human rights—human rights as the by-product of public policy and international diplomacy. The United States can act to secure human rights only in situations in which it appears that the United States can readily secure its objectives in concert with a broad-based international coalition. More usually, the most the United States can do is quietly encourage other governments to respect human dignity. He worries that strong human rights rhetoric and unilateral humanitarian intervention may turn out to be counterproductive. Instead, he favors facilitating the conditions within states and creating the international conditions that can allow for political and economic liberties to take hold within foreign countries and make it less likely that foreign heads of state would feel the need to suppress human rights.[235]

Other critics have found him unimaginative as a strategic thinker. One former NSC official speaks of Scowcroft's "conformity" and "middle-of-the-road" policy making, for instance, and Elliott Abrams (among other neocons) regarded Scowcroft as taking a managerial view of the NSC process and believed that the George H. W. Bush administration had no vision. Some on the both left and right wings of the political spectrum see him as taking conventional, pro-establishment positions on the issues.[236]

There is something to this critique. Many of Scowcroft's positions have been well within the policy mainstream. And for much of his adult life he has gone along with conventional wisdom; his support of the Vietnam War, of a strong US deterrence against the Soviet Union, and of NAFTA are cases in point. He is famously reticent, and once he makes his case—sometimes quite forcefully—he doesn't insist on own position. Never once did Scowcroft protest decisions by leaking to the press or threatening to resign, and he is rightly regarded as being loyal and a team player.

Scowcroft's instincts and actions are those of a political insider. He believes in working with other influential people, out of public view. Somewhat wary of Congress, skeptical of the media, and uncertain about the wisdom of the public, he believes in a national security policy made by mandarins—a hierarchical approach to leadership that is characteristic of several of the institutions which Scowcroft has been a part of, such as the Air Force, the Department of Defense, the presidency, and the Mormon Church. As a natural insider, moreover, he is drawn to positions that reflect the views of experienced and worldly leaders of differing perspectives. As the journalist James Mann said about the membership of the Aspen Strategy Group, "Above all, they were respectable." The "Aspen participants were not too far to the left or right; there was no radical critic of the United States such as, say, the late Chalmers Johnson, inveighing against American empire, or isolationists like, say, Pat Buchanan or Ron Paul, urging that all U.S. troops simply be brought home," Mann reports. On the contrary, they "shared similar assumptions; they were senior practitioners, practical people who dwelt within the realm of the possible."[237]

Is this conformism? Of a sort. Scowcroft would identify it as bipartisanship or nonpartisanship instead, however, since Republicans, neoconservatives, liberals, and Democrats all attend the Aspen summer meetings. Furthermore, Scowcroft himself, as well as Joseph Nye and the culture itself of the Aspen Strategy Group meetings has done much to appeal to reasonable and responsible dialogue and to foster purposeful deliberation. Scowcroft often says little at the meetings and in other situations, but by virtue of his roles he has often been able to shape the agendas of policy discussions and by virtue of the respect he commands to lead by example.

He can be seen as a conformist in another important sense, though: his support for American business, consistent with his family's roots, his long-standing identity with the Republican Party, his role in Republican administrations, his work as a strategic consultant, and his membership on corporate boards. And yet this general support for US-based companies can itself be seen as a kind of nationalism or patriotism. The promotion of foreign investment, the encouragement of foreign trade, and the support of international institutions that promote economic growth such as the IMF, the WTO, and NAFTA, among others, serve to make US companies more competitive globally. Thriving US companies can provide the revenues, the raw materials, the skilled workforce, the energy needs, and the other goods and services that protect and promote the United States' international position and Americans' well-being.

"Some of the consulting he does, actually does advance the US national interest," Arnold Kanter said. "If [The Scowcroft Group] can help an American company [do] business in China, in a way that further strengthens US-China relations, that a good thing, and if we get paid to do it, so much the better."[238] Scowcroft agrees that he seeks to protect and help the interests of US companies, encourage research and development, aid weapons development, further American science and education, and safeguard the United States' preeminent status in the world. It is "basically who I am," he says.[239] As he wrote Missouri senator Republican Kit Bond in 1992 on the sale of new F-15s to Saudi Arabia, "You can feel certain that the economic viability of the American aerospace industry as well as its place in our defense industrial base are significant factors in our deliberations."[240]

Yet to say that Scowcroft is "predictable, unimaginative," "very timid," and a "cautious player," as the former NSC official quoted above said and some neocons contend, is misleading. A number of Scowcroft's actions, including his willingness to work with China after Tiananmen Square, his 1989 proposal to radically reduce force-levels in central Europe, his insistence that President Bush attend the 1992 world environmental summit in Rio de Janeiro (contrary to nearly all of Bush's other advisers), and his dissent against George W. Bush's plans to go to war against Iraq, reveal qualities other than a lack of boldness. They reveal a quiet confidence instead, an independent judgment, a consistent focus on the long term, and an understated courage.

To assert that Scowcroft did "everything within the forty-yard lines" also conflates different stages of his career.[241] Scowcroft *was* cautious when he was an Air Force officer and first started working for the Nixon administration; he accepted Nixon's and Kissinger's foreign policy, just as he had earlier followed the directives of his military bosses. Even so, he took considerable initiative as a military officer as we have seen and, less visibly, showed initiative as Kissinger's deputy. Once he became de facto national security advisor under presidents Nixon and Ford, and then national security advisor outright under presidents Ford and Bush 41, his independent leadership became more apparent, as seen with the handling of the evacuation of South Vietnam, the rescue of the British pound, and the orchestration of German reunification within NATO.

On some occasions Scowcroft himself moved the goalposts, as when he recommended the MX missile package to Congress and the Reagan White House in 1983, when in late 1991 and early 1992 he proposed that the United States unilaterally eliminate its tactical nuclear weapons among other measures, when he called for negotiations with Iran on its nuclear program during the George W. Bush administration, and with his repeated calls for a two-state solution in Israel—notwithstanding the opposition of many in Congress, many political analysts and media commentators, and even his colleagues in the Bush administration and US officials in later administrations.

However, it must be said that Scowcroft's insider perspective with its natural gravitation toward the foreign policy mainstream was ill-suited to the new era of the early 1990s. Confronted by the utterly transformed world that he, Baker, George H. W. Bush, and others in the administration had helped to bring about—a reunified Germany, a soundly defeated Iraq, a dissolved Soviet Union, a Europe whole and free, and an emerging China—Scowcroft and Bush remained conservative Cold Warriors, unhappy with Yeltsin, uneasy with Ukrainian independence, dubious about self-determination in Yugoslavia, silent on the democratic voices in China, and skeptical about other portents of impending change. And it may be that they simply didn't have enough time. Even so, over their last two years in office Scowcroft, the president, and their colleagues were unable to formulate a new approach to global relations commensurate with the revolutionary changes that they had helped bring about.

Scowcroft and Bush are more men of action than philosophers. But it would be a mistake to call them "stewards not visionaries, technocrats not philosophers," as Andrew Bacevich does in his book *American Empire*.[242] The two friends share a worldview that they articulated—if not always to the greatest effect—and worked to put into practice in Eastern Europe, China, and North America. It is a vision of a world shaped by open markets, US leadership, and international institutions, one bending toward democracy and human rights. And it rests on an underlying philosophy of old-fashioned Burkean conservatism that is cognizant of human dignity, protective of private property, and skeptical about ambitious plans for human progress. Still, it assumes that political leaders are capable of reasoned negotiation and intelligent cooperation. Hence Scowcroft's emphasis on rigorous discussion of issues in the NSC process and his faith that quiet conversations and timely writings are capable of persuading presidents, their advisers, and other policy makers to think through the possible consequences of their actions and consider alternative options.

Scowcroft's deep and long-standing influence on US national security policy, his ability to be highly effective across military, political, commercial, and intellectual dimensions of national security policy, and the confidence he inspires in others place him in rare company. In many ways, he resembles Elihu Root, who at the turn of the twentieth century served as secretary of war, chairman of the Republican Party, and US senator from New York. Root reformed the US Army and was a principal architect of the United States' expansion into the Caribbean and Western Pacific. Like Scowcroft, Root was a strategist, a writer, an insider, an intellectual, and comfortable at the highest levels of the political and business worlds.

Root was also at once an internationalist and a dedicated patriot. He worked with President Woodrow Wilson on behalf of the League of Nations; he helped establish the International Court of Justice; he participated in the Washington Naval Conference; he became the first president of the Carnegie Endowment for International Peace; and he received the Nobel Peace Prize in 1912. Even so, Root believed in the potential of the United States as a great power and strove to improve US military capabilities. When he agreed to put aside his private law practice to become secretary of war, it was to serve "the greatest of all our clients," Henry Stimson commented, "the government of our country."[243]

Henry Stimson himself is a second statesman with whom Scowcroft can be compared, as the historian David F. Schmitz observes. A lawyer by training, like Root, Stimson was secretary of state under President Hoover, governor-general of the Philippines under President Calvin Coolidge, and secretary of war under presidents William Howard Taft, Franklin D. Roosevelt, and Harry Truman. Stimson followed up on Root's reforms of the War Department and then supervised the great mobilization of personnel and supplies for the Second World War. He was "the consummate American statesman," Schmitz writes, who "personified the bipartisanship and practical idealism" that shaped US foreign policy and containment.[244]

Like Scowcroft, both Root and Stimson were among the closest advisers to several different American presidents and both were superb at working within the federal bureaucracy and with their White House colleagues. Root and Stimson also got along well with important members of Congress and the press, and both were liked and respected by others in Washington and abroad. Although Republicans, neither was viewed as partisan. More than merely insiders, they, like Scowcroft, came to be Washington institutions essential to the United States' international successes.

Scowcroft has been less of a public figure than either Root or Stimson were, though. It is hard to imagine Scowcroft running for public office or becoming the national spokesman for the Republican Party, as did Root. Self-effacing and unpretentious, Scowcroft doesn't think he necessarily knows more than the next person; "I don't expect to be right," he says.[245] And for someone who is impatient by those driven by their egos, he does not want the attention that running for office would bring. Campaigning for elected office calls for emotional appeals at the expense of logical persuasion, for disingenuousness and sophistry at the expense of sincerity, and for egocentrism at the expense of humility—none of which appeals to Scowcroft.

Electoral candidates have to project certitude to opinionated and fickle members of the press and the public, a self-presentation that flies in the face of Scowcroft's typically nuanced and sophisticated understanding of the issues and that contradicts the provisional qualities of judgments and decisions. "The process of running for public office is fairly abhorrent to me," Scowcroft admits. "I've watched [campaigns] close up, and it's demeaning." And while he "wouldn't mind being in public office," he says, he wouldn't want to do what's necessary to get there.[246] So Scowcroft has always remained a presence behind the throne, an éminence grise even before his hair turned gray.

In the end, we come back to Scowcroft the man and the human qualities that have made him an extraordinary person and policy maker. The late wife of Lawrence Eagleburger, Marlene Eagleburger, said that underneath his objectivity, practicality, and lack of sentimentality, Scowcroft is "a man of great faith," one who believes that any misfortune is "God's plan, and you deal with it."[247] When things don't go his way, he isn't prone to self-pity, second-guessing, or worrying about what might have been.[248] Instead, he remains focused on causes and institutions that transcend any single individual life. "There's nothing greater than to be working for something greater than you are," he says. "I think that the notion of duty, honor, country, as the motto by which you live and conduct your affairs, helps in so many ways: helps separate truth from error, right from wrong, all those sorts of things if you keep that in mind."[249]

Many have referred to Scowcroft as the last of his kind. Perhaps, particularly since his non-partisan approach to US foreign policy, his personal qualities, and the fact that his internationalism stands increasingly at odds with the main currents of the Republican Party. But it's more likely the case that people of his kind have always been uncommon: people dedicated to thinking and acting on behalf of the United States' long-term interests; people who are gifted with the analytical skills, intellectual talent, leadership ability, emotional intelligence, and tough-mindedness that allow them to translate their thoughts into actions; and people who are at once warm, modest, and considerate. Though these would seem to be simple-enough qualities, they are vanishingly rare. Especially in combination, and especially among those occupying the highest positions of power.

Brent Scowcroft: A Timeline

1925   Brent Scowcroft born in Ogden, March 19
Calvin Coolidge inaugurated

1944   Scowcroft arrives at West Point, July 1
D-Day
FDR reelected

1947   Graduates from the US Military Academy, June 3
Joins Army Air Corps, begins flight school in San Antonio
Truman Doctrine proclaimed for the containment of the Soviet Union
Voice of America begins broadcasts to Eastern Europe and the Soviet Union

1949   Crashes his F-51 fighter plane on a New Hampshire training mission, January 6
James Scowcroft, his father, dies, February 12
North Atlantic Treaty signed, forming NATO
Soviets detonate first atomic bomb
Communist revolution in China
Alger Hiss trial

1951   Marries Marian Horner, September 17
Truman fires General Douglas MacArthur
European Coal and Steel Community formed
Julius and Ethel Rosenberg are convicted of spying for the Soviets

1952   Begins graduate study at Columbia University, January
United States detonates first hydrogen bomb; Eisenhower elected president

1954   Joins USMA faculty at West Point, August
        Soviets test first hydrogen bomb
        French withdraw from Vietnam
        US Navy launches USS Nautilus, *first nuclear submarine*

1959   Begins two years at US embassy in Belgrade as assistant air
            attaché, May
        Cuban revolution; Nixon and Khrushchev engage in "Kitchen Debate"

1962   Starts teaching at the US Air Force Academy, January
        Cuban missile crisis

1964   Staff assistant to Maj. Gen. Richard Yudkin, USAF Headquarters,
            September
        Gulf of Tonkin Resolution
        Brezhnev succeeds Khrushchev

1968   Graduates from the National War College, May 31
        Completes doctoral thesis from Columbia University
            (PhD awarded 1967)
        Tet Offensive
        USS Pueblo *captured by North Korea*
        Prague Spring

1971   Appointed military assistant to President Richard Nixon,
            December 15
        *UN General Assembly recognizes the People's Republic of China as
            the sole legitimate government of China; "Ping Pong diplomacy";
            Kissinger visits China*

1972   Goes to China for advance work to facilitate Nixon's
            famous visit, February
        Travels to Moscow for the United States–Soviet Union
            summit, May
        Strategic Arms Limitation Treaty (SALT I) signed
        Nixon begins B-52 "Christmas bombing" campaign against Hanoi

1973   National security advisor Henry Kissinger selects Brig. Gen.
            Scowcroft as deputy assistant for national security affairs, January
        Kissinger becomes secretary of state, stays national
            security advisor, September
        Paris Peace Accords; Chilean coup deposes Allende; Yom Kippur War

1975   President Ford appoints Scowcroft national security advisor,
            November 3
        Lt. Gen. Scowcroft retires from the US Air Force, effective
            December 31
        Khmer Rouge seize power in Cambodia, April 18
        South Vietnam falls, April 30
        Mayaguez *seized, May 12*
        *The United States, the Soviet Union, Canada, and Western European
            and Eastern European countries alike sign the Helsinki Final Act,
            August 1*

1976   Manages US response to the "Korean tree incident," August 18
        Orchestrates IMF package for the United Kingdom, fall
        George Bush becomes director of central intelligence
        Zhou Enlai and Mao Zedong die, reemergence of Deng Xiaoping
        Cuban and Soviet forces help install a communist government in Angola
        Jimmy Carter defeats Gerald Ford in presidential election

1977   Scowcroft leaves the White House and establishes
            International Six Inc.
        President Carter pursues a US foreign policy based on human rights

1982   Cofounds Kissinger Associates, Inc. and becomes vice chairman
        British defeat Argentina in the Falklands
        Alexander Haig resigns as secretary of state
        Leonid Brezhnev dies, replaced by Yuri Andropov

1983   President Reagan appoints Scowcroft as chairman of the President's
            Commission on Strategic Forces (the Scowcroft Commission),
            January 3
        Reagan announces the Strategic Defense Initiative
        Shootdown of Korean Airlines flight 007
        Operation Able Archer war games, Soviets fear US attack

1986   Reagan appoints Scowcroft to the Tower Commission,
            November 26
        Reagan-Gorbachev Cold War Summit in Reykjavik
        Iran-Contra affair breaks
        Chernobyl disaster

1989	Scowcroft begins his position as national security advisor, January 20

Soviet Union withdraws last forces from Afghanistan, February 15

Tiananmen Square massacre, June 4

Poland establishes first noncommunist government in Eastern Bloc, August 24

Hungary creates multiparty system of government, October 18

Breech of the Berlin Wall, November 9

Malta summit, December 2

US invasion of Panama, December 19

Romanian president Ceausescu and his wife executed, December 25

1990   *Boris Yeltsin elected president of Russia, May 29*

US-Soviet Washington summit, May 31

Iraq invades Kuwait, August 2

Germany reunifies, October 3

Conventional Forces in Europe treaty signed, November 19

UN Security Council passes Resolution 478, which authorizes the use of "all necessary means" against Iraq, November 29

1991   *Congress authorizes war against Iraq, January 12*

Air war against Iraq begins, January 16

Ground war against Iraq begins, February 25

Slovenia and Croatia declare independence from Yugoslavia, June 25

Scowcroft receives Presidential Medal of Freedom, July 3

Warsaw Pact officially dissolved, Bush, Gorbachev sign START, July 31

Coup attempt against Gorbachev, August 19

United States recognizes Estonia, Latvia, and Lithuania, September 2

Ukraine population passes referendum for independence from USSR, December 1

Soviet Union disestablished; Gorbachev resigns as president, December 25

1992   *End of Najibullah regime in Afghanistan, civil war in Afghanistan*

War in Bosnia begins, April 6

Bush agrees to sell 150 F-16 aircraft to Taiwan, September 2

Bill Clinton elected US president, November 3

US Marines land at Mogadishu, Somali, December 8

President Bush, Canadian prime minister Mulroney, and Mexican president Carlos Salinas sign NAFTA, December 17

1993	Scowcroft and colleagues establish the Forum for International Policy, June
	United States and Russia sign START II, January 3
	Congress approves NAFTA
	"Black Hawk Down" incident in Somalia
	Oslo accords signed by Israel and the Palestinian Liberation Organization
1994	Scowcroft founds the Scowcroft Group, June
	Yasser Arafat dies
1995	Coauthors *A World Transformed* with George H. W. Bush
	Becomes a member of Qualcomm board of directors
	Dayton accords
2001	George W. Bush appoints Scowcroft as chairman of the NSPD 5 external study of the intelligence community, May 9
	President Bush appoints Scowcroft as chairman of PFIAB, October 5
	Terrorist attacks on the World Trade Towers and the Pentagon, September 11
	US and NATO forces invade Afghanistan and, with the Northern Alliance, begin their assault to overthrow the Taliban, October 7
2002	Writes *Wall Street Journal* op-ed, "Don't Attack Saddam," August 15
	President Bush delivers "axis of evil" State of the Union address to Congress
	Congress authorizes President Bush to use military force in Iraq
	Bush asserts a US foreign policy based on the unilateral preemption by the United States against any enemy it considers an imminent threat
	Downing Street memo: presidential administration committed to military action
2008	Coauthors *America and the World* with Zbigniew Brzezinski and David Ignatius
	Receives Andrew J. Goodpaster Award
	Iraqi government agrees to US withdrawal by 2011
	Conflict in South Ossetia, August 7–12
	Beijing Summer Olympics, August 8–24
	Barack Obama elected president, November 4

2010   Cochairs The Blue-Ribbon Commission on America's Nuclear
       Future

       Google threatens to leave China over Internet censorship, January 13
       Deepwater Horizon drilling well explodes in Gulf of Mexico, April 20
       Tunisian man sets himself on fire, igniting Arab Spring, December 17

2013   Begins writing his memoirs
       Elected into the National Defense University Hall of Fame
       Receives the Gerald R. Ford Foundation Medal for Distinguished
       Public Service

       *Edward Snowden begins leaking classified information from the NSA,
       June 5*
       Iran Nuclear Deal, November 22

Acknowledgments

The name Brent Scowcroft—as austere, old-fashioned, and flinty a name as they come—first caught my attention in the mid-1970s. I remember reading of General Scowcroft in newspaper and magazine articles about the Ford administration, yet the articles had little about Scowcroft beyond mentioning his titles as deputy national security advisor and then national security advisor. He seemed to be playing an important role, while the lack of sustained press attention he received stood in stark contrast to the voluminous press and often harsh criticism that Henry Kissinger and later Zbigniew Brzezinski attracted.

Scowcroft's name reappeared in the national news when in 1983 he was appointed as the chairman of the President's Commission on Strategic Forces—the eponymous Scowcroft Commission—and then one of three members of the Tower Commission, right after the Iran-Contra scandal broke. Again, the news stories contained little on Scowcroft himself. This changed in 1988, when president-elect George Bush again appointed him as national security advisor. Scowcroft made the headlines more often this time, occasionally appeared on television, and attracted some criticism in the press. He nonetheless mostly escaped personal attacks—an impressive feat, considering the fierce and bitter politics characteristic of presidential administrations and the nation's capital. Nearly ten years after leaving the Bush White House, Scowcroft regained national prominence in August 2002 with his controversial dissent in the *Wall Street Journal.*

As a student of the United States' international relations and of the executive branch, I found my curiosity sparked by this history. Here was someone whose fingerprints were all over the last four decades of American foreign relations, and yet few journalists, historians, or other political analysts had lifted those prints and investigated General Scowcroft's long record of achievement. The more I read about Scowcroft and the more I spoke to others, the more interesting and important his life seemed to be. For me to translate this developing interest into a book took far more than my own initiative, however; it took the extensive and repeated help and cooperation of many others.

I never would have proceeded with the biography, or at least not in any form resembling the present book, were it not for General Scowcroft's generous cooperation and the assistance of his colleagues at the Scowcroft Group, especially that of Gail Turner, his personal assistant, and Virginia Mulberger, managing director of the Scowcroft Group. Dozens of other friends and colleagues of Scowcroft likewise generously devoted their time to talk to me about Scowcroft and US national security in the late twentieth and early twenty-first centuries. Although I do not cite all of my interviewees in the text, they provided me with the context, details, and color that gave me a fuller sense of Scowcroft's contributions and the world of which he has been part. Among those I talked to were Elliott Abrams, Don Bailey, James A. Baker III, Richard Barth, Reginald Bartholomew (deceased), Jean Becker, Lance Betros, David Boren, Jack Brennan, Zbigniew Brzezinski, R. Nicholas Burns, George H. W. Bush, Frank Carlucci, David Carney, Sandra Charles, Daniel Christman, Dick Cheney, Mrs. Frank (Bethine) Church, Carl Colby, Timothy Deal, David Demarest, Joan Dempsey, John Deutch, Blair Dorminey, Lawrence Eagleburger (deceased), Marianne Eagleburger (deceased), Charles Ferguson, Marlin Fitzwater, Sherman Fleek, Florence Gantt, Robert Gates, Jake Garn, Toby Gati, Leslie Gelb, Robert A. Goldwin (deceased), Larry Goodson, Michael Gordon, Paul Gorman, Clinton Granger, Alan Greenspan, Deb Gullett, Bill Gulley (deceased), Stephen Hadley, Lee Hamilton, Robert Hathaway, Richard Haass, Carla Hills, David Hoffman, Robert Hormats, Jonathan Howe, Robert Hutchings, David Ignatius, Bobby Ray Inman, Karl Jackson, Irwin Jacobs, David Jeremiah (deceased), Amos Jordan, Robert Jordan, Walter Kansteiner, Arnold Kanter (deceased), Frederick Kempe, Bobbie Kilberg, Robert Kimmitt, Henry Kissinger, Susan Koch, William Kristol, David Lake, James Langdon, Jan Lodal, Catherine Lotrionte, Winston Lord, Hans Mark, Jack Matlock, Robert McFarlane, Michael Meese, Eric Melby, Andrea Mitchell, Virginia Mulberger, Sam Nunn, Phyllis Oakley, Robert Oakley, Douglas Paal, Jay Parker, George Perkovich, Thomas Pickering, Daniel Poneman, Walter Pincus, Richard Pipes, Roman Popadiuk, Colin Powell, Jonathon Price, Condoleezza Rice, Nicholas Rostow, J. Stapleton Roy, Kevin Scheid, Bob Schieffer, Michael Shifter, George Shultz, Thomas Simons, William Sittmann, William Y. Smith, William Smyser, William Stearman, James Steinberg, John Sununu, Paul Thompson, Margaret Tutwiler, Craig Unger, Marvin Weinbaum, James Woolsey, and Philip Zelikow. I am also appreciative of the cooperation of Scowcroft's grandnephew James Hinckley, his nephew Robert Hinckley, his grandniece Catie Hinckley Kelley, his niece Sheri Piergeorge, and his daughter, Karen Scowcroft. My apologies to any whose names have been inadvertently omitted.

I owe special thanks to those who read parts of chapters, one or more chapters, or the entire text of my manuscript. They saved me from many errors and forced me to be more precise. I am fortunate to have received comments from Timothy Brook, Sherman Fleek, Jim Hornfischer, Robert Kimmitt, Kenneth Kitts, Susan Koch, Mark Atwood Lawrence, Patricia Maclachlan, Paula Newberg, Peter Osnos, Richard C. Roberts, David Schmitz, Ted Sparrow, Robert Strong, Robert Suettinger, Guillermo Velasco, and Ralph Wetterhahn.

I am also very appreciative to the contributions of acquaintances, colleagues, and friends who answered questions, explained events, pointed me in helpful directions, or assisted me in other ways: Lance Betros, Philip Bobbitt, Janet Bogue, H. W. Brands, Bruce Buchanan, Michael Desch, Jeffrey Engel, Frank Gavin, Christine Fair, Stephen Holmes, Seymour Hersh, William Inboden, Don Inbody, Bryan Jones, Paul Kens, W. Roger Louis, Patrick McDonald, Robert Moser, Michael Nelson, Shannon O'Brien, Patrick Roberts, Elspeth D. Rostow (deceased), Mary Elise Sarotte, Jeremi Suri, and Mark Updegrove. I also want to thank Kit Belgum, Jason Brownlee, Patrick Conge, George Forgie, Rod Hart, Timothy Naftali, Gwenn Okruhlik, Molly and Skip Silloway, Dan Sterneman, and P. Hartley Walsh.

I am very grateful to the Woodrow Wilson International Center for Scholars for a residential fellowship, to the George Bush and Gerald Ford presidential libraries for travel allowances, to the College of Liberal Arts and the Office of the Vice President for Research at the University of Texas at Austin for indispensable leave time, and to Gary Freeman and Robert Moser, chairs of the Department of Government at the University of Texas, for their long-standing support.

Administrators, archivists, and librarians affiliated with the above institutions and other government and nonprofit institutions also offered invaluable assistance: the Bush Presidential Library in College Station (Zachary Roberts in particular), the Gerald R. Ford Presidential Library, the Richard Nixon Presidential Library, the Ronald Reagan Presidential Library, Ray Wilson, the US Military Academy, the Woodrow Wilson International Center for Scholars (Janet Spikes), Columbia University (Kay Achar), Lafayette College (Pamela Murray), the George Marshall Foundation (Paul Barron), the Library of Congress, the Hoover Institution, the Air Force Historical Research Agency, the Dolph Briscoe Center for American History, the Hinckley Institute of Public Affairs, the LBJ Presidential Library, and the University of Texas Department of Government.

For help with the photographs, I thank Amy Bowman, Ed Brouder, Carolyn Brierley, Kenneth Hafeli, Mary Finch, John Fletcher, Aryn Glazier, Tom Hildreth, Melissa Johnson, Jessica Pappathan, Brent Scowcroft, and

Lee Witten. Oxford University Press granted me permission to publish material (mostly from Chapter 17) previously published in "Bartholomew H. Sparrow, 'Realism's Practitioner: Brent Scowcroft and the Making of the New World Order, 1989–1993,' *Diplomatic History* (2010) 34 (1): 141–175.

Several University of Texas undergraduates—undergraduates no longer and who have moved on to bigger things—helped me transcribe interviews, find facts, trace sources, and complete other tasks. Hannah DeMartini, Taylor Perk, Elizabeth Resendez, and Heather Winkle, in particular, were terrific. Edgar Walters helped with translation of German-language documents.

Jim Hornfischer, my agent, was encouraging, supportive, and offered valuable feedback throughout, from soon after I approached him in 2008 through the manuscript's completion.

At PublicAffairs, I have been lucky to work with editor and now publisher Clive Priddle, his predecessor and the founder of PublicAffairs, Peter Osnos—who, to my good fortune, took a personal interest in the project—managing editor Melissa Raymond, and others on the PublicAffairs team. I could not have asked for a more professional, quicker, or more helpful editor than Karl Weber. Karl helped me focus the manuscript, eliminate extraneous material (painfully!), and write as concisely and directly as possible.

John Padgett, my former PhD adviser and friend, encouraged me to be thorough and not to rush. His advice dovetailed with my own sense: that Brent Scowcroft's life warranted an extensive study. The result was that this project took longer to complete than I envisioned. So I thank PublicAffairs and Clive Priddle, in particular, for his forbearance. I am also thankful for the continued interest shown by my parents, brothers and sisters, and in-laws. They persistently, but never impatiently, inquired about the book and never seemed to tire of my invariable answer of "Soon," to their repeated questions of "When are you going to be done?"

Polly Lanning Sparrow has been my invaluable partner. Besides her patience and willingness to take care of most of the home front while I spent hours on end in my office working on "the book," as a former journalist and editor, Polly contributed a needed perspective on various aspects of the project, answered questions about phrasing and tone, and helped immensely with her good judgment.

I have been blessed to have had so much support.

Source Notes

Abbreviations

SWPPR	Scowcroft West Point Personnel Records
SPR	Scowcroft Personnel Records
BOHP	Bush Oral History Project
ADST	Foreign Affairs Oral History Collection of the Association for Diplomatic Studies and Training
Nixon Project	Richard Nixon Presidential Materials Project
WHCF	White House Central Files
DNSA	Digital National Security Archive
FRUS	*Foreign Relations of the United States*
BPR	Bush Presidential Records, Bush Presidential Library

Preface

1. Brent Scowcroft, "Don't Attack Saddam," *Wall Street Journal*, August 15, 2002.

2. Leslie Gelb interview, April 9, 2014.

3. James A. Baker, "The Right Way to Change a Regime," *New York Times*, August 25, 2002; see Thomas E. Ricks, *Fiasco: The American Military Adventure in Iraq* (New York: Penguin, 2006), 48.

4. Todd S. Purdum and Patrick E. Tyler, "Top Republicans Break with Bush on Iraq Strategy," *New York Times*, August 16, 2002; Tony Karon, "Iraq: GOP War With Itself," *Time*, August 21, 2002.

5. Iraq Hearing, US Senate Foreign Relations Committee, Thursday, February 1, 2007; Scowcroft interview, November 3, 2009.

6. See James Mann, *The Obamians: The Struggle Inside the White House to Re-define American Power* (New York: Viking, 2012).

7. Arnold Kanter interview, March 24, 2009.

8. Scowcroft interview, December 2, 2009; Lee Hamilton interview, May 5, 2009.

9. Scowcroft interview, August 22, 2012.

10. John Lewis Gaddis, *George F. Kennan: An American Life* (New York: Penguin, 2012); Nicholas Thompson, *The Hawk and the Dove: Paul Nitze, George Kennan, and the History of the Cold War* (New York: Henry Holt, 2009).

11. Lt. Gen. Brent Scowcroft, foreword, in *The National Security Enterprise: Navigating the Labyrinth*, eds. Roger Z. George and Harvey Rishikof (Washington, DC: Georgetown University Press, 2011), xii.

12. Amos A. Jordan interview, July 6, 2010; Leslie Gelb interview, April 9, 2014; Jonathan Howe interview, January 12, 2012.

13. See Victor W. Turner, *Forest of Symbols: Aspects of Ndembu Ritual* (Ithaca, NY: Cornell University Press, 1967).

14. Nicholas Rostow interview, April 26, 2009; William Kristol interview, March 2009; David Lauter, "Brent Scowcroft," in *Fateful Decisions: Inside the National Security Council*, eds. Karl F. Inderfurth and Lock K. Johnson (New York: Oxford University Press, 2004), 204; Arnold Kanter interview, March 24, 2009.

15. Karl Jackson interview, June 11, 2009; Jordan interview, July 6, 2010.

16. But see Jeffrey Goldberg, "Breaking Ranks: What turned Brent Scowcroft against the Bush Administration?," *New Yorker*, October 31, 2005; David F. Schmitz, *Brent Scowcroft: Internationalism and Post-Vietnam Foreign Policy* (Lanham, MD: Rowman and Littlefield, 2011).

17. Scowcroft's books with Bush and Brzezinski are both "river books," meaning that each book alternates portions of Scowcroft's text, usually taken from tape transcriptions and then edited, with the other text, whether that of a second author, jointly written text with George Bush in *A World Transformed*, or that written by Bush and Brzezinski's interlocutor, David Ignatius, in *America and the World*.

18. Condoleezza Rice interview, August 17, 2009.

19. Schmitz, *Brent Scowcroft*.

Part I: Air Force Officer

Chapter 1: Junction City

1. C. Wright Mills, *The Power Elite* (New York: Oxford University Press, 1956), 199.

2. Mark Twain, *Roughing It*, in *The Works of Mark Twain*, eds. Harriet Elinor Smith and Edgar Marguess Branch, Robert H. Hirst (Berkeley: University of California Press, 1993), 2, 76; "Job Pingree Company," *Mormon Pioneer Overland Travel, 1847–1868*, http://history.lds.org/overlandtravels/companyDetail?lang=eng&companyId=236, www.lds.org/churchhistory/library/narrative/0,18046,4981-1-236,00.html.

3. Conway Sonne, *Knight of the Kingdom* (Salt Lake City: Deseret Press, 1989).

4. John G. Turner, *Brigham Young: Pioneer Prophet* (Cambridge, MA: Belknap Press, 2012), 314.

5. See John D. Unruh Jr., *The Plains Across: The Overland Emigrants and the Trans-Mississippi West, 1840–60* (Urbana: University of Illinois Press, 1979), 302–323; also see Michael L. Tate, *Indians and Emigrants: Encounters on the Overland Trails* (Norman: University of Oklahoma Press, 2006).

6. Milton R. Hunter, *Beneath Ben Lomond's Peak: A History of Weber Country 1824–1900*, 2nd ed. (Salt Lake City: Deseret News Press, 1945), 399, 404. Pingree was also a trustee of the local school district and treasurer of the Veteran Firemen's Association. On the ZCMIs in general, see Turner, *Brigham Young*, 354–356.

7. Ogden City Commission, *A History of Ogden*, The Utah Historical Records Survey Project Division of Professional and Service Projects, Works Projects Administration (Ogden, UT: Utah State Historical Records Survey, 1940), 54.

8. Hunter, *Beneath Ben Lomond's Peak*, 531.

9. For further information, see Frank MacLynn, *Wagons West: The Epic Story of America's Overland Trails* (London: Jonathan Cape, 2002), 371–394.

10. See "Richard Ballantyne Company," *Mormon Pioneer Overland Travel, 1847–1868*, http://history.lds.org/overlandtravels/companyDetail?lang=eng&companyId=59, www.lds.org/chuchhistory/library/narrative/0,18946,4981-1-59,00 .html.

11. Sonne, *Knight of the Kingdom*.

12. Hunter, *Beneath Ben Lomond's Peak*, 398.

13. "Biography of Richard Ballantyne," microfilm, Mormon Church Archives, Salt Lake City, Utah; Conway B. Sonne, *Ships, Saints, and Mariners* (Salt Lake City: University of Utah Press, 1987).

14. Hunter, *Beneath Ben Lomond's Peak*, 386, 442–443; J. Hugh Baird, "Richard Ballantyne," *Encyclopedia of Mormonism*, vol. 1 (New York: Macmillan, 1992); Andrew Jenson, ed., *Latter-Day Saint Biographical Encyclopedia* (Salt Lake City: Andrew Jenson History Company, 1901), 1: 705.

15. Turner, *Brigham Young*, 353–354.

16. Ogden *Standard-Examiner*, May 1939, cited in Hunter, *Beneath Ben Lomond's Peak*, 7, 419; Issac Goeckeritz, *Ogden: Junction City of the West* (IG Films, 2007); Steven D. Cornell, "Ogden High School and the Embodiment of Craft" (2011), http://utah-rchitecture.blogspot.com/2011/05/ogden-high-school-and -embodiment-of.html.

17. Goeckeritz, *Ogden*; Richard W. Sadler and Richard C. Roberts, *Weber County's History* (Ogden, UT: Weber County Commission, 2000), 245.

18. "Historic Union Station & Ogden 25th Street," Utah.com, n.d., www.utah .com/culture/ogden.htm.

19.Sadler and Roberts, *Weber County's History*, 123; Richard C. Roberts and Richard W. Sadler, *A History of Weber County*, Utah Centennial County History Series (Salt Lake City: Weber County Commission, Utah Historical Society, 1997), 140; Lynn Arave, "Major Ogden Streets Have Presidential Ring," *Deseret News*, December 10, 2007.

20. US Bureau of the Census, US Government Printing Office, various years.

21. Sadler and Roberts, *Weber County's History*, 131, 210–216; Dale L. Morgan and Elizabeth M. Tillotson, *A History of Ogden* (Ogden: Ogden City Commission, 1940), 64–65; Scowcroft interview, March 4, 2009.

22. Hunter, *Beneath Ben Lomond's Peak*, 365; Sadler and Roberts, *Weber-County's History*, 131–132.

23. Scowcroft interview, July 12, 2010.

24. Scowcroft interview, November 17, 2007; "Ballantyne-Scowcroft," *Ogden Standard Journal*, August 21, 1915, city ed., 9.

25. Scowcroft interview, June 22, 2010.

26. Scowcroft interviews, July 27, 2009, and August 12, 2010; David Lauter, "Brent Scowcroft," in *Fateful Decisions: Inside the National Security Council*, eds. Karl F. Inderfurth and Loch K. Johnson (New York: Oxford University Press, 2004), 204; Brent Scowcroft scrapbook, n.p., courtesy of Brent Scowcroft.

27. Associated Press, "Breaks Spoil Ogden Victory," *Ogden State Tribune*, April 18, in Scowcroft scrapbook; Scowcroft interview, March 4, 2009.

28. Scowcroft interviews, November 17, 2007, and March 27, 2012; "Polk School Drum Corps Report," 1938–1939, L. E. "Ray" Minter, Director, "Brent Scowcroft" scrapbook, n.p., courtesy of Brent Scowcroft.

29. Scowcroft interviews, March 4, 2009, July 27, 2009, and August 13, 2010; "Personal and School History Sheet," application to the US Military Academy, July 2, 1944, 2, from Brent Scowcroft cadet file, provided by Joanna Rera, Chief Clerk, Graduate Records, Office of the Dean, US Military Academy, March 10, 2009 (henceforth Scowcroft West Point Personnel Records [SWPPR]).

30. Scowcroft interview, September 14, 2011; Scowcroft scrapbook.

31. Sarah Barringer Gordon, *The Mormon Question* (Chapel Hill: University of North Carolina Press, 2002), 234; James Hinckley interview, November 10, 2009.

32. Scowcroft interviews, July 27, 2009, and August 12, 2010.

Chapter 2: Surviving Hell on the Hudson

33. Kendall Banning, *West Point Today* (New York: Funk & Wagnalls, 1937); Scowcroft interviews, November 18, 2007, and July 27, 2009.

34. David Lipsky, *Absolutely American: Four Years at West Point* (Boston: Houghton Mifflin, 2003), 6.

35. Lt. Gen. Brent Scowcroft, "Window to the Oval Office: A Diplomatic View of the American Presidency (Part 1 of 2)," West Point Center for Oral History, March 12, 2012, 2 of 30.

36. Banning, *West Point Today*; Scowcroft interviews, July 27 and December 2, 2009.

37. "Our America," n.d., Brent Scowcroft scrapbook, courtesy of Brent Scowcroft.

38. Scowcroft interview, March 4, 2009.

39. Scowcroft interview, March 4, 2009; *Annual Report of the Superintendent, United States Military Academy* (West Point: USMA Printing Office, 1944), 1–2; letter, Jim Scowcroft to Adjutant, United States Military Academy, June 3, 1943, SWPPR; letter, Col. S. Wittle to Mr. Jim Scowcroft, June 6, 1943, SWPPR; telegram, Elbert Thomas, US Senate, to Academic Board, US Military Academy, June 15, 1943, SWPPR); letter, Maj. Gen. F. B. Wilby, Superintendent, to Honorable Elbert Thomas, June 15, 1943, SWPPR.

40. Elbert Thomas, US Senate, to Adjutant General's Office, West Point Section, War Department, August 16, 1943, SWPPR.

41. Lance A. Betros, *Carved from Granite: West Point Since 1902* (College Station: Texas A&M University Press, 2012), 89.

42. Scowcroft interview, November 18, 2007.

43. Albert W. Gendebien, *Biography of a College: A History of Lafayette College 1927–78* (Easton, PA: Lafayette College, 1986), 166–171; Betros, *Carved from Granite*, 89; Matthew F. Ingoffo, "A Brief History of USMAPS," *Assembly* 34, no. 1 (June 1975): 13; Scowcroft interviews, November 18, 2006, and June 22, 2010.

44. Photograph of Vickie from Brent Scowcroft scrapbook, courtesy of Brent Scowcroft; Major General Edwin W. Robertson II, US Air Force oral history interview, April 24–25, 1989, Air Force Historical Research Agency, Maxwell Air Force Base, Alabama, K239.0512-1862.

45. Louis E. Keefer, *Scholars in Foxholes: The Story of the Army Training Program in World War II* (Jefferson, NC: McFarland & Company Inc., 1988), 56, 99–100; Gendebien, *Biography of a College*, 166.

46. Keefer, *Scholars in Foxholes*, 40, 70; Gendebien, *Biography of a College*, 165–172; Scowcroft interview, June 22, 2009.

47. Banning, *West Point Today*, 13.

48. See, for example, James T. Sparrow, *Warfare State: World War II Americans and the Age of Big Government* (New York: Oxford University Press, 2011); Bartholomew H. Sparrow, *From the Outside In: World War II and the American State* (Princeton: Princeton University Press, 1996); Studs Terkel, *The Good War* (New York: Vintage Books, 1984).

49. Rick Atkinson, *The Long Gray Line: The American Journey of West Point's Class of 1966* (Boston: Houghton Mifflin, 1989), 39.

50. *Annual Report of the Superintendent, United States Military Academy* (West Point: USMA Printing Office, 1943), 1. There were 1,843 cadets in 1940.

51. Act of October 1, 1942; Theodore J. Crackel, *West Point: A Bicentennial History* (Lawrence: University Press of Kansas, 2002), 208; see *Annual Report of the Superintendent, 1943* (West Point, NY: US Military Academy Printing Office), 1943.

52. *Annual Report of the Superintendent, 1943.*

53. Crackel, *West Point*, 208; Johannes Vazulik, "German POWs at West Point During World War II," paper presented at "Making History: West Point at 200 Years," United States Military Academy, March 8, 2002.

54. Scowcroft interview, March 4, 2009.

55. Brent Scowcroft, "Report of Physical Examination of Candidate for Admission to the United States Military Academy, West Point, N.Y.," March 22, 1944, Form 0164, SWPPR.

56. Banning, *West Point Today*, 25, 30; Gen. William T. Smith interview, May 20, 2009; Atkinson, *The Long Gray Line*, 30.

57. Smith interview, May 5, 2009; Banning, *West Point Today*, 26–27; Atkinson, *The Long Gray Line*, 25–26; Scowcroft interview, July 20, 2012; Robertson, US Air Force oral history interview; Scowcroft, "Window to the Oval Office," 3.

58. Smith interview, May 20, 2009; "Form 53, U.S.C.C.—Individual Delinquency Record," Air Force Personnel Records, San Antonio, "Scowcroft Personnel Records" (henceforth Scowcroft Personnel Records [SPR]).

59. Memorandum for the 201 File of Cadet Scowcroft, B, Cadet Lieutenant, Company B-2, USCC, May 15, 1947, Department of Tactics, United States Military Academy, SPR; Scowcroft interview, October 6, 2010.

60. Scowcroft interviews, September 1, 2009, and July 12, 2010.

61. Scowcroft interview, June 6, 2012; "Athletic Record," (Form 41, USCC), n.d., SWPPR.

62. Smith interview, May 20, 2009; Scowcroft interview, August 13, 2010.

63. Scowcroft interview, November 18, 2006.

64. Transcript, SPR; Scowcroft interviews, March 29 and August 13, 2010.

65. Transcript, SPR; Scowcroft interviews, March 29 and August 13, 2010; "Athletic Record," SWPPR.

66. Scowcroft interview, March 4, 2009.

67. Scowcroft interview, July 27, 2009. The Army Air Corps officially became the Army Air Forces in 1947, but the personnel within the AAF were still called the Army Air Corps.

68. Virginia Mulberger interview, October 5, 2011.

69. Scowcroft interview, September 1, 2009.

Chapter 3: Crash Landing

70. This account draws from Scowcroft interview, August 14, 2010; "Grenier Pilot Has Close Call: Escapes Death in Londonderry Crash," Manchester *Evening Leader*, city edition, January 7, 1949, 1–2, courtesy of Manchester City Library; Lt. Gen. Brent Scowcroft, "Window to the Oval Office: A Diplomatic View of the American Presidency (Part 1 of 2)," West Point Center for Oral History, March 12, 2012, 5; Jeffrey Goldberg, "Breaking Ranks: What turned Brent Scowcroft against the Bush Administration?," *New Yorker*, October 31, 2005; Scowcroft gives a slightly different account in an interview with Mark Warren, "Brent Scowcroft," *Esquire*, January 2009, 96.

71. Scowcroft, "Window to the Oval Office," 6.

72. Scowcroft interview, November 18, 2006, and August 14, 2010; Scowcroft, "Window to the Oval Office," 6; "Change of Physical Qualification Affecting Flying Status," May 11, 1949, SPR; "Report of Proceedings of FEB [Flying Evaluation Board], 1st Lt. Brent Scowcroft, May 7, 1951, SPR; "Report of Disability for Insurance Purposes," January 17, 1950, Form SG 700, SPR; "Medical Certificate," Julius M. Koralsky, Captain, MC (USAF), Flight Surgeon, January 11, 1949, Station Hospital Grenier Air Force Base, SPR; caption of official USAF photo accompanying "Grenier Pilot Has Close Call," 2.

73. Scowcroft, "Window to the Oval Office (Part 1 of 2)," 5; Scowcroft interview, February 11, 2013.

74. Major C. R. Melzer to Flight Surgeon, Station Hospital Grenier AFB, Manchester, NH, April 8, 1949, SPR; Scowcroft interview, March 4, 2009.

75. Scowcroft interviews, July 27, 2009, and June 22, 2010.

76. Scowcroft interviews, November 18, 2006, and August 13, 2010; James Hinckley interview, November 10, 2009.

77. Scowcroft interviews, July 12 and August 10, 2010; "Prominent Woman Dies at 79," Ogden *Standard-Examiner*, September 4, 1971, 14, courtesy of the Weber County Library.

78. Scowcroft interview, August 13, 2010.

79. Scowcroft interviews, March 4, 2009, and June 24, 2010.

80. "Summary of Hospitalization," Capt. Lucas C. Hollister Jr., March 13, 1950, SPR.

81. Clinical Record, Narrative Summary, Standard Form 502, January 22, 1951, SPR; Scowcroft interviews, July 29, 2009, and June 22, 2010. Scowcroft was unable to remember the date when he received the letter.

82. Theodore J. Crackel, *West Point: A Bicentennial History* (Lawrence: University Press of Kansas, 2002), 214.

83. Michael Meese interview, May 15, 2009; William Y. Smith interview, May 5, 2009; Gen. Amos "Joe" Jordan interview, July 5, 2010; Scowcroft interview, September 27, 2012.

84. Jordan interview, July 19, 2010; Meese interview, May 15, 2009.

85. Scowcroft interviews, March 4 and July 27, 2009.

86. "Marian Horner Scowcroft," obituary, *Washington Post*, July 18, 1995; Scowcroft interview, April 10, 2009.

87. Scowcroft interview, April 10, 2009.

88. Major C. R. Melzer to Flight Surgeon, Station Hospital, Grenier Air Force Base, July 6, 1949, SPR; "Report of Medical Examination," May 4, 1950, Mitchel Air Force Base [form number illegible], SPR.

89. Scowcroft interview, June 22, 2010.

90. Scowcroft interviews, April 10, 2009, July 12, 2010, and November 10, 2012.

91. Armand L. Tremblay, USAF Captain, to President of the Flying Evaluation Board, Mather AFB, Mather Field, California, "Flight Check," May 2, 1951, SPR. Scowcroft interview, May 5, 2010.

92. Scowcroft interviews, April 10, 2009, and July 12, 2010; Officer Effectiveness Report, October 31, 1951, SPR.

93. Scowcroft interview, December 2, 2009.

94. Brent Scowcroft transcript, Columbia University, courtesy of Brent Scowcroft and Columbia University.

95. Scowcroft interview, May 5, 2010; Scowcroft interview, November 12–13, 1999, Bush Oral History Project, Miller Center, University of Virginia, (henceforth BOHP), 3.

96. Scowcroft interviews, March 29 and August 13, 2010; Scowcroft interview, BOHP, 7–8.

97. Michael Meese interview, May 15, 2009; Scowcroft interview, BOHP, 3, 7.

98. Letter, Col. George A. Lincoln to Brig. Gen. R. J. Wood, West Point Correspondence Files, January 1955, File 1, USMA Files, Official Correspondence, January 1955–September 1955, Lincoln Collection, US Military Academy, West Point, NY; Fred Kaplan, *The Wizards of Armageddon* (New York: Simon & Schuster, 1983), 19–23. Also see Nicolas Guilhot, ed., *The Invention of International Relations Theory: Realism, the Rockefeller Foundation, and the 1954 Conference on Theory* (New York: Columbia University Press, 2011).

99. Scowcroft interviews, November 18, 2007, May 13, 2009, and October 20, 2011.

100. Scowcroft interviews, November 18, 2007, and May 13, 2009; Scowcroft interview, BOHP, 4; also see Zbigniew Brzezinski and Brent Scowcroft, *America and the World: Conversations on the Future of American Foreign Policy*, Moderated by David Ignatius (New York: Basic Books, 2008), 243.

101. Scowcroft interview, BOHP, 4.

102. Letter, Lincoln to Wood; William T. R. Fox, Memorandum for the Department of Public Law, Columbia University in the City of New York, May 26, 1953; Scowcroft records, Columbia University, Department of Public Law and Government [Department of Political Science], courtesy of Brent Scowcroft.

Chapter 4: Soldier-Scholar

103. Officer Effectiveness Report, November 4, 1953, SPR; Jordan interview, July 6, 2010.

104. Officer Effectiveness Report, May 7, 1954, SPR.

105. *Annual Report of the Superintendent, United States Military Academy* (West Point: USMA Printing Office, 1955), 102; Officer Effectiveness Report, November 4, 1953, SPR; Zbigniew Brzezinski interview, June 21, 2009; Jordan interview, July 6, 2010.

106. Scowcroft interview, August 13, 2010; Paul T. Gorman interview, June 18, 2010; Jordan interview, July 6, 2010; Scowcroft address, Hinckley Institute Hall of Fame, October 23, 2008.

107. Gorman interview, June 18, 2010.

108. USAF Officer Effectiveness Reports, May 7, 1954, April 30, 1955, and April 2, 1956, SPR.

109. Jordan interview, July 6, 2010; Scowcroft interview, September 1, 2010.

110. Jordan interview, July 6, 2010; Gorman interview, June 18, 2010.

111. Officer Effectiveness Report, November 4, 1953, SPR.

112. Officer Effectiveness Report, May 7, 1954, SPR.

113. Cited in Joseph Ellis and Robert Moore, *School for Soldiers: West Point and the Profession of Arms* (New York: Oxford University Press, 1974), 137–138.

114. John P. Lovell, *Neither Athens nor Sparta? The American Service Academies in Transition* (Bloomington: Indiana University Press, 1979), 51; Michael Meese interview, June 23, 2010.

115. Gorman interview, June 18, 2010.

116. David Cloud and Greg Jaffe, *The Fourth Star: Four General and the Epic Struggle for the Future of the United States Army* (New York: Crown, 2009), 58–59. Lovell, *Neither Athens nor Sparta?*, 51. Ellis and Moore, in *School for Soldiers* (153, 156–157), make explicit what Cloud and Jaffe, as well as Lovell, leave implicit: that other West Point departments, particularly the humanities, didn't share the intellectualism of the Department of Social Sciences. And if the Social Sciences Department tolerated if not nurtured dissent and debate, the same didn't hold for other departments, where the watchword was administration and the officers were strongly aware of the need to conform in order to get the positive efficiency-reports needed for good placement back in "the real Army."

117. Daniel Christman interview, May 12, 2009; Cloud and Jaffe, *The Fourth Star*, 54; Meese interview, June 23, 2010.

118. Lovell, *Neither Athens Nor Sparta?*, 51; Scowcroft interview, September 1, 2009; Jay Parker interview, May 8, 2009.

119. "An Oral History Interview with Brent Scowcroft" by Timothy Naftali, Richard Nixon Oral History Project, Richard Nixon Presidential Library and Museum, Yorba Linda, CA, June 29, 2007, 10; see Lincoln Papers.

120. Andrew J. Goodpaster, "National Technology and International Politics," PhD dissertation, Princeton University, May 1952, 3; attachment to fax from Andy Goodpaster, Eisenhower Institute, to Ed Deagle, April 22, 2004, folder 6, "1995–2005," Correspondence, Box 1 Andrew J. Goodpaster Collection, #231-A., George C. Marshall Library, Lexington, VA.

121. Cloud and Jaffe, *The Fourth Star*, 54, 55–56; Lovell, *Neither Athens nor Sparta?*, 50–51.

122. Scowcroft interview, September 27, 2012.

123. *Annual Report of the Superintendent, United States Military Academy* (West Point: USMA Printing Office, 1954), 33–34; *Annual Report of the Superintendent, United States Military Academy* (West Point: USMA Printing Office, 1955), 24.

124. Gorman interview, June 18, 2010.

125. *Annual Report of the Superintendent 1954, United States Military Academy* (West Point: USMA Printing Office), 37; *Annual Report of the Superintendent 1956, United States Military Academy* (West Point: USMA Printing Office, 1956), 30.

126. See Official Correspondence files, USMA files, George A. Lincoln Collection, US Military Academy, West Point, NY.

127. Scowcroft interviews, September 1, 2009, February 23, 2010, and August 13, 2010; letter, Lincoln to Brig. Gen. William Stone, Air Staff, Department of the Air Force, September 9, 1955, West Point correspondence files, September 1955, file 9, Official Correspondence, January 1955–September 1955, Box 16, USMA Files, Lincoln Collection.

128. Scowcroft interviews, March 4 and September 1, 2009; letter, George Lincoln to Paul Nitze, February 11 and November 10, 1955, Nitze, Official Correspondence, USMA files, Box 17, Lincoln Collection; letter to Henry A. Kissinger, February 6, 1956, Kissinger, Official Correspondence, USMA files, Box 18, Lincoln Collection; letter to Frank Barnett, 4 June 1956, "Barnett," Official Correspondence, USMA files, Box 18, Lincoln Collection.

129. Robert S. Jordan, *An Unsung Soldier: The Life of Gen. Andrew Goodpaster* (Annapolis, MD: Naval Institute Press, 2013), 6.

130. Scowcroft interviews, September 1, 2009, February 23, 2010, and August 13, 2010.

131. Scowcroft interview, November 18, 2006; Officer Effectiveness Report, December 20, 1958, SPR.

132. Scowcroft interview, January 6, 2012; Lt. Col. Jay N. Fisher, USAF, Deputy Director, Civilian Institutions Progress, Training Report, December 31, 1958, SPR. Although the Navy had a similar intelligence training program, the US military didn't have joint-service intelligence school analogous to the other joint-service postgraduate programs offered by the National Defense University, contrary to what had been initially proposed by the Joint Chiefs of Staff in 1946. See John W. Masland and Laurence I. Radway, *Soldiers and Scholars: Military Education and National Policy* (Princeton, NJ: Princeton University Press, 1957), 134–137.

133. Officer Effectiveness Report, September 30, 1959, SPR.

134. Scowcroft interviews, March 4 and December 2, 2009.

135. Lawrence S. Eagleburger interview, Foreign Affairs Oral History Collection of the Association for Diplomatic Studies and Training, Foreign Service Institute, Arlington, VA, August 13, 1988, http://adst.org/oral-history/oral-history-interviews (henceforth ADST).

136. Scowcroft interview, BOHP, 6, 7.

137. Officer Effectiveness Report, October 3, 1960, SPR.

138. Officer Effectiveness Report, July 26, 1961, SPR.

139. Scowcroft interview, December 2, 2009; Officer Effectiveness Reports, September 29, 1959, October 3, 1960, and July 26, 1961, SPR.

140. George F. Kennan, *Memoirs: 1950–1963* (Boston: Little, Brown, 1972), 274–275.

141. Scowcroft interview, February 11, 2013.

142. Scowcroft interview, September 1, 2010; Officer Military Record, "Scowcroft, Brent FR 17607 (Lt. Col.)," n.d.; Frank Lichtenheld, M.D. "Clinical Record, Narrative Summary," December 20, 1960, Standard Form 502; USAF Officer Effectiveness Report, September 29, 1959, SPR.

143. Kennan, *Memoirs*, 279–280.

144. Ibid., 293–294; also see John Lewis Gaddis, *George F. Kennan: An American Life* (New York: Penguin, 2011), 552–568; Scowcroft interview, July 20, 2012.

145. Scowcroft interview, January 6, 2012.

146. Scowcroft interview, January 6, 2012; Scowcroft interview, BOHP, 8.

147. Scowcroft interview, July 27, 2009; Scowcroft interview, BOHP, 7; Lt. Gen. Brent Scowcroft, "Window to the Oval Office (Part 1 of 2)," 9.

148. Masland and Radway, *Soldiers and Scholars*, 307–316; Arthur A. Ageton with William P. Mack, *The Naval Officer's Guide*, 8th ed. (Annapolis: United States Naval Institute, 1970), 403–404.

149. Aeronautical Orders, Number 196, Form 110, October 16, 1961, SPR; Training Report, January 19, 1962, SPR; Scowcroft interviews, August 13 and September 1, 2010.

150. Officer Effectiveness Report, December 20, 1958, and July 13, 1960, SPR; Personal Clothing and Equipment Record, AF Form 538, n.d., SPR; Scowcroft interview, July 12, 2010.

151. Scowcroft interview, August 13, 2010.

152. Scowcroft interview, August 12, 2009.

153. Officer Effectiveness Report, September 8, 1964, SPR.

154. Officer Effectiveness Report, September 8, 1964, SPR. On Col. Robert F. McDermott and the low morale at the US Air Force Academy, see Vance O. Mitchell, *Air Force Officers Personnel Policy Development 1944–1974* (Washington, DC: Air Force History and Museums Program, United States Air Force, 1996), 223–227.

155. Citation to Accompany the Award of the Air Force Commendation Medal to Brent Scowcroft, Special Order G-89, September 16, 1964, USAF Academy, SPR.

156. Scowcroft interviews, May 13, 2009, and February 23, 2010.

157. Scowcroft interviews, May 13 and August 12, 2009.

158. Scowcroft interviews, May 13, 2009, and September 1, 2010; Karen Scowcroft interview, March 19, 2009; Sherri Piergeorge interview, June 1, 2011.

159. Major General Edwin W. Robertson II, US Air Force oral history interview, Air Force Historical Research Agency, Maxwell Air Force Base, Alabama, K239.0512-1862.

160. Scowcroft interviews, March 4 and July 27, 2009; also see Scowcroft interview, BOHP, 5.

161. Scowcroft interview, BOHP, 11; Scowcroft interview, April 10, 2009. See, generally, Jordan, *An Unsung Soldier*.

162. The term "blue suiter" is from Robert Corum, *Boyd: The Fighter Pilot Who Changed the Art of War* (Boston: Little, Brown and Company, 2002).

Chapter 5: Blue Suiter

163. Scowcroft interviews, September 1 and October 6, 2010; Richard A. Yudkin, Oral History Interview by Dr. Edgar F. Puryear, Air Force Consultant, IRIS No. 01053505, July 30, 1979, US Air Force Historical Research Agency, Maxwell Air Force Base, Montgomery, AL, 9; also see Maj. Gen. Richard A. Yudkin, "American Armed Strength and Its Influence," *Annals of the American Academy of Political and Social Science* 384 (July 1969): 1–13.

164. Scowcroft interview, August 13, 2010; Fred Kaplan, *The Wizards of Armageddon* (New York: Simon & Schuster, 1983), 356–358. Also see William Burr, "The Nixon Administration, the 'Horror Strategy,' and the Search for Limited Nuclear Options, 1969–1972: Prelude to the Schlesinger Doctrine," *Journal of Cold War Studies* 7, no. 3 (Summer 2005): 34–78.

165. See Richard Rhodes, *Arsenals of Folly: The Making of the Nuclear Arms Race* (New York: Knopf, 2007); Scowcroft, "Window to the Oval Office (Part 1 of 2)," 13.

166. Scowcroft interview, August 13, 2010.

167. Scowcroft interview, March 4, 2009; Officer Effectiveness Report, January 21, 1966, SPR; Scowcroft interview, BOHP, 11.

168. Officer Effectiveness Report, August 17, 1966, SPR.

169. Officer Effectiveness Report, August 7, 1967, SPR.

170. Major General Edwin W. Robertson II, US Air Force Oral History Interview, Air Force Historical Research Agency, Maxwell Air Force Base, Alabama, K239.0512-1862, 70–71; Scowcroft interview, January 3, 2014.

171. Maj. Gen. Edwin W. Robertson II, *U.S. Air Force Oral History Interview*, 72.

172. See H. R. McMaster, *Dereliction of Duty: Lyndon Johnson, Robert McNamara, the Joint Chiefs of Staff, and the Lies That Led to Vietnam* (New York: HarperCollins, 1997), 156–158, 163, 306–308; Thomas E. Ricks, *The Generals: American Military Command from World War II to Today* (New York: Penguin, 2012); also see Robert Dallek, *Camelot's Court: Inside the Kennedy White House* (New York: Harper, 2013). Scowcroft interview, January 3, 2014.

173. Scowcroft interview, August 12, 2009.

174. Jeanne W. Davis, "The Role of the Coordinative Staff Officer," typescript, V-2, "Davis, Jeanne W.—Coordinating Staff Work (typescript) (2)," Box 84,

US NSC Internal Files, 1974–1977, Gerald R. Ford Presidential Library, Ann Arbor, MI.

175. "Citation to Accompany the Award of the Legion of Merit to Brent Scowcroft," n.d., SPR; Special Order GB-393, October 30, 1967, Department of the Air Force, SPR; Colonel William B. Sandlin, Joint Chiefs of Staff, "Announcement of Award of the Joint Chiefs of Staff Identification Badge," March 23, 1971, SPR.

176. Yudkin interview by Puryear, 3–4; Scowcroft interviews, March 4, 2009, and October 6, 2010.

177. Scowcroft interview, November 3, 2009.

178. Scowcroft interview, BOHP, 9; Scowcroft interviews, August 13, 2010, and September 1, 2010.

179. Scowcroft interviews, April 10, 2010, and November 28, 2012; Scowcroft, "Window to the Oval Office," 13–14.

180. Scowcroft interviews, November 3 and December 2, 2009; Scowcroft interview, BOHP, 9.

181. Scowcroft interview, August 13, 2010.

182. Scowcroft interviews, May 13, 2009, August 12, 2009, and September 1, 2010.

183. Brent Scowcroft, "Congress and Foreign Policy: An Examination of Congressional Attitudes Toward the Foreign Aid Programs to Spain and Yugoslavia," Ph.D. dissertation, Department of Political Science, Columbia University, 1967.

184. Ibid.

185. Brent Scowcroft, transcript, Columbia University in the City of New York.

186. Officer Effectiveness Reports, August 5, 1965, January 21, 1966, and August 7, 1967, SPR.

187. Scowcroft, "Window to the Oval Office (Part 1 of 2)," 14.

188. John W. Masland and Laurence I. Radway, *Soldiers and Scholars: Military Education and National Policy* (Princeton, NJ: Princeton University Press, 1957), 344; Scowcroft interview, November 4, 2010.

189. Ageton, *The Naval Officer's Guide*, 404; Scowcroft, "Window to the Oval Office (Part 1 of 2)," 15.

190. See "Curriculum," Folders 4–12, Boxes 30–31, Record Group 231, VIII National War College (1930–1997), Andrew J. Goodpaster Papers, George C. Marshall Library, Lexington, VA.

191. "Trip II Middle East," folder "Curriculum-Coursework-Course IV-Memoranda," 30/16, Box 30, Record Group 231, Goodpaster Papers; Scowcroft interview, November 4, 2010.

192. Scowcroft interview, November 4, 2010.

193. Ibid. Forty-five years later, Scowcroft couldn't recall any specific names of NWC classmates when asked.

194. Training Report, June 14, 1968, SPR; letters of Wm. E. Creer to General McConnell, June 4, 1968, and of J. P. McConnell to Assistant Secretary of Defense

(International Security Affairs), July 1968 [exact date illegible], SPR; Brent Scow-croft, "Deterrence and Strategic Superiority," *Orbis* 13, no. 2 (Summer 1969): 435–454.

195. Scowcroft interviews, July 29, 2009, August 13, 2010, and November 4, 2010; Robert S. Jordan interview, February 15, 2011.

196. Scowcroft interview, February 24, 2011; see, for instance, "The Atlantic Council," Folder 9, Box 41, Record Group 231, Projects, XI Retirement, Good-paster Papers.

197. Officer Effectiveness Reports, February 7 and December 2, 1969, SPR.

198. Jeffrey Kimball, *Nixon's Vietnam War* (Lawrence: University Press of Kan-sas, 1998), 73; Willard J. Webb, *The Joint Chiefs of Staff and the War in Vietnam 1969–1970*, History of the Joint Chiefs of Staff (Washington, DC: Office of Joint History, Office of the Chairman of the Joint Chiefs of Staff, 2002).

199. Jacob Van Staaveren, "The Air Force in Southeast Asia: Toward a Bombing Halt 1968," Office of Air Force History, September 1970, 47, Document 6, "Fighting the War in Southeast Asia, 1961–1973," *National Security Archive Elec-tronic Briefing Book* No. 248, www2.gwu.edu/~nsarchiv/NSAEBB/NSAEBB248.

200. Officer Effectiveness Report, February 24, 1970, SPR.

201. Van Staaveren, "The Air Force in Southeast Asia," 45; Maj. Gen. Nguyen Duy Hinh, *Vietnamization and Cease Fire*, Indochina Monographs (Washington, DC: US Army Center of Military History, 1980), 44–45, 60.

202. Webb, *The Joint Chiefs of Staff and the War in Vietnam*, 123–124, 251; also see Van Staaveren, "The Air Force in Southeast Asia," 45–47.

203. See James N. Willbanks, *Abandoning Vietnam: How America Left and South Vietnam Lost Its War* (Lawrence: University Press of Kansas, 2004), 204–207; Ar-nold Isaacs, *Without Honor: Defeat in Vietnam and Cambodia* (Baltimore: Johns Hopkins University Press, 1983), 102–114; also see Kimball, *Nixon's Vietnam War*, 161.

204. Webb, *The Joint Chiefs of Staff and the War in Vietnam*, 252–254; Wil-liam J. Crowe Jr. with David Chanoff, *The Line of Fire: From Washington to the Gulf, the Politics and Battles of the New Military* (New York: Simon & Schuster, 1993), 80; also see Michael Eggleston, *Exiting Vietnam: The Era of Vietnamization and American Withdrawal Revealed in First-Person Accounts* (Jefferson, NC: McFar-land & Company, 2014).

205. Robert Dallek, *Nixon and Kissinger: Partners in Power* (New York: Harper-Collins, 2007), 619.

206. Ibid.; Scowcroft interview, October 20, 2011.

207. Kimball, *Nixon's Vietnam War*, 182; Eric Van Marbrod quoted in John Prados, *Keepers of the Keys* (New York: William Morrow, 1991), 364.

208. Scowcroft interview, August 12, 2009.

209. Scowcroft interview, October 20, 2011; Officer Effectiveness Report, Feb-ruary 16, 1970, SPR.

210. Scowcroft interview, August 13, 2010; Officer Effectiveness Report, June 3, 1971, SPR; Scowcroft interview, BOHP, 13.

211. "Citation to Accompany the Award of the Distinguished Service Medal to Brent Scowcroft," n.d., SPR.

212. Scowcroft interview, September 1, 2010.

213. Officer Effectiveness Report, December 16, 1971, SPR.

214. Robertson, US Air Force oral history interview, 71.

215. Officer Effectiveness Report, December 16, 1971, SPR.

216. Scowcroft interview, August 12, 2009.

217. Ibid.

218. Scowcroft interview, August 3, 2011.

219. "Washington: For the Record," *New York Times*, November 17, 1971, 19; Bill Gulley interview, February 11, 2009. In his oral history of the Bush administration, however, Scowcroft states that there "was no notion that Al Haig would ever leave" (Scowcroft interview, BOHP, 10).

220. Bill Gulley interview, February 11, 2009.

221. Scowcroft interview, November 18, 2006; Gulley interview, February 11, 2009.

222. Bill Gulley with Mary Ellen Reese, *Breaking Cover* (New York: Simon & Schuster, 1980), 144; Dallek, *Nixon and Kissinger*, 350–351; Peter Rodman, *Presidential Command: Power, Leadership, and the Making of Foreign Policy from Richard Nixon to George W. Bush* (New York: Knopf, 2009), 66–67.

223. Gulley, *Breaking Cover*, 144; Dallek, *Nixon and Kissinger*, 350–351; Rodman, *Presidential Command*, 66–69; Walter Isaacson, *Kissinger: A Biography* (New York: Simon & Schuster, 1992), 380–385; Ivo Daalder and I. M. Destler, *In the Shadow of the Oval Office: Profiles of the National Security Advisers and the Presidents They Served—from JFK to George W. Bush* (New York: Simon & Schuster, 2009), 84–85.

224. Bill Gulley interview, February 11, 2009; also see Scowcroft, "Window to the Oval Office (Part 1 of 2)," 20.

Part II: The Nixon and Ford Administrations, 1972–1977

Chapter 6: Military Assistant to the President

1. Bill Gulley interviews, February 11, 2009, April 13, 2009, and July 22, 2011; Request and Authorization for Permanent Change of Status, Special Order AA-2123, Form 899, November 8, 1971, SPR.

2. Scowcroft interview, March 4, 2009; Scowcroft address, Hinckley Institute Hall of Fame, Salt Lake City, Utah, October 23, 2008.

3. Scowcroft interview, March 4, 2009; Gulley interviews, February 11, 2009, April 13, 2009, and July 22, 2011; Lawrence Eagleburger interview, May 19, 2009;

Frank Carlucci interview, September 29, 2011; Lee Hamilton interview, May 5, 2009.

4. Jack Brennan interview, February 24, 2009; Gulley interviews, February 11, 2009, April 13, 2009, and July 22, 2011.

5. Brennan interview, February 24, 2009; Gulley interviews, February 11, 2009, April 13, 2009, and July 22, 2011.

6. Gulley interviews, February 11, 2009, April 13, 2009, and July 22, 2011. Also see Crowe, *The Line of Fire*, 39, and Bradley Patterson Jr., *The Ring of Power: The White House Staff and Its Expanding Role in Government* (New York: Basic Books, 1988), 321–327.

7. Gulley, *Breaking Cover*, 29–43.

8. Gulley, *Breaking Cover*, 75–76, 89–92. Also see transcript of Jack Albright oral history interview I, December 11, 1980, by Michael L. Gillette, 80–83; transcript of Jewel Malachek Scott oral history interview II, December 20, 1978, by Michael L. Gillette, 7–9; transcript of Arthur B. Krim oral history interview VI, October 13, 1983, by Michael L. Gillette, 28–30, all in LBJ Presidential Library, Austin, TX.

9. Gulley, *Breaking Cover*, 19, 23–33; Gulley interviews, February 11 and April 13, 2009.

10. Arthur M. Schlesinger Jr., *The Imperial Presidency* (Boston: Houghton Mifflin, 1973); Richard E. Neustadt, *Presidential Power: The Politics of Leadership from FDR to Carter* (New York: John Wiley & Sons, 1980), 181; Gulley, *Breaking Cover*.

11. See, for instance, Memorandum for H. R. Haldeman, March 7, 1972, from Brigadier General Brent Scowcroft, "Operation at Key Biscayne," File "General Hughes [Gen. Brent Scowcroft] March 1972," Box 94, White House Special Files, Haldeman Files, Richard Nixon Presidential Materials Project, National Archives and Records Administration, College Park, MD (henceforth Nixon Project); Nixon's papers were subsequently relocated to the Nixon Presidential Library in Yorba Linda, CA).

12. Memorandum for Mr. H. R. Haldeman from General Brent Scowcroft, October 10, 1972, "*Sequoia* Cruises," file "General Hughes [Gen. Brent Scowcroft] October 1972," Box 104, White House Special Files, Haldeman Files, Nixon Project; memorandum for Brigadier General Scowcroft, military assistant to the President, from Department of Army, Paul C. Miller, chief, Ceremonies & Special Events, December 18, 1972, "General Hughes [Gen. Brent Scowcroft] January 1973," Box 108, White House Special Files, Haldeman Files, Nixon Project; memorandum for Brent Scowcroft from Al Haig, July 28, 1972, subject "Soviet Hydrofoil," NSC Files, Henry A. Kissinger Office Files, Box 7, Nixon Project; Florence Gantt interview, November 2, 2009.

13. Scowcroft interviews, July 29 and August 12, 2009.

14. Scowcroft interviews, July 29 and August 12, 2009.

15. Memcon, Israeli Ambassador Simcha Dinitz, Minister Shalev, Major General Brent Scowcroft, Major R. C. McFarlane, December 12, 1973, "Dec. 12, 1973—Scowcroft, Israeli Ambassador Simcha Dinitz," Memcons, Box 3, Ford Library.

16. Scowcroft interviews, April 10, 2009, and June 24, 2011.

17. Scowcroft interview, April 10, 2009. In general, see Michael J. Allen, *Until the Last Man Comes Home* (Chapel Hill: University of North Carolina Press, 2009). As Allen points out, Scowcroft was later involved with the POW-MIA issue in the Ford and then Bush administrations, if in different capacities.

18. See, for instance, letter from Brent Scowcroft to Mr. Frank Ray, February 3, 1972, and letter from Brent Scowcroft to Mrs. Sadler, same date, White House Central Files (henceforth WHCF), Subject 1969–74, National Security–Defense file, ND 18-3, Nixon Project. Also see letters to Mary McCain, June 26, 1972, Mrs. Donnie Collins, June 28, 1972, and others in "Gen. ND 18-3/CO-1 6/1/72–6/30/72," in "Gen ND 18-3/CO 165-1" folder, "National Security—Defense (ND)," Box 10, Subject Files, 1969–74, Nixon Presidential Materials Staff, WHCF, Nixon Project.

19. Scowcroft interview, April 10, 2009.

20. Gulley interviews, February 11, 2009, and April 13, 2009.

21. Ibid.

22. Neil Sheehan, *A Bright Shining Lie: John Paul Vann and America in Vietnam* (New York: Random House, 1988), 25–32.

23. Scowcroft interview, September 27, 2012.

24. Bush quoted in Nancy Gibbs and Michael Duffy, *The President's Club: Inside the World's Most Exclusive Fraternity* (New York: Simon & Schuster, 2012), 378.

25. See correspondence by Scowcroft, as well as letters drafted by Col. Joseph Ulatoski and Col James S. Murphy, in "Gen ND 18-3/3CO 165-1 5/1/72–5/31/72," "Gen ND 18-3/3CO 165-1 6/1/72–6/30/72," and "Gen ND 18-3/3CO 165-1 7/1/72–7/31/72," Box 10, "National Security—Defense (ND)," Subject Files, 1969–74, Nixon Presidential Materials Staff, WHCF, Nixon Project. Also, Scowcroft interviews, July 27, 2009, and January 4, 2011; Thomas Mallon, "Wag the Dog," *New Yorker*, February 4, 2013.

26. Scowcroft interview, May 13, 2009; Scowcroft interview, BOHP, 17–18. Gerald Ford recalled how moody Richard Nixon could be when both were members of the House of Representatives: sometimes Nixon would be extroverted and friendly, other times sad and withdrawn. See Gibbs and Duffy, *The President's Club*, 295.

27. Scowcroft interviews, March 4, 2009, May 13, 2009, and January 4, 2011; Scowcroft interview, BOHP, 6.

28. The White House Communications Agency was originally known as the White House Signal Detachment and was officially formed in 1942, during the Roosevelt administration.

29. Sig Rogich interview, BOHP, 93.

30. Gulley interview, July 22, 2011.

31. Robert Dallek, *Nixon and Kissinger: Partners in Power* (New York: Harper-Collins, 2007), 330 (October 20–25); J. Stapleton Roy, quoted in "China Policy and the National Security Council," Oral History Roundtables, National Security Council Project, Ivo H. Daalder and I. M. Destler, moderators, Center for International and Security Studies at Maryland, Brookings Institution, November 4, 1999, 20; Gantt interview, November 2, 2009.

32. Memorandum for HAK/Haig from Winston Lord, March 17, 1972, Top Secret/Sensitive Exclusively Eyes Only, and "Checklist of Undertakings with the PRC," Attachment, June 17, 1972, Subject "Undertakings with the PRC," Henry A. Kissinger Office File, "Country File—Far East," Box 87, NSC Files, Nixon Project.

33. Memorandum for the Deputy Secretary of State from HAK, "Transfer of Major Items of Military Equipment to the Republic of China: 100 M-48 Tanks," March 21, 1974, "McFarlane Chron–Jan-March 1974" [1 of 2], Telcon files, Nixon Project; William Safire, *Before the Fall: An Inside View of the Pre-Watergate White House* (Garden City, NY: Doubleday, 1975), 411.

34. Scowcroft interview, BOHP, 15.

35. Safire, *Before the Fall*, 412. For a timeline of Watergate, see Bob Woodward and Carl Bernstein, *The Final Days* (New York: Simon & Schuster, 1976), appendix.

36. See letter, Kissinger to Scowcroft, September 18, 1972, Name Files, "Scowcroft, Brent Col. 1973–1974," National Security Council (NSC) Files, Box 833, White House Special Files, Nixon Project.

37. "Citation to Accompany the Award of the Distinguished Service Medal (First Oak Leaf Cluster) to Brent Scowcroft," n.d., SPR; Special Order GB-825, December 27, 1972, Department of the Air Force, Washington, DC, SPR.

Chapter 7: Kissinger's Deputy

38. Henry A. Kissinger, *Years of Renewal* (New York: Simon & Schuster, 1999), 182–183; Scowcroft interview, April 12, 2011.

39. Joseph Ellis and Robert Moore, *School for Soldiers: West Point and the Profession of Arms* (New York: Oxford University Press, 1974), 196; Scowcroft interview, BOHP, 14; also see Walter Isaacson, *Kissinger: A Biography* (New York: Simon & Schuster, 1992), 386–387, 493; Woodward and Bernstein, *The Final Days*, 197; Gulley interview, December 21, 2011.

40. Henry A. Kissinger, *Years of Upheaval* (Boston: Little, Brown, 1982), 107; Alexander M. Haig Jr., interview by Martha Kumar, December 22, 1999, White House Interview Program, www.archives.gov/presidential-libraries/research/transition-interviews/pdf/haig.pdf.

41. Roger Morris, *Haig: The General's Progress* (New York: Playboy Press, 1982), 224; John Prados, *Keepers of the Keys: A History of the National Security Council from Truman to Bush* (New York: William Morrow, 1991), 339; Winston Lord interview, March 29, 2011.

42. Prados, *Keepers of the Keys*, 325.

43. Kissinger, *Years of Renewal*, 182–183; Kissinger interview, April 28, 2009.

44. Kissinger interview, April 28, 2009; Gulley interview, February 11, 2009; Scowcroft interview, April 10, 2009. Gulley reported that he got the story from President Nixon's personal secretary, Rose Mary Woods. Scowcroft didn't deny the story when asked. Also see Scowcroft interview, BOHP, 12; "Up from Anonymity," *Newsweek*, November 17, 1975, 44; Isaacson, *Kissinger*, 493; Goldberg, "Breaking the Ranks," 63.

45. Nixon White House Tapes 801 A, October 17, 1972, at 37:00, Nixon Project; Safire, *Before the Fall*, 11; Woodward and Bernstein, *The Final Days*, 187; Scowcroft interview, March 4, 2009.

46. Scowcroft interview, BOHP, 13; February 11, 2009. Bill Gulley, as a retired Marine sergeant with thirty years' service, would become the first noncommissioned officer to become military assistant when Ford's chief of staff Cheney appointed him military assistant (Gulley interview, July 22, 2011).

47. Kissinger interview, April 28, 2009; Gulley interviews, February 11 and April 13, 2009.

48. Scowcroft interview, March 3, 2009.

49. Isaacson, *Kissinger*, 493.

50. Haldeman, cited in John P. Burke, *Honest Broker? The National Security Advisor and Presidential Decision Making* (College Station: Texas A&M Press, 2009), 154; Scowcroft interview, BOHP, 13.

51. Robert McFarlane interview, April 3, 2009.

52. Lawrence Eagleburger interview, May 19, 2009.

53. Scowcroft interview, April 10, 2009; Jack Brennan interview, February 24, 2009; Scowcroft interview, BOHP, 13; Eagleburger interview, May 19, 2009. On Kissinger's abuse of his subordinates, see Dallek, *Nixon and Kissinger*, 329; Safire, *Before the Fall*, 158; Woodward and Bernstein, *The Final Days*, 193–195; Gantt interview, November 2, 2009.

54. Gulley interviews, February 11 and April 13, 2009; Joseph A. Sisco, "Ford, Kissinger and the Nixon-Ford Foreign Policy," in *The Ford Presidency: Twenty-Two Intimate Perspectives of Gerald Ford*, ed. Kenneth W. Thompson, Portraits of American Presidents, vol. 7 (Lanham, MD: University Press of America, 1988), 331.

55. Kissinger interview, April 28, 2009.

56. Eagleburger interview, May 19, 2009; McFarlane interviews, April 3 and April 23, 2009.

57. John Hersey, *The President* (New York: Knopf, 1975), 120, quoted in Christopher Jon Lamb, *Belief Systems and Decision Making in the Mayaguez Crisis*

(Gainesville: University of Florida Press, 1989), 76–77; Robert McFarlane with Zofia Smardz, *Special Trust* (New York: Cadell and Davies, 1994), 154.

58. Winston Lord interview, March 29, 2011; Florence Gantt interview, November 2, 2009.

59. Henry Kissinger interview, April 28, 2009; also see Isaacson, *Kissinger*, 506.

60. See, for example, David J. Rothkopf, *Running the World: The Inside Story of the National Security Council and the Architects of American Power* (New York: PublicAffairs, 2005), 155.

61. McFarlane, *Special Trust*, 154–155; William Smyser interview, February 24, 2009.

62. McFarlane, *Special Trust*, 153–154; Jussi Hanhimäki, *The Flawed Architect: Henry Kissinger and American Foreign Policy* (New York: Oxford University Press, 2004), 488. Also see Seymour Hersh, *The Price of Power: Kissinger in the Nixon White House* (New York: Summit Books, 1983), although Hersh's study ends before Scowcroft began working for Kissinger, and Christopher Hitchens, *The Trial of Henry Kissinger* (London: Verso, 2001).

63. McFarlane, *Special Trust*, 154; William Safire quoted in John Osborne, *White House Watch: The Ford Years* (Washington, DC: New Republic Books, 1977), 80. Also see Dallek, *Nixon and Kissinger*, 610; Hanhimäki, *The Flawed Architect*, 458, 488; Burke, *Honest Broker?*; Robert D. Schulzinger, *Henry Kissinger: Doctor of Diplomacy* (New York: Columbia University Press, 1999).

64. Scowcroft interview, BOHP, 17; McFarlane, *Special Trust*, 152; Isaacson, *Kissinger*, 760; Scowcroft interview, February 24, 2011.

65. Kissinger interview, April 28, 2009; Ambassador Robert Oakley interview, ADST, July 7, 1992, 61; Walter Pincus interview, October 5, 2010; Scowcroft interview, November 4, 2010; Scowcroft quoted in Priscilla Painton, "Brent Scowcroft: Mr. Behind-the-Scenes," *Time*, October 7, 1991, 24–26, cited in David Lauter, "Brent Scowcroft," in *Fateful Decisions: Inside the National Security Council*, eds. William Inderfurth and Loch K. Johnson (New York: Oxford University Press, 2004) 178; also see Peter W. Rodman, *Presidential Command: Power, Leadership, and the Making of Foreign Policy from Richard Nixon to George W. Bush* (New York: Knopf, 2009), 70.

66. Bob Schieffer interview, June 6, 2009.

67. "Telephone conversations—Chron File 1972 1–4 Feb.," February 1, 1972, Henry A. Kissinger Telecons, Box 14; "Telephone conversations—Chron File 1972 25–30 Apr.," April 25, 1972, Henry A. Kissinger Telecons, Box 14; "HAK Telephone conversations—Chron File 1973 21–31 July," July 21, 1973, Henry A. Kissinger Telecons, Box 21, Nixon Project.

68. Scowcroft interview, BOHP, 40.

69. Isaacson, *Kissinger*, 760–761; Lord interview, March 29, 2011; Oakley interview, ADST, 61; Scowcroft interview, April 12, 2011; John P. Leacacos, "Kissinger's Apparat," in *Fateful Decisions*, eds. William Inderfurth and Loch K. Johnson, 91;

Hanhimäki, *The Flawed Architect*, 299; Jack Brennan interview, February 24, 2009; Robert Hormats interview, November 9, 2009; Osborne, *White House Watch*, 311.

70. Isaacson, *Kissinger*, 762–763; Hanhimäki, *The Flawed Architect*, 364.

71. Marvin Kalb and Bernard Kalb, *Kissinger* (Boston: Little, Brown and Company, 1974) 96. On Kissinger's playfulness, see Safire, *Before the Fall*. Also see transcripts of his conversations with foreign leaders.

72. Safire, *Before the Fall*; Jeremi Suri, *Henry Kissinger and the American Century* (Cambridge, MA: Belknap Press, 2009); Isaacson, *Kissinger*.

73. Osborne, *White House Watch*, 273; Isaacson, *Kissinger*, 735; Gantt interview, November 2, 2009.

74. David Callahan, "The Honest Broker: Brent Scowcroft in the Bush White House," *Foreign Policy Journal* 69, no. 2 (February 1992): 29.

75. Isaacson, *Kissinger*, 766–777.

76. Brandon Toropov, "Scowcroft, Brent," *Encyclopedia of Cold War Politics* (New York: Facts on File, 2000), 181; Robert T. Hartmann, *Palace Politics: An Inside Account of the Ford Years* (New York: McGraw-Hill, 1980), 371; Sheehan, *A Bright Shining Lie*, 30; Pincus interview, October 5, 2010; Osborne, *White House Watch*, 218. Walter Isaacson, in *Kissinger*, and John Osborne, in *White House Watch*, treat Scowcroft more extensively than most writers. Examples of well-regarded historical accounts that essentially ignore Scowcroft include Schulzinger, *Henry Kissinger*, and Suri, *Henry Kissinger and the American Century*. For "Kissinger clone," Hedrick Smith quotes the weekly *Human Events* (Smith, "Allen's Operation Examined by Meese," *New York Times*, December 4, 1981). But see Robert Oakley interview, ADST, 62.

77. Robert S. Jordan, *An Unsung Soldier: The Life of Gen. Andrew Goodpaster* (Annapolis: Naval Institute Press, 2013), 131; Scowcroft interview, February 24, 2011.

78. Gulley interviews, February 11 and April 13, 2009; McFarlane interviews, April 3 and April 23, 2009; Richard C. Head, Frisco W. Short, and Robert C. McFarlane, *Crisis Resolution: Presidential Decision Making in the* Mayaguez *and Korean Confrontations* (Boulder: Westview Press, 1978), 78; Lord interview, March 29, 2011; Isaacson, *Kissinger*, 507; Scowcroft interview, April 10, 2009; Kissinger interview, April 28, 2009.

79. Scowcroft interview, April 10, 2009.

80. Telcon, General Scowcroft/Sec. Kissinger, April 17, 1974, 10:10 A.M., "HAK Telephone Conversations—Chron File 1974, 10–14 April," Henry A. Kissinger Telcons, Box 25, Nixon Project.

81. Telcon, Gen. Scowcroft/Sec. Kissinger, November 25, 1974, 12:50 P.M., "HAK Telephone Conversations—Chron File 1974, 20–30 December," Box 25, Nixon Project.

82. Memorandum of conversation, March 25, 1975, President Ford, Kissinger, Scowcroft, "Mar 24, '75—Ford, Kissinger," Box 10, "National security advisor Memoranda of Conversations, 1973–1977," Ford Presidential Library.

83. Memcon, "December 3, 1974—Ford, Kissinger," Ford, Kissinger, and Scowcroft, Box 7, "National security advisor Memoranda of Conversations, 1973–1977," Nixon Project; Kissinger disparaged Schmidt for being "unbelievably vain."

84. Robert Oakley interview, ADST, 69, 76; Robert Oakley interview, February 4, 2014.

85. Jeanne Davis, "The Role of the Coordinative Staff Officer," typescript, V-3, "Davis, Jeanne W.—Coordinating Staff Work (typescript) (2)," Box 84, US NSC Internal Files, 1974–1977, Ford Presidential Library; "Advance Man in Moscow: Brent Scowcroft," *New York Times*, April 21, 1972.

86. Kissinger interview, April 29, 2009; Henry Kissinger, *White House Years* (Boston: Little, Brown, 1979), 1156n. Winston Lord thought Kissinger was being polite and meant "invaluable" or "essential" rather than an equal partner (Winston Lord interview, March 29, 2011).

87. Woodward and Bernstein, *The Final Days*,184.

88. Prados, *Keepers of the Keys*, 30.

89. Rothkopf, *Running the World*, 19; National Security Act of 1947, Section 101(c), (h)(2). The SWNCC was formed in December 1944 for the purpose of coordinating the positions of the State, War, and Navy Departments on issues in which they had a common stake. From late 1947 until June 1949, the SWNCC was called the State, Army, Navy, Air-Force Coordinating Committee. For histories of the NSC, see Prados, *Keepers of the Keys*; Rodman, *Presidential Command*; Ivo Daalder and I. M. Destler, *In the Shadow of the Oval Office: Profiles of the National Security Advisers and the Presidents They Served—from JFK to George W. Bush* (New York: Simon & Schuster, 2009); Burke, *Honest Broker?*; Inderfurth and Johnson, eds., *Fateful Decisions*.

90. See Burke, *Honest Broker?*, 19–22; Inderfurth and Johnson, eds., *Fateful Decisions*, 31; Daalder and Destler, *In the Shadow of the Oval Office*, 3–5; Alan G. Whittaker, Shannon A. Brown, Frederic C. Smith, and Elizabeth McKune, *The National Security Policy Process: The National Security Council and Interagency System* (Washington, DC: Industrial College of the Armed Forces, National Defense University, US Department of Defense, 2011), 7.

91. Daalder and Destler, *In the Shadow of the Oval Office*, 5–6; Whittaker, Brown, Smith, and McKune, *The National Security Policy Process*, 7; also see Scowcroft interview, BOHP, 14.

92. Inderfurth and Johnson, eds., *Fateful Decisions*; Daalder and Destler, *In the Shadow of the Oval Office*, 14.

93. Prados, *Keepers of the Keys*, 108; see Daalder and Destler, *In the Shadow of the Oval Office*, 35.

94. Daalder and Destler, *In the Shadow of the Oval Office*, 51–56.

95. Jonathan Howe interview, January 12, 2012.

96. Matthew Dickenson, "The Executive Office of the President: The Paradox of Politicization," in *Institutions of American Democracy: The Executive Branch*, eds.

Joel D. Aberbach and Mark A. Peterson (New York: Oxford University Press, 2005), 149; Burke, *Honest Broker?*, 114–115.

97. Jussi Hanhimäki, *The Flawed Architect*, 487.

98. Burke, *Honest Broker?*

99. Gantt interview, October 18, 2010; Gulley interviews, February 11 and April 13, 2009.

100. Gantt interview, November 2, 2009; Gulley interviews, February 11 and April 13, 2009; Jan Lodal interview, May 11, 2009; Scowcroft interview, March 29, 2010; McFarlane interviews, April 3 and April 23, 2009; Hormats interview, October 29, 2009; "Brent Scowcroft," *Facts on File*, 582, Hoffman Collection, George BPR, College Station, TX.

101. Scowcroft interview, April 25, 2013.

102. Gantt interview, October 18, 2010.

103. Gantt interview, November 2, 2009; Gulley interviews, February 11 and April 13, 2009; Scowcroft interview, November 3, 2009.

104. Woodward and Bernstein, *The Final Days*, 184.

105. Gantt interview, November 4, 2009.

106. McFarlane interview, April 23, 2009; Head, Short, and McFarlane, *Crisis Resolution*, 79; Robert M. Gates, *From the Shadows: The Ultimate Insider's Story of Five Presidents and How They Won the Cold War* (New York: Simon & Schuster, 1996).

107. Gantt interviews, November 2 and November 4, 2009.

108. Gantt interview, November 4, 2009; Gulley interview, February 11, 2009.

109. Gulley interviews, February 11 and April 13, 2009; "Up from Anonymity," *Newsweek*, November 17, 1975, 44; Ron Nessen, *Making the News, Taking the News: From NBC to the Ford White House* (Middletown, CT: Wesleyan University Press, 2011), 116; Bob Schieffer interview, June 6, 2009; Maria Downs, "Book, Mostly Wine and Roses (1)," Box 1, Maria Downs Papers, 1975–77, Ford Presidential Library.

110. McFarlane interviews, April 4 and April 23, 2009.

111. Gantt interview, November 2, 2009; Gulley interviews, February 11 and April 13, 2009.

112. Scowcroft interview, April 10, 2009.

113. Scowcroft interview, July 12, 2011; Gen. William T. Smith interview, May 20, 2009; "Advance Man in Moscow: Brent Scowcroft," *New York Times*, April 21, 1972; Gantt interviews, November 2, 2009, and October 18, 2010.

Chapter 8: White House Under Siege

114. Bob Woodward and Carl Bernstein, *The Final Days* (New York: Simon & Schuster, 1976), 308–309, 314.

115. John Prados, *Keepers of the Keys: A History of the National Security Council from Truman to Bush* (New York: William Morrow, 1991), 339, 340–341; Woodward and Bernstein, *The Final Days*, 200; Alexander M. Haig, interview by Martha Kumar, December 22, 1999, White House Interview Program, www.archives.gov /presidential-libraries/research/transition-interviews/pdf/haig.pdf; William G. Hyland, *Mortal Rivals: Superpower Relations from Nixon to Reagan* (New York: Random House, 1987), 194–195.

116. William Lloyd Stearman interview, 1998, ADST, 62; Lou Cannon, "Not Always in Control," *Politics Daily*, February 21, 2010.

117. Scowcroft interview, May 5, 2010; Haig interview, White House Interview Program, 9.

118. Gulley interview, February 11, 2009; Woodward and Bernstein, *The Final Days*, 184–185; Isaacson, *Kissinger*, 503.

119. Scowcroft interview, July 17, 2012; Jonathan Howe interview, January 12, 2012. On the USMA tactical officer, see "About the Brigade Tactical Department," USMA website, www.usma.edu/btd/SitePages/About.aspx.

120. It was because of Watergate that Kissinger wanted to go over to the State Department in first place, Sonnenfeldt said. The national security advisor wanted to be appointed to a position that had a firm institutional base; he didn't want to be in a job that depended on Nixon's personal involvement for its effectiveness.

121. Scowcroft interview, BOHP, 14–15.

122. Ibid., 17–18.

123. Scowcroft interview, February 23, 2010; Rodman, *Presidential Command*, 71–73; Helmut Sonnenfeldt interview, ASDT, 2004.

124. Gulley interview, April 13, 2009. Woodward and Bernstein doubt this story, but they provide no factual evidence to suggest it is untrue. In their telling, Kissinger's logic for keeping Scowcroft was that the secretary of state needed his own man in the West Wing (Scowcroft), since Haig and Nixon's press secretary, Ron Ziegler, were both against him and since he had few other friends in the White House. But Rose Mary Woods had nothing to gain by saying that Nixon initially wanted Scowcroft. While she may have liked Scowcroft and disliked Kissinger, such a difference would hardly be grounds for her to misinform others about Nixon's first choice as his new chief of staff. After he resigned, moreover, the former president gave Gulley the same account of how he hired Haig. Walter Isaacson's version of this story is that since Kissinger no longer trusted Haig, he didn't want him to become chief of staff. So Kissinger suggested that the president appoint Scowcroft as his chief of staff, and Nixon rejected the idea (Isaacson, *Kissinger*, 503). Yet Kissinger had something to lose if Woods's version of events were true (and Kissinger had a track record of telling the press self-serving stories). John Prados, for his part, writes that Nixon very much liked Haig and that he and Haldeman both thought Haig would be excellent; he doesn't mention Scowcroft (Prados, *Keepers of the Keys*, 340).

125. Woodward and Bernstein, *The Final Days*, 390.

126. Lt. Gen. Brent Scowcroft, "Window to the Oval Office (Part 1 of 2)," West Point Center for Oral History, March 12, 2012, 22–23.

127. Woodward and Bernstein, *The Final Days*, 422–424, 457.

128. Scowcroft, "Window to the Oval Office (Part 1 of 2)," 25–26; Woodward and Bernstein, *The Final Days*, 388–389.

129. See John Robert Greene, *The Presidency of Gerald R. Ford* (Lawrence: University Press of Kansas, 1988); Yanek Mieczkowski, *Gerald Ford and the Challenges of the 1970s* (Lexington: University of Kentucky Press, 2005); but see Woodward and Bernstein, *The Final Days*, 326.

130. Woodward and Bernstein, *The Final Days*; Safire, *Before the Fall*, 373, 657.

131. Safire, *Before the Fall*, 167, 169; Prados, *Keepers of the Keys*, 338, 351; Rothkopf, *Running the World*, 138.

132. Scowcroft interview, December 2, 2009; Gerald R. Ford, *A Time to Heal: The Autobiography of Gerald R. Ford* (New York: Harper & Row, 1979), 129.

133. Scowcroft interview, December 2, 2009; McFarlane interviews, April 3 and April 23, 2009; Ford, *A Time to Heal*, 121; Head, Short, and McFarlane, *Crisis Resolution*, 77.

134. Prados, *Keepers of the Keys*, 376. Also see Burke, *Honest Broker?*, 154–155.

135. Mieczkowski, *Gerald Ford and the Challenges of the 1970s*, 52; Brent Scowcroft, "Ford as President and His Foreign Policy," in *The Ford Presidency: Twenty-Two Intimate Perspectives of Gerald Ford*, ed. Kenneth W. Thompson, Portraits of American Presidents, vol. 7 (Lanham, MD: University Press of America, 1988), 310.

136. McFarlane interview, April 3, 1999; Rodman, *Presidential Command*, 83–84; John Osborne, *White House Watch: The Ford Years* (Washington, DC: New Republic Books, 1977), xvi, xix.

137. Ford, *A Time to Heal*, 326, 404; Osborne, *White House Watch*, 218; also see Burke, *Honest Broker?*, 154.

138. McFarlane interviews, April 3 and April 23, 2009; Scowcroft interview, April 10, 2009; Lt. Gen. Brent Scowcroft, "Window to the Oval Office: A Diplomatic View of the American Presidency (Part 2 of 2)," West Point Center for Oral History, March 12, 2012, 2; Joseph A. Sisco, "Ford, Kissinger, and the Nixon-Ford Foreign Policy," in *The Ford Presidency: Twenty-Two Intimate Perspectives of Gerald Ford*, ed. Kenneth W. Thompson, Portraits of American Presidents, vol. 7 (Lanham, MD: University Press of America, 1988), 327.

139. University of Michigan National Election Study, www.gallup.com/poll/5392/trust-government.aspx, accessed May 20, 2013. The one exception is a brief period in late 2001, when trust climbed back above 50 percent, higher than the proportion expressing the view that they could trust the government "only some of the time" or "never." But it quickly dropped off again.

140. Nessen, *Making the News*, 113.

141. Isaacson, *Kissinger*, 516–519.

142. Kissinger, *Years of Upheaval*, 492, 496; Isaacson, *Kissinger*, 517–518; Avner Cohen, "The Last Nuclear Moment," *New York Times*, October 6, 2003.

143. "An Oral History Interview with Brent Scowcroft," by Timothy Naftali, Richard Nixon Oral History Project, Richard Nixon Presidential Library and Museum, Yorba Linda, CA, June 29, 2007, 16.

144. Ibid.; Isaacson, *Kissinger*, 524–527.

145. "An Oral History interview with Brent Scowcroft," 20; Isaacson, *Kissinger*, 531–532; Gates, *From the Shadows*, 40–41.

146. "An Oral History interview with Brent Scowcroft," 22.

147. Memcon, "Umar al-Saqqaf, Minister of State for Foreign Affairs, Saudi Arabia," with Henry A. Kissinger and Lt. Gen. Brent Scowcroft, file "June 15, 1974—Kissinger, Saudi Foreign Minister Umar al-Saqqaf," Box 4, National security advisor Memoranda of Conversations, 1973–1977, Nixon Project.

148. Memorandum of Conversation, Schlesinger, Kissinger, Scowcroft, April 23, "April 23, 74–Kissinger/Schlesinger," Box 3, Ford Presidential Library.

149. "HAK Telephone conversations—Chron File 1973 1–9 August," telcon, Mr. Kissinger/Mr. Schlesinger, August 4, 1973, 10:05 A.M. Henry A. Kissinger Telecons, Box 21, Nixon Project.

150. "HAK Telephone conversations—Chron File 1974 5–9 March," telcon, March 6, 1974, 9:30 P.M. Henry A. Kissinger Telecons, Box 25, Nixon Project.

151. McFarlane interview, April 23, 2009.

152. Memorandum of conversation, Ford, Kissinger, Rumsfeld, Scowcroft, "March 17, 1976—Ford, Kissinger, Rumsfeld," Box 18, Ford Presidential Library.

153. NSSM 219, Working Group Nuclear Cooperation Agreement with Iran, Digital National Security Archive (henceforth DNSA), George Washington University, April 22, 1975, www2.gwu.edu/~nsarchiv/nukevault/ebb268/doc05a.pdf.

154. NSDM 238, February 13, 1976, "U.S. Policy Toward the Persian Gulf," PD 01489, DNSA.

155. "Meeting with Carlos P. Romulo, Foreign Secretary of the Republic of the Philippines," April 13, 1976, PH 00855, DNSA.

156. McFarlane interview, April 23, 2009. Also see "113. Telegram from Secretary of State Kissinger to the Department of State," Dacca, October 3, 1974, 0130Z, *Foreign Relations of the United States* (henceforth *FRUS*), 1969–1976, vol. 26, *Arab-Israeli Dispute, 1974–1976*, ed. Adam M. Howard (Washington, DC: US GPO, 2012), 452; Memorandum of conversation, Ford, Kissinger, Scowcroft, Monday, December 13, 1976, "December 13, 1976—Ford, Kissinger, Scowcroft," Box 21, Ford Presidential Library.

157. Memorandum of conversation, Ford, Kissinger, Scowcroft, Sunday, October 3, 1976, "October 3, 1976–Ford, Kissinger, Scowcroft," Box 21, Ford Presidential Library.

158. Executive Summary/NSSM 231: "244. Study Prepared by the National Security Council Ad Hoc Group," undated, "Israeli Military Requests," *FRUS*, 1969–1976, 26:858; "254. Minutes of the National Security Council Meeting," January 13, 1976, *FRUS*, 1969–1976, 26:885.

159. Gantt interview, November 2, 2009.

160. Gulley interview, February 11, 2009.

161. Memorandum of conversation, Monday, July 7, 1975, 9:15 A.M., Ford, Kissinger, Scowcroft, "July 7, 1975—Ford-Kissinger," Box 13, Ford Presidential Library.

162. Memorandum of conversation, Ford, Rumsfeld, Scowcroft, "April, 1976—Ford, Rumsfeld," Box 18, Ford Presidential Library.

Chapter 9: SALT, Détente, and the Intelligence Wars of the Seventies

163. "Address at the Industrial College of the Armed Forces," March 4, 1974, "January–March 1974 [2 of 2]," McFarlane Chronological File, Henry A. Kissinger, NSC Administration and Staff Records, Nixon Project.

164. Ford, *A Time to Heal*, 216–217, 219.

165. Memorandum of conversation, Ford, Kissinger, Rumsfeld, Scowcroft, "November 26, 1975—Ford, Kissinger, Rumsfeld," Box 16, Ford Presidential Library.

166. Schmitz, *Brent Scowcroft*, 44; John Robert Greene, *The Presidency of Gerald R. Ford* (Lawrence: University Press of Kansas, 1988), 125–126; also see Jan M. Lodal, "SALT II and American Security," *Foreign Affairs* (Winter 1978/79).

167. John Lewis Gaddis, *The Cold War: A New History* (New York: Penguin, 2005), 182–183.

168. See "Jackson-Vanik Amendment," *The YIVO Encyclopedia of Jews in Eastern Europe*, www.yivoencyclopedia.org/article.aspx/Jackson-Vanik_Amendment.

169. Greene, *The Presidency of Gerald R. Ford*, 151–152; Ford, *A Time to Heal*, 297–298; Nessen, *Making the News*, 166.

170. Richard Cheney with Liz Cheney, *In My Time* (New York: Simon & Schuster, 2011), 81.

171. Ford, *A Time to Heal*, 298; Greene, *The Presidency of Gerald R. Ford*, 152–153.

172. Scowcroft interview, August 22, 2012; Kissinger quoted in Schmitz, *Brent Scowcroft*, 45; telecon, Mr. Buckley/The Secretary, July 21, 1975, "Document 12," National Security Archive, "The Kissinger State Department Telcons," www.gwu .edu/~nsarchiv/NSAEBB/NSAEBB135/index.htm.

173. Office of Current Intelligence, CIA, "The CSCE and Western Europe—Plusses and Minuses," July 18, 1975, "Conference on Security and Cooperation in Europe, 1975 (1) NSC," Box 44, NSC Europe, Ford Presidential Library.

174. See Mieczkowski, *Gerald Ford and the Challenges of the 1970s*, 296–297.

175. Greene, *The Presidency of Gerald R. Ford*, 152–153.

176. Schmitz, *Brent Scowcroft*, 45.

177. Ibid., 46.

178. Burke, *Honest Broker?*, 161; Greene, *The Presidency of Gerald R. Ford*, 152–153; Scowcroft quoted in Schmitz, *Brent Scowcroft*, 48.

179. Ford quoted in Greene, *The Presidency of Gerald R. Ford*, 153.

180. Osborne, *White House Watch*, 174; Ford, *A Time to Heal*, 299 (emphasis in original).

181. Schmitz, *Brent Scowcroft*, 49–50.

182. Brent Scowcroft, "Signing Ceremony for S. 2679 Establishing a Commission on Security and Cooperation in Europe," Thursday, June 3, 1976, "Conference on Security and Cooperation in Europe, 1976 (2)," Box 44, NSC Europe files, Ford Presidential Library; Brent Scowcroft, "Memorandum for the President, Implementation of the Final Act of Conference on Security and Cooperation in Europe," August 28, 1976, "Conference on Security and Cooperation in Europe, 1976 (3)," Box 44, NSC Europe files, Ford Presidential Library.

183. Quoted in Arnaud de Borchgrave, "Euro Byliner," attached to Jerry H. Jones, "Memorandum for the Honorable Henry A. Kissinger," May 6, 1975, "Scowcroft, Brent (NSC) 1975 (1)," J. E. Connor Papers, Box 30, Ford Presidential Library.

184. James A Schlesinger, "The Continuing Challenge to America," *Reader's Digest*, April 1976, 61–66, in "Defense—Schlesinger Interviews," Box 7, Ron Nessen Papers, 1974–1977, Ford Presidential Library.

185. "Memorandum, Eugene Rostow to Participant in the March 12 meeting at the Metropolitan Club," March 19, 1976, subject file, "Committee on Present Danger Miscellaneous, 1976–79," Box 70, Nitze Papers, Library of Congress.

186. Scowcroft interview, November 4, 2010.

187. William Colby, *Honorable Men: My Life in the CIA* (New York: Simon and Schuster, 1978), 15, 391; see John Ranelagh, *The Agency: The Rise and Decline of the CIA* (New York: Simon & Schuster, 1988).

188. William E. Colby to the President, December 24, 1974, "Investigation of the US Intelligence Community," Box 11, America Since Hoover Collection, Ford Presidential Library; James A. Wilderotter, "CIA Matters," Memorandum for the File, January 3, 1975, "Intelligence—President's Meeting with Richard Helms, 1/75," Box 7, Cheney Files, Ford Presidential Library.

189. Ranelagh, *The Agency*, 629–630.

190. Kissinger quoted in Kenneth Kitts, *Presidential Commissions & National Security: The Politics of Damage Control* (Boulder, CO: Lynne Rienner Publishers, 2004), 51; Rhodri Jeffreys-Jones, *The CIA and American Democracy* (New Haven: Yale University Press, 1989), 195.

191. Kitts, *Presidential Commissions*, 53–54; Memcon, February 21, 1975, "Feb. 21, 1975—Ford, Kissinger, Rumsfeld, March," Box 9, Memcons, Ford Presidential Library.

192. Jeffreys-Jones, *The CIA and American Democracy*, 201–202.

193. Nessen, *Making the News*, 141–143; Kitts, *Presidential Commissions*, 61–63.

194. Osborne, *White House Watch*, 281–282. Scowcroft made the "perhaps 25 to 30 percent extra time" comment in a TV interview with ABC's Ann Compton; Memorandum of conversation, Lt. General Brent Scowcroft, Assistant to the President for National Security Affairs, Ms. Ann Compton, ABC TV, Ms. Margi Vanderhye, Note Taker, Saturday, December 13, 1975, "Chron File, Nov.-Dec., 1975," NSC Press-Cong. Liaison, Box 7, Ford Presidential Library.

195. Brent Scowcroft, Memcon, "May 27, 1975—Ford, Schlesinger, Colby, Rumsfeld, Ingersoll," Box 12, Memcons, Ford Presidential Library.

196. Colby, *Honorable Men*, 16–17; memorandum of conversation, June 16, 1975, President Ford, Kissinger, Scowcroft, "June 16, 1975—Ford, Kissinger," Box 12, Ford Presidential Library.

197. *The Man Nobody Knew: In Search of My Father, William Colby*, Carl Colby, director and producer, 2011.

198. Scowcroft interview, July 17, 2012. Scowcroft acknowledged that Colby's family disagreed with him and that he hadn't drawn any conclusions about Colby's mysterious death.

199. McFarlane, *Special Trust*.

200. Walter Pincus, Donald Rumsfeld, and Bob Woodward, quoted in *The Man Nobody Knew*.

201. Carl Colby interview, June 26, 2012.

202. Colby, *Honorable Men*, 16–17.

203. Scowcroft interview, August 12, 2009.

204. Memorandum of conversation, Ford, Kissinger, Scowcroft, October 13, 1975, "October 13, Ford, Kissinger," Box 16, Ford Presidential Library.

205. Stephen Hadley interview, April 7, 2009; memorandum of conversation, Ford, Kissinger, Schlesinger, Levi, Lynn, Colby, Buchan, Marsh, Rumsfeld, Scowcroft, Raoul-Duval, October 13, 1975, "October 13, Ford, Kissinger," Box 16, Ford Presidential Library.

206. Colby, *Honorable Men*, 436–437.

207. McFarlane interview, April 23, 2009.

208. Nessen, *Making the News*, 146; Ford, *A Time to Heal*, 297–298; Jeffreys-Jones, *The CIA and American Democracy*, 200, 208; also see John Prados, *The Family Jewels: The CIA, Secrecy, and Presidential Power* (Austin: University of Texas Press, 2013).

209. Osborne, *White House Watch*, 284–285.

210. See "Issues," attached to Jack Marsh, "Meeting on Intelligence Community," January 10, 1976, "Intelligence—Meeting to Review Intelligence Community Decision Book, 1/10/76," Box 6, Cheney files, 1974–77, Ford Presidential Library.

211. Gerald R. Ford, "Special Message to the Congress Proposing Legislation to Reform the United States Foreign Intelligence Community," February 18, 1976,

Online by Gerhard Peters and John T. Woolley, *The American Presidency Project*, www.presidency.ucsb.edu/ws/?pid=5590.

212. "The President's Actions Concerning the Foreign Intelligence Community," Office of the White House Press Secretary, February 17, 1976, "Intelligence—President's Actions (1)" Box 7, Cheney files. Ford Presidential Library.

213. "Ford's CIA Shake-Up," *Newsweek*, March 1, 1976.

214. Ibid.

215. Richard Pipes, "Team B: The Reality Behind the Myth," *Commentary* 30 (October 1986); Anne Hessing Cahn, *Killing Détente: The Right Attacks the CIA* (University Park, PA: Pennsylvania State University Press, 1998), 127–130.

216. Scowcroft interview, February 24, 2011; Scowcroft interview, BOHP, 25.

217. Cahn, *Killing Détente*, 154–155, 159.

218. Memorandum of conversation, President Ford, Henry Kissinger, Brent Scowcroft, January 4, 1977, The Oval Office, "Jan. 4, 1977—Ford, Kissinger," Box 21, Memcon files, Ford Presidential Library; Scowcroft interview, BOHP, 25.

219. Scowcroft interview, BOHP, 24.

220. Brent Scowcroft, "American Attitudes Toward Foreign Policy," *Naval War College Review* 32, no. 2 (1979): 11–19, 16–17.

Chapter 10: Managing Failure

221. Osborne, *White House Watch*, 321–322; Arnold R. Isaacs, *Without Honor* (Baltimore: Johns Hopkins University Press, 1983), 435; Nessen, *Making the News*, 10; Robert D. Schulzinger, *A Time for War: The United States and Vietnam, 1941–1975* (New York: Oxford University Press, 1999), 325; Hartmann, *Palace Politics*, 321–322.

222. Scowcroft interviews, August 22, 2012, and January 3, 2014; Greene, *The Presidency of Gerald Ford*, 139–140; Hanhimäki, *The Flawed Architect*, 393–395; Lt. Gen. Brent Scowcroft, "Window to the Oval Office (Part 2 of 2)," 1, 3.

223. Scowcroft interview, March 4, 2009; John Robert Greene, *The Presidency of Gerald R. Ford* (Lawrence: University Press of Kansas, 1988), 161; "The Tactical Thinker Shaping Nuclear Strategy," *Business Week*, April 11, 1983, 111.

224. Scowcroft interview, June 6, 2012.

225. Scowcroft, "Window to the Oval Office (Part 2 of 2)," 2.

226. Tim Weiner, *Legacy of Ashes: The History of the CIA* (New York: Anchor Books, 2008), 397.

227. Richard D. Johnston, "Summary of the Evacuation of Saigon, South Vietnam Under Operation Frequent Wind (U)," Operations Analysis Group Report No. 2–75, Headquarters of the Commander in Chief Pacific Operations Analysis Group, Department of Defense, May 16, 1975, 96; Schlesinger quoted in "Memorandum of Conversation," April 17, 1975, 4:30 P.M., Cabinet Room, White House, Subject: Vietnam Evacuation Transcript," "April 17, 1975—Ford, Kissinger,

Schlesinger, Rumsfeld, Marsh," Box 11, Memcon Files, Ford Presidential Library; Olivier Todd, *Cruel April: The Fall of Saigon*, trans. Stephen Becker (New York: W. W. Norton, 1987), 371.

228. See, for instance, "Memorandum for Secretary Kissinger," from Jeanne W. Davis, subject "Minutes of the NSC Meeting March 28, 1975," DNSA 01346, 1–14.

229. Eyes only via Martin Channel, to General Scowcroft from Chargé Lehmann, March 17, 1975, DNSA, No. 01328; Lien-Hang T. Nguyen, *Hanoi's War: An International History of the War for Peace in Vietnam* (Chapel Hill: University of North Carolina Press, 2012).

230. Charles Henderson, *Goodnight Saigon* (New York: Penguin, 2005), 320; Frank Snepp, *Decent Interval* (New York: Random House, 1977), 447–448; Johnston, "Summary of the Evacuation of Saigon," 96; Schlesinger quoted in "Memorandum of Conversation," April 17, 1975, 4:30 P.M., Cabinet Room, White House, Subject: Vietnam Evacuation Transcript," "April 17, 1975—Ford, Kissinger, Schlesinger, Rumsfeld, Marsh," Box 11, Memcon Files, Ford Presidential Library; Todd, *Cruel April*, 371; Hanhimäki, *The Flawed Architect*, 391.

231. "Memorandum for the Record of National Security Council Meeting," Washington, April 24, 1975, 4:35 P.M., *FRUS*, 1969–1976, 10:899–900; Prados, *Keepers of the Keys*, 361–362, 366; Henry Kissinger, *Crisis: The Anatomy of Two Major Foreign Policy Crises* (New York: Simon & Schuster, 2003), 482–483, 497–499; Anatoly Dobrynin, *In Confidence: Moscow's Ambassador to America's Six Cold War Presidents* (New York: Times Books, 1995), 343–344; Todd, *Cruel April*, 277; Snepp, *Decent Interval*, 417–418, 478, 534.

232. Walter Boyne, "The Fall of Saigon," *Air Force Magazine*, April 2000, 73–74; Snepp, *Decent Interval*, 408, 533, 566; Johnston, "Summary of the Evacuation of Saigon," 61; Prados, *Keepers of the Keys*, 366–367; George J. Veith, *Black April: The Fall of South Vietnam 1973–1975* (New York: Encounter Books, 2012); Richard Smyser interview, February 24, 2009.

233. Snepp, *Decent Interval*, 413.

234. See National Security Council Memorandum to General Scowcroft from W. R. Smyser, April 16, 1978, DNSA 01411; George S. Springsteen, Executive Secretary, Department of State, "Memorandum for Lieutenant General Brent Scowcroft, The White House," Subject: "Study of Evacuation Planning Issues and Options for Viet-Nam," April 17, 1975, DNSA 01417, 15, 16; Henry Kissinger, *Ending the Vietnam War: A History of America's Involvement In and Extrication from the Vietnam War* (New York: Simon & Schuster, 2003), 542–543; Snepp, *Decent Interval*, 418–419, 447–448.

235. See Snepp, *Decent Interval*; Evan Thomas, "The Last Days of Saigon," *Newsweek*, May 1, 2000; Johnston, "Summary of the Evacuation of Saigon," 67–70.

236. Cable from Ambassador Martin to General Brent Scowcroft, April 7, 1975, DNSA 01376; statement by Kissinger to the Senate Foreign Relations Committee

in "Memorandum of Conversation, Washington, April 14, 1975," *FRUS*, 1969–1976, 10:818; Memorandum for General [Scowcroft] from Bud [McFarlane], April 15, 1975, DNSA 01406; "Memorandum for Lieutenant General Brent Scowcroft the White House," Subject: Study of Evacuation Planning Issues and Options for Viet-Nam, Department of State, April 17, 1975, DNSA 01417.

237. The total number of potential evacuees was inflated because of the South Vietnamese and US governments' disinformation on the grisly fates that awaited the South Vietnamese after their capture by the communists (Springsteen, "Memorandum for Lieutenant General Brent Scowcroft, the White House," Subject: "Study of Evacuation Planning Issues and Options for Viet-Nam," 3; Isaacs, *Without Honor*.

238. See Snepp, *Decent Interval*, 566–567, 569–570; Isaacs, *Without Honor*, 94–95, 450–451; Memorandum for Secretary Kissinger from W. R. Smyser, Clinton E. Granger, and William L. Stearman, "WSAG Meeting on the Evacuation of South Vietnam, National Security Council, April 16, 1975," "WSAG, April 17, 1975, Evacuation," Box 25, NSC East Asian Files, Ford Presidential Library. Also see Johnston, "Summary of the Evacuation of Saigon."

239. Isaacs, *Without Honor*, 480; Todd, *Cruel April*, 351; Snepp, *Decent Interval*, 404–405.

240. Mark Atwood Lawrence, *The Vietnam War: A Concise International History* (New York: Oxford University Press, 2008), 168; Snepp, *Decent Interval*, 569.

241. Quoted in Robert Dallek, *Nixon and Kissinger: Partners in Power* (New York: HarperCollins, 2007), 154; Scowcroft, "Window to the Oval Office (Part 2 of 2)," 3; Isaacson, *Kissinger*, 246.

242. Hanhimäki, *The Flawed Architect*, 385.

243. See Memorandum for Mr. Kissinger from William L. Stearman, Subject: "Alleged U.S. and GVN Cease-fire Violations," May 14, 1973, "Nixon—NSC-Henry Kissinger," Country Files, Far East–Vietnam, Box 116, "Vol. I Meeting Book, May 1973, General Scowcroft Top Secret," Nixon Project; "Rebuttal to Charges of USG Violations," Nixon, NSC Files, Henry A. Kissinger Office Files, Country Files-Far East-Vietnam," Volume I—Meeting, Box 116, Book "December 26, 1973–75," Nixon Project; William Lloyd Stearman interview, 1998, ADST, 40.

244. On Haig's role in the war see, for instance, Kimball, *Nixon's Vietnam War*; Tad Szulc, *Illusion of Peace* (New York: Viking Press, 1978); "An Oral History interview with Brent Scowcroft."

245. Robert Hartmann, "A War That Is Finished as Far as America Is Concerned," in *Tears Before the Rain: An Oral History of the Fall of South Vietnam*, ed. Larry Engelmann (New York: Oxford University Press, 1990), 149.

246. McFarlane interview, April 3, 2009.

247. There is no mention of General Scowcroft in Lien-Hang T. Nguyen's fine history of the war from the perspective of the North Vietnamese, *Hanoi's War*, for

example, and Scowcroft came to the NSC too late to be included in Jeffrey Kimball's revealing volume of annotated documents, *The Vietnam War File: Uncovering the Secret History of Nixon-Era Strategy* (Lawrence: University Press of Kansas, 2004). And there is only one reference in Arnold Isaacs's comprehensive and engrossing account, *Without Honor.*

248. William Shawcross, *Sideshow: Kissinger, Nixon, and the Destruction of Cambodia*, rev. ed. (New York: Cooper Square Press, 1987), 95, 269, 340.

249. "Memorandum from the President's Deputy Assistant for National Security Affairs (Scowcroft) to the President's Assistant for National Security Affairs (Kissinger)," Washington, April 11, 1973, *FRUS*, 1969–1976, 10:186–188.

250. "Minutes of Washington Special Actions Group Meeting," Washington, DC, November 29, 1973, 3:21–3:49 P.M., *FRUS*, 1969–1976, 10:464.

251. Scowcroft in "Meeting at Noon, March 24, on Indochina," DNSA 015471, 6; "Memorandum of Conversation, Tuesday, October 2, 1973, 1:15–2:55 [Luncheon]," 2, file "October 2, 1973—Kissinger, Schlesinger, Colby, Moorer," Box 2, Ford Presidential Library; "Memorandum of Conversation," Monday, January 13, 1975, DNSA KT 01475, 2.

252. Brent Scowcroft to Roy Ash, January 13, 1975, "Additional 1975 Foreign Aid Requests for South Vietnam." DNSA 01283.

253. See "Memorandum of Conversation," August 7, 1973, Tuesday, 12:00 noon, NSC Deputies, DNSA KT 00786.

254. See, for example, "Conversation Between President Nixon and the President's Deputy Assistant for National Security Affairs (Scowcroft)," Washington, June 12, 1973, *FRUS*, 1969–1976, 10:331–337; Scowcroft interview, November 4, 2010.

255. Lloyd Gardner, "Harry Hopkins with Hand Grenades?" in *Behind the Throne: Servants of Power to Imperial Presidents, 1898–1968*, eds. Thomas J. McCormick and Walter LaFeber (Madison: University of Wisconsin Press, 1993), 221–222.

256. Scowcroft quoted in Christopher Jon Lamb, *Belief Systems and Decision Making in the Mayaguez Crisis* (Gainesville: University of Florida Press, 1989), 77.

257. Also see Hanhimäki, *The Flawed Architect*, 388–389.

258. Quoted in "Meeting at Noon, March 24, on Indochina," March 24, 1975, DNSA 01547, 4; Kissinger quoted in *FRUS*, 1969–1976, 10:718.

259. Brent Scowcroft to Roy Ash, January 13, 1975, "Additional 1975 Foreign Aid Requests for South Vietnam," DNSA 01283.

260. James H. Willbanks, *Abandoning Vietnam: How America Left and South Vietnam Lost Its War* (Lawrence: University Press of Kansas, 2008), 229–230; Veith, *Black April*, 310.

261. See comments by Ambassador Graham Martin and Mr. William Hyland in "Meeting at Noon, March 24, on Indochina," DNSA 01547; Engelmann, ed., *Tears Before the Rain*, 302–303.

262. William Colby, Jeanne W. Davis, "Memorandum for Secretary Kissinger," Minutes of NSC Meeting, March 28, 1975, DNSA 01346; Thomas, "The Last Days of Saigon," 2; Boyne, "The Fall of Saigon," 72.

263. Boyne, "The Fall of Saigon," 70–71; Snepp, *Decent Interval*, 567–568.

264. "Memorandum for Secretary Kissinger," from Jeanne W. Davis, Subject: "Minutes of the NSC Meeting March 28, 1975," DNSA 01346, 17; Scowcroft interview, August 22, 2012.

265. Johnston, "Summary of the Evacuation of Saigon," 57; Thomas, "The Last Days of Saigon"; also see Isaacs, *Without Honor*, 453–454.

266. Hanhimäki, *The Flawed Architect*, 384–385, 387–388.

267. Scowcroft interview, August 12, 2012.

268. Dobrynin, *In Confidence*, 343; Scowcroft interviews, March 4, 2009, and August 22, 2012.

269. Scowcroft interview, March 4, 2009; Scowcroft, "Window to the Oval Office (Part 2 of 2)," 4.

270. Snepp, *Decent Interval*, 374; Telecon, General Scowcroft/The Secretary, April 15, 1975, KA 13492, DNSA.

271. Memorandum of conversation, Ford, Kissinger, Scowcroft, December 18, 1975, "Dec. 18, 1975—Ford, Kissinger, Scowcroft," Memcon Files, Box 17, Ford Presidential Library.

272. Hanhimäki, *The Flawed Architect*, 383.

273. Larry Berman, *No Peace, No Honor: Nixon, Kissinger, and Betrayal in Vietnam* (New York: Free Press, 2001), 261.

274. Boyne, "The Fall of Saigon," 72; see, generally, Veith, *Black April*; Isaacs, *Without Honor*, 393.

275. Snepp, *Decent Interval*, 416; Veith, *Black April*, 454, 537n23.

276. Kennerly quoted in Isaacs, *Without Honor*, 405; Prados, *Keepers of the Keys*, 362–363.

277. Snepp, *Decent Interval*, 358–359; Springsteen, "Memorandum for Lieutenant General Brent Scowcroft," 10, 11; also see Memorandum for Secretary Kissinger from W. R. Smyser, Clinton E. Granger, and William L. Stearman. Also see "Categories of Evacuees," Tab M, "WASG, April 19, 1975, Evac (3)," Box 25, NSC East Asian Files, Ford Presidential Library.

278. See "Memorandum of Conversation," Washington, April 14, 1975, *FRUS*, 1969–1976, 10:817–822; "Minutes of the Washington Special Actions Group Meeting," Washington, April 17, 1975, 3:28–4:10 P.M., *FRUS*, 1969–1976, 10:837–838; Springsteen, "Memorandum for Lieutenant General Brent Scowcroft"; Dean Brown quoted in "Minutes of Washington Special Actions Group Meeting," Washington, April 19, 11:05 A.M.–12:02 P.M., Subject: Vietnam Evacuation, *FRUS*, 1969–1976, 10:853.

279. Scowcroft interview, August 22, 2012.

280. See Scowcroft's statements in "Memorandum of Conversation," Washington, March 24, 1975, noon, *FRUS*, 1969–1976, 10:692–693.

281. Springsteen, "Memorandum for Lieutenant General Brent Scowcroft," 3.

282. "The Situation in Vietnam," DCI Briefing for April 17 WSAG Meeting, "WSAG, April 17, 1975, Evac," Box 25, NSC East Asia Files, Ford Presidential Library, 1–8.

283. See remarks by President Ford in "Memorandum of Conversation," Washington, April 14, 1975, 3:30 P.M., *FRUS*, 1969–1976, 10:817–822.

284. Scowcroft interview, July 17, 2012; General Brent Scowcroft, "Ford as President and His Foreign Policy," in *The Ford Presidency*, 148–149.

285. See cable from Ambassador Martin to General Brent Scowcroft, April 7, 1975, DNSA 01376, 3; Scowcroft interview, August 22, 2012; also see Memorandum for General Scowcroft from W. R. Smyser, April 15, 1975, DNSA 01405, attachment, Cable to Henry A. Kissinger from Graham Martin, April 25, 1975, 1–2; "Memorandum of Conversation," Washington, April 14, 1975, 3:30 P.M., *FRUS*, 1969–1976, 10:817–822; Kissinger, *Ending the Vietnam War*, 540; Kissinger, *Crisis*, 510; Snepp, *Decent Interval*, 386.

286. Memorandum of Conversation, August 7, 1973, Tuesday, 12:00 Noon— NSC Deputies, DNSA 00786; Todd, *Cruel April*, 274–275; Scowcroft interview, April 10, 2009.

287. Scowcroft interview, April 10, 2009.

288. Cable from Brent Scowcroft to Ambassador Graham Martin, April 19, 1975, DNSA 01432.

289. Snepp, *Decent Interval*, 346.

290. Henderson, *Goodnight Saigon*, 328; Snepp, *Decent Interval*, 489–490; Greene, *The Presidency of George Bush*, 140–141.

291. Snepp, *Decent Interval*, 363; Boyne, "The Fall of Saigon," 74.

292. McFarlane, *Special Trust*, 146.

293. Scowcroft and Martin quoted in David Butler, *The Fall of Saigon: Scenes from the Sudden End of a Long War* (New York: Simon & Schuster,1985), 438–439. Also see Snepp, *Decent Interval*, 421.

294. Martin quoted in Butler, *The Fall of Saigon*, 441.

295. Graham Martin, "Walking Around with My Head in a Basket," in *Tears Before the Rain*, 58.

296. Ibid.; Isaacs, *Without Honor*, 470–471.

297. Martin, "Walking Around with My Head in a Basket," 58; Todd, *Cruel April*, 367.

298. Snepp, *Decent Interval*, 562; Isaacs, *Without Honor*, 468–477.

299. Todd, *Cruel April*, 368; Snepp, *Decent Interval*, 561–562.

300. Isaacs, *Without Honor*, 481–483; Snepp, *Decent Interval*, 568. For detailed and often firsthand accounts of those final hours, see Snepp, *Decent Interval*; Butler,

The Fall of Saigon; Isaacs, *Without Honor*; Engelmann, ed., *Tears Before the Rain*; Henderson, *Goodnight Saigon*; and Todd, *Cruel April*. The lead vehicle was tank No. 843.

301. To Graham Martin from Henry Kissinger, April 30, 1975, "Sent via Military Channels," DNSA, 01515.

302. See, for instance, Memorandum of Conversation, November 14, 1974, 6:00 P.M., White House, "Gayler, Noel A. M. (Admiral)," National security advisor files, President Nixon Files, Box 1, Ford Presidential Library.

303. See Springsteen, "Memorandum for Lieutenant General Brent Scowcroft"; Prados, *Keepers of the Keys*, 367.

304. Prados, *Keepers of the Keys*, 367; Nessen, *Making the News,* 10.

305. For Kissinger's worsening moods, see "Minutes of Washington Special Actions Group Meeting," Washington, April 28, 1975, 10:38–11:14 A.M., *FRUS*, 1969–1976, 10:914–920; Hartmann, *Palace Politics*, 324; Hanhimäki, *The Flawed Architect*, 396.

306. Scowcroft interview, March 4, 2009.

307. Isaacs, *Without Honor*, 401; also see Memorandum of conversation, Friday, February 8, 1974, 2:37–3:35 P.M., Cabinet Room, White House, National security advisor Collection, folder "February 8, 1974—Nixon, President's Foreign Intelligence Advisory Board," Nixon Project.

308. Kissinger, *Crisis*, 542; Snepp, *Decent Interval*, 452.

309. Scowcroft interview, August 12, 2009.

310. Snepp, *Decent Interval*, 579.

311. "245. Minutes of Washington Special Actions Group Meeting," April 19, 1975, *FRUS*, 1969–1976, 10:855.

312. Osborne, *White House Watch*, 124.

313. Hartman, "A War That Is Finished as Far as America Is Concerned," 151. Also see Isaacs, *Without Honor*, 434–435.

314. Osborne, *White House Watch*, 124.

315. David Elliott, "Senior Scholars' Interpretations of the American Experience in Southeast Asia," East Auditorium, George C. Marshall Conference Center, Washington, DC. September 29, 2010, http://history.state.gov/conferences/2010-southeast-asia/senior-scholars.

316. John Prados, "Senior Scholars' Interpretations of the American Experience in Southeast Asia," East Auditorium, George C. Marshall Conference Center, Washington, DC. September 29, 2010, http://history.state.gov/conferences/2010-southeast-asia/senior-scholars.

317. Scowcroft interviews, April 10, 2009, October 6, 2010, and February 11, 2013; William Lloyd Stearman interview, 1998, ADST, 37, 45; Eagleburger interview, August 13, 1988, ADST; "An Oral History interview with Brent Scowcroft," 25.

318. Hanhimäki, *The Flawed Architect*, 383, 386.

319. Kissinger, *Ending the Vietnam War*, 556–560.

320. Also see Nguyen, *Hanoi's War*, on the determination of the North Vietnamese.

321. George S. Springsteen, "Memorandum for Lieutenant General Brent Scowcroft, The White House," Subject: Lessons of Viet-Nam, May 9, 1975, Department of State, DNSA 01542; Secret Action memorandum, William Smyser to Secretary Kissinger, "Lessons of Vietnam," May 12, 1975, 11 pages, DNSA, VW01539.

Chapter 11: We Mean Business

322. Osborne, *White House Watch*, 136–137; John Guilmartin, *A Very Short War* (College Station: Texas A&M Press), 26.

323. Memorandum of conversation, Ford, Kissinger, Scowcroft, May 12, 1975, "May 12, '75—Ford, Kissinger," Box 11, Ford Library; see Robert J. Mahoney, *The Mayaguez Incident: Testing American's Resolve in the Post-Vietnam Era* (Lubbock: Texas Tech University Press, 2011), 19; "Capture and Release of SS Mayaguez by Khmer Rouge Forces in May 1975," www.usmm.org/Mayaguez.html; Head, Short, and McFarlane, *Crisis Resolution*, 103–104.

324. "285. Minutes of National Security Council Meeting," Washington, May 12, 1975, 12:03–12:50 P.M., *FRUS*, 1969–1976, 10:977–985; Head, Short, and McFarlane, *Crisis Resolution*, 102–103.

325. "285. Minutes of National Security Council Meeting"; Head, Short, and McFarlane, *Crisis Resolution*, 102–104; Kissinger, *Years of Renewal*, 550.

326. McFarlane interviews, April 3, April 23, 2009; Ford, *A Time to Heal*, 275.

327. Ford, *A Time to Heal*, 275–277, 280; Kissinger, *Years of Renewal*, 550–551; Mahoney, *The Mayaguez Incident*, 26–29; also see Admiral William J. Crowe Jr. with David Chanoff, *The Line of Fire: From Washington to the Gulf, the Politics and Battles of the New Military* (New York: Simon & Schuster, 1993), 63–74.

328. "Minutes of the National Security Council Meeting," Washington, May 13–14, 1975, 10:40 P.M.–12:25 A.M., *FRUS*, 1969–1976, 10:1015. Also see Head, Short, and McFarlane, *Crisis Resolution*, 117, and Mahoney, *The Mayaguez Incident*.

329. Scowcroft quoted in Head, Short, and McFarlane, *Crisis Resolution*, 79.

330. Kissinger, *Years of Renewal*, 550–551; Guilmartin, *A Very Short War*, 37; Mahoney, *The Mayaguez Incident*, 28–29.

331. Letter from Lawrence Eagleburger to Elmer B. Staats, Comptroller General of the United States, March 5, 1976, "Unclassified with Secret Attachment," "7600658—Comments on GAO Mayaguez Study (1)," Box 32, President NSC Logged Documents, Ford Presidential Library.

332. "295. Minutes of the National Security Council Meeting."

333. Ibid.; also see Mahoney, *The Mayaguez Incident*, 74.

334. Mahoney, *The Mayaguez Incident*, 31.

335. McFarlane interviews, April 3 and April 23, 2009.

336. "291. Minutes of the National Security Council Meeting," Washington, May 13, 10:22 A.M.–11:17 P.M., *FRUS*, 1969–1976, 10:991–1001.

337. "295. Minutes of the National Security Council Meeting," Washington, May 13–14, 1975, 10:40 P.M.–12:25 A.M., *FRUS* 10:1004–1013.

338. Memorandum for the President from Henry A. Kissinger, Subject: Debrief of the MAYAGUEZ Captain and Crew, May 19, 1975, "Cambodia-Mayaguez Seizure (3)," Box 1, Kissinger-Scowcroft West Wing Office Files, 1969–77, Ford Presidential Library; Head, Short, and McFarlane, *Crisis Resolution*, 116.

339. "295. Minutes of the National Security Council Meeting," 1004–1013.

340. Head, Short, and McFarlane, *Crisis Resolution*, 120; Guilmartin, *A Very Short War*, 60–62; Mahoney, *The Mayaguez Incident*, 94–97.

341. Mahoney, *The Mayaguez Incident*, 96–100.

342. Guilmartin, *A Very Short War*, 60–61; Ford, *A Time to Heal*, 282.

343. Mahoney, *The Mayaguez Incident*, 59.

344. See Guilmartin, *A Very Short War*, 63–64, 167–187; Mahoney, *The Mayaguez Incident*, 59–60.

345. "Military Operations Which Resulted in the Successful Recovery of the SS Mayaguez and Crew," "Cambodia–Mayaguez Seizure (3)," Box 1, Kissinger-Scowcroft West Wing files, 1974–77, Ford Presidential Library; footnote 4 of "301. Minutes of the National Security Council Meeting," Washington, May 14, 4:02 P.M.–4:20 P.M., *FRUS*, 1969–1976, 10:1039–1043, identifies the date of this Department of Defense report as May 20, 1975. Also see Mahoney, *The Mayaguez Incident*, 161–180.

346. "Capture and Release of SS Mayaguez by Khmer Rouge Forces in May 1975," www.usmm.org/Mayaguez.html.

347. Mahoney, *The Mayaguez Incident*, 179–180; see generally Ralph Wetterhahn, *The Last Battle: The Mayaguez Incident and the End of the Vietnam War* (Cambridge, MA: Da Capo Press, 2001).

348. "298. Minutes of the National Security Council Meeting," Washington, May 14, 3:52 P.M.–5:42 P.M." *FRUS*, 1969–1976, 10:1021–1036.

349. "295. Minutes of the National Security Council Meeting," 1004–1013.

350. Ford, *A Time to Heal*, 280; Memorandum of Conversation, President Ford, Dr. Henry A. Kissinger, and Lt. General Scowcroft, Wednesday, May 14, 1975, 11:45 A.M., Oval Office, "May 14, 1975—Ford-Kissinger," Mayaguez file, Box 11, Ford Presidential Library.

351. Ford, *A Time to Heal*, 280.

352. Mahoney, *The Mayaguez Incident*, 155; Wetterhahn, *The Last Battle*, 190.

353. Mahoney, *The Mayaguez Incident*, 155–156.

354. Transcript of telephone conversation between President Ford and the President's Deputy Assistant for National Security Affairs, Washington, DC, May 13,

1975, 8:10 P.M., "Cambodia, Mayaguez Seizure (1)," Box 1, National security advisor, Kissinger-Scowcroft West Wing Office Files, Ford Presidential Library.

355. "The President/General Scowcroft," 9:50 P.M., May 13, 1975, "Cambodia, Mayaguez Seizure (1)," Box 1, National security advisor, Kissinger-Scowcroft West Wing Office Files, Ford Presidential Library.

356. "298. Minutes of the National Security Council Meeting"; also see Ford, *A Time to Heal*, 281.

357. "298. Minutes of the National Security Council Meeting."

358. Greene, *The Presidency of Gerald R. Ford*, 148.

359. "295. Minutes of the National Security Council Meeting," 1004–1013.

360. "298. Minutes of the National Security Council Meeting."

361. Ibid.

362. McFarlane, *Special Trust*, 163; Ford, *A Time to Heal*, 283.

363. Quoted in Wetterhahn, *The Last Battle*, 206; also see Greene, *The Presidency of Gerald R. Ford*, 143–155.

364. Mahoney, *The Mayaguez Incident*, 156; Wetterhahn, *The Last Battle*, 206–207; Memcon, "May 16, 1975—Ford, Kissinger," Box 11, Ford Presidential Library.

365. "Capture and Release of SS Mayaguez by Khmer Rouge Forces in May 1975," www.usmm.org/Mayaguez.html.

366. See Wetterhahn, *The Last Battle*, 197–198; Mahoney, *The Mayaguez Incident*, 79–81.

367. Memorandum for the President from Henry A. Kissinger, Subject: Debrief of the MAYAGUEZ Captain and Crew, May 19, 1975, "Cambodia-Mayaguez Seizure (3)," Box 1, Kissinger-Scowcroft West Wing Office Files, 1969–77, Ford Presidential Library.

368. Kissinger, *Years of Renewal*, 565.

369. Hersh, *The Price of Power*, 639–640.

370. "285. Minutes of National Security Council Meeting."

371. Ford, *A Time to Heal*, 283; letter from Lawrence Eagleburger to Elmer B. Staats, Comptroller General of the United States, March 5, 1976, "Unclassified with Secret Attachment," "7600658—Comments on GAO Mayaguez Study (1)," Box 32, President NSC Logged Documents, Ford Presidential Library. See also Greene, *The Presidency of Gerald Ford*, and Mahoney, *The Mayaguez Incident*, 194–203.

372. Mahoney, *The Mayaguez Incident*, 192–193, 194–203; Greene, *The Presidency of Gerald R. Ford*, 151; Schulzinger, *Henry Kissinger*, 203–204; Prados, *Keepers of the Keys*, 371.

373. Mark J. Rozell, *The Press and the Ford Presidency* (Ann Arbor: University of Michigan Press, 1992), 98–101; Wetterhahn, *The Last Battle*, 257; Osborne, *White House Watch*; Mieczkowski, *Gerald Ford and the Challenges of the 1970s*, 295.

374. Wetterhahn, *The Last Battle*, 311–312; McFarlane interviews, April 9 and 23, 2009; William Lloyd Stearman, April 15, 1992, ADST, 43.

375. Gerald R. Ford, "Memorandum for the Assistant to the President for National Security Affairs," Subject: "The Rescue of the SS Mayaguez and Its Crew," May 18, 1975, "Cambodia-Mayaguez Seizure (2)," Box 1, Kissinger-Scowcroft West Wing Office Files, 1969–77," Ford Presidential Library.

376. "301. Minutes of the National Security Council Meeting"; Kissinger, *Years of Renewal*, 571; "298. Minutes of the National Security Council Meeting"; also see Mahoney, *The Mayaguez Incident*, 185–186.

377. Memorandum for General Scowcroft from Thomas J. Barnes, Subject: "*Mayaguez* Post-Mortem," October 16, 1975, "Draft Report to the President, October 16, 1975 (1)" Box 29, National Security Council East Asia files, Ford Presidential Library; also see Ford, *A Time to Heal*, 284.

378. Memorandum for General Scowcroft from Thomas J. Barnes, Subject: "*Mayaguez* Post-Mortem"; also see Mahoney, *The Mayaguez Incident*, 85–100.

379. "The Daily Diary of President Gerald R. Ford," May 15, 1975, White House, Washington, DC, "5/9–15/75 (work copy)," Box 14, President's Daily Diary, Ford Presidential Library.

380. Also see Nessen, *Making the News*, 161–165.

381. Kennerly quoted in Wetterhahn, *The Last Battle*, 123–124; Ford, *A Time to Heal*, 279–280; Ron Nessen, *It Sure Looks Different from the Inside* (New York: Playboy Press, 1979), 122; Scowcroft interview, February 23, 2011.

382. Nessen quoted in Wetterhahn, *The Last Battle*, 205.

383. "291. Minutes of the National Security Council Meeting."

384. Scowcroft interview, October 20, 2011.

385. "295. Minutes of the National Security Council Meeting"; Kissinger, *Years of Renewal*, 562–563.

386. Nessen, *Making the News*, 162.

387. Wetterhahn, *The Last Battle*, 191; Kissinger, *Years of Renewal*, 569; Mahoney, *The Mayaguez Incident*, 127; Nessen, *Making the News* 162.

388. Gerald R. Ford, "Memorandum for the Assistant to the President for National Security Affairs," Subject: "The Rescue of the SS Mayaguez and Its Crew," May 18, 1975, "Cambodia-Mayaguez Seizure (2)," Box 1, Kissinger-Scowcroft West Wing Office Files, 1969–77," Ford Presidential Library.

389. Richard A. Gabriel, *Military Incompetence: Why the American Military Doesn't Win* (New York: Hill and Wang, 1985), 61–83, cited in James R. Locher, *Victory on the Potomac: The Goldwater-Nichols Act Unifies the Pentagon* (College Station: Texas A&M University Press, 2003), 30; McFarlane quoted in Locher, *Victory on the Potomac*, 279, 278.

390. Amy Zegart, *Flawed by Design: The Evolution of the CIA, JCS, and NSC* (Chicago: University of Chicago Press, 1989), 144–145; Dick Cheney interview, BOHP, 39.

391. See Crowe, *The Line of Fire*, 146–147; Mahoney, *The Mayaguez Incident*, xv, 260; Sam Nunn, foreword, in Locher, *Victory on the Potomac*, xi–xii.

392. Zegart, *Flawed by Design*, 141; Locher, *Victory on the Potomac*.

393. *US Statutes at Large* 1989, 1005, quoted in Zegart, *Flawed by Design*, 141.

394. Scowcroft interview, November 3, 2009; Locher, *Victory on the Potomac*, 170–171, 348, 398.

395. Attachment, Memorandum for Colonel Keith McCartney from Colonel Kenneth R. Bailey, Office of the Secretary of Defense, June 10, 1975, Name File, "Scowcroft, Brent," WHCF, Box 2848, Ford Presidential Library.

396. Ibid.

397. Guilmartin, *A Very Short War*, xxi, 28; Kissinger, *Years of Renewal*, 575.

398. Mahoney, *The Mayaguez Incident*, 207, 202.

Chapter 12: National Security Advisor

399. Scowcroft quoted in *The Man Nobody Knew*; Memorandum of conversation, June 16, 1975, President Ford, Kissinger, Scowcroft, "June 16, 1975—Ford, Kissinger," Box 12, Ford Presidential Library.

400. On Colby's experience, see William Colby, *Honorable Men: My Life in the CIA* (New York: Simon and Schuster, 1978), 8–12; Cheney, *In My Time*, 91; Cheney interview, BOHP, 22–23; Stephen F. Hayes, *Cheney: The Untold Story of America's Most Powerful and Controversial Vice President* (New York: HarperCollins, 2007), 96–97.

401. Scowcroft interview, BOHP, 16; Osborne, *White House Watch*, 219–220; Hartmann, *Palace Politics*, 364–365; Scowcroft interview, April 10, 2009.

402. Bob Schieffer interview, June 6, 2009.

403. Osborne, *White House Watch*, 228, 298; Ford, *A Time to Heal*, 330; Henry Kissinger, *On China* (New York: Penguin, 2011), 313–314.

404. Ford, *A Time to Heal*, 329–330.

405. "President Nixon and Bob Haldeman Discuss Donald Rumsfeld," March 9, 1971, conversation no. 464-12, http://whitehousetapes.net/clips/rmn_rumsfeld.html; Henry A. Kissinger, *Years of Upheaval* (Boston: Little, Brown, 1982), 175.

406. Osborne, *White House Watch*, 228; Scowcroft interview, April 10, 2009.

407. Victor Gold, *Invasion of the Party Snatchers: How the Holy-Rollers and the Neo-Cons Destroyed the GOP* (Naperville, IL: Sourcebooks, 2007), 88.

408. George H. W. Bush interview, December 18, 2009.

409. Mieczkowski, *Gerald Ford and the Challenges of the 1970s*, 322.

410. Burke, *Honest Broker?*, 155; Hyland, *Mortal Rivals*; Kissinger, *Years of Renewal*, 837.

411. Scowcroft interview, September 1, 2009; Sen. Henry Jackson, 42/29, "Firing of James Schlesinger," n.d., Speeches and Writing, AC No. 3560–012 Campaign Papers, 1952–82, Henry Jackson Papers, University of Washington Libraries; Roger Morris, *Haig: The General's Progress*, 224; Scowcroft interview, December 20, 2012; Senator Byrd quoted in UPI, "Ford Helped by Rocky's Decision," *The*

Pocono Record, Tuesday, November 4, 1975; George Will, "Dampening Dissent, . . ." *Washington Post*, November 5, 1975; Joseph Kraft, "The Crumbling Administration," *Washington Post*, November 4, 1975, in "Cabinet Reorganization," Box 78, Robert Goldwin Papers, Ford Presidential Library.

412. Gaylord Shaw, "Scowcroft: Out of the Shadows and Into the Security Spotlight," *Los Angeles Times*, November 4, 1975.

413. Ambassador Dobbins quoted in Rothkopf, *Running the World*, 153; Osborne, *White House Watch*, 218–219, 227–228, 272–273; Hyland, *Mortal Enemies*, 149; Joseph A. Sisco, "Ford, Kissinger and the Nixon-Ford Foreign Policy," in *The Ford Presidency*, 327.

414. Memorandum of conversation, Ford, Kissinger, Scowcroft, "October 16, 1975—Ford, Kissinger," Box 16, Ford Presidential Library.

415. Ford, *A Time to Heal*, 320; Dallek, *Nixon and Kissinger*, 573; Leslie H. Gelb, "Ford Discharges Schlesinger and Colby and Asks Kissinger to Give Up His Security Post," *New York Times*, November 3, 1975; Greene, *The Presidency of Gerald Ford*, 158–163.

416. Hartmann, *Palace Politics*, 377–378, Osborne quoted on 379; Memcon, Wednesday, November 19, 1975, 9:15 A.M., Oval Office, DNSA, KT01832; also see Kissinger, *Years of Renewal*, 841–844; Hyland, *Mortal Enemies*.

417. Sen. Henry Jackson, 42/29, "Firing of James Schlesinger," n.d., Speeches and Writing, AC No. 3560-012 Campaign Papers, 1952–82, Henry Jackson Papers, University of Washington.

418. Scowcroft interviews, August 12, 2009, and April 25, 2013.

419. Jeremiah O'Leary, "Scowcroft's Commission in Air Force Questioned," *Washington Star*, November 9, 1975.

420. L. Niederlehner, Acting General Council, to Rep. John E. Ross, May 29, 1973, "Personal—White House: Appointment of Military Personnel to Staff," Buchen Files, Box 41, Ford Presidential Library.

421. Dick Cheney interview, BOHP, 31; Arnold Kanter interview, March 24, 2009; Scowcroft interview, August 12, 2009.

422. O'Leary, "Scowcroft's Commission in Air Force Questioned"; Scowcroft interview, March 4, 2009; Gulley interviews, April 13 and February 11, 2009; also see L. Niederlehner, Acting General Counsel, to Representative John A. Moss, May 29, 1973, "Personal—White House; Appointment of Military Personnel to Staff," Buchen Papers, Box 41, Ford Presidential Library.

423. Brent Scowcroft quoted in "The Role of the National Security Advisor," Oral History Roundtables, 11.

424. Prados, *Keepers of the Keys*, 376; Head, Short, and McFarlane, *Crisis Resolution*; Jonathan Howe interview, January 12, 2012.

425. On issues Kissinger neglected as national security advisor, see, for example, Daalder and Destler, *In the Shadow of the Oval Office*, 72–73.

426. Memorandum of conversation, Ford, Kissinger, Scowcroft, Tuesday, October 19, 1976, "October 19, 1976—Ford, Kissinger, Scowcroft," Box 21, Ford Presidential Library.

427. Memorandum of conversation, Ford, Kissinger, Scowcroft, "November 11, 1975—Ford, Kissinger," Box 16, Ford Presidential Library; James Dobbin quoted in Rothkopf, *Running the World*, 154.

428. Memorandum of conversation, Monday, July 19, 1975, 3:31–4:15 P.M., President Ford, Kissinger, Scowcroft, "July 19, 1975—Ford-Kissinger-Scowcroft," Box 20, Ford Presidential Library.

429. Memorandum of conversation, Thursday, August 7, 1975, 9:30–10:21 A.M., Ford, Kissinger, Scowcroft, "August 7, 1975—Ford, Kissinger, Scowcroft," Box 14, Ford Presidential Library; Howe interview, January 12, 2012.

430. Burke, *Honest Broker?*, 114–115.

431. David Callahan, "The Honest Broker: Brent Scowcroft in the Bush White House," *Foreign Policy Journal* 69, no. 2 (February 1992): 27–32, 29. Also see Schmitz, *Brent Scowcroft*, 50–51.

432. Memorandum for General Scowcroft from Clinton E. Granger, November 4, 1975, "Outside of the System Chronological File, 11/3/75–11/11/75," Box 2, Ford Presidential Library.

433. Daniel Christman interview, May 12, 2009.

434. Memorandum of conversation, Ford, Kissinger, Scowcroft, "November 3, 1975—Ford, Kissinger, Scowcroft," Box 16, Ford Presidential Library.

435. Burke, *Honest Broker?*, 148; Prados, *Keepers of the Keys*, 376–377.

436. Burke, *Honest Broker?*, 154, 157; Scowcroft interview, March 4, 2009; Prados, *Keepers of the Keys*, 376–377.

437. Press Office staff meeting, Sunday June 29, 1975, 3–5, "Press Office Improvement Meeting, 6/26–29/75 (3)," Box 28; "Press Office Improvement Meeting," October 18, 1975; "Press Office Improvement Meeting, 10/18/75 (2)," Box 23, Nessen Papers, 1974–77, Ford Presidential Library.

438. Memorandum of conversation, Lt. General Brent Scowcroft, Assistant to the President for National Security Affairs, Ms. Ann Compton, ABC TV, Ms. Margi Vanderhye, Note Taker, Saturday, December 13, 1975, "Chron File, Nov.-Dec., 1975," NSC Press-Cong. Liaison, Box 7, Ford Presidential Library.

439. Brent Scowcroft, "Ford as President and His Foreign Policy," in *The Ford Presidency*, 311; also see Burke, *Honest Broker?*, 155, 158.

440. Prados, *Keepers of the Keys*, 376; Callahan, "The Honest Broker," 30; Burke, *Honest Broker?*, 156.

441. Head, Short, McFarlane, *Crisis Resolution*, 78–79; Howe interview, January 12, 2012.

442. McFarlane interview, April 3, 2009; also see Scowcroft quoted in "The Role of the National Security Advisor," 11.

443. Scowcroft quoted in "The Role of the National Security Advisor," 11.

444. Rothkopf, *Running the World*, 154.

445. David Gompert quoted in Burke, *Honest Broker?*, 157; Scowcroft, "Ford as President," 311; Rodman, *Presidential Command*, 102–103; Scowcroft interview, April 25, 2013. But to say that Kissinger "destroyed the State Department," as this critic did, that the "Foreign Service lost most of its power in that period," and that he gutted their morale are overstatements. Kissinger elevated the State Department from where it had been under Secretary of State Rogers—acknowledging that that degraded status was partly Kissinger's own doing. He was able to give Foreign Service officers more of a feeling of participation and to provide firmer and more forceful leadership, thereby empowering the State Department.

446. Burke, *Honest Broker?*, 156–157; David Gompert, quoted in "The Bush Administration National Security Council," 3, 13; McFarlane interviews, April 3 and April 23, 2009; Prados, *Keepers of the Keys*, 376. But see Rodman, *Presidential Command*, 77–78.

447. Burke, *Honest Broker?*, 149, 154–155, 159; Kissinger, *Years of Renewal*, 183–184.

448. Kissinger, *Years of Renewal*, 183–184.

449. Scowcroft quoted in Burke, *Honest Broker?*, 156–157; emphasis in original.

450. Burke, *Honest Broker?*, 149; Rodman, *Presidential Command*, 78.

451. Kenneth Rush, "Ford and the Economy: National and International," in *The Ford Presidency*, 148–149.

452. Rothkopf, *Running the World*, 139; Burke, *Honest Broker?*, 147; Hyland, *Mortal Rivals*, 188, 190.

453. See, for example, Rothkopf, *Running the World*, 141; Daalder and Destler, *In the Shadow of the Oval Office*, 92–93.

454. Daalder and Destler, *In the Shadow of the Oval Office*, 57–93; Burke, *Honest Broker?*, 148.

455. Larry Eagleburger, "Interview with Lawrence S. Eagleburger," ADST; Hyland, *Mortal Rivals*, 196–198.

456. William Lloyd Stearman, April 15, 1992, ADST, 39.

457. Prados, *Keepers of the Keys*, 341, 355.

458. Also see Schulzinger, *Henry Kissinger*, 239–241.

459. *Chicago Tribune*, November 11, 1984, 13; also see Osborne, *White House Watch*, 302.

460. Karen Scowcroft interview, March 19, 2009; Gulley interviews, February 11, 2009, and April 13, 2009.

Chapter 13: The Fixer

461. See Douglas Wass, *Decline to Fall: The Making of British Macro-Economic Policy and the 1976 IMF Crisis* (New York: Oxford University Press, 2008;

Mark D. Harmon, *The British Labour Government and the 1976 IMF Crisis* (New York: St. Martin's Press, 1997); Kathleen Burk and Alec Cairncross, *Goodbye, Great Britain: The 1976 IMF Crisis* (New London: Yale University Press, 1992).

462. Also see Memcon, "Dec. 3, 1976—Ford, Kissinger," Box 21, Ford Presidential Library.

463. For the British prime minister's more detailed but somewhat different account, see James Callaghan, *Time and Change* (London: Collins, 1987), 413–444.

464. Robert Hormats interview, October 29, 2009.

465. Hormats interview, October 29, 2009.

466. Scowcroft interviews, October 6, 2010, and February 24, 2011.

467. Burk and Cairncross, *Goodbye, Great Britain*, 62–63.

468. Ibid., 77.

469. McFarlane interview, April 3, 2009; Hormats interview, October 29, 2009.

470. Alan Greenspan interview, October 5, 2010; Scowcroft quoted in Burk and Cairncross, *Goodbye, Great Britain*, 38.

471. Hormats interview, October 29, 2009.

472. Hormats interview, October 29, 2009; Robert McFarlane interview, April 3, 2009; Scowcroft interview, October 6, 2010.

473. Burk and Cairncross, *Goodbye, Great Britain*, 79.

474. Ibid., 115.

475. Dominic Sandbrook, "Crisis, What Crisis?" *New Statesman*, October 2, 2008.

476. Brent Scowcroft, Memorandum for the President, April 14, 1976, "Outside the System Chronological Files, 4/11/76–4/14/76," Box 4, National Security Advisor Files, Ford Presidential Library.

477. "A Follow-on to the Summit," "Economic Summit—Puerto Rico (1)," Box 3, IEASF (1973), 1975–1976, National Security Advisor Files, Ford Presidential Library; "Second Session of Summit Meeting," June 28, 1978, "Memcon—Puerto Rico Summit, June 27 and 28, 1976," "Economic Summit in Puerto Rico (7)," Box 4, IEASF (73), 1975–76, National Security Advisor Files, Ford Presidential Library.

478. Memcon, June 29, 1976, "Puerto Rico Economic Summit," "June 26, 1976, Cabinet Meeting," Box 20 Memcons, Ford Presidential Library.

479. Robert Hormats, Memorandum for Secretary Kissinger, "Scenario for Economic Summit," October 24, 1975, "Economic Summits—Rambouillet (3)," Box 4, IEASF (73), 1975–76, NSC files, Ford Presidential Library.

480. Ford, *A Time to Heal*, 345.

481. See Jeffrey T. Richelson, *The U.S. Intelligence Community*, 2nd ed. (New York: Harper Business, 1989), 338.

482. Greene, *The Presidency of Gerald Ford*, 112–114.

483. Memcon, "Nov. 11, 1975—Ford, Kissinger," Box 16, Ford Presidential Library.

484. Memorandum of conversation, Ford, Kissinger, Scowcroft, "November 28, 1975—Ford, Kissinger, Scowcroft," Box 16, Ford Presidential Library.

485. Brent Scowcroft, "I. Soviet Dynamics: Rapporteur's Summary," in *Soviet Dynamics—Political Economic Military* (World Affairs Council of Pittsburgh, 1978), 2–8, 4.

486. Margi Vanderhye to General Scowcroft, February 26, 1976, "President's Recent Remarks on Angola," "Chron File, Jan.-Feb. 1976," Box 7, NSC Presidential and Congressional Liaison Collection, Ford Presidential Library; "Memorandum of Conversation, Lt. General Brent Scowcroft, Arthur House, John McGoff, Les Devilliers," White House, January 21, 1976, "Jan. 21, 1976—Scowcroft, Arthur House, John McGoff, Les Devilliers," Box 17, A/Africa, NSC files, Ford Presidential Library.

487. Margi Vanderhye to General Scowcroft, February 26, 1976, "President's Recent Remarks on Angola," "Chron File, Jan.-Feb. 1976," Box 7, NSC Presidential and Congressional Liaison Collection, Ford Presidential Library; "Memorandum of Conversation, Lt. General Brent Scowcroft, Arthur House, John McGoff, Les Devilliers," White House, January 21, 1976, "Jan. 21, 1976—Scowcroft, Arthur House, John McGoff, Les Devilliers," Box 17, A/Africa, NSC files, Ford Library.

488. Greene, *The Presidency of Gerald R. Ford*, 115.

489. Associated Press, "Money Funneled," *Fort Scott Tribune*, February 2, 1976.

490. Mieczkowski, *Gerald Ford and the Challenges of the 1970s*, 286–287.

491. NSSM 241, April 21, 1976, PI01490, DNSA.

492. Richelson, *The U.S. Intelligence Community*, 343.

493. Ford, *A Time to Heal*, 397–398; Osborne, *White House Watch*, 378–379.

494. Brent Scowcroft, "American Attitudes Toward Foreign Policy," *Naval War College Review* 32, no. 2 (1979): 11–19, 17.

495. Scowcroft interview, BOHP, 82–84.

496. Reagan and Thatcher quoted in John Lewis Gaddis, *The Cold War: A New History* (New York: Penguin, 2005), 216–217.

Part III: The Carter and Reagan Years, 1977–1989

Chapter 14: Out on the Street

1. Brent Scowcroft interview, November 12–13, 1999, BOHP, 21.

2. Carla Hills interview, January 6, 2004, BOHP, 35.

3. Ibid., 5.

4. Scowcroft interview, September 1, 2009; John Osborne, *White House Watch: The Ford Years* (Washington, DC: New Republic Books, 1977), 415–416.

5. Scowcroft interview, September 1, 2009.

6. Ibid.

7. Ibid.

8. See Richard Head, Frisco W. Short, and Robert C. McFarlane, *Crisis Resolution: Presidential Decision-Making in the Mayaguez and Korean Confrontations* (Boulder, CO: Westview Press, 1978), 149–215; William G. Hyland, *Mortal Rivals: Superpower Relations from Nixon to Reagan* (New York: Random House, 1987), 168–171.

9. Brent Scowcroft, "American Attitudes Toward Foreign Policy," *Naval War College Review* 32, no. 2 (1979): 11–19, 17–18.

10. Hyland, *Mortal Rivals*, 169; Head, Short, and McFarlane, *Crisis Resolution*, 172. This account draws mostly from the comprehensive treatment of the crisis by Head, Short, and McFarlane.

11. See Head, Short, and McFarlane, *Crisis Resolution*, 172, 179; Hyland, *Mortal Rivals*, 169.

12. See Head, Short, and McFarlane, *Crisis Resolution*, 196–201.

13. Scowcroft interview, BOHP, 79; Robert McFarlane interview, April 23, 2009.

14. Yanek Mieczkowski, *Gerald Ford and the Challenges of the 1970s* (Lexington: University Press of Kentucky, 2005), 332–333.

15. Walter Isaacson, *Kissinger: A Biography* (New York: Simon & Schuster, 1992), 702; Osborne, *White House Watch*, 415–416; Jussi Hanhimäki, *The Flawed Architect: Henry Kissinger and American Foreign Policy* (New York: Oxford University Press, 2004), 453; McFarlane interview, April 23, 2009.

16. Isaacson, *Kissinger*, 702; Hyland, *Mortal Rivals*, 178.

17. Osborne, *White House Watch*, 415–416; Hanhimäki, *The Flawed Architect*, 453; McFarlane interview, April 23, 2009; Office of the White House Press Secretary, October 6, 1978, White House, The Holiday Inn, San Francisco, "Ford, Gerald R., Speeches by Advocates," Phelan Papers, Box 3, Ford Presidential Library.

18. Mieczkowski, *Gerald Ford and the Challenges of the 1970s*, 333.

19. Ron Nessen, *It Sure Looks Different from the Inside* (New York: Playboy Press, 1979), 268–277; John Robert Greene, *The Presidency of Gerald R. Ford* (Lawrence: University Press of Kansas, 1988), 183–186; Isaacson, *Kissinger*, 702–703; Osborne, *White House Watch*, 54; Hyland, *Mortal Rivals*, 179; Mark J. Rozell, *The Press and the Ford Presidency* (Ann Arbor: The University of Michigan Press, 1992), 146–148.

20. Memorandum of Conversation, Ford, Kissinger, Scowcroft, Monday, October 11, 1976, "October 11, 1976—Ford, Kissinger, Scowcroft," Box 21, Ford Presidential Library; Hanhimäki, *The Flawed Architect*, 453; Osborne, *White House Watch*, 417.

21. Scowcroft interview, September 1, 2009.

22. Nancy Gibbs and Michael Duffy, *The President's Club: Inside the World's Most Exclusive Fraternity* (New York: Simon & Schuster, 2012), 299.

23. Ibid., 316–318; Mieczkowski, *Gerald Ford and the Challenges of the 1970s*, 312–313; also see Osborne, *White House Watch*, 301–302.

24. Isaacson, *Kissinger*, 719–720, 721.

25. Letter, Ford to Lt. Gen. Scowcroft, November 1, 1976, Name File, "Scowcroft, Brent," Box 2848, WHCF, Ford Presidential Library.

26. Robert Timberg, *A Nightingale's Song* (New York: Free Press, 1996), 251.

27. See, for instance, Mieczkowski, *Gerald Ford and the Challenges of the 1970s*, 325–337.

28. Memorandum of Conversation, Ford, Kissinger, Scowcroft, Thursday, November 4, 1976, "Nov. 4, 1976—Ford, Kissinger, Scowcroft," Box 21, Ford Presidential Library.

29. Scowcroft interview, September 1, 2009.

30. Scowcroft interview, June 20, 2013.

31. Scowcroft interview, April 10, 2009.

32. Scowcroft interview, October 20, 2011; Jack Brennan interview, February 24, 2009; Bill Gulley interview, April 13, 2009.

33. Bill Gulley interview, December 21, 2011; Lt. Gen. Brent Scowcroft, "Window to the Oval Office: A Diplomatic View of the American Presidency (Part 1 of 2)," West Point Center for Oral History, March 12, 2012, 19, 28–29.

34. Scowcroft interview, January 4 and October 20, 2011.

35. Scowcroft interview, April 10, 2009; Gulley interviews, April 13, 2009, and December 21, 2011; Maxine Cheshire, "VIP: The Mysterious Business of the 'International Six,'" *Washington Post*, February 3, 1980.

36. Gulley interview, December 21, 2011; Scowcroft interview, April 10, 2009.

37. Gulley interview, April 13, 2009; Scowcroft interviews, April 10, 2009, and January 3, 2014.

38. Gulley interview, December 21, 2011; Brennan interview, February 24, 2009.

39. Gulley interviews, February 11, 2009, and December 21, 2011; Scowcroft interview, April 10, 2009.

40. FBI 302 report, cited in Joseph J. Trento, *Prelude to Terror: The Rogue CIA and the Legacy of America's Private Intelligence Network* (New York: Carroll & Graf, 2005), 303.

41. Scowcroft interview, March 14, 2013; Isaacson, *Kissinger*, 733–734; Seymour Hersh, *The Price of Power* (New York: Summit Books, 1983), 642; Hanhimäki, *The Flawed Architect*, 467–468.

42. David Lauter, "Brent Scowcroft," in *Fateful Decisions: Inside the National Security Council*, eds. Karl F. Inderfurth and Loch K. Johnson (New York: Oxford University Press, 2004), 207; Isaacson, *Kissinger*, 744; Scowcroft interview, May 13, 2009.

43. See Isaacson, *Kissinger*, 745; Jeff Gerth, "Scowcroft Sold Military Holdings a Month Before Persian Gulf War," *New York Times*, January 18, 1991; Jeff Gerth and David Van Natta, "Threats and Responses: The Adviser; Still Very Much a

Player, Scowcroft Straddles the Worlds of Business and Government," *New York Times*, September 20, 2002.

44. Douglas Kellner, *The Persian Gulf TV War* (Boulder, CO: Westview Press, 1992), 39–40, 53. On US assistance to both Iran and Iraq, see Jeffrey T. Richelson, *The U.S. Intelligence Community* (New York: Harper Business, 1989), 344–346.

45. Hanhimäki, *The Flawed Architect*, 468–469.

46. Lawrence Eagleburger interview, April 19, 2009.

47. Isaacson, *Kissinger*, 714; Gulley interview, December 21, 2011.

48. Gulley interview, December 21, 2011; Scowcroft interview, May 13, 2009.

49. The Atlantic Council's Special Working Group on the Middle East, *Oil and Turmoil: Western Choices in the Middle East*, John C. Campbell, rapporteur, Andrew J. Goodpaster and Brent Scowcroft, cochairmen (Washington, DC: Atlantic Council of the United States, 1979); The Atlantic Council's Special Working Group on the Credibility of the NATO Deterrent, *Strengthening Deterrence: NATO and the Credibility of Western Defense in the 1980s*, Kenneth Rush and Brent Scowcroft, cochairmen, Joseph J. Wolf, rapporteur and editor (Cambridge, MA: Ballinger, 1982); The Atlantic Council's Special Working Group on the Caribbean Basin, *Western Interests and U.S. Policy Options in the Caribbean Basin*, James R. Greene and Brent Scowcroft, cochairmen, Richard E. Feinberg, rapporteur, Robert Kennedy, co-rapporteur, Joseph W. Harned, projects director (Washington, DC: The Atlantic Council of the United States, 1983); The Atlantic Council's Special Working Group on Strategic Stability and Arms Control, *Defending Peace and Freedom: Toward Strategic Stability in the Year 2000*, Brent Scowcroft and R. James Woolsey, cochairmen, and Thomas H. Etzold, rapporteur (Lanham, MD: University Press of America, 1988); Brent Scowcroft, ed., *Military Service in the United States* (Englewood Cliffs, NJ: Prentice-Hall, Inc., 1982).

50. "Address at the Industrial College of the Armed Forces," March 4, 1974, "January-March 1974 [2 of 2]," McFarlane Chronological File, Henry A. Kissinger, NSC Administration and Staff Records, Nixon Presidential Library.

51. Jan Lodal interview, May 11, 2009.

52. Scowcroft interview, BOHP, 22.

Chapter 15: The Scowcroft Commission

53. See "Missile Impossible," editorial, *New York Times*, January 6, 1983, "Scowcroft, Brent, June 1973 to" [clippings file], "Early Bird Files," Box 380, WGBH Interviews Collection, National Security Archive, George Washington University.

54. James McCartney, "A Defense That Would Depend on Offense," *Philadelphia Inquirer*, September 26, 1982; Les Aspin, interview, UBIT 12135, "The Nuclear Age (MX)," 1, 7, MX Transcripts, Copy 2, Vol. 3, WGBH Interviews Collection, Box 3, National Security Archive, George Washington University. Also see Russell Warren Howe, "MX Panel to Sift All Missile Options," *Washington*

Times, January 3, 1983; R. Jeffrey Smith, "A Doomsday Plan for the 1990's," *Science*, April 23, 1982, 388–390; Gregg Harken, *Counsels of War* (New York: Knopf, 1985), 331–332; Hedrick Smith, *The Power Game: How Washington Works* (New York: Ballantine Books, 1988), 530.

55. James Woolsey, oral history, UBIT A21008 "The Nuclear Age," MX Transcripts, Box 2, Copy 2, Vol. 5, WGBH Interviews Collection.

56. James Woolsey interview, May 7, 2009; "Dense Pack and SALT II," 1, Folder 29, Box 48, Accession Number 3560-S, Henry Jackson Papers, University of Washington Libraries; Scowcroft interview, UBIT A12044, "The Nuclear Age (MX)," 9, WGBH Interviews Collection. See, generally, Kenneth Kitts, *Presidential Commissions and National Security: The Politics of Damage Control* (Boulder, CO: Lynne Rienner Publishers, 2006); Gregg Harken, *Cardinal Choices: Presidential Science Advising from the Atomic Bomb to SDI* (New York: Century Foundation, 2000), 206–207; David C. Morrison, "ICBM Vulnerability," *Bulletin of the Atomic Scientists*, November 1984, 22–29; Smith, *The Power Game*, 529–543.

57. Scowcroft interview, UBIT A12044, 7.

58. Scowcroft interview, November 2, 2012; Scowcroft interview, UBIT A12044, 7–8.

59. Charles Townes interview, UBIT A12146, "The Nuclear Age (MX)," 1–2, MX Transcript, Copy 2, Vol. 5, WGBH Interviews Collection, Box 2; John Deutch interview, UBIT A12112, "The Nuclear Age (MX)," MX transcripts, Copy 2, Vol. 3, WGBH Interviews Collection, Box 3.

60. John Deutch interview, April 17, 2009; Robert McFarlane interview, April 23, 2009.

61. Robert McFarlane with Zofia Smardz, *Special Trust* (New York: Cadell and Davies, 1994), 223–224; also see "The Tactical Thinker Shaping Nuclear Strategy," *Business Week*, April 11, 1983, 111; Lou Cannon, *President Reagan: The Role of a Lifetime* (New York: Simon & Schuster, 1991), 324; Frances FitzGerald, *Way Out There in the Blue Yonder* (New York: Simon & Schuster, 2000), 192; Brent Scowcroft interview, UBIT A12043, "The Nuclear Age (MX)," 2, MX Transcripts, Copy 2, Vol. 1, WGBH Interview Collection, Box 2; Scowcroft interview, September 1, 2009.

62. Kitts, *Presidential Commissions and National* Security, 78–80; Cannon, *President Reagan*, 324; Brent Scowcroft, I, October 10, 1986, Page 1, "Reagan Years," WGBH Interview Collection, Box 4; Scowcroft interview, UBIT A12043, 7; Cohen quoted in McFarlane, *Special Trust*, 224; "The Tactical Thinker Shaping Nuclear Strategy." On McFarlane's role in both the Scowcroft Commission and SDI, see FitzGerald, *Way Out There in the Blue Yonder*, 191–209.

63. Scowcroft interview, November 2, 2012; Fitzgerald, *Way Out There in the Blue Yonder*, 193.

64. Deutch interview, UBIT 12112, 7–8; Scowcroft interview, November 2, 2012.

65. Kitts, *Presidential Commissions*, 81.

66. Scowcroft interview, September 1, 2009; Townes interview, UBIT A12146, 7.

67. Walter Pincus, "Will You Defense Mavens Open Reagan's Window of Reality on the MX?" *Washington Post*, January 17, 1983; Deutch interview, UBIT A12112, 6; "The Tactical Thinker Shaping Nuclear Strategy."

68. Brent Scowcroft interview, UBIT A12043, 4–5.

69. Deutch interview, UBIT 12112, 3.

70. Brent Scowcroft, I, October 10, 1986, 1, "Reagan Years," WGBH Interview Collection, Box 4, National Security Archive, George Washington University.

71. "Brent Scowcroft on Arms Control and the MX," *The Inter Dependent*, May–June 1983, 1, 6; Brent Scowcroft interview with Sam Donaldson, *This Week with David Brinkley*, ABC News, Sunday, June 17, 1984, in "Scowcroft, Brent, June 1973 to" [clippings file], in "Early Bird Files," Box 380, WGBH Interviews Collection.

72. See Oberdorfer, *The Turn*, 65–68; Benjamin B. Fischer, "A Cold War Conundrum: The 1983 Soviet War Scare," CIS, www.cia.gov/library/center-for-the-study-of-intelligence/csi-publications/books-and-monographs/a-cold-war-conundrum/source.htm.

73. Les Aspin, interview, UBIT 12135, 2.

74. Ibid., 3; Fred Kaplan, *The Wizards of Armageddon* (New York: Simon & Schuster, 1983), 387.

75. Woolsey interview, May 7, 2009; also see R. James Woolsey, "Introduction," in *Nuclear Arms: Ethics, Strategy, Policy*, ed. R. James Woolsey (San Francisco: Institute for Contemporary Studies, 1984), 2–3; Les Aspin, interview, UBIT 12135, 1.

76. See generally, [Brent Scowcroft,] "Address to the Industrial College of the Armed Forces," Wednesday, March 6, 1974, in "McFarlane, June–March 1974 [2 of 2]," Administration and Staff Files, Henry A. Kissinger, Henry A. Kissinger Office Files, National Security Council files, Nixon Project; Brent Scowcroft, "I. Soviet Dynamics: Rapporteur's Summary," 2, "Soviet Dynamics—Political Economic Military, World Affairs Council of Pittsburgh (1978), in "Scowcroft, Brent, June 1973 to" [clippings file], in "Early Bird Files," Box 380, WGBH Interviews Collection; "A Military Report," *Atlantic Community Quarterly* 17, no. 4 (1980), 411–412; Brent Scowcroft, "Understanding the U.S. Strategic Accord," in *Nuclear Arms: Ethics, Strategy, Policy*, ed. R. James Woolsey (San Francisco: Institute for Contemporary Studies, 1984), 65–86.

77. Scowcroft, "Understanding the U.S. Strategic Accord," 74. On the Soviets' advantages, as detailed by Senator Jackson's staff (unattributed), see "Key Measures of U.S.-Soviet Military Balance," in "Arguments Against the MX and Points for Rebuttal, May 25 [1983]," and "Dense Pack and SALT II," Folder 29, Box 48, Accession Number 3560-S, Henry Jackson Papers, University of Washington Libraries.

78. Quoted in Brian Reppert, "Warning: Soviets Set to Win," *Philadelphia-Inquirer*, January 25, 1981; Scowcroft, "I. Soviet Dynamics: Rapporteur's Summary," 2.

79. Scowcroft, "A Military Report," 411–412; "The Tactical Thinker Shaping Nuclear Strategy."

80. Brent Scowcroft interview, UBIT A12045, "The Nuclear Age (MX)," 6–7; "Interview with Lt. Gen. Brent Scowcroft," "Two Views: How to Avert an Atomic War," *U.S. News & World Report*, December 5, 1983, 31–32; Scowcroft, "A Military Report," 411–416; also see "Shevchenko Tapes," 27–28, 32, CBS Walter Cronkite Unit, "Hiroshima," Tape 44, WGBH Interview Collection, Box 2, "Walter Cronkite, CBS," National Security Archive, George Washington University.

81. Scowcroft, "A Military Report," 411–416; "Interview with Lt. Gen. Brent Scowcroft," "Two Views: How to Avert an Atomic War," *U.S. News & World Report*, December 5, 1983, 31–32.

82. Brent Scowcroft interview, UBIT A12046, "The Nuclear Age (MX)," 8; Scowcroft, "I. Soviet Dynamics: Rapporteur's Summary," 5–6.

83. General Scowcroft interview, "MX 'Important to Demonstrate National Will'," *U.S. News & World Report*, April 19, 1983, 25; also see Brent Scowcroft, "Understanding the U.S. Strategic Arsenal," in *Nuclear Arms: Ethics, Strategy, Policy*, ed. R. James Woolsey (San Francisco: Institute for Contemporary Studies, 1984), 78.

84. Scowcroft interview, October 20, 2011.

85. Woolsey interview, May 7, 2009; Deutch interview, April 17, 2009; Scowcroft interview, UBIT A12043, 2.

86. McFarlane, *Special Trust*, 223–224.

87. Ibid.

88. Scowcroft interview, UBIT A12043, 5, 9–10; Woolsey interview, UBIT A12007, 16, "The Nuclear Age (MX)," MX Transcript Copy 2, Vol. 5, WGBH Interview Collection, Box 2.

89. John Deutch interview, UBIT A12113, "The Nuclear Age (MX)," 4–5, MX transcripts, Copy 2, Vol. 3, WGBH Interviews Collection, Box 3.

90. Woolsey interview, UBIT A12008, 6–7; also see Woolsey interview, UBIT A12009, 1–2.

91. Woolsey interview, May 7, 2009; Woolsey interview, UBIT A12008, 1.

92. Scowcroft, "Understanding the U.S. Strategic Arsenal," 76.

93. Woolsey interview, May 7, 2009; Woolsey interview, UBIT A12008, 1; Les Aspin interview, UBIT A12135, 4; also see Elizabeth Drew, "A Political Journal," *New Yorker*, June 20, 1983, 49–50.

94. Scowcroft interview, UBIT A12043, 8.

95. Woolsey interview, May 7, 2009; Scowcroft interview, November 2, 2012; Kitts, *Presidential Commissions*, 85.

96. Deutch interview, April 17, 2009.

97. Scowcroft interview, May 13, 2009.

98. Deutch interview, UBIT A12113, 15–17; Woolsey interview, UBIT A12007, 17–18.

99. Woolsey interview, UBIT A12007, 17–18.

100. Les Aspin interview, UBIT A12135, 4; also see Drew, "A Political Journal," 49–50.

101. Les Aspin, interview, UBIT A12135, 4; Kenneth Kitts, personal communication, December 31, 2012.

102. Deutch interview, UBIT A12113, 14–15; Scowcroft interview, UBIT A12043, 7; Drew, "Political Journal"; Scowcroft interviews, April 10, 2009, and November 2, 2012.

103. Woolsey interview, May 7, 2009; Woolsey interview, UBIT A12008, 2.

104. Scowcroft interview, November 28, 2012.

105. Margot Hornblower and George C. Wilson, "Recommendation on MX Basing 'Has a Chance' for Hill Approval," *Washington Post*, April 12, 1983.

106. See "Scowcroft, Brent, June 1973 to" [clippings file], "Early Bird Files," Box 380.

107. Dr. Richard Garwin interview, UBIT A12163, "The Nuclear Age (MX)," 15–18, MX Transcripts, Copy 2, Vol. 5, WGBH Interviews Collection, Box 2, National Security Archive, George Washington University. See R. James Woolsey, "The Politics of Vulnerability: 1980–83," in *Nuclear Arms*, ed. Woolsey, 251–266; Kaplan, *The Wizards of Armageddon*, 379–385.

108. Garwin interview, UBIT A12163, 15–18; Townes panel quoted in R. Jeffrey Smith, "An Alternative to the MX," *Science*, May 21, 1982, 828. See, generally, Woolsey, "The Politics of Vulnerability."

109. Robert G. Kaiser, "Crazy Assumptions and the MX," *Washington Post*, April 17, 1983; James Schlesinger, "Press Briefing by General Brent Scowcroft on the MX Commission Report," April 11, 1983, The White House, Office of the Press Secretary, "Press Secretary: Press Releases: Briefing, 4/11/83," #4167, Box 54, Reagan Presidential Library.

110. Scowcroft, "Understanding the U.S. Strategic Accord," 78, 80–81; also see Woolsey interview, UBIT A12008, 10–12; Michael Getler, "MX Advisory Panel May Have Opened New Threat Debate," *Washington Post*, April 12, 1983; Kaiser, "Crazy Assumptions and the MX."

111. "MX D-Day Delay," *Time*, February 21, 1983, 18; "What's the Right Rx for Troubled MX?" *U.S. News & World Report*, February 21, 1983, 13.

112. Drew, "A Political Journal," 55.

113. Stephen Chapman, "The MX: Walking the Last Mile," *Chicago Tribune*, April 17, 1983. On the stakes the members had in the MX, see Kitts, *Presidential Commissions*, 81–82; Harken, *Counsels of War*, 333–334.

114. Drew, "A Political Journal," 55–56, 66; Scowcroft interview, UBIT A12044, 5.

115. See, for example, Cannon, *President Reagan*; Julian Zelizer, *Arsenal of Democracy: The Politics of National Security—From World War II to the War on Terrorism* (New York: Basic Books, 2011).

116. FitzGerald, *Way Out There in the Blue Yonder*, 195–206.

117. McFarlane, *Special Trust*, 228; Gregg Harken, *Cardinal Choices: Presidential Science Advising from the Atomic Bomb to SDI* (New York: Century Foundation, 2000), 208–209.

118. McFarlane, *Special Trust*, 231; Kitts, *Presidential Commissions*, 85–86.

119. Kitts, *Presidential Commissions*, 86.

120. John Deutch interview, UBIT A12113, 7–8.

121. Ibid.; Deutch interview, April 17, 2009.

122. Deutch interview, April 17, 2009, emphasis in original; Woolsey interview, May 7, 2009.

123. Scowcroft interview, UBIT A12045, 11; "Brent Scowcroft on Arms Control and the MX," 1, 6; Woolsey interview, May 7, 2009; Woolsey interview, UBIT A12009, 17–18.

124. Scowcroft interview, BOHP, 22.

125. Brent Scowcroft, I, Oct 10, 1986, 1, "Reagan Years," WGBH Interview Collection, Box 4, National Security Archive, George Washington University.

126. Don Oberdorfer, *The Turn: From the Cold War to a New Era* (New York: Touchstone Books, 1991), 209, also see 169–209.

127. President's Commission on Strategic Forces, *Report of the President's Commission on Strategic Forces*, April 1983, Washington, DC.

128. Smith, *The Power Game*, 533.

129. President's Commission on Strategic Forces, *Report*.

130. Scowcroft interview, May 13, 2009.

131. Kitts, *Presidential Commissions*, 92.

132. Drew, "Political Journal," 64.

133. Drew, "Political Journal"; Kitts, *Presidential Commissions*, 90.

134. Kitts, *Presidential Commissions*, 91–93; Les Aspin interview, UBIT A12135, 8.

135. Kitts, *Presidential Commissions*, 92–93.

136. Scowcroft interview, UBIT A12044, 2–3; Townes interview, UBIT 12149, "The Nuclear Age (MX)," 4–5, Copy 2, Vol. 5, WGBH Interviews Collection, Box 2.

137. Scowcroft interview, UBIT A12044, 11–12.

138. Les Aspin interview, UBIT A12135, 18; Woolsey interview, UBIT A21008, 3; Drew, "A Political Journal."

139. Scowcroft interviews, March 29, 2010, and November 28, 2012.

140. Kitts, *Presidential Commissions*; "Statement by Edward Rowny, Ambassador to the START Talks," June 1, 1983, The White House, Office of the Press Secretary, #4476, Box 58, Press Secretary: Press Releases: Briefings, Reagan Presidential Library.

141. McFarlane, *Special Trust*, 298; McFarlane interview, April 23, 2009; Scowcroft interview, November 2, 2012; also see Serge Schmemann, "Soviet Says It Offered Talks to Reagan Envoy," *New York Times*, March 28, 1984.

142. Editorial, *Chicago Tribune*, November 11, 1984, 13; Leslie H. Gelb, "Reagan Initiative on Arms Control Is Hinted," *New York Times*, November 3, 1984. Also see Smith, *The Power Game*, 615.

143. Woolsey interview, May 7, 2009; Scowcroft interview, November 2, 2012; Kitts, *Presidential Commissions*, 85; Deutch interview, April 17, 2009; "The Tactical Thinker Shaping Nuclear Strategy."

144. "The Tactical Thinker Shaping Nuclear Strategy."

145. John Deutch interview, April 17, 2009; Paul Nitze IV interview, January 6, 1987, 2, "WGBH, Box 4, "Carter Administration," WGBH Interview Collection.

146. McFarlane, *Special Trust*, 270–271.

147. Scowcroft interview, UBIT A12044, 1; Les Aspin interview, UBIT A12135, 10; Scowcroft interview, UBIT A12043, 11–12; Deutch interview, April 17, 2008.

148. Drew, "Political Journal," 46.

149. "The Tactical Thinker Shaping Nuclear Strategy," 111–112.

150. Deutch interview, UBIT A12113, 14–15; Scowcroft interview, UBIT A12043, 7.

151. See "Flexo #35 MX Missile," June 9, 1983, Folder 34, Box 217, Accession Number 3560-S, and "Arguments Against the MX and Points for Rebuttal, May 25 [1983]," and "Dense Pack and SALT II," Folder 29, Box 48, Accession Number 3560-S, Henry Jackson Papers.

152. Deutch, UBIT A12113, 16; Drew, "A Political Journal," 58; Harken, *Counsels of War*, 325–326.

153. Scowcroft interview, UBIT A12044, 12.

154. Brent Scowcroft, John Deutch, and R. James Woolsey, "Midgetman: Keep It on Track," *Washington Post*, April 1, 1986.

155. Brent Scowcroft, John Deutch, and R. James Woolsey, "A Way Out of Reykjavik," *New York Times Magazine*, January 25, 1987.

156. Brent Scowcroft, John Deutch, and R. James Woolsey, "The Danger of Zero Option," *Washington Post*, March 31, 1987; Brent Scowcroft, "INF: Fewer Is Not Better," *Washington Post*, April 20, 1987.

157. Brent Scowcroft, John Deutch, and R. James Woolsey, "The Survivability Problem," *Washington Post*, December 3, 1987; Brent Scowcroft, John Deutch, and R. James Woolsey, "Come and Get Us: Reagan's Nuclear Strategy," *New Republic*, April 19, 1988. Also see Brent Scowcroft, John Deutch, and R. James Woolsey, "Verify but Survive," *Washington Post*, June 14, 1988.

158. Woolsey interview, May 7, 2009; Michael Mawby cited in James McCartney, "MX Missile Champion Says $25 Billion 'Wasted,'" *Philadelphia Inquirer*, August 28, 1986.

Chapter 16: A Watergate-Type Problem

159. *The Tower Commission Report: The Full Text of the President's Special Review Board*, Introduction by R. W. Apple (New York: New York Times, 1987), xv, xvi.

160. McFarlane, *Special Trust*, 98; John Prados, *The Family Jewels: The CIA, Secrecy, and Presidential Power* (Austin: University of Texas Press, 2013); Peter

Rodman quoted in "The Bush Administration National Security Council," Oral History Roundtables, National Security Council Project, Ivo H. Daalder and I. M. Destler, Moderators, Center for International and Security Studies at Maryland, Brookings Institution, November 4, 1999, 16.

161. Theodore Draper, *A Very Thin Line: The Iran-Contra Affairs* (New York: Hill & Wang, 1991), 537–541.

162. McFarlane, *Special Trust*, 98; Prados, *The Family Jewels*, 298.

163. Kitts, *Presidential Commissions and National Security*, 102–104; John Tower, *Consequences: A Personal and Political Memoir* (Boston: Little, Brown, 1991), 273.

164. Dennis Thomas, "Random Thoughts—Iran," December 1, 1986, "Regan Memorandum 1986 October–December [2 of 4]," Box 18, Dennis Thomas Files, Reagan Presidential Library; The Communications Group, Memorandum for Donald T. Regan, Subject: Iran—A Strategy/General Observations, December 5, 1986, "Regan Memorandum 1986 October–December [2 of 4]," Box 18, Dennis Thomas Files, Reagan Presidential Library; David Chew/Dennis Thomas to Donald T. Regan, "Memorandum—Dealing with Iran/Advancing the 1987 Agenda," n.d., "Regan Memorandum (Jan. '87) [2 of 2]," Box 18, Dennis Thomas Files, Reagan Presidential Library; Sam Nunn interview, April 23, 2012.

165. Thomas quoted in Kitts, *Presidential Commissions*, 105; Reagan quoted in Tower, *Consequences*, 273; Ronald Reagan, Executive Order 12575—President's Special Review Board, December 1, 1986.

166. Reagan quoted in Tower, *Consequences*, 273; Reagan, Executive Order 12575.

167. Ronald Reagan, "President's Special Review Board for the National Security Council," IC 03991, DNSA.

168. Reagan, Executive Order 12575.

169. Kitts, *Presidential Commissions*, 106–107.

170. Quoted in Tower, *Consequences*, 273.

171. Scowcroft interview, November 2, 2012.

172. Scowcroft interview, September 27, 2012; Scowcroft quoted in Joanne Omang and Walter Pincus, "Security Experts Differ on Effects of CIA Mining," *Washington Post*, April 21, 1984.

173. Scowcroft interview, September 27, 2012; John Prados, *Keepers of the Keys: A History of the National Security Council from Truman to Bush* (New York: William Morrow, 1991), 537.

174. McFarlane, *Special Trust*, 338–339.

175. McFarlane, *Special Trust*, 91; Kitts, *Presidential Commissions*, 111, 112; Prados, *Keepers of the Keys*, 507. On McFarlane's difficult relationship with Regan, see John Burke, *Honest Broker?* (College Station: Texas A&M Press, 2009), 215–217.

176. McFarlane interview, April 3, 23, 2009; Tower, *Consequences*, 278–279.

177. Scowcroft interview, November 28, 2012.

178. Tower, *Consequences*, 274–275; emphasis added.

179. McFarlane, *Special Trust*, 346.

180. "Summary and Recommendations from Special Review Board Interview With Richard Allen," n.d., and "Summary and Recommendations from Special Review Board Interview With William Colby," January 8, 1987, "Case Studies: Summaries Wise Men—Lessons Learned Scowcroft, 2/2," Box 93222, President's Special Review Board (Tower Commission) 1986–87, Reagan Presidential Library.

181. Kitts, *Presidential Commissions*, 110; Scowcroft interview, September 27, 2012.

182. Scowcroft interview, September 27, 2012; Lt. Gen. Brent Scowcroft, "Window to the Oval Office: A Diplomatic View of the American Presidency (Part 2 of 2)," West Point Center for Oral History, March 12, 2012, 14.

183. Scowcroft interviews, November 3, 2009, and September 27, 2012.

184. Tower, *Consequences*, 276; Kitts, *Presidential Commissions*, 114–115; Scowcroft interview, September 27, 2012.

185. See "Case Studies: Summaries Wise Men—Lessons Learned Scowcroft, 1/2," Box 93222, President's Special Review Board (Tower Commission) 1986–87, Reagan Presidential Library.

186. See, for example, Alexander L. George, "The Case for Multiple Advocacy in Making Foreign Policy," *American Political Science Review* 66, no. 3 (September 1972): 751–785.

187. Tower, *Consequences*, 285; Scowcroft interview, September 27, 2012; Rostow interview, April 28, 2009.

188. Cannon, *President Reagan*, 729, 733.

189. Ibid.

190. Ibid., 736–738.

191. "The President's Special Review Board Interview of Richard Armitage, Washington, D.C., December 18, 1986," Tab 13, 6, "Tower Board: 12/07/1985 White House Meeting (1)," Box 5, Howard H. Baker Jr. Files, Series I: Subject File, Reagan Presidential Library; Tower, *Consequences*, 286–287.

192. Scowcroft quoted in Prados, *Keepers of the Keys*, 537.

193. *Tower Commission Report*, 4–5.

194. Ibid., 88–99.

195. Nicholas Rostow interview, April 28, 2009; Stephen Hadley interview, April 7, 2007.

196. "Summary and Recommendations from Special Review Board Interview with Henry Kissinger, January 23, 1987, 3, "Case Studies: Summaries Wise Men—Lessons Learned Scowcroft, 2/2," Box 93222, President's Special Review Board (Tower Commission) 1986–87, Reagan Presidential Library. Also see Morton Abramowitz interview, April 10, 2007, ADST, 105.

197. Stephen Hadley interview, April 7, 2009.

198. Associated Press, Editorial Reaction to the Tower Commission Report, February 27, 1987, www.apnewsarchive.com/1987/Editorial--Reaction-to-the-Tower-Commission-Report/id-508e2ebf5b8edc165788f772233e4e2e; Tower, *Consequences*, 288–289.

199. Pincus interview, October 5, 2010.

200. Herbert S. Parmet, *George Bush: The Life of a Lone Star Yankee* (New York: Scribner, 1997), 307–314; Murray Waas and Craig Unger, "In the Loop: Bush's Secret Mission," *New Yorker*, November 2, 1992. See Maura Dolan, "The Tower Commission Report: Bush Largely Spared from Blame; Regan Story Buttressed," *Lost Angeles Times*, February 27, 1987; statements by Richard Secord, Michael Ledeen, and editorial in *The Nation* quoted in Kitts, *Presidential Commissions*, 120; also see C. J. Mixtter to Judge Walsh, "Criminal Liability of President Bush," March 21, 1991, 9, 19, 65, 83–84, 86, National Security Archive, George Washington University.

201. Parmet, *George Bush*, 313–314; Pincus interview, October 5, 2010.

202. Cannon quoted in Ivo Daalder and I. M. Destler, *In the Shadow of the Oval Office: Profiles of the National Security Advisers and the Presidents They Served—from JFK to George W. Bush* (New York: Simon & Schuster, 2009), 160.

203. Prados, *Keepers of the Keys*, 356; Lou Cannon, *President Reagan: The Role of a Lifetime* (New York: Simon & Schuster, 1991), 714; Waas and Unger, "In the Loop."

204. See *Report of the Congressional Committees Investigating the Iran-Contra Affair: With Supplemental, Minority, and Additional Views*, Lee H. Hamilton, Chairman, Daniel K. Inouye, Chairman, 100th Congress, 1st Session, H. Rept. No. 100-433, S. Rept. No. 100-216 (Washington, DC: US Government Printing Office, 1987); Lawrence E. Walsh, *Firewall: The Iran-Contra Conspiracy and Cover-Up* (New York: Norton, 1997).

205. Scowcroft interview, February 23, 2010; Arthur Liman, *Lawyer: A Life of Counsel and Controversy* (New York: PublicAffairs, 1998), 306.

206. Scowcroft interview, February 23, 2010; Parmet, *George Bush*, 713; Liman, *Lawyer*, 306.

207. Waas and Unger, "In the Loop," 65; Rostow interview, April 28, 2009.

208. Kitts, *Presidential Commissions*, 120. Also see Harold Hongju Koh, *The National Security Constitution: Sharing Power After the Iran-Contra Affair* (New Haven, CT: Yale University Press, 1990), 13–16.

209. Rostow interview, April 28, 2009; Paul B. Thompson interview, October 2, 2009.

210. Koh, *The National Security Constitution*, 15.

211. Robert Parry, "Lost History: Newsweek's Convenient Lies," The Consortium, www.consortiumnews.com/archive/lost5.html, retrieved on March 19, 2012.

212. Pincus interview, October 5, 2010.

213. "Deposition of John M. Poindexter," Saturday, May 2, 1987, United States Senate, Select Committee to Investigate Covert Arms Transactions with Iran, 126, Tab 10, "Tower Board: 12/07/1985 White House Meeting (1)," Box 5, Howard H. Baker Jr. Files, Series I: Subject File, Reagan Presidential Library.

214. See Howard Means, *Colin Powell: Soldier/Statesman, Statesman/Soldier* (New York: Donald I. Fine, 1992), 215–231; Thompson interview, October 2, 2009.

215. McFarlane, *Special Trust*, 364.

216. Kitts, *Presidential Commissions*, 124; Abrams interview, October 6, 2010.

217. Stephen Hadley interview, April 7, 2009.

218. For an overview of Bush's involvement, see Timothy Naftali, *George H. W. Bush: The 41st President* (New York: Times Books, 2007), 44–51.

219. Brent Scowcroft quoted in "The Role of the National Security Advisor," Oral History Roundtables, October 25, 1999, 32.

220. Fox Butterfield, "The White House Crisis; Tower Commission Feared Analysis Was Compromised," *New York Times*, February 28, 1987; Nunn interview, April 23, 2012.

Part IV: The Bush Administration, 1989–1993

Chapter 17: *Organizing Security*

1. Claude Monnier cited in "The World Looks at the 'New World Order,'" August 16, 1991, "Media Analysis," USIA, Foreign Media Relations, file, "New World Order," Nancy Bearg Dyke files, NSC Collection, Bush Presidential Records, George BPR (henceforth BPR).

2. Herbert S. Parmet, *George Bush: Life of a Lone Star Yankee* (New York: Scribner, 1997), 364; Michael Duffy and Dan Goodgame, *Marching in Place: The Status Quo Presidency of George Bush* (New York: Simon & Schuster, 1992), 50; Elliott Abrams interview, October 6, 2010.

3. Scowcroft interview, October 6, 2010; Scowcroft interview, BOHP, 27–28.

4. Scowcroft interview, October 6, 2010; Brent Scowcroft quoted in "The Role of the National Security Advisor," Oral History Roundtables, The National Security Council Project, Ivo H. Daalder and I. M. Destler, moderators, Center for International and Security Studies at Maryland, Brookings Institution, October 25, 1999, 26–27; Russell L. Riley, "History and George Bush," in, *41: Inside the Presidency of George H. W. Bush*, eds. Michael Nelson and Barbara A. Perry (Ithaca, NY: Cornell University Press, 2014), 1–24, 9–11.

5. Frank Carlucci interview, Miller Center, University of Virginia, Ronald E. Reagan Oral History Project, Miller Center, 49–51; Robert Oakley interview, the Foreign Affairs Oral History Collection of the Association for Diplomatic Studies and Training, Foreign Service Institute, ADST, 124–126.

6. Elliott Abrams interview, October 6, 2010.

7. George Bush and Brent Scowcroft, *A World Transformed* (New York: Knopf, 1998), 47; Robert Gates interview, April 17, 2012.

8. Margaret D. Tutwiler, ADST, May 4, 1999.

9. Dennis Ross interview, BOHP, 5, 18, 19, 21, 41; Peter W. Rodman, *Presidential Command: Power, Leadership, and the Making of Foreign Policy from Richard Nixon to George W. Bush* (New York: Knopf, 2009), 186–187.

10. George Bush and Brent Scowcroft, *A World Transformed* (New York: Knopf), 18; James A. Baker III, *The Politics of Diplomacy* (New York: G. P. Putnam's Sons, 1995), 18–20; Rodman, *Presidential Command*, 186; Ivo Daalder and I. M. Destler, *In the Shadow of the Oval Office: Profiles of the National Security Advisers and the Presidents They Served—from JFK to George W. Bush* (New York: Simon & Schuster, 2009), 175–176; Maureen Dowd and Thomas L. Friedman, "The Fabulous Bush and Baker Boys," *New York Times Magazine*, May 6, 1990, 34; Arnold Kanter interview, March 24, 2009. Baker reveals that Bush offered the job to him two days before the election. The same day that Bush announced Baker's appointment, the day after the election, Bush also announced that Boyden Gray would serve as his counsel and Chase Untermeyer as director of presidential personnel.

11. Dowd and Friedman, "The Fabulous Bush and Baker Boys," 59; Philip D. Brady interview, BOHP, 23; Timothy Naftali, *George H. W. Bush* (New York: Times Books, 2007), 59.

12. Reginald Bartholomew interview, May 5, 2010; Nicholas Burns interview, April 4, 2009.

13. Robert Gates, *From the Shadows: The Ultimate Insider's Story of Five Presidents and How They Won the Cold War* (New York: Simon & Schuster, 1996), 456; Gates interview, April 17, 2012; Daniel Poneman interview, April 10, 2009; Lawrence Eagleburger interview, April 19, 2009; Kanter interview, March 24, 2009.

14. Burns interview, April 4, 2009; Dowd and Friedman, "The Fabulous Bush and Baker Boys," 60.

15. Dowd and Friedman, "The Fabulous Bush & Baker Boys," 60; Eagleburger interview, April 19, 2009.

16. Bush and Scowcroft, *A World Transformed*, 24–24; Scowcroft interview, December 20, 2012; Kimmitt interview, BOHP, 41.

17. Bush and Scowcroft, *A World Transformed*, 20–21; Daalder and Destler, *In the Shadow of the Oval Office*, 177.

18. Zbigniew Brzezinski, "NSC's Midlife Crisis," *Foreign Policy* 69 (Winter 1987–88): 80–99, and Baker, *Politics of Diplomacy*, 26, cited in, "Transformation: Editors' Introduction" in *Fateful Decisions: Inside the National Security Council*, eds. Karl F. Inderfurth and Loch K. Johnson, (New York: Oxford University Press, 2004) 77, 79 (see also 74–79, Editors' Introduction,137–138).

19. See John Prados, *Keepers of the Keys: A History of the National Security Council from Truman to Bush* (New York: William Morrow, 1991); Daalder and Destler, *In*

the Shadow of the Oval Office, 164–167; Carlucci interview, September 29, 2011; Carlucci interview, BOHP; Colin Powell with Joseph E. Persico, *My American Journey* (New York: Random House, 1999), 368.

20. Rodman, *Presidential Command*, 345; Michael Meese interview, May 15, 2009.

21. Powell, *My American Journey*, 368.

22. Scowcroft interview, BOHP, 19; Bush and Scowcroft, *A World Transformed*, 19.

23. Scowcroft interview, BOHP, 38; Bush and Scowcroft, *A World Transformed*, 19.

24. Scowcroft interview, BOHP, 86.

25. Scowcroft interview, BOHP, 14.

26. Arnold Kanter interview, March 24, 2009.

27. Parmet, *George Bush*, 387; Duffy and Goodgame, *Marching in Place*, 46–47, 138.

28. David Lauter quoted in Rodman, *Presidential Command*, 182. See, generally, Barbara Bush, *Barbara Bush: A Memoir* (New York: Scribner, 1994) and Maureen Dowd's coverage of the White House in the *New York Times*.

29. Bush and Scowcroft, *A World Transformed*, 36. Brent Scowcroft quoted in "The Role of the National Security Advisor," Oral History Roundtables, October 25, 1999, 6, 34; also see Brent Scowcroft, "Ford as President and His Foreign Policy," in *The Ford Presidency: Twenty-Two Intimate Perspectives of Gerald Ford*, ed. Kenneth W. Thompson, Portraits of American Presidents, vol. 7 (Lanham, MD: University Press of America, 1988), 310.

30. Scowcroft interview, BOHP, 29; Richard Haass interview, BOHP, May 27, 2004; Bush and Scowcroft, *A World Transformed*, 26; Prados, *Keepers of the Keys*, 548.

31. Scowcroft interview, September 14, 2011.

32. Scowcroft interview, BOHP, 13, 19; Scowcroft interview, September 14, 2011.

33. Scowcroft interview, September 14, 2011; Scowcroft interview, BOHP, 14, 19, 39. Also see Dennis Ross interview, BOHP, 13.

34. James A. Baker interview, September 2, 2009.

35. Baker interview, September 2, 2009; Zelikow quoted in "The Bush Administration National Security Council," Oral History Roundtables, October 25, 1999, 5; Abrams interview, October 6, 2010.

36. Baker interview, September 2, 2009; Zelikow quoted in "The Bush Administration National Security Council," Oral History Roundtables, April 29, 1990, 5; Abrams interview, October 6, 2010; Baker, *Politics of Diplomacy*, 25.

37. Kissinger quoted in Daalder and Destler, *In the Shadow of the Oval Office*, 183; Richard N. Haass, *War of Necessity, War of Choice: A Memoir of Two Iraq Wars* (New York: Simon & Schuster, 2009), 83; Baker interview, September 2, 2009.

38. Kanter interview, March 24, 2009.

39. Dan Quayle, *Standing Firm: A Vice Presidential Memoir* (New York: HarperCollins, 1994), 101, 102.

40. Baker interview, II, BOHP, 26–27; Bush and Scowcroft, *A World Transformed*, 26; also see Daalder and Destler, *In the Shadow of the Oval Office*, 183.

41. Scowcroft interview, BOHP, 30; Daalder and Destler, *In the Shadow of the Oval Office*, 182.

42. Scowcroft interview, BOHP, 37–38.

43. Quayle, *Standing Firm*, 102.

44. Ibid., 101, 102; Gates interview, April 17, 2012.

45. Quayle interview, BOHP, 30; Scowcroft interview, August 3, 2011.

46. Quayle interview, BOHP, 30.

47. Scowcroft interview, BOHP, 26–27.

48. Ibid., 41.

49. Gates interview, BOHP, 8; Burns interview, April 4, 2009.

50. Zelikow quoted in "The Bush Administration National Security Council," Oral History Roundtables, 37.

51. Scowcroft interview, BOHP, 26; Gates interview, BOHP, July 23–24, 2000; Kanter interview, March 24, 2009; Prados, *Keepers of the Keys*, 550.

52. Timothy Deal interview, June 9, 2009.

53. Scowcroft interview, January 6, 2012; January 27, 2010; Richard C. Barth interview, May 26, 2009; Gates interview, April 17, 2012.

54. Gates interview, BOHP, 7; Scowcroft interview, December 20, 2013.

55. Gates interview, BOHP, 7; also see Daalder and Destler, *In the Shadow of the Oval Office*, 186.

56. Robert Kimmitt quoted in Steve A. Yetiv, "Testing the Government Politics Model: U.S. Decision Making in the 1990–91 Persian Gulf Crisis," *Security Studies* 11, no. 2 (Winter 2001/2): 50–84, 77.

57. Gates interview, BOHP, 7; Scowcroft interview, March 29, 2010; "The Modern NSC: Editors' Introduction," *Fateful Decisions*, 99.

58. Gates interview, April 17, 2012.

59. "National Security Advisers: Profiles: Editors' Introduction," *Fateful Decisions*, 178–189.

60. Marcus Mabry, *Twice as Good: Condoleezza Rice and Her Path to Power* (Emmaus, PA: Modern Times, 2007), 112.

61. Ibid., 111; Antonia Felix, *Condi: The Condoleezza Rice Story* (New York: Newmarket Press, 2002), 137; "National Security Advisers: Profiles: Editors' Introduction," *Fateful Decisions*, 179; Bush and Scowcroft, *A World Transformed*, 36n.

62. Mabry, *Twice as Good*; Elisabeth Bumiller, *Condoleezza Rice: An American Life* (New York: Random House, 2007); Felix, *Condi*.

63. Ann Reilly Dowd, "Is There Anything This Woman Can't Do?" *George* 5, no. 5 (June 2000): 86–90, 101–103; Parmet, *George Bush*, 38; Mabry, *Twice as Good*.

64. Bumiller, *Condoleezza Rice*, 94; Mabry, *Twice as Good*, 111; Condoleezza Rice, *Extraordinary, Ordinary People: A Memoir of a Family* (Crown Archetype, 2010), 242.

65. Gates interview, BOHP, 18, 20.

66. Scowcroft interview, September 14, 2011; Burns interview, April 4, 2009; Gates, *From the Shadows*, 460.

67. Daniel Poneman interview, April 10, 2009; Burns interview, April 6, 2009; Marlin Fitzwater interview, February 27, 2008.

68. Burns interview, April 4, 2009.

69. Quayle interview, BOHP, 26; Scowcroft interview, BOHP, 30; Scowcroft interview, September 27, 2012. See Robert A. Strong, "Character and Consequence: The John Tower Confirmation Battle," in *41: Inside the Presidency of George H. W. Bush*, eds. Michael Nelson and Barbara A. Perry (Ithaca: Cornell University Press, 2014), 122–139.

70. Scowcroft interview, BOHP, 30; Parmet, *George Bush*, 372.

71. John Robert Greene, *The Presidency of George Bush* (Lawrence: University Press of Kansas, 2000), 52; Sam Nunn interview, April 23, 2012; Bob Schieffer interview, June 6, 2009.

72. Chase Untermeyer interview, BOHP, 87; Greene, *The Presidency of George Bush*, 52.

73. Bush and Scowcroft, *A World Transformed*, 20–21; Bush, *A Memoir*, 271–272; Strong, "Character and Consequence," 135.

74. Scowcroft interview, BOHP, 32.

75. Scowcroft interview, BOHP, 32, 35; Scowcroft interview, September 14, 2011; Bush and Scowcroft, *A World Transformed*, 22; Baker, *Politics of Diplomacy*, 23; Maureen Dowd, "How Cheney's Name Came Up Again," *New York Times*, March 12, 1989; Cheney interview, BOHP, 32; Cheney interview, May 13, 2009; Douglas Paal interview, March 5, 2009.

76. Cheney interview, BOHP, 39.

77. Bush and Scowcroft, *A World Transformed*, 24.

78. Colin Powell in "The Role of the National Security Advisor," Oral History Roundtables, October 25, 1999, 57.

79. Peter Rodman quoted in "The Bush Administration National Security Council," Oral History Roundtables, 16; Chase Untermeyer interview, BOHP; also see Rodman, *Presidential Command*, 346.

80. Quayle interview, BOHP, 56; John Sununu quoted in Bobbie Kilberg interview, BOHP, 73.

81. Thomas Pickering interview, BOHP, 8.

82. Rodman, *Presidential Command*, 180–181; Duffy and Goodgame, *Marching in Place*, 51–52.

83. Cheney interview, BOHP, 45.

84. Quayle interview, BOHP, 56.

85. Gates interview, BOHP, 11.

86. Frank Carlucci interview, September 29, 2011.

87. See Roman Popadiuk, *The Leadership of George Bush: An Insider's View of the Forty-First President* (College Station: Texas A&M University Press, 2009), 58–61.

88. Scowcroft quoted in "The Role of the National Security Advisor," 9.

89. Cheney interview, BOHP, 36; Kimmitt quoted in David J. Rothkopf, *Running the World: The Inside Story of the National Security Council and the Architects of American Power* (New York: PublicAffairs, 2005), 268, 271.

90. Richard Haass interview, BOHP, 45; Bush and Scowcroft, *A World Transformed*, 25; Rothkopf, *Running the World*, 271; Popadiuk, *The Leadership of George Bush*, 83–85; Poneman interview, April 10, 2009.

91. Maureen Dowd, "Washington Talk: Remorseless Dozing Gets Presidential Nod," *New York Times*, November 10, 1989; Gates interview, BOHP, 12, 13.

92. Duffy and Goodgame, *Marching in Place*, 182.

93. Baker interview II, BOHP, 14; Gates, *From the Shadows*, 456; Andy Card quoted in "The Bush Administration National Security Council," Oral History Roundtables, 23.

94. Burns interview, April 4, 2009.

95. Deal interview, June 9, 2009.

96. Scowcroft interview, BOHP, 38, 41. Scowcroft would also get his "geographic principals"—that is, the principal officials in the NSC area directorates—reading the cables going out from State and Defense Departments, since policy is made by the outgoing cables from the State and Defense.

97. Scowcroft interview, BOHP, 41; Roger Porter quoted in "The Bush Administration National Security Council," Oral History Roundtables, 36.

98. Scowcroft interview, BOHP, 18; Fred McClure interview, BOHP, 84.

99. Paal interview, March 5, 2009.

100. Roman Popadiuk, "White House Interview Program," Martha Kumar interviewer, November 2, 1999, www.archives.gov/presidential-libraries/research/transition-interviews/pdf/popadiuk.pdf; William Sittmann interview, May 12, 2009.

101. Scowcroft interview, May 5, 2010.

102. Scowcroft interview, November 4, 2010.

103. Roman Popadiuk, "White House Interview Program"; Fitzwater interview, February 27, 2008.

104. Fitzwater interview, February 27, 2008; Schieffer interview, June 2009; Walter Kansteiner interview, May 18, 2009; Nicholas Rostow interview, April 28, 2009.

105. See Parmet, *George Bush*, 420.

106. Rostow interview, April 28, 2009.

107. Scowcroft interview, October 6, 2010; also see Daalder and Destler, *In the Shadow of the Oval Office*, 164–165.

108. Scowcroft, author interview, October 6, 2010; Scowcroft interview, BOHP, 32.

109. Bush quoted in Rodman, *Presidential Command*, 183; Robert Kimmitt quoted in "The Bush Administration National Security Council," 7.

110. Scowcroft interview, BOHP, 32.

111. Scowcroft interview, BOHP, 34; See Alexander L. George, "The Case for Multiple Advocacy in Making Foreign Policy," *American Political Science Review* 66, no. 3 (September 1992), 763–765. The "Group of Eight" or "Big Eight" of the Desert Shield period and Desert Storm was but a slightly expanded Core Group. (In actuality, it was a group of nine since press secretary Marlin Fitzwater routinely sat in, but Fitzwater's name was purposely not included on the circulation lists).

112. Baker interview II, BOHP; Baker, *Politics of Diplomacy*; Cheney interview, May 13, 2009.

113. Cheney interview, BOHP, 36.

114. Robert S. Hutchings, *American Diplomacy and the End of the Cold War* (Baltimore: Johns Hopkins University Press, 1997), 23; Alan G. Whittaker, Shannon A. Brown, Frederick C. Smith, and Elizabeth McKune, *The National Security Policy Process: The National Security Council and Interagency System*, Research Report, August 15, 2011, Annual Update (Washington, DC: Industrial College of the Armed Forces, National Defense University, US Department of Defense, 2011),10, 24.

115. Scowcroft interview, BOHP, 31.

116. Baker interview II, BOHP, 9.

117. Gates interview, BOHP, 7; Vice President Quayle also attended the meetings, but with his lesser experience in national security affairs, he wasn't as active (Quayle interview, BOHP, 56).

118. Scowcroft interview, BOHP, 39.

119. Scowcroft interview, BOHP, 39.

120. Karl Jackson interview, June 11, 2009.

121. Scowcroft interview, January 6, 2012; Gates interview, BOHP, 6.

122. Florence Gantt interview, November 2, 2009.

123. Gates interview, BOHP, 7.

124. Rostow interview, April 29, 2009.

Chapter 18: The Pause

125. Bush and Scowcroft, *A World Transformed*, 161–162; Sigmund Rogich interview, BOHP, 67; Naftali, *George H. W. Bush*, 87; Popadiuk, *The Leadership of George Bush*, 86; Scowcroft interview, August 3, 2011; Bush and Scowcroft, *A World Transformed*, 133. US-Soviet summits had been held on a rotating capital-and-capital basis. The Soviet Union was due to host, but Gorbachev didn't want to hold the summit in Moscow. Preston Bush, the president's brother, suggested having the summit in Malta and passed along the idea.

126. See, for instance, "Document No. 57: National Intelligence Estimate 11-4-89, "Soviet Policy Toward the West: The Gorbachev Challenge," April 1989, in *Masterpieces of History: The Peaceful End of the Cold War in Europe, 1989*, eds.

Svetlana Savranskaya, Thomas Blanton, and Vladislav Zubok (New York: Central European University Press, 2010), 442–445.

127. Cheney interview, BOHP, 92; Marlin Fitzwater, *Call the Briefing! Reagan and Bush, Sam and Helen: A Decade with Presidents and the Press* (New York: Times Books, 1995), 232–233.

128. Scowcroft interview, August 3, 2011.

129. Scowcroft, BOHP, 77.

130. ABC News, "World News Tonight Sunday," January 22, 1989.

131. Scowcroft interview, BOHP, 73–74.

132. Scowcroft interview, BOHP, 25; also see Gates, *From the Shadows*, 460; Oberdorfer, *The Turn*, 329, 332.

133. James Woolsey interview, UBIT A12010, "The Nuclear Age (MX)," Box 2, Copy 2, Vol. 5, WGBH Interviews Collection, National Security Archive, George Washington University, 11.

134. Robert Gates interview, BOHP, 23; Don Oberdorfer, *The Turn: The Cold War to the New Era* (New York: Poseidon Press, 1991), 244.

135. Scowcroft quoted in David Schmitz, *Brent Scowcroft: Internationalism and Post-Vietnam War American Foreign Policy* (Lanham, MD: Rowman & Littlefield: 2011), 94; Scowcroft interviews, October 6, 2010, and April 4, 2011.

136. Brent Scowcroft, "I. Soviet Dynamics: Rapporteur's Summary," *Soviet-Dynamics—Political Economic Military* (World Affairs Council of Pittsburgh, 1978), 2–8, 5; Lt. Gen. Brent Scowcroft, "American Attitudes Toward Foreign Policy," *Naval War College Review* 32, no. 2 (1979), 11–19, 14.

137. General Brent Scowcroft, *Der Spiegel*, October 1988.

138. Scowcroft interview, October 6, 2010.

139. Bush and Scowcroft, *A World Transformed*, 61.

140. Ibid., 37.

141. Ibid.; Michael Meyer, *The Year That Changed the World* (New York: Scribner, 2012), 60; Scowcroft interview, August 3, 2011; Parmet, *George Bush*, 384.

142. Bush and Scowcroft, *A World Transformed*, 38–39; Scowcroft interview, BOHP, 36.

143. Priscilla Painton and Michael Duffy, "Brent Scowcroft: Mr. Behind-the-Scenes," *Time*, October 7, 1991, 24; Gates interview, April 17, 2012; Bush and Scowcroft, *A World Transformed*, 132–133; Gates, *From the Shadows*, 481.

144. "National Security Directive 23," "The United States Relations with the Soviet Union," September 22, 1989, BPR (online documents).

145. Bush and Scowcroft, *A World Transformed*, 47; Meyer, *The Year That Changed the World*, 63; Oberdorfer, *The Turn*, 346–347; David E. Hoffman, *The Dead Hand: The Untold Story of the Cold War Arms Race and Its Dangerous Legacy* (New York: Anchor Books, 2009), 312–319; David E. Hoffman interview, June 11, 2009; "Russian Voices: A Fly on the Diplomatic Wall: Thursday, December 10, 1987: The White House," (editorial) *Los Angeles Times*, March 21, 1993,

http://articles.latimes.com/1993-03-21/books/bk-13220_1_white-house. See generally, Derek H. Chollet and James M. Goldgeier, "Once Burned, Twice Shy? The Pause of 1989," in *Cold War Endgame: Oral History, Analysis, Debates*, ed. William C. Wohlforth (State College: Pennsylvania State University Press, 2003), 141–173.

146. Nicholas Burns interview, April 4, 2009.

147. Ibid.

148. Ibid.

149. Scowcroft interview, May 5, 2010.

150. Bush and Scowcroft, *A World Transformed*, 39.

151. Scowcroft interview, BOHP, 74; Scowcroft, interview, August 13, 2010; Schmitz, *George Bush*, 94–96.

152. Bush and Scowcroft, *A World Transformed*, 47. ·

153. Ibid., 40–41.

154. Scowcroft interview, BOHP, 36; Bush and Scowcroft, *A World Transformed*, 44–45; Dennis Ross interview, BOHP, 9; Demarest interview, BOHP, 15.

155. Alfred Dregger quoted in Mary Elise Sarotte, *1989: The Struggle to Create Post–Cold War Europe* (Princeton, NJ: Princeton University Press 2009), 27.

156. Scowcroft interview, October 11, 2010; Scowcroft interview, BOHP, 24.

157. Scowcroft interview, BOHP, 22.

158. Scowcroft interview, BOHP, 24.

159. Robert Hutchings, "American Diplomacy and the End of the Cold War in Europe," in *Foreign Policy Breakthroughs: Case Studies in Successful Diplomacy*, eds. Robert Hutchings and Jeremi Suri (New York: Oxford University Press, 2015, forthcoming), 2.

160. "Remarks to Citizens in Hamtramck, Michigan," April 17, 1989, *Public Papers of the Presidents of the United States: George Bush: 1989* (Washington, DC: US GPO, 1990), 1:430–433; Bush and Scowcroft, *A World Transformed*, 53.

161. Bush and Scowcroft, *A World Transformed*, 52–53.

162. Scowcroft interview, BOHP, 80. Also see Sarotte, *1989*, 25.

163. Scowcroft interview, BOHP, 79; Gates, *From the Shadows*, 465.

164. Schmitz, *Brent Scowcroft*, 100.

165. Bush and Scowcroft, *A World Transformed*, 50–51.

166. "Remarks at the Boston University Commencement Ceremony in Massachusetts," May 21, 1989, *Public Papers of the Presidents of the United States: George Bush: 1989* (Washington, DC: US GPO, 1990), 1:582–585; Bush and Scowcroft, *A World Transformed*, 54–55.

167. Bush and Scowcroft, *A World Transformed*, 55–56; Oberdorfer, *The Turn*, 349.

168. "Remarks at the United States Coast Guard Commencement Ceremony in New London, Connecticut," May 24, 1989, *Public Papers of the Presidents of the United States: George Bush: 1989* (Washington, DC: US GPO, 1990), 1:600–604.

169. Ibid.

170. Baker, *The Politics of Diplomacy*, 92–93, 96; Bush and Scowcroft, *A World Transformed*, 83.

171. Bush and Scowcroft, *A World Transformed*, 83.

172. Baker, *The Politics of Diplomacy*, 92–93, 96; Bush and Scowcroft, *A World Transformed*, 83; George Bush, "Remarks to the Citizens of Mainz, Federal Republic of Germany," May 31, 1989, *Public Papers of the Presidents of the United States: George Bush: 1989* (Washington, DC: US GPO, 1990), 1:650–654.

173. Bush, "Remarks to the Citizens of Mainz, Federal Republic of Germany."

174. Bush and Scowcroft, *A World Transformed*, 135.

175. Ibid., 136–137.

176. Kanter interview, March 24, 2009.

177. Gates, *From the Shadows*, 480–481; Baker, *The Politics of Diplomacy*, 156–158.

178. Bush and Scowcroft, *A World Transformed*, 127–129.

179. "Russian Voices: A Fly on the Diplomatic Wall," *Los Angeles Times*, March 21, 1993; Bush and Scowcroft, *A World Transformed*, 128–129.

180. Gates, *From the Shadows*, 478–479; Bush and Scowcroft, *A World Transformed*. 141–143; Timothy J. Colton, *Yeltsin: A Life* (New York: Basic Books, 2012), 171–172.

181. Gates, *From the Shadows*, 479; Gates interview, BOHP, 9.

182. Beschloss and Talbott, *At the Highest Levels*, 479; Gates, BOHP, 9.

183. Bush and Scowcroft, *A World Transformed*, 147; John Lewis Gaddis, *The Cold War: A New History* (New York: Penguin, 2005), 247.

184. Gaddis, *The Cold War*, 245.

185. Memorandum of Telephone Conversation, The President, Helmut Kohl, October 23, 1989, 9:02–9:26 A.M. The Oval Office. Telcons 1989 (CD), BPR.

186. Bush and Scowcroft, *A World Transformed*, 148–149.

187. Scowcroft interview, BOHP, 83.

188. Bush and Scowcroft, *A World Transformed*, 149–151.

189. "Document No. 15: Diary of Anatoly Chernyaev regarding the Collapse of the Berlin Wall," November 10, 1989, *National Security Archive Electronic Briefing Book* No. 293, Posted—November 7, 2009. Svetlana Savaranskaya and Thomas Blanton, eds., National Security Archive, George Washington University.

190. Ibid., 161.

191. Marlin Fitzwater interview, February 27, 2008.

192. Fitzwater interview, February 27, 2008.

193. Bush and Scowcroft, *A World Transformed*, 163.

194. Ibid., 173; Gates, *From the Shadows*, 482–483.

195. Mikhail Gorbachev, *Memoirs* (New York: Doubleday, 1995), 513.

196. Bush and Scowcroft, *A World Transformed*, 173–174.

197. Baker interview II, BOHP, 10.

198. Gorbachev, *Memoirs*, 537; Baker interview II, BOHP, 10.

199. Memorandum of Conversation, "First Expanded Bilateral Session with Chairman Gorbachev of the Soviet Union," December 2, 1989, 10:00–11:55, Maxim Gorky [sic], Cruise Liner, Malta, "Summit at Malta December 1989: Malta Memcons [1]," CF00718-006, Soviet Union/USSR Subject Files, Condoleezza Rice Files, NSC Collection, BPR.

200. Memorandum of Conversation, "Second Expanded Bilateral Session with Chairman Gorbachev of the Soviet Union," December 3, 1989, 4:35–6:45 P.M., Maxim Gorkii Cruise Liner, Malta, "Summit at Malta December 1989: Malta Memcons [1]," CF00718-006, Soviet Union/USSR Subject Files, Condoleezza Rice Files, NSC Collection, BPR.

201. Scowcroft interview, BOHP, 51.

Chapter 19: Gardening in a Tempest

202. Scowcroft interview, August 3, 2011; George Bush, "Remarks Upon Returning From a Trip to the Far East," February 27, 1989, *Public Papers of the Presidents of the United States: George Bush: 1989* (Washington, DC: US GPO, 1990), 150–151.

203. Ezra Vogel, *Deng Xiaoping and the Transformation of China* (Cambridge, MA: Harvard University Press, 2011), 618.

204. Chinese officials sought to downplay the number of casualties, and hospital and morgue figures ignored the bodies friends and family members took away as well as the bodies that had been burned on-site. The International Red Cross estimated twenty-six hundred deaths; the US government estimated at least seven hundred dead. See Timothy Brook, *Quelling the People: The Military Suppression of the Beijing Democracy Movement* (New York: Oxford University Press, 1992), 161–162; James Lilley with Jeffrey Lilley, *China Hands: Nine Decades of Adventure, Espionage, and Diplomacy in Asia* (New York: PublicAffairs, 2004), 321–322; James Mann, *About Face: A History of America's Curious Relationship with China, from Nixon to Clinton* (New York: Knopf, 1999), 192. But see Robert L Suettinger, *Beyond Tiananmen: The Politics of US-China Relations, 1989–2000* (Washington, DC: Brookings Institution Press, 2003), 61.

205. Bush and Scowcroft, *A World Transformed*, 179; Lampton, *Same Bed, Different Dreams*, 30, 31; Patrick Tyler, *A Great Wall: Six Presidents and China: An Investigative History* (New York: PublicAffairs, 1999), 371; Henry Kissinger, *On China* (New York: Penguin, 2010), 436; Cheng Chu-yuan, *Behind the Tiananmen Massacre: Behind the Social, Political, and Economic Ferment in China* (Boulder, CO: Westview Press, 1990), 193–194; Qian Qichen, *Ten Episodes in Chinese Diplomacy* (New York: HarperCollins, 2005), 143–144; Douglas Paal interview, March 5, 2009; Vogel, *Deng Xiaoping*, 654–655.

206. Kissinger, *On China*, 411–428; Paal interview, March 5, 2009; Stapleton Roy interview, March 27, 2009.

207. Paal interview, March 5, 2009.

208. Bush and Scowcroft, *A World Transformed*; Scowcroft interview, August 3, 2011, Scowcroft interview, BOHP, 55.

209. Scowcroft interview, August 3, 2011; Bush and Scowcroft, *A World Transformed*, 91; Parmet, *George Bush*, 378; J. Stapleton Roy interview, March 27, 2009.

210. Memorandum of Conversation, "Meeting with Ambassador Han Xu," January 28, 1989, Situation Room, Karl Jackson Files, "China 1989 [3]," CF00306-005, NSC Collection, BPR.

211. Cable, American Embassy, Beijing, to Sec. State, Wash. DC, "President's Banquet—Chinese Guest List," February 18, 1989, Department of State, DNSA, Parmet, *George Bush*, 378; Roy interview, March 27, 2009.

212. Kathy Wilhelm, "China Steps Up Criticism of United States over Fang Incident," Associated Press, March 1, 1989; "China Again Assails U.S. over Dissident," *St. Louis Post-Dispatch*, March 2, 1989; Pei Minxin, "The Man Who Didn't Come to Dinner," *St. Louis Post-Dispatch*, March 3, 1989.

213. Winston Lord interview, April 28, 1998, ADST; US Embassy Beijing Cable, "President's Banquet—Chinese Guest List," February 18. 1989, Department of State, "The US 'Tiananmen Papers,'" in *National Security Archive Electronic Briefing Book*, ed. Michael L. Evans, June 4, 2001; also see Mann, *About Face*, 180–181.

214. Nancy Bernkopf Tucker, *China Confidential: American Diplomats and Sino-American Relations, 1945–1996* (New York: Columbia University Press, 2003), 408; Winston Lord interview, April 18, 2011; Mann, *About Face*, 177–178; Roy interview, March 27, 2009.

215. "Banquet Incident Angers Beijing," *Sydney Morning Herald*, March 2, 1989, 12; Roy interview, March 27, 2009.

216. R. W. Apple, "'Blunder' at Beijing Dinner: U.S. Chides Embassy," March 3, 1989; Tucker, *China Confidential*, 408.

217. Tucker, *China Confidential*, 408.

218. Mann, *About Face*, 178.

219. Bush and Scowcroft, *A World Transformed*, 91.

220. Scowcroft interview, June 24, 2011; Parmet, *George Bush*, 377.

221. Scowcroft interviews, April 12 and June 24, 2011; "China Again Assails U.S. over Dissident," *St. Louis Post-Dispatch*, March 2, 1989; Pei, "The Man Who Didn't Come to Dinner"; interviews with Scowcroft, April 12 and June 24, 2011.

222. Scowcroft interview, December 2007; Lord interview, April 18, 2011; Roy interview, March 27, 2009; Paal interview, March 30, 2011; Barbara Bush, *Barbara Bush: A Memoir* (New York: Scribner, 1994), 270; Tucker, *China Confidential*, 407; Parmet, *George Bush*, 375–376.

223. Parmet, *George Bush*, 376–377.

224. Apple, "'Blunder' at Beijing Dinner"; Tucker, *China Confidential*, 408–409; Mann, *About Face*, 178–179; Kissinger, *On China*, 428; Lord oral history.

225. "China Again Assails U.S. Over Dissident," *St. Louis Post Dispatch*, March 2, 1989, 18D; Pei, "The Man Who Didn't Come to Dinner"; Mann, *About Face*, 179; Scowcroft interviews, April 12 and June 24, 2011.

226. Lord interview, April 18, 2011; Parmet, *George Bush*, 377–378.

227. Lord interview, April 18, 2011; Paal interview, March 30, 2011; Parmet, *George Bush*, 377–378.

228. Paal interview, March 30, 2011; Scowcroft interview, December 2007; Kissinger, *On China*, 430; Bush and Scowcroft, *A World Transformed*; Tyler, *A Great Wall*, 346–347; David M. Lampton, *Same Bed, Different Dreams: Managing U.S.-China Relations, 1989–2000* (Berkeley: University of California Press, 2001); Lord interview, April 18, 2011.

229. David Hoffman, "China's Objection to Dissident Didn't Reach Key Bush Officials, U.S. Says," *Washington Post*, March 3, 1989; Apple, "'Blunder' at Beijing Dinner"; Lord interview, March 29, 2011; Paal interviews, March 5 and March 30, 2011; Scowcroft interviews, May 13, 2009, and April 12, 2011.

230. Lord interview, ADST; Lord interview, April 18, 2011; Roy interview, March 27, 2009; Tucker, *China Confidential*, 410. The lack of advance notice prevented the trip from reaching the status of an official state visit.

231. See Memorandum, Brent Scowcroft to POTUS, "Meeting with Asia Scholars," February 17, 1989, Subject File—C. F. WHORM, BPR, OA/ID 00002-001, BPR; also see Mann, *About Face*, 178, and Scowcroft interview, BOHP, 61.

232. "White House On-the-Record Briefing," Subject: President Bush's Trip to Asia, Briefer: General Brent Scowcroft, February 21, 1989, Federal News Service; Lord interview, ADST; Scowcroft interview, BOHP, 61.

233. Karl Jackson interview, June 23, 2011; Scowcroft interview, June 24, 2011; Roy interview, March 27, 2009; Barbara Bush, *A Memoir*, 270–271.

234. Kissinger, *On China*, 429.

235. Lord interview, March 29, 2011; Tucker, *China Confidential*, 410; Mann, *About Face*, 182.

236. Scowcroft interview, December 2007; Tyler, *A Great Wall*, 347.

237. Lord interviews, March 29 and April 18, 2011; Lord interview, ADST; Scowcroft interview, April 12, 2011; Tucker, *China Confidential*, 410; Mann, *About Face*, 183; Roy interview, March 27, 2009.

238. Winston Lord, "China and America: Beyond the Big Chill," *Foreign Affairs*, Fall 1989; Lord, "Misguided Mission," *Washington Post*, December 19, 1989.

239. Tucker, *China Confidential*, 453–455; Roy interview, April 9, 2009.

240. Scowcroft interview, June 24, 2011. Kissinger, in contrast, also very much disagreed with Lord's political position—siding with Scowcroft and President Bush on how to handle the US-China relationship—but he remained socially close to Lord; both men were former colleagues and both lived in New York City (Lord interview, April 18, 2011).

241. Bush and Scowcroft, *A World Transformed*; Lilley, *China Hands*; Vogel, *Deng Xiaoping*. But see Parmet, *George Bush*.

242. Kissinger, *On China*, 428.

243. Roy interview, March 27, 2009. On Bush's year in Beijing, see *The China Diary of George H. W. Bush: The Making of a Global President*, ed. Jeffrey A. Engel (Princeton, NJ: Princeton University Press, 2008).

244. "Memorandum of Conversation," President Bush's Meeting with Chairman Deng Xiaoping of the People's Republic of China, Great Hall of the People, Beijing, China, February 26, 1989, MemCons, BPR.

245. Vogel, *Deng Xiaoping*, 649.

246. See, for example, Bette Bao Lord, *Legacies: A Chinese Mosaic* (New York: Knopf, 1990); Scowcroft interview, August 3, 2011.

247. Scowcroft interview, April 12, 2011; Tucker, *China Confidential*, 403; Lord interview, ADST; Lord interview, April 18, 2011.

248. Memcons, Bush visit to China February 25, 26, 1989, BPR.

249. Scowcroft interview, December 2007.

250. Scowcroft interview, April 12, 2011; Lord interview, March 29, 2011; see Mann, *About Face*, 182–183.

251. Lord interview, ADST. Also see Tucker, *China Confidential*, 452–453.

252. On engagement vs. nonengagement, see, for example, Quayle, *Standing Firm*, 121–122; Lord interview. Also see Tucker, *China Confidential*, 452–453.

253. Elliott Abrams interview, October 6, 2010.

254. See Suettinger, *Beyond Tiananmen*, 20–21; Lord interview, ADST; Zhao Ziyang, *Prisoner of the State: The Secret Journal of Zhao Ziyang*, ed. and trans. Bao Pi, Renee Chang, and Adi Ignatius (New York: Simon & Schuster, 2009), 161–182; Vogel, *Deng Xiaoping*, 574–585.

255. Memorandum for Brent Scowcroft through Karl Jackson from Douglas Paal, "U.S. Posture During Current Unrest in China," April 20, 1989, Karl Jackson Files, "China 1989 [3]" CF00306-005, NSC Collection, BPR.

256. Suettinger, *Beyond Tiananmen* 12, 16–17; Tyler, *A Great Wall*, 347–348; Vogel, *Deng Xiaoping*, 599–603; Lord interview, ADST.

257. See Zhao, *Prisoner of the State*, 8–9; Vogel, *Deng Xiaoping*, 603–609.

258. "It Is Necessary to Take a Clear-Cut Stand Against Disturbances," Foreign Broadcast Information Service, April 25, 23–24, cited in www.tsquare.tv/chronology-/April26ed.html; Roy interview, March 27, 2009; also see Brook, *Quelling the People*, 29; Vogel, *Deng Xiaoping*, 604–605.

259. Suettinger, *Beyond Tiananmen*, 34; Vogel, *Deng Xiaoping*, 605;

260. Vogel, *Deng Xiaoping*, 611–612; Suettinger, *Beyond Tiananmen*, 35–57.

261. Vogel, *Deng Xiaoping*, 614–615.

262. Ibid., 617.

263. Roy interview, March 27, 2009; Vogel, *Deng Xiaoping*, 618.

264. Lilley, *China Hands*, 316; Vogel, *Deng Xiaoping*, 620–621; Suettinger, *Beyond Tiananmen*, 51.

265. US Embassy Beijing Cable, "PLA Ready to Strike," May 21, 1989, Department of State, "The US 'Tiananmen Papers'"; Mann, *About Face*, 190.

266. Letter from President Bush to Chairman Deng Xiaoping, May 27, 1989, from American Embassy in Beijing to Secretary of State, OA/ID CF00316-004, Doug Paal series, China-US, January–July 1989 [4], NSC Collection, BPR.

Chapter 20: Cold War Relics

267. Michael R. Gordon, "U.S. Troops Move in Panama in Effort to Seize Noriega: Gunfire Is Heard in Capital," *New York Times*, December 20, 1989; Frederick Kempe, *Divorcing the Dictator* (New York: Putnam, 1990), 12. Also see Bob Woodward, *The Commanders* (New York: Simon & Schuster, 1993), 119–131; Parmet, *George Bush*; Naftali, *George H. W. Bush*; Baker, *The Politics of Diplomacy*; Fitzwater, *Call the Briefing!*; and Colin Powell, *My American Journey*.

268. Rodman, *Presidential Command*, 170–180; Baker, *The Politics of Diplomacy*, 182.

269. Associated Press, "Bush and Noriega," *New York Times*, September 28, 1988; Morton Abramowitz interview, ADST, 111–112f; see Robert A. Strong, "Tipping Point: George H. W. Bush and the Invasion of Panama," George H. W. Bush Oral History Symposium, October 14–15, 2011, Miller Center of Public Affairs, University of Virginia, 7–10; Kempe, *Divorcing the Dictator*.

270. Parmet, *George Bush*, 330; Baker, *Politics of Diplomacy*, 184; Naftali, *George H. W. Bush*, 71.

271. "Statement for Television on Panama Election by Former President Jimmy Carter," Telemundo, May 10, 1989, in Dyke, Nancy Bearg, Subject Files, "Panama," OA/ID CF01076-010, BPR; Scowcroft interview, BOHP, 43.

272. Memorandum for the Vice President et al. [from President George Bush], n.d [August 1989], Eric Melby Files, NSC Collection, BPR.

273. Baker, *Politics of Diplomacy*, 184; Naftali, *George H. W. Bush*, 71; Scowcroft interview, BOHP, 45.

274. Fitzwater, *Call the Briefing!*, 203.

275. Fitzwater, *Call the Briefing!*, 203; Panamanian Situation Update #2, "Situation Room Note," October 3, 1989, 1300 EDT, William T. Pryce Files Latin American Directorate Staff Files, NSC Collection, BPR.

276. Fitzwater, *Call the Briefing!*, 207; Kempe, *Divorcing the Dictator*.

277. See Mark J. Rozell, *The Press and the Bush Presidency* (Westport, CT: Praeger Publishers, 1996), 51; Woodward, *The Commanders*, 127.

278. "World News Tonight Sunday—ABC," ABC News Transcripts, October 8, 1989.

279. Ibid., David Boren interview, February 2, 2012.

280. Boren quoted in Bob Burke and Von Russell Creel, *Oklahoma Statesman: The Life of David Boren* (Oklahoma City: Oklahoma Heritage Association, 2009), 326; Boren interview, February 2, 2012.

281. Boren interview, February 2, 2012; Burke and Creel, *Oklahoma Statesman*, 327. The two accounts are not identical; in his interview with the author, Boren said Scowcroft wasn't there and Cheney was; Burke and Creel report that Scowcroft was there and Cheney wasn't.

282. Kempe, *Divorcing the Dictator*; Fitzwater, *Call the Briefing*, 203; Woodward, *The Commanders*, 121–122.

283. Scowcroft interview, BOHP, 44.

284. Parmet, *George Bush*, 413; Powell, *My American Journey*, 419; Naftali, *George Bush*; Kempe, *Divorcing the Dictator*; Baker, *The Politics of Diplomacy*, 185–186.

285. Scowcroft interview, BOHP, 48.

286. Kempe, *Divorcing the Dictator*; Woodward, *The Commanders*, 124; Morton Abramowitz interview, ADST, 112.

287. Popadiuk, *The Leadership of George Bush*, 122; Scowcroft interview, BOHP, 44, 48, emphasis added.

288. Scowcroft interview, BOHP, 48.

289. Woodward, *The Commanders*, 128–129; Kempe, *Divorcing the Dictator*, 386.

290. Fitzwater, *Call the Briefing*, 207, 210–211; Scowcroft interview, BOHP, 48–50.

291. Burke and Creel, *Oklahoma Statesman*, 327; Scowcroft interview, BOHP, 44; Memorandum for PCC Chairman Bernard Aronson et al. from William T. Price, Director for Latin America and the Caribbean, NSC, October 12, 1989, Eric Melby Files, NSC Collection, BPR; Baker cited in Parmet, *George Bush*, 414. Colin Powell gives Thurman and himself credit for deciding to plan an attack against Panama; he was right that they did the actual planning, wrong to suggest that he and Thurman originated the suggestion (Powell, *My American Journey*, 420). On the existing military plans, see "Operation Just Cause: The Incursion into Panama," www.history.army.mil/brochures/Just Cause/Just Cause.htm, 5–6.

292. Cheney interview, BOHP, 124.

293. Scowcroft interview, BOHP, 44; Powell, *My American Journey*, 418.

294. Robert Gates interview, April 17, 2009.

295. Daniel Poneman interview, April 10, 2012.

296. Scowcroft interview, BOHP, 48–50; Cheney interview, BOHP, 132; also see Quayle, *Standing Firm*, 136–140.

297. Baker, *Politics of Diplomacy*, 179–180; Strong, "Tipping Point"; Kempe, *Divorcing the Dictator*; James A. Baker interview II, BOHP, 25.

298. See Strong, "Tipping Point," 2; also see Greene, *The Presidency of George Bush*, 101. Scowcroft interview, March 14, 2013; Baker, *Politics of Diplomacy*, 179–180; Scowcroft interview, BOHP, 42.

299. Lt. Gen. Carl W. Stiner, "Oral History Interview JCIT 24," Joint Task Force South in Operation Just Cause, December 20, 1989–January 12, 1990, Department of the Army, XVIII Airborne Corps, www.history.army.mil/documents/panama/JCIT/JCIT24.htm; "Operation Just Cause: The Incursion into Panama," 2.

300. Bush and Scowcroft, *A World Transformed*, 62–63; Baker interview I, BOHP, 25; Scowcroft interview, BOHP, 44.

301. Powell, *My American Journey*, 432.

302. Ibid.

303. Baker, *Politics of Diplomacy*, 191.

304. Powell, *My American Journey*, 432; also see Cheney interview, BOHP, 128.

305. Powell, *My American Journey*, 432–433.

306. Ibid., 425.

307. Powell, *My American Journey*, 425.

308. Poneman interview, April 10, 2009; Colin Powell interview, March 24, 2009.

309. Scowcroft interview, BOHP, 42–48; Thomas Pickering interview, BOHP, 27.

310. "Statement on the Bipartisan Accord on Central America," March 24, 1989, *Public Papers of the Presidents of the United States: George Bush: 1989*, 309; "Bipartisan Accord on Central America," March 24, 1989, *Public Papers of the Presidents of the United States: George Bush: 1989* (Washington, DC: US GPO, 1990), 1:307.

311. Scowcroft interview, BOHP, 42.

312. Sergii Plokhy, *The Last Empire: The Final Days of the Soviet Union* (New York: Basic Books, 2014), 202–203; Kimmitt, personal communication, August 26, 2014.

313. Larry P. Goodson, *Afghanistan's Endless War: State Failure, Regional Politics, and the Rise of the Taliban* (Seattle: University of Washington Press, 2001).

314. The population figure is from the World Bank online database, which clusters the years 1989–1993. Also see Rizwan Hussain, *Pakistan and the Emergence of Islamic Militancy in Afghanistan* (Aldershot, UK: Ashgate, 2005), 147; United Nations statistics on refuges quoted by Selig Harrison, cited in Peter W. Rodman, *More Precious than Peace: The Cold War and the Struggle for the Third World* (New York: Scribner's, 1994), 357.

315. Selig S. Harrison, "Afghanistan," in Anthony Lake, *After the Wars* (New Brunswick, NJ: Transaction, 1990), 51; Rodman, *More Precious than Peace*, 336–340; Oberdorfer, *The Turn*, 239, 337; Abramowitz interview, ADST, 106–108; also see George Crile, *Charlie Wilson's War: The Extraordinary Story of the Largest Covert Operation in History* (New York: Atlantic Monthly Press, 2003).

316. Riaz M. Khan, *Untying the Afghan Knot: Negotiating Soviet Withdrawal* (Durham, NC: Duke University Press, 1991), 293–294.

317. Steve Coll, *Ghost Wars: The Secret History of the CIA, Afghanistan, and Bin Laden, from the Soviet Invasion to September 10, 2001* (New York: Penguin, 2004),

171; Dennis Kux, *The United States and Pakistan 1947–2000: Disenchanted Allies* (Washington: Woodrow Wilson Center Press; Baltimore: Johns Hopkins University Press, 2001), 297; Diego Cordovez and Selig S. Harrison, *Out of Afghanistan: The Inside Story of the Soviet Withdrawal* (New York: Oxford University Press, 1995), 339; Marvin Weinbaum interview, July 1, 2013; Harrison, "Afghanistan," 51; Barnett Rubin, *The Search for Peace in Afghanistan: From Buffer State to Failed State* (New Haven: Yale University Press, 1995), 99.

318. Riaz Mohammad Khan, *Afghanistan and Pakistan: Conflict, Extremism, and Resistance to Modernity* (Baltimore: Johns Hopkins University Press, 2011), 3.

319. Robert Oakley interview, ADST, 152.

320. "National Security Review-1," February 7, 1989, Haass Working Files, "Afghanistan 1989–1992 [2]," ID: 1304-011, NSC Collection, BPR.

321. Bush and Scowcroft, *A World Transformed*; Oberdorfer, *The Turn*, 333; Robert Oakley interview, February 12, 2014.

322. Thomas Pickering interview, March 27, 2014; Pickering interview, BOHP, 12.

323. Riaz, *Afghanistan and Pakistan*, 22; Rubin, *The Search for Peace in Afghanistan*, 108–109, 111 (also generally 102–111); Robert Oakley interview, ADST, 133.

324. Cordovez and Harrison, *Out of Afghanistan*, 383.

325. Rubin, *The Search for Peace in Afghanistan*, 122; Marvin Weinbaum interview, July 1, 2013.

326. Edmund McWilliams interview, ADST, 69; Sandra Charles interview, July 1, 2013; the White House received letters from President Najibullah on March 19, March 16, and May 20, 1989, August 16, September 27, October 2, October 16, and November 20, 1991.

327. Coll, *Ghost Wars*, 179–180; Zia quoted in Hussain, *Pakistan and the Emergence of Islamic Militancy in Afghanistan*, 123; Rodman, *More Precious than Peace*, 352; Cordovez and Harrison, *Out of Afghanistan*, 258–259; Phyllis and Robert Oakley interview, January 28, 2014; McWilliams interview, ADST, 75; Weinbaum interview, July 1, 2013.

328. Cordovez and Harrison, *Out of Afghanistan*, 375–378.

329. Najibullah, President of the Republic of Afghanistan, to His Excellency, George Bush, March 10, 1989, CO 002-17185, WHORM files, BPR; Memcon, "Plenary Meeting with Prime Minister Bhutto of Pakistan," June 6, 1989. When President Najibullah invited a US congressional delegation to visit to advance "the rehabilitation of Afghanistan and investment here" and "promote Afghan-US joint cooperation against narcotic drugs, education, and the resumption of the U.S. former projects," for example, an NSC staff member jotted down "no action required" on the cover sheet of the written invitation (Mr. Abdul Ghafoor Jawshan, "Forwards an Excerpt of the Speech by His Excellency Najibullah, President of the Republic of Afghanistan, on the Occasion of the Afghan New Year," March 27, 1991, CO 002-224315, WHORM files, BPR). Also see letter of Jimmy Carter to President Bush,

January 25, 1990, writing that the United States could help promote peace by supporting a peace-keeping force under the UN Security Council and the response by President Bush on February 22, 1990, CO 002-108027, WHORM files, BPR).

330. Brent Scowcroft to Mr. Agha K. Saeed, September 2, 1989, CO 002-05242, WHORM files, BPR.

331. James A. Baker, "White House Meeting Agendas, 1989," November 14, 1989, "1989 November," folder 11, Box 108, Baker Papers, Princeton University; Rodman, *More Precious than Peace*, 354; Bush and Scowcroft, *A World Transformed*, 134.

332. See "NSC and Deputies Committee meetings," BPR, http://bushlibrary. tamu.edu/research/pdfs/nsc_meetings_1989-1992-declassified.pdf, http://bush library.tamu.edu/research/pdfs/nsc_and_dc_meetings_1989-1992-declassified.pdf; Bruce Riedel, *What We Won: America's Secret War in Afghanistan, 1979–1989* (Washington, DC: Brookings Institution Press, 2014), 132. The Deputies Committee and the NSC sometimes met to discuss covert operations, and it's very possible that Afghanistan or Pakistan may have been the subject of one of those meetings. The number of NSC and DC meetings in the text is not the same as those in the Bush Presidential Library, because the Bush Presidential Library website relies on the official number of the meetings, not on the actual number of times the committees met (sometimes on the same day). Neither do the numbers differentiate when the meetings addressed only one subject or when they addressed multiple subjects (such as both Afghanistan and Panama in the same meeting).

333. Scowcroft interview, June 20, 2013; Coll, *Ghost Wars*, 217.

334. Also see Parmet, *George Bush*; Naftali, *George H. W. Bush*; Popadiuk, *The Leadership of George Bush*; Gates, *From the Shadows*; Rothkopf, *Running the World*; John P. Burke, *Honest Broker?* (College Station: Texas A&M Press, 2009); Daalder and Destler, *In the Shadow of the Oval Office*.

335. Crile, *Charlie Wilson's War*, 514; Rubin, *The Search for Peace in Afghanistan*, 110–111.

336. James A. Baker, "White House Meeting Agendas, 1989," November 14, 1989, "1989 November," folder 11, Box 108, Baker Papers; Bush and Scowcroft, *A World Transformed*, 134; Coll, *Ghost Wars*, 190–195.

337. Coll, *Ghost Wars*, 190.

338. Peter Tomsen, *The Wars of Afghanistan: Messianic Terrorism, Global Conflicts, and the Failures of Great Powers* (New York: PublicAffairs, 2011); Coll, *Ghost Wars*, 198.

339. Memorandum of Conversation, "Meeting with Secretary General Javier Perez de Cuellar of the United Nations," September 23, 1991, 1:15–2:30 P.M., The Indonesian Lounge at the United Nations, New York City, MemCon files, BPR.

340. Coll, *Ghost Wars*, 180.

341. Hussain, *Pakistan and the Emergence of Islamic Militancy in Afghanistan*, 180; Crile, *Charlie Wilson's War*, 521.

342. Coll, *Ghost Wars*, 182–181, 206; McWilliams interview, ADST, 74–79; also see Larry Wright, *The Looming Tower*.

343. Crile, *Charlie Wilson's War*, 518–519.

344. Christine Fair interview, May 21, 2013; Coll, *Ghost Wars*, 220; Robert A. Hathaway interview, July 24, 2013.

345. Kux, *The United States and Pakistan 1947–2000*, 299; Robert Oakley interview, ADST, 144; Robert Oakley interview, January 29, 2014.

346. Memorandum of Conversation, "Plenary Meeting with Prime Minister Bhutto of Pakistan," June 6, 1989, Haass Working Files, "Presidential Visit with Prime Minister Benazir Bhutto, June 6–7, 1989," OA/ID CF01404-020, NSC Collection, BPR; Feroz Hassan Khan, *Eating Grass: The Making of the Pakistani Bomb* (Stanford: Stanford University Press, 2012), 254; Robert Oakley interview, ADST, 144.

347. Kux, *The United States and Pakistan 1947–2000*, 306–308; Haass, *War of Necessity, War of Choice*, 91.

348. Hussain, *Pakistan and the Emergence of Islamic Militancy in Afghanistan*, 145–146.

349. Kux, *The United States and Pakistan 1947–2000*, 308, 310; Haqqani, *Magnificent Delusions*, 280–281.

350. Ibid.

351. Bruce Riedel, *Deadly Embrace: Pakistan, America, and the Future of Global Jihad* (Washington, DC: Brookings Institution Press, 2011), 28–35.

352. Rubin, *The Search for Peace in Afghanistan*, 111; John Holzman quoted in Kux, *The United States and Pakistan 1947–2000*, 317.

353. Harrison, "Afghanistan," 45; Oberdorfer, *The Turn*, 337; McWilliams interview, ADST, 114; Rodman, *More Precious than Peace*, 340; Baker, "Proposed Agenda for meeting with the President, April 15, 1992," White House Meeting Agendas, 1992, Box 115, Folder 9, Baker Papers.

354. Harrison, "Afghanistan," 45; Oberdorfer, *The Turn*, 337; McWilliams interview, ADST, 114; Rodman, *More Precious than Peace*, 340; Baker, "Proposed Agenda for meeting with the president, April 15, 1992.

355. Scowcroft interview, 2013; Gates, *From the Shadows*, 485; McWilliams interview, ADST, December 1, 2005, 64.

356. Gates quoted in Andrew Spring, "Did the U.S. 'Abandon' Afghanistan in 1989?" *The Atlantic*, December 2009; Phyllis Oakley interview, ADST, 86.

357. McWilliams interview, ADST, 114.

358. Scowcroft interview, June 20, 2013; Zia quoted in Cordovez and Harrison, *Out of Afghanistan*, 259.

359. Kux, *The United States and Pakistan 1947–2000*, 311, 324–325.

360. Rubin, *The Search for Peace in Afghanistan*, 101; Barnett R. Rubin, *The Fragmentation of Afghanistan: State Formation and Collapse in the International System* (New Haven: Yale University Press, 2012), 251; Hussain, *Pakistan and the*

Emergence of Islamic Militancy in Afghanistan, 141; Kux, *The United States and Pakistan 1947–2000*, 302–303; Robert Oakley interview, ADST, 149; Phyllis Oakley interview, ADST, 91.

361. Khan, *Afghanistan and Pakistan*, 54.

362. Haass, BOHP, 19–21, 63.

363. Haass, BOHP, 19.

Chapter 21: Blood on the Stones

364. Suettinger, *Beyond Tiananmen*, 51, 60.

365. Cable from US Embassy Beijing, to: Department of State, Wash DC, "SITREP No. 32: The Morning of June 4," "Tiananmen Square, 1989: The Declassified History," *National Security Archive Electronic Briefing Book*.

366. Secretary of State's Morning Summary for June 5, 1989, "China after the Bloodbath," "Tiananmen Square, 1989: The Declassified History," *National Security Archive Electronic Briefing Book*; Lord, *Legacies*, 229; Brook, *Quelling the People*; Tyler, *A Great Wall*, 358–359; Baker, *The Politics of Diplomacy*, 103.

367. Tyler, *A Great Wall*, 360–361; Lilley, *China Hands*, 322–323; Memorandum from US Embassy Beijing to Douglas Paal, "China and the U.S.A. Protracted Engagement," July 11, 1989, OA/ID CF00316-002, Doug Paal Series, 1989–1990 China Files, "January–July 1989 [2]," NSC Collection, BPR.

368. Lilley, *China Hands*, 321–322; Lord, oral history, ADST; Brook, *Quelling the People*, 166–168; "Hearing of the Foreign Affairs Committee," December 13, 1989, Federal News Service, 20.

369. Henry Kissinger, *On China* (New York: The Penguin Press, 2010), 410; Scowcroft interview, August 3, 2011.

370. Kissinger, *On China*, 410.

371. Brook, *Quelling the People*; memorandum from Douglas Paal to Robert M. Gates, "Update on the Situation in China," June 8, 1989, "China-US," "January–July 1989 [4]," OA/ID: CF00316-004, Doug Paal Series, NSC Collection, BPR.

372. Brook, *Quelling the People*; Gates interview, BOHP, 28; Ezra Vogel, *Deng Xiaoping and the Transformation of China* (Cambridge: Harvard University Press, 2011).

373. Tyler, *A Great Wall*, 354.

374. Lord, *Legacies*, 210; Bruce Gilley, *Tiger on the Brink: Jiang Zemin and China's New Elite* (Berkeley: University of California Press, 1998), 140–141; Nancy Bernkopf Tucker, *China Confidential: American Diplomats and Sino-American Relations, 1945–1996* (New York: Columbia University Press, 2003), 448–449; Scowcroft interview, BOHP, 57. Also see Suettinger, *Beyond Tiananmen*, 32–33.

375. Gilley, *Tiger on the Brink*, 145–146; Vogel, *Deng Xiaoping*, 622, 644–646.

376. Vogel, *Deng Xiaoping*, 627.

377. Scowcroft interview, BOHP, 58.

378. Brook, *Quelling the People*, 196, 199; Scowcroft interview, August 3, 2011; also see Michael Yahuda, "Deng Xiaoping: The Statesman," in *Deng Xiaoping: Portrait of a Chinese Statesman,* ed. David Shambugh (New York: Oxford University Press, 1995), 143–164.

379. Brook, *Quelling the People*. As of June 8, however, the NSC found "no convincing evidence of serious dissension with the army or security forces, and the regime probably has no reason to fear imminent attack from renegade military units" (Memorandum from Douglas Paal to Robert M. Gates, "Update on the Situation in China," June 8, 1989, "China-US," "January–July 1989 [4]," OA/ID: CF00316-004, Doug Paal Series, NSC Collection, BPR).

380. Brook, *Quelling the People*, 188–191.

381. Ibid., 178–180.

382. Ibid., 198–199, 203; Vogel, *Deng Xiaoping*, 631.

383. Brook, *Quelling the People*, 203.

384. Scowcroft interview, August 3, 2011; Scowcroft interview, BOHP, 55.

385. Bette Bao Lord quoted in Tyler, *A Great Wall*, 359. Also see Lord, *Legacies*, 229–231; Vogel, *Deng Xiaoping*, 617.

386. For inconsistent descriptions of the massacre, see Brook, *Quelling the People*, 108–169; Lilley, *China Hands*, 311–332; Tyler, *A Great Wall*, 356–359; Vogel, *Deng Xiaoping*, 624–632.

387. Tucker, *China Confidential*, 449.

388. Scowcroft interview, BOHP, 59; Duffy and Goodgame, *Marching in Place*, 184.

389. Scowcroft interview, BOHP, 56; see Suettinger, *Beyond Tiananmen*, 79.

390. George H. W. Bush interview, December 18, 2009.

391. Tyler, *A Great Wall*, 359; ABC News/*Washington Post* Poll, February 1989; *Los Angeles Times* Poll, June 1989 (www.ropercenter.uconn.edu).

392. Scowcroft interview, May 13, 2009; Bush and Scowcroft, *A World Transformed*, 99.

393. Richard Nixon letter to Brent Scowcroft, "China: Post-Tiananmen" (October 1990), Post-Tiananmen files, China Chronological files, Brent Scowcroft Collection, OA/ID 91133-003, BPR.

394. Douglas Mulholland to Secretary of State Baker, "Re: China's Attitude Toward the U.S.," July 1, 1989, "China-U.S." files, "January–July 1989 [3]," Doug Paal series, NSC Collection, BPR; Scowcroft, BOHP, 63.

395. American Embassy, Beijing, to Sec. State Wash. DC, July 12, 1989, "January–July 1989 [2]," OA/ID CF00316-002, "1989–1990 China Files," Doug Paal Series, NSC Collection, BPR; Lilley, *China Hands*, 352–358.

396. Leslie Gelb interview, April 9, 2014.

397. Mann, *About Face*, 201–204; Fang Lizhi, "My 'Confession,'" *New York Review of Books*, June 23, 2011, 23.

398. Lampton, *Same Bed, Different Dreams*, 28; Suettinger, *Beyond Tiananmen*, 90–91.

399. Scowcroft interview, BOHP, 58.

400. Scowcroft interview, BOHP, 58–59.

401. Memorandum for Brent Scowcroft through Karl Jackson from Douglas Paal, "State's Views on Ambassador Lilley's Recommendations on China," June 5, 1989, OA/ID CF00316-004, Doug Paal Series, NSC Collection, BPR; Suettinger, *Beyond Tiananmen*, 79; Schmitz, *Brent Scowcroft*, 109.

402. Scowcroft interview, BOHP, 56; Qian, *Ten Episodes in China's Diplomacy*, 132; Bush and Scowcroft, *A World Transformed*, 104–105.

403. Bush interview, December 18, 2009.

404. Mann, *About Face*, 206–207; Tucker, *China Confidential*, 446; Richard H. Solomon quoted in "China Policy and the National Security Council," Oral History Roundtables, November 4, 1999, 22. Also see Douglas Paal, "Re: China's Attitude Toward the U.S. (4 pp.)," June 27, 1989, OA/ID CF00316-003, Doug Paal Series, NSC Collection, BPR.

405. Suettinger, *Beyond Tiananmen*, 79; Qian Qichen, *Ten Episodes in China's Diplomacy*, 131–132; Mann, *About Face*, 205–206; Bush and Scowcroft, *A World Transformed*; Am. Embassy Beijing to Sec. State Wash. DC, July 12, 1989, "January–July 1989 [2]," OA/ID CF00316-002, Doug Paal Series, "1989–1990 China Files," NSC Collection, BPR.

406. Qian, *Ten Episodes in China's Diplomacy*, 132–133.

407. Ibid., 133. Bush and Scowcroft, *A World Transformed*, 105–106; Kissinger, *On China*, 418. Qian Qichen disputes Scowcroft's claim that the Chinese military was not aware of the plane, saying that the Chinese knew of the time and route of the incoming aircraft (see Qian, *Ten Episodes in China's Diplomacy*, 133).

408. Qian, *Ten Episodes in China's Diplomacy*, 134–136; Kissinger, *On China*, 418–419; Scowcroft interview, BOHP, 59; Vogel, *Deng Xiaoping*, 650; Schmitz, *Brent Scowcroft*, 110.

409. Vogel, *Deng Xiaoping*, 651.

410. Ibid.

411. Suettinger, *Beyond Tiananmen*, 81; Qian, *Ten Episodes in China's Diplomacy*, 134.

412. Qian, *Ten Episodes in China's Diplomacy*, 136; Kissinger, *On China*, 418–420; Bush and Scowcroft, *A World Transformed*; Mann, *About Face*, 207–208; Scowcroft interview, BOHP, 59.

413. Scowcroft interview, August 3, 2011; Scowcroft interview, BOHP, 56–57; Vogel, *Deng Xiaoping*, 650; Suettinger, *Beyond Tiananmen*, 82–83.

414. Mann, *About Face*, 208–209.

415. Am. Embassy Beijing to SecState WashDC, July 12, 1989, "January–July 1989 [2]," OA/ID CF00316-002, Doug Paal Series, "1989–1990 China Files," NSC Collection, BPR.

416. Kissinger, *On China*; Qichen, *Ten Episodes in China's Diplomacy*, 136–139; Mann, *About Face*, 408.

417. Scowcroft interview, BOHP, 55.

418. "China's Attitude Toward the U.S.," May 27, 1989, OA/ID CF00316-003, Doug Paal Series, NSC Collection, BPR; Memorandum to Secretary of State Baker from Douglas Mulholland, July 1, 1989, OA/ID CF00316-003, Doug Paal Series, NSC Collection, BPR. Also see Memorandum for Paal from American Embassy Beijing, "China and the U.S.—A Protracted Engagement," July 11, 1989, OA/ID CF00316-002, Doug Paal Series, 1989–1990 China Files, "January–July 1989 [2]," NSC Collection, BPR.

419. Am. Embassy Beijing to SecState WashDC, July 12, 1989, "January–July 1989 [2]," OA/ID CF00316-002, Doug Paal Series, "1989–1990 China Files," NSC Collection, BPR.

420. Kissinger, *On China*; Scowcroft interview, August 3, 2011; Scowcroft interview, BOHP, 62.

421. Walter Isaacson, *Kissinger: A Biography* (New York: Simon & Schuster, 1992), 750.

422. Suettinger, *Beyond Tiananmen*, 97; Vogel, *Deng Xiaoping*, 653.

423. Bush and Scowcroft, *A World Transformed*, 157; Scowcroft interview, BOHP, 60.

424. Isaacson, *Kissinger*, 751–752.

425. Bush and Scowcroft, *A World Transformed*, 99.

426. Ibid., 158; Vogel, *Deng Xiaoping*, 653; Suettinger, *Beyond Tiananmen*, 97–98.

427. Baker, *The Politics of Diplomacy*, 100–101; Tucker, *China Confidential*, 446–447, 453; Mann, *About Face*, 209. Also see Daalder and Destler, *In the Shadow of the Oval Office*, 77; Richard H. Solomon quoted in "China Policy and the National Security Council," Oral History Roundtables, November 4, 1999, 22.

428. Mann, *About Face*, 215; Kerry Dumbaugh, "China's Most-Favored Nation (MFN) Status: Congressional Consideration," *CRS Report for Congress*, August 1, 1998, 6.

429. Scowcroft, interview, October 2007; Suettinger, *Beyond Tiananmen*, 95.

430. Chase Untermeyer interview, BOHP, July 27–28, 22–23.

431. Scowcroft interview, BOHP, 60.

432. Qian, *Ten Episodes in China's Diplomacy*, 140; Bush and Scowcroft, *A World Transformed*, 158.

433. Bush and Scowcroft, *A World Transformed*.

434. Tyler, *A Great Wall*, 370; Mann, *About Face*, 219.

435. Scowcroft interview, BOHP, 60.

436. Kissinger, *On China*, 437; Douglas Paal interview, March 5, 2009.

437. Bush and Scowcroft, *A World Transformed*, 174; Fang, "My 'Confession,'" 23; Scowcroft interview, August 3, 2011.

438. See "Proposed Toast for Gen Scowcroft Banquet," December 8, 1989, Department of State, DNSA, CH01242.

439. "Hearing of the International Economic Policy & Trade Subcommittee of the House Foreign Affairs Committee," Subject: "Recent Administration Visit to China," December 13, 1989, Federal News Service, 3, 4; Mitch McConnell quoted in *The Congressional Quarterly*, December 16, 1989, 3435, in Kerry Dumbaugh, "China's Most-Favored Nation (MFN) Status: Congressional Consideration," *CRS Report for Congress*, August 1, 1998, 6.

440. Mary McCrory, "Patting the Dragon," *Washington Post*, December 12, 1989; "Back to Beijing, Head Bowed," *St. Louis Post-Dispatch*, December 12, 1989; "Disgrace at Beijing," (editorial) *St. Petersburg Times*, December 12, 1989; A. M. Rosenthal, "On My Mind: Betrayal in Beijing," *New York Times*, December 12, 1989; Richard Cohen, "China Card Too Dear to Bush, Scowcroft," *St. Louis Post-Dispatch*, December 13, 1989; Scowcroft interview, BOHP, 61. Also see Jim Hoagland, "The Descent of American Diplomacy," *Washington Post*, December 17, 1989.

441. "Toast by the Honorable Brent Scowcroft," Beijing, December 9, 1989, CH01245, DNSA; Scowcroft interview, BOHP, 65.

442. Fang, "My 'Confession,'" 23; Scowcroft interview, May 5, 2010; Scowcroft interview, BOHP, 65; also see Suettinger, *Beyond Tiananmen*, 99–100.

443. Winston Lord, "Misguided Mission," *Washington Post*, December 19, 1989; J. Stapleton Roy interview, March 27, 2009; Kathy Wilhelm, "China Steps Up Criticism of United States over Fang Incident," Associated Press, March 1, 1989.

444. Roy interview, April 9, 2009; Robert Gates interview, April 17, 2012.

Chapter 22: One Germany

445. Letter from Richard Nixon to George Bush, November 17, 1989, folder 10, POTUS Notes, 1989–1992, Box 115 folder 10, Baker Papers, emphasis in original.

446. Scowcroft interview, BOHP, 51; Zelikow and Rice, *Germany Unified and Europe Transformed*, 27.

447. Bush quoted in Arnaud de Borchgrave, "Bush Would Love 'Reunited Germany,'" *Washington Times*, May 16, 1989, cited in Jeffrey Engel, "Bush, Germany, and the Power of Time," *Diplomatic History* 37, no. 4 (September 2013), 639–663; Zelikow and Rice, *Germany Unified*, 28–29; also see Scowcroft interview, BOHP, 81.

448. Bozo, *Mitterrand, the End of the Cold War, and German Reunification*, 95; Sigal, *Hang Separately*, 47.

449. Gates interview, BOHP, 33.

450. Bush and Scowcroft, *A World Transformed*, 154–155. On the Baker-Shevardnadze relationship see James A. Baker III, *The Politics of Diplomacy* (New York: G. P. Putnam's Sons, 1995).

451. Robert Kimmitt interview, March 2, 2010; Kimmitt personal communication, August 26, 2014; Elizabeth Pond, *Beyond the Wall*, 315n31.

452. Hutchings, "American Diplomacy," 17; Stent, *Russia and Germany Reborn*, 99.

453. Memorandum of Conversation, "Second Expanded Bilateral Session," December 3, 1989, 4:35–6:45 P.M., Maxim Gorkii Cruise Liner, Malta, "Summit at Malta December 1989: Malta Memcons [1], CF00718-006, Soviet Union/USSR Subject Files, Condoleezza Rice Files, NSC Collection, BPR.

454. Gates, *From the Shadows*, 484–485; Zelikow and Rice, *Germany Unified*, 130.

455. Gates, *From the Shadows*, 484–485; Scowcroft interview, BOHP, 81–82; Sarotte, *1989*, 64, 79.

456. Baker, Meeting Notes, November 12, 1989, "1989 November," folder 11, Box 108, Meeting Notes, Baker Papers; Zelikow and Rice, *Germany Unified*, 158–159.

457. Bush and Scowcroft, *A World Transformed*, 241.

458. Ibid., 241; Sarotte, *1989*, 121.

459. Bush and Scowcroft, *A World Transformed*, 236–237; Zelikow and Rice, *Germany Unified*, 174–177.

460. Bush and Scowcroft, *A World Transformed*, 236.

461. "National Security Directive 50," October 12, 1990, "Decisions on START and CFE Issues," 4, NSD online, BPR.

462. Baker, *The Politics of Diplomacy*, 173, 527; Hutchings, *American Diplomacy and the End of the Cold War*, 162, 194–195, 296–300; "The Organization for Security and Cooperation in Europe," Icelandic Human Rights Centre, www.humanrights.is/the-human-rights-project/humanrightscasesandmaterials/humanrightsconceptsideasandfora/humanrightsfora/theorganizationforsecurityandcooperationineurope; Brent Scowcroft, Memorandum for the President, "Scope Paper—Helsinki Summit," n.d., folder "Briefing Book—President's Visit to Warsaw, Poland; Munich, Germany; and Helsinki, Finland" (Economic Summit/CSCE Summit) July 5–10, 1992 [4], [Helsinki, Finland—July 8–10, 1992]," Trip Files, Walter H. Kansteiner Files, NSC Collection, BPR, OA/ID CF015549. Also see Sarah Snyder, *Human Rights Activism and the End of the Cold War*.

463. Hutchings, *American Diplomacy and the End of the Cold War*, 102–103.

464. Bozo, *Mitterrand, the End of the Cold War, and German Reunification*, 246.

465. Bush and Scowcroft, *A World Transformed*, 233–234; Robert L. Hutchings, Memorandum for Brent Scowcroft, "Managing the German Question," n.d., "German Reunification—2+4," Hutchings, Robert file, NSC, OF/IF CF01414-007; Zelikow and Rice, *Germany Unified*, 154–155, 159; Sarotte, *1989*, 80.

466. Gates, *From the Shadows*, 485; Bush and Scowcroft, *A World Transformed*, 234.

467. Philip Zelikow interview, 2009; Zelikow and Rice, *Germany Unified*, 195; Scowcroft interview, January 27, 2009.

468. Zelikow and Rice, *Germany Unified*, 194–195.

469. Scowcroft interview, February 23, 2010.

470. Baker, *The Politics of Diplomacy*, 214; Bush and Scowcroft, *A World Transformed*, 255; Sarotte, *1989*, 197.

471. Bush and Scowcroft, *A World Transformed*, 257; Zelikow and Rice, *Germany Unified*, 190.

472. Bush and Scowcroft, *A World Transformed*, 259.

473. Memorandum from Brent Scowcroft to the President, "Preparing for the Six Power German Peace Conference," Non-log item [February 19, 1990], [German Reunification 11/89–6/90] [1], Robert Blackwill series, NSC Collection, BPR.

474. Kimmitt interview, BOHP II, 35.

475. Manfred Woerner quoted in Bush and Scowcroft, *A World Transformed*, 243; Zelikow and Rice, *Germany Unified*, 169.

476. Bush and Scowcroft, *A World Transformed*, 268; Sigal, *Hang Separately*, 38–40; Bozo, *Mitterrand, the End of the Cold War, and German Reunification*, 249–250; Zelikow and Rice, *Germany Unified*, 169.

477. Bush and Scowcroft, *A World Transformed*, 268; Sigal, *Hang Separately*, 38–40; Bozo, *Mitterrand, the End of the Cold War, and German Reunification*, 249–250; Zelikow and Rice, *Germany Unified*, 169; Kimmitt interview, BOHP II, 37.

478. Hubert Védrine quoted in Sarotte, *1989*, 210, italics in original.

479. Scowcroft interview, BOHP, 82–84; also see Bush and Scowcroft, *A World Transformed*, 280–283; Zelikow and Rice, *Germany Unified*, 278–280.

480. Scowcroft interview, BOHP, 82–84; Bush and Scowcroft, *A World Transformed*, 288, 298; Zelikow and Rice, *Germany Unified*, 328–329.

481. Zelikow and Rice, *Germany Unified*, 282–283.

482. Gorbachev, *Memoirs*; Bush and Scowcroft, *A World Transformed*, 283–286.

483. Bush and Scowcroft, *A World Transformed*, 288.

484. Dubcek, Sharansky, and Kashlev, quoted in Snyder, *Human Rights Activism and the End of the Cold War*, 242.

485. Scowcroft interview, BOHP, 84; Bush and Scowcroft, *A World Transformed*, 299; Hutchings, *American Diplomacy and the End of the Cold War*, 137–138.

486. Daalder and Destler, *In the Shadow of the Oval Office*, 187–188.

487. Bush and Scowcroft, *A World Transformed*, 297–298; Zelikow and Rice, *Germany Unified*, 335–337, 339.

488. "Notes from Jim Cicconi re: 7/3/90 pre-NATO Summit briefing at Kennebunkport," "July 1990," Folder 3, Box 109, Baker Papers.

489. Scowcroft letter to Teltschik, June 30, 1990, title, 1285.

490. Beschloss and Talbott, *At the Highest Levels*, 237; Stent, *Russia and Germany Transformed*, 131.

491. Memorandum of Conversation, "Meeting with Manfred Woerner, Secretary-General of NATO," June 25, 1991, 2:45–3:15, Oval Office, Memcons, BPR; Memorandum of Conversation, "Meeting with Prime Minister Gro Harlem Brundtland

of Norway," September 24, 1991, 2:00–2:30 P.M., EST, Waldorf Astoria Hotel, New York City, MemCons, BPR; Memorandum of Conversation, "The President's Meeting with Manfred Woerner, Secretary-General of NATO," October 11, 1991, 11:30–12:00, The Oval Office, MemCons, BPR.

492. Bush and Scowcroft, *A World Transformed*, 294; Sarotte, *1989*, 175.

493. Scowcroft letter to Teltschik, June 30, 1990, *Deutsche Einheit Sonderedition aus den Akten des Budeskanleramtes 1989/90*, Dokumente zur Deutschlandpolitik, Hanns Jürgen Küsters und Daniel Hofman (München: R. Oldenbourg Verlag, 1998), 1285, trans. Edgar Walter.

494. Baker, *The Politics of Diplomacy*, 258; Memorandum of Conversation, "Meeting with Manfred Woerner, Secretary-General of NATO," June 25, 1991, 2:45–3:15, Oval Office, MemCons, Bush Library; Memorandum of Conversation, "The President's Meeting with Manfred Woerner, Secretary-General of NATO," October 11, 1991, 11:30–12:00, The Oval Office, MemCons, BPR.

495. Scowcroft interview, May 9, 2014; Scowcroft interview, November 28, 2012. The "prefab" image is from Sarotte, *1989*.

496. Bush and Scowcroft, *A World Transformed*, 261–262; Helmut Kohl letter to President Bush, June 28, 1989, 321. Hanns Jürgen Küsters, "Introduction," *Deutsche Einheit Sonderedition aus den Akten des Budeskanleramtes 1989/90*, 91; Horst Teltschik, "Saturday, Feb. 3, 1990," *329 Tage*, trans. Edgar Walter; Stent, *Russia and Germany Reborn*, 118–119.

497. Bush and Scowcroft, *A World Transformed*, 298–299; Sarotte, *1989*, 178.

498. Zelikow and Rice, *Germany Unified*, 353.

499. Memorandum from Robert D. Blackwill to Brent Scowcroft, "The Beginning of the Big Game," February 7, 1990, "[German Reunification 11/89–6/90] [1]," Robert D. Blackwill Series, NSC Collection, BPR.

500. Stent, *Russia and Germany Reborn*, 102, 113.

501. James A. Baker notes from meetings on November 11, 1989, and November 12, 1989, emphasis in original, "1989 November," folder 11, Box 108, Subseries 8c, Monthly notes, Baker Papers, emphasis in the original.

502. Bush and Scowcroft, *A World Transformed*, 299.

503. Robert Hutchings, "American Diplomacy and the End of the Cold War in Europe," manuscript, 4–5; Pond, *Beyond the Wall*, 112–120.

504. See Sarotte, *1989*, 199–200; Angela E. Stent, *Russia and Germany Reborn* (Princeton: Princeton University Press, 1999), 121, 212; Anatoly Dobryinin, *In Confidence*, 630–631.

505. Zelikow and Rice, *Germany Unified*, 329, 366–368; Sarotte, *1989*, 200–201.

506. John Sununu interview, BOHP.

507. Beschloss and Talbott, *At the Highest Levels*, 471; Andrew Bacevich, *American Empire: The Realities and Consequences of U.S. Diplomacy* (Cambridge, MA: Harvard University Press, 2002), 57. For highly favorable judgments on Scowcroft

as national security advisor see Daalder and Destler, *In the Shadow of the Oval Office*; Rothkopf, *Running the World*; Burke, *Honest Broker?*.

508. Bush and Scowcroft, *A World Transformed*, xiii.

509. General Brent Scowcroft, *Der Spiegel*, October 1988, trans. Edgar Walter.

510. Alexander Moens, "American Diplomacy and German Unification," *Survival* 33, no. 6 (November/December 1991): 531, cited in Robert Hutchings, "American Diplomacy and the End of the Cold War in Europe," in *Foreign Policy Breakthroughs*, 9.

511. Gates quoted in Sarotte, *1989*, 203.

Chapter 23: On-Ramp

512. Bush and Scowcroft, *A World Transformed*, 302–303.

513. David Lauter, "25% of Kuwaitis May Be Casualties, U.S. Believes," *Los Angeles Times*, February 26, 1991.

514. Bush and Scowcroft, *A World Transformed*, 302–303; Nicholas Rostow interview, April 29, 2009; Maureen Dowd, "The Guns of August Make a Dervish Bush Whirl Even Faster," *New York Times*, August 7, 1990.

515. Jeffrey Goldberg also makes this point in "Breaking Ranks: What Turned Brent Scowcroft Against the Bush Administration," *New Yorker*, October 31, 2005.

516. On the confidentiality of calls, see Presidential Call to Prime Minister Nawaz of Pakistan on February 2, 1991, 10:30–10:50 A.M., Camp David, 1991 Telcons, BPR; Telephone Conversation with King Hussein of Jordan, August 13, 1990, 6:18–6:20 P.M., Kennebunkport, 1990 Telcons, BPR.

517. Bush and Scowcroft, *A World Transformed*, 302–304; Duffy and Goodgame, *Marching in Place*, 131; Quayle, *Standing Firm*, 205.

518. Bush and Scowcroft, *A World Transformed*, 304, 314; Quayle, *Standing Firm*, 205.

519. Rothkopf, *Running the World*, 294–295; Bush and Scowcroft, *A World Transformed*, 314; Thomas Pickering interview, BOHP, 11; Duffy and Goodgame, *Marching in Place*, 139.

520. Bush and Scowcroft, *A World Transformed*, 315–317.

521. Gates interview, BOHP, 71; Haass, *War of Necessity, War of Choice*, 61–62; Scowcroft quoted in Rothkopf, *Running the* World, 295–296; Bush and Scowcroft, *A World Transformed*, 317–318; Robert Gates interview, April 17, 2012; Duffy and Goodgame, *Marching in Place*, 140.

522. Scowcroft interview, September 1, 2009.

523. Lawrence Freedman and Efraim Karsh, *The Gulf Conflict 1990–1991: Diplomacy and War in the New World Order* (Princeton, NJ: Princeton University Press, 1993), 214–215; Scowcroft quoted in Karen DeYoung, *Soldier: The Life of Colin Powell* (New York: Knopf, 2006), 193. With respect to the worries over oil,

also see Department of Energy, "Draft on Medium Term Measures to Mitigate the Energy Effects of the Middle East Situation," September 7, 1990, Issues Files "Persian Gulf War 1991 [4]," John H. Sununu series, Office of the Chief of Staff to the President," BPR.

524. Michael R. Gordon and General Bernard E. Trainor, *The Generals' War: The Inside Story of the Conflict in the Gulf* (Boston: Little, Brown, 1995), 25.

525. Roman Popadiuk, *The Leadership of George Bush: An Insider's View of the Forty-First President* (College Station: Texas A&M University Press, 2009), 82; Bush and Scowcroft, *A World Transformed*, 317–318.

526. Bush and Scowcroft, *A World Transformed*, 318–319; "Presidential Calls During Iraq-Kuwait Crisis," August 1, 1990–August 7, 1990, "Kuwait-Iraq, Middle East [7]" folder, (1988-0099F) OA/ID CF00703-007, BPR; Telcon with King Hussein of Jordan and President Mubarak of Egypt, August 2, 1990, 12:17–12:31 P.M., Aboard Air Force One en route Aspen, Colorado, 1990 Telcons, BPR; Telcon with King Fahd of Saudi Arabia, August 2, 1990, 6:43–7:21 P.M., [Aspen, Colorado], 1990 Telecons, BPR.

527. Bush and Scowcroft, *A World Transformed*, 319.

528. Freedman and Karsh, *The Gulf Conflict*, 77–79; Maureen Dowd, "Confrontation in the Gulf," *New York Times*, August 9, 1990. Also see Bush and Scowcroft, *A World Transformed*, 307.

529. Memorandum from Brent Scowcroft to George Bush, August 2, 1990, cited in Bush and Scowcroft, *A World Transformed*, 322.

530. Minutes, National Security Council Meeting, August 3, 1990, "Iraq—August 2, 1990–December 1990 [8]," Richard N. Haass Working Files, NSC Collection, BPR.

531. Ibid.

532. Ibid.

533. Cheney interview, BOHP, 134.

534. Ibid.; Robert Gates, oral history, "The Gulf War," *Frontline*, PBS, www .pbs.org/wgbh/pages/frontline/gulf/oral/gates/1.html.

535. Colin Powell with Joseph E. Persico, *My American Journey* (New York: Random House, 1999), 464, 465–466.

536. Scowcroft quoted in DeYoung, *Soldier*, 193.

537. Haass, *War of Necessity, War of Choice*, 69–70; Kenneth R. Timmerman, *The Death Lobby: How the West Armed Iraq* (Boston: Houghton Mifflin, 1991), 466.

538. Bob Woodward, *The Commanders* (New York: Simon & Schuster, 1993), 261; also see Bush and Scowcroft, *A World Transformed*, 333.

539. Woodward, *The Commanders*, 237; Haass, *War of Necessity, War of Choice*, 73; Popadiuk, *The Leadership of George Bush*, 82.

540. George H. W. Bush interview, December 18, 2009.

541. Woodward, *The Commanders*, 302.

542. Bush and Scowcroft, *A World Transformed*, 330; Haass, *War of Necessity, War of Choice*, 67; Duffy and Goodgame, *Marching in Place*, 144–145; Memorandum for James A. Baker and Brent Scowcroft from Virginia Lampley, "Persian Gulf Legislative Issues," September 20, 1990, OA/ID CF01361, Virginia Lampley Series, NSC Collection, BPR.

543. See Haass, *War of Necessity, War of Choice*, 66, 72–73; Cheney interview, BOHP, 73; Gates interview, BOHP, 54–55; also see Telcon with King Fahd of Saudi Arabia, August 4, 1990, 1:50–2:42 P.M., Camp David, 1990 Telcons, BPR; Telcon with King Hassan of Jordan, August 7, 1990, 12:52–12:56 P.M., The Oval Office, 1990 Telcons, BPR.

544. George Bush, "National Security Directive 45," August 10, 1990, DNSA; John E. Robson, "Memorandum for the Honorable Brent Scowcroft," August 14, 1990, "Report of the Economic Analysis Group on the Oil Supply Situation," "Persian Gulf War 1991 [4]" folder, John H. Sununu series, Office of the Chief of Staff to the president, BPR.

545. Bush and Scowcroft, *A World Transformed*, 340–341; Haass, *War of Necessity, War of Choice*, 63; David Schmitz, *Brent Scowcroft: Internationalism and Post-Vietnam War American Foreign Policy* (Lanham, MD: Rowman & Littlefield, 2011), 146.

546. Scowcroft interview, July 25, 2013.

547. Burke, *Honest Broker?*, 175; Marlin Fitzwater interview, February 27, 2008; Colin Powell interview, March 26, 2009.

548. George Bush, "Remarks at the Presentation Ceremony for the Presidential Medals of Freedom and Presidential Citizen's Medals," July 3, 1991, *Public Papers of the Presidents: George Bush: 1991* Book II (Washington, DC: US Government Printing Office, 1992), 816–819; Haass interview, March 16, 2009; Kimmitt personal communication, August 26, 2014; also see Haass, *Wars of Necessity, Wars of Choice*.

549. Haass quoted in Rothkopf, *Running the World*, 297–298.

550. See Woodward, *The Commanders*, 290–296; Richard Cheney with Liz Cheney, *In My Time* (New York: Simon & Schuster, 2011), 196–197; DeYoung, *Soldier*, 243.

551. Freedman and Karsh, *The Gulf Conflict*, 205; Scowcroft interview, July 27, 2009; Bush and Scowcroft, *A World Transformed*, 341; Lawrence Eagleburger interview, April 19, 2009.

552. DeYoung, *Soldier*, 199.

553. Gates interview, BOHP, 52.

554. Bush and Scowcroft, *A World Transformed*, 431; Haass, *War of Necessity, War of Choice*, 96–97.

555. "Janet Mullins," folder 4, Box 173, [book notes],7–8, Baker Papers.

556. Dave Carney interview, June 15, 2009; Walter Kansteiner interview, May 18, 2009.

557. See, for example, "Background Briefing by Senior Administration Official," August 9, 1990, OA/ID CF00703-015, "Middle East Gulf Crisis [6]," Roman Popadiuk files, NSC Collection, BPR.

558. David Lauter, "Brent Scowcroft," in *Fateful Decisions*, 204.

559. Schmitz, *Brent Scowcroft*, 147.

560. Steven Mufson, "The Privatization of Craig Fuller," *Washington Post Magazine*, August 2, 1992; John R. MacArthur, *Second Front: Censorship and Propaganda in the Gulf War* (New York: Hill & Wang, 1992), 49; Carney interview, June 15, 2009.

561. Bush and Scowcroft, *A World Transformed*, 341.

562. See Michael Massing, "The Way to War," *New York Review of Books*, March 28, 1991; Douglas Kellner, *The Persian Gulf TV War* (Boulder, CO: Westview Press, 1992), 68.

563. John Stauber and Sheldon Rampton, *Toxic Sludge Is Good For You* (Monroe, ME: Common Courage Press, 1995).

564. Duffy and Goodgame, *Marching in Place*, 155.

565. David Demarest interview, August 18, 2009; also see Memorandum from the President to John Sununu, Brent Scowcroft, November 23, 1990 (Cairo), Issues Files, "Persian Gulf Working Group," John Sununu Files, OA/ID CF00472, BPR.

566. One of those on the Iraq Working Group, Deb Amend—whose surname is now Gullett—was "special assistant to the president for communications." She reports: "When David Souter was nominated to the Supreme Court, we figured out which states I needed to work on to generate support in states where would matter for the senators voting on the nomination. We complemented the regular press office. Where senators were iffy or where we wanted to persuade them, that's where we worked. We would look at media markets, usually in response to legislative initiatives, and figure out here are the six states (for example) we are worried about and we would focus on garnering support in those states and come up with a menu of things to focus on. Local media interviews, talk radio, not like today where everything is available by satellite hookup. . . . The Press Office do their thing, and we would give resonance, worked mostly with public affairs and congressional liaison shops. [The administration] had different working group, depend[ing]" (Deb Gullett interview, February 20, 2009).

567. Gullett interview, February 20, 2009; Demarest interview, February 29, 2009. Demarest said that the next five weeks were the most fun he ever had in the White House.

568. Memorandum for Sununu from Demarest, November 28, 1990, OA/ID CF006670, Issues file, "Persian Gulf Working Group," John Sununu Series, BPR.

569. Memorandum for David Demarest from Deb Amend, "Working Group Report," December 4, 1990, OA/ID CF006567, Issues Files, "Persian Gulf Working Group," John Sununu Series, BPR.

570. Memorandum for David Demarest from Deb Amend, "Gulf Working Group Status Report," December 5, 1990; Demarest interview, August 8, 2009. Like Vietnam, too, the administration tracked the antiwar protests both on and off campuses. See Memorandum for Deb Amend from Lisa Battaglia, "Student Activism Against U.S. Involvement in the Gulf," December 20, 1990, OA/ID CF006573, Issues file, "Persian Gulf Working Group," John Sununu Series, BPR.

571. Gullett interview, February 20, 2009. "General Scowcroft and his staff were consistently nice, pleasant, and this was a reflection of General Scowcroft," she recalled. Demarest also attested to the fact that Scowcroft was "quietly effective." He held his counsel, rarely tried to dominate conversations—indeed, as national security advisor he didn't see it as his role to be outspoken—and "chose his battles wisely" (Demarest interview, August 8, 2009).

572. Memorandum for David Demarest, from Deb Amend, December 11, 1990, "Pending Projects," OA/ID CF006677, Issues file, "Persian Gulf Working Group," John Sununu Series, BPR.

573. Memorandum for Governor Sununu through David Demarest from Deb Amend, December 20, 1990, CF00468, John Sununu Series, "Communication (Demarest) (1991) [3]," BPR; Bush and Scowcroft, *A World Transformed*, 426–427. Also see Haass, *War of Necessity, War of Choice*, 105; Haass describes himself as conducting "public diplomacy" when he met with the *New York Times* editorial board, a group of prominent Jewish leaders, and the Council of Foreign Relations.

574. Scowcroft quoted in Schmitz, *Brent Scowcroft*, 152–153.

575. MacArthur, *Second Front*, 49–50.

576. Demarest interview, August 8, 2009.

577. Memorandum for David Demarest from Deb Amend, "Working Group Report," December 4, 1990, OA/ID CF006567, Issues file, "Persian Gulf Working Group," John Sununu Series, BPR.

578. See, for example, Memorandum for Governor Sununu from Ed Rogers, FYI, December 2, 1990, Issues Files, "Persian Gulf War 1991 [7]," Sununu Files, OA/ID CF00472, BPR. Attached to Rogers' memorandum was a "National Tracking Summary," Citizens for a Free Kuwait, November 27, 1990, Wirthlin Group, #5332-12. (Rogers was the deputy chief of staff.) Pickering interview, BOHP, 25.

579. Mufson, "The Privatization of Craig Fuller"; Kellner, *The Persian Gulf TV War*, 67–71; MacArthur, *Second Front*.

580. Mufson, "The Privatization of Craig Fuller."

581. See Parmet, *George Bush*, 310–311; Woodward, *The Commanders*, 343–344. Neither does Woodward bring up Hill & Knowlton or its chairman, Robert Gray, who ran the Citizens for a Free Kuwait account and who cochaired Reagan's inaugural committee in 1981, in his discussion of the incubator baby story or of Iraqi human rights violations—many of them atrocities, to be sure—in Kuwait.

582. Bob Schieffer interview, June 2009.

583. Bush and Scowcroft, *A World Transformed*, 417–418; Duffy and Goodgame, *Marching in Place*, 157.

584. Am. Embassy Muscat for USIA Ed Bernier, "Public Affairs Strategy for the Kuwait/Iraq Crisis," 141258Z Aug 90, "File Kuwait Iraq-Middle East" file, OA/ID CF00703-005 [3], Popadiuk Papers, NSC Collection, BPR; "Three Scenarios to End the Gulf Crisis," "Iraq-December 1990 [6]," Haass Working File, NSC Collection, BPR.

585. "Presidential Calls During Iraq-Kuwait Crisis," "File Kuwait Iraq-Middle East [3]" file, OA/ID CF00703-005, Popadiuk Papers, NSC Collection, BPR.

586. Rothkopf, *Running the World*, 298; also see Bush and Scowcroft, *A World Transformed*, 303–304; US General Accounting Office, Report to the Chairman, Committee on Armed Forces, House of Representatives, "Persian Gulf Allied Burden Sharing Efforts," December 1991, GAO/NSIAD-92-71.

587. Jean Edward Smith, *George Bush's War* (New York: Henry Holt, 1992), 232–233.

588. Memorandum for James Cicconi from William F. Sittmann, "Changes to President's Address to Jt. Session of Congress," September 11, 1990, "Address to Joint Session of Congress 9/11/90, [2]," OA/ID 5376, "Speech Draft" file, David Snow records, Speechwriting Series, BPR,.

589. Bush and Gorbachev quoted in Schmitz, *Brent Scowcroft*, 146; Baker, *The Politics of Diplomacy*, 266.

590. Bush and Gorbachev quoted in Schmitz, *Brent Scowcroft*, 146.

591. Schmitz, *Brent Scowcroft*, 147–148.

592. Jeffrey Engel, "The Gulf War at the End of the Cold War and Beyond," in *Into the Desert: Reflections on the Gulf War*, ed. Jeffrey Engel (New York: Oxford University Press, 2012), 43. Cheney, BOHP, 149; Bush and Scowcroft, *A World Transformed*, 338, 362.

593. Scowcroft cited in Sigal, *Hang Separately*, 99.

594. Sigal, *Hang Separately*, 100; Baker, *Politics of Diplomacy*, 282–283, 292–293.

595. Bush interview, December 18, 2009.

596. Gates interview, BOHP, 71; Freedman and Karsh, *The Gulf Conflict*, 147–149; Bush and Scowcroft, *A World Transformed*, 351–352; Duffy and Goodgame, *Marching in Place*, 149.

597. Telcon with President Turgut Özal of Turkey, January 12, 1991, 6:55–6:59 P.M., Camp David, 1991 Telcons, BPR.

598. Gibbs and Duffy, *The Presidents Club*, 406–408.

599. Ibid..

600. Ibid..

601. Baker, *The Politics of Diplomacy*, 348–353.

602. Kimmitt, personal communication, August 26, 2014; Bush and Scowcroft, *A World Transformed*, 420.

603. Baker, *The Politics of Diplomacy*, 353–354.

604. Friedman and Karsh, *The Gulf Conflict*, 236; Bush and Scowcroft, *A World Transformed*, 437.

605. Friedman and Karsh, *The Gulf Conflict*, 241; Cheney interview, BOHP, 71.

606. Bush and Scowcroft, *A World Transformed*, 442–443.

607. Philip Zelikow quoted in Cheney, BOHP, 70; Cheney interview, BOHP, 71.

608. Schmitz, *Brent Scowcroft*, 154.

609. Freedman and Karsh, *The Gulf Conflict*, 224; Bush and Scowcroft, *A World Transformed*, 420–421.

610. Scowcroft interview, February 23, 2010; Cheney interview, BOHP, 87.

611. Haass, *War of Necessity, War of Choice*; Bush and Scowcroft, *A World Transformed*; Duffy and Goodgame, *Marching in Place*, 159.

612. "Janet Mullins," folder 4, Box 173 [book notes], Baker Papers, 18–23.

613. Freedman and Karsh, *The Gulf Conflict*, 211; Cheney interview, BOHP, 88; Paul Nitze and Michael F. Stafford, "War Whether We Need It or Not? A Blockade—Plus Bombs—Can Win," *Washington Post*, January 6, 1991.

614. Bush and Scowcroft, *A World Transformed*, 444–446.

615. "Janet Mullins," folder 4, Box 173 [book notes], Baker Papers, 18–23.

616. Cheney interview, BOHP, 88. Nunn later said that the Bush administration "could have done much better" and said he still thought it was the right decision (Nunn interview, April 24, 2012).

617. Friedman and Karsh, *The Gulf Conflict*, 202, 203–204; Smith, *George Bush's War*, 187–188; Cheney interview, BOHP, 57.

618. Bush and Scowcroft, *A World Transformed*, 437–438.

619. Freedman and Karsh, *The Gulf Conflict*, 224; Bush and Scowcroft, *A World Transformed*, 433; Warren H. Donnelly, "Iraq and Nuclear Weapons," Updated December 21, 1990, *CRS Issue Brief*, DNSA, IG 01607, 5, 8; also see Telcon with Prime Minister Felipe Gonzalez of Spain, January 21, 1991, 7:48–8:02 A.M., Camp David, 1991 Telcons, BPR; Richard L. Russell, "CIA's Strategic Intelligence in Iraq," in *Strategic Intelligence: Windows into a Secret World*, eds. Loch Johnson and James J. Wirtz (Los Angeles: Roxbury, 2004), 148.

620. Philip Zelikow quoted in Cheney interview, BOHP, 70.

621. Bush and Scowcroft, *A World Transformed*, 447.

622. Schmitz, *Brent Scowcroft*, 1546.

Chapter 24: War in the Gulf

623. Maureen Dowd, "Storm's Eye: Bush Decides to Go to War," *New York Times*, August 9, 1990, A16.

624. Cheney interview, BOHP, 143–144.

625. Gates interview, BOHP, 65; Freedman and Karsh, *The Gulf Conflict 1990–1991*, 333–341.

626. Telephone conversation with Prime Minister Brian Mulroney of Canada, January 18, 1991, 10:10 A.M.–10:20 A.M., Oval Office, Telcons 1991, BPR.

627. Gates interview, BOHP, 65; Freedman and Karsh, *The Gulf Conflict*, 333–341. Also see President's Phone Call to King Fahd of Saudi Arabia on January 20, 1991, January 20, 1991; 3:45–4:05 P.M., Camp David, 1991 Telcons, BPR.

628. Telephone conversation with Prime Minister Brian Mulroney of Canada, January 18, 1991, 10:10 A.M.–10:20 A.M. Oval Office, 1991 Telcons, BPR; Haass, *War of Necessity, War of Choice*, 91–92.

629. President's Phone Call to King Fahd of Saudi Arabia on January 20, 1991, January 20, 1001; 3:45–4:05 P.M., Camp David, 1991 Telcons, BPR.

630. Telecon to President François Mitterrand of France, October 11, 1990, 3:41–4:00 P.M., The Oval Office, Telcons 1990, BPR; Thomas Pickering interview, March 27, 2014.

631. Roger Hilsman, *George Bush v. Saddam Hussein: Military Success! Political Failure?* (Novato, CA: Presidio Press, 1992), 98.

632. Telephone Conversation with President Mikhail Gorbachev of the Soviet Union, January 18, 1991, 9:23–10:34 A.M., The Oval Office, 1991 Telcons, BPR.

633. *Israel: Foreign Assistance Facts*, Congressional Research Service, March 15, 1990; www.merip org/mer/mer164–165/us-aid-israel?ip_login_no_cache=9e640 ef695ca7d615332202d37f47881.

634. Elliott Abrams interview, October 6, 2010; Nicholas Rostow interview, April 28, 2009; Leslie Gelb interview, April 9, 2014; Duffy and Goodgame, *Marching in Place*, 163.

635. Thomas L. Friedman and Patrick E. Tyler, "After the War: A Reconstruction," *New York Times*, March 2, 1991.

636. Brent Scowcroft, Memorandum for Philip Brady, "Talking Points for President's Meeting with Jewish Leaders," January 31, 1991, Chron file, BPR.

637. See "Telephone Call with President François Mitterrand of France," February 16, [1991], 10:18–10:27 A.M., Kennebunkport, Maine, 1991 Telcons, BPR; Telcon with President Turgut Özal of Turkey on February 19, 1991, February 19, 1991, 5:03–5:16 P.M., The Oval Office, 1991 Telcons, BPR; Telcon with President Mikhail Gorbachev of the USSR on February 22, 1991, February 22, 1991, 11:31–12:43 P.M., The Oval Office, 1991 Telcons, BPR.

638. Telephone Conversation with President Mikhail Gorbachev of the Soviet Union," February 22, 1991, 11:31 A.M.–12:43 P.M., The Oval Office, 1991 Telcons, BPR; also see Telephone Conversation with President Mikhail Gorbachev of the Soviet Union," February 22, 1991, 11:31 A.M.–12:43 P.M., The Oval Office, 1991 Telcons, BPR.

639. "Telephone Conversation with President Mikhail Gorbachev of the Soviet Union," January 18, 1991, 9:23–10:34 A.M., The Oval Office, 1991 Telcons, BPR (there was a ten-minute interruption of the call at 10:10 to 10:20 (at which time

Bush spoke to Prime Minister Mulroney), so it was sixty-one, not seventy-one, minutes in length; Freedman and Karsh, *The Gulf Conflict*, 382–383.

640. "US-USSR and the Persian Gulf," US Department of State *Dispatch*, 2, no. 5 (February 4, 1991).

641. Gates interview, BOHP, 63; Bush and Scowcroft, *A World Transformed*, 432; Dick Cheney interview, May 13, 2009.

642. Gates interview, BOHP, 63; Bush and Scowcroft, *A World Transformed*, 432.

643. Cheney interview, BOHP, 142; Scowcroft interview, June 30, 2013; Russell, "CIA's Strategic Intelligence in Iraq," 149.

644. Brent Scowcroft, February 23, 1991, "Handwritten Notes (of meetings/calls, etc.) 1991 [3]," Handwritten Meeting Notes Files, Meetings files, Brent Scowcroft Collection, BPR.

645. See President's Call to the King of Saudi Arabia, February 2, 1991, 3:03–3:35, Camp David, 1991 Telcons, BPR; Scowcroft interview, March 20, 2014.

646. "America's Wars," Department of Veterans Affairs, May 2013, www.va.gov /opa/publications/factsheets/fs_americas_wars.pdf (August 28, 2014).

647. Gates interview, BOHP, 61. Scowcroft quoted in Rothkopf, *Running the World*, 299.

648. Powell, *My American Journey*, 521, 522.

649. Scowcroft interview, August 12, 2009; Duffy and Goodgame, *Marching in Place*, 150–151.

650. Cheney interview, BOHP, 66.

651. Gates interview, BOHP, 34.

652. Richard Haass, "US (Coalition) War Objectives and War Termination Working Paper," January 1991, cited in Michael R. Gordon, "The Last War Syndrome: How the United States and Iraq Learned the Wrong Lessons from Desert Storm," in *Into the Desert: Reflections on the Gulf War*, ed. Jeffrey Engel (New York: Oxford University Press, 2012), 128–129; Scowcroft interview, January 27, 2010. Also see Telcon with Helmut Kohl, March 21, 1991, 3:02–3:23 P.M., The Oval Office, 1991 Telcons, BPR; Duffy and Goodgame, *Marching in Place*, 166.

653. Powell, *My American Journey*, 527; Rothkopf, *Running the World*, 299.

654. Telephone Conversation with President Turgut Ozal of Turkey, February 5, 1991, 10:02–10:17 A.M., The Oval Office, 1991 Telcons, BPR; Telephone Call with Prime Minister Gonzalez of Spain, February 9, 1991, 7:20–7:40 A.M., Camp David, 1991 Telcons, BPR; also see Ricks, *Fiasco*, 5–6; Thomas E. Ricks, *The Generals: American Military Command from World War II to Today* (New York: Penguin, 2012), 374–385; Hilsman, *Saddam Hussein v. George Bush*, 103.

655. Thomas G. Mahnken, "A Squandered Opportunity? The Decision to End the Gulf War," in *The Gulf War of 1991 Reconsidered*, eds. Andrew J. Bacevich and Efraim Inbar (London: Frank Cass, 2003), 126–136; also see Michael Sterner, "Closing the Gate: The Persian Gulf War Revisited," *Current History* 96, no. 606

(January 1997): 13–19; Gordon and Trainor, *The General's War*, 412–416, 419–420.

656. Powell, *My American Journey*, 527; Rothkopf, *Running the World*, 299.

657. Hilsman, *Saddam Hussein vs. George Bush*, 209, 211–212.

658. Michael Gordon, "The Last War Syndrome," *Into the Desert*, 136–137.

659. Rostow interview, April 28, 2009.

660. Cheney interview, BOHP, 145; Gates interview, BOHP, 64.

661. Scowcroft interview, December 2007.

662. Duffy and Goodgame, *Marching in Place*, 166; Joseph Trento, *Prelude to Terror* (New York: Carroll & Graf, 2005), 349–350; Bush and Scowcroft, *A World Transformed*, 463–464.

663. Kimmitt interview, March 2, 2010; Haass, *War of Necessity, War of Choice*, 135–137; Scowcroft interviews, December, 2007. Also see William J. Crowe Jr. *The Line of Fire: From Washington to the Gulf, the Politics and Battles of the New Military* (New York: Simon & Schuster, 1993), 322, 339.

664. John Podhoretz, "Beyond Bush 41," *New York Post*, August 20, 2002; William Kristol, "Interviews—William Kristol," *Frontline*, PBS, January 14, 2003, www.pbs.org/wgbh/pages/frontline/shows/iraq/interviews/kristol.html.

665. Gordon and Trainor, *The Generals' War*, xiii.

666. "National Security Directive 26: Subject: U.S. Policy Toward the Persian Gulf," October 2, 1989, www.fas.org/irp/offdocs/nsd/nsd26.pdf.

667. Michael Massing, "The Way to War," *New York Review of Books*, March 28, 1991.

668. Duffy and Goodgame, *Marching in Place*, 133.

669. Bush and Scowcroft, *A World Transformed*, 309, 312; Jeffrey Engel, "The Gulf War at the End of the Cold War and Beyond," in *Into the Desert*, 31–33; Gates interview, BOHP, 48.

670. Tutwiler quoted in Martin Yant, *Desert Mirage* (Buffalo, NY: Prometheus Books, 1991), 85.

671. Gordon and Trainor, *The General's War*, 85.

672. J. Stapleton Roy, Executive Secretary, Department of State, "Memorandum for Brent Scowcroft," May 16, 1990, IG01379, DNSA; Freedman and Karsh, *The Gulf Conflict*, 36–37.

673. Gordon, "The Last War Syndrome," 122–123.

674. Kaleem Omar, "Is the State Department Still Keeping April Glaspie Under Wraps?" *News International* (Pakistan), www.informationclearinghouse.info/article 11376.html; Robert Gates, "The Gulf War," Oral History, *Frontline*, PBS, www .pbs.org/wgbh/pages/frontline/gulf/oral/gates/1.html.

675. Gordon, "The Last War Syndrome," 127, 139–140; Bob Zoellick, 1993, Folder 8, Box 173, Baker Papers; Robert Gates, "The Gulf War," *Frontline*.

676. John E. Robson to Brent Scowcroft, "Report to the Economic Analysis Group and the Oil Supply Situation," OA/ID CF00472, "Persian Gulf War 1991

[4], August 14, 1990, John Sununu Series, Office of the Chief of Staff, BPR; "Loss of Iraqi Crude," "Persian Gulf War 1991 [6]," n.d., John Sununu Series, Office of the Chief of Staff, BPR

677. Toryali Hemat quoted in Roy Gutman, *How We Missed the Story: Osama bin Laden, the Taliban, and the Hijacking of Afghanistan* (Sterling, VA: Potomac Books, 2007), 15.

678. Baker, *The Politics of Diplomacy*; Telcon with Turgut Özal, President of Turkey on April 2, 1991, 11:49–11:56 A.M., Islamorada Island, Florida, 1991 Telcons, BPR; Telephone Conversation with President François Mitterrand of France, April 11, 1991, 1:45–2:00 P.M., The Oval Office, 1991 Telcons, BPR.

679. Haass, *Wars of Necessity, Wars of Choice*; Studs Terkel, *The Good War* (New York: Vintage Books, 1984); Ryan C. Crocker, foreword, in *Into the Desert: Reflections on the Gulf War* (New York: Oxford University Press, 2012), xii. The wording "war of necessity" and "war of choice" was previously used by Anthony Lewis in the *New York Times* in a column of 1983 in reference to Israel's wars (William Safire, "On Language," *New York Times*, May 10, 2009).

680. Telephone conversation with F. W. de Klerk of South Africa on February 4, 1991, 9:45–10:05 A.M., 1991 Telcons, BPR; Telcon with President Mubarak of Egypt on February 22, 1991, The Oval Office, 1991 Telcons, BPR.

681. See President George Bush 1990 Telcons, 1991 Telcons, BPR, http://bush library.tamu.edu/research/memcons_telcons.php.

682. Maureen Dowd, "Washington Goes to War, Besieging the TV Set," *New York Times*, January 29, 1991, A13.

683. Zelikow quoted in Cheney interview, BOHP, 68–69.

684. Phillip D. Brady interview, BOHP, 33.

685. Goldberg, "Breaking Ranks"; Freedman and Karsh, *The Gulf Conflict*.

686. Schmitz, *Brent Scowcroft*, 162.

687. Bobbie Kilberg interview, March 9, 2009. Kilberg headed the Office of Public Liaison, and was ranked as a "deputy assistant to the president," the same as Demarest; Scowcroft and Sununu were "assistants to the president."

688. Gates, *From the Shadows*, 458.

689. "Presidential Medal Ceremony White House State Floor," White House Briefing, Federal News Service, July 3, 1991.

690. Goldberg, "Breaking Ranks."

691. Bush and Scowcroft, *A World Transformed*, 505.

692. "To White House via Cabinet Office Channels Only," "Personal for General Scowcroft from Prime Minister Thatcher," September 29, 1990.

693. Gates interview, BOHP, 11; also see Haass, *War of Necessity, War of Choice*, 68.

694. Gates interview, BOHP, 11.

695. Dowd, "Washington Goes to War, Besieging the TV Set."

696. Jack Brennan interview, February 24, 2009; Dave Carney interview, June 15, 2009.

697. Schmitz, *Brent Scowcroft*, 162; Bush and Scowcroft, *A World Transformed*, 487.

698. Haass, *War of Necessity, War of Choice*, 83.

699. Virginia Mulberger interview, July 8, 2013.

Chapter 25: End of Empire

700. John Sununu interview, BOHP, 101; also see Bush and Scowcroft, *A World Transformed*, 286; Quayle, *Standing Firm*, 167.

701. "Mikhail Gorbachev Reflects on Working Toward Peace," Markkula Center for Applied Ethics, Santa Clara University, www.scu.edu/ethics/architects-of -peace/Gorbachev/essay.html.

702. "Meeting with Eduard Shevardnadze, Foreign Minister of the Soviet Union," September 21, 2:00 P.M.–3:05 P.M., The Oval Office," Memcons, BPR.

703. John Lewis Gaddis, *The Cold War: A New History* (New York: Penguin, 2005), 257.

704. "Telcon with Brian Mulroney, Prime Minister of Canada," May 15, 1991, 9:39 A.M.–9:46 A.M., The Oval Office, 1991 Telcons, BPR.

705. Popadiuk interview, BOHP, 29; Bush and Scowcroft, *A World Transformed*, 563.

706. James M. Goldgeier and Michael McFaul, *Power and Purpose: U.S. Policy Toward Russia After the Cold War* (Washington, DC: Brookings Institution Press, 2003), 21. Also see Sigal, *Hang Separately*, 181.

707. Scowcroft interview, BOHP, 85.

708. "The Conventional Armed Forces in Europe (CFE) Treaty and the Adapted CFE Treaty at a Glance," Arms Control Organization, August 2012, www.arms control.org/print/4458.

709. "Treaty Between the United States of America and the Union of the Soviet Socialist Republics on Strategic Offensive Reductions (START I)," Nuclear Threat Initiative, www.nti.org/treaties-and-regimes/treaties-between-united-states-america -and-union-soviet-socialist-republics-strategic-offensive-reductions-start-i-start-ii.

710. Memorandum Scowcroft to Secretary of State et al., "The U.S. Economic Relation with the Soviet Union," May 31, 1991, "Meeting with General Scowcroft, Situation Room, re: U.S. Economic Relationship with Soviet Union," A/ID CF01113-051, Michael Boskin files, Council of Economic Advisers, BPR; James Woolsey interview, May 7, 2009; "A Deal for You," *Washington Times*, March 26, 1992; "Soviet Noncompliance with Arms Control Agreements," March 16, 1992, "Report to Congress, Soviet Non-Compliance, March 1992 [1]," CFO1639-006, John A. Gordon Files, NSC Collection, BPR.

711. Beschloss and Talbott, *At the Highest Levels*, 395.

712. Hutchings, *American Diplomacy and the End of the Cold War*, 329; Marlin Fitzwater interview, February 27, 2008; Naftali, *George H. W. Bush*, 138–139.

713. Hutchings, *American Diplomacy and the End of the Cold War*, 329.

714. Bush and Scowcroft, *A World Transformed*, 516.

715. Kitty Kelley, *The Family: The Real Story of the Bush Dynasty* (New York: Doubleday, 2004), 485.

716. Bush and Scowcroft, *A World Transformed*, 518–536; Scowcroft interview, December 2007; Duffy and Goodgame, *Marching in Place*, 173; Brent Scowcroft interview with Timothy Naftali, Director, Richard Nixon Presidential Library and Museum, "HBO History Maker Series: Brent Scowcroft," October 3, 2007. Also see Quayle, *Standing Firm*, 174; Beschloss and Talbott, *At the Highest Levels*, 422–441; Baker, *The Politics of Diplomacy*, 514–523; Naftali, *George H. W. Bush*, 137; Hutchings, *American Diplomacy and the End of the Cold War*, 329–330.

717. Beschloss and Talbott, *At the Highest Levels*, 430–433.

718. Scowcroft interview, BOHP, 75.

719. Scowcroft interview, September 1, 2009.

720. "Telephone Conversation with President Boris Yeltsin of Russia," December 17, 1991; 10:45–11:15 A.M., Oval Office, 1991 Telcons, BPR; Hutchings, *American Diplomacy and the End of the Cold War*, 336.

721. "Telephone Conversation with President Boris Yeltsin of Russia," December 17, 1991; 10:45–11:15 A.M. Oval Office, 1991 Telcons, BPR; Hutchings, *American Diplomacy and the End of the Cold War*, 336; Plokhy, *The Last Empire*, 263.

722. Bush and Scowcroft, *A World Transformed*, 563.

723. Beschloss and Talbott, *At the Highest Levels*, 448–449; Sigal, *Hang Separately*, 252–256.

724. Memorandum of Conversation, "NATO Summit," November 7, 1991, 5:35–6:00 P.M., Sheraton Hotel, Conference Center, Rome, Memcons, BPR.

725. Memorandum of Conversation, "Luncheon Meeting with President Gorbachev," October 29, 1991, Memcons, BPR.

726. Beschloss and Talbott, *At the Highest Levels*, 412–413, 441, 444.

727. Ann Devroy, quoted in Beschloss and Talbott, *At the Highest Levels*, 438–444; Plokhy, *The Last Empire*, 145.

728. Bush and Scowcroft, *A World Transformed*, 542, 543–544.

729. Popadiuk, BOHP, 29; also see Goldgeier and McFaul, *Power and Purpose*, 35; Plokhy, *The Last Empire*, 199–201.

730. Beschloss and Talbott, *At the Highest Levels*, 447, 455.

731. Ibid., 455.

732. National Security Council, October 22, 1991, 12:13 EDT, "USSR Contingency Papers (Past)," Burns, R. Nicholas, NSC, OA/ID CF01498-008, BPR; Bush and Scowcroft, *A World Transformed*, 556–557.

733. "Beschloss and Talbott, *At the Highest Levels*, 402–405; Scowcroft interview, December 2007; Naftali, *George H. W. Bush*, 136.

734. Sam Nunn interview, April 23, 2012; Susan Koch interview, August 31, 2014.

735. Kanter interview, March 24, 2009; Daalder and Destler, *In the Shadow of the Oval Office*, 188–190.

736. Daalder and Destler, *In the Shadow of the Oval Office*, 188–189; Kanter interview, March 24, 2009.

737. Kanter quoted in Daalder and Destler, *In the Shadow of the Oval Office*, 189; Kanter interview, March 24, 2009.

738. Scowcroft interview, April 25, 2013; Kanter interview, March 24 and 27, 2009; Brent Scowcroft, Memorandum for D. Allan Bromley, February 22, 1992, "International Fund to Aid Basic Science in Russia," Russia files, WHORM 325472 CO165, Bush Library; Brent Scowcroft, "Meeting with President of the Russian Federation Boris Yeltsin," February 1, 1992, Camp David, 10:00 A.M., Russia files, WHORM 324647 CO165; John A. Gordon, "Concrete Progress on Nuclear Initiatives," February 2, 1992, "June 1992 [U.S.-Russian] Summit—March 1992], John A. Gordon Files, NSC Collection, BPR. Also see Brent Scowcroft to George Bush, "Re: Foreign Minister Kozyrev's Appeal to Secretary Baker to Help Save Russian Science," January 31, 1992, OA/ID CF01939, "Brain Drain—February 1992 [2 of 2]," John Gordon Files, NSC Collection, BPR.

739. See, for example, Ray S. Cline, "Technology Proliferation from the Soviet Republics: Threat and Opportunity," United States Global Strategy Council, n.d., [circa October 25, 1991], OA/ID CF01343, "CIS-Folder #1 [3 of 3] Daniel Poneman Files," NSC Collection, BPR; Memorandum, Graham Allison to General Brent Scowcroft, November 21, 1991, OA/ID CF01343, "CIS-Folder #1 [3 of 3]," Daniel Poneman Files, NSC Collection, BPR, Daniel Poneman Memorandum for Jonathan Howe, "Combating the Spread of Militarily-Useful Technology from the Former Soviet Union," March 16, 1992, "Brain Drain—March 1992," John A. Gordon files, NSC Collection, BPR.

740. Susan Koch interview, personal communication, September 4, 2014; also see Sigal, *Hang Separately*, 232–233.

741. Susan Koch interview, February 2009; Kanter interview, March 24, 2009; Kimmitt personal communication, August 25, 2014.

742. See "Nunn-Lugar Revisited," *National Security Archive Electronic Briefing Book* No. 447, Tom Blanton and Svetlana Savranskaya with Ann Melyakova, November 23, 2013, www2.gwu.edu/~nsarchiv/NSAEBB/NSAEBB447.

743. Goldgeier and McFaul, *Power and Purpose*, 51.

744. Gates, *From the Shadows*, 525–527; Brent Scowcroft, Memorandum for the President, "Turmoil in the Soviet Union and U.S. Policy," August 18, 1990, NSC PA Files, Document Number 9006249, NSC Collection, BPR.

745. Scowcroft quoted in Goldgeier and McFaul, *Power and Purpose*, 42–43; see Bush and Scowcroft, *A World Transformed*, 543–545; also see Sigal, *Hang Separately*, 232–233.

746. Memo from Daniel Poneman to Jonathan Howe, "Re: DC Meeting on the Spread of Militarily-Useful Technologies from the Former Soviet Union," March 16, 1992, OA/ID CFO1637-005, "Brain Drain—March 1992," John A. Gordon series, NSC Collection, BPR.

747. Memorandum from Ed A. Hewett for Brent Scowcroft, "Discussion at the B-C-S Breakfast on Planning for Soviet Contingencies," November 25, 1991, OA/ID CFO 1656-006, "Contingency Group, December 1991," John A. Gordon records, NSC Collection, BPR; also see Memorandum for the Record from Daniel Poneman, "FSU Hemorrhage Working Group," December 18, 1991, OA/ID CF01656-002, "Brain Drain," John A. Gordon records, NSC Collection, BPR.

748. Susan J. Koch, "The Presidential Nuclear Initiatives of 1991–1992," Center for the Study of Weapons of Mass Destruction Case Study 5 (Washington, DC: National Defense University Press, September 2012), 14–15. Bush and Scowcroft, *A World Transformed*, 542, 544–546; Cheney interview, BOHP, 115.

749. Susan J. Koch, "The Presidential Nuclear Initiatives of 1991–1992," 19.

750. Koch, "The Presidential Nuclear Initiatives of 1991–1992," 19–20.

751. Baker, *The Politics of Diplomacy*, 669–671.

752. "START II and Its Extension Protocol at a Glance," Arms Control Association, January 2003, www.armscontrol.org/factsheets/start2; Susan J. Koch, personal communication, September 4, 2014.

753. Nicholas F. Brady, Memorandum for the President, "Visit to the Soviet Union, September 18–20, 1991," OA/ID CFO1498-010, "USSR Economic Assistance [2]," subject file, R. Nicholas Burns and Ed Hewitt Series, NSC Collection, BPR.

754. Scheid interview, January 26, 2009.

755. Scowcroft interview, February 23, 2010; Kanter interview, March 24, 2009; Andrew Futter, *Ballistic Missile Defence and US National Security Policy: Normalisation and Acceptance after the Cold War* (New York: Routledge, 2013), 15. See John Newhouse, *War and Peace in the Nuclear Age* (New York: Knopf, 1989).

756. US Mission US NATO to US Secretary of State, "Intervention by Secretary Baker at the NAC Ministerial, December 19, 1991," file "Commonwealth, December 1991," OA/ID CF01956-005, John A. Gordon Series, NSC Collection, BPR.

757. "The President's News Conference Following the North Atlantic Treaty Organization Summit in London, United Kingdom," *Public Papers of the Presidents of the United States: George Bush: 1990*, Book II, 972.

758. Brent Scowcroft to President Bush, "Proposed Presidential Letters to the London Summit Participants Concerning the Meeting with Gorbachev," n.d., "USSR Chron File: July 1991," OA/ID CF01407-006, Chronological Files, R. Nicholas Burns and Ed Hewitt Series, NCS Collection, BPR; Brent Scowcroft, "Meeting on Soviet Economic Issues and the London Economic Summit," June 21, 1991, Cabinet Room, 8:30–9:30 A.M., "G-7," OA/ID CFO1486-019, R. Nicholas Burns and Ed Hewitt Series, NSC Collection, BPR.

759. Timothy Deal interview, June 9, 2009; Scowcroft interview, November 4, 2010; Plokhy, *The Last Empire*, 330–332. See also Brent Scowcroft, "Meeting on Soviet Economic Issues and the London Economic Summit," June 21, 1991, Cabinet Room, 8:30–9:30 A.M., "G-7," OA/ID CFO1486-019, R. Nicholas Burns and Ed Hewitt Series, NSC Collection, BPR.

760. Beschloss and Talbott, *At the Highest Levels*, 381–392; Sigal, *Hang Separately*, 220–224.

761. Timothy Deal interview, June 9, 2009; Scowcroft interview, November 4, 2010.

762. Scowcroft, May 2, 1991, "Handwritten Notes (of meetings/calls, etc.) 1991 [3]," "Handwritten Meeting Notes Files," Meetings files, Brent Scowcroft Collection, BPR; Memo Brent Scowcroft to Secretary of State, et al., "The U.S. Economic Relation with the Soviet Union," May 31, 1991, "Meeting with General Scowcroft, Situation Room, re: U.S. Economic Relationship with Soviet Union," OA/ID CF01113-051, Michael Boskin files, Council of Economic Advisers, BPR,.

763. Ibid.; Goldgeier and McFaul, *Power and Purpose*, 61; Halberstam, *War in a Time of Peace*, 75.

764. Gates, *From the Shadows*, 504; Beschloss and Talbott, *At the Highest Levels*, 407.

765. Beschloss and Talbott, *At the Highest Levels*, 407; Sigal, *Hang Separately*, 225.

766. See Daniel L. Bond, "The Role of Export Credit Agencies in the 'New East,'" 384–386, and Patricia A. Wertman, "The External Financial Position of the Former Soviet Union: From Riches to Rags?" 398–400, in Joint Economic Committee, *The Former Soviet Union in Transition*, Vol. 1, US 103d Congress, 1st Session, S. Print 103–111 (Washington, DC.: US GPO, 1993).

767. Goldgeier and McFaul, *Power and Purpose*, 61; Michael Parks, "Soviet Union Granted Billions in Debt Relief," *Los Angeles Times*, November 22, 1991, http://articles.latimes.com/1991–11–22/news/mn-47_1_soviet-union; Toby Gati interview, May 12, 2014. Also see Memorandum from Under Secretary Mulford to Secretary Brady, "Preparing Russia's Rescheduling," August 31, 1992, in Paul Wonnacott files, Council of Economic Advisers, "USSR(CIS & NIS)" OA/ID CF01111012, BPR; Memorandum David Mulford (Treasury), Robert Green (Agriculture), Paul Wonnacott (CEA) to General Scowcroft, September 4, 1992, OA/ID CF01111012, Paul Wonnacott files, Council of Economic Advisers, "USSR (CIS & NIS)" BPR.

768. "U.S. Assistance to Russia," June 17, 1992, Press Release, The White House, Office of the Press Secretary, OA/ID CF01339, in "[Bush/Yeltsin Washington] Summit [2], [June 15–16] 1992, Susan Koch files, NSC Collection, BPR; Goldgeier and McFaul, *Power and Purpose*, 77–78; Plokhy, *The Last Empire*, 237.

769. Brent Scowcroft, "Meeting with President of the Russian Federation Boris Yeltsin," February 1, 1992, Camp David, 10:00 A.M., OA/ID CO165 324647, "Russia" file, WHORM, BPR.

770. Goldgeier and McFaul, *Power and Purpose*, 79, 81. Also see Gates, *From the Shadows*, 504.

771. See Monica Crowley, *Nixon in Winter* (New York: Random House, 1998). Crowley recounts the frequent contact Nixon had with his former military assistant and deputy national security advisor.

772. "Statement on Signing the FREEDOM Support Act," October 24, 1992, *Administration of George Bush, 1992* (Washington: GPO 1993), 1973–1974 "FREEDOM" stood for the "Freedom for Russia and Emerging Eurasian Democracies and Open Markets."

773. Memorandum of Conversation, "Lunch with President Mikhail Gorbachev of the USSR," July 30, 1991, 1:28–2:07 P.M., Official Residence Dining Hall, Kremlin, Memcons, BPR.

774. "Role of the American Private Sector in the Economic and Democratic Development of the Soviet Union and Its Constituent Republics" [n.a.], October 21, 1991, "USSR Economic Assistance [2]," Nick Burns, Ed Hewitt," CFO1498-010, NSC, BPR.

775. Memcon, "Private Plenary Session, 1992 Munich Economic Summit, July 7, 1992, 10:20 A.M.–12:30 P.M.," Residencz—Vierschlimmelsaal, Munich, OA/ID CF00971, "Munich Economic Summit [1]," Economic Summit Files, Eric Melby Files, NSC Collection, BPR,.

776. Memcon, "Joint Plenary Session, 1992 Munich Economic Summit," Wednesday July 8, 1992, Munich, OA/ID CF00971, "Munich Economic Summit [1]," Economic Summit Files, Eric Melby Files, NSC Collection, BPR; Sigal, *Hang Separately*, 229.

777. Baker, *The Politics of Diplomacy*, 635; Bush, quoted in Frances Fitzgerald, *Way Out in the Blue: Reagan, Star Wars and the End of the Cold War* (New York: Simon & Schuster, 2000), 464; Scowcroft interview, December 2007.

778. "Private Plenary Session, 1992 Munich Economic Summit, July 7, 1992, 10:20 A.M.–12:30 P.M.," Residencz—Vierschlimmelsaal, Munich, OA/ID CF00971, "Munich Economic Summit [1]," Economic Summit Files, Eric Melby Files, NSC Collection, BPR,; Goldgeier and McFaul, *Power and Purpose*, 84–86. Also see Sigal, *Hang Separately*.

779. Beschloss and Talbott, *At the Highest Levels*, 447; Baker, *Politics of Diplomacy*, 583; Goldgeier and McFaul, *Power and Purpose*, 49; Gates, *From the Shadows*, 536. Also see "Telcon with President Boris Yeltsin of the Republic of Russia, USSR," August 20, 1991, 8:18–8:15 A.M., The Oval Office, 1991 Telcons, BPR; "Memorandum of Telephone Conversation with President Boris Yeltsin of the Russian Republic, USSR," August 21, 1991, 8:30–9:05 A.M, Kennebunkport, 1991 Telcons, Bush Library; Memorandum of Telephone Conversation, Telcon with Boris Yeltsin, President of the Republic of Russia, USSR," September 27, 1991, 12:30–12:36 P.M, Oval Office, 1991 Telcons, BPR.

780. Bush and Scowcroft, *A World Transformed*, 563–564.

781. "Welcome Back Professor Rice," Interview with Condoleezza Rice, *Newsletter*, Spring 1991, Center for Russian & Eastern European Studies, Stanford University, 8.

782. Scowcroft interview, BOHP, 84.

783. Ibid.

784. Scowcroft interview, BOHP, 85.

785. Richard Holbrooke, *To End a War* (New York: Random House, 1998), 26–28.

786. Central Intelligence Agency, "NIE 15-90: Yugoslavia Transformed, 18 Oct. 1990," 656–659, in Patrick S. Roberts and Robert P. Saldin, "On a Need to Know Basis: The President's Desire for Intelligence Opacity," manuscript, Policy History Conference, June 4–7, 2014.

787. See Halberstam, *War in a Time of Peace*, 81–84, 127; Baker, *Politics of Diplomacy*, 643.

788. Halberstam, *War in a Time of Peace*, 94.

789. Lenard J. Cohen, *Broken Bonds: Yugoslavia's Disintegration and Balkan Politics in Transition*, 2nd ed. (Boulder, CO: Westview Press, 1999), 219.

790. Ibid., 221.

791. Memorandum of Conversation, "Meeting with Manfred Woerner, Secretary-General of NATO," June 25, 1991, 2:45–3:15 P.M., Oval Office, MemCons, BPR.

792. Ibid.

793. Ibid., 228–230.

794. Memorandum of Conversation, "NATO Summit," November 7, 1991, 5:35–6:00 P.M., Sheraton Hotel, Conference Center, Rome, 1991 MemCons, BPR.

795. Arnold Kanter, in Oral History Roundtables, "The Bush Administration National Security Council," April 29, 1999.

796. Kimmitt II, BOHP, 23–24.

797. David C. Gompert, "The United States and Yugoslavia's Wars," in *The World and Yugoslavia's Wars*, ed. Richard H. Ullman (New York: Council on Foreign Relations, 1996).

798. Phyllis E. Oakley interview, ADST, 98; Holbrooke, *To End a War*, 22–23.

799. Lawrence Eagleburger interview, April 9, 2009; Kanter and Haass quoted in "The Bush Administration National Security Council," 26–27; Halberstam, *War in a Time of Peace*, 148.

800. Warren Zimmermann, *Origins of a Catastrophe: Yugoslavia and Its Destroyers—America's Last Ambassador Tells What Happened and Why* (New York: Times Books, 1996), 215; Baker, *Politics of Diplomacy*, 648–650.

801. Halberstam, *War in a Time of Peace*, 125; Thomas G. Weiss, "Collective Spinelessness: U.N. Actions in the Former Yugoslavia," in *The World and Yugoslavia's Wars*, ed. Richard H. Ullman (New York: Council on Foreign Relations, 1996), 59–96, 59–60.

802. Halberstam, *War in a Time of Peace*, 133–135; William Safire, "On Language," *New York Times*, March 14, 1993.

803. Louis Sell, *Slobodan Milosevic and the Destruction of Yugoslavia* (Durham, NC: Duke University Press, 2003), 265.

804. Ibid., 264.

805. Ibid.

806. Ibid., 266–267; Cheney interview, BOHP, 154; Richard H. Ullman, "The Wars in Yugoslavia and the International System After the Cold War," in *The World and Yugoslavia's Wars*, 9–41.

807. See, for example, Gorbachev, *Memoirs*, 548–549.

808. David Gompert, "The United States and Yugoslavia's Wars," in *The World and Yugoslavia's Wars*, 128.

809. Zimmermann, *Origins of a Catastrophe*, 217–218, 237–239.

810. Scowcroft interview, December 2007 (n.d.).

811. "The United States Army in Somalia 1992–1994," Prepared by Richard W. Stewart, U.S. Army Center of Military History, CMH Pub 70-81-1, 8, www.history .army.mil/brochures/Somalia/Somalia.htm.

812. John L. Hersh and Robert B. Oakley, *Somalia and Operation Restore Hope: Reflections on Peacemaking and Peacekeeping* (Washington, DC: United States Institute of Peace Press, 1995), 25.

813. Valerie J. Lofland, "Somalia: U.S. Intervention and Operation Restore Hope," 54, 57–58, www.au.af.mil/au/awd/awcgate/navy/pmi/somalia1.pdf, accessed June 20, 2014.

814. Ibid., 56.

815. Marianne K. Cusimano, "Operation Restore Hope: The Bush Administration's Decision to Intervene in Somalia," Case 463, *Pew Case Studies in International Affairs* (Washington, DC: The Institute for the Study of Diplomacy), 8.

816. Walter S. Poole, *The Effort to Save Somalia, August 1992–March 1994* (Washington, DC: Joint History Office, Office of the Chairman of the Joint Chiefs of Staff, 2005), 10; Don Oberdorfer, "The Path to Intervention; A Massive Tragedy 'We Could Do Something About,'" *Washington Post*, December 6, 1992; Jonathan Howe interviews, June 20 and June 27, 2014.

817. Poole, *The Effort to Save Somalia*, 10; John L. Hersh and Robert B. Oakley, *Somalia and Operation Restore Hope: Reflections on Peacemaking and Peacekeeping* (Washington, DC: United States Institute of Peace Press, 1995) 43; Halberstam, *War in a Time of Peace*, 251; Howe interview, June 20, 2014.

818. Lofland, "Somalia," 60.

819. Poole, *The Effort to Save Somalia*, 20–21; Colin Powell with Joseph E. Persico, *My American Journey* (New York: Random House, 1999), 565; Howe interview, June 20, 2014; Oberdorfer, "The Path to Intervention."

820. Oberdorfer, "The Path to Intervention"; "Appendix A, UN Security Council Resolution 794," December 3, 1992, in Hersh and Oakley, *Somalia and Operation*

Restore Hope, 177–181 (also see 45); Robert Baumann and Lawrence A. Yates with Versaille F. Washington, *"My Clan Against the World": US and Coalition Forces in Somalia 1992–1994* (Fort Leavenworth, KS: Combat Studies Institute Press, 2011), 30.

821. Poole, *The Effort to Save Somalia*, 23.

822. James L. Woods, "U.S. Decisionmaking During Operations in Somalia," in *Learning from Somalia: The Lessons of Armed Humanitarianism*, eds. Walter S. Clarke and Jeffrey Herbst (Boulder: Westview Press, 1997), 159; Baumann and Yates, *"My Clan Against the World,"* 18.

823. Howe interview, June 27, 2014.

824. Hersh and Oakley, *Somalia and Operation Restore Hope*, x–xiii, 19; Halberstam, *War in a Time of Peace*, 254.

825. Poole, *The Effort to Save Somalia*, 70.

826. Lofland, "Somalia," 53.

Chapter 26: China Rising and the International Economy

827. Scowcroft interview, August 3, 2011.

828. Scowcroft interview, BOHP, 60.

829. Cheng Chu-yuan, *Behind the Tiananmen Massacre: Behind the Social, Political, and Economic Ferment in China* (Boulder, CO: Westview Press, 1990), 194; Gilley, *Tiger on the Brink*, 61–62.

830. Lilley, *China Hands*, 327; Tyler, *A Great Wall*, 361.

831. Mann, *About Face*, 256; James Mann, "US-China Relations Reach an Unhappy Upcoming Anniversary," *Los Angeles Times*, March 18, 1990.

832. Lampton, *Same Bed, Different Dreams*, 30; Tyler, *A Great Wall*, 371; Mann, "US-China Relations Reach an Unhappy Upcoming Anniversary"; Dan Quayle quoted in Mann, *About Face*, 235.

833. Mann, *About Face*, 239–240.

834. "Brent Scowcroft to POTUS," Re: China—Economic Effects of the Loss of MFN, May 18, 1990, "China: Non-Tiananmen (May 1990)," OA/ID 91134-004, Non-Tiananmen files, China Chronological Files, Brent Scowcroft Series, BPR; Fred McClure interview, BOHP, 104; James A. Baker, "Points to be made with Republican Senators on China," 1990 January, Box 108 Folder 13, Baker papers.

835. Suettinger, *Beyond Tiananmen*, 113–114; Qian, *Ten Episodes*, 147–149. For a somewhat slightly different account, see Kimmitt II, BOHP, 13–14.

836. Suettinger, *Beyond Tiananmen*, 113–114; Qian, *Ten Episodes*, 147–149.

837. Suettinger, *Beyond Tiananmen*, 119.

838. Ibid., 130; Mann, *About Face*, 251; Qian, *Ten Episodes*, 147–149.

839. Gilley, *Tiger on the Brink*, 184; Tyler, *A Great Wall*, 375; Kissinger, *On China*, 441.

840. Gantt interview, November 4, 2009; Barbara Bush, *A Memoir*, 97, 140, 287.

841. Carl E. Walter and Fraser J. T. Howie, *Red Capitalism: The Fragile Financial Foundation of China's Extraordinary Rise* (New York: John Wiley & Sons, 2011), 31–33.

842. Ibid., 115; Parmet, *George Bush*, 375. One of the benchmarks in the rise of capitalism in China was when Shenzhen Development Bank, one of the Chinese state owned enterprises, began to pay a dividend and declared a two-for-one stock split. And SDB's shares ran from RMB40 to RMB120 just before June 4, 1991, and then backed down to RMB90.

843. J. Stapleton Roy interview, March 27, 2009; Gilley, *Tiger on the Brink*, 240; Tyler, *A Great Wall*, 375.

844. Peter Morici, "Barring Entry? China and the WTO," *Current History*, September 1997; Carla Hills interview, BOHP, 70.

845. Gilley, *Tiger on the Brink*, 187; Walter and Howie, *Red Capitalism*, 144–145.

846. Walter and Howie, *Red Capitalism*.

847. Kissinger, *On China*, 467–469. See Lampton, *Same Bed, Different Dreams*, 33–43.

848. Douglas Paal interview, March 5, 2009; Scowcroft interview, BOHP, 66.

849. Suettinger, *Beyond Tiananmen*, 139–143; Mann, *About Face*, 271; Tyler, *A Great Wall*, 377–378; Paal interview, 5 March 2009; Scowcroft interview, August 3, 2011; Scowcroft interview, BOHP, 65–66.

850. Mann, *About Face*, 259, 271–272.

851. Ibid.

852. Ibid., 186–187; Scowcroft interview, August 3, 2011.

853. George Lardner Jr., "U.S. Began Lifting Business, Military Sanctions on China Months Ago," *Washington Post*, December 12, 1989, A20.

854. Scowcroft interview, BOHP, 64.

855. Bush and Scowcroft, *A World Transformed*, 176; Vogel, *Deng Xiaoping*, 713–714.

856. Scowcroft interview, BOHP, 54–55.

857. Tyler, *A Great Wall*, 404.

858. Bao Tong quoted in Jamil Anderlini, "Interview: Tanks Were Roaring and Bullets Flying," *Financial Times*, May 30/31, 2009.

859. Andrew Bacevich, *American Empire: The Realities and Consequences of U.S. Diplomacy* (Cambridge, MA: Harvard University Press, 2002), 64–68.

860. Scowcroft interview, BOHP, 62.

861. Brent Scowcroft and Richard N. Haass, "Bringing Foreign Affairs Back into Clearer Focus," *Washington Times*, February 15, 1996.

862. Scowcroft interview, January 27, 2010.

863. Scowcroft interview, May 10, 2010.

864. Sandra Kristoff quoted in "China Policy and the National Security Council," Oral History Roundtables, November 4, 1999, 28; Robert Suettinger quoted in "China Policy and the National Security Council," 30–31.

865. James R. Lilley quoted in "China Policy and the National Security Council," Oral History Roundtables, November 4, 1999, 21.

866. Also see J. Stapleton Roy, Director, Kissinger Institute on China and the US, Woodrow Wilson Center International Center for Scholars, "China Since June 4, 1989: What Has Changed? Panel II," Thursday June 4, 2009, Carnegie Endowment for International Peace, Transcript by Federal News Service Washington, DC.

867. "Memorandum of Conversation," President Bush's Meeting with General Secretary Zhao Ziyang of the People's Republic of China, Great Hall of the People, Beijing, China, February 26, 1989, 1991 MemCons, BPR.

868. Scowcroft interview, May 10, 2010.

869. Karl Jackson interview, June 11, 2009.

870. Scowcroft interview, BOHP, 66–68; Jackson interview, June 11, 2009.

871. Scowcroft interview, May 5, 2010; also see George A. Lincoln, *Economics of National Security*, planned and edited by George A. Lincoln, William S. Stone, and Thomas H. Harvey (New York: Prentice-Hall, 1950).

872. Eric Melby interview, May 14, 2009; Carla Hills interview, October 9, 2009; Carla Hills interview, BOHP, 26.

873. Timothy Deal interview, June 9, 2009; Hills interview, October 9, 2009.

874. Scowcroft interview, BOHP, 34.

875. Hills interview, BOHP, 22.

876. Duffy and Goodgame, *Marching in Place*, 107; Hills interview, October 9, 2009.

877. Kimmitt personal communication, August 26, 2014; "About Us," Asia-Pacific Economic Cooperation, www.apec.org/About-Us/About-APEC/History.aspx; www.transatlanticbusiness.org/about-us/history-mission.

878. Melby interview, May 14, 2009; William Reilly interview, October 6, 2010.

879. Melby interview, May 14, 2009.

880. Ibid.

Chapter 27: A New World Order—or the Resumption of History?

881. Bush and Scowcroft, *A World Transformed*, 353–355; Don Oberdorfer, "Bush's Talk of a 'New World Order': Foreign Policy Tool or Mere Slogan?" *Washington Post*, May 26, 1991; Doyle McManus, "Bush's Vision of a 'New World Order,' Still Unclear," *Los Angeles Times*, February 18, 1991; Hutchings, *American Diplomacy and the End of the Cold War*, 145; Popadiuk, *The Leadership of George Bush*, 151–152; Scowcroft interview, May 23, 2011. One report has the two men catching three fish, another, none. Scowcroft interview, BOHP, 52.

882. Scowcroft quoted in Oberdorfer, "Bush's Talk of a 'New World Order.'"

883. See Memorandum of Dan Jahn to Tony Snow, Speechwriters, Researchers, "Presidential References to New World Order," June 26, 1991, "A New World Order, 1990–1991 [1]," OA/ID 08487, Speech Files, Backup Files, Alpha File 1987–1991, White House Office of Speechwriting, BPR; Fax from Michael Schneider, USIA, to Nancy Bearg Dyke, "New World Order-References," July 18, 1991, Nancy Bearg Dyke Series, NSC Collection, BPR.

884. Toby Gati interview, May 12, 2014.

885. Bush and Scowcroft, *A World Transformed*, 354–355. Also see Derek Chollet and James Goldgeier, *America Between the Wars: From 11/9 to 9/11* (New York: PublicAffairs, 2008), 7.

886. Bush and Scowcroft, *A World Transformed*, 354–355. Also see Chollet and Goldgeier, *America Between the Wars*, 7; Nicholas Rostow, "Toward a New World Order," draft March 28, 1991, "New World Order" file, Nicholas Rostow Papers, NSC Collection, BPR.

887. President George Bush, "Remarks and a Question-and-Answer Session at a Meeting of the Economic Club in New York, New York," February 6, 1991, *Public Papers of the Presidents: George Bush, 1991* (Washington, DC: US GPO, 1992), 123–124; Popadiuk, *The Leadership of George Bush*, 138. Also see Brent Scowcroft, "Remarks to the Graduating Class of the Citadel," Charleston, South Carolina, Saturday May 11, 1991, "New World Order" file, Nancy Bearg Dyke Series, NSC Collection, BPR.

888. Robert Gates interview, April 17, 2012; memorandum for Brent Scowcroft from Nicholas Rostow, Subject: New World Order, January 25, 1991. "New World Order," Nancy Bearg Dyke Series, NSC Collection, BPR.

889. Henry Kissinger, "False Dreams of a New World Order," *Washington Post*, February 26, 1991, A21.

890. Walter Russell Mead, "The 'New World Order': Will We Be Its Arsenal— or Its Infantry," *Washington Post*, February 17, 1991. But see Charles Krauthammer, "Bless Our Pax Americana," *Washington Post*, March 22, 1991; Charles Krauthammer, "The Unipolar Moment," *Foreign Affairs* 70, no. 1 (1991): 23–33.

891. A. M. Rosenthal, "On My Mind: The New World Order Dies," *New York Times*, January 15, 1991; William Pfaff, "The Illusion of Founding a New World Order," *The Sun* (Baltimore), January 28, 1991; Kissinger, "False Dreams of a New World Order"; "New World Order: What's New? Which World? Whose Orders? *The Economist*, February 23, 1991; Stanley R. Sloan, "The US Role in a New World Order: Prospects for George Bush's Global Vision," *CRS Report for Congress* (Washington: Congressional Research Service, March 28, 1991), 26. Also see Freedman and Karsh, *The Gulf Conflict 1990–1991*, 215–216; Kellner, *The Persian Gulf TV War*, 99.

892. Walter Russell Mead, "Germany and Japan—Dragging Their Boots," *New York Times*, February 3, 1991; Kissinger, "False Dreams of a New World Order";

Jeane Kirkpatrick quoted in McManus, "Bush's Vision of a 'New World Order' Still Unclear"; Pfaff, "The Illusion of Finding a New World Order"; "New World Order: What's New? Which World? Whose Orders?" *The Economist*, February 23, 1991, 25; Sloan, "The US Role in a New World Order," 28–30.

893. See, for instance, John Steinbruner, "The Rule of Law," *Bulletin of the Atomic Scientists*, June 1991, 20.

894. A. M. Rosenthal, "The New World Order Dies," *New York Times*, January 15, 1991; Sloan, "The US Role in a New World Order," 27–28.

895. See, for instance, "New World Order: What's New?," 25.

896. George Bush, "Remarks and a Question and Answer Session at a Meeting of the Economic Club in New York, New York," February 6, 1991, *Public Papers of the Presidents: George Bush: 1991* (Washington, DC: US GPO, 1992), 123–124.

897. David Gergen, "Bye-Bye to the New World Order," *U.S. News & World Report*, July 8, 1991, 21; Scowcroft interview, April 10, 2009; Bush and Scowcroft, *A World Transformed*, 355.

898. Don Oberdorfer, "Bush's Talk of a 'New World Order': Foreign Policy Tool or Mere Slogan?" *Washington Post*, May 26, 1991.

899. Gergen, "Bye-Bye to the New World Order"; Richard Haass interview, March 16, 2009.

900. Scowcroft interview, BOHP, November 12–13, 1999.

901. Scowcroft interview, May 23, 2010.

902. "Remarks by the President to the United Nations General Assembly," September 23, 1991, United Nations, New York.

903. Scowcroft interviews, December 2, 2009, and May 23, 2011.

904. Scowcroft interview, June 22, 2009; Roy, April 9, 2009.

905. Dowd and Friedman, "The Fabulous Bush and Baker Boys," 61.

906. See, for instance, Dennis Ross, BOHP, 28; Scowcroft interview, September 1, 2009; Kimmitt personal communication, August 26, 2014.

907. Scowcroft interview, May 23, 2011; Fitzwater, *Call the Briefing!*, 274ff, 283.

908. See George Bush Memcons and Telcons, BPR.

909. Brent Scowcroft in "The Role of the National Security Advisor," Oral History Roundtables, October 25, 1999, 20.

910. See Chollet and Goldgeier, *American Between the Wars*, 43–47; Stephen Hadley interview, April 7, 2009.

911. Scowcroft interview, May 5, 2010.

912. Bush and Scowcroft, *A World Transformed*, 400.

913. Rep. Les Aspin, Chairman, House Armed Services Committee, "The Bush Quick Fix Foreign Policy: Winning the War But Forgetting the Peace," paper presented to the Center for National Policy, Washington, DC, December 19, 1991, OA/ID CF 01343, "CIS [4 folders]," Daniel Poneman Series, NSC Collection, BPR

914. Scowcroft interview, BOHP, 85.

915. Scowcroft interview, June 22, 2010; Kanter interview, March 24, 2009.

916. Scowcroft interview, May 5, 2010; Acheson quoted in Nicholas Rostow, "Toward a New World Order," draft 3/28/91, "New World Order" file, Nicholas Rostow Papers, NSC Collection, BPR.

917. George H. W. Bush interview, December 18, 2009.

918. Dave Carney interview, June 15, 2009.

919. Burns interview, April 4, 2009; Cheney interview, May 11, 2009.

920. James A. Baker III interview II, March 17, 2011, BOHP, 15.

921. David Gompert quoted in "The Bush Administration National Security Council," Oral History Roundtables, October 29, 1999, 35.

922. See John P. Burke, *Honest Broker? The National Security Advisor and Presidential Decision Making* (College Station: Texas A&M Press, 2009).

923. Kimmitt interview, March 2, 2010.

924. Gelb interview, April 9, 2014.

925. Andrea Mitchell interview, May 18, 2009. Also see Editors' Introduction, "National security advisors: Profiles," in *Fateful Decisions*, 182; Rodman, *Presidential Command*.

Part V: Citizen-Statesman

Chapter 28: An Independent Voice

1. Brent Scowcroft, "Build a Coalition," *Washington Post*, October 16, 2001.

2. Bush quoted in Colin Powell with Joseph E. Persico, *My American Journey* (New York: Random House, 1999), 561.

3. Richard Thornburgh interview, BOHP, 125; Dan Quayle interview, BOHP, 71.

4. Dave Carney interview, June 15, 2009.

5. Scowcroft interview, BOHP, 73.

6. Ibid.; Sigmund Rogich interview, BOHP, 106.

7. Nicholas Rostow interview, April 28, 2009.

8. Scowcroft interview, January 3, 2014.

9. Timothy Naftali, *George H. W. Bush* (New York: Times Books, 2007), 143–144; Scowcroft interview, January 3, 2014; Parmet, *George Bush*, 321.

10. Quayle interview, BOHP, 75, 79; Herbert S. Parmet, *George Bush: Life of a Lone Star Yankee* (New York: Scribner, 1997), 500–507; Leslie Gelb interview, April 9, 2014.

11. Michael Boskin interview, BOHP, 77; Philip A. Brady interview, BOHP, 58; Quayle interview, BOHP, 73.

12. Scowcroft interviews, December 2007 (n.d.) and March 14, 2013.

13. Center for Media and Democracy, "Forum for International Policy," *Source-watch*, www.sourcewatch.org/index.php?title=Forum_for_International_Policy, accessed March 3, 2012; Arnold Kanter interview, March 24, 2009.

14. Center for Media and Democracy, "Forum for International Policy"; Kanter interview, March 24, 2009.

15. Forum for International Policy, 900 17th Street, N.W., Washington, DC, 2006, Form 990-PF, "Return of Private Foundation," 2002, 2003, and 2007 (Guidestar). Virginia Mulberger interview, December 18, 2013; Rostow interview, April 28, 2009; Stephen Hadley interview, April 17, 2014.

16. Kanter interview, March 27, 2009.

17. Brent Scowcroft, "Who Can Harness History?" *New York Times*, July 2, 1993.

18. Brent Scowcroft and Arnold Kanter, "Foreign Policy Straitjacket," *Washington Post*, October 20, 2003, emphasis added.

19. Scowcroft interviews, May 13, 2009, and April 12, 2011.

20. Center for Media and Democracy, "Forum for International Policy"; Mulberger interview, July 6, 2013.

21. J. Stapleton Roy interview, April 9, 2009.

22. Ibid.

23. Scowcroft interview, July 12, 2010.

24. Ibid.

25. Scowcroft interview, May 13, 2009.

26. Kanter interview, March 27, 2009; Mulberger interviews, February 13 and December 18, 2013; Daniel Poneman interview, April 10, 2009.

27. Poneman interview, April 10, 2009; Mulberger interview, December 18, 2013; Scowcroft interview, May 13, 2009.

28. The Scowcroft Group, www.scowcroft.com/html/clients.html, accessed March 3, 2012 [page no longer active]; Hadley interview, April 7, 2009.

29. Mulberger interview, February 13, 2013.

30. Scowcroft interview, April 12, 2011.

31. Leslie H. Gelb, "Kissinger Means Business," *New York Times*, April 20, 1986.

32. Bobby Ray Inman interview, May 31, 2012.

33. Mulberger interview, February 13, 2013; Thomas Pickering interview, April 1, 2014; Bobby Ray Inman interview, May 31, 2012.

34. See Ken Silverstein, "The Mandarins: American Foreign Policy, Brought to You by China," *Harper's Magazine*, August 2008.

35. David Jeremiah interview, March 14, 2013; Inman interview, May 31, 2012; Kanter interview March 27, 2009.

36. Mulberger interview, February 13, 2013; Kanter interview, March 24, 2009; Brent Scowcroft, "Getting the Middle East Back on Our Side," *New York Times*, January 4, 2007.

37. Jeffrey Goldberg, "Breaking Ranks: What Turned Brent Scowcroft Against the Bush Administration?" *New Yorker*, October 31, 2005, 3.

38. David Ignatius interview, April 6, 2009; Jan Lodal interview, May 11, 2009.

39. Ignatius interview, April 6, 2009; Lodal interview, May 11, 2009.

40. Scowcroft interview, April 12, 2011; Willow Darsie, "Politics Stops at the Water's Edge (at Least in Aspen)," *Aspen Idea*, Summer 2006, 46–51; Jonathon Price interview, June 21, 2013.

41. Darsie, "Politics Stops at the Water's Edge."

42. James Mann, "Brzezinski and Iraq: The Makings of a Dove," in *Zbig: The Strategy and Statecraft of Zbigniew Brzezinski*, ed. Charles Gati (Baltimore, MD: Johns Hopkins University Press, 2013), 167.

43. Irwin Mark Jacobs interview, May 31, 2011; "China Tips the Balance," Forbes.com, November 27, 2000; Richard Ernsberger Jr., with Meredith Thompson in Beijing, "Qualcomm's Long March," *Newsweek*, Atlantic Edition, June 25, 2001; David Mock, *The Qualcomm Equation: How a Fledgling Telecom Company Forged a New Path to Big Profits and Market Dominance* (New York: American Management Association, 2005), 194–198.

44. Jacobs interview, May 31, 2011.

45. Virginia Mulberger, personal communication, June 24, 2013; David Halberstam, *War in a Time of Peace: Bush, Clinton, and the Generals* (New York: Scribner, 2001), 138.

46. Scowcroft interview, September 27, 2010; "Scene in D.C.: Kissinger, Rometty, Tillerson, Scowcroft," *Bloomberg News*, March 14, 2013; Bill Gulley interview, December 21, 2011.

47. Mulberger interview, February 13, 2013; Catie Hinckley Kelly interview, November 6, 2009; James Hinckley interview, November 10, 2009.

48. Barbara Bush, *Barbara Bush: A Memoir* (New York: Scribner, 1994), 52; Monica Crowley, *Nixon off the Record* (New York: Random House, 1996), 214.

49. Scowcroft interviews, January 6, 2012, and April 25, 2013.

50. Karen Scowcroft interview, March 19, 2009; Scowcroft interview, December 2, 2009; Robert Gates interview, April 17, 2012.

51. George H. W. Bush interview, December 18, 2009; Lodal interview, May 11, 2009.

52. Lawrence Eagleburger interview, April 19, 2009; James Langdon interview, November 14, 2009.

53. Florence Gantt interview, November 2, 2009; William Sittmann interview, May 12, 2009.

54. Eagleburger interview, April 19, 2009; Florence Gantt interview, November 2, 2009.

Chapter 29: The Broken Process

55. Jacob Weinberg, *The Bush Tragedy* (New York: Random House, 2008); Frank Rich, *The Greatest Story Ever Sold* (New York: Penguin, 2006); Evan Thomas

and Richard Wolffe, "Bush in a Bubble," *Newsweek*, December 19, 2005; J. Stapleton Roy interview, March 27, 2009; Bob Schieffer interview, June 2009; Timothy Naftali, *George H. W. Bush* (New York: Times Books, 2007), 150–151.

56. Ivo Daalder and I. M. Destler, *In the Shadow of the Oval Office: Profiles of the National Security Advisers and the Presidents They Served—from JFK to George W. Bush* (New York: Simon & Schuster, 2009), 258–262; John P. Burke, *Honest Broker? The National Security Advior and Presidential Decision Making* (College Station: Texas A&M University Press, 2009), 244–251, 255–257; Bumiller, *Condoleeza Rice*, 135–135; Marcus Mabry, *Twice as Good: Condoleezza Rice and Her Path to Power* (Emmaus, PA: Modern Times, 2007), 207–209.

57. Craig Unger, *The Fall of the House of Bush: The Untold Story of How a Band of True Believers Seized the Executive Branch, Started the Iraq War, and Still Imperils America's Future* (New York: Scribner, 2007), 4; David Boren interview, February 7, 2012.

58. Scowcroft interviews, January 27 and February 23, 2010; Roy interview, March 27, 2009; Mabry, *Twice as Good*, 177–178; Brent Scowcroft, "New Directions for American Foreign Policy," 9/11 a Year On: America's Challenges in a Changed World, United States Institute of Peace Conference, September 5, 2002.

59. Federation of American Scientists, "NSPD-5: Review of U.S. Intelligence," May 9, 2001, www.fas.org/irp/offdocs/nspd/nspd-5.htm. Also see Philip Zelikow, "Evolution of Intelligence Reform," *Studies in Intelligence* 56, no. 3 (September 2012): 1–20, 5–6.

60. Kevin Scheid interview, January 26, 2009; David Jeremiah interview, March 14, 2013. Also see Unger, *The Fall of the House of Bush*, 225–226; Ron Suskind, *The One Percent Doctrine: Deep Inside America's Pursuit of Its Enemies Since 9/11* (New York: Simon & Schuster, 2006), 30.

61. Scowcroft interviews, August 12, 2009, and June 24, 2011; Lt. Gen. Brent Scowcroft, "Window to the Oval Office: A Diplomatic View of the American Presidency (Part 2 of 2)," July 5, 2012, The West Point Center for Oral History, West Point, NY, 18.

62. Joan Dempsey interview, October 7, 2009; also see David E. Kaplan, "Mission Impossible: The Inside Story of How a Band of Reformers Tried—and Failed—to Change America's Spy Agencies," *U.S. News & World Report*, July 25, 2004.

63. Dempsey interview, October 7, 2009; Scheid interview, January 26, 2009.

64. Scheid interview, January 26, 2009; Roy interview April 9, 2009.

65. Suskind, *The One Percent Doctrine*, 32.

66. Scheid interview, January 26, 2009.

67. Scowcroft interview, April 10, 2009; Zbigniew Brzezinski and Brent Scowcroft, *America and the World* (New York: Basic Books, 2008), 17.

68. Scowcroft interview, April 10, 2009; Joe Dejka, "Inside StratCom on Sept. 11 Offutt Exercise Took Real-Life Twist," *Omaha World Herald*, February

27, 2002; Joe Dejka, "Admiral: StratCom in Midst of Change," *Omaha World Herald*, February 22, 2002.

69. Scowcroft interview, April 10, 2009.

70. Richard A. Clarke, *Against All Enemies* (New York: Free Press, 2004), 7.

71. Scowcroft interview, April 10, 2009.

72. Scowcroft interview, March 30, 2007; Remarks by Brent Scowcroft, "New Direction for American Foreign Policy," 9/11 a Year On: America's Challenges in a Changed World, United States Institute of Peace conference, September 5, 2002.

73. Mabry, *Twice as Good*, 175–178; George S. Tenet with Bill Harlow, *At the Center of the Storm: My Years in the CIA* (New York: HarperCollins, 2007), 306.

74. Unger, *The Fall of the House of Bush*, 202.

75. Richard Perle, James Colbert, Charles Fairbanks Jr., Douglas Feith, Robert Loewenberg, David Wurmser, and Meyrev Wurmser, "A Clean Break: A New Strategy for Securing the Realm," Institute for Advanced Strategic and Political Studies, 1996, www.informationclearinghouse.ino/article1438.htm; Unger, *The Fall of the House of Bush*, 146–148. Also see Stephen Walt and John Mearsheimer, "The Israeli Lobby," *London Review of Books*, March 2006.

76. Victor Gold, *Invasion of the Party Snatchers: How the Holy-Rollers and Neo-Cons Destroyed the GOP* (Novato, CA: Sourcebooks, 2008), 90; also see Jacob Weisberg, *The Bush Tragedy* (New York: Random House, 2008) and Frank Rich, *The Greatest Story Ever Sold* (New York: Penguin, 2006).

77. Rich, *The Greatest Story Ever Sold*; Weisberg, *The Bush Tragedy*; Unger, *The Fall of the House of Bush*, 138; Scowcroft quoted in Andrew Rice, "Brent Scowcroft Calls Iraq War 'Overreaction,'" *New York Observer*, September 5, 2004.

78. Suskind, *The One Percent Doctrine*, 22; Tenet, *At the Center of the Storm*, 303–304; Unger, *The Fall of the House of Bush*, 213.

79. Dempsey interview, October 7, 2009; Scheid interview, January 26, 2009.

80. Suskind, *The One Percent Doctrine*, 20, 32; Jeremiah interview, March 14, 2013.

81. "Post 9/11 Reforms Haven't Fixed Intelligence Failings," *USA Today*, April 16, 2004. For other appraisals and reforms of the intelligence community, see Bruce Berkowitz, "Better Ways to Fix US Intelligence," *Orbis* 45, no. 4 (September 22, 2001); Craig R. Eisendrath and Melvin A. Goodwin, "Reforming US Intelligence After the Terrorist Attack," *USA Today*, November 1, 2001; "Time for a Rethink—American Intelligence Services—Reforming American Spies," *The Economist*, April 20, 2002.

82. Jeremiah interview, March 14, 2013; Scheid interview, January 26, 2009; Suskind, *The One Percent Doctrine*, 34.

83. Jeremiah interview, March 14, 2013.

84. Ibid.; Scheid interview, January 26, 2009.

85. Bill Gulley interview, February 11, 2009; Catherine Lotrionte interview, May 3, 2012; Zelikow, "Evolution of Intelligence Reform," 7.

86. Unger, *The Fall of the House of Bush*, 226.

87. Gulley interviews February 11 and April 13, 2009; Kanter interview, March 27, 2009.

88. But see Condoleezza Rice, *No Higher Honor: A Memoir of My Years in Washington* (New York: Crown, 2011), 264–266, for a favorable view of the newly created position.

89. Jeremiah interview, March 14, 2013.

90. Ishmael Jones, *The Human Factor: Inside the CIA's Dysfunctional Intelligence Culture* (New York: Encounter Books, 2008), 239.

91. Ibid.; James Langdon interview, November 14, 2009.

92. Dempsey interview, October 7, 2009; Scheid interview, January 26, 2009.

93. Peter Baker, *Days of Fire: Bush and Cheney in the White House* (New York: Doubleday, 2013), 9–10; Evan Thomas and Richard Wolffe, "Bush in the Bubble," *Newsweek*, December 19, 2005.

94. Unger, *The Fall of the House of Bush*, 168–169.

95. Richard Haass, *Wars of Necessity, Wars of Choice* (New York: Simon & Schuster 2009), 212–216; Mabry, *Twice as Good*, 184–185; Tenet, *At the Center of the Storm*, 307–309.

96. Brent Scowcroft quoted in *Face the Nation*, CBS, August 4, 2002.

97. Bob Schieffer interview, June 6, 2009; Scowcroft interview, August 12, 2009.

98. Bob Woodward, *Plan of Attack* (New York: Simon & Schuster), 149–152; Hadley interview, April 17, 2009.

99. "Interview with Dennis Ross," *Fox News Sunday*, August 11, 2002; "Boxer, Hutchison Discuss Possible War with Iraq," *CNN Late Edition with Wolf Blitzer*, August 11, 2002; "Senator Lugar Discusses Iraq," CBS News Transcripts, August 11, 2002; Virginia Mulberger interview, February 9, 2012.

100. Arnold Kanter interview, March 24, 2009; Goldberg, "Breaking Ranks: What Turned Brent Scowcroft Against the Bush Administration?."

101. Kanter interview, March 24, 2009; Unger, *The Fall of the House of Bush*, 242–243; Mark Warren, "Brent Scowcroft," *Esquire*, January 2009, 96.

102. Unger, *The Fall of the House of Bush*, 4–6; Boren interview, February 7, 2012.

103. Boren interview, February 7, 2012; see Unger, *The Fall of the House of Bush*, 242.

104. Scowcroft quoted in Andrew Rice, "Brent Scowcroft Calls Iraq War 'Overreaction,'"; also see Scowcroft, "Window to the Oval Office (2)," 19.

105. Kanter interview, March 24, 2009; Mulberger interview, February 9, 2012; also see Haass, *Wars of Necessity, Wars of Choice*, 217; Elisabeth Bumiller, *Condoleezza Rice: An American Life: A Biography* (New York: Random House, 2007), 187–188.

106. Unger, *The Fall of the House of Bush*, 244.

107. Peter Schweizer and Rochell Schweizer, *The Bushes: Portrait of a Dynasty* (New York: Random House), 535, cited in Unger, *The Fall of the House of Bush*, 244; Haass, *Wars of Necessity, Wars of Choice*, 216–218; Goldberg, "Breaking Ranks"; Bumiller, *Condoleezza Rice*, 188; Baker, *Days of Fire*, 209; Mulberger interview, February 9, 2012.

108. Scowcroft interview, August 12, 2009; Haass, *Wars of Necessity, Wars of Choice*, 217.

109. This description of the *Wall Street Journal*'s editorial pages is from Thomas E. Ricks, *Fiasco: The American Military Experience in Iraq* (New York: Penguin Press, 2006), 47.

110. Elliott Abrams interview, October 6, 2010; Rice, *No Higher Honor*, 178–179.

111. George W. Bush, *Decision Points* (New York: Crown, 2010), 238.

112. This deduction coincides with one former intelligence official's view (Lotrionte interview, May 3, 2011); Lawrence Eagleburger interview, April 19, 2009.

113. Unger, *The Fall of the House of Bush*, 243.

114. Woodward, *Plan of Attack*, 160; Abrams interview, October 6, 2010.

115. Ricks, *Fiasco*, 49; Mabry, *Twice as Good*, 175–178.

116. Bush, *Decision Points*, 238.

117. Scowcroft interview, March 30, 2007; Boren interview, February 7, 2012; Sidney Blumenthal, "A State of Chaos," *The Guardian*, December 30, 2004. See Weisberg, *The Bush Tragedy*.

118. Robert Hormats interview, October 29, 2009.

119. Mulberger interview, February 9, 2012; Michael R. Gordon and Bernard E. Trainor, *The Endgame: The Inside Story of the Struggle for Iraq, from George W. Bush to Barack Obama* (New York: Pantheon Press, 2013), 9; Goldberg, "Breaking Ranks."

120. Lee Hamilton interview, May 5, 2009.

121. Abrams interview, October 6, 2010.

122. Baker, *Days of Fire*, 217; see Woodward, *Plan of Attack*.

123. Fred Barnes, *Special Report*, Fox News, August 15, 2002.

124. William Kristol, "The Axis of Appeasement," *Weekly Standard*, August 26, 2002; William Kristol interview, March 2009, n.d.; John Podhoretz, "Beyond Bush 41," *New York Post*, August 20, 2002.

125. Bill Keller, "The Loyal Opposition," *New York Times*, August 24, 2002.

126. William Safire, "Tying Saddam to Terrorist Organizations," *Seattle Post-Intelligencer*, August 25, 2002.

127. Henry Kissinger, *Capital Report*, CNBC, August 15, 2002.

128. "Warning Shots on Iraq" (editorial), *New York Times*, August 16, 2002; Leslie Gelb interview, April 9, 2014.

129. Morton Kondracke, *Special Report*, Fox News, August 15, 2002.

130. Robert Gates, *Duty*, 6.

131. Dempsey interview, October 7, 2009; Rice, "Brent Scowcroft Calls Iraq War 'Overreaction.'"

132. Hamilton interview, May 5, 2009; Andrea Mitchell interview, May 18, 2009.

133. Blumenthal, "A State of Chaos"; Mitchell interview, May 18, 2009; James Langdon interview, November 9, 2009.

134. Scowcroft quoted in Bumiller, *Condoleezza Rice*, 188.

135. Scowcroft interview, December 2, 2012; Antonia Felix, *Condi: The Condoleezza Rice Story* (New York: Newmarket Press, 2002), 12, 128–130, 198; Robert Gates interview, April 17, 2012.

136. Condoleezza Rice interview, August 17, 2009.

137. Felix, *Condoleezza Rice*, 150.

138. Unger, *The Fall of the House of Bush*, 162; James Mann, *Rise of the Vulcans: The History of Bush's War Cabinet* (New York: Penguin 2004), 251–252.

139. See Barton Gellman, *Angler: The Cheney Vice Presidency* (New York: Penguin Press, 2009), 328–342; Daalder and Destler, *In the Shadow of the Oval Office*, 257–258; Donald Rumsfeld, *Known and Unknown: A Memoir* (New York: Sentinel, 2011), 321–330; Alexander Cockburn, *Rumsfeld: His Rise, Fall, and Catastrophic Legacy* (New York: Scribner, 2007), 134–138; Jane Mayer, *The Dark Side* (New York: Doubleday, 2008), 187–188.

140. Gold, *Invasion of the Party Snatchers*, 91; Baker, *Days of Fire*, 230–231.

141. Bumiller, *Condoleezza Rice*, 220–222.

142. David J. Rothkopf, *Running the World: The Inside Story of the National Security Council and the Architects of American Power* (New York: PublicAffairs, 2005), 407–414; Kissinger quoted in Daalder and Destler, *In the Shadow of the Oval Office*, 276; Unger, *The Fall of the House of Bush*, 213, 226; Haass, *Wars of Necessity, Wars of Choice*, 185–186; Burke, *Honest Broker?*, 257–261.

143. William Perry quoted in Rothkopf, *Running the World*, 415.

144. Nora Ephron quoted in Francine Prose, "Being Nora Ephron," *New York Review of Books*, November 21, 2013; Bumiller, *Condoleezza Rice*, 134–135.

145. Rumsfeld cited in Baker, *Days of Fire*, 232.

146. Gellman, *Angler*, 339–342; Bumiller, *Condoleezza Rice*, 223; Rothkopf, *Running the World*, 414.

147. Rothkopf, *Running the World*, 422; Unger, *The Fall of the House of Bush*, 199.

148. See Gellman, *Angler*, 50–60; Rothkopf, *Running the World*, 413–414; Daalder and Destler, *In the Shadow of the Oval Office*, 253.

149. Unger, *The Fall of the House of Bush*, 221.

150. Gellman, *Angler*, 50; Rothkopf, *Running the World*, 407–408.

151. Bumiller, *Condoleezza Rice*, 136–137; Richard Haass quoted in Rothkopf, *Running the World*, 241; Brzezinski and Scowcroft, *America and the World*, 263; Unger, *The Fall of the House of Bush*, 206; Rothkopf, *Running the World*, 420–425; Daalder and Destler, *In the Shadow of the Oval Office*, 252–253.

152. Brent Scowcroft quoted in Goldberg, "Breaking Ranks"; Dick Cheney interview, May 13, 2009.

153. Bernard Lewis quoted in Goldberg, "Breaking Ranks"; Martin Frost quoted in Stephen F. Hayes, *Cheney: The Untold Story of America's Most Powerful and Controversial Vice President* (New York: HarperCollins 2007), 287.

154. This was also Powell's concern, Bob Woodward reports: that Cheney "was not the steady, unemotional rock he had witnessed a dozen years earlier" (Woodward, *Plan of Attack*, 175).

155. Goldberg, "Breaking Ranks"; Haass, *Wars of Necessity, Wars of Choice*, 220.

156. Goldberg, "Breaking Ranks."

157. Brzezinski and Scowcroft, *America and the World*, 259, 263.

158. Bumiller, *Condoleezza Rice*, 215–216; Tenet, *At the Center of the Storm*, 426–428.

159. Burke, *Honest Broker?*, 267–273; Peter W. Rodman, *Presidential Command: Power, Leadership, and the Making of Foreign Policy from Richard Nixon to George W. Bush* (New York: Knopf, 2009), 260–266; Tenet, *At the Center of the Storm*, 430–431; also see Haass, *Wars of Necessity*, 254–263.

160. Bush, *Decision Points*, 258; Scowcroft interview, July 27, 2012. Also see Gordon and Trainor, *The Endgame*, 13–17.

161. Daalder and Destler, *In the Shadow of the Oval Office*, 276–277.

162. Rothkopf, *Running the World*, 406.

163. Eagleburger interview, April 19, 2009; Abrams interview, October 6, 2010.

164. Bumiller, *Condoleezza Rice*, 217; Rothkopf, *Running the World*, 419.

165. Bumiller, *Condoleezza Rice*, 221–222; Gates interview, April 17, 2012; William Sittmann interview, May 12, 2009.

166. Dick Cheney interview, BOHP, 25.

167. Scowcroft interview, May 8, 2014; Sam Nunn interview, April 23, 2012.

168. Mabry, *Twice as Good*, 203, 207.

169. Scowcroft, quoted in Mabry, *Twice as Good*, 203.

170. Brent Scowcroft, "Ford as President and His Foreign Policy," in *The Ford Presidency: Twenty-Two Perspectives of Gerald R. Ford*, ed. Kenneth W. Thompson, Portraits of American Presidents, vol. 2 (Lanham, MD: University Press of America, 1988), 314.

171. Ibid.

172. Scowcroft quoted in Mabry, *Twice as Good*, 207; Brzezinski and Scowcroft, *America and the World*, 262.

173. Scowcroft interview, October 6, 2010.

174. Ibid.

175. Scowcroft quoted in Mabry, *Twice as Good*, 178; Randy Bean quoted in Glenn Kessler, *The Confidante: Condoleezza Rice and the Creation of the Bush Legacy* (New York: St. Martin's Press, 2007), 18.

176. Bumiller, *Condoleezza Rice*, 134; Rice quoted in Thomas and Wolffe, "Bush in the Bubble."

177. Goldberg, "Breaking Ranks."

178. Bumiller, *Condoleezza Rice*, 108; Gold, *Invasion of the Party Snatchers*, 107; Scowcroft interview, July 25, 2013.

179. Felix, *Condi*, 12–13; generally see Clarence Lusane, *Colin Powell and Condoleezza Rice: Foreign Policy, Race, and the New American Century* (Westport, CT: Praeger Press, 2006); Mabry, *Twice as Good*; Bumiller, *Condoleezza Rice*.

180. Thomas and Wolffe, "Bush in the Bubble"; Nicholas Rostow interview, April 28, 2009.

181. Scowcroft interview, September 1, 2009; Lotrionte interview, May 3, 2012.

182. Robert Litwak interview, May 18, 2009; Rostow interview, April 28, 2009; Scowcroft interview, September 1, 2009.

Chapter 30: Elder Statesman

183. Bob Woodward, *Plan of Attack* (New York: Simon & Schuster, 2004), 160.

184. Brent Scowcroft, "Stalling on the Road Map," *Washington Post*, August 20, 2003.

185. Richard Armitage and Marc Grossman refused to resign, and Bob Blackwill was forced to resign (Sidney Blumenthal, "A State of Chaos," *The Guardian*, December 30, 2004); David Ignatius interview, April 6, 2009.

186. Stephen Hadley interview, April 7, 2009; Burke, *Honest Broker?*, 363–365; Daalder and Destler, *In the Shadow of the Oval Office*, 293–298.

187. Scowcroft interview, February 24, 2011; Robert Gates interview, April 17, 2012; Robert Gates, *Duty* (New York: Knopf, 2014).

188. See especially Baker, *Days of Fire*, and Gelman, *Angler*.

189. Zbigniew Brzezinski and Brent Scowcroft, *America and the World* (New York: Basic Books, 2008), 82.

190. James Langdon interview, November 14, 2009; Brent Scowcroft, "Window to the Oval Office (Part 2 of 2)," July 5, 2012, 19.

191. Paul Krugman, "They Told You So," *New York Times*, December 8, 2006.

192. Carl Colby interview, June 26, 2012; Boren interview, February 7, 2012.

193. Scowcroft interview, December 20, 2012.

194. Samuel R. Berger and Brent Scowcroft, "The Right Tools to Build Nations," *Washington Post*, July 27, 2005; Brent Scowcroft, "The Dispensable Nation?" *National Interest*, July 1, 2007; Brent Scowcroft, "A Sit-Down with Brent

Scowcroft," *National Interest*, January 1, 2009; and Brent Scowcroft, "A World in Transformation," *National Interest*, May 1, 2012.

195. Brent Scowcroft and Daniel Poneman, "It's Time for a New Policy on Korea," *Asian Wall Street Journal*, November 4, 2002; Brent Scowcroft and Daniel Poneman, "Korea Can't Wait," *Washington Post*, February 16, 2003; Brent Scowcroft and Arnold Kanter, "A Surprising Success on North Korea," *Washington Post*, May 1, 2003; Ashton Carter, Arnold Kanter, William Perry, and Brent Scowcroft, "Good Nukes, Bad Nukes," *New York Times*, December 22, 2003; Brent Scowcroft, "A Critical Nuclear Moment," *Washington Post*, June 24, 2004; Brent Scowcroft and Daniel Poneman, "An Offer that Iran Cannot Refuse," *Financial Times*, March 9, 2005; Brent Scowcroft, "Confront North Korea," *Wall Street Journal*, May 26, 2005; Brent Scowcroft, "Don't Get Belligerent about Iran," *The Australian*, April 13, 2006; Brent Scowcroft, "Nuclear Guarantees," *The Advertiser*, April 29, 2006; William J. Perry, Brent Scowcroft, and Charles D. Ferguson, "How To Reduce the Nuclear Threat; North Korea's Test is a Troubling Development," *Wall Street Journal*, May 28, 2009.

196. Brent Scowcroft, " . . . And the Tools for Peace," *Washington Post*, May 17, 2002; Zbigniew Brzezinski and Brent Scowcroft, "A 'Road Map' for Israeli-Palestinian Amity," *Wall Street Journal*, February 13, 2003; Brent Scowcroft, "No Stalling on the Road Map," *Washington Post*, August 20, 2003; Brent Scowcroft, "A Middle East Opening," *Washington Post*, November 12, 2004; Brent Scowcroft, "Beyond Lebanon; This Is the Time for a U.S.-Led Comprehensive Settlement," *Washington Post*, July 30, 2006; Brent Scowcroft, "Getting the Middle East Back on Our Side," *New York Times*, January 4, 2007; Brent Scowcroft and Zbigniew Brzezinski, "Middle East Priorities For Jan. 21," *Washington Post*, November 21, 2008; Brent Scowcroft, "It Is Time for Obama to Risk All for a Middle East Peace Deal," *Financial Times*, April 14, 2011.

197. Brent Scowcroft and Bob Graham, "Quick Aid to Colombia—For Our Sake," *Los Angeles Times*, April 26, 2000; William J. Perry and Brent Scowcroft, "Merits of the Middle; Caution Is a Virtue in Our Approach to Taiwan," *Washington Post*, May 1, 2000.

198. Jonathon Price interview, June 22, 2013; Willow Darsie, "Politics Stops at the Water's Edge (at Least in Aspen),," 50.

199. Virginia Mulberger interview, February 13, 2013; Nicholas Burns interview, April 4, 2009; Jonathon Price interview, June 22, 2013.

200. Scowcroft interviews, December 2, 2009, August 3 and September 14, 2011, August 22 and September 27, 2012, April 25, 2013, and January 3, 2014.

201. Lawrence Eagleburger interview, April 19, 2009; Catie Hinckley Kelly interview, November 9, 2009.

202. Scowcroft interview, August 22, 2012; Mulberger interview, February 13, 2013; USAFA Department of Political Science homepage, www.usafa.edu/df/dfps /indexDFPS.cfm?catname=dfps; Price interview, June 22, 2013.

203. Daniel Christman interview, May 12, 2009; Michael Meese interview, June 23, 2010.

204. Christman interview, May 12, 2009; Meese interview, June 23, 2010.

205. Mulberger interview, February 13, 2013; Scowcroft interview, August 22, 2012; USAFA Department of Political Science homepage, www.usafa.edu/df/dfps /indexDFPS.cfm?catname=dfps; Price interview, June 22, 2013.

206. Don Bailey interview, January 21, 2014.

207. Mulberger interview, July 6, 2013.

208. Arnold Kanter interview, March 24, 2009; Major General Edwin W. Robertson II, US Air Force Oral History Interview, April 24–25, 1989, Air Force Historical Research Agency, Maxwell Air Force Base, Alabama.

209. Ignatius interview, April 6, 2009.

210. Brzezinski and Scowcroft, *America and the World*, 3–4, 13–14. Scowcroft also made many of these and the points below on WBUR in NPR's *On Point* with Tom Ashbrook, September 25, 2008.

211. Brzezinski and Scowcroft, *America and the World*, 25.

212. Ibid., 29–30, 150–151, 253–254.

213. Ibid., 228–229, 230–231.

214. George P. Shultz, William J. Perry, Henry A. Kissinger, and Sam Nunn, "A World Free of Nuclear Weapons," *Wall Street Journal*, January 4, 2007.

215. Brent Scowcroft in "Playing Percentages: An Interview with Brent Scowcroft," *eJournal*, U.S. Department of State, Vol. 15, no. 2 (February 2010), 9–12. [Aug 14]; Kanter interview, April 27, 2009.

216. Scowcroft, "Playing Percentages."

217. Charles Ferguson interview, June 6, 2012; Brent Scowcroft and William Perry, cochairs, "US Nuclear Weapons Policy," Council of Foreign Relations, 2009.

218. Charles Ferguson interview, June 6, 2012; Brent Scowcroft and William Perry, cochairs, "US Nuclear Weapons Policy," Council of Foreign Relations, 2009; Michael Shifter interview, June 1, 2012; Bob Graham and Brent Scowcroft, cochairs, "Toward Greater Peace and Security in Columbia: Forging a Constructive U.S. Policy," Report of an Independent Task Force (New York: Council of Foreign Relations, 2000); James Woolsey interview, May 7, 2009; John Deutch interview, April 17, 2009; Scowcroft interview, December 20, 2012.

219. Mulberger interview, February 13, 2013; Scowcroft interview, February 24, 2011; James Langdon interview, November 14, 2009.

220. Scowcroft interview; James Mann, *The Obamians: The Struggle Inside the White House to Redefine American Power* (New York: Viking, 2012).

221. Scowcroft interviews, October 6, 2010, and February 24, 2011; Mulberger interview, February 13, 2013.

222. Scowcroft interview, February 24, 2011.

223. Scowcroft interview, April 25, 2013; Scowcroft address, Hinckley Institute Hall of Fame, University of Utah, Salt Lake City, October 23, 2008.

224. Andrea Mitchell interview, May 18, 2009; John Deutch interview, April 17, 2009; Stephen Hadley interview, April 7, 2009; Amos "Joe" Jordan address, Hinckley Institute Hall of Fame, University of Utah, Salt Lake City, October 23, 2008; Eagleburger interview, April 19, 2009.

225. Carl Colby interview, June 26, 2012.

226. George Shultz interview, August 17, 2009; William Kristol interview, March 2009, n.d.; Elliott Abrams interview, October 6, 2010.

Chapter 31: The Strategist

227. Brent Scowcroft and Daniel Poneman, "It's Time for a New Policy on Korea," *Asian Wall Street Journal*, November 4, 2002.

228. Thomas Pickering interview, BOHP, 35.

229. Rothkopf, *Running the World*, 298.

230. Martin Tolchin, "Ford Aides Weigh Charging Reporters," *New York Times*, June 14, 1978; Letter of Jeff Gerth to Roman Popadiuk, April 19, 1989, "Presidential [illegible]—January–June 1989 [1]," Roman Popdiuk files, NSC BPR, OA/ID CF 00899; David Lauter, "Brent Scowcroft," in *Fateful Decisions*, 204.

231. David Halberstam, *War in a Time of Peace: Bush, Clinton, and the Generals* (New York: Scribner, 2001), 243.

232. Daniel Poneman interview, April 10, 2009; Scowcroft interviews November 18, 2006, and December 20, 2013.

233. Lawrence Eagleburger interview, April 19, 2009; Marlene Eagleburger sat in on the interview.

234. Lodal interview, May 11, 2009; Scowcroft interview, August 22, 2012.

235. Scowcroft interview, October 6, 2010.

236. Paul Thompson interview, October 2, 2009; Abrams interview, October 6, 2010.

237. Scowcroft interview, May 13, 2009; Mann, *The Obamians*, 56. Also see Willow Darsie, "Politics Stops at the Water's Edge (at Least in Aspen): The Non-Partisan Aspen Strategy Group Informs US Foreign Policy," *The Aspen Idea*, Summer 2006, 46–51.

238. Arnold Kanter interview, March 27, 2009.

239. Scowcroft interview, November 28, 2012; also see John Deutch, Arnold Kanter, and Brent Scowcroft, "Saving NATO's Foundation," *Foreign Affairs* 78, no. 6 (November/December 1999): 54–67.

240. Scowcroft to Senator Bond, August 3, 1992, "Saudi Arabia [1]," Virginia Lampley Files, NSC, BPR.

241. Paul Thompson interview, October 2, 2009; Abrams interview, October 6, 2010).

242. Andrew J. Bacevich, *American Empire: The Realities and Consequences of U.S. Diplomacy* (Cambridge, MA: Harvard University Press, 2002), 56.

243. Henry Stimson quoted in *Addresses Made in Honor of Elihu Root*, 25, www. nobelprize.org/nobel_prizes/peace/laureates/1912/root-bio.html.

244. David F. Schmitz, *Brent Scowcroft: Internationalism and Post-Vietnam War American Foreign Policy* (Lanham, MD: Rowman & Littlefield, 2011), 64; also see David F. Schmitz, *The First Wise Man* (Wilmington, DE: Scholarly Resources, 2001).

245. Scowcroft interviews, May 13, 2009, and August 22, 2012.

246. Scowcroft interviews, May 13, 2009, and February 13, 2013.

247. Eagleburger interview, April 19, 2009.

248. Scowcroft interview, January 6, 2010; Frank Carlucci interview, February 4, 2010.

249. Lt. Gen. Brent Scowcroft, "Window to the Oval Office (Part 2 of 2)," 23; Scowcroft interview, July 17, 2012.

Index

Bartholomew Sparrow is professor in the department of government at the University of Texas at Austin, where he teaches American political development. He has received fellowships from the Woodrow Wilson International Center for Scholars, the Joan Shorenstein Center on the Press, Politics,  and Public Policy at Harvard University, and the Harry S. Truman Presidential Library, and has been awarded the Leonard D. White and the Franklin L. Burdette/Pi Sigma Alpha awards from the American Political Science Association. He is the author of *Insular Cases and the Emergence of the American Empire; Uncertain Guardians;* and *From the Outside, In: World War II and the American State.*

PublicAffairs is a publishing house founded in 1997. It is a tribute to the standards, values, and flair of three persons who have served as mentors to countless reporters, writers, editors, and book people of all kinds, including me.

I. F. STONE, proprietor of *I. F. Stone's Weekly*, combined a commitment to the First Amendment with entrepreneurial zeal and reporting skill and became one of the great independent journalists in American history. At the age of eighty, Izzy published *The Trial of Socrates*, which was a national bestseller. He wrote the book after he taught himself ancient Greek.

BENJAMIN C. BRADLEE was for nearly thirty years the charismatic editorial leader of *The Washington Post*. It was Ben who gave the *Post* the range and courage to pursue such historic issues as Watergate. He supported his reporters with a tenacity that made them fearless and it is no accident that so many became authors of influential, best-selling books.

ROBERT L. BERNSTEIN, the chief executive of Random House for more than a quarter century, guided one of the nation's premier publishing houses. Bob was personally responsible for many books of political dissent and argument that challenged tyranny around the globe. He is also the founder and longtime chair of Human Rights Watch, one of the most respected human rights organizations in the world.

•   •   •

For fifty years, the banner of Public Affairs Press was carried by its owner Morris B. Schnapper, who published Gandhi, Nasser, Toynbee, Truman, and about 1,500 other authors. In 1983, Schnapper was described by *The Washington Post* as "a redoubtable gadfly." His legacy will endure in the books to come.

Peter Osnos, *Founder and Editor-at-Large*